Whole House Catalog

By The Editors Of Consumer Guide®

A Fireside Book Published by Simon and Schuster

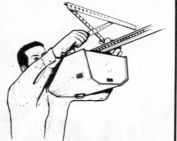

Contents

Welcome To Your Home! 4

Plumbing

How Plumbing Works 6
Plumbing Emergencies 9
Pipe Leaks 10
Dripping Faucets 12
Clogged Drains 14
Toilet Tank Repairs 16
Clogged Toilets 18
Changing a Toilet Seat 19
Thawing Frozen Pipes 20

Electrical

Power Failure 22
Replacing a Wall Switch 24
Replacing a Lamp Socket 26
Replacing a Wall Outlet 27
Fix a Faulty Doorbell 28
Replacing a Plug 29
Fluorescent Fixtures 30
Changing a Ceiling Fixture 31
Repairing Appliance Cords 32

Structural

Load-Bearing Walls 33
Sagging Support Beams 34
Foundation Care and Repairs 35
Damp Basements 36

Floors

Squeaking Floors 38
Fixing a Loose Tile 39
Squeaky Stairs 40
Laying a Tile Floor 42
Removing Spots from Resilient Floors 44
Refinishing Hardwood Floors 45
Laying Tacked Down Carpet 46
Installing Bathroom Carpet 47
Carpet Cleaning 48
Repairing Burns in Carpeting 50

Walls

Replacing a Ceramic Tile 51
Regrouting Tiles 52
Recaulking a Tub or Sink 53
Framing for a Wall 54
Installing Wallboard 56
Fabrics on Walls 59
Patching Holes in Wallboard 60
Paneling a Wall 62
Installing Pegboard 64
Applying an Artificial Brick or Stone Wall 66
Papering a Wall 68
Replacing Molding 70
Wallpaper Patching 73
Hanging Things on Walls 74
Framing a Picture 76

Ceilings

Tile Ceilings 78
Suspended Ceilings 80
Installing Artificial Beams 82
Papering a Ceiling 84

Windows

Unsticking Windows 85
Replacing a Broken Pane 86
Glass Cutting 88
Cleaning Windows 89
Replacing a Sash Cord 90
Screen Replacement 92
Screen Repairs 94
Stained Glass Work 95
Weatherstripping 96
Window Shades 97
Drapery Hardware 98
Venetian Blinds 99
Caulking 100

Doors

Hanging Various Types of Doors 102
Installing an Automatic Garage Door Opener 105
Garage Doors 106
Unsticking a Door 108
Weatherstripping 110

Copyright© 1976 by Publications International, Ltd.
All rights reserved
including the right of reproduction
in whole or in part in any form.
A Fireside Book
Published by Simon and Schuster
A Gulf+Western Company
Rockefeller Center, 630 Fifth Avenue
New York, New York 10020

Manufactured in the United States of America
1 2 3 4 5 6 7 8 9 10

Library of Congress Cataloging in Publication Data
Main entry under title:
Whole house catalog.

  1. Dwellings—Maintenance and repair—Amateurs'
manuals. 2. Dwellings—Remodeling—Amateurs'
manuals. I. Consumer guide.
TH4817.3.W5   643'.7   76-14453
ISBN 0-671-22636-3
ISBN 0-671-22416-6 pbk.

Publications International, Ltd., has made every effort to ensure accuracy and reliability of the information, instructions, and directions in this book; however, it is in no way to be construed as a guarantee, and Publications International, Ltd., is not liable in case of misinterpretations of the directions, human error or typographical mistakes.

Painting

Interior Painting 112
Exterior Painting 114
Paint Failures 116
Painting Doors, Windows, and Shutters 118
Paintbrush Care 120
Painting Metal 122
Cleaning Metal 123
Painting Masonry 124

Furniture

Loose Chair Rungs 125
Broken Parts 126
Wobbly Table Legs 128
Casters 129
Unsticking Drawers 130
First Aid 132
Stripping 134
Tack Rags 136
Staining 137
Finishing 138
Antiquing 140
Decorating Furniture 141
Fixing Cane Chairs 142
Care of Marble 143

Security

Security Tips 144
Installing a Lock 146
Electronic Systems 148

Storage

Storage Walls 150
Bookcase 152
Bookcase with Cabinet Beneath 154
Installing a Plastic Laminate Counter Top 156
Peninsula Kitchen Storage 158
Fruit and Vegetable Cabinet 160
Revolving Utensil Rack 162
Kitchen Storage Above Cabinets 163
Extra Kitchen Shelf 164
Hanging Overhead Utensil Rack 165
Adding Shelves 166
Between-Stud Storage 168
Bathroom Cabinet 170
Installing a Medicine Chest 172
U-Shaped Closet Shelf 173
Sewing Door 174
Stairway Cabinet 176
Building a Cedar Closet 177
Wine Racks 178
Cleaning Closet 179
Lift-Out Tray 180
Tilt-Out Wall Bin 181
Overhead Screen and Storm Window Rack 182
Overhead Closet in Garage 183
House Plant Center 184

Pesky Problems

Mildew 185
Insect Control 186
A Word About Insecticides 188
Rodents 189
Noise and Sound Dampening 190

Children and Pets

Childproofing Your House 192
Child's Closet 193
Teenager's Desk and Storage Wall 194
Bicycle and Tricycle Storage 196
Providing for Pets 198
Making a Blackboard 200

Workshop

Workshop Safety 201
Planning a Workshop 202
Building a Workbench 204
Tool Storage and Protection 206
Tool Rack 208

Tool Safety 209
Keeping Tools Sharp 210
What to Oil and When 212

Outdoors

Minimum Maintenance Landscaping 213
Planting a Lawn 214
Power Mowers (Gasoline) 216
Pruning Trees 218
Garbage Can Enclosures and Racks 219
Compost Heap 220
Garden Tool Storage in a Fence 221
Building a Fence 222
Chain Saws 224
Yard Tool Safety 226
Outbuildings 227
Pouring a Patio 228
Building a Mortarless Patio 230
Building an Outdoor Cooker 231
Swimming Pool Care 232

Roofs

Leaks and Repairs 234
Valleys and Flashing 236
Installing Gutters and Downspouts 238
Care of Gutters and Downspouts 240
De-icing 242
Roof Safety 243

Brick and Masonry

Primer on Concrete Mixing and Finishing 244
Patching Holes in a Concrete Slab 246
Patching Concrete Steps 248
Cracks in Concrete 250
Repairing Blacktop Surfaces 251
Building a Brick Wall 252
Tuckpointing Loose Mortar Joints 254
Replacing a Brick 255

Heating and Cooling

Central Heating and Air Conditioning 256
Gas Burners 259
Oil Burners 260
Checking and Changing a Thermostat 262
Electric Baseboard Units 263
Window Air Conditioning Units 264
Insulation 266
Ventilation 268
Storm Windows 270
Humidity Control 272
Be Your Own Chimney Sweep 274

Mechanical Monsters

Pilot Lights 275
Appliance Motors 276
Garbage Disposer 278
Vacuum Cleaners 280
Washers 282
Dryers 284
Dishwashers 286
Refrigerators 288
Ranges (Gas) 290
Ranges (Electric) 292
Hot Water Heater Maintenance 294
Replacing V-Belts 296
Sewing Machines 297

Whole House Knowledge Miscellany

Adhesives 298
Abrasive Chart 299
Plywood Grading 300
Woods 301
Screw Chart 302
Think Metric 303
Our Catalog of Catalogs 304
Whole House Phone Directory 306

Directory and Index

Directory of Manufacturers 307
Index of Recommended Products 313

Welcome To Your Home!

YOU CALL IT home. You spend more time there than you spend anywhere else. Be it ever so humble, it is nonetheless your castle. And, most likely, it represents the largest expenditure you've ever made or ever will make.

But chances are you know very little about the place you call home. And the full measure of how little you know becomes alarmingly apparent when some aspect of the physical structure itself, or something inside (furnishings, appliances, etc.) needs fixing. Then you run to the telephone to call in the professional repairman, thereby acknowledging your inability to cope with the place you call home.

That's why the WHOLE HOUSE CATALOG welcomes you to your home. A unique publishing achievement, the WHOLE HOUSE CATALOG is your guide to curing the ailments that can afflict your property. Simple step-by-step instructions carry the most inexperienced person

from start to finish in fixing, maintaining, and improving everything in and around the home.

There are a host of excellent repair and maintenance manuals available today. What sets the WHOLE HOUSE CATALOG apart from the rest lies not only in its well-written, easy-to-follow, expert instructions, or in its outstanding line drawings illustrating the crucial phases of each project. What truly sets the WHOLE HOUSE CATALOG apart from every other guide to home maintenance is the presentation of the name-brand tools, materials, and supplies a person needs to perform specific repair projects efficiently and professionally.

Only CONSUMER GUIDE® could produce such a unique volume. With years of experience in guiding buyers to wise purchases, CONSUMER GUIDE® testers examined the do-it-yourself market and culled those tools and other home repair products that merited the atten-

tion of people who like to take care of their own property themselves. Then, in consultation with leading experts in the home repair field, the editors of CONSUMER GUIDE® linked these quality products with appropriate home repair, maintenance, and improvement instructions.

What can the WHOLE HOUSE CATALOG do for you? For the novice, it can be the most reliable guide to the hardware store, lumberyard, and home center available. No longer need these retailers be the only source of advice to people who do not know a miter box from a masonry bit. All one needs to do is look up the relevant project in the table of contents; the border area surrounding the instructional material contains capsule descriptions of precisely what is needed to complete the task—including brand names!

But the WHOLE HOUSE CATALOG is not confined to the novice do-it-yourselfer. Even the home handypersons who have spent

years in the workshop and would never dream of calling in professional assistance when something breaks down will find plenty of interesting items to peruse in the WHOLE HOUSE CATALOG. The enormous breadth of home projects covered means that there is bound to be some instructional material here for everyone. The person who handles his or her own plumbing, painting, patching, paneling, papering, and pest problems may well need some expert directions on fixtures, furnaces, fans, foundations, floors, and framing. Moreover, the most experienced do-it-yourselfer can still enjoy and profit from reading about the fascinating name-brand tools and materials that have just arrived on the market. Thus, the WHOLE HOUSE CATALOG deserves a place in every home.

The WHOLE HOUSE CATALOG is organized to make using it as easy as possible. The major areas of homeowner responsibility stand as major chapters, with the specific projects relating to the particular area listed under that heading as subchapters. Each subchapter is complete unto itself, containing its own instructional copy and illustrations and — in the border space surrounding the how-to material — its own recommended products.

Naturally, certain basic tools (hammers, saws, screwdrivers, etc.) have such versatile applications that a particular model could as easily be linked with several other projects as with the one it appears. If you care to learn about and review all of the recommended screwdrivers, for example, you can do so easily without examining each and every subchapter throughout the book. Merely look under "Screwdrivers" in the product index, and you will find name-brand listings of all the screwdrivers that appear in the WHOLE HOUSE CATALOG.

Although every item in the WHOLE HOUSE CATALOG carries the hallmark of a CONSUMER GUIDE® recommendation, readers are advised that in many cases tools, materials, and supplies of equivalent quality are available. If you cannot locate the specific product recommended, therefore, read the description carefully and then go shopping. You may well be able to find comparable products at your local retailer.

As you might expect, your nearby hardware store, lumberyard, and home center are the most logical places to find and buy the products recommended in the WHOLE HOUSE CATALOG. In a small number of instances the item described is available by mail-order only; in such instances, you should write to the address provided for further information regarding prices and shipping policy. Manufacturers whose products are in wide distribution—and such distribution was one of the factors weighed in selecting products for recommendation—generally will not sell to consumers directly. If you cannot track down a particular product nor one of comparable quality, however, you can write to the manufacturer and ask where you can obtain the item in your locale. The WHOLE HOUSE CATALOG provides a directory of manufacturers' addresses covering the makers of all recommended products.

Maintenance By The Calendar

IF YOU DO maintenance chores on a calendar basis, you can keep your home in top shape and prevent small problems from growing into major ones. By establishing a schedule of tasks to accomplish during each season, you can fix the damage done by the previous season and take

steps to prevent any ill effects from the upcoming elements.

Another big plus to your doing home repairs at various times throughout the year is that you spread the expense over twelve months. If you wait until your fix-it tasks become critical, you might discover that several projects need doing all at the same time. Then your financial position could suddenly become in need of repair as well.

Naturally, the maintenance calendar that you establish will be different from those of homeowners in different parts of the country. Nevertheless, the following season-by-season guide should be of some help when you set up your own schedule. Why not read through the guide and then make up your maintenance calendar before another day goes by in which you say "I wish I had done it earlier"?

Autumn: The fall season is generally one in which you should prepare for winter. The protective measures you take during the mild autumn weather may well prevent having to deal with emergency conditions when the temperature dips below freezing.

The first thing to check is your heating system. Make sure it is working well before the time you actually need it. If you have a central heating system, make sure that all components are clean. Dirt is your heating system's worst enemy. If you have the disposable type filters, purchase enough to last you through the winter. Furnace filters are so inexpensive that you could install a fresh one every month without ever feeling a financial pinch. If you have the permanent type filters, take them out and clean them well before the mercury starts plummeting.

The fan or blower in a forced air system needs to be cleaned and lubricated annually. If the blower is of the squirrel-cage type, use a vacuum cleaner and a stiff brush to get all the dirt out from between the blades. Once these fins get clogged, the blower cannot move as much air, and the efficiency of your heating system goes way down while the cost of its operation goes way up. Remember, of course, that before you do any furnace cleaning you should turn off the gas and electrical power to the unit.

Check the thermostat as well. Remove the face plate, and gently blow away any lint that may have collected there. Just a little lint can destroy the accuracy of this delicate instrument. Inspect the pilot and burners for accumulated dirt, and if you find any, brush and vacuum it away. The registers for the forced hot air and for the cool return air must also be clean. Usually brushing and vacuuming will do the job.

Now that you have the heating

unit clean, inspect the area around it. Make sure that there are no items near the furnace that could pose a potential fire hazard or that might restrict the free flow of air to the system. Wall heater units must also have a free flow of air or they could become hazardous. Turn both the pilot and the burner off, and use a vacuum cleaner to remove all lint from all accessible surfaces. While you are vacuuming, check for any soot marks. Soot deposits are an indication that insufficient air is going to the heating unit, and you must correct the situation yourself or call in a heating professional to service the heater.

That should take care of your heating problems. Now move to your roof and check for any loose or missing shingles. Inspect the flashing for leaks, and look for signs of water spots in the attic.

Once you are confident that the trees are finished shedding their leaves, clean all gutters and downspouts. Inspect the weatherstripping around all doors and windows, and replace the screens with storm doors and windows. Then make a complete tour all around the house to be sure that all caulking is sound. Bring in the garden tools, and drain and store the hoses. You should clean all the tools, protecting metal parts with a coating of oil or grease and rubbing wooden handles with a light coat of linseed oil. Power mowers and edgers should be drained and winterized.

Install covers over all window air conditioning units and over all crawl space vents. Inspect all trees and remove any limbs too weak to withstand the weight of heavy ice and snow. Be sure that all outside faucets are turned off or properly protected so that they will not freeze, and check the main water cutoff to make certain you can shut it off should a plumbing emergency arise.

Winter: Now is the time to keep busy doing all the inside repairs. Clean, repair, and repaint your patio furniture. Take care of any cracks or holes in your home's interior walls. If you have been wanting to panel some walls or install a suspended ceiling, winter is a good time to get the job(s) done.

Check your heating system on a regular basis during the winter. Make sure that motors are running properly and that they are well lubricated. There should be a clean filter in the heating unit at all times. Keep your home's humidity up to a comfortable level, but eliminate any condensation problems as they arise.

Spring: This is the time to repair all the damage done by winter weather and to prepare for the onset of summer.

Examine all masonry and brick work, walls, patios, the foundation, driveways, and all other ex-

terior areas for cracks and holes. Repair any damage immediately. Inspect the roof once again for loose shingles, and look for potential problems that might crop up in your gutters or downspouts. Remove any rust and refinish all bare spots.

Repair and replace screens as you take down and store storm windows and doors. Store the storm windows and doors carefully to prevent any breakage.

Since spring is also the time when insects abound, keep a watchful eye for wasps starting nests in or near your home. Make certain that there are no unwanted openings in your home's exterior through which bugs could enter.

Spring is the best time to paint the outside of the house. Do it as soon as the weather turns warm enough but before the temperature gets too hot.

Inspect trees and shrubs, and cut off any broken limbs. Consult your nurseryman or county agent about proper spring feeding of your lawn, and plant seeds in any bare spots. Prepare your power mower and edger for a season of hard work. If you have been thinking about planting a vegetable garden, spring is the time to start.

Inspect the air conditioning system and get it ready for the hot days ahead. Remove all covers from window units and from crawl space vents. Clean out the fireplace, close the damper, and inspect the chimney to see whether it needs cleaning. Move all leftover firewood out away from the house before it can become a haven for bugs.

Summer: The good old summertime is a fine time for interior painting because you can keep the windows open. But try not to paint on excessively hot or humid days.

Check the basement for sweating pipes, and wrap any that might prove troublesome. Remove any standing water around your house before it can become a breeding ground for mosquitoes, and launch your program to combat the insects that can ruin your garden.

Be sure to keep your lawn, trees, and plants watered. If you are planning a vacation, arrange for a neighbor to water while you are away. Speaking of vacations, take steps to assure your home's security when you are gone. Arrange for mail and papers to be picked up, for the lawn to be mowed regularly, and for the neighbors to watch your place during your absence.

By observing this annual checklist you will find that home maintenance need never become a crushing burden. If you take care of your home's season-by-season requirements, you can save plenty of money and reduce your annual quota of homeowner headaches.

Plumbing

Copper Is Still Popular In Home Plumbing

Copper pipe and tubing is still very popular, although joining pieces of copper requires a somewhat complicated process called sweat soldering. A good, sweat-soldered joint starts with a clean, straight cut. This can best be done with a tube cutter similar to the Bonney model from the Utica Tool Company. The arrow on the Bonney Tube Cutter is a reamer to remove any burrs from inside the tubing. Next, the copper must be cleaned with either steel wool or an abrasive such as Carborundum Company's emery cloth. Buy this abrasive in rolls for maximum usefulness. Use a paste flux like Canfield's Copper-Mate and a solid wire solder such as the Canfield Quality solder roll. Heat the pipe or tubing with a propane torch or with one of the newer Mapp gas torches like the Spitfire Turbotorch from Wingaersheek Company. Make sure that the tubes and fittings are totally dry before you begin sweat soldering, and always direct the flame toward the fitting and not at the solder. After the fitting starts to heat, keep touching the tip of the wire to the seam to be soldered; the solder will eventually melt, and capillary action will draw the molten solder into the cavity.

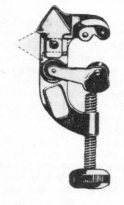

Stillson Wrench Is Basic For Plumbing Work

The Stillson wrench, like the one bearing the Classic brand from the Indestro Manufacturing Company, is strictly a plumber's tool. Available in five sizes (sized according to pipe diameters they fit), the Classic Stillson wrenches feature handles and heads made of special steel that has been heat treated. The jaw teeth are deep milled, uniformly spaced, and scientifically hardened, while the head itself has a machine-ground finish.

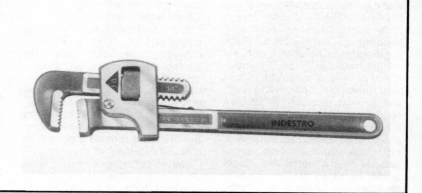

How Plumbing Works

ALTHOUGH THE entire plumbing system may seem like a mystery, it is more misunderstood than mysterious. The plumbing in your house operates on some very basic laws of nature—laws like gravity, water pressure, and the fact that water seeks its own level.

There are two separate and distinct plumbing systems in your home—one for incoming, and one for outgoing. Total separation is an absolute must between these two plumbing systems. Let's take a look at the way a typical home receives and disposes of water.

Water Supply System

NO MATTER what the source of water to your house may be, it is delivered under pressure. If you live in a typical city, the community water department pumps water into a storage tank or water tower, and usually gravity provides the pressure because the tower is higher than the outlets in the homes. In some cases, pump pressure is needed.

The water to your home is supplied through a water main. The water main usually goes through a water meter which is located very near the point where the supply line enters your property. The meter may be underground outside the house with a metal cover for access, or it may be inside at the point where the supply pipe comes in the house. The meter records the number of gallons brought into the house. If you can see it easily, look at the meter's dials spin when you have several outlets open at one time.

If you have your own well, you are probably using a pump to supply the water and add the pressure. Except for the fact that you lack a meter, all the rest of the information here concerning your water supply is the same.

Very close to the meter is a main cutoff valve which shuts off all the water coming into the house. You must know how to find and use the main cutoff in a plumbing emergency. The cutoff may be a stop and waste valve that drains the water from the pipes as well as shuts off the supply. Most fixtures have—or should have—individual shut-off valves.

All water comes into your house as cold water. It is piped directly to all fixtures that use unheated water through the cold water main; offshoots to individual fixtures are called branches. The water can travel upstairs, around corners, or wherever needed because it is under pressure. The pipes that run vertically and extend upward a story or

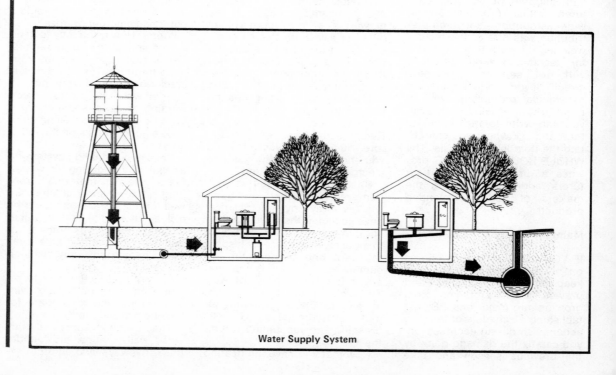

Water Supply System

Support Your Local Pipes

Extra support for plumbing pipes is available for easy installation in the plastic-coated wire pipe hooks marketed by Western Wire Products Company. The U-shaped hangers have two sharp points that you drive into the joists; the pipe rests in the bottom of the plastic-coated cradle. By supporting your pipes in this way, you reduce the bouncing and vibration to which they are subjected as water travels through them under pressure.

Pipes Have Their Own Vises

Pipe vises have specially-shaped jaws with teeth to hold pipe firmly without bending it. The Columbian Long Jaw hinged vise comes in four sizes to accommodate a wide range of pipe sizes. The purpose of the hinge is to allow you to put in pipe from the side; the locking lever is there to hold the top part down when the jaws grip the pipe. Columbian Vises are part of the Warren Group of tool manufacturers.

Polybutylene Plumbing Parts Prove Plastic Is Here To Stay

Polybutylene plumbing systems offer many unique advantages. Flexible tubing, of course, is much easier for the do-it-yourselfer to install, and polybutylene can be used for both hot and cold supply lines. If your local code permits, therefore, you could install polybutylene plumbing throughout the entire house. Its flexibility means that fewer fittings are required, and that precise pipe measurement and cutting are things of the past. With such a system, moreover, connections are made with no special tools. The Qest Magic Seal cone and ring, for example, can be hooked onto copper, galvanized steel, rigid plastic, or to itself. Most connections can be made in less than a minute. Another system, called Cinch-Pipe, comes in three different tubing sizes. There are fittings for all three sizes as well as adapters to hook Cinch-Pipe onto other types of pipe. The Magic Seal cone and ring are from Qest Products, and Cinch-Pipe is made by Cerro Copper Products.

Qest Magic Seal

Where To Buy Plumbing Supplies

Home centers, lumberyards, plumbing supply houses, and hardware stores generally carry what you need for most repairs. Sears, Montgomery Ward, and J.C. Penney also carry a wide selection of plumbing products, and they can be relied upon to sell quality goods. If you live far from any of these retailers, you can order plumbing supplies through the Sears, Ward, and Penney mail-order catalogs. The plumbing section in the Penney catalog is not quite as complete as the other two.

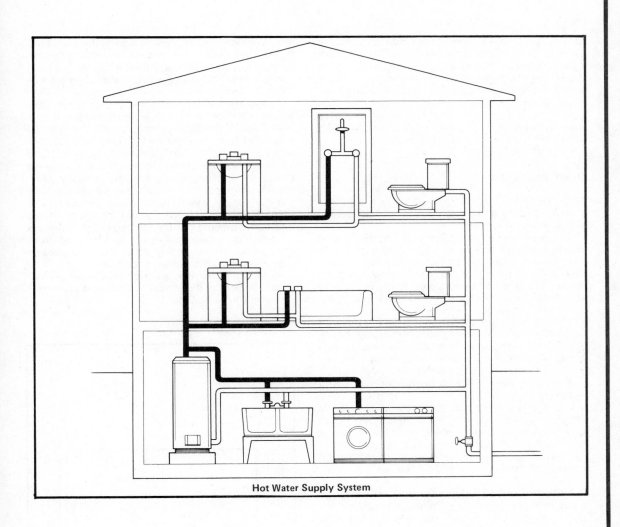

Hot Water Supply System

Plastic Pipe Fulfills Do-It-Yourselfers' Dreams

Although some local plumbing codes forbid plastic pipe, it makes a good deal of sense to use it wherever the law allows. Genova offers rigid vinyl pipe for both supply and drainage systems. The drain system, including fittings and the vent stack, are PVC DWV pipe. The water supply pipes—both hot and cold—are CPVC as are the fittings. Genova's Nova-weld Solvents join all types of plastic pipe. Genova also makes a number of plastic specialty items for the plumbing field, including a sump pump called the Sump Witch. All Genova products are widely distributed.

more are called risers.

One part of the cold water system carries water to the heater. From the water heater, a hot water main carries hot water to all the fixtures, outlets, or appliances that require hot water.

All faucets, hot or cold, should have some sort of air chamber. The air chamber serves as a cushion to stop the shock waves that occur when water moving rapidly under pressure is suddenly shut off.

Water Pressure

YOU CAN no doubt see the value of water pressure, but too much of a good thing can be bad. Too much pressure causes your pipes to bang around, and it may even cause joints and connections to break. Too much pressure is also a water waster. In addition, it can strain your fixtures and cause faucets to leak. Pressure that fluctuates, of course, can be uncomfortable in the shower.

Residential water pressure that reaches or exceeds 60 psi (pounds per square inch) is too much of a good thing. You can test the pressure in your house by attaching a pressure gauge to any threaded faucet. If the gauge shows 60 psi or more, you ought to install a pressure-reducing valve. Of course, be sure to test the pressure at several times during the day to find a good average. In addition, make sure that no water is running in your home besides the outlet with the gauge attached.

A pressure-reducing valve is a fairly inexpensive unit, and installation is an easy do-it-yourself project. Most of the valves work best when installed on a horizontal pipe, and the valve has union
(Continued on following page)

Plumbing

Plumbing Books

If you want to learn more details of how a home plumbing system works and what to do when it doesn't, any one of several inexpensive books can tell you all you need to know. *Home Guide To Plumbing, Heating And Air Conditioning* by George Daniels does a good job of explaining how plumbing works, and it shows how to make all kinds of repairs. *The Practical Handbook Of Plumbing And Heating* by Richard Day, is profusely illustrated with art that really shows how everything works and what goes on inside many plumbing gadgets. The text isn't as complete as Daniels' book, but the pictures make up for any lack as far as the layman is concerned. *Plumbing Repairs Simplified* by Donald R. Brann is not as complete as either Daniels' or Day's books, but it is widely distributed in hardware stores and home centers. So if you can't find the others, buy this one.

Get A Complete Bath Drain System In Kit Form

All the material to run drains from the tub, the toilet, and the lavatory of a new bathroom is available in one easy-to-install kit. The Nibcoware kit includes all of the elbows, tees, fittings, solvent, primer, and even the vent stack with its flashing—everything you need to connect a three-piece bathroom. The kits are available in either ABS or PVC plastic. Nibcoware solvents are easy to use. Just brush on the primer, put on the solvent, and then push the pipe into the fitting with a slight twist. You must, however, position the pipe and fitting immediately because in a matter of seconds, the joint is fixed and ready for a lifetime of use. Nibcoware is from the Consumer Product Division of Nibco, Inc.

Plumbing Tasks Call For Special Tools

Although some of your regular tools can be used in plumbing chores, you'll find that special plumber's wrenches—like those from Ridgid Tools—work much better. The Ridgid strap wrench, made for use on any polished pipe, has a woven nylon strap that can be adjusted easily around the pipe; it gives you a tight grip without marring the pipe's surface. The Ridgid chain wrench is a heavy-duty tool with ratchet ac-

 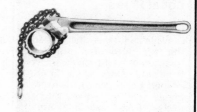

tion that lets you work from either side in close quarters. Ridgid, brand name of the Ridge Tool Company, offers plumbing wrenches for just about every plumbing problem.

(Continued from previous page)

fittings for an easy connection. You can set the valve to provide the pressure that best suits your needs. Once set, the valve lowers the pressure to the setting, and steadies it at that level.

While too much pressure can be tamed inexpensively, too little pressure is something you may have to accept. Trying to increase pressure may require such major endeavors as building your own water tower or completely replacing all the pipes in your home.

Drainage System

NOW THAT we have all that water in the house, how do we get rid of it after we use it? The answer is the drainage system.

The drainage system operates on the law of gravity, with all the waste pipes going downhill. The water drains out of the house and into a sewer line that continues the downhill flow, carrying away the waste and used water. There is more to the system than that, however. There are vents, traps, and cleanouts.

The vents are open pipes that stick out the roof of the house and allow air to enter the drain pipes. The vents sometimes are just extensions of a drain pipe. Proper venting is a must. The introduction of air pressure helps the water to flow out. Air from the vents also prevents a syphoning action at the traps.

If the vents were not there—or if they were clogged up—the lack of air in the drain could cause the rush of water going out to syphon out too much of the water in the trap, leaving a gap. The gap would mean no more seal, and that would mean that sewer gas could back up into your house.

The curved pipes you can see under the drain of every sink are called traps. When a basin is emptied, the water flows out with enough force to push through the trap and out through the drain pipe. When it runs out, however, there is still water left in the trap to protect you; the trapped water provides a seal against the backup of sewer gas. If you had no seal there, bad odors and dangerous gases could enter your home. Every fixture must have a trap.

Toilets are self trapped, and do not require an additional trap in the drain. Frequently, bathtubs have a drum trap which provides the same safeguards, but also traps hair and dirt to prevent clogging. In some kitchens, grease traps collect grease that goes down the sink. Grease and hair are the prime offenders in the clogging department, but the clean-out plugs on these traps allow for a direct shot at any clogs.

Fixtures

THE BRIDGE between the two systems—supply and drainage—is the point of having the plumbing in the first place: the fixture. Plumbing jargon refers to any outlet—whether it be an outside hydrant or a twelve-cycle automatic washing machine—as a fixture.

Those are the basics of the plumbing in your house. The fact that it is usually hidden in the walls, under the floors, and beneath the ground may make the plumbing seem mysterious, but it is really a simple and logical system. Now that you know how it works, take a look at the pipes in your basement or crawl space. The larger heavy pipes are for drainage. You should also be able to pick out the supply lines. Try to locate the clean-out plugs. If you can see up on your roof, you will have no trouble picking out the vent stacks. It is always a good idea, moreover, to tag as many different lines as possible so that you can know what each pipe does should an emergency arise.

Knowing how the plumbing system works should make the diagnosis of your next plumbing problem a little easier.

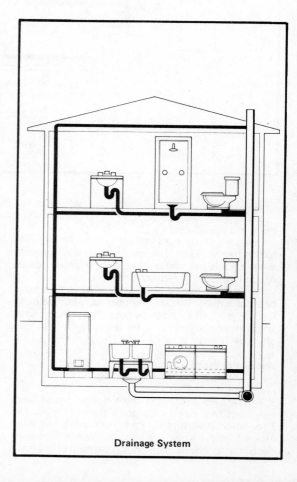

Drainage System

Collar Can Keep Your Cool

Although you know that the water cutoffs in your home are in good working order, at the time you discover a burst pipe and your house seems to be floating away, you may lose your cool and forget which valve to turn or which way to turn it. A handy panic preventer can be made from the bottom of an empty plastic bleach bottle. Cut the bottom off and put a hole

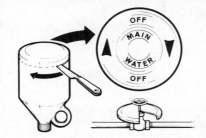

in the center, creating a collar that will fit over the stem of the valve. Use India ink to identify the valve,

and put a large arrow indicating the direction you must turn the valve to shut off the water supply.

Cutoff Key Can Prevent Disaster

In an emergency, the main cutoff for your water supply may be inaccessible or it might be frozen in its open position. What can you do? You can shut off the water supply at the meter cutoff. Some meters are underground, locked behind a sort of manhole cover. If your meter is of this type, you must have a key in order to remove the cover. Some utility companies forbid—or at least discourage—homeowners from having such a key; but if possession of such a key is allowable, you would be wise to have one and know where to find it in a hurry . . . just in case.

Plumbing Emergencies

I T IS A sad fact but a true one: By the time you get a call through to the plumber, a burst pipe can pour thousands of gallons of water into your house. Untamed water, of course, can do thousands of dollars in damage to your house and its furnishings. Now, while there is no emergency, is the time to learn what to do in the event of a major plumbing disaster.

1. The first thing everyone should know is how to shut off the flow of water. Take the entire family on a tour of your home to see where the cutoffs are located. Each sink, basin, tub, and appliance should have its own cutoff, but you will find that many do not have them. Everyone must, therefore, know the location of the main cutoff.
2. Usually located very close to where the water supply enters the house, the main cutoff may be a gate valve or it may be an "L"-shaped rod. If the meter is in the basement, you could have a meter valve that requires a wrench to turn. An underground meter would have the same type of valve, but a buried pipe means that you must dig to find the cutoff.
3. Once you locate the main cutoff valve, find out exactly how it works and, most importantly, if it works. Little-used valves have a way of corroding, and it is better to find out now that the valve needs replacement than when you are struggling in a panic situation. In the case of the "L"-shaped rod, the actual valve is usually underground. If the valve malfunctions, you must dig down and treat the valve with penetrating oil to free it.
4. Make sure that you know which way to turn the valve to shut off the water. It might even be a good idea to tag the cutoff with a drawing that indicates what the valve is and which way to turn it. You can use the occasion to acquaint the family with gas and electricity cutoffs as well. As for preventive maintenance, it is a good idea to turn the water cutoff valve off and then on again once every six months or so to keep it in working order.
5. One word of caution: Remember that the flooding waters can come in contact with electrical components. Make sure that you do not complete the fatal triangle. If there is any chance of electrical contact, always throw the main switch to your household

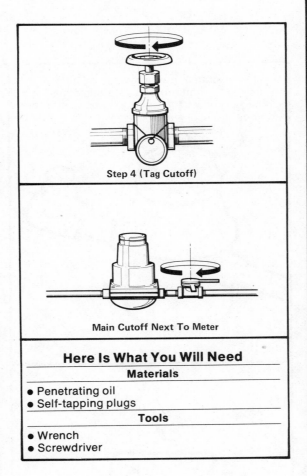

Step 4 (Tag Cutoff)

Main Cutoff Next To Meter

Here Is What You Will Need
Materials
- Penetrating oil
- Self-tapping plugs

Tools
- Wrench
- Screwdriver

current before you go wading around in the water.

6. If the flood emanates from a leaky tank, try one of the self-tapping plugs that are designed to go into the hole. When tightened down, the screw applies enough pressure to stop the leak. If the tank rotted through in one place, however, it may well do so in another. The plugs, nonetheless, may buy you enough time to shop around for the best replacement tank while preventing damage to your home.

The most important thing to remember in a plumbing emergency is to keep a cool head. Stop the flow of rising water to minimize damage. Once you get the water shut off, there is no reason to panic; you even have time to figure out your next move. You may decide that the time has come to call in professional help, but you may conclude that this emergency is merely one of the many plumbing projects that you can tackle yourself.

Flooded Basement Can Pose Emergency Situation

The same drain in the center of the basement floor that lets water run out can also let water back in when the sewers fail to handle a large volume of water. A homeowner feels helpless watching the basement fill with water, but the problem can generally be remedied. If flooding is a regular event, you should have a sump pump standing guard. But if the water backup is an occasional problem, install a unit like the Flood Guard marketed by the General Wire Spring Company. Flood Guard lets water flow out the drain, but when the drain backs up, the potential flood water lifts a float in the Flood Guard that seals the opening. A similar product, also widely distributed, is called Drain Guard.

Plugs For Tank Leaks

Any tank that springs a leak can cause panic, and with good reason. A tank leak can be as disastrous as any pipe leak. Tank plugs, though, may solve the problem. Brand name is not much of a factor in selecting tank plugs. The primary consideration is getting the right size plugs. Hancock-Gross' Boiler Repair Plugs are self-tapping and come with washers.

Plumbing

Pipe Leaks

WHEN A PIPE bursts, it can do tremendous damage to your home. But there are measures you can take to prevent major destruction. If you act quickly and follow these steps, you can turn a potential disaster into an easy do-it-yourself repair job.

1. Cut off the water. If there is a cutoff for just that section of pipe, shut it off. If not, go to the main water cutoff for your home and turn it off.
2. Locate and examine the leaky section.
3. If the leak is in the middle of a length of

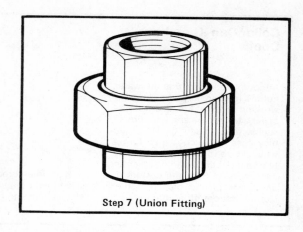

Step 7 (Union Fitting)

galvanized pipe, there are several ways to clamp a patch over the hole. You can buy a kit at the hardware store that includes a pair of clamps, a rubber pad, and bolts. Or you

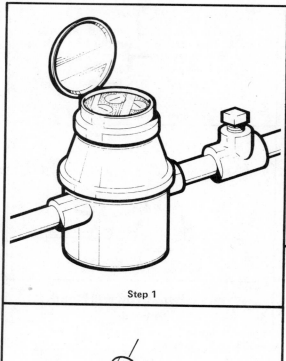

Step 1

Here Is What You Will Need

Materials

- Pipe patching kit (clamps, rubber pad and bolts) or inner tube scrap and worm gear hose clamp
- Waterproof tape
- Epoxy metal
- Pipe joint compound
- Solder
- New pipe
- Union fitting
- Solvent weld compound

Tools

- Pipe wrench
- Propane torch
- Hacksaw

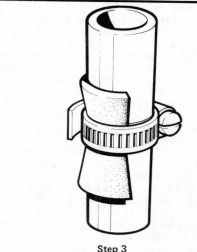

Step 3

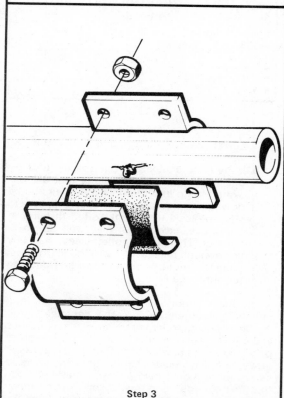

Step 3

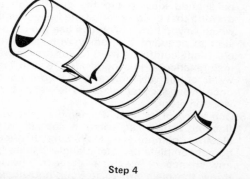

Step 4

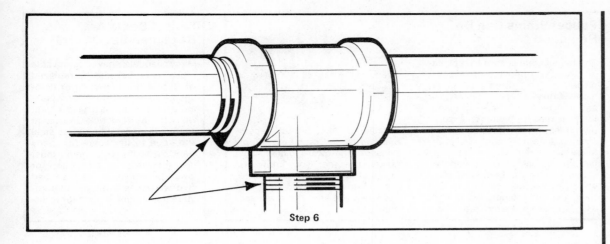

Step 6

can apply the same sort of patch with a scrap of inner tube and a worm gear hose clamp.

4. For a temporary repair of a small leak, you can wrap waterproof tape around any type of pipe. The tape should cover several inches to either side of the hole.

5. You can apply epoxy metal to any metal pipe. Be sure to allow the pipe to dry completely, and then follow the directions for curing time.

6. Leaks around pipe joints are more common than burst pipes. Galvanized pipe joints are threaded, and sometimes they just need to be tightened. If tightening fails to stop the leak, loosen the fitting, apply pipe joint compound, and retighten. A compression fitting that leaks probably just needs a slight tightening; but joints in copper tubing that leak must be removed, all the old solder cleaned away, the tubing dried completely, and then the joint resoldered.

7. A bad section of pipe should be replaced rather than patched. Cut the bad part out, and replace it with two shorter pipe sections joined by a fitting—called a union.

8. If the leak is in plastic pipe, try to use solvent weld compound to seal the leak. If the compound does not do the job, replace the bad section of pipe.

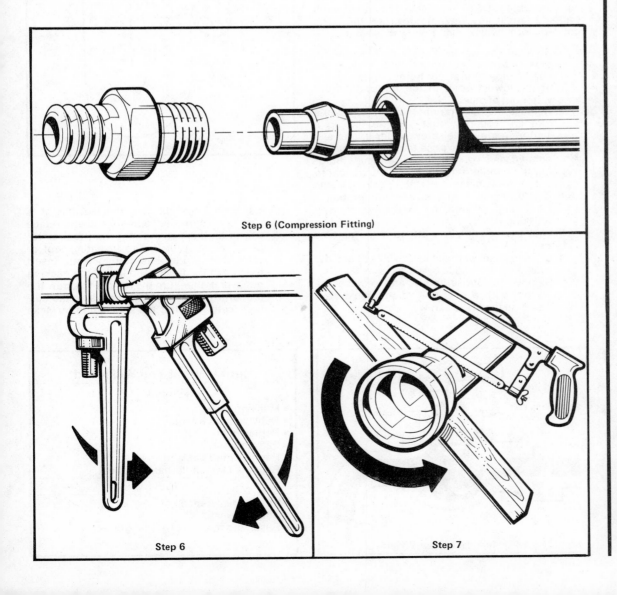

Step 6 (Compression Fitting)

Step 6

Step 7

11

Plumbing

Multi-Adjustment Pliers Help Fix Drips

To get to the spindle, and thus to the washer, the faucet's packing nut must first be removed. Packing nuts come in various sizes, and many people find that large slip-joint pliers handle the job best. The Channellock Model 415 is a top quality tool and quite popular. The 415's smooth jaws are kind to plated fittings, and—like all of Channellock's tongue-and-groove pliers—the 415 features undercut mated non-slip channels.

Faucet Stems Can Be Replaced

The faucet stem is easy to replace . . . once you find the proper replacement part. Stems come in many different sizes and styles, and you must find the right one for your faucet. A plumbing supply house is your best bet when seeking a replacement. Most of these suppliers have charts showing the actual sizes of various stems for various brands of faucets. Private-label stems offered by Sears, Montgomery Ward, and J.C. Penney, however, are com-

parable to most brands recommended by the plumbing supply house or hardware dealer. Just make sure that you know the brand of faucet you have, and remember to take the old stem with you when you shop for a replacement.

Faucet Seats Are Replaceable

Many faucets have removable brass seats that can be replaced when they become worn or damaged. The tool required for replacing a faucet seat is called a seat wrench. The Hancock-Gross seat wrench is made of hardened steel and—due to its taper—fits many standard seats. This model must be used with a wrench or pliers for leverage, but there are L-shaped seat wrenches available that require no additional tools for leverage.

Kits Make Single-Handle Faucet Repairs A Snap

Complete kits containing all the repair parts for a single-lever faucet make fix-it tasks quick and easy. Most kits are carded with illustrations and instructions on the back of the packet. All you have to do is know the brand of single-lever faucet, and then find a store that carries the specific kit for that faucet brand.

Handles Give Faucet A Face Lift

Sometimes, an old faucet still works satisfactorily, but it looks terrible. New handles may be just the touch needed to give the faucet an attractive appearance. There are many types of handles available, and all hardware, plumbing, and builder's supply stores offer a wide assortment. The ones pictured here are inexpensive handles from Bowers. The faucet handles are designed to fit all stems and come with an installation wrench.

Dripping Faucets

AMONG THE MORE harmless of household problems is the dripping faucet. Most people reason that a drip just amounts to a few drops of wasted water, so why worry? Yet, if you stop to add up how much water is wasted in a year, the cost can mount up to around $50 right down the drain. If you call for a plumber to fix it, of course, he will charge you $15 to $25, but you can repair a dripping faucet in a few minutes, and the parts cost no more than a dollar. Follow these steps.

1. Shut off the water at the cutoff below the sink or at the main cutoff where the water supply pipe enters your home. Open a faucet at the lowest point in the house to drain water out of pipes.
2. Remove the packing nut with an adjustable wrench. You may first have to flip up a button, remove the screw under it, and slip the handle off to expose the packing nut. In some cases, you will find a set screw holding the handle; remove it and the handle to get at the packing nut. If the packing nut is highly visible or made of chrome, protect it from the wrench by wrapping it with masking tape.
3. With the packing nut off, turn the spindle out.
4. At the bottom of the spindle you will see the washer held in place by a brass screw.
5. Remove the brass screw, and replace the washer with a new one of the same size. Reinstall the brass screw.

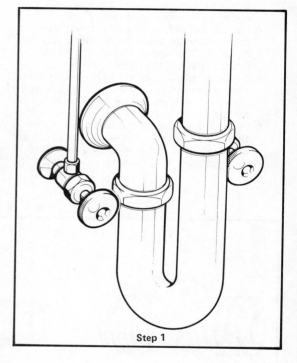

Step 1

6. Inspect the seat down in the faucet. If it is scarred or corroded, either clean and reface it with an inexpensive reseating tool or replace the seat itself. The reseating tool or valve seat grinder has cutting teeth. Insert the tool in the faucet and install the packing nut over it; then turn the handle to screw the tool down against the seat, causing the cutting teeth to grind the seat smooth. Make

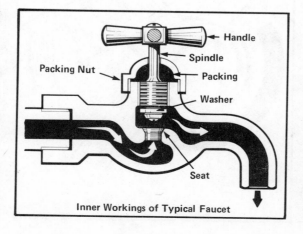

Inner Workings of Typical Faucet

Here Is What You Will Need

Materials

- Masking tape
- Replacement washer
- Replacement seat
- Petroleum jelly
- Replacement packing
- Repair kit for single-handle faucet

Tools

- Adjustable wrench
- Screwdriver
- Reseating tool or valve seat grinder

Fewer Parts Mean Fewer Problems

A new single-lever faucet designed with the idea in mind that fewer parts mean less trouble, Bradley Corporation's Bradtrol faucet valve—with one moving part that is kept completely isolated from the water—carries a 1000-month guarantee against leaks. With no washers, springs, or gaskets, no metal parts to corrode, and fewer moving parts, the permanently lubricated Bradtrol

valve is unlikely to cause problems. The Bradtrol valve is offered on Bradley faucets for both bath and kitchen.

Washer Sizes And Shapes

Hancock-Gross' assortment pack, a plastic carton filled with 100 washers, contains a number of different sized faucet washers. Smaller assortment packs are available, and most hardware stores can sell you the single washer you need. Often a packet of washers includes replacement brass screws as well, and it is generally wise to install a new screw with the new washer.

Getting The Nuts Out Of Those Recessed Shower Faucets

The nut that holds the spindle in a recessed shower faucet is set so far back that you need a special tool, a socket wrench, to get it out. The Hancock-Gross socket wrench set includes seven different deep-set wrenches, and should handle any situation a homeowner is likely to face.

Tips For Faucet Work

If you find it difficult to remove a handle from a faucet, squirt penetrating oil at the point where the stem and handle are joined, and then give it time to do its work. Remember, too, that when using any tool against chrome faucet parts, be sure to pad the parts to prevent scratches and mars.

O'Malley Reseating Kit Features Guide Cone

Among the many faucet seat dressing tools available, the one from O'Malley comes in kit form with new washers, brass screws to hold the washers in place on the spindle, self-forming packing, and a guide cone for easier dressing of faucets without cap nuts. The No. 31 O'Malley Drip Stopper Kit, just one of many offered by the company, has three different cutter heads for various sized faucets and comes with an extra long stem so that the tool may be used for recessed faucets in tubs and showers.

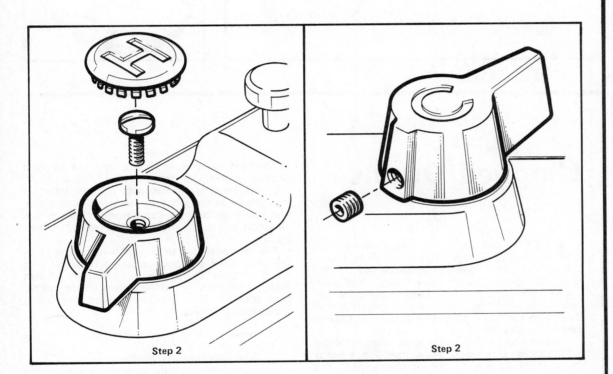

Step 2

Step 2

sure that the seat is smooth and shiny after using the tool.
7. Coat the threads of the spindle with petroleum jelly.
8. Reassemble the faucet, and turn the water back on.
If your faucet leaks around the handle only when the water is turned on, you need to replace the packing. Here is how to do that simple repair procedure.
△ 1. Remove the spindle as in steps 1, 2, and 3.
△ 2. If you have not already removed the handle

to get to the packing nut, remove the handle now.
△ 3. Slide the packing nut up off the spindle.
△ 4. The blob under the packing nut is the packing. It may be a solid piece, or it may be a string of black graphite material that is self forming. Replace the old packing with new packing of the same type.
△ 5. Coat the threads of the spindle with petroleum jelly.
△ 6. Reassemble the faucet and turn the water back on.

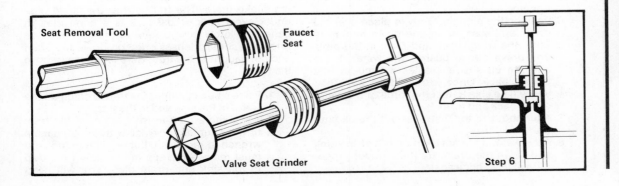

Seat Removal Tool Faucet Seat Valve Seat Grinder Step 6

Plumbing

Hair Snare Snares Hair

Hair that would otherwise go into the drain to cause possible problems can be kept out of drains with this simple device, the Hair Snare from O'Malley. The model shown has a cap to fit over the screen to act as a stopper, but basically the Hair Snare is a simple screen designed to trap all hair and other particles. The Hair Snare fits over almost every sink, tub, or shower drain, and can even go into lavatories with pop-ups.

Snake Container Cuts Down Mess

While the conventional plumber's auger gets the job done, the snake that is coiled in a housing makes the job easier and neater. Spin-Thru Drain Cleaners come in 10-, 15-, and 25-foot lengths. The model with the "T"-grip handle is a bit easier to use than the model with the wood grip, but both units save you from touching the mess that emerges with the snake from the pipe, and both keep the mess away from sink, tub, floor, and other clean surfaces. In addition, a plumber's auger in a housing is easier to store.

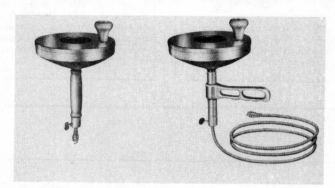

Ribbon Rids Rubbish

The flat sewer auger, often referred to as the plumber's ribbon, resembles a large clock spring. It is lightweight and, therefore, easy to handle despite its great length. The U-Plumb-It model comes in 25-, 50-, and 100-foot versions. The longer the ribbon, of course, the deeper you can probe into the sewer lines. Extremely flexible, the ribbon can follow the various turns in the pipes.

Aerosol Plungers Blast Clogs Away

The plumber's friend creates an up-and-down force to work against clogs in drains. If you want to avoid the tedious exercise involved in using a plumber's friend, though, try one of the aerosol drain cleaners such as Drano Instant Plunger from the Drackett Company. Just close off all other drain outlets, place the canister top down into the drain opening, and press. A blast of propellent shoots down through the pipe to dislodge the clog. Drano Instant Plunger has a two-piece cap that adapts to most drains, even those with grids and strainers that might restrict the use of other such products. A similar aerosol drain opener is called Drain Power, and both products can be found in grocery and hardware stores.

Clogged Drains

IT IS NOT surprising that home drain lines get clogged up. People put all kinds of things down the sink: grease, followed by coffee grounds, leftover salad, table scraps, and even cigarette butts. Once these items wash down the drain and disappear, who worries about them? Then one day, the kitchen sink goes on strike and refuses to take any more.

You should be able to clear the clogged drain with a plumber's friend or plunger. Since many clogs are close at hand, the plumber's friend can usually build up enough force and direct it against the clog to solve the problem. There are aerosol drain openers on the market that do the same thing, but they are no more effective than the plunger and are considerably more expensive. Just make sure that the rubber cup is big enough to cover the opening in the sink, and then follow these directions.

1. Cover any other openings to the drain pipe such as the other side of a double sink or an overflow drain.
2. Remove the stopper and/or strainer.
3. Brush aside the garbage around the drain opening.
4. Have at least an inch of water standing in the sink.
5. Place the cup of the plunger over the drain opening.
6. Position the plunger firmly in place over the drain, and start an up-and-down motion to force the water back and forth in the pipe. The down stroke pushes the water down, and the up stroke creates a vacuum that pulls it back. Once you build up a rhythm, you will be able to feel the force of the water going back and forth.
7. After about 15 to 20 strokes, lift the plunger up.
8. If the water does not swirl on out of the sink and down the drain, try the plunger procedure at least once again.

The next thing most people try on a clogged drain is a chemical drain cleaner. These chemicals are caustic and they can be dangerous. If they fail to do the job, they remain in your pipes, and you must be very careful not to splash this water on you or on anything that could be damaged.

The next best step to take after using the plunger is to drive a plumber's snake or auger into the drain pipe. The tool is so flexible that it can make its way around all the curves inside a drain pipe until it reaches the clog. Here is how to use the plumber's snake.

△ 1. Remove the stopper and/or strainer in the sink.
△ 2. Feed the snake into the drain.
△ 3. When it hits a turn, slide the handle up to within a few inches of the opening, tighten it, and start turning the snake until it negotiates the turn.
△ 4. Loosen the handle and slide it back out of the way.
△ 5. Keep feeding the snake in until it hits either another turn or the clog. Set the handle once more.
△ 6. When you finally do hit the clog, work the snake back and forth while at the same time turning the handle.
△ 7. When you feel the clog break loose, pull the snake back and forth a few more times, and then remove it from the drain pipe.
△ 8. Flush the line with hot water.

If you cannot get the snake down the sink drain, you can remove the trap under the sink and insert the snake there. The trap is that U-shaped pipe under every sink or basin. It is a good idea in general to know how to remove the trap because rings and contact lenses often go down the drain and get caught in the trap. Here is how to remove the trap.

○ 1. Place a bucket under the trap to catch all the water in the sink and in the trap.
○ 2. If you see a plug in the bottom of the trap, turn it counterclockwise with an adjustable wrench to remove it. If there is no plug, you must remove the slip nuts holding the trap to the sink and drain pipe. You will need

Plumber's Plunger Still A Good Friend

The old standby in the clogged drain department is the rubber force cup, commonly called the plumber's friend or plunger. Brand names are fairly insignificant; just be sure that the rubber is live and solid and that the cup is big enough to cover the drain opening. The U-Plumb-It plunger is fully adequate for handling most clogged drains in homes and apartments. Incidentally, the plumber's friend still offers an advantage over the new aerosol decloggers; it not only exerts force against the clog on the down stroke, but it also creates a vacuum on the up stroke that pulls at the clog. Often this pulling is more effective than the downward pressure in breaking up the mess.

Auger Attachment For Power Drills

Meet the electric snake, a plumber's auger designed to fit any size electric drill. Drill power—rather than your muscle power—does all the twisting to make the snake curve around bends in the pipe. A variable-speed drill operating at a very slow speed works best, and very short bursts of power from any drill are recommended for maneuvering the snake through the pipes. The Drainmaster Power Drain Auger from Chicago Specialty Manufacturing Company comes in 15- and 25-foot lengths.

Solvent Solves Stoppage Safely

Since most drain-cleaning chemicals are acids or caustics, they can be dangerous if handled improperly. CPM (Chemical Preventive Maintenance) is a solvent that safely dissolves grease, soap, and fat, the substances most responsible for clogs in drains. Deposits of grease, soap, and fat form in pipes and then collect hair and food stuffs to build into a clog. CPM transforms the deposits into a free-flowing liquid that will not solidify at another point in the drain. Of course, dissolving the grease and soap scum allows the other clogging material to wash away as well. Until recently, CPM was only available to industry and professional plumbers, but it is now being sold to consumers. If you cannot locate CPM at plumbing supply retailers, write

to the CPM Corporation (Arlington, N.J. 07032) to find out who distributes the product in your area. Once you purchase CPM, be sure to read the instructions on the can carefully; the solvent comes as a concentrate, and to use it undiluted is a waste.

---

either large pliers or a large adjustable wrench to turn the nuts counterclockwise. Make sure that you do not lose the washers under the nuts.

○ 3. Check to see if the clog is in the trap itself. If so, clean it out with a piece of wire or with the plumber's snake.

○ 4. If the clog is not in the trap, run the snake in at the cleanout plug or into the pipe leading

into the wall, following the same procedures as above.

○ 5. When replacing the trap or plug, smear some pipe joint compound (available at the hardware store) or some petroleum jelly on the threads.

○ 6. Run the water for a few minutes to make sure that you have the trap all back together properly so that it will not leak.

Snake Slithers To Problem

The Tuffy Drain Cleanout Auger, a product of Wrightway Manufacturing Company, is a typical plumber's snake. The handle can be moved to the most convenient spot and then locked in place with a thumbscrew. Tuffy comes in 6-, 8-, 10-, 15-, and 25-foot lengths, while other manufacturers offer models as long as 50 feet. Beyond that length, an auger becomes heavier and longer than most homeowners can handle and is better suited to industrial purposes.

Chemical Warfare

There are many chemical drain cleaners on the market, most of which do a good job of clearing slow-running drains; often they can even cure a completely clogged drain. Liquid-Plumr, a product of the Clorox Company, is available at grocery and hardware stores as well as in plumbing supply outlets. It is among the easiest of the chemical drain cleaners to apply, but like all such drain cleaners, it must be handled cautiously. Be sure to read and follow all of the safety instructions provided on the bottle.

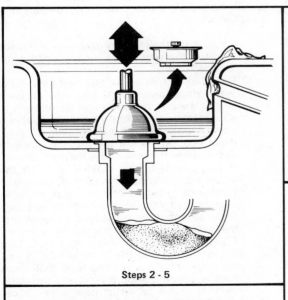

Steps 2 - 5

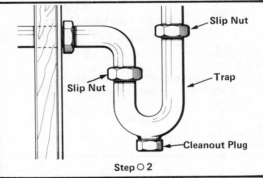

Step ○ 2

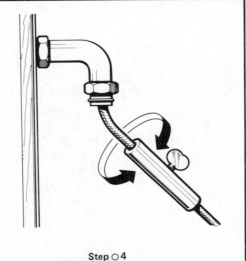

Step ○ 4

Here Is What You Will Need

Materials

- Aerosol drain opener
- Chemical drain cleaner
- Pipe joint compound or petroleum jelly

Tools

- Plumber's friend (plunger)
- Plumber's snake (auger)
- Adjustable wrench

Plumbing

Replace Tank Troublemakers

The Flusher Fixer Kit—a product of Fluidmaster, Inc.—does away with the conventional tank ball, lift wires, and guide. It features a vinyl type flapper and a non-corrosive stainless steel replacement seat. The installation requires no tools, and the new seat does not require removal of the tank, a tedious chore that often ends in a cracked tank. The unit is bonded to the existing flush valve seat with a watertight sealant, and since the flapper is hinged directly to the seat, there can be no mis-alignment.

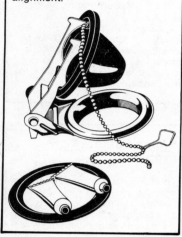

Keep John Quiet

Some ballcock units get to the point where they proclaim loudly to the entire neighborhood each time the toilet is flushed. Corrosion, worn parts, or faulty washers can cause all sorts of noises. The Fluidmaster 400-A is a replacement ballcock that promises quiet operation and long life. By eliminating the float ball and arm, the 400-A does away with two possible problem causers. When the Fluidmaster valve opens to let water into the tank, the valve remains wide open until the tank is full and then shuts off completely. The old-style ballcock, in contrast, gradually shuts off the supply as the float ball rises, and that gradual process can be a noisy one. The 400-A also is height adjustable so that it can fit any toilet tank. Installation is very easy and requires no special tools.

Shutoff Valve Easy To Install

A properly working shutoff supply valve is a must for a toilet or any other fixture. If the valve is defective, you can buy a replacement. Complete instructions are included in the packet. If the water supply comes out of the wall, you need an angled type of shutoff valve; if the supply pipe comes from the floor, get the straight type. The size of the valve, of course, is determined by the size of the supply pipe.

Complete Toilet Installation Kit

Installation of a replacement toilet is much easier when you use a kit like the one available from EZ Plumb. This kit contains everything you need for the installation, plus a very valuable extra—a well-illustrated instruction sheet. Included in the kit are the riser (water supply pipe), the wax gasket that seals the bottom of the unit where it connects to the drain, screws and bolts for mounting, the water cutoff, all the fittings needed for connections, the escutcheon plates that go around the entry into the floor, and even a roll of Teflon tape to seal all the threaded connections. EZ Plumb (like other manufacturers catering to the do-it-yourselfer) also offers kits for installing lavatories, sinks, and many appliances.

Toilet Tank Repairs

A FAULTY TOILET tank can send thousands of gallons of water down the drain and take a great deal of money out of your pocket to pay for the wasted water. In addition, the noise of the ever-flowing toilet can get on your nerves. Although the insides of a toilet tank may look very complicated, you can figure out how it works with no difficulty whatsoever.

Here is the way a toilet works.

1. You push the handle to flush.

2. The handle raises the trip lever inside the tank.
3. Since the trip lever is attached to the lift wires, they go up too.
4. The lift wires raise the tank ball from where it rests in an outflow hole, allowing water in the tank to run out into the bowl and clean it.
5. Meanwhile, the float ball—which had been floating on the top of the water in the tank—drops as the water in the tank rushes out.
6. The float arm moves down with the float ball, opening the valve which lets new water flow into the tank.
7. The tank ball falls back in place in the outflow hole, causing the new water to fill the tank.
8. As the water rises in the tank, it picks up the float ball and moves the float arm back up until the valve closes and no more water can enter.

Now that you know how the tank works, you can follow the procedure for fixing a continually running toilet.

△ 1. Remove the tank lid very carefully, and place it out of the way where it cannot fall or be stepped upon.
△ 2. Reach in and lift up on the float arm. If the water stops running, you know the problem is that the arm does not rise far enough to shut off the valve. Merely bend the float arm down slightly to correct the situation.
△ 3. If the float arm is not the problem, look to see whether the tank ball is properly seated. If you cannot tell by looking, turn off the water supply under the tank. A toilet that continues to run is one in which water is seeping out around the outflow opening. Make sure that the guide is in place so that the wires are directly above the opening. Rotate the guide until the tank ball falls straight down into the outflow hole. If you see any bent wires or a trip lever that is not exactly where it should be, bend the parts back in shape or install new ones. Occasionally the tank ball wears out, but it is easy to replace too. If all the parts seem to be in good shape, inspect the valve seat for corrosion on its lip. Such corrosion may be preventing the tank ball from sealing the opening. You can remove the residue with wet-dry emery paper, steel wool, or even a knife.
△ 4. If the toilet continues to run, then something is probably wrong with the valve in the ballcock assembly. This valve has one or more washers (often including a split leather washer) that can be replaced. To get at

Here Is What You Will Need

Materials

- Replacement guide wires or trip lever
- Replacement tank ball
- Wet-dry emery paper or steel wool
- Replacement washers for valve of ballcock assembly

Tools

- Knife

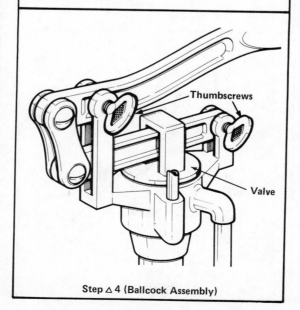

Thumbscrews

Valve

Step △ 4 (Ballcock Assembly)

Guides Lead Way To Less Trouble

The guide through which the wires move when the tank ball is raised up or dropped back in place can mean the difference in a properly working tank. If the guide becomes corroded or broken, it must be replaced promptly. Be sure to cut off the water supply and flush the tank before making the change; then align the guide properly after attaching it to the overflow tube. The guide from Plumb Craft, like other good models available, is quite inexpensive.

Flapper Flush Ball Eliminates Wires And Guides

While conventional type tank balls are still popular, more and more people are electing to do away with the wires and guide and install a flapper type replacement. The flapper's fewer parts often mean fewer problems. The Korky Flapper is typical of the good units available; others include the ones from Water Master Company, Wal-rich Corp., and the Sealmaster from Radiator Specialty Company.

Plastic Float Balls Popular

The metal float balls that were once the standard type have largely been replaced by plastic floats, such as the Supreme line made by the Schaul Manufacturing Company. Whether you opt for plastic or metal, though, be sure to replace a defective float ball promptly. The float ball is so inexpensive that attempting to patch a leaking ball makes very little sense.

Kits Include All Tank Parts

If all the parts within the toilet tank are causing problems, you can buy a kit like the one from U-Plumb-It that contains a ballcock unit, a tank ball, lift wires, a float ball, and the float rod. No special tools are needed to replace the troublesome tank parts, and most of the packaged kits offer excellent instructions.

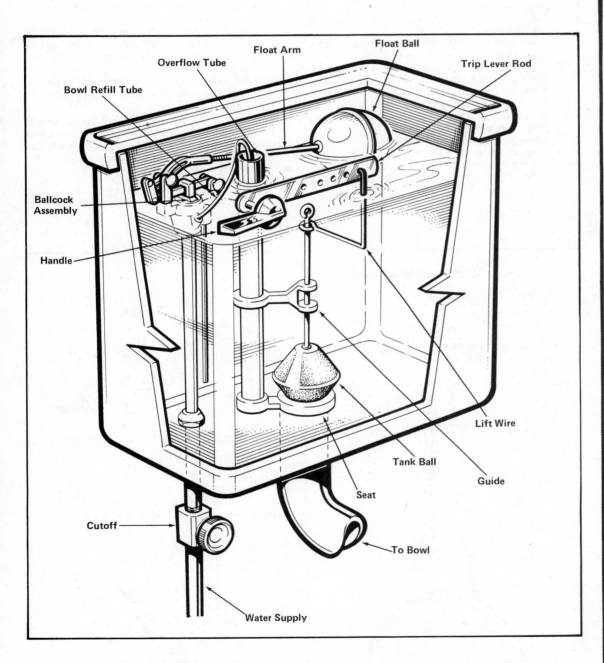

Ballcock Unit Senses Water Level From Tank Bottom

The Exelon FillValve is a compact unit that rests near the bottom of the toilet tank and shuts off the flow of water when its diaphragm senses (via water pressure) that the water level is right. The water level can be adjusted easily with a knob on the unit. Since the FillValve is so small, it fits all tanks; and since it is constructed almost entirely of plastic and other non-corrosive parts, Exelon offers a three-year guarantee. The Exelon FillValve does away with the float ball and its arm, and the unit can be easily installed without any special tools. Generally, the hardest part of the installation is removing the old ballcock.

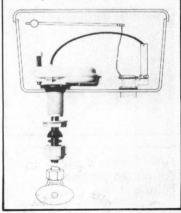

Free Folder Fights Faulty Flusher

A new homeowner's booklet about toilet repairs, "Troubleshooter's Guide to a Noisy Toilet Tank" is available from Fluidmaster, Inc., 1800 Via Burton, Anaheim, CA 92805. The booklet explains the causes of toilet tank problems and tells about the Fluidmaster products that can solve them.

---

the washers, remove the two thumbscrews and lift the valve out. Replace any and all faulty washers.

Here are some other basic repair procedures for toilet tanks.

○ 1. If the toilet makes a screaming noise as it fills, but works properly otherwise, replace the washers in the ballcock assembly valve.

○ 2. If the flush is inadequate, make certain that the level of water in the tank is sufficient; it should be about a half inch below the top of the overflow tube. If the water level is too low, bend the float arm up slightly. An inadequate flush might also result from the tank ball not going up far enough. Raise the guide to give the tank ball more room.

Plumbing

Convert Regular Snake For Toilet Clogs

Although a standard plumber's snake can often clear a toilet clog, the addition of an accessory guide tube—as found on a regular closet auger—usually makes the job much easier. Toilet tube attachments, such as the one from Wrightway Manufacturing Company, convert many snakes so that they are more manageable for countering closet clogs.

Special Plunger For Toilet Troubles

While the conventional plumber's friend generally works well on most toilet clogs, there are specially shaped plungers that do a better job. The Toilaflex is a good example. Its tapered sleeve fits into the toilet opening to prevent any loss of force from the cup. Made by the Water Master Company, the Toilaflex design also resists splash back as it concentrates full pressure toward the clog.

Replaceable Wax Ring Seals Toilet At Floor

Sometimes efforts at unclogging a toilet fail, and the bowl must be removed from the floor in order for the clogging object to be extracted from underneath. In such cases, the ring of plumber's putty or the wax ring that was there before must be replaced to seal the area where the bowl attaches to the floor. Packaged wax gaskets, which are far easier and less messy to work with than plumber's putty, are available with or without an imbedded plastic sleeve; the sleeve provides added security to the wax seal. The Seep-Seal shown is from the Galaxy Chemical Company.

Tuffy Closet Auger Tough On Clogged Toilets

The Tuffy closet auger, made by Wrightway Manufacturing Company, features a heat-tempered rod and a heavy-duty guide tube. It also has a rubber bowl guard which, considering how easy it is to crack the porcelain on toilet bowls, is a good feature to look for when buying a closet auger.

Clogged Toilets

FOR SOME REASON, children have a tendency to put things in the toilet—like toys, teddy bears, etc.—that clog up the john. Adults can be guilty as well, placing items on the tank lid that then accidentally get knocked into the bowl. The good old plumber's friend, or plunger, will usually clear the clog. You should be aware, though, that there is a plunger made especially for toilets. It has a special tapered lip that fits down snugly into the bowl. If you have frequent toilet clog troubles in your home, invest in a toilet plunger and then follow these steps.

1. Make sure that there is enough water in the bowl to cover the plunger, and then place the plunger over the outlet in the bottom. Keep in mind that you must allow room for the extra water the plunger will bring back into the bowl.
2. Push down on the plunger's handle, and start a steady up and down motion.
3. When you can feel that the force created by the plunger has the water rocking back and forth, lift the plunger out and check to see if any matter has been dislodged. If you unclog the drain, some of the water will probably rush out. If you dislodge a big wad of paper, use a wire coat hanger to break it up.
4. Pour some water from another source into the bowl; do not trip the handle to flush the toilet. Flushing the toilet while the clog is still present will produce an overflow, while pouring in some water from another source will tell you whether your work with the plunger did the job.

Stubborn clogs often require the use of a closet snake, a shorter version of the plumber's snake. Sometimes referred to as a closet auger, the closet snake has a crank at one end with a hollow metal tube housing the snake itself. You do not need a long snake for toilets, since the blockage cannot be very far away. Just be careful not to bang the auger against the bowl; it could break the porcelain. Here is what to do with the closet auger.

△ 1. Insert the snake into the outflow opening.
△ 2. Push it in until it hits the clog.
△ 3. Turn the crank, forcing the snake to move forward into the clog.
△ 4. Reverse the direction of the crank every few turns to prevent compacting whatever is causing the clog.
△ 5. Once the snake works its way through the clog, keep advancing and reversing the tool to be sure you remove everything that once blocked the drain.
△ 6. Pour water in the bowl from another source to make sure that the toilet drain is clear.

Another useful thing for clearing toilet clogs is one you can make yourself. Just straighten a wire coat hanger, but leave the hook at the end. You can generally fish out paper clogs, teddy bears, and whatever else is blocking the drain with the coat hanger hook.

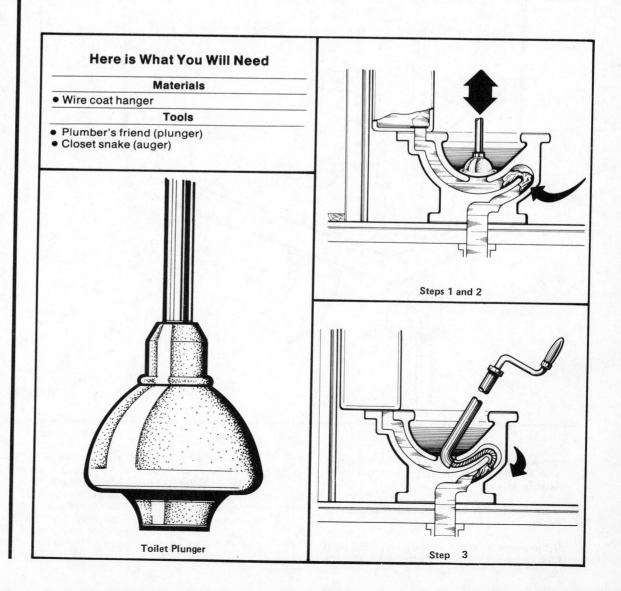

Here is What You Will Need

Materials
- Wire coat hanger

Tools
- Plumber's friend (plunger)
- Closet snake (auger)

Toilet Plunger

Steps 1 and 2

Step 3

New Top-Mount Seat Makes Installation Easy

If you've ever had to lie on the bathroom floor trying to fasten the nuts holding a toilet seat in place, you'll love the new top-mount system from Magnolia Products. The Magnolia seat mounts from above, and the only tool needed is a screwdriver. Just tighten the bolt and then flip the attached snap cap over to hide the bolt and protect it from dirt and moisture.

Of course, the Magnolia top-mount system is of no help in removing an old traditionally mounted toilet seat, but the new method makes future replacements a snap.

Complete Seat Hinge Units Available

If the toilet seat itself is still in good condition but the hinge is shot, you can buy a complete replacement hinge unit from the Chicago Specialty Manufacturing Company. These hinge replacement units come in both plastic and metal, and they fit most standard size bowls.

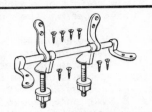

Church Changes Seat Shape

Toilet seats need not conform to a single conventional shape in order to fit a conventional toilet. The Church Four Hundred Series —available in several patterns and colors—is an example of a decorator shape that fits all regular toilets. Church seats (a product of American Standard) come with the company's exclusive Pop-Pins, which can be pulled out to allow both cover and seat ring to to be lifted off for easier cleaning. Church also offers top-mounting hinges on the Four Hundred Series and on many other toilet seat models.

Changing a Toilet Seat

THERE ARE so many styles of replacement toilet seats on the market that you should find it easy to match any bathroom color scheme or motif. Since most toilets are standard size, you will have no difficulty in getting a new seat and lid that fit. If your toilet is extra wide or very old, however, you may not be able to use a standard size replacement. You would probably have to place a special order with a firm that deals in plumbing fixtures.

1. The problem for most people is not in getting the new seat, but in removing the old one. Removal sounds simple. Remove the two nuts and lift the old unit up and out. What could go wrong? Wait until you try to loosen those two nuts. Usually, they are rusted or corroded, and sometimes they are recessed and practically inaccessible. Penetrating oil should help loosen the nuts. Give the oil plenty of time to work, and do not use too much muscle on the stubborn nuts. If your wrench were to slip, you could crack the tank or bowl or whatever else the wrench were to strike.

2. The inaccessible nuts may require a deep throated socket wrench, but if all else fails, a hacksaw inserted under the hinge can saw through the bolts. Start sawing, however, only after you are convinced that nothing is going to break the nuts loose. Again, be extremely cautious so as not to hit anything with the hacksaw.

3. Once the old seat is off, the new one goes on simply by replacing the bolts and tightening the nuts. Be careful not to overtighten the nuts.

4. If the lid and seat are still in good condition, but the little rubber bumpers are shot, your hardware dealer can sell you replacements. Some of these bumpers are screw-ins, while others are nailed in. Try to install the new ones in new holes that are close enough to the old holes so that the new bumpers cover the old holes.

Here Is What You Will Need

Materials
- Replacement seat
- Penetrating oil
- Replacement bumpers

Tools
- Wrench
- Socket wrench
- Hacksaw

5. If you live in an apartment and put on a new mod seat and lid unit, be sure to keep the old one. When you are ready to leave, put the old toilet seat back on and take your fancy new one along with you to your next abode.

Step 1

Soft Seats

Several toilet seat makers offer padded units. National Seat Manufacturing Company's So-Soft seat is a popular replacement. National's extra-heavy gauge vinyl covering is heat sealed and comes in more than 150 patterns and colors to match any bathroom decor.

Seat Bumpers

Both the toilet seat's outside cover and seat ring usually have bumpers which frequently become lost or damaged. Replacement sets like the ones from Jiffy are available at all plumbing supply retailers, and in most cases installation of replacement seat bumpers is quick and easy.

Plumbing

Heat Tapes Have Thermostats

Some heat tapes, like Thermwell Products' Frost King Automatic Electric Heat Cable, come with a built-in thermostat. Merely wrap the cable around the pipe and then plug it into regular house current. The built-in thermostat then prevents the pipe temperature from falling below the freezing level. Frost King Automatic Electric Heat Cables are available in lengths from three to 60 feet, while the company's heat tapes without thermostats come in lengths up to 30 feet.

Prevent Problems With Electric Heat Tape

Did you know that you can protect pipes from freezing down to minus 50 degrees Fahrenheit? Wrap-On Heat Tape, from Wrap-On Company, comes in several lengths and plugs right into the house current. Just wrap the Heat Tape around the pipe and then leave it on year-round, unplugging it during warmer times. Other major companies marketing similar products include Cox and Co., Wirekraft, York Home Products, GE, Edwin L. Wiegand, and Hancock-Gross.

Thawing Frozen Pipes

WHEN WINTER sets in, the water in unprotected pipes can freeze. Of course, it is a great inconvenience not to have water, but that is only a temporary problem. The expansion caused by freezing can rupture the pipe, and then you really have a major plumbing problem on your hands.

The best time to fight frozen pipes is before the freeze sets in. By taking the proper preventative steps, you may never have to worry about thawing frozen pipes. Here are some freeze-fighting tips.

1. If you are building a new house or adding pipes underground, be sure to bury them below the frost line if possible. Since this depth is different in different parts of the country, check with your local United States Weather Bureau to learn about the frost line in your community.
2. Make sure that new pipes are as well insulated as is practical. Run the pipes along your home's inner walls instead of along the outside walls.
3. Install frost-free faucets outside, and when the cold weather sets in, cut off the outside faucets and open the tap to drain the exposed pipe and faucet.
4. If you have a stretch of pipe that is subject to freezing, invest in heat tape (sometimes called heat cable). You can buy tape that has an automatic thermostat to start the heat when the temperature outside drops to about 35 degrees.

The suggestions above will be of little value or consolation when you wake up to find a pipe frozen solid. Here are some hints on thawing frozen pipes.

△ 1. Before applying any heat to the pipe, open the tap so that the steam produced by the thawing can escape. Start your heat at the tap and work back toward the source of the freeze. This way, as the ice melts, the water and/or steam will come out the open tap. If you were to start in the middle, the expansion as the ice melts and becomes steam could build up enough pressure to burst the pipe.

△ 2. One very popular and safe heat source for thawing pipes is simply hot water. The heat can be concentrated by wrapping the pipe with a heavy towel or burlap bag; the towel holds the heat and lets it surround the pipe. Pour very hot water over the towel. Since most of the water runs off, be sure to have a bucket on hand to avoid one heck of a mess.

△ 3. A less messy way to heat pipes is with a propane torch, but you must be extremely careful to insure that the heat does not ignite a wall behind the pipe. A scrap of asbestos siding or some other fireproof material behind the flame can help, but never leave the flame in one spot. Keep it moving back and forth. Above all, pass over any

Here Is What You Will Need

Materials
- Frost-free faucets
- Heat tape or cable
- Hot water
- Heavy towel or burlap bag
- Bucket
- Asbestos scrap

Tools
- Propane torch
- Heat lamp
- Electric iron
- Garden hose
- Funnel

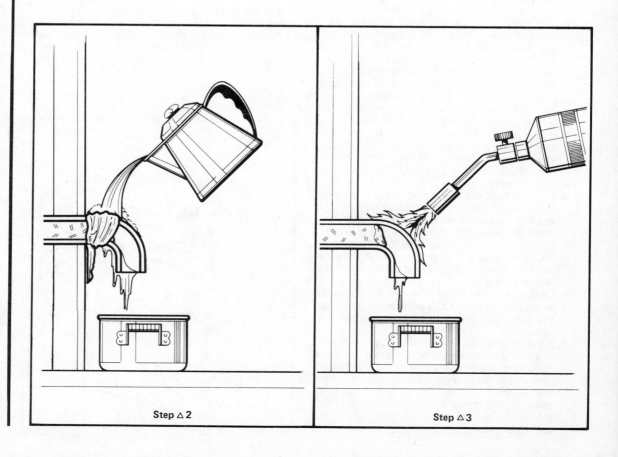

Step △ 2

Step △ 3

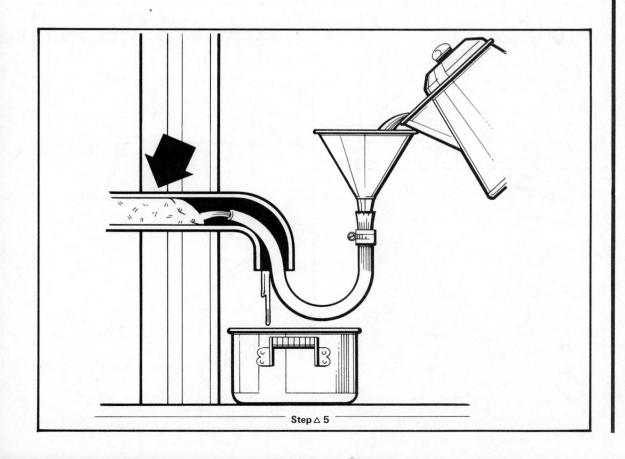

Step △ 4

Step △ 4

soldered joints very quickly; otherwise, you could cause an even bigger problem than you already have.

△ 4. Other heat sources include heat lamps, hair blowers, and electric irons. They are very slow, but are safe.

△ 5. In the case of a frozen drain pipe, the best way to go is to put hot water down the drain. Sometimes, however, you may need to get the water closer to the actual ice blockage. In such cases, remove the trap and insert a short length of garden hose into the pipe. When the hose gets to the solid ice and can no longer be pushed through, raise the outside end and — with the aid of a funnel — feed the hot water in. This is the best way to get the hot water to the problem area. Of course, until the ice melts and drains down the pipe, the hot water you insert will back up at you. Have a bucket ready under the pipe, and be careful not to scald yourself when the back-flow process begins.

Step △ 5

Propane Torch Thaws Pipes Fast

When used with caution, a propane torch makes a fine heat source for thawing a frozen pipe quickly. While there are many excellent torches available, one of the better ones is the Tornado, a product of the Turner Company. The HT-99 seven-piece propane Gas Torch Kit comes in a metal chest and has many uses in addition to thawing frozen pipes.

Blow Out Ice Blocks

Try attaching the hose and crevice tool to the vacuum cleaner's blower end and directing the air flow at the frozen pipe.

Fiberglass Covers Heat Tape

Frost King is offering pipe protection kits comprising fiberglass pipe wrap and a plastic outer wrap. Manufactured by Thermwell Products Company, Inc., the various kits contain three- and six-inch wrap in lengths from 25 to 50 feet. This kind of additional wrapping material is especially valuable when placed over thermostatically controlled electric heat tapes, keeping heat loss to a minimum and thus consuming less energy. In moderate climates, the Frost King wrap alone is often adequate protection against frozen pipes, and the wrap is also very handy in preventing pipes from sweating and in minimizing the heat loss from hot water pipes.

Electrical

Cartridge Fuses

Cartridge fuses come in several sizes to handle a wide variety of amperages. They also come in two styles: the knife blade type and the ferrule type. Read the size and type from the side of the old fuse to get the proper replacement. Like Type S fuses, cartridge fuses are also available in time-delay versions. There are also renewable cartridge fuses in which the old link can be replaced with a new link after an end cap is removed.

Fuse That Can Tell You What's Wrong

Eagle's "O.K." fuse tells you at a glance whether it is still good, and, if not, why it blew. If the "O.K." is intact, the fuse is still good. An overloaded circuit causes part of the "O.K." to disappear, while a dead short eliminates all of the "O.K." These handy Eagle glass plug type fuses come in all the standard sizes.

Put An End to Fuse Changing

The Mini-Breaker Fuse from Montgomery Ward is typical of the reset type fuses that can replace ordinary plug fuses. When the circuit becomes overloaded or when a short develops, the button pops out. All you need do to reset the fuse is push the button back in. Mini-Breaker Fuses come in 15-, 20-, and 30-amp sizes. While they cost more than regular fuses, they are certainly much more convenient.

Power Failure

ALTHOUGH IT IS annoying when the electricity goes out, most people just flip the circuit breaker or put in a new fuse and forget about it. That may be all that is necessary. On the other hand, you should know that a tripped circuit breaker switch or a blown fuse is a warning that something is wrong within your electrical system. Fuses blow and circuit breakers trip when there is too much heat in the wires of a particular circuit; the fuse or circuit breaker then acts as a safety device to keep a fire from starting. The excessive heat can be caused by an overload or by a short circuit.

An overload generally means that you have too many devices operating on that one circuit, but it can also mean that you have a temporary overload that occurs when a large appliance motor (like a refrigerator) comes on. It takes about three times as much current to get a motor started as it does to keep it going. A short circuit occurs when a bare wire touches either another wire or something metal. The short can be in an appliance, a lamp, or in the house wiring itself.

If you have fuses, you will keep blowing new ones every time you put them in, if you fail to find the cause. Here is how to track down the reason for a fuse blowing or a circuit breaker switch tripping.

1. The first thing to do is check everything on that particular circuit. Test each outlet by plugging in a lamp, and be sure to check all the overhead lights too. Make a list of everything on the blown circuit.
2. Now turn off or disconnect every appliance or light on that circuit.
3. Go to the service entry box (fuse box), and locate the blown fuse or tripped circuit breaker switch.

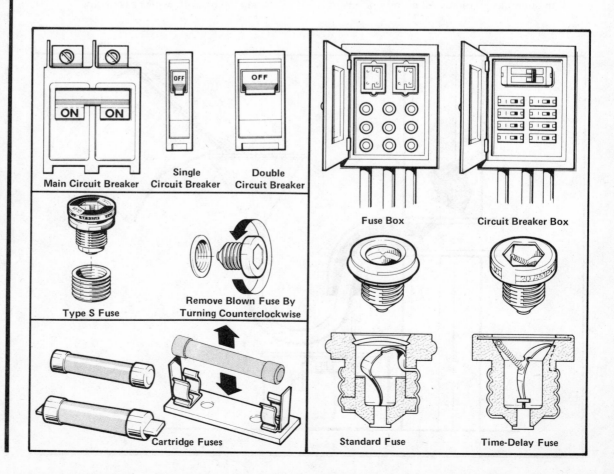

Main Circuit Breaker

Single Circuit Breaker

Double Circuit Breaker

Type S Fuse

Remove Blown Fuse By Turning Counterclockwise

Cartridge Fuses

Fuse Box

Circuit Breaker Box

Standard Fuse

Time-Delay Fuse

Your Own Power Plant Fights Blackouts

Just think of the things in your home that depend on electrical power. Then think about what would happen should a storm, flood, accident, mechanical breakdown, or other unforeseen event knock out that power. You can protect your home from such a calamity with a standby power system, which can be installed for home use without rewiring your house. The Onan Standby System mounts near the base of your electric utility meter and takes up

no more room than an air conditioner condenser. A small connection is made to the meter box, and the unit itself is covered with attractive sound-reducing fiberglass. A qualified electrician should be called in to handle certain aspects of the installation (as described in Onan's literature), and the completed installation should be examined by a representative of the local electrical utility company. If you experience frequent power failures in your area, you may find that the Onan Standby System is a very useful—though costly—addition to your home.

Tamper-Proof Fuses

Some people are foolish enough to cancel the protection a fuse provides by installing a fuse designed to carry a bigger load than the circuit should properly handle. To prevent such an installation from occurring by mistake, you can insert an adapter in your fuse box that converts the regular Edison base fuse holder into one that will hold only the right Type S fuse. You screw the fuse into the adapter and then screw both into the fuse box. The adapter then becomes locked in place because a small metal spur sticks out to prevent its removal. The Buss Fustat Type S fuse (a time-delay fuse to handle temporary overloads without blowing) and adapter are quite popular, but there are several other quality models available.

4. Replace the fuse or push the switch back to the "on" position. If the fuse blows or the switch trips immediately, you know that there must be a short in the wiring since no lights or appliances are hooked to the circuit. Check light fixtures, outlets, and wall switches for shorts. Look for either a loose connection or a frayed or bare wire. If you cannot locate any such problem after checking all the wiring you can find, the problem is probably within the walls. Unless you have some electrical expertise, this is the time to call in the professional electrician.

5. If the fuse did not blow or the switch did not trip, go back in and start plugging in or turning on each appliance or light one at a time. When you get to the one that has a short, the circuit will blow again. Unplug that light or appliance and get it fixed. Now you can plug everything back in and restore the power once more.

6. If nothing you plugged in or turned on in-

dicates a problem, go back and plug in all of the things that were on at the time of the blackout. If you have a blackout again, you know that the circuit is overloaded. All you need do is move some of the devices to another circuit.

7. If the fuse blows often and you notice that it occurs when a motor (such as an air conditioner or a refrigerator) comes on, you know you have a temporary overload. Replace the regular fuse with a time-delay fuse. A time-delay fuse can withstand a short-term overload without blowing, but it still gives you the protection you need.

Never replace a fuse with one that is rated to carry more amps than the one you took out. In addition, never put a penny behind a fuse or try to bypass it in any other way; you would be asking for an electrical fire. One more thing: respect the service entry box. Stand on a dry board, have dry hands, and use only one hand to trip switches or change fuses.

Fuse Pullers Enhance Safety

If your cartridge fuses are hard to reach, you would be wise to invest in an inexpensive fuse puller. Made of nonconducting materials, the holders come in various sizes to match the different sizes of cartridge fuses, although several models can handle more than one size fuse. Any homeowner who must change cartridge fuses would do well to attach a fuse puller to a string and hang the string on the wall next to the fuse box. The two different types of fuse pullers shown here are made by Bussman Manufacturing.

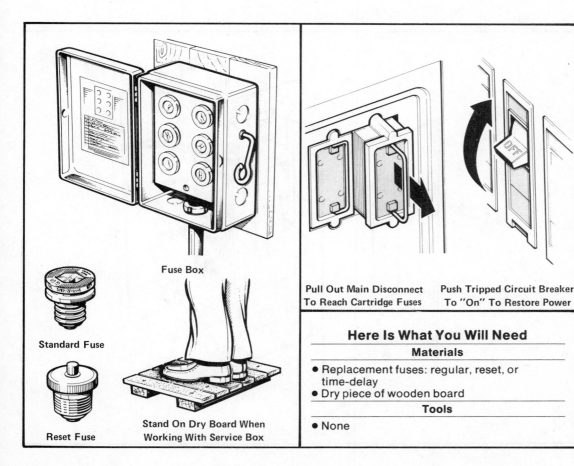

Fuse Box

Standard Fuse

Reset Fuse

Stand On Dry Board When Working With Service Box

Pull Out Main Disconnect To Reach Cartridge Fuses

Push Tripped Circuit Breaker To "On" To Restore Power

Here Is What You Will Need
Materials
- Replacement fuses: regular, reset, or time-delay
- Dry piece of wooden board

Tools
- None

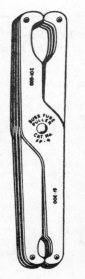

Electrical

Aluminum Wiring Needs Special Fixtures

Periodic copper shortages have resulted in certain homes being wired with aluminum. Since aluminum is not as good a conductor as copper, larger sized wires are required. Moreover, aluminum expands and contracts at a greater rate than copper, loosening the wires in the connections. Loose wires constitute a definite safety hazard, creating the possibility of a fire. If your receptacles and switches are of the CO/ALR variety, however, the special gripping surfaces on the terminals will prevent wires from loosening. CO/ALR fixtures (these are from GE and Eagle) are plainly marked. If you have aluminum wiring, it would be a good idea to check all connections annually, but be sure to cut off all current before working with any switches or outlets. When you need to replace any of these fixtures, do so with CO/ALR units.

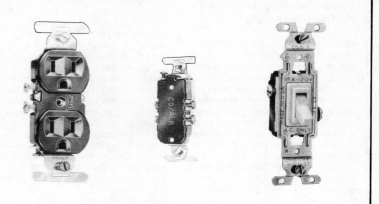

Turn On And Off Quietly

Anytime that you have to replace a light switch, spend a little more and buy the silent-operating type. Eagle's Quiet Switch boasts a dust apron that has an internal baffle to keep dust from getting into the switch. Your old wall plate will fit around the toggle and its dust apron. Featuring E-Z Wired connections, Eagle's Quiet switch can also be connected with regular side screws. There are several methods for manufacturing a switch that operates noiselessly, and some—like the mercury switch—are more expensive than others.

Dimmer Switches Replace Regular Wall Units

Hemco's dimmer switches are typical of the moderately priced units found in hardware stores, home centers, and even in the larger drug and variety stores. Full-range dimmers allow you to dial the illumination you want from completely off to fully on. Hi-lo controls mean there are but two settings—bright or dim. Either type fits into the space occupied by a conventional wall switch, making changeover simple. Even a rectangular switch plate opening can be covered by the round dimmer dial, although many dimmers come with their own switch plates.

Replacing a Wall Switch

WHEN YOU WALK into a dark room, flip the switch, and nothing happens, your first impulse is to change the bulb. Usually that is the problem, but one of these days you just might discover that the switch has gone bad. Never fear, replacing a broken wall switch is an inexpensive and easy do-it-yourself repair job.

If the switch is the only one that controls the fixture, it is called a single-pole switch. If there are two switches that control the same light, then it is called a three-way switch. Here is how to replace a single-pole switch.

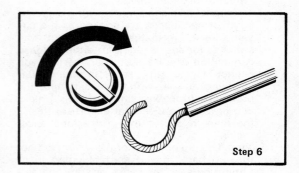

Step 6

1. Cut off the power to the switch; unscrew the appropriate fuse or trip the appropriate circuit breaker switch.
2. Remove the cover plate by turning the

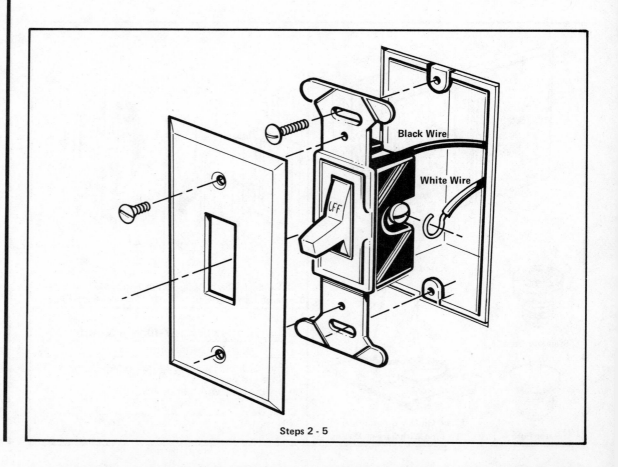

Steps 2 - 5

24

GE's Dimmer With Lighted Dial

General Electric's Premier full-range dimmer features a lighted dial that adjusts brightness to any level. The Premier, GE's finest home dimmer, can be wired for either single-pole or three-way application. It features a push switch, advanced high attenuation filtering of radio interference, 600-watt capacity, and enhanced surge resistance for cooler operation.

Switches Go Mod

The light switches in your home need not conform to an old-fashioned style. Many companies are marketing decorator switches that are installed in the same way as conventional units. Leviton's new Decora Designer line of its rocker switches, receptacles, and wall plates prove how attractive the new styles can be. You can also achieve a new look without changing the entire switch apparatus. There are hundreds of easily installed decorator wall plates made of various metals, plastics, and woods in all sorts of colors, textures, and shapes.

No Installation Plug-In Dimmer

You can convert any plug-in incandescent light fixture into a full-range dimmer light without any wiring work whatsoever. The attractive table-top dimmer from Leviton plugs into a wall outlet, and then the light fixture merely plugs into the dimmer unit. That's all there is to this noninstallation.

---

screws on its face counterclockwise.
3. Remove the two screws holding the switch to the junction box.
4. Grasp the switch and pull it out from the box. It should come out several inches. Observe the way the switch is hooked up. Most will have two wires connected to the switch. Some will be wired as below.
5. Remove the two wires to the switch by turning the screws counterclockwise.
6. The new switch has two screws. Put the wires under the screws with the curls going in the same direction—clockwise—you turn the screws to tighten them. Tighten the screws.
7. Push the wires back into the junction box, and press the switch back against the box. Reinstall the screws that hold the switch in place.
8. Replace the cover plate with its face screws.
9. Restore the power.

Here Is What You Will Need
Materials
● Replacement single-pole or three-way switch
Tools
● Screwdriver

If you have a three-way switch, very little more is involved. The difference is that a three-way switch has an extra wire, usually a red one. All of the same safety precautions apply to changing such a switch. All you do differently is make a note of where each wire is attached to the old switch, and then attach the wires the same way to the new three-way switch.

Stick-On Switch

Switchpack Systems, Inc., of Del Mar, California, has introduced a system that allows for the addition of a wall switch without having to cut a hole in the wall. The self-sticking wiring is so thin that it can be wallpapered or painted over; two coats completely hide the paper-thin wires. A transformer steps down the current that passes through the stick-on wires to a mere two volts. If you opt for the plug-in version of the Surface Switch, you don't even have to shut off the power during the installation. Just mount the outlet to the wall right next to a wall outlet, plug it in, and then plug the lamp or appliance you wish to control into the Surface Switch receptacle.

In-Line Dimmer Switch

Plug-type pole or swag lamps can easily be changed to full-range dimmer lamps. This feed-through switch, a product of Leviton Manufacturing Company, Inc., can be installed easily into the lamp cord. Leviton's Kwikwire pins make contact through the wires and connect the switch automatically; no tools are necessary to install this switch.

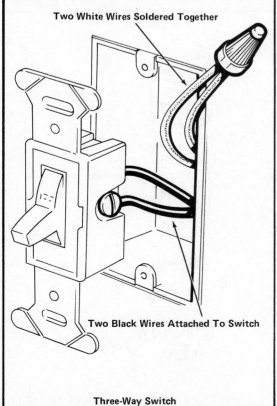

Two White Wires Soldered Together

Two Black Wires Attached To Switch

Three-Way Switch

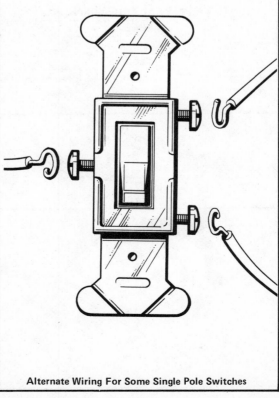

Alternate Wiring For Some Single Pole Switches

Electrical

Socket Replacements

Standard socket replacement units—like these from Eagle—come in keyless (no switch), keyed, pull chain, and push-through types. All are interchangeable. Three-way sockets, which of course require three-way bulbs, are also interchangeable with standard sockets. You can also buy just the interior part of the socket alone.

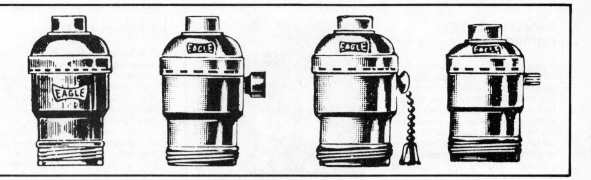

Wire Stripper-Electrician's Pliers

A pair of electrician's pliers is a necessary tool for the home handyman who plans to do any wiring. Most electrician's pliers also serve as wire strippers and terminal crimpers. The tool pictured is from the Stanley Tools Division of the Stanley Works and can be found in many retail outlets that carry electrical repair supplies. A quality tool for home use, it features insulated grips for comfort and safety, and it can cut several sizes of small bolts or screws cleanly with minimal effort. Since a good pair of electrician's pliers is relatively inexpensive and can last a lifetime, be sure to stick with brand name tools which are well known for quality.

Dimmer Lamp

A special socket replacement will add a new dimension to any lamp. The Leviton dimmer socket is installed just like the conventional socket, but it converts any incandescent lamp into an energy-saving, mood-enhancing dimmer lamp.

Replacing a Lamp Socket

DO YOU HAVE a lamp that flickers, one that refuses to come on until you jump up and down on a certain board in the floor, or one that just will not work no matter what you do? The problem could be a defective bulb, plug, wiring, or socket. If you find that the socket is the culprit, you can repair it easily and safely. Socket repairs are made without any electrical current flowing to the lamp. It makes no difference whether your lamp has a pull chain, a push button switch, or no switch at all; all conventional sockets are installed in the same manner. Even three-way sockets hook up the same way.

1. Unplug the lamp.
2. Remove the bulb.
3. Remove the old socket from its base or cap. Usually all you have to do is press on the brass outer shell with your thumb and forefinger, but stubborn sockets may require that you will pry them out with a screwdriver. Usually, the base from the old socket will still be good and can be used.
4. Slide off the cardboard insulating sleeve.
5. Loosen the screws that hold the two wires to the socket.
6. Check the wires. The tiny strands must be twisted to form a single unit with no stray strands. If the ends are in disarray, snip them off and strip the insulation back to expose about 3/4 of an inch of bare strands. Twist the strands into one neat wire.
7. Curl the wire ends in a clockwise direction to fit around the screws of the new socket.
8. Tighten the screws.
9. Replace the insulating sleeve and outer shell back over the socket.
10. Snap the entire unit back into the lamp base, and check to make sure that it is in good and tight.
11. Install the bulb, plug in the lamp, and take a moment to marvel at your repair skills.

Many ceiling and wall fixtures possess the same type of sockets as found on standard table lamps. The installation is just about the same, but since you cannot unplug a wall or ceiling fixture, you must unscrew the fuse or trip the circuit breaker to make certain that no current goes to the fixture while you are working on it.

Here Is What You Will Need

Materials
- Replacement socket

Tools
- Screwdriver
- Wire cutters
- Insulation stripper or knife

Step 6

Step 7

Brass Outer Shell

Cardboard Insulating Sleeve

Socket

Base Or Cap

Pliers For Electrical Work

Generally, the same tools you use for other home fix-it chores can be used for electrical repairs. One special tool, though, can come in very handy for forming loops when connecting wires to screws. Long-nosed pliers, such as this pair from Indestro's Classic tool line, feature thin jaws that are cross grooved for better holding power. This tool also has cutting edges for electrical wire cutting, and the handles have bonded vinyl plastisol grips.

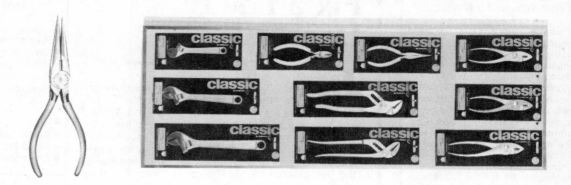

Screwdriver Strips And Cuts Electrical Wiring

The Stanley Tools division of the Stanley Works offers a screwdriver called the Strip-Driver. It is designed to cut wire and strip off insulation with little effort and great speed. Merely insert the wire in the tool's slot until it protrudes from the proper hole, and then press down on the handle while the screwdriver tip is on a solid surface. The Strip-Driver gives a clean cut on wire up to 12 gauge. Stripping is accomplished by inserting the wire into the lower part of the slot and out of the bottom

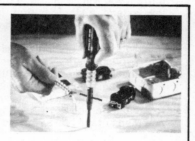

hole. Then set the knurled dial to the correct number for the wire gauge. Again place the screwdriver tip on a solid work surface and press down on the handle;

then pull the wire out of the tool to strip the insulation off the wire. Naturally, the tool can also be used as a conventional screwdriver.

A Tool Tip

You can add insulation to your pliers by slipping a length of small diameter rubber hose on each handle and wrapping other metal parts with electrician's tape. The shank of a screwdriver can be insulated by slipping a section of rubber or plastic tubing over it. Cut the tubing so that it extends from the handle down to the blade. The best "insulation," of course, is a trip to the fuse or circuit breaker box to shut off the current for the circuit you're working on.

Replacing a Wall Outlet

VERY OFTEN, PEOPLE plug in an appliance and when nothing happens they mistakenly blame the appliance for malfunctioning when the real culprit is the wall outlet. If you have a faulty outlet, the first thing you need to determine before trying to replace it is whether you need to buy a grounded or ungrounded receptacle. It is easy to tell the difference. The grounded outlet has a third hole for a three-pronged plug. Once you purchase the proper replacement, just follow these steps to install it.

1. Cut off the power to that circuit by either unscrewing the fuse or tripping the circuit breaker.
2. Remove the single screw in the middle of the face plate that holds the plate to the wall.
3. With the face plate off, remove the two screws that hold the outlet to the junction box.
4. Pull the outlet from the box. The outlet's wires will allow it to come out several inches.
5. Before loosening the screws to remove the wires, take note of how each wire is connected. You must attach the new outlet the same way. Hook any black wires to the side with the brass screws, and white wires to the side with the silver screws. Attach the green or uninsulated wire to the green screw of a grounded outlet.
6. Push the unit back in place in the junction box and secure it with the two screws.
7. Reattach the face plate with its screw.
8. Restore the power.

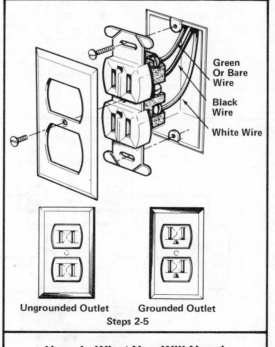

Green Or Bare Wire

Black Wire

White Wire

Ungrounded Outlet   Grounded Outlet
Steps 2-5

Here Is What You Will Need
Materials
- Replacement grounded or ungrounded receptacle

Tools
- Screwdriver

Grounded Receptacles Are Easy To Replace

If your grounded outlet goes bad, you can put in a new one yourself without much trouble. You must, however, buy a grounded replacement unit, and be sure to shut off the current before you start working. The installation follows the same procedure as that for installing an ungrounded outlet except for the additional attachment of the ground wire to the green screw at the bottom of the receptacle. This Eagle grounded duplex receptacle (accommodates two plugs) can be connected by pushing the wire into special holes (E-Z Wire) or by wrapping the wire around screws in the traditional manner. Remember your electrical system is not automatically grounded by merely installing a grounded receptacle. There must be a ground wire in the system that is actually grounded.

Electrical

From Noise To Music

If you have an annoying buzzer to announce visitors at your door, you could probably change to a musical chime system without much difficulty. The existing wiring and the outside push button would probably accommodate the new unit. In most cases, however, a new transformer would be required. Attractive chime units—the elaborate Monticello design, which comes with or without long chime tubes, and the very simple Accent model for the contemporary home—are available from Nu-Tone.

All Kinds Of Buttons

The most frequent source of difficulty affecting doorbells and chimes is the push button. Fortunately, a faulty push button is easy to replace. Brand names are relatively unimportant; just select a button that will fit in the same opening as the old one and that blends well with the exterior of your home. GE's Sculpturesque lighted decorator buttons are quite popular. There are also buttons with a slot for your name.

Transformers Lower Doorbell Voltage

Almost every doorbell, chime, and buzzer operates on low voltage. Some are battery-powered, but most, by far, run off of house current that is transformed from 110-120V to the 10-16V required. The little gadget that handles this conversion is the transformer. Name brands are generally not important; just make sure you buy a transformer of the proper size. It must match the primary voltage (the voltage going in your house current) and the secondary voltage (the voltage required by the bell or chime unit). The other important thing to consider is how the transformer will be mounted. The Eagle Handi-Mount transformer not only can be mounted on the surface with screws holding the four pronged feet, but it can also be mounted to the side of a metal junction box through a knockout hole. It features a thermal safety control and comes with instructions and wiring diagram.

Fix a Faulty Doorbell

IT IS AMAZING how many people shy away from even trying to fix a faulty doorbell, considering what a simple hookup is involved. There are only four components to check, and the first one you look at—the push button—is usually the problem. Fortunately, the button is also the easiest component to fix. The other components are the bell or chime unit, the transformer, and the wiring.

You should be aware of how much electric current you will be facing. A doorbell runs on very low voltage. A single button unit may operate on only 12 volts, while a unit with separate buttons at the front and back may involve from 16 to 24 volts. Most doorbell repair experts will tell you that these voltages are too low for you to bother cutting the power to the circuit, but even though none of these voltages can harm you, 24 volts is enough to make you feel the shock. Therefore, try to avoid touching the wires while troubleshooting, and then cut the power while doing the repairs.

1. First, check the button. Buttons wear out and go bad before any of the other components in most cases. To check the push button, remove its face plate.
2. Disconnect the wires to the button unit.
3. Touch the two wires together. If the bell rings, you know that everything else is in good shape. The trouble is in the button itself.
4. Scrape the ends of the wires and sand the contact points on the button to get rid of any corrosion.
5. Hook up the wires again and try the button. If it still fails to work, go buy a new button.
6. On the other hand, if the bell failed to ring when you touched the wires together, you know that the problem lies elsewhere. The next part to check is the buzzer or chime unit. Check the connections going into the unit to make sure that the wires are clean and that the terminals are tight. Inspect the bell clapper to make certain that it is close enough to the bell to hit it. If you have a set of chimes, clean the striker rods carefully with a solvent. After cleaning and checking the connections, disconnect the bell unit from its circuit and hook up a 12-volt test light (you can make one with a 12-volt auto bulb in a socket with two wires coming from it) to check the bell unit itself. If the light glows when you push the doorbell, you need a new bell. With a unit that has a back door button, remove only the wire marked "transformer" and one other—either the one marked "front" or "rear"—and hook them to the light. If the doorbell button lights the bulb, you can be doubly certain that the trouble is in the bell unit.
7. If the unit checks out, meaning the light fails to go on when you push the door buttons, you must next test the transformer. Keep in mind that there are 110 volts on one side of the transformer; therefore, be sure to unscrew the fuse or trip the circuit breaker before you touch the transformer.
8. With the power turned off, hook the test light to the low voltage side of the transformer. Restore the power. If the light comes on, you know that the transformer is all right. If not, you will need a standard electrical testing light to check the other side of the transformer for current flow from the power source.
9. If the transformer checks out, then the trouble must be in the wiring. When you locate the bad section, inspect it to see if it can be repaired. If not, replace the faulty wire. To run new wire inside the walls, splice the new to the old wire. As you pull the old wire out from the other end, it will pull the new wire through the walls and into position.

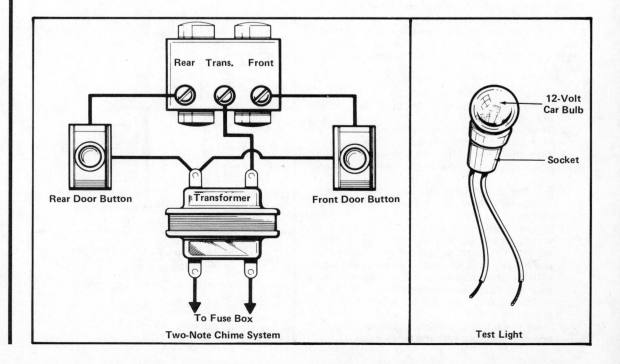

Rear   Trans.   Front

Rear Door Button   Front Door Button

Transformer

To Fuse Box

Two-Note Chime System

12-Volt Car Bulb

Socket

Test Light

Replacing a Plug

Here Is What You Will Need

Materials

● Electrical plug

Tools

● Wire cutters
● Screwdriver

A FAULTY PLUG can put your lamp or appliance into the "on again - off again" category. It should be changed, and the repair is quite simple. It is also totally safe because the plug has to be disconnected to be replaced.

If the plug is on a lamp cord nicknamed zip cord (so named because the two inner wires can be separated with the zip of a thumbnail), the new plug can be the clamp-on type. Clamp-on plugs work in different ways, but many require that you do nothing but snip off the old plug. No stripping or separating the wires is necessary. The wires are inserted into the plug case, and then into the plug unit. The prongs are separated for the insertion, and when the wire is in place, they are pulled together. Sharp points go through the insulation on the wire and make separate contact with each wire inside. We suggest using this type of plug if your lamp or appliance has a zip cord.

For items with larger wire, a regular plug is required. It is almost as easy to replace, and should be wired using an underwriter's knot. Here is how to replace such a plug.

1. Cut off the old plug.
2. Insert the wire through the new plug.
3. Strip away about 3 inches of the outer insulation exposing the two inner wires.
4. Strip the insulation from the two inner wires exposing the bare strands of wire. Twist the ends of each wire so the strands become like a solid wire.
5. Tie the two wires into a knot. Then pull the knot tight.
6. Pull the wire so the knot goes down into the recess of the plug. Properly done, the knot takes the pressure from tugging on the cord instead of the pressure being at the connecting screws.
7. Bring each wire around a prong of the plug and attach it under the screw. The best way is to loop the end of the wire around the screw in a way in which it will turn (clockwise) to tighten. This prevents the movements of the screw from pushing the loop out. Instead, it pulls it in.
8. Replace the cardboard insulating disc that fits over the prongs.

Faster Wiring With Kwiklok Plugs And Connectors

Heavy-duty wires require heavy-duty plugs, and the quick and easy clamp-on type plugs won't do. Eagle's Kwiklok principle, though, makes such plugs as easy to replace as possible. The only connection is to the terminal screws inside. Then a turn of the end cap locks and seals the cord into the device. Almost every type of heavy-duty plug and connector is available in a Kwiklok version. Moreover, all are made of bright yellow nylon that can really take a beating.

Clamp-On Plugs Make Replacement A Snap

Most companies that manufacture small electrical supplies offer clamp-on plugs designed for use with two-conductor parallel lamp cords. These plugs install in seconds, requiring no tools, no stripping, and no splitting of the wires. Typical of what is available are the GE Quick Clamp devices: a regular plug, a Wall Hugger that fits flat against the receptacle, a single connector, and a Quick Clamp Triple Tap. Other companies offer kits containing both a plug and connector, permitting you to tailor-make your own extension cords. A good example is the Eagle Jiffy Push-Pull system.

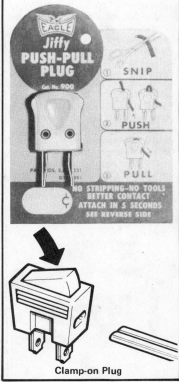

Clamp-on Plug

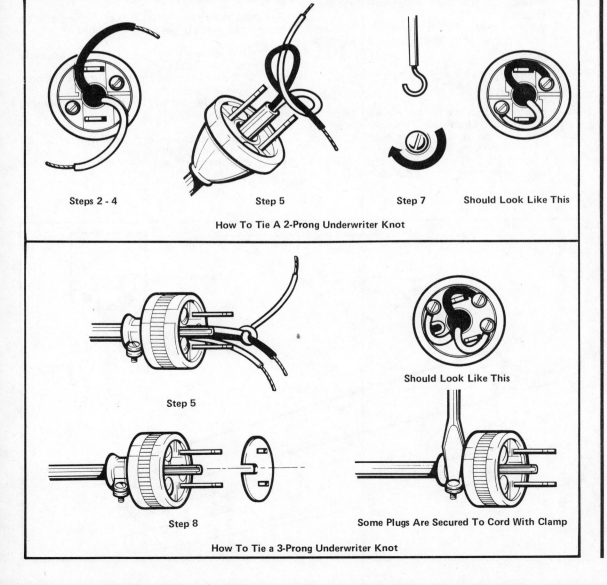

Steps 2 - 4

Step 5

Step 7

Should Look Like This

How To Tie A 2-Prong Underwriter Knot

Step 5

Should Look Like This

Step 8

Some Plugs Are Secured To Cord With Clamp

How To Tie a 3-Prong Underwriter Knot

Electrical

Fluorescent Starters

Starters, those inexpensive silver gadgets, are the cause of many fluorescent failures. When buying replacements, just make sure that you get the proper size; all the brands we examined are comparable. But we did find one starter that offers some advantages. GE's Watch Dog features automatic cut-off of failing tubes, which eliminates annoying blinking and protects both the ballast and the fixture wiring. It also has a manual reset button.

Fluorescent Fixtures Light Up Under-Cabinet

If you have a spot under a cabinet that is crying for light, install the easy-to-mount 18-inch fluorescent fixture from L&L Manufacturing. It comes with a six-foot plug-in cord, and the switch is right on the fixture as is an extra outlet. The package contains all the mounting hardware.

Screw-In Fluorescent Replacement

Fluorescent lighting consumes at least 40 percent less energy than incandescent bulbs, but changing over to fluorescent fixtures can be expensive. Recently, the American Fluorescent Corporation introduced the Convert-A-Lite unit, a fluorescent replacement bulb that screws into the standard socket of an incandescent ceiling fixture. No installation is required. The Convert-A-Lite unit is complete in itself, and you need not buy anything else. The 22-watt round fluorescent tube not only costs approximately 38 percent less to operate and probably lasts ten times longer, but it also produces greater light output than the 60-watt incandescent bulb it replaces.

Fluorescent Fixtures

FLUORESCENT LIGHT fixtures are quite popular these days because they burn much cooler and consume less electrical current. There are three basic types of fluorescents: the pre-heat, the rapid start, and the instant start. Pre-heat units use a starter mechanism, while the other two types do not. Every fluorescent unit, though, contains a component called a ballast, a sort of transformer that converts house current into a current of its own that produces light. The type of ballast is also your guide to purchasing all replacement components—tubes, starters, or the ballast itself. You must have the exact replacement parts or you will never enjoy properly working fluorescent light fixtures.

If you get no light at all from your fluorescent fixture, follow these basic steps.

1. Make sure that the house current is on and that the circuit is live by checking the fuse or circuit breaker box.
2. Next, make sure that the fluorescent tube is inserted properly in the lamp holder.
3. If you have another fluorescent fixture that is working, try the nonfunctioning tube in the good fixture to see whether the tube is burned out.
4. If the tube is still good, replace the starter—provided you have a pre-heat fluorescent fixture. The starter is an inexpensive and easy component to replace. Just be sure to buy the right replacement for your fixture.
5. If a new starter fails to make the light work, replace the tube. Again, be sure to get the proper size.

If the light blinks off and on, here is the procedure to follow.

△ 1. Make sure that the temperature in the room is more than 65 degrees Fahrenheit.
△ 2. Check to be sure that the tube is seated firmly in the lamp holder.
△ 3. Inspect the pins on the ends of the tube to see that they are free of dirt or corrosion. If they are not, sand them lightly. If the pins are bent, use a pair of pliers to straighten them gently.
△ 4. Cut the current to the fixture at the fuse or circuit breaker box, and inspect the wiring for loose connections.
△ 5. If none of the above steps stop the light from blinking off and on, replace the starter and then the tube.

If the tube is dark in the middle but the ends light up, or if the ends are discolored to more than just a brownish tinge, these steps should restore the lamp to proper working order.

○ 1. Be sure that the room temperature is high enough. It should be 65 degrees or higher.
○ 2. Replace the starter.
○ 3. Remove the tube and reverse it in the holder end for end.
○ 4. Cut off the circuit that supplies current to the fixture, and check the wiring inside the unit.

If there is a pronounced flicker in the light, try these basic steps to get it working right.

□ 1. If it is a new tube, the flicker will go away soon. New tubes often flicker at first.
□ 2. Shut the fixture off and then turn it back on.
□ 3. Replace the starter.
□ 4. Cut off the current and check the wiring inside the fixture.

If you experience any problems right after you replace parts, check the legend on the ballast to verify that the parts are the right ones for the fixture.

Here Is What You Will Need

Materials

- Replacement starter
- Replacement tube
- Sandpaper
- Replacement ballast

Tools

- Pliers

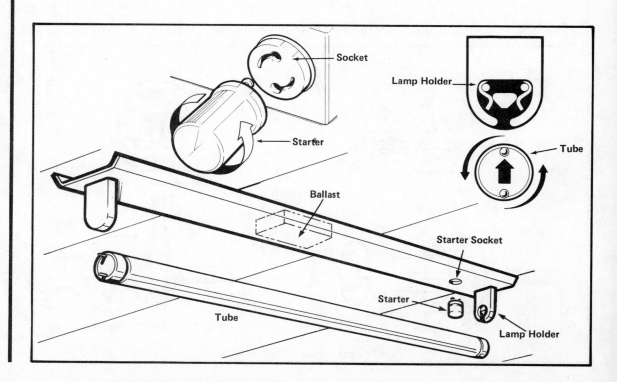

Changing a Ceiling Fixture

Here Is What You Will Need

Materials

- Light fixture
- Wire nuts

Tools

- Screwdriver
- Wire cutters

WITH ALL THE fantastic new types of fixtures around, you may wish to replace one that is too plain for your current tastes. In most cases, it will be a simple changeover. From a wiring standpoint, here is how it goes:

1. Turn off the power at the entry box by either flipping the proper circuit breaker switch or by removing the fuse. If there is any doubt, throw the main switch.
2. Remove the plate or canopy covering the hole in the ceiling.
3. Disconnect the old fixture. Notice how it is wired, and if there is anything other than a white wire and a black wire coming out of the ceiling, make a note of how it is hooked up. A 3-way or 4-way hook-up would be different. Outlets or other lights on the same switch would also cause it to be different.
4. Strip back about one inch of insulation from the wires on the new fixture.
5. Use wire nuts to connect the wires from the ceiling box to the wires from the new fixture; white wire to white, and black to black unless you observed a different wiring setup.
6. Fix the new canopy in place and restore power. If it is all done right, you should have light.

So much for the wiring. There are other factors that enter into the installation of a new fixture. For instance, they have to hang from something. Different fixtures will have different modes of mounting, depending sometimes on the weight of the fixture.

The simplest way is with a mounting bracket called a strap which is attached to the ceiling box by screws through the ears, small tabs with threaded holes. The fixture will then have screws going through the canopy and into threaded holes in the strap.

If the fixture has a threaded collar, it will need additional hardware to secure the fixture to the ceiling. The collar has to screw onto something, and this is called a stud. It is threaded and will stick down from the ceiling box. It will be held by a long hanger bar on the attic side of the box. If it does not extend down long enough, a connector called a hickey and a small threaded piece called a nipple are needed to bring it all together.

These are just the basics of how fixtures are secured. There are variations, and when you select a new fixture, if it does not fall into these categories, ask what special supplies will be needed to be sure the new fixture will not come crashing down.

Solderless Connectors

The pigtail type splice can be completed quickly and easily with solderless connectors. The one pictured here is a rigid plastic type from Eagle, but solderless connectors (also called wire nuts) are also available in soft plastic with metal or spring cores and in porcelain. Most are threaded inside so that as they are twisted around the wires to be joined, they bite into and hold the wires firmly in place. Brand names are of relatively little importance in selecting solderless connectors.

Helpful Books On Electricity

There are several books on the market that can help you when it comes to electrical wiring. No matter what the books say, however, remember that you must follow your local building code in any wiring you do. Both Sears and Montgomery Ward offer good books on wiring. Another good book, *Wiring Simplified*, by H.P. Richter is based on the National Electrical Code; each time the National Code is revised, Richter does another revision of his book. It is now in its 31st edition and is available at hardware stores, home centers, and electric supply stores.

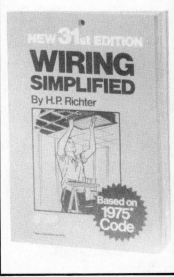

Step 2

Step 3

Step 4

Step 5

Step 6

Mounting Bracket

Electrical

What Does UL Mean?

Perhaps you've noticed an appliance cord tag, sticker, or label with the initials "UL" on it. This indicates that the merchandise is Listed by Underwriters Laboratories Inc., an independent, not-for-profit testing laboratory. UL tests products and materials submitted by the manufacturer to see that they meet nationally recognized safety requirements. Listing by UL does not mean that all products in the same category are of equal quality; one may just meet

the minimum requirement, while another may be truly superior. UL Listed means that the merchandise meets the minimum standards for the purpose for which it was intended. If used for some other purpose or under a different set of circumstances, the product may not be safe at all.

Appliance Cords

There are several types of appliance cords, and it is most important that you have the right one for your appliance. The end of the cord that connects to the appliance can come with a connector or can have what is called a "free end" that must be wired into the appliance. Belden and General Electric are among many major manufacturers producing a wide variety of appliance cords for the do-it-yourselfer.

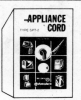

Appliance Cord Connectors

Appliance cord connectors, used to connect small household heat-generating appliances, come in two basic sizes: standard and miniature. The standard has 111-inch terminal spacing, and the miniature has ½-inch spacing. The standard connector is for most irons and toasters, while the miniature connector is for such appliances as coffee makers, skillets, and corn poppers. Cord connectors—like these from Eagle—come in a wide variety of styles, and some include on-off switches. All have some means of cord protection, usually in the form of a coil spring cord protector. The old cord is attached to the new connector by fastening the terminals on the wire to the terminal screws in the connector.

Tapes For Splices

Always cover bare wires at splices with electrical tape. Plastic, rubber, or friction tape is a neat clean way to cover and insulate wires safely. There are dozens of popular brands on the market, including Scotch (3M), Arno, GE, Gold Seal, Snapit, and Eagle. You should be able to find a wide selection in variety and grocery stores, as well as in home repair supply outlets.

Repairing Appliance Cords

ONE OF THE MOST common reasons why an appliance is not working properly is a faulty appliance cord. If the appliance works intermittently, or if it works when you jiggle the cord, the problem is in the cord. Often a visual inspection will uncover the problem.

The most common spots for wires to break or separate is where the cord enters the appliance or where the cord enters the plug. These are the points where most of the flexing of the wires takes place. Often when there is no visible sign of a break in the wire, jiggling the wire at these two points will indicate where the trouble is.

Here are the steps to take to track down and correct the problem.

1. Disconnect the appliance.
2. If there are visible breaks, these spots must be eliminated. If it is next to the plug, clip off the plug a few inches beyond the break and replace it. If it is where the cord enters the appliance, open the housing and disconnect the cord. Shorten the cord to eliminate the bad section and reconnect it to the appliance.
3. If there were no visible signs, look inside to see that the connection between the cord and the appliance is secure. If not, tighten it. If it has a female plug-in at the appliance, remove the cover plates and check the connections there. Inspect the contact points for corrosion, and clean if necessary.
4. If this is not the problem, disconnect the cord and use an inexpensive battery powered continuity tester. If a wire is whole, it will complete the circuit through the tester and turn on the light. Since there are two current carrying wires in an appliance cord, both must be checked. The tester will have a wire coming out of it with an alligator clip on the end. Clip this to one of the prongs on the plug. Now go to the other end of the cord where the two wires or connectors are. Touch each of the two wires separately with the probe tip. The tester light should come on when you touch one of these wires. Move the clip to the other prong on the plug and test it.
5. If the tester fails to light, snip off the plug and test the wires. If they test out all right, then the plug is faulty and must be replaced.
6. If the wires do not test out, then you need a new appliance cord. In selecting a new one,

be sure the replacement cord is the right size wire to handle the load required by the appliance. If it has a female type plug to connect to, be sure it is the same type. If the appliance is connected to the cord inside, be sure it has the same type of connectors, if any. Sometimes you will have to add crimp-on connectors to the ends of wires to make the connection.

Here Is What You Will Need

Materials

- Appliance cord
- Electrical plug

Tools

- Wire cutters
- Screwdriver
- Continuity tester

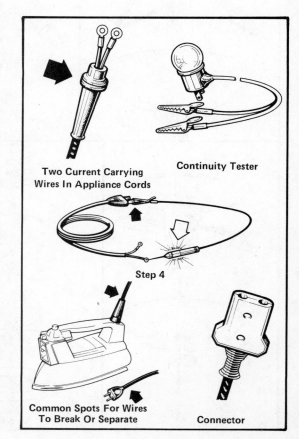

Two Current Carrying Wires In Appliance Cords

Continuity Tester

Step 4

Common Spots For Wires To Break Or Separate

Connector

Ring-Shanked Nails Increase Header Holding Power

The popularity of ring-shanked and screw-shanked nails for framing and general carpentry has grown due to their increased holding power. Armco Steel now makes common nails in ring-shank and the screw-shank versions, and markets these fasteners under the A to Z Brand. When you put a header into a load-bearing wall, use the same size ring- or screw-shanked nails as if you were using plain common nails.

Lightweight Aluminum Ladder Works Well For Structural Tasks

An aluminum stepladder is ideal when working on many household projects, the only exception being work involving electrical wiring. Lightweight yet sturdy, the Bauer ladder has a foldout shelf plus tool-holder holes in the top step. Available in several sizes (the four- and five-foot sizes are the most popular for general household purposes), the Bauer aluminum ladder is braced for extra stability and strength and features Shur-grip safety shoes. Bauer also makes ladders of all types in wood and fiberglass as well as in aluminum.

Framing Anchors Reduce Framing Chores

Anything that can make wall framing both easier and stronger is a product worth some attention. The F.D. Kees Manufacturing Company markets Timberlock Framing Anchors that not only eliminate toe-nailing, notching, and bridging, but also yield stronger connections than ordinary nailing methods. Made of 18-gauge zinc-coated sheet steel, Timberlock Anchors are available in five different forms, all of which have four nailing faces instead of the conventional three. They can make a great deal of difference in every wall framing project you tackle.

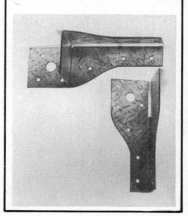

Load-Bearing Walls

Here Is What You Will Need

Materials
- Framing lumber
- Nails
- Door

Tools
- Saw
- Hammer
- Measuring tape
- Plumb bob

SOME WALLS in your home may only be partitions, and if knocked out completely, their loss would have no effect on what is above them. Other walls, however, support the floor or roof above; remove such a wall, and the structure may come tumbling down.

You can, though, remove part of such a wall to put in a door or window. But you must offset the loss of support with double studs and strong horizontal pieces of heavy timber or metal called headers. In most areas, the local building code specifies the size of headers you must install.

Here is an idea of what would be needed in a load-bearing wall to offset the weakening of the structure due to the installation of a door.

1. First of all, determine whether the wall is in fact a load-bearing wall. How? If it is an exterior wall, you know it must be load bearing, and if the joist ends rest on the plate of the wall, then it is definitely load bearing.
2. Make sure that the portion of the wall you plan to rip out does not contain wiring or ducts or plumbing pipes.
3. Start the opening next to an existing stud if possible.
4. Remove 2½ inches more of the wall than the door width from both sides of the wall. Leave only the studs and framing. Continue the removal to the next stud.
5. Cut four cripple studs out of 2x4-inch framing lumber to reach from the top of the floor or soleplate to the bottom of the header which you will install. Cripples are studs that do not reach all the way from the floor plate to the ceiling plate. The header should be installed at 1¾ inches higher than the height of the door as measured from the floor.
6. Nail one cripple to the stud you started from and another to the stud beyond the opening. Then nail the two extra cripples together and attach them to the soleplate at a point 2½ inches beyond the width of the door.
7. Use 2x8s (or whatever the code specifies for headers) to cut two pieces that span from the beginning stud to the ending one. Nail the two pieces together.
8. Remove the original wall studs that now stand in the doorway.
9. Nail the double header in place from the beginning stud to the ending stud.
10. Use a plumb bob to make sure that the double cripple marking the edge of the door

frame is right, and then nail it to the header. Cut short cripples to go up from the header to the ceiling or top plate.
11. Saw out and remove the soleplate where the door will go.

Your new opening is now properly framed and ready to accept the new door unit without diminishing the supporting role of the wall. You would follow the same procedure in creating an opening for a new window, except that the opening—instead of going to the floor—would end at a double-framed sill consisting of cross pieces under the window.

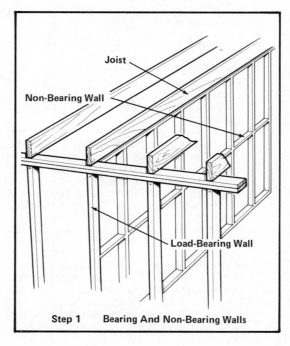

Joist

Non-Bearing Wall

Load-Bearing Wall

Step 1   **Bearing And Non-Bearing Walls**

Tapeless Measure Features Metric Readout

ENM Company now makes a metric version of its popular Tapeless Measure. A scratch-proof, skip-free measuring wheel revolves as the handheld measuring instrument glides over any surface, producing a direct digital readout in centimeters up to 1000 centimeters (10 meters) or the equivalent of approximately 33 feet. The wheel is geared to measure, accumulate, and automatically record a magnified readout in centimeters and tenths of centimeters without computation or conversion. The new metric Tapeless Measure may be recycled beyond the 1000-centimeter limit or snapped back instantly to zero by pressing the reset button. Able to measure on a straight line, around corners, and even over irregular or contoured surfaces, the pocket-size ENM Tapeless Measure is made of rugged, highly impact-resistant plastic and is completely non-conductive. It is also available with an adjustable, removable 32-inch handle.

Structural

Telescoping Post Takes Sag Out Of Supports

By installing a Telescopic Adjusta-Post, you can cure sagging support beams and have a permanent post to prevent future problems. The Sturdy "R" Series offers a 15,000-pound capacity and a safe load of 10,000 pounds. The posts are ball-and-socket jointed and have a half-inch turning bar. They use a one-inch screw with six inches of threads, and feature two pins in the adjustment holes for greater strength. Your local building supply outlet can order the Adjusta-Posts you need and may even carry the telescoping supports in stock.

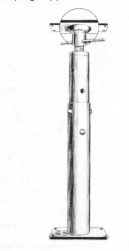

Jack Screws Fight The Sags

Montgomery Ward's Heavy-Duty Jack Screw is available in four sizes to handle weights from five to 18 tons. Short and stubby, the Heavy-Duty Jack Screw is best used in a crawl space where a standard jack post could not fit. It is made of a high-tensile iron for strength and painted to resist rust. The wide bell bottom gives the Jack Screw a firm footing, and the hot-forged one-piece steel turn screw (you'll need a wrecking bar to turn it) has precision cut threads. Heavy-Duty Jack Screws are available at Montgomery Ward stores and through the catalog.

Level Tells You When Support Job Is Done

The 24-inch aluminum level made by Skokie Saw and Tool Company features aluminum "I" beam construction, which means that it is warp-proof, corrosion-proof, and very lightweight. The three bubble vials—providing vertical, horizontal, and 45-degree readings—are protected by plastic windows. Skokie also makes an 18-inch version with two vials as well as a popular nine-inch pocket-size level, but the longer level would be the one to choose if you are planning to work on sagging support beams.

Tiger Mauls Foundation Faults

Tiger Brand Jack Posts, from the Jack-Post Corporation, come in two popular series. The Super "S" posts possess an 18,000-pound capacity with a 14,000-pound safe load, while the Tiger Cub (or "C" Series) posts are designed to support smaller loads. All Tiger Jack Posts are made of heavy-gauge tubing painted inside and out for total protection against rust, and all are self aligning.

Sagging Support Beams

Here Is What You Will Need

Materials

- Nails
- 4x4's
- Steel columns or adjustable jack posts
- Concrete mix

Tools

- Screw jack
- Saw
- Hammer
- Measuring tape
- Carpenter's level
- Chisel
- Trowel

MANY TIMES, a cracked wall or a sticking door upstairs—or even a roof leak—is actually caused by a problem in the basement. The problem is that the joists under the first floor are sagging. Once the joists give a little, the sag continues on up the line. Before you start trying to remedy the results upstairs, therefore, you need to take care of the cause in the basement. Although the cure is simple, you first must check your local building code to see that what you do conforms to the law. Once you get that aspect of the problem cleared up, just follow these steps to remedy your sagging supports.

1. Buy or rent a screw-type house jack (commonly called a screw jack).
2. Place a 4x4 timber directly under the center of the sag to serve as a support base for the screw jack.
3. Cut another 4x4 timber to run across the sagging joists and beyond to several non-sagging joists on each side. Nail this beam in place across the joists.
4. Place the screw jack on the support base.
5. Measure from the top of the lowered screw jack to the bottom of the beam you nailed up and cut a third 4x4 to this length.
6. Install this third piece as a vertical between the jack and the beam. Since it must be plumb, use a level to set it.
7. Turn the handle of the screw jack until you feel resistance, and **STOP.** The leveling process must be very gradual; otherwise, you can crack your walls and do great damage to the house.
8. Wait a full 24 hours, and then turn the screw jack handle only one quarter of a turn. The handle will probably be very easy to turn, and you will be tempted to turn more, but be patient. Continue to make no more than a quarter turn every 24 hours. If you miss a day, do not compensate for it with additional turning.
9. When the sagging beams begin to straighten out, start checking them with your level every day.
10. When they are all level, install columns at each end of each beam to secure them. You can buy steel lally columns or you can cut 4x4's; there are also adjustable jack posts that work like the screw jack and are the easiest supports to set.
11. No matter what kind of supports you decide to install, you must make sure that the footing below is sound. The common concrete basement floor is not reliable enough. You should remove a two-foot section of the old floor where each support post will go, pour a concrete footing that is at least a foot thick, and make it level with the rest of the floor. When it has cured, you can put the support posts on the footing and know that the floor will not give way.

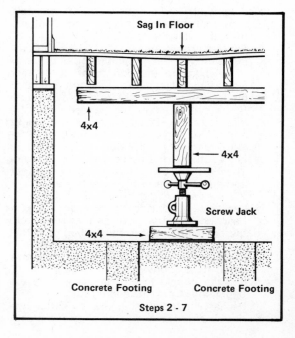

Sag In Floor

4x4

4x4

Screw Jack

4x4

Concrete Footing   Concrete Footing

Steps 2 - 7

Heavy-Duty Level Is Shockproof

Just to give it a test, try dropping the Johnson Shockproof Extruded Aluminum Level more than 500 times on a concrete floor. That's what Johnson Products Company did, and the result was no damage to the vials, windows,

or the setting. Available in all the popular lengths up to 72 inches, Johnson levels feature a permanent anodized finish over the specially tempered frame as well as patented snap-in vial holders that grip the vials securely while cushioning them against impact. You should be able to find a large selection of Johnson levels at your local hardware store.

Fill Foundation Cracks The Easy Way

Most foundation cracks have little bearing on the structural soundness of your home. The house will not fall down due to a small crack in the foundation. On the other hand, once moisture gets in and the temperature changes radically from one season to the next, the crack will enlarge and may well lead to more serious damage. The quickest way to patch cracks is by applying a good cement patch like Stay-Tite. Available in cartridges

for use with a caulking gun, Stay-Tite's hanger spout makes it easily recognizable.

Foundation Care and Repairs

FAULTS IN THE foundation can be due to poor construction, but in most cases the problems stem from subsequent movement of the soil on which the foundation was built. And moisture is generally the chief culprit in shifting soil. Too much or too little moisture causes enough expansion or contraction of the soil to move the entire house. If the movement is uniform throughout the structure, the foundation may not suffer. It is unequal movement that causes twisting, bending, and other problems in your home's foundation.

Since unequal movement usually is the product of changes in the moisture content of the soil, be aware of the possible harmful effects on your foundation of plumbing leaks, excessive watering of flower beds adjacent to the house, poor drainage away from the house, or anything that lets water collect in one spot. Here are some preventive maintenance procedures to follow to minimize the risk of foundation woes.

1. Check the grade around the house to be sure it slopes away from the foundation.
2. Make sure that the natural channels for drainage haven't been dammed or filled. These low places (they shouldn't be ditches) were either created when the property was originally graded or they formed naturally,

Here Is What You Will Need
Materials
- Concrete patching compound
Tools
- Hammer
- Cold chisel
- Trowel or putty knife

but uninformed homeowners often fill in the needed lows in order to make their lawns totally level.
3. Inspect gutters and downspouts to be certain that they are effective and that the water is being deposited far enough away from the foundation so as not to cause a problem.
4. Check flower beds next to the house to be sure they are sloped and that the curb or edging does not act as a trap for the water.
5. Avoid planting shrubs and trees right next to the house. They take quite a bit of moisture out of the soil, and too little moisture can lead to foundation problems as well.
6. Be sure to water lawns and, particularly, flower beds uniformly—even to the extent of watering where there may be no plants—so that the moisture content will be as equal as possible.
7. Never allow a plumbing problem to go unrepaired any longer than absolutely necessary.

Evidence of unequal settling or upheaval shows itself in spaces developing between the walls and the doors and the windows, cracks in the inside walls, doors that suddenly fail to fit their frames properly, and, of course, cracks in the foundation itself. You can let problems inside the house slide for a while, but take care of exterior cracks and spaces at once. Fill in foundation cracks and caulk spaces around doors and windows before additional moisture can get in and cause more damage.

If your foundation problems continue to worsen after you correct the moisture imbalance, call in a professional repairman. Slab foundations may have to be raised and shored with a process called mud-jacking, which involves pumping soil cement grout under pressure to lift the slab and chemically stabilize the soil. Doing a foundation leveling and repair job correctly requires engineering skill, experience, and equipment. Done properly, this kind of foundation repair should not have to be repeated.

Down Spout-O-Matic Carries Water Away From Your Foundation

When you attach a Down Spout-O-Matic to the end of a downspout, you can say farewell to worries about rain water possibly damaging your home's foundation. The Down Spout-O-Matic coils up at the end of the spout until the weight of the water automatically makes it uncoil. It then rolls out to its full 48-inch length, sprinkles the water harmlessly away from the foundation, and recoils automatically when the rain stops. Made of heavy-gauge durable vinyl with a stainless steel spring coiling mechanism, the Down Spout-O-Matic is a product of the H.D. Campbell Company.

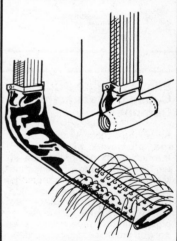

Chisel And Point Clean Concrete Cracks

Whenever you patch cracks in concrete, you first should chip out enough of the old concrete to undercut the crack and create a good surface to which the patch can adhere. The Dasco Cold Chisel and Dasco Concrete Point are specially made of heat treated high-grade steel to handle concrete work. The chisel comes in sizes from 4⅞ to 12 inches in length, while the concrete point features an edge that starts easier, cuts faster, and lasts longer than most competitive makes. Dasco tools are made by Damascus Steel Products.

Hot Bituminous Waterproofing
Gravel Fill
Foundation (Poured)
Cove
Drain Pipe
Basement Floor
Compacted Earth
Concrete Base
Keyed Footing
Footing

Structural

USG Waterproofing Coating Brightens As It Protects

Durabond Waterproofing Coating from the United States Gypsum Company brightens porous masonry walls while it protects against water penetration. Available in white to brighten basement walls, Durabond Waterproofing Coating can be tinted to suit individual tastes. It comes ready-mixed for do-it-yourself application right from the can, and it goes on quickly and easily by roller or brush to interior or exterior walls above or below grade. This heavy-bodied coating stops water seepage through concrete and cinder block, stucco, brick, and other porous masonry surfaces. Sold in one-gallon and five-gallon pails, Durabond Waterproofing Coating dries in a few hours and is backed by a five-year limited guarantee.

Eliminate Pipe Drips As Cause Of Basement Dampness

Since most basements have all the plumbing pipes running through them, dampness can often be attributed to condensation. Mortell markets two products that put a stop to pipe condensation. NoDrip Tape is a 100-percent moisture-proof, self-adhering pipe insulating tape that will not dry out, crack, shrink, rot, or deteriorate. NoDrip Plastic Coating is a self-bonding seamless insulation that can be brushed, troweled, or sprayed around pipes, tanks, valves, or anything else subject to condensation. It will also adhere to concrete, brick, tile, wood, or surfaces previously painted or galvanized.

Pick Up Puddles With Your Pump

While a pump can rid your basement of dangerous flood waters, it can do nothing about the puddles. But if you add a Pud-L-Scoop from the Simer Pump Company, you can pick up the rest of the water on your basement floor. The Pud-L-Scoop has a special threadless rubber connector, and all you need do is push in a section of ¾-inch pipe or regular garden hose to create an attachment for your suction pump that works

much like a vacuum cleaner attachment except that the Pud-L-Scoop sucks up water instead of dirt.

Waterproof Paint Can Stop Some Dampness Problems

By applying a waterproof paint to your basement walls, you can often stop the seepage and leaks. Pliolite resin-based paints are moisture-proof, resistant to alkali (a natural problem in concrete) and resistant to mildew (an outgrowth of dampness), but, at the same time, they let the coating breathe. Thus, they not only stop water, but also permit moisture to escape.

Damp Basements

THERE IS A tremendous amount of wasted floor space in this country; it is not being used because it happens to be in basements that suffer from a dampness problem. In some cases, the usable floor space in a home could almost be doubled if the basement were dry.

The first step toward solving the dampness problem is to ascertain where the moisture is coming from. Assuming that there is no plumbing problem, the dampness must result from leakage, seepage, or condensation. Leakage is outside water that comes in through cracks. Seepage is also outside water, but it is in such abundance that it makes its way through pores in the concrete. Condensation is inside water that exists as humidity in the air until it condenses on the cool masonry walls or cold water pipes.

You should be able to tell when the problem is leakage because the moisture will only be around cracks. Seepage and condensation may appear much alike, however. To find out which one it is, tape a hand mirror against the wall in the middle of a damp spot, and leave it there overnight. If the mirror is fogged over the next day, you have condensation. If not, you have seepage.

1. The first step to take for leakage is to patch the crack. Buy a special hydraulic cement, the kind that is quick setting and can actually set up with water coming in through the crack.
2. Anything other than a hairline crack should be undercut. That means taking a hammer and chisel and making the crack wider beneath than the crack is on the surface. Undercutting lets the cement lock itself in place.
3. Clean away all the loose debris, and then hose out the cavity.
4. Mix the patching compound according to directions.
5. Push the mixture into the crack with your trowel, making sure to fill all cavities.
6. Smooth the surface and let it cure according to directions.

That takes care of the cracks, but you are not through yet. You should try to divert the outside water that has been attacking your foundation. Here is what to look for and what to do about the water outside.

△ 1. Check your gutters and downspouts. They

Here Is What You Will Need

Materials

- Hand mirror
- Hydraulic cement
- Patching compound
- Concrete mix
- Clay tile pipe drains
- Waterproofing compound
- Pipe insulation
- Dehumidifier
- Exhaust fan

Tools

● Hammer	● Trowel
● Chisel	● Shovel
● Garden hose	● Stiff brush

must be free of debris, pitched properly to carry the water off, and the ground on which the downspouts spill should be sloped to carry the water away from the house. If it is not, install concrete splash blocks.

△ 2. Inspect the ground around the house to be sure it slopes away all the way around. If not, fill it in until there is good run off, and then roll and seed (or sod) to prevent the soil from washing away.

△ 3. Examine the flower beds to be sure they are not trapping the water that should be running off.

△ 4. Be sure patios and walks butting against the house are sloped away, and check the joints to see that they are sealed and curved properly. If they are not, use a chisel and hammer to undercut the joints, and then fill them with a mortar mix.

Some outside conditions can be cured only by digging down around the foundation and laying drains. This is not a do-it-yourself project for someone lacking experience in such work. If you want to tackle it, though, you must dig down to a level below the basement floor (but not below the footing), set a drain alongside each wall, and extend the drain out to carry the water away. The drain is made of sections of clay tile pipe covered with about two feet of gravel. While you have the outside wall exposed, coat it with a waterproofing compound. There are several good ones on the market.

There are also companies that have a process for pumping a special sealing compound into the ground under pressure. The compound flows along the same paths that the water takes and then seals the wall. Be sure to check with your Better Business Bureau, though, before con-

Thoro System Waterproofs Inside And Out

The Thoro System—a creation of Standard Dry Wall Products—consists of two coatings in powder form: Waterplug and Thoroseal. Waterplug, applied first to all cracks and joints, is quick setting and effective even against running water. In fact, Waterplug becomes harder when exposed to water. The next step is Thoroseal, a heavy cement-base waterproof coating that seals pores. Painted

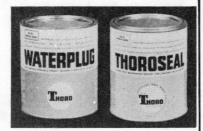

on, Thoroseal comes in white, gray, and assorted other colors to decorate as it seals your basement walls.

Silicone Rubber Patches Basement Wall Leaks

Now there is a brush-on/roll-on silicone rubber coating that can patch cracks in masonry and concrete as well as handle a host of other sealing jobs around the house. Use it to seal around joints inside and out, protect wooden posts against rot, and to coat flashings. Dow Corning's Silicone Rubber Coating is easy to use; just stir and then apply right from the can. Flexible enough to withstand future expansion and con-

traction, it can adjust to any temperature. You can even put it in a sprayer to apply a waterproofing sealant to your roof.

E-Pox-E Stops Leaks

The family handyman can now professionally waterproof the basement at a fraction of what a professional waterproofing job costs. With the Duro E-Pox-E Waterproofing Kit, the do-it-yourselfer can seal leaks in basements, swimming pools, brick, block, and masonry. An epoxy formulation—not just a paint coating—it dries to an iron-like bond that can withstand extreme water pressure without seepage. Once it dries, the Duro E-Pox-E Waterproofing Kit is unaffected by temperature, age, alkalies, or acids. The Duro E-Pox-E Waterproofing Kit, manufactured by Woodhill Chemical Sales Corporation, contains enough material to waterproof 50 square feet.

Causes Of Dampness (Condensation, Leakage, Seepage)

Buried Drain Solves Some Outside Problems (Waterproofing Compound, Clay Drain Pipe)

Step 2

Step △ 4 (Wall, Curved Seam At Joint, Floor)

---

tracting for such a treatment because there are some dishonest companies in the field.

Another way to deal with the seepage problem is to coat the inside of your basement with a waterproofing compound. There are many good ones on the market. Such compounds will not eliminate your seepage problem, however, unless you reduce the amount of water outside your house. Once you take care of the outside problem, follow these directions to waterproof your basement walls.

- ○ 1. Clean the walls.
- ○ 2. Wet the surface.
- ○ 3. Mix the waterproofing compound according

to directions.
- ○ 4. Apply the mixture with a stiff brush to cover the walls completely.
- ○ 5. Apply a second coat if necessary; usually it is.

Condensation results from too much moisture in the air combining with a cold surface. A dehumidifier can take much of the excess moisture out of the air, and you should also try to provide better ventilation in the basement. If you cannot air it out regularly, you might consider installing an exhaust fan. In addition, be sure to wrap exposed cold water pipes with the type of insulation made especially to stop pipes from sweating.

Floors

Elmer's Bonds Stronger Than Wood Itself

Elmer's two-part Waterproof Glue is an excellent adhesive, bonding stronger than the wood itself in most cases. A resorcinol adhesive made especially for outdoor furniture, sports equipment, and other items susceptible to moisture (even boats), it withstands both freezing and boiling water, solvents, and fungus.

S-K Tools Are The Mechanics' Choice

The S-K Division of Dresser Industries has achieved an enviable reputation producing tools for mechanics. Why bring in a mechanic's tools for a floor squeaking project? Because if you need a screwdriver, the S-K Round Cabinet Blade Screwdriver in either a four- or six-inch length is ideal for your purposes. Buying quality screwdrivers is always a smart investment. Poorly made screwdrivers not only have a short life span, but they also botch up screw heads.

Metal Bridging Can Help Stop Squeaks

If the joists under your floors move and cause floor squeaks, consider placing bridging between the joists to stiffen them and create a better floor. Stur-D ribbed steel cross bridging, made by F.D. Kees Manufacturing Company, can be either nailed or screwed in place between the joists. Made from 16-gauge galvanized V-ribbed steel, the bridging pieces are stronger than wood bridging, yet they can be worked in around pipes and wiring. Stur-D bridging is available in two lengths to handle differences in beam sizes and spacing. F.D. Kees products, which include Timberlock Framing Anchors as well as Stur-D bridging, are sold in building materials supply stores.

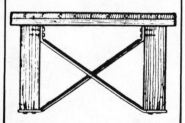

Dry White Lubricant Silences Squeaks

A powdered lubricant can often stop the rubbing that creates squeaks in floors and stairs. Lub-A-Lite, a dry white lubricant that comes in a squeeze type container-appplicator, is stainless, greaseless, and nonoily. Unlike regular graphite powders, moreover, it does not appear gray on the wood. Available in two plastic puffer sizes—⅛ ounce and 1⅛ ounce sizes—Lub-A-Lite can also be used on locks, drawers, zippers, and any other place where a dry powdered lube is called for and where you want no traces of the lubricant to show. Lub-A-Lite is one of several home lubricating products made by Panef Manufacturing Company, Inc.

Squeaking Floors

NEARLY ALL floor squeaks are the result of two pieces of wood rubbing against each other. If you know where the loose boards are, you can step over these spots; but if you want to stop the squeaks without having to resort to this broken field running, there are some simple remedies you can try.

If you have exposed hardwood floors and if the rubbing occurs between boards of this top flooring, an easy way to stop the noise is to sprinkle talcum powder over the area and sweep it back and forth until you get the powder to go down between the cracks. Talc acts as a dry lubricant, and even though the boards will still move, there will be no more squeaks. Liquid floor wax or glue will accomplish the same thing as the talc, but there are more permanent ways to stop squeaks—and they are almost as easy. The best way to attack floor squeaks is from underneath.

1. Go to the basement or crawl space under the floor, and have someone on the floor above step on the squeaky spot. If you can see any movement in the subfloor, mark the spots with chalk.
2. Drive wedges in between the joists and the subflooring to stop the boards from moving. You can fashion wedges from scrap shingles or other scrap lumber.
3. If the wedges are no help, use wood screws to pull the subflooring and surface flooring together. Make sure, however, that the screws are not so long as to go all the way through the floor and stick up into the room above.
4. If you cannot reach the floor from underneath, drive sixpenny finishing nails through the cracks of the hardwood flooring at points around the squeaking boards. Drive the nails in at an angle so that each nail goes through both of the two adjoining boards. Be sure to drill a pilot hole first, before you drive a nail into hardwood. Then, after the nails are in, drive them below the surface with a nailset and hide them with wood filler.
5. You also attack from above if the movement is between the top flooring and the subfloor. Drive tenpenny finishing nails through the center of hardwood planks and on into the subfloor below. Again, drive the nails at a slight angle, and then countersink and hide them as mentioned above.
6. If the floors are covered with carpet, vinyl, or

some other such covering—and if there is no way to work from underneath—you may have to tolerate the squeaks or else learn how to dodge the bad spots. Nevertheless, there is one thing you can try: Put padding over the floor, and then pound a block of wood with a hammer to reseat the loose nails. Move the block in an area about two or three feet all around the squeak, tapping sharply with the hammer. If the floor still squeaks, then wait until it is time to recover the floors. With the old flooring out of the way, you can drive wood screws in to pull the subflooring tight against the joists.

Here Is What You Will Need

Materials
- Talcum powder, liquid floor wax, or glue
- Chalk
- Wooden wedges
- Wood screws
- Finishing nails
- Wood filler
- Padded wood block

Tools
- Hammer
- Screwdriver
- Drill
- Nailset

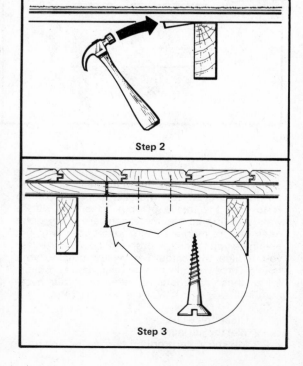

Step 2

Step 3

Fixing a Loose Tile

Here Is What You Will Need

Materials

- Aluminum foil
- Dry ice or metal pot filled with ice, water, and ice cream salt
- Sandpaper
- Floor tile mastic
- Replacement tile
- Weights (i.e., heavy books)

Tools

- Propane torch or electric iron
- Putty knife

Steps 2 and 7

PERHAPS YOU HAVE seen the commercials that show how easy it is to lay floor tiles yourself. Although it really is easy to lay new tiles, it is something else again to fix loose ones. If for some reason a tile should get loose and start to curl up at the ends—or if you happen to drop something sharp on the floor and gouge out a chunk—you could find yourself with one heck of a job removing that one tile and either regluing it or replacing it . . . unless you know the secrets.

1. If the tile is loose just around the edges, try to heat the mastic; sometimes you can then press the tile back down for keeps. The best way to heat the mastic is to play the flame of a propane torch across the tile. You must be careful, of course, not to leave the flame in any one spot, and you must not overheat. If you want a less hazardous method, you can place aluminum foil over the square and use a warm iron. Press the edges of the loose tile with the iron, and then place weights over the tile to clamp it in place until the mastic sets up fully.
2. If there seems to be insufficient mastic to glue the tile back down, apply heat again and peel back the edges. Then clean out the old mastic as completely as you can. Apply new floor tile mastic, but be careful not to put so much down that mastic will squeeze out when you press down on the tile. Replace the tile and weight it down until the mastic has cured. Check the label for the prescribed drying time.
3. If the tile is botched up and needs to be replaced, you can use either heat or cold to remove the bad tile. If you do not have a propane torch, try placing dry ice or a metal pot filled with ice, water, and ice cream salt over the tile. After about five to ten minutes, the cold will make both the tile and the mastic very brittle, allowing you to flip the tile out in chips with a putty knife. Tap the putty knife with a hammer as you go, and the tile will shatter.
4. Once you remove the tile, clean away all the old mastic. Scraping with a wide putty knife is probably the best way to clean the entire area.

5. Now you are ready to lay the new tile. Place it down in the opening before you apply any mastic. This enables you to match up the pattern. You may find that the new tile does not fit exactly. If such is the case, sand down the new tile until it fits.
6. Apply the floor tile mastic (be sure it is the kind made for your type of tile) directly to the floor, following the instructions on the label. Now warm the new tile, using either the propane torch or the electric iron, and press the tile firmly in place.
7. Put weights on the tile, and leave them there for the prescribed drying time. Volumes A through L of the encyclopedia should do the job nicely.

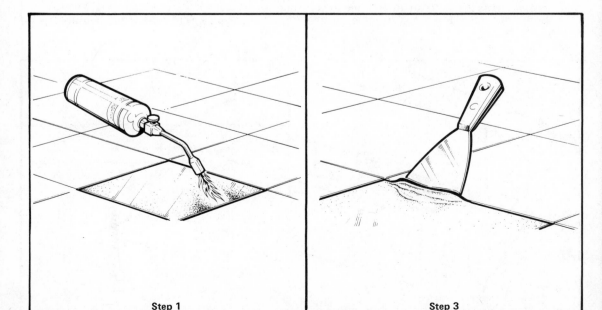

Step 1   Step 3

Torch Can Help Remove Old Tiles

The heat from a torch can usually soften the adhesive under floor tiles sufficiently to allow the tiles to come up easily. Ronson's handy and compact Varaflame Torch does not get as hot as a propane torch, but it gets more than hot enough for any tile task. Quite inexpensive itself, the Ronson Varaflame Torch burns inexpensive butane gas, and each butane cylinder lasts for hours.

Electric Paint Remover Softens Mastic

Hyde Tool Company makes an electric paint remover that can quickly soften the adhesive holding a floor tile. The tool plugs into regular house current and has a heating element much like that of an electric range. Of course, the Hyde Electric Paint Remover also does an excellent job of softening paint for removal with a scraper.

Wide Putty Knife Aids In Old Tile Removal

Any putty knife can lift old tiles off your floor, but a wide scraper type like the Warner six-inch flexible blade gets old floor tiles up quicker. The Warner blade is hardened, tempered, and ground, and it can be a big help in many other chores around the house. Warner also makes an electric paint remover as well as several other scrapers and putty knives.

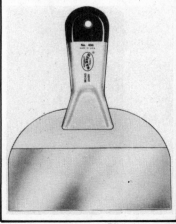

Floors

Ball Peen Hammer Can Drive Wedges Home

The ball peen (often spelled pein) hammer is never used to drive nails, but it can be quite useful in driving wedges to stop stair and floor squeaks. Generally used for striking cold chisels in masonry work, for shaping metal, and for riveting, ball peen hammers come in different weights and with different shaped faces. The Vaughan model has a fiberglass handle with a neoprene grip for comfort, and it features Vaughan's exclusive hollow-core design that absorbs more shock and provides better balance.

VSI Wood Screws Come Packaged For Convenience

Quite often all you need to do to stop squeaks is pull the moving stair components together with wood screws. No movement will mean no more squeaking. VSI Fasteners make a complete line of screws, bolts, washers, and nuts, and VSI offers assortment packs of all these items.

Philstone Nails Down Your Stair Problem

Consider using threaded nails to end your stair squeaks. Annular and spiral threaded nails hold wood better than unthreaded nails. Philstone packages threaded nails in one- and five-pound boxes. The Philstone 1⅝-inch annular threaded nail can frequently do the job when driven down from the top of the stairs, but generally you'll need to use longer nails.

Squeaky Stairs

THE STAIRWAY that squeaks when you walk up or down is caused by the same thing that causes your floor to squeak; two pieces of wood rubbing together. It is usually the tread rubbing against either the riser or the stringer because these boards are not fastened down securely. Stop their movement, and you stop the squeak. If you can work from under the stairs, here is how to cure the problem.

1. Have someone walk on the stairs, going back and forth on the step that squeaks, while you try to spot movement from below. Look especially for loose nails, split boards, or anything else that could cause the movement.
2. The best way to stop the movement is to drive wedges between the rubbing members. Cut the wedges from scrap shingles.
3. Coat the wedges with glue (white polyvinyl or any wood glue) on the side that will press against a flat surface.
4. Drive the wedges into the seam, making them go in as tight as possible.
5. When you get them in place, secure the wedges with nails. Use small nails, and blunt the points to avoid splitting the wedges.
6. If the seams are too small to admit wedges, cut wood blocks (1x2) to fit into the joints under the stairs. Put a coat of glue on the

Here Is What You Will Need

Materials
- Wooden wedges or blocks
- White polyvinyl or any wood glue
- Finishing nails
- Graphite powder or talcum powder
- Wood putty

Tools
- Hammer
- Nailset

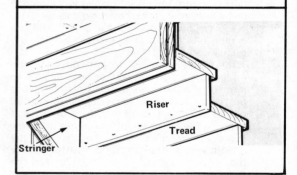

sides that will touch the stairs, and then—as you hold the blocks in place—secure them with nails. Be sure your nails do not go through the stairs and protrude from the top.

If there is no way to work from under the stairs,

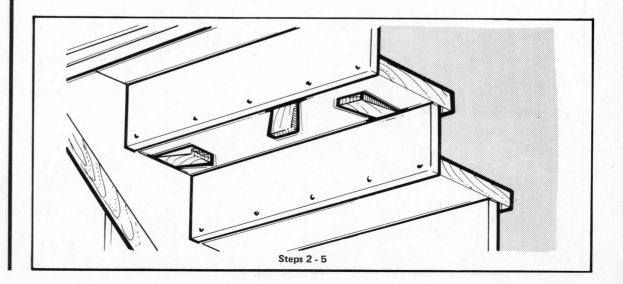

Steps 2 - 5

Shape Wedges With Quality Pocket Knife

Pocket knives used to be common carry-along items, but that situation is not true today. Nevertheless, the pocket knife can be very handy in shaping the wedges you need to get the squeaks out of stairs. If you want a top quality pocket knife that you can use for hundreds of different projects and then pass along to a grandchild, look at the line from Buck Knives, one of the few really good knife makers in the country.

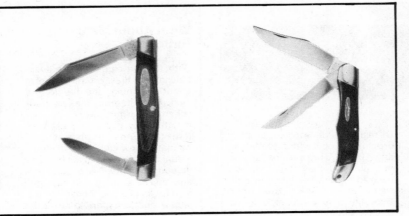

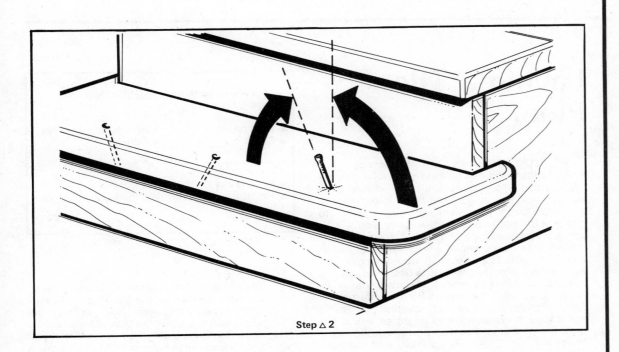

Step △ 2

you have to try to find the movement from topside. Unfortunately, you frequently cannot spot the problem and must guess where the trouble is by listening to the squeak. After you track down the squeak, here is what to do.

△ 1. Buy a tube of graphite powder and squeeze the graphite into the joints all around the

squeak. You can also use talcum powder in a plastic squeeze bottle with a spout.

△ 2. If the powder fails to stop the squeak, drive finishing nails into the tread at such an angle that they will go into the riser or the stringer where you think the movement is. Use a nailset to sink the heads below the surface, and cover the holes with wood putty.

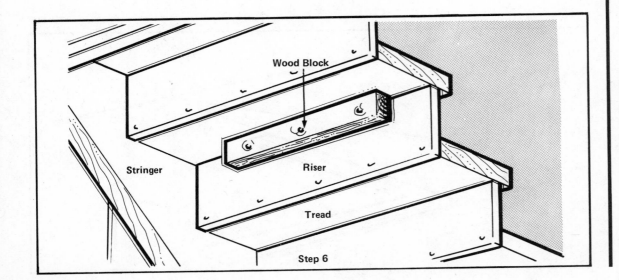

Wood Block

Stringer

Riser

Tread

Step 6

Dry Film Lubricant Stops Wood Squeaks

The Cling-Surface Company's TFE Dry Film Lubricant contains DuPont Teflon and is available in six- and 16-ounce aerosol cans. When sprayed between rubbing boards, TFE's long-lasting film prevents noise. Spray the lubricant from underneath the stairs if possible; any surface film on top of the steps could create a dangerously slippery situation. TFE has many other uses. It bonds to metal, plastic, glass, rubber, and other clean substances to render instantly lubricated surfaces.

Corner Braces Or Shelf Brackets Can Silence Stair Squeaks

Metal corner braces or shelf brackets may be the answer to eliminating the noise in your stairs. Since the braces or brackets will not be visible, finish is unimportant; the most important thing is to get a sturdy brace or bracket of the correct size. Hager corner braces come in lengths up to eight inches, with the smaller sizes carded and the larger ones in bins without screws. The Hager shelf brackets, made of gray wrought steel, are designed so that their two sides are of different lengths; one arm is an inch or two longer than the other. Just make sure that one arm is the right size for your stairs.

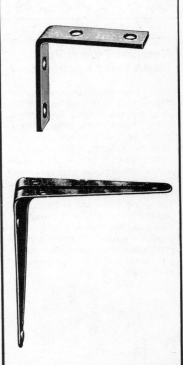

Floors

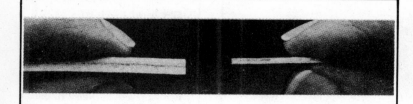

GAFSTAR Has Foam Backing

The foam backing on GAF'S GAFSTAR really does provide a more comfortable feel as you walk across it. Much thicker than old-fashioned flooring, GAFSTAR is so resilient that you can actually drop dishes on it without breaking any. GAFSTAR never needs waxing, but you may find that you have to restore the gloss in high traffic areas. GAF's Brite-Bond floor finish is formulated to do precisely that.

What About Matching Patterns?

With the intricate patterns available in floor tiles, you might worry about matching one tile to the next. Most flooring makers have taken the guesswork out of matching by producing tile patterns that automatically match up no matter how you place the individual components. Aztec by Congoleum Industries is a good example. The striking sunburst design looks like you'd have to be a jigsaw puzzle expert to put it together, but each tile matches all the others around it for an easy installation.

Pour A Floor

Once used only for industrial purposes, pouring an epoxy onto the floor and then adding chips of color for depth and beauty can now be done in the home. For a tough seamless floor covering, check out a Dur-A-Flex installation. The density and color of the chips let you vary the effect to suit your surroundings. Dur-A-Flex, Inc., also markets the epoxy in a number of solid colors.

Notched Trowel Puts Down Floor Adhesive

When applying floor covering adhesive, you need a trowel with the proper notch pattern. Since different patterns serve different purposes, be sure to check the can of adhesive to find out which pattern best suits your needs. Harrington Tools makes the Throw Away Spreader, ideal for the one time floor project, in several patterns. Featuring a 6⅜-inch wide toothed area, the Throw Away Spreader is made of heavy-gauge steel with a rigidity crimp for extra strength. Harrington also makes fine notched trowels for the professional craftsmen.

Laying a Tile Floor

IF YOU REALLY want to amaze your friends—and maybe even yourself—with the professional appearance of a do-it-yourself project, put down a resilient tile floor. In a matter of only a few hours, you can change a drab floor into one that will perk up the entire room. You will be amazed at how easily and quickly the work goes.

Floor tiles now come in a wide range of prices and materials. The two most popular types are asphalt tiles and vinyl tiles. The use to which you put the room, the type of subflooring that is already down, and the availability of patterns will have much to do with your selection of tile. Spend some time in choosing; you might as well get it right the first time. Purchasing right adhesive is important too. Different materials and different subfloors require different mastics. No matter what type of tiles you choose, however, the procedures for installation are about the same. Here are the steps to follow.

1. The first step—preparation—is the most important one of all. Pry up the moldings; remove all wax and dirt from the floor surface; search for and sand down any high spots; and make sure there are no nails sticking up. Since resilient tiles are flexible and will conform to whatever is under them, any irregularities in the subfloor will eventually show through. And unless the subflooring is solid, the tiles will loosen.
2. Next, find the exact center of each wall and snap a chalk line from these points across the floor. Where the two lines intersect is the center of the room.
3. Lay a full run of loose (uncemented) tiles from the center of each wall within one quarter of the room. If the last tile in either direction is less than half the width of a full tile, draw a new chalk line beside the actual center line, moving the original line half a tile in either direction. This technique will give you even-sized end tiles at both ends of the room.

Here Is What You Will Need

Materials	
● Sandpaper	● Asphalt or vinyl tiles
● Chalk line	● Adhesive

Tools
● Heavy-duty scissors
● Rolling pin
● Paintbrush or roller or thin-notched flooring trowel

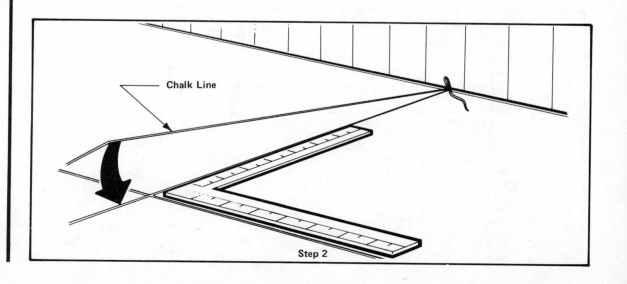

Chalk Line

Step 2

Give Your Tile Floor A Wall-To-Wall Effect

The Almiera pattern by Flintcoat is a self-sticking tile that utilizes three-color embossing to hide the seams between the tiles. The result is a wall-to-wall effect that you might have thought you could attain only with sheet goods.

Brick Look Is Really Vinyl Tile

Not all floor tiles need look like resilient flooring. The Hampshire Brick pattern made by Azrock Floor Products is an example of how tile can be made to look just like brick. Other patterns from this and other companies simulate terrazzo, marble, stone, and ceramic substances, allowing you to create a great number of different effects with the installation ease of resilient floor tiles.

Place 'N Press Is The Easy Way To Go

What could be easier and less messy than to peel off a paper backing and stick self-adhering tiles on the floor. Armstrong's Solarian flooring comes in convenient Place 'N Press tiles. Although the easy installation is an attractive feature, it is probably Solarian's Mirabond finish—the no-wax finish—that has made it so popular.

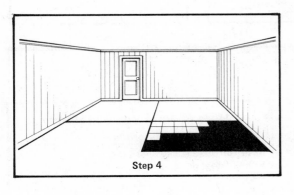
Step 4

8. Follow the same procedures for the other three quarters, and then be prepared to receive pats on the back for doing such professional-looking work.

Here are some tips that will make the job easier. Make sure that the temperature of the room is at least 70 degrees before you start, put all the boxes of tile in this room for at least 24 hours prior to putting them down, and keep the temperature at that level for about a week afterward. Then wait at least a week after installation before washing the floor.

Elmer's Gets A Good Grip

There are special mastics made for almost every type of resilient flooring, but Elmer's Heavy Grip Cement is a good all-purpose fast-grabbing solvent-type adhesive that works well with most types of tile. Be sure to follow all the directions and observe the caution notices on the container. Elmer's Heavy Grip is also good for bonding metal, ceramics, brick, masonry, and other substances found around the home.

4. Now you are ready to start cementing the tiles down. Work on a quarter of the room at a time. Be sure that you check the back of each tile to see that all of the arrows are aimed in the same direction. This keeps the pattern, if any, aligned. If you are using a mixed tile pattern, you should lay it out without mastic before putting the tiles in place. If you have tiles with the adhesive already on the backing, peel off the release paper. Start at the center point, and place the tile down precisely on both lines. It will not slide into place; once down, it is down for good. If you have tiles without mastic, spread the cement over the first quarter only, bringing it right up to the lines. Be sure to use the proper mastic, and follow the directions regarding how long to wait before setting the tiles in place. Usually, you are instructed to wait until the adhesive is tacky.

5. After you get the first center tile in place, lay tiles alternately toward each wall, building a sort of pyramid until the entire quarter is covered except for the tiles along the edges.

6. To cut and fit the border tiles, first place a loose tile (#1) on the last tile in the row. Then butt another loose tile (#2) against the wall, with its sides aligned with those of the #1 tile. Now, make a mark on the #1 tile, along the edge of #2 where the two tiles overlap. If you then cut the #1 tile along the line, you will have an exact fit for the border tile. If you have any irregularities (such as pipes) to fit tiles around, make a paper pattern of the obstacle, trace it onto the tile, and then cut along the line. You should be able to cut most tiles with ordinary heavy-duty scissors.

7. Go over the tiles with a rolling pin.

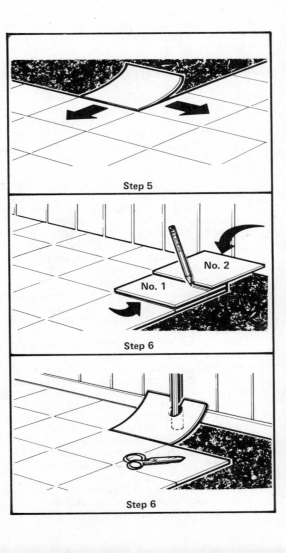
Step 5
Step 6
Step 6

Take Your Pick Of Installation Methods

Many manufacturers of resilient flooring give the do-it-yourselfer a choice of application methods. Kentile's Delhi tiles, for example, are available in both self-adhering and regular versions. These vinyl asbestos tiles come in 12x12-inch squares, the most popular size for do-it-yourselfers, because such tiles are easy to handle, go down quickly, and make figuring much easier.

Floors

Spray Cleaners Handle Floor Spots With A Spritz

Most spots on resilient flooring can be removed with a spritz from one of the many fine spray cleaners available at grocery and hardware stores. Formula 409, for example, is a popular all-purpose cleaner that quickly rids floors of food and grease stains, heel marks, and other spots and substances that can attack your floors. It works on linoleum as well as vinyl flooring, but like most spray cleaners, Formula 409—a product of Clorox Company—will remove wax if left on for a long period of time. Thus, the key to spot removal is spray on and wipe off immediately. Other popular spray cleaners include Fantastik, Top Job, and Whistle.

String-Type Floor Mop Is Still Hanging Around

Although the sponge mop is currently more popular, the old-fashioned string mop has a definite place in the care of resilient flooring. Zephyr Manufacturing Company makes both types, as well as many other floor cleaning tools. The Zephyr Deck Mop is well made and, of course, takes replacement mopheads quickly and simply. If you opt for a string mop over a sponge mop, you should really have a wringer bucket. Of the many currently on the market, Mr. Twister from Federal Housewares Company is unusually effective and easy to use.

Stainless Steel Wool Can Zap Floor Spots

Although more expensive than the regular type, stainless steel wool is much better for long-term wet usage. Several companies market stainless steel wool, including the International Steel Wool Corporation, producers of Elephant Steel Wool, in poly bags or sleeves. Elephant Steel Wool is a high quality product that is carefully graded.

Good Floor Waxes Are Plentiful

There are so many good floor waxes and wax-cleaners on the market that it's difficult to pick one over another. For example, S.C. Johnson and Son markets Beautiflor, Bravo, Future, Glo-Coat, Klear, and Step Saver, all of which can be found in grocery and hardware stores as well as in the housewares sections of department stores. The key to finding the proper wax lies in reading the recommendations from the maker of your floor covering and then reading the labels on the various wax and wax-cleaner products. Knowing the nature of your flooring will help you pick the right wax for it. Some of the other good, widely distributed waxes include Simoniz Non-Scuff Floor Wax, Aero Wax Floor Finish, Formica Floor Shine, Mop and Glo, Bruce Wash N Wax, White Magic Acrylic, Treewax Vinyl Finish, and Mirasheen.

Removing Spots from Resilient Floors

THOSE STURDY and beautiful resilient floors that are so popular in modern kitchens receive a great deal of punishment. Although you can usually just mop them clean, there are some stains that will not respond to the mop. Rather than letting such a floor become so unattractive that you must replace it, follow these tips for removing spots from your resilient floor.

1. Remember, you can prevent spills from turning into stains by treating them immediately. In many cases, a damp cloth removes the spill and the possibility of a stain.
2. Know the material the flooring is made of; it could be vinyl, asphalt, rubber, or linoleum.
3. Treat heel marks, probably the most common problem, with an all-purpose spray cleaner. If the cleaner fails to get rid of the marks, use 0000 steel wool dipped into liquid wax. Then go over the area with a damp cloth. When dry, wax the floor.
4. Tar, chewing gum or candle wax will get brittle if you hold an ice cube against the substance. Then use a metal spatula or some other such dull tool to scrape away the brittle matter. If there is residue left, try a dry cleaner and 0000 steel wool. Wash the area, and wax it when dry.
5. Ink stains should be covered for a few minutes with a rubbing alcohol compress. Then—unless the floor is linoleum—wipe the area with an ammonia dampened rag.
6. You can often scrape up paint spots with a spatula. If not, try wearing them away with 0000 steel wool and liquid wax.
7. Rust stains should be treated by rubbing on a dilute solution of oxalic acid with 0000 steel wool. Oxalic acid is available at paint stores, but you must observe all the caution notices when using it on your floors.
8. Mustard will sometimes leave a stain if

Here Is What You Will Need

Materials

- All-purpose spray cleaner
- 0000 steel wool
- Liquid wax
- Ice
- Dry cleaner
- Rubbing alcohol
- Ammonia
- Oxalic acid
- Hydrogen peroxide
- White vinegar

Tools

- Metal spatula
- Mop

Step 4

allowed to dry. After removing all the dried matter with a spatula or damp cloth, make a compress soaked with hydrogen peroxide and leave it on the stain for several minutes. Then wash, let dry, and wax.

9. Drain cleaners are caustics and should be neutralized with white vinegar as soon as possible. Wash, let dry, and wax.
10. Fruit stains and coffee stains that you cannot wipe up should first be rubbed with 0000 steel wool and liquid wax. Then, remove all the wax and make a compress soaked with hydrogen peroxide. Leave the compress on for several minutes. Wash, let dry, and wax.

Sanding Discs Reach Floor's Edges

The disc sander is the tool to use for getting into the edges and corners the big sander cannot reach. 3-M makes coated abrasives for every type of sander and for every sanding function, and the 3-M Resinite Sanding Discs are as good as you will find. They come in all the popular grits in discs made to fit all makes and sizes of machines from five to 16 inches in diameter. Be sure to buy enough sanding discs so that you can replace spent ones readily. Trying to stretch the life of a worn-out disc results in bad sanding, and bad sanding produces an unattractive floor finish.

Refinishing Hardwood Floors

DESPITE ALL OF the fantastic new easy-to-apply flooring materials, there are few that can beat the beauty of hardwood floors—when they are in good condition, that is. By the same token, a hardwood floor in bad condition can look terrible. If you now have ugly hardwood floors, you can either cover them with carpet or you can restore their beauty.

The best way to remove the old worn-out finish is to sand it off. When you look at an average-size room, though, and think about how long it will take to sand, you may wish to give up and forget about refinishing. Fortunately, you can rent a large drum sander that does the job quickly. When you go to the rental company, have the dealer show you how to operate the unit properly. The same holds true for the other sander you will need for the edges. This tool is a disc sander, commonly called a floor edger.

1. Move all of the furniture out of the room, and take down any wall hangings.
2. Tape over all heating and air conditioning ducts.
3. Carefully remove the shoe molding.
4. Check the entire floor for nail heads. If you find any, use a nailset to drive them below the surface.
5. When you finish all of the preparatory steps, open all the windows and close the doors to adjoining rooms.
6. For the initial sanding, place coarse (20 grit) open coat sandpaper on the drum sander. Go over the entire floor with the sander, sanding with the grain. Since the sander works in both directions, you make one pass pushing and another pulling. You must tilt the unit to raise the drum at the beginning and ending of each pass. Lower it back slowly each time to prevent it from digging into the floor. Proceed slowly; never let the machine run away with you. Go over the edges with the disc sander, using the same grit abrasive. To get right up in the corners, however, you must use a sanding block equipped with the same grit sandpaper.
7. When you finish the first sanding, change to a medium sandpaper, a 40 grit. Repeat the same sanding procedure.
8. Next comes the final sanding. Use a fine or 100 grit sandpaper.
9. Return the rented equipment.
10. Vacuum the room to get all of the dust out.
11. The next step is optional; it is a matter of personal taste whether to stain the floor or leave it natural. For a pretty good idea of how the natural wood will look without a stain but with a finish, take a rag and rub turpentine over a small section of the floor. What you see is quite close to the way the floor will look with just a finish on it. If you think it lacks character or is too light, then staining is the answer.
12. After you stain the floor or decide against staining, you must apply the finish. The most popular finishes today are synthetic varnishes—such as polyurethane—but you should consult your paint dealer and let him show you samples of how each finish will look on your floor. Whatever type you decide to apply, be sure to follow the directions on the label. Put down at least two coats of the finish on your floor.
13. Most finishes wear better when given a periodic waxing. Wax the floor and then buff the new finish when it is completely dry.

Here Is What You Will Need

Materials

- Tape
- Coarse (20 grit) open coat sandpaper
- Medium (40 grit) sandpaper
- Fine (100 grit) sandpaper
- Wood stain
- Turpentine
- Rags
- Synthetic varnish or other floor finish
- Wax

Tools

- Drum sander
- Disc sander
- Nailset
- Vacuum cleaner
- Paintbrush
- Buffer

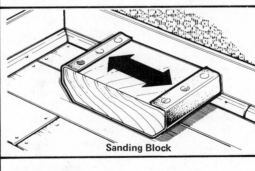

Sanding Block

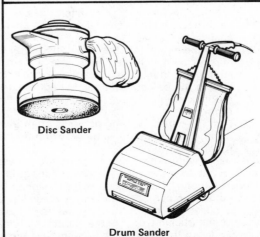

Disc Sander

Drum Sander

Trewax Plus Elbow Grease Equal Beautiful Floors

Trewax Paste, like any paste wax, requires more work to apply than the easy-to-use liquids on the market. But, when applied properly, Trewax can produce such excellent results that you will never question the value of your labor. Over half of the wax solids in Trewax are Brazilian carnauba, which produce an exquisitely shiny floor (though UL-approved for slip-resistance) and one that allows the true tone of the wood to show through without discoloration. The Trewax Company markets a wide assortment of wood care products for floors and furniture.

Fabulon Finishes Refinished Floors

One of the most popular finishes to put on floors after you sand and smooth them is Fabulon from the Pierce & Stevens Chemical Company. Available in several different forms, the original Fabulon is a fast-drying easy-to-apply floor finish that is ready to use with no stirring or mixing. It can be brushed or rolled on, and when applied to a well-sanded floor during the day, Fabulon can be ready for a party that night. Although the original Fabulon provides a hard finish, try Fabulon's Epoxy Gym Finish or Polyurethane Heavy Duty if you want your floors to have a truly tough and durable covering.

Dustless Belt Sander Cuts Finish Fast

The Skil three-inch Dustless Belt Sander is a lightweight, easy-to-handle tool that provides a fast way to cut down any surface. The built-in dust pickup means that no dust falls on you or your work; it all stays in the bag. Efficient for sanding wood, composition material, and metal, the Skil Dustless Belt Sander features a flush design for sanding right up to a vertical surface. Belt changing is quick and easy, and the unit is competitively priced.

Floors

Knee Kicker Is Key To Stretching Carpet Tight

The knee kicker, or stretcher as the device is properly called, pulls the carpet and hooks it tightly over the teeth on the tack strips. Since the tool's usefulness is so limited, however, you may encounter some difficulty in tracking one down. It is certainly not the type of tool you can find at your neighborhood hardware store. Try your carpet retailer and ask whether he will rent one to you. If not, call one of the regular tool rental services. You probably will want to buy a knee kicker only as a last resort, but if you do, the C.S. Osborne Company makes a good one.

Wooden Tack Strips Cover Perimeter

For tacked-down carpet installations, you must cover the perimeter of the room with wooden tack strips. Sears offers tack strips in four-foot lengths, packaging them in boxes of 25 strips. You merely tack the strips to the floor, and then the concealed teeth grab and hold the carpet taut around the edges of the room. Sears carpet departments have a complete line of everything the do-it-yourselfer needs for carpeting and padding installations. Of course, all of these items may also be ordered through the Sears catalog.

Free Folder Tells How To Install Carpet Tiles And Rolls

Armstrong Cork Company offers a pamphlet describing how to install both carpet rolls and carpet tiles. It incorporates diagrams and easy instructions, along with a chart to help the do-it-yourselfer estimate how much carpeting is needed to complete a room. There is even a section illustrating how to match patterned carpeting at the seams.

Making A Knee Kicker

A homemade knee kicker is simple to put together. Since the padded part must be thick enough for comfort when you hit it with your knee, glue a thick scrap of foam upholstery to one side of an eight-inch square of scrap lumber. Make the body of the kicker out of a pair of 2x4s about a foot long, and use nails driven through another eight-inch square of scrap lumber as the stretcher pins. Be sure to angle the nails (hardened steel nails work best) so that they will grab the carpet when pushed down. Put all the wooden pieces together with wood screws, and your knee kicker is finished. Swift knee movement against the foam pad stretches the carpet. Then, when the forward push stops, the carpet hooks over the angled spikes in the tack strip.

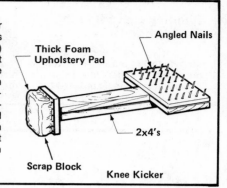

Laying Tacked Down Carpet

TACKED DOWN wall-to-wall carpeting can enhance the beauty and comfort of just about any room in your house. It makes for a warmer room, cuts noise, and feels comfortable under foot. Installing wall-to-wall carpeting is really not difficult, but you must know the tricks and techniques to getting the job done right.

1. Move all furniture out of the room.
2. Remove the door (or doors) to the room.
3. Prepare the floor by removing all the tacks remaining from previous carpet installations, by eliminating any squeaks in the floor (use nails and/or countersunk screws to pull the subflooring tight to eliminate movement), and by filling in wide cracks with wood putty.
4. Nail carpet tack strips to the floor all the way around the room, leaving a quarter-inch space between the edge of the strip and the wall.
5. Install the padding by stapling it to the subflooring. Make sure that the padding goes right up to the edge of the tack strips; you can trim it with a utility knife or scissors after you get it properly stapled.
6. If you wish, many carpet sellers will cut and seam the carpet before delivery. If you don't wish to have them do the cutting and seaming, you can do your own seaming easily with carpet tape; you can use either the regular sticky tape or the kind that must be activated by a special heat device available from carpet dealers and tool rental firms. The heat-activated tape usually works better. If you do decide to handle your own seaming, make sure you match the carpet pattern and pile direction carefully to create an invisible seam.
7. Bring the carpet into the room and unroll it, making sure it is centered. Use a carpet stretcher (often called a knee kicker) to stretch the carpet and hook the edges over the tack strips around the perimeter of the room.
8. Trim the carpet, leaving about ⅜ of an inch beyond the tack strip all the way around the room.
9. Use a wide putty knife to poke the excess carpet down between the wall and the strip.
10. Install one of the special strips designed to hold down carpet at doorways. These strips are like the tack strips in that they have points sticking up for the carpet to hook over, but they also have a decorative metal

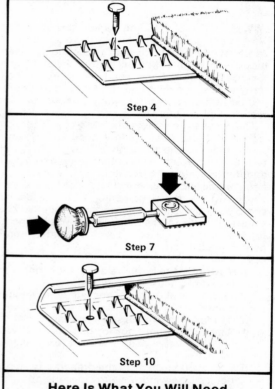

Step 4

Step 7

Step 10

Here Is What You Will Need

Materials

- Carpet
- Padding
- Tack strips
- Nails
- Countersunk screws
- Staples
- Carpet tape
- Doorway strip
- Wood putty

Tools

- Hammer
- Screwdriver
- Putty knife
- Tape measure
- Staple gun
- Utility knife or scissors
- Carpet tape heater
- Carpet stretcher (knee kicker)

lip which can be bent flat against the carpet. If the new carpet and pad are much thicker than the previous floor covering, you may have to trim off part of the door for it to clear the carpet.

Padding Makes A Big Difference

You can make inexpensive carpet feel several times thicker and plushier by placing good padding beneath it. Installation is easy. For padding under a bathroom carpet, try one of the rubberized types since fiber padding is too susceptible to moisture in such circumstances. If you plan to carpet over resilient flooring, you can use doubled-faced carpet tape to hold the padding down.

Rug Shears Cut Carpets Cleanly

While you can cut most bathroom carpeting with nearly any good pair of heavy-duty scissors, you can see at a glance that the Clauss Rug Shears offer one big advantage: their shape. The offset handles make carpet cutting much easier. Made of hammer-forged molybdenum steel with double-plated chrome over nickel, the Clauss Rug Shears boast exceptionally sharp eight-inch knife

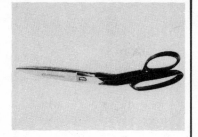

blade edges. Clauss Cutlery Company enjoys a fine reputation as manufacturers of top quality scissors and shears.

Entry Edging Is Finishing Touch

Even with carpet that is taped in place, there always exists the possibility that someone will catch a heel on the edge when entering the room. You can prevent such accidents by installing one of the many different types of edging strips, some metal and some plastic, made to accommodate both the carpet and the flooring in the adjoining room or hall. Mercer Plastics Company, Inc., offers a wide variety of such edgings, including the universal joiner for use where carpets in two adjoining rooms meet.

Installing Bathroom Carpet

ONLY A FEW years ago, laying a carpet in the bathroom was strictly a job for the professional—and that cost money. Now the situation is completely different. In a single afternoon you can lay wall-to-wall carpeting in your bathroom that will look great, feel great, and leave your budget in better shape than you probably think. Here is how to do it.

1. Measure the bathroom to figure out the square footage. Then draw a floor plan.
2. Now you are ready to shop. You will find packaged bathroom carpets that come in several sizes with a paper pattern included. They make installation easy. You can also buy carpet remnants on sale, but just remember that the carpet will get wet; therefore, be sure to buy a synthetic material that will stand up to the use it will receive.
3. After you buy your carpet, you must make a pattern. You can buy rolls of brown paper at the variety store, or you can tape sheets of newspaper together. The pattern is easier to handle if you use several small sections at first, and then put them together when you finish the entire bathroom.
4. To make the pattern for around the toilet, fold the paper in half and place it beside the toilet. Press the pattern against the toilet with your hand to give you an outline, and then use a scissors to cut along the line.
5. Now cut a straight line in the paper from the part that goes against the back wall to the opening for the toilet.
6. Fit the pattern around the toilet and trim.
7. Use the same technique around any other immovable objects.
8. When you get all the sections cut out, piece them together on the floor to make sure they fit the room precisely. Then add extra tape to prevent the separate pieces from pulling loose. Mark the pattern "TOP."
9. In another room, lay the carpet face down on the floor.
10. Turn the pattern face down on the carpet and tape it to the backing. Mentally check the pattern as it rests on the carpet to be sure that the cutouts will be in the right parts of the room for the toilet, etc.
11. Carefully trace the pattern onto the backing with a ball point pen.
12. Use a heavy-duty pair of scissors to cut along the lines.

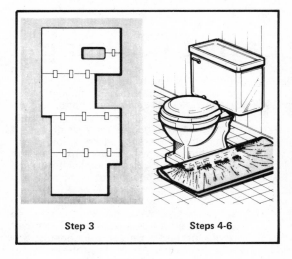

Step 3   Steps 4-6

13. Place carpet tape (sticky on both sides) around the perimeter of the room and around any cutouts. If you must have seams in the carpet, use tape to keep joints together.
14. Put the carpet down in place and press it against the carpet tape. If later you need to move the carpet, you can peel it up from the tape and then stick it back down again.

Here Is What You Will Need
Materials
- Bathroom carpet
- Brown paper or newspaper
- Tape
- Carpet tape

Tools
- Measuring tape
- Heavy-duty scissors
- Ball point pen

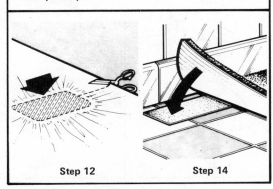

Step 12   Step 14

Quality Rules

Disston's 20-foot retractable steel rule is a quality measuring device. It offers a positive locking system that engages with just a push of your thumb, and its smooth power return automatically retracts just as easily. The mylar blade has red and black markings on white or yellow, and a belt clip is attached for your carrying convenience.

Tape Anchors Carpet Securely

Double-faced tapes, those that are sticky on both sides, have changed many carpet installations from have-it-done jobs to do-it-yourself projects. Carpetak Tape from Arno is one of the best of the double-faced tapes, and it is especially good with indoor-outdoor carpets. You can use this tape to anchor loose rugs, hold down hall runners, fix bath mats in place, and keep your door mat where it belongs. In fact, you can use Carpetak wherever you would otherwise have to tack, sew, or staple to keep your carpet in place.

Floors

Blue Lustre For Any Color Carpets

Blue Lustre's rental shampooers are lightweight and easy to use. The electric shampooer massages the Blue Lustre foam cleaner into the carpet; once the foam dries, you just vacuum up the dirt and cleaner residue. Blue Lustre carpet shampoo can also be used on upholstery, and there is a squeeze bottle applicator with a brush head that lets you hand massage the foam into the fabric. Of course, you should always test this or any other fabric cleaner on an obscure area to make sure that it won't affect the carpet or uphol-

stery colors. Blue Lustre products are distributed by the Earl Grissmer Company, Inc.

Bissell Shampooer Is A Featherweight

With regular carpet cleaning and care, you may never need to call in the professionals or rent one of the heavy-duty carpet cleaning machines. Bissell markets inexpensive home shampooers that make such care and cleaning possible. The lightweight (seven pounds) Spinfoam Electric Rug Shampooer gently massages foam into the carpet fibers; when the shampoo dries, you just vacuum it and the dirt away. Easy to operate, the Bissell Spinfoam Shampooer holds enough shampoo to clean about 50 square feet without refilling.

Sweep Up The Daily Dirt

The Bissell Century II Carpet Sweeper features two small brushes at the front corners of the unit to get dirt that is right up against the wall, dirt that other sweepers might miss. The unit adjusts in height to be effective on any floor surface from bare floors to shag carpets. Bissell also markets several carpet cleaning compounds, including the Dry Carpet Cleaner that eliminates all possibility of staining or fading.

Don't Let Your Carpets Shock You

If you get a jolt every time you walk across the room and reach for a door knob, you should try one of the sprays that minimize and often eliminate this static electricity. D'Stat from Vigilant Products Company, Inc., is an aerosol spray that does just that. Other good sprays for static electricity include Stat-O-Cide, End Stat, and Merix Anti-Static.

Carpet Cleaning

PROBABLY NOTHING in your home is subjected to as much abuse as your carpeting. And when the carpeting gets dirty or stained it detracts from the appearance of the whole room. Of course, there is no way to prevent carpeting from getting dirty, but you can clean it yourself and keep your floors looking great. Here is what to do.

1. Treat spots and stains as soon as you see them, but before you use any spot remover formula, pretest it on some inconspicuous area of the carpet. Apply the spot remover to the carpet and let it remain there for a few moments; then dab at the area with a white cleansing tissue. If the formula is harmful to the dye in the carpet, you will know it now.
2. Go over the carpet daily with a nonpowered sweeper.
3. Vacuum once or twice a week, depending on the traffic over your carpets. Make seven to eight passes over each section to remove imbedded dirt as well as to pick up surface particles.
4. If your carpets are not tacked down, turn them annually to spread the effects of wear. If you have wall-to-wall carpeting, rearrange the furniture from time to time, and place throw rugs over high traffic areas.

5. Shampoo your carpets at least once a year, before they get really dirty. You can rent an electric shampooer, and there are several good shampoos on the market. Vacuum thoroughly before shampooing, and be sure to avoid soaking the carpet or using too much shampoo. Move all of the furniture out of the way, and if you have to put it back before the carpet is completely dry, place squares of aluminum foil under the furniture legs. Vacuum again after shampooing.

Here Is What You Will Need

Materials

- Spot remover
- Cleansing tissues
- Carpet shampoo
- Aluminum foil
- White vinegar
- Dry carpet cleaner
- Ammonia
- Sponge

Tools

- Nonpowered sweeper
- Vacuum cleaner
- Electric shampooer
- Stiff brush
- Scissors

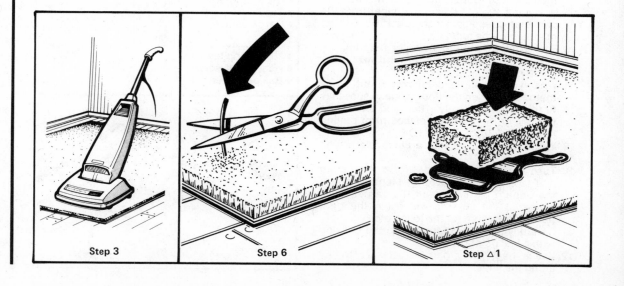

Step 3

Step 6

Step △1

Out, Damn Spot

When a spot appears on your otherwise clean carpet, reach for a good spot remover instead of the carpet shampoo. There are some good spot removers available; some of the best include Renuzit from the Drackett Company, Rid-Spot from Coastal Chemical, and Rug-Mate (a stain-removing shampoo) from Zynolyte Products Company. Before applying any spot remover, always test first under a couch or in a corner to be sure the chemicals won't take the color out of your carpet. In addition, follow the manufacturer's caution notices to the letter.

Heavy-Duty Steam Carpet Cleaner Pumps Out Dirt

Steamex, made by U.S. Floor Systems, Inc., is a heavy-duty carpet cleaner that injects streams of hot cleaning solution deep into the carpet pile. Almost simultaneously, it extracts the moisture, cleaner residue, and suspended soil from the full depth of the carpet. In fact, a Steamex unit actually consists of two separate systems, one to pump out and one to vacuum in. When you rent a Steamex, you receive complete operating instructions which are quite simple. You just add water and cleaner; the machine is pre-set and almost trouble-free. Before you clean your carpets with a Steamex, however, you should go over them with your regular vacuum cleaner, spot clean any grease or food stains, and pre-treat heavy traffic areas.

6. Never pull loose carpet threads. Always snip them off even with the rest of the carpet.

Here are the best ways to get rid of various spots and stains. Once again, remember to treat the spot immediately and to pretest any solution on an inconspicuous area of the carpet before you apply it in the middle of the room.

△ 1. Blot all spilled liquids with a white paper towel, sponge, or cleansing tissue.
△ 2. Scrape up all semi-solids which fall on the carpet.
△ 3. Always work from the outer edge of the stain toward the center.
△ 4. Take care not to overmoisten. Use small amounts of spot remover and blot.
△ 5. After removing the excess, treat any greasy or oily stain with a dry cleaning solution. Be sure to read the caution notice on the label and to provide adequate ventilation. Follow with shampoo, but if you do not have any carpet shampoo in the house, you can use a detergent that is mild enough for lingerie.
△ 6. Coffee and tea stains require carpet shampoo. If the stains are still visible after you shampoo them, blot with a white vinegar solution—one part vinegar to two parts water—or apply a dry cleaner.
△ 7. Dampen blood stains with cold water, and then use a concentrated solution of carpet shampoo. When dry, apply a dry cleaner and then shampoo once again.
△ 8. Treat milk, gravy, or ice cream stains as you would blood stains, following the procedure in step 7.
△ 9. Ink stains fall in three categories: ball point pen marks respond to a dry cleaner; washable ink should come up with a concentrated solution of carpet shampoo; but indelible ink is a lost cause. Try to minimize the damage with carpet shampoo.
△ 10. Usually, alcoholic beverages respond well to blotting, but it is best to play it safe and apply carpet shampoo. Red wines must be shampooed.
△ 11. Hold an ice cube against chewing gum and candle wax until they become brittle enough to be chipped off. A dry cleaner can soften them and allow you to scrape them away.
△ 12. Chocolate responds to a concentrated solution of carpet shampoo or to a very mild ammonia solution (one tablespoon per cup of water).
△ 13. Crayon marks can be removed with a dry cleaner followed by shampooing.
△ 14. Fingernail polish could be removed with polish remover, but this procedure often

removes carpet dye and damages some fibers. Try a dry cleaner.
△ 15. Mud should be allowed to dry, and then loosened with a stiff brush and vacuumed away.

Carpet Sweeper

Electric Shampooer

Wet-Dry Vacuum Cleaner Helps Shampoo Carpets

Although the Aqua-Vac Wet-Dry Vacuum Cleaner is made for heavy-duty shop use, it can do a great job of removing wet shampoo from your carpet. Able to pick up almost six gallons of straight liquid, the Aqua-Vac has a float shut-off so the water level can never get near the motor. Aqua-Vac is a product of the Shop-Vac Corporation.

Floors

Tape A Patch Or Whole Carpet With CarpeTape

My-Ro Products, Inc., markets a good double-faced tape called CarpeTape, which does all the things carpet tape should do and does them well. In addition, you will probably discover a multitude of other uses for My-Ro Carpe-Tape around the house. For example, it does a great job of holding posters to a teenager's wall, leaving no ugly holes or unsightly residue. My-Ro also makes bathtub seam-sealing tapes, bathtub safety treads, and other adhesive products.

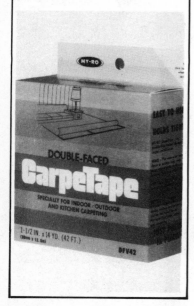

Carpet Edges Stick Together With Mr. Quick

Instead of trying to bind the edges of a carpet patch with needle and thread to prevent raveling, try the specially prepared binding adhesive called Mr. Quick. It comes in a plastic squeeze bottle with a handy spout that lets you run along the carpet edge with good speed. Since it dries clear, Mr. Quick is great for carpet burn repairs. Available wherever carpet products are sold, Mr. Quick is manufactured by Carpet Products Company of Central Square, New York.

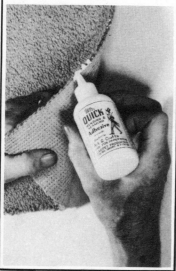

Carpet Cutter Cuts Carpet Quickly

The American Safety Razor Company markets an inexpensive Carpet Cutter knife that is much like a utility knife except that its handle is shaped to provide a better angle for cutting carpet. The American Carpet Cutter comes carded with the special handle and a package of ten blades. American also makes strippers, scrapers, and other bladed tools, as well as extra blades for shop use.

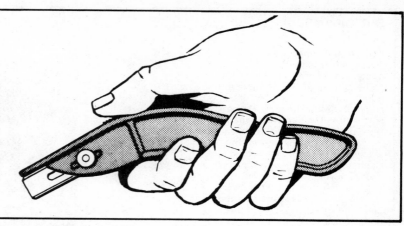

Repairing Burns in Carpeting

Here Is What You Will Need
Materials
● Carpet scrap
● Glue
● Carpet tape
Tools
● Fingernail scissors

AFTER EVERY party you find some evidence of totally careless people, but one of the worst sights you can spot is the cigarette burn in the living room carpet. Although you cannot repair the damage completely without having the carpet rewoven, there are several ways to hide the burned spot very effectively. Here are the steps to take.

1. Use a pair of fingernail scissors to clip away all the blackened fibers. If the burn failed to go down all the way to the backing, you may not have to do anything else; the one low spot generally is not noticeable. If the burn did go to the backing, however, scrape the charred matter away.
2. If the backing shows, clip new fibers from a carpet scrap and glue them in place over the hole. First put glue on the hole, and then as the glue gets tacky enough to support the fibers, carefully place a few of them at a time upright in the glue.
3. If the damage is even more severe, cut an entire square out of the carpet and replace it with a scrap piece. Use carpet tape that is sticky on both sides to hold the patch in place, and make sure that the nap of the new carpet scrap lays the same way as the nap of the carpet already down.

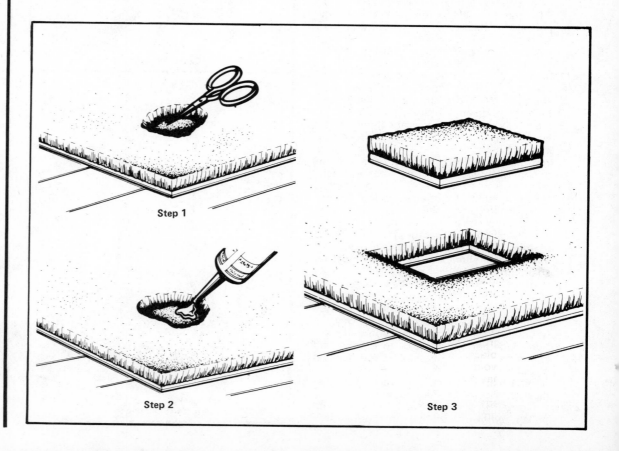

Step 1

Step 2

Step 3

Mastic Reseats New Tile

Although the old tile you take out may have been set in mortar, the easiest and most efficient way to seat its replacement is with an adhesive. Although there are a number of products on the market that would do the job, be sure that the one you select is waterproof and made specifically for ceramic tile. One such product that fulfills all the criteria is Quick Set Ceramic Tile Adhesive from the United States Ceramic Tile Company. No matter what type of mastic you use under the tile, though, be sure to remove all the dirt and dust from the work surface, make the new tile level with the others, and be careful not to apply so much mastic that it squeezes out into the grout lines.

Carbide-Tipped Masonry Bit Goes Through Ceramic Tile

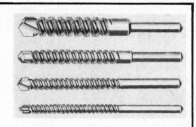

General Hardware's drill bit set contains five tungsten-carbide tipped bits for use with a quarter-inch drill. In addition to drilling ceramic tiles, these bits can cut through concrete, brick, and stone, and they are spiral fluted to assure fast dust removal without clogging. Since you only need the smallest bit in the set for drilling out a ceramic tile, you may wish to buy these General Hardware drill bits individually; on the other hand, once you own the set you will probably find plenty of uses for the other sizes.

Replacing a Ceramic Tile

GENERALLY, the hardest part about replacing a cracked ceramic tile is tracking down a new tile that matches. Some colors are not easy to find. If your tile is very old, you may have to go to a wrecking yard to find a match. Once you have the right tile, however, just follow these directions for removing the cracked one and putting in its replacement.

1. The best method for removing the old tile is to drill a hole in its middle with a carbide bit in your power drill.
2. Next, score an "X" in the tile with a glass cutter.
3. With a cold chisel and hammer break away the tile without damaging any of the surrounding tiles.
4. Clean the bed on which the old tile rested, removing all the bumps to make the surface as smooth as possible. Then remove any loose grout around the opening.
5. Purchase tile mastic at a hardware store, and spread it over the back of the new tile. Keep the mastic about a half inch away from all four edges.
6. Hold the tile by its edges and ease it into place. Press until the new tile is flush with the surrounding tiles.
7. Position the tile to provide an even space all around it, and then either tape it in place or insert broken toothpicks to keep gravity from pulling the tile down before the mastic sets up.
8. Allow enough time for the mastic to cure, and then mix tile grout according to the directions on the package. Be sure to mix the grout until it is completely smooth.
9. Fill in the space all the way around the tile with the grout mix. Dip either a sponge or your finger into the mix, and apply it so as to fill the space entirely. You will do no harm if you get the grout on other tiles.
10. After the grout has set for about a quarter of an hour, take a damp terry cloth towel and gently remove any excess on the other tiles. Just be careful not to dig out any of the grout from between the tiles.
11. Wait until the next day, and then rub the damp towel more vigorously to remove all traces of grout and to polish the tile. If the tile you replaced is in a shower, make sure that you avoid getting any water on it until the grout has set up completely.

You can remedy loose tiles the same way, except that you eliminate steps 1, 2, and 3. Use a

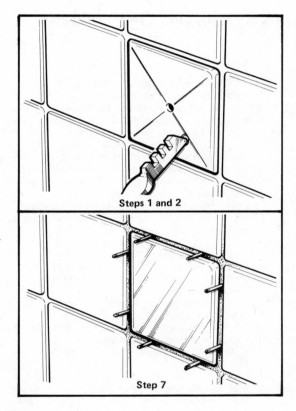

Steps 1 and 2

Step 7

knife to scrape out all the grout around the loose tile, and then gently pry out the tile with a putty knife. Follow all of the steps above to replace it.

While you are working on the one tile, check all the others to see if they are loose. Loosened tiles usually are caused by shifting in the foundation, and, therefore, several tiles often come loose at the same time. Light tapping on the tiles with a putty knife handle will show you where any loose ones are.

Here Is What You Will Need
Materials
- Replacement tile
- Tile mastic
- Tape or wooden toothpicks
- Tile grout
- Sponge
- Terry cloth towel

Tools
- Power drill with carbide tip
- Glass cutter
- Cold chisel
- Hammer
- Knife
- Putty knife

Powdered Grout Just Needs Water

Bondex Tile Grout from Bondex International (makers of a wide line of paint and patch products) comes in powder form, and you just add water according to the directions. Be sure to mix until all the lumps dissolve. When replacing only one tile, you can probably get away without wearing rubber gloves; but the grout does have lime in it and is, therefore, a skin irritant. In addition, if you plan to work on several tiles, you would be wise to spread a plastic sheet over the drain since the grout that you drop as you are working could clog the drain. Similarly, never wash your grouting tools and mixing container in the sink or tub.

Easy-Set System Goes On Over Existing Ceramic Tile

If you find yourself with a ceramic tile wall that is too far gone to be helped by replacing one or two tiles—or if you cannot find the replacement tiles to match—you have no choice but to install new ceramic tile over the entire surface. Before you rip out the whole wall and start over, however, you should know that the Easy-Set System from the American Olean Tile Company can make your work much easier. Easy-Set is a modular system that goes on over your old tiles. Each block of nine tiles is pre-grouted to form one square foot of tile wallcovering. All you do is spread the adhesive over a sound surface, put the sections in place, and then grout the seams between the sections with the same silicone rubber grout (available in a cartridge for use with a caulking gun) previously applied between the individual tiles.

Ready-To-Use Grout Saves Time And Mess

If you want to avoid mixing powdered grout, merely seek out one of the ready-mixed preparations available. Gibson-Homans Tile Grout with Silicone is ideal for either ceramic or mosaic tile. It dries white and resists stains and mildew. G-H is known for producing top quality items for the home, and the company's Tile Grout with Silicone is easy to apply, attractive, and durable.

Keep Grout Lines Clean

One of the biggest problems with tile is keeping the grout lines clean. The lines start off gleaming white, but they fade and yellow as time goes by. Magic American Chemical Company markets a special Tile 'N Grout Spray (the cap is a handy brush/sponge combination) that not only cleans and whitens the grout but also polishes the tiles. Most household cleaners can clean surface stains off ceramic tile, but a product that can both clean tiles and whiten the grout is a real find.

Sealer Helps Keep Grout White

You can prolong your new grout's gleaming white condition by applying a sealer over it. There are several good brands of silicone grout sealer on the market; they all penetrate and seal the grout against dirt, soil, mildew, and yellowing soap scum. In addition, these colorless coatings protect the tiles as well by resisting soap film and water spotting. H.B. Fuller Silicone Sealer and Polish is an aerosol grout sealer that provides approximately six months protection per application. Sears markets a similar product under the Sears label in the ceramic tile department.

Decorative Appliques Rescue Mismatched Tiles

What can you do if you cannot find a replacement tile that exactly matches the others? Look upon that problem as an opportunity to do something decorative. Tile Appliques from Con-Tact are transparent peel-and-stick squares sized to fit standard ceramic tiles. Available in nine different designs, the appliques are washable, waterproof and stain- and mildew-resistant. While their transparency permits the tile color to show through, the appliques' colorful design obscures any mismatch. When spaced tastefully on a tile wall they can produce a truly attractive decor . . . even if all the tiles match. Con-Tact Tile Appliques, products of the Comark Plastics Division of United Merchants, Inc., come in packages of a dozen.

Regrouting Tiles

Here Is What You Will Need

Materials

- Tile cleaner
- Grout
- Rubber gloves
- Coarse towel
- Silicone tile grout spray

Tools

- Putty knife, kitchen knife, or ice pick
- Sponges

NOT ONLY DOES the absence of grout between ceramic tiles look bad, but pockets between can be an invitation to mildew. These openings acquire and collect dirt and soap scum which, of course, are what mildew needs to thrive. If the loss of grout is deep enough, moreover, water can get in behind the tiles, causing them to fall out before long. Prolonged water penetration behind the tiles can even rot wooden supports or ruin a ceiling below.

You can prevent such calamities easily by regrouting whenever and wherever you see trouble starting. Here is how to do it.

1. Use a sharp tool—a putty knife, an old kitchen knife, or an ice pick will do—to dig away all the loose grout from between the tiles.
2. Flush out all the debris.
3. Clean the tiles to remove all soap scum. Rinse thoroughly.
4. Mix the grout according to the directions on the package. It should be about the consistency of cake batter. Make sure there are no lumps.
5. Jab the grout into the joints. A sponge dipped into the mixture and then pushed into the cracks often works well. Don't worry about getting the grout on the tiles, but do worry about getting it on your hands. Grout is caustic, and you should wear rubber gloves. Use a gloved finger to push the grout into gaps between corner tiles.
6. Use a clean, damp sponge to smooth the grout lines and remove excess mixture.
7. If any gaps remain, add more grout and smooth again. Stop only when the grout lines look the way you want them to look.
8. Let the grout dry.
9. Now is the time to take the grout off the tiles. If you rub the tiles with a coarse dry towel, it will come off.
10. When the grout has cured thoroughly (as specified in the directions on the grout package), seal the grout lines with a silicone tile grout spray.

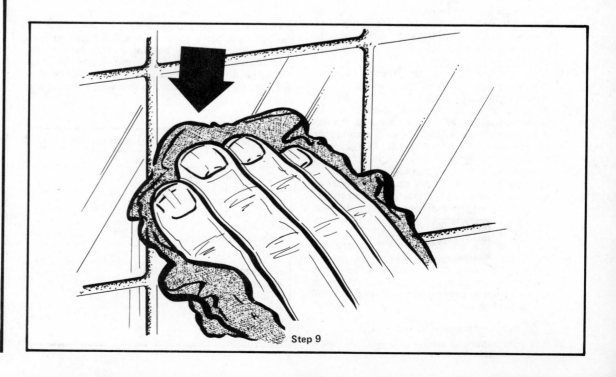

Step 9

Mico Tools Make Caulking Neat

the Mico Master Calker which smooths the seam and trims the The key to a great caulking job is making the seams look as neat as possible. You can own that key in the Mico Master Calker which smoothes the seam and trims the excess caulk all in one stroke. Once the excess is separated from the bead, you can either scrape it away with a putty knife or peel it off after the caulk is partially cured. Mico also makes a tool called the Calk Router, which is

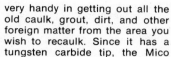

very handy in getting out all the old caulk, grout, dirt, and other foreign matter from the area you wish to recaulk. Since it has a tungsten carbide tip, the Mico

Calk Router can even rout out concrete. Both tools are available via mail order from Modern Industries Inc., 515 Olive Avenue, Vista, California 92083.

Caulking In A Roll Cuts Mess

If caulking with a gun or tube sounds like too much work, consider solving your caulking problems with My-Ro Tub 'N Wall Seal-A-Crack. Pre-shaped vinyl tape that comes in a roll, Seal-A-Crack is self adhering and merely needs to be pressed in place. Since Seal-A-Crack strips can go on right over old caulk, no routing out is required. The 15-foot-roll is more than enough for the average tub caulking situation, and each package contains two pre-cut corner pieces to make your work even neater. Seal-A-Crack comes in white, yellow, green, beige, pink and blue and is available at hardware and paint outlets.

Recaulking a Tub or Sink

WHEN CAULKING breaks loose, the crack that forms around the tub may not look terrible, but you should fix it immediately. As long as there is a gap between the tub and wall, you are letting water seep in. The seepage can rot the walls, cause mildew with its musty odors to form inside, damage the ceiling below, and even loosen the tiles around the tub. Here is how to fix the crack.

1. Purchase a tube of the caulk made especially for bathtubs; it differs from the regular caulk. Some manufacturers of tub caulk offer their product in colors, allowing you to match the color of the tub. If you cannot find the right color, white caulk will look fine no matter what color the tub is.
2. Remove all of the old caulk. Use a putty knife, and be careful not to chip the surface of the tub or the edges of the bottom row of tiles.
3. Use a solvent to clean away any soap residue.
4. Rinse away the solvent with water.
5. Make sure that the surface is completely dry by wrapping a cloth around the putty knife

Here Is What You Will Need
Materials
- Bathtub caulking
- Cleaning solvent
- Rags

Tools
- Putty knife
- Knife
- Razors

blade and running it through the seam.
6. Cut the nozzle of the tub caulk tube at an angle and at a point where the size bead that comes out will be slightly wider than the cavity around the tub.
7. Squeeze the caulk in one continuous bead all around the tub.
8. Wrap a rag around your index finger, dip your finger into a glass of water, and then press the caulk into the cavity. Keep dipping as you go whenever the rag loses its moisture. Smooth the caulk as you push it in.

Done correctly, a caulk job should last for a long time. Quality caulk has elasticity, allowing it to stretch and compress as the weight in the tub changes.

The Cadillac Of Caulking Guns

The Albion 139-3 is the caulking gun against which all standard caulking guns must be compared. It features Albion's ¼-inch Square Piston Rod with thumb-activated instant pressure release. In addition, the gun offers a stroke adjustment so you can regulate the stroke to fit the size of your hand. All in all, the Albion caulking gun is a pleasurable tool to use; it does, however, cost several times the price of more ordinary caulking guns. Albion Engineering Company makes several other caulking tools and accessories.

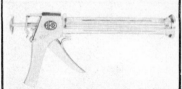

Plenty Of Quality Tub Caulks On The Market

There are many high quality caulks made especially for use around the top of the bathtub. GE Silicone Bathtub Caulk & Seal comes with a screw-on spout, which has the advantage over spouts that must be snipped in that snipped spouts often cannot be capped properly after use. GE's pure white caulk is guaranteed for 10 years. U.S. Gypsum's Durabond Tub Caulk is another good one, as is Macco's Liquid Seal Tub & Tile Caulk. A pure white flexible latex compound that is treated with a fungicide to resist mildew, Macco Liquid Seal Tub & Tile Caulk comes in cartridges for use with a caulking gun as well as in tubes. Of course, you must always get rid of all mildew before recaulking no matter what type of caulk you apply.

Step 6

Step 7

Walls

Careful Measuring Leads To Better Framing

Measuring carefully before cutting framing members will help you end up with a better wall. Generally, a zigzag or folding rule is tops for a framing project, but if you plan to invest in just one measuring device, a retractable steel tape unit would be best. All the units shown are from Lufkin. In front is Lufkin's 25-foot Mezurlok Power Tape with automatic return; it can be locked in any extended position. The 50-foot White Tape model in the center features a pointed end-hook so you won't need someone to hold the tape as you unroll it. The Lufkin Folding Tape at the rear provides a short extension piece to prevent unnecessary unfolding.

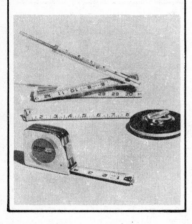

Extra Heft In Framing Hammer

The Stanley Framing Hammer is a little heavier (it has a 22-ounce mill checkered face) than an all-purpose hammer, but you need the extra heft when framing a wall. All Stanley hammers with fiberglass handles feature tapered assembly design to eliminate the possibility of the head flying off. The head, forged of high carbon steel, is secured with epoxy resin adhesive. The comfortable grip is made of vinyl.

Level Keeps Framing On The Up And Up

As you install each stud, you should check to be sure it goes up plumb. A good level can make this task a quick one. Lightweight aluminum levels are easy to handle and generally outlast the wooden models. For example, the Tuflite Level from Rathbone Chesterman Ltd., of Birmingham, England, comes in lengths of 24, 30, 36, 40, and 48 inches. The body is

made of an extruded heavy-duty alloy with end caps for extra strength, and the plastic tubes are shockproof and protected by plastic cover plates. Tuflite Levels are widely distributed in the United States.

Common Nails Do It All

Most framing is done with common nails, and 16d nails are usually the choice. Sheffield Nails, made by Armco Steel, are available either in bulk or in boxes. Usually, you need so few nails when framing a wall that the convenience of getting them in a box is worth the difference in cost. If you buy in bulk, though, figure on getting approximately 15 16d common nails in a pound.

Framing for a Wall

IF YOU PLAN to convert your basement or attached garage into living space, you will probably get into framing, which refers to putting up partitions for walls. Even if you have never done many carpentry chores, you will find that framing is fairly easy.

The basic components of the frame include the top plate, the sole plate, and the studs. The studs are usually on 16-inch centers, which means that the distance from the center of one stud to the center of the next stud measures 16 inches. All framing lumber for a project is of the same size, usually 2x4s.

The framing described here is for a wall that is non-load bearing. Since it is not designed to support the ceiling or the floor above, you need not worry about the roof caving in because of your amateur workmanship. All you have to strive for is

Here Is What You Will Need
Materials
● 2x4s
● 8d Nails
● Shims
Tools
● Measuring Tape
● Straightedge
● Level
● Hammer
● Saw
● Chalk line

making the finished wall look as attractive as possible. Remember, too, that minor cosmetic faults in the framing will be covered over by the wallboard that goes on after the framing is complete.

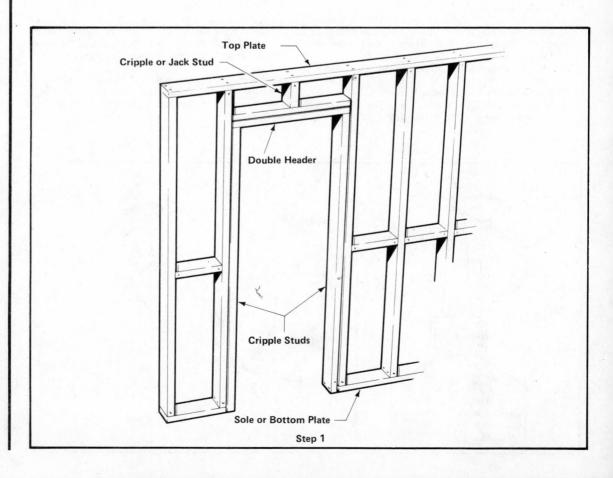

Top Plate

Cripple or Jack Stud

Double Header

Cripple Studs

Sole or Bottom Plate

Step 1

Power Saw Cuts Studs

A circular saw, like this Black & Decker 7¼-inch model, can cut all the studs for your framing job in a matter of minutes. The combination blade does both cross-cutting and ripping. Though not an expensive saw, this Black & Decker unit with its 1½ horse-power motor will do nicely for the average home handyman. When you buy power tools, always select a brand that you can trust from a company that stands behind the tools it makes.

The Carpentry Connection

Teco Carpentry Connectors make framing a snap. The metal clips, which join the studs to the plates at the floor and ceiling, come packaged with nails and instructions for the entire installation. Teco makes connectors for almost every type of framing joint; all are easy to use, quick in application, and render a strong joint. Be sure, though, to check your local building code to make sure that this sort of installation conforms with the law.

A Good Handsaw Is Fine For Framing

A good cross-cut handsaw works fine for cutting studs, plates, cripples, headers, etc. Moreover, a well-made top quality saw will last almost forever. The Nicholson Professional Silver Steel cross-cut saw is just what you need for framing tasks, but it can also handle many other cutting chores around the house. Called a cross-cut saw because it is made to cut across the grain of the wood—which is the way you cut studs for framing—a good cross-cut saw should be 26 inches long and have 10 teeth per inch. Nicholson saws enjoy an excellent reputation for first-rate quality.

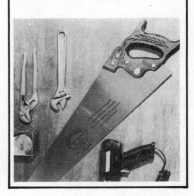

Here are the basic steps for framing:

1. Plan the wall, making sure that you consider all the uses the rooms will be put to and what furniture or equipment will go in them. Think about the best place for doors, and make sure that they will be large enough to allow you to bring in everything you want in the room.
2. When the planning is done, cut the top plate and sole plate. Use long lumber to make these long stretches of wall all of one piece, if possible. Remember that the sole plate does not run under the door.
3. When these plates are cut, lay them side by side and mark them for stud locations.
4. If the wall runs across the joists in the ceiling above, nail the top plate to each joist. If the wall runs parallel to the joists and cannot be positioned so that the top plate can be nailed to a joist, then you must install bridging of 2x4s to provide solid nailing for the top plate. Space the bridging pieces on 16-inch centers, and nail them to the joists with two nails through each end of each bridging piece.
5. Snap a chalk line on the floor where the sole plate is to go.
6. Install the sole plate, shimming under the plate to compensate for any unlevel sections of flooring.
7. With the sole plate in place, use a straight, long 2x4 to ascertain where the top plate should go so that it will be directly above the sole plate. Place the straightedge against the 2x4, and use a level to make it plumb.
8. If the floor and ceiling are even, assemble the studs and top plate on the floor as a unit and then raise the unit in place. This allows you to nail through the plate and straight into the top of each stud. If the studs must vary in length, however, install the top plate, cut each stud to fit, and then toenail each stud in place. Toenailing consists of driving 16d nails into the side of the stud at about a 45-degree angle so that the nails penetrate the top plate. Drive two nails into each broad side of the stud, plus one nail into the narrow side.
9. Toenail the studs in place to the sole plate as well.
10. Openings for doors in the framing must be about three inches wider and about two inches higher than the actual size of the door. Nail extra 2x4s—called cripples or jack studs—on both sides of the door opening and a header at the top. Then place shorter cripples between the header and the top plate, and nail them in place too.

That completes the essentials of your wall framing. Now you can put up the wallboard, hang the doors, and decorate with paint or paper to finish your new wall.

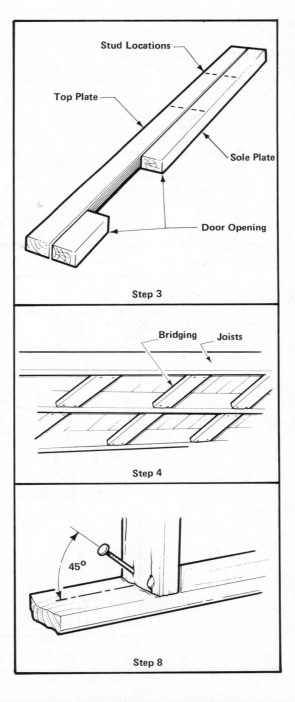

Step 3

Step 4

Step 8

A Stud Of Steel

Who says that studs must be made of wood? Metal stud systems for framing walls, such as United States Gypsum's Steel Stud Drywall Partitions, make sense from many standpoints. They can be placed on 24-inch centers instead of the 16 inches with wooden studs. They never warp or shrink, and, of course, they do not attract termites. With most of these systems for non-load bearing walls, the studs snap into previously installed metal floor and ceiling runners. The sheetrock panels are then attached with screws to each side of the partition. Sears also offers a wall-framing kit with metal studs and floor and ceiling plates.

Wide-Blade Knife Aids In Taping Wallboard

The Iowa Broad Knife is the Marshalltown Trowel Company's medium-priced taping knife. Excellent for the home handyman, the stiff 10-inch blade and handle are fuse welded into a one-piece tool that gets drywall jobs finished quickly. A higher quality model carrying the Marshalltown brand comes in 8-, 10-, and 12-inch widths. Its tempered blade is fashioned from the highest grade blue clock steel, and it presents no exposed rivets or ridges. If you do a great deal of drywall work, you should consider buying this more expensive model.

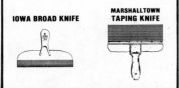

IOWA BROAD KNIFE   **MARSHALLTOWN TAPING KNIFE**

Backed Into A Corner?

For working on inside corners, you need a special tool like the Red Devil Corner Taping Tool. A rugged precision-angled tool of stainless steel with just the right amount of flex to handle those difficult inside corners, it features a hefty handle for a firm and comfortable grip. Red Devil's Dry Wall Hawk, designed to hold a supply of mud while you trowel it on, has a ring at the end of the handle as a callous preventer. The Finishing Trowel from Red Devil has a blade that is bowed for perfect shearing, while the company's Mud Pan is angled for easy access to the compound. Red Devil also makes taping knives for drywall use.

Installing Wallboard

IF YOU EVER decide to finish a room where presently there are exposed studs, the easiest way to accomplish the task is to attach wallboard to the studs. After the wallboard is up, you can paint, paper, or texture it. Wallboard (also known as sheetrock, plasterboard, and gypsum board) possesses excellent insulating and sound deadening qualities.

Although it is a snap to figure how much wallboard to buy (just compute the square footage of the walls and ceilings), it takes some planning to end up with as few joints as possible. The standard size sheets for walls are 4x8 feet. You normally place them with the long side running from floor to ceiling, but you can place them horizontally if by doing so you eliminate a joint. You can buy longer sized sheets for the ceiling. All wallboard sheets are four feet wide, but most lumberyards offer 12 foot lengths.

As to the number of nails, rolls of tape, and the amount of joint compound you will need, consult the table at your local lumberyard to learn how much of each is required for the square footage involved. For example, 1000 square feet of 1/2-inch thick wallboard (the most popular home thickness) requires about 5¼ pounds of coated nails, a five-gallon pail of joint compound in mixed form, and a 500-foot-roll of tape. Each outside corner requires a metal cornerbead.

Once you buy all the materials you need for the project, just follow these steps to install your new wallboard walls.

1. Install the ceilings first. If possible, try to span the entire width with a single sheet of wallboard to reduce the number of joints. Before you can work on the ceilings, though, you need to construct a pair of T-braces from 2x4's about an inch longer than the distance from floor to ceiling. Nail lighter boards about three feet long to the 2x4's to form the T's, and then position and wedge the braces against the wallboard sheet to hold it in place until you finish nailing.

2. Drive nails at seven-inch intervals into all the joints covered by the sheet. Start in the center of the wallboard panel and work out.

3. After you drive each nail in, give it one extra hammer blow to dimple the surface slightly. Take care, though, not to break the face paper.

4. When you need to cut panels to complete the coverage, use a wallboard knife along a straightedge. All you want to do with the knife is cut the face paper. After you make the cut, place the board over the edge of a sawhorse (or some other type of support) and bend it down. The gypsum core will snap along the line you cut. Then turn the

Here Is What You Will Need

Materials

- Wallboard sheets
- Coated nails
- Joint tape
- Joint compound
- Metal cornerbeads
- 2x4's
- Wooden boards
- Sandpaper
- Molding and baseboards
- Sealer or primer
- Paint

Tools

● Measuring tape	● Sanding block
● Hammer	● Drill
● Wallboard knife	● Keyhole saw
● Straightedge	● Putty knife
● Sawhorse or other support	● Metal float
	● Paintbrush

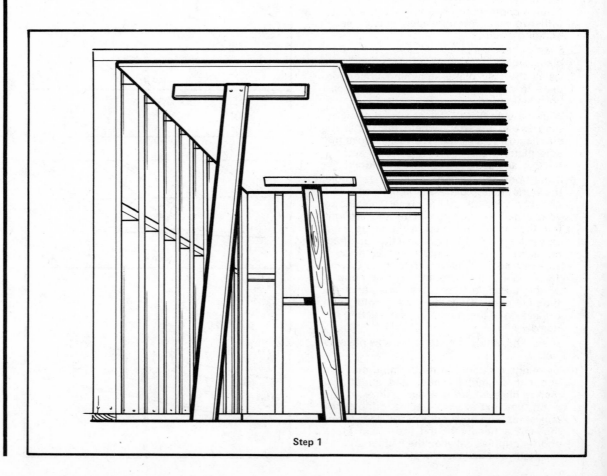

Step 1

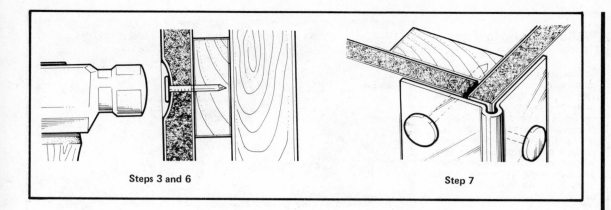

Steps 3 and 6   Step 7

panel over, cut the paper on the other side, and smooth the rough edges with a very coarse sanding block.

5. When the ceiling is finished, put up the walls. Again space the nails seven inches apart, but start nailing seven inches from the ceiling. Butt the wall panels against the ceiling sheets.
6. Dimple all nails.
7. If outside corners are involved, nail the cornerbeads in place.
8. Be sure to measure carefully for any cutouts such as electrical outlets, switches, or light fixtures. To make cutouts in the wallboard, first draw a pattern of the cutout, drill a hole, and then use a keyhole saw to follow the pattern around.

Once you are through applying the board to the walls, you face the problem of covering up all the nails and joints. This is where you use the joint compound and the tape in a technique called taping and bedding.

△ 1. Use a wide putty knife to spread joint compound into the slight recess created by the tapered edges of the wallboard sheets. Smooth the compound until it is even with the rest of the surface.
△ 2. Next, center the wallboard tape over the joint and press it firmly into the compound. Since some compound will squeeze out,

you should make sure that there is still a good bed underneath.
△ 3. When you get the tape imbedded into the

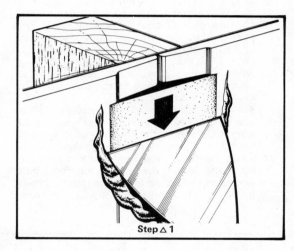

Step △ 1

compound all along the joint, smooth it with your putty knife.
△ 4. When the compound is completely dry (usu-

(Continued on next page)

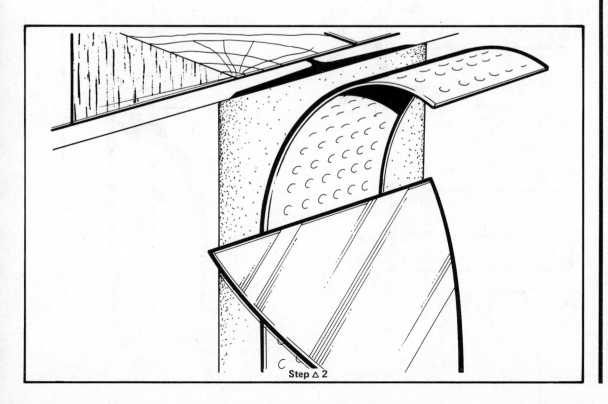

Step △ 2

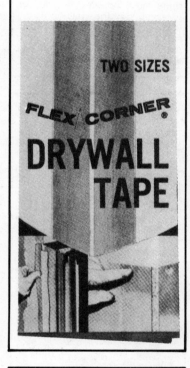

Walls

The Right Nails Can Make A Difference

There are many types of nails and screws used to fasten different thicknesses of wallboard in different situations. One popular type is the annular threaded nail like the one made by Nails Unlimited from Wilmod Company, Inc. Available in lengths of 1¼, 1⅜, and 1⅝ inches and in 12½ and 13 gauges, these nails have a long and sharp diamond point, and their annular rings resist popping out. At the time you buy the wallboard, tell your dealer the exact circumstances of the installation you are planning; he will make sure you buy the proper fastener.

Drywall Finishing In A Kit

Everything you need to finish a drywall installation is contained in The Durabond Wallboard Kit from United States Gypsum Company. The kit contains a gallon of Durabond Wallboard Compound (enough to cover about five 4x8-foot panels—approximately 160 square feet), 60 feet of reinforcing tape, a wide-blade tape knife applicator, and a handy little book that tells how to finish drywall.

Ready-To-Use Compounds Are Popular

USG's All-Purpose Crater-Free Joint Compound—part of an entire line of non-asbestos drywall compounds formulated to comply with the recent Occupational Safety and Hazards Act—is already mixed so that you can apply it immediately. Six gallons of this compound will cover approximately 1000 square feet of wall; by comparison, you would need about 60 pounds of the dry powder type compound to cover that much wall.

Wall Texturing In Dry Form

Compounds for drywall texturing come either dry or ready mixed. The Denswall Wall Texture in dry form is from Georgia-Pacific. Also shown is a pamphlet available at Georgia-Pacific dealers that explains the step-by-step procedures for texturing and finishing walls. In addition, Georgia-Pacific offers booklets on the use of joint compound and on the installation of gypsum board.

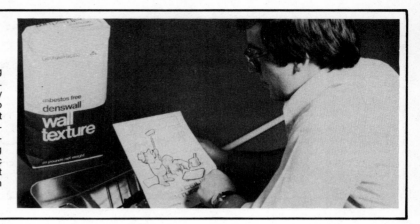

(Continued from previous page)

ally 24 hours later), apply a second very thin coat of compound which extends out a few inches to either side of the first coat.

△ 5. After the second coat dries completely, apply a third coat, extending it out to about six inches to either side. A metal float will do better than the putty knife at this stage.

△ 6. When the third coat is dry, feather all the edges with a sanding block covered with medium grit paper.

△ 7. Fill all the dimples with compound. They also require three coats as well as drying time in between. After the final coat, sand to feather and smooth the dimpled spots.

△ 8. Inside corners, including spots where the walls and ceiling meet, must also be taped and bedded. Cut the tape to length and then fold it in half. After laying the bed of compound, press the folded tape into the compound and then feather the compound out at least 1½ inches to each side. The corners require three coats, and the last coat should extend out about eight inches to each side. Sanding is required here too.

△ 9. If you have any outside corners, apply three coats that taper up to the bead. The last coat should extend the compound on each wall to about eight inches wide. Sand here too.

△ 10. If there are cracks at the floor and ceiling, install molding to hide them. Always attach baseboards at the floor.

After you are sure that the compound is completely dry, wait at least another couple of days before applying the sealer or primer coat and any subsequent decorative treatment.

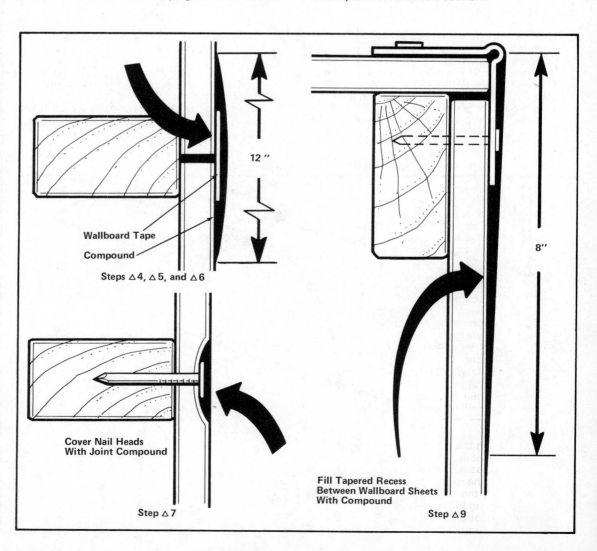

Wallboard Tape

Compound

Steps △4, △5, and △6

12"

Cover Nail Heads With Joint Compound

Step △7

Fill Tapered Recess Between Wallboard Sheets With Compound

Step △9

8"

Heavy Wall Fabric Requires Heavy-Duty Scissors

The household scissors you now have may not do the job on fabrics used for wallcoverings. If they don't quite "cut it," so to speak, you'll end up not only with sore and aching hands but probably with a sloppy job as well. The new precision-made Contura-lite shears by Wiss are what you need. Though extremely lightweight, they make a sharp clean cut in all types of fabrics. Made in eight- and nine-inch versions, the Wiss

Contura-lite shears are the only featherweight scissors in which the steel blades extend fully into the cushioned, contoured handles, providing extra strength with maximum comfort.

Special Glue Helps In Fabric Work

There is a white fabric cement called Val-A Tehr-Greeze Fabric Cement that glues fabrics of all kinds, from delicates to tarps. It is ready to use, it dries in seconds, and just a few drops from the plastic squeeze bottle are all you need. In addition to holding fabrics on walls, Tehr-Greeze can handle many fabric mending chores: clothing, tents, even leather. A product of the Val-A Company, Tehr-Greeze has been on the market for many years.

Plumb Bob Is A Must For Fabric Hanging

Anytime you want something straight up and down, you should use a plumb bob. For putting fabric on walls or hanging wallpaper, it's a must. Some plumb bobs are no more than a weight on a string, while others are almost precision instruments. One handy version is the combination plumb bob and chalk line called the Strait-Line Chalk Line Reel, a product of the Irwin Auger Bit Company. The unit consists of the line, a container from which the line unreels, a handle to reel it back in, and the chalk dust. The container, which is pointed at the bottom, acts as the weight for the plumb bob. There is a small trap door on the container through which the chalk dust is poured, and blue chalk dust refills are available at hardware and paint stores.

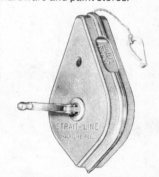

Fabrics on Walls

IF PAINTING sounds too messy and wallpapering is more work than you care to tackle, you should consider covering your walls with fabric. Before you decide that such a fashionable project is restricted to the professionals, just look at these simple steps.

1. Select fabric in rolls as wide as possible. Remember when picking a pattern that the panels must match adjacent panels.
2. Since it is unlikely that the last panel will match the first one after you go all around the room, pick out the most obscure corner in which to start.
3. Use a plumb bob chalk line as a guide for getting the first panel straight up and down.
4. Cut each panel to the height of the room plus one inch extra at both top and bottom.
5. Take the first panel, turn an inch of fabric under at the top, and staple the top of the panel to the wall so that the side edge lines up with the chalkline. Unless you plan to cover the top and bottom with molding or ribbon, place the staples as near and as in line with the ceiling as possible. Try to use only as many staples as are required to prevent the fabric from sagging; you can also run a bead of glue across the top to guard against sagging.
6. Staple down both sides of the first panel about 1/4 of an inch in from the edges.
7. Fold the inch under at the bottom, pull the fabric tight, and staple the panel along the baseboard.
8. For the second panel, place the edge face to face with the first panel. In other words, the reverse side of the second panel faces out.
9. Staple the second panel at several spots about 1/2 inch in from where the edges of the two panels meet.
10. Now staple strips of cardboard (1/2-inch wide) all along the edges you just stapled together. Make sure that the cardboard strips are straight.
11. When you pull the second panel of fabric over into position, you will find you have a hidden seam that is stapled securely in place.
12. Staple down the other edge about 1/4 inch in from the edge.
13. Repeat the same procedure as you continue on around the room.
14. Rough cut the panels for doors and windows, turning the excess under and stapling them as close to the frames as possible. Keep the number of staples to a minimum,

Step 3

using glue wherever possible. With some fabrics, you can glue the entire job.
15. Turn under and glue the last panel in place over the staples you left showing along the edge of the first panel.
16. If you wish to hide the staples at the top and bottom, you can glue a band of the fabric—or even a wide contrasting ribbon—around these seams. You can also attach molding strips to cover the staples.

Here Is What You Will Need

Materials

- Fabric
- Staples
- Shirtboard
- Glue
- Molding strips
- Nails

Tools

- Plumb bob chalkline
- Scissors
- Staple gun
- Hammer

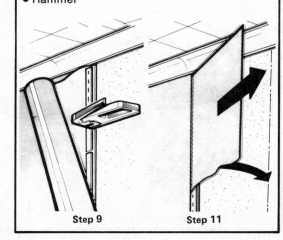

Step 9   Step 11

Staple Gun Is A Staple Tool

Every home tool kit should include a staple gun. For putting fabric on walls you can, in most cases, get by without having a heavy-duty gun, and Swingline's Decorator 101 is a good high-compression gun at a moderate price. Able to accommodate two different staple sizes—the ¼-inch and ⁵⁄₁₆-inch legs—the Decorator 101 is both lightweight and maneuverable. Since it can staple within a sixteenth of an inch from corners, this Swingline unit is great for a host of tacking jobs around the house. The Decorator 101 comes with a locking system and a built-in staple extractor.

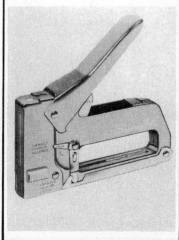

Walls

Special Patch For Recurring Cracks

Some cracks come back again and again no matter how well you patch them, but Krack-Kote can put an end to these recurring cracks. Krack-Kote employs a fiberglass fabric in tape form; the tape is placed over the crack and held in place by a special fiberglass adhesive. The finished patch then has enough "give" so that cracks will not reappear as they would with a rigid patching system. You can buy Krack-Kote in kit form, or you can buy the rolls of fabric and cans of adhesive separately. A companion product, called Tuff-Kote, is made for exterior patching, both are products of the Tuff-Kote Company, Inc.

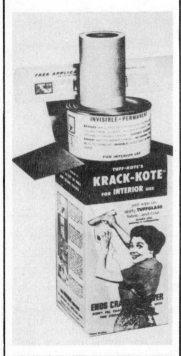

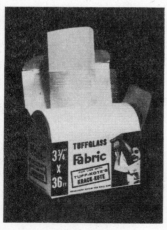

A Special Saw Handles Those Tricky Wallboard Jobs

The Plasplugs Mini Hacksaw is a handy tool for cutting wallboard. The comfortable plastic handle holds the blade in your choice of two positions, either straight in line with the handle or at an angle, and the seven-inch blade cuts metal, wood, plastic, and hardboard as well as wallboard. The

entire line of Plasplugs tools—file handles, laminate trimmers, edging trimmers, scrapers, several knife styles, and other small tools—boasts exceptional design at modest prices. Created in Great Britain, Plasplugs tools are distributed in the United States by Landers Import-Export Company, Inc.

Patching Holes in Wallboard

THE EASE AND economy of dry wall construction are marred only by the fact that wallboard can develop holes the first time someone slams a door knob against it or gets mad and punches a fist through it. These holes may look like complete disasters, but you will be amazed at how easily you can patch them up. Small holes require one kind of backing, while larger ones may necessitate another. First, here is what to do for the smaller hole that needs a backing.

1. Remove any loose material around the hole.
2. Select a tin can lid that is bigger than the hole and measure across the lid. Then use a keyhole saw to cut a slit extending out from both sides of the hole so that you can slip the lid into the hole sideways.
3. Punch two holes in the center of the lid and run a wire through them.
4. Now slip the lid through the slit, holding onto the wire. With the lid inside, pull the wire until the lid is flat against the inside of the wall.
5. Twist the wire around a stick which is long enough to span the hole. This technique will hold the lid in place.
6. You can now plaster over the hole with spackling compound (available at paint or hardware stores in either ready mixed or powdered form). Cover all of the backing plate, the slit, and the edges, but avoid trying to make the main body of the patch level with the rest of the wall.
7. When the first patch dries, remove the stick and snip the wire off flush with the patch.
8. Apply a second coat of spackling compound, bringing the surface up level with the rest of the wall. This coat will, of course, cover the remaining tip of wire.
9. Use a brush or trowel to texture the patch so that it matches the rest of the wall.
10. Let the patch dry overnight before applying the primer coat for repainting.

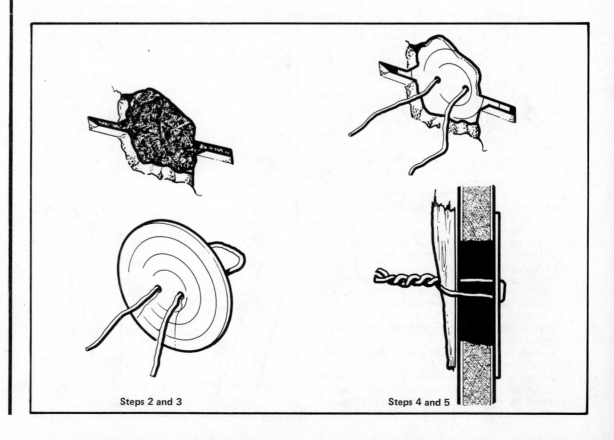

Steps 2 and 3

Steps 4 and 5

Two Tips For Patching Plaster

Since most patching jobs require only a small amount of mix, an excellent albeit off-beat container to use for the mixing is the plumber's friend—the rubber suction cup. The plunger is the right size, and after the mixing is done, you have an ideal handle underneath to carry patching compound.

If your patching mix always dries out too soon, add about a tablespoon of white vinegar along with the water when mixing.

Cover Hairline Cracks With A Stick

There are sticks for filling hairline cracks in plaster or drywall that do the job quickly and easily. Plaster-Stick—from Murray Black—is an example of such a stick that can also fill cracks in wood, stone, or any hard surface that will be painted over. All you do is work the stick back and forth over the crack in a circular motion. Usually, there is no need for sanding as any excess can be removed with a putty knife or even with your fin-

ger. After 24 hours you can paint over the patched crack with any kind of paint.

The Patcher Upper

Plaster or drywall patching is really simple once you get one of the patching compounds that are ready to use. Macco-Spacko, a product of the Glidden Coatings and Resins Company, is just such a compound. Ready to use, the almost odorless self-sealing latex patching compound does not shrink, and it can be cleaned easily from tools and hands with warm soapy water. Macco-Spacko becomes tack free in ten minutes and can be sanded within two hours, often less. Be sure it is completely dry before sanding, however. When the patch is finished, clean and prime it and then paint the area with either oil or latex paint.

Here Is What You Will Need
Materials
- Tin can lid
- Wire
- Wooden stick
- Spackling compound
- Paint
- Scrap wallboard
- Wooden board
- Countersunk screws

Tools
- Keyhole saw
- Wire cutters or scissors
- Brush or trowel
- Screwdriver

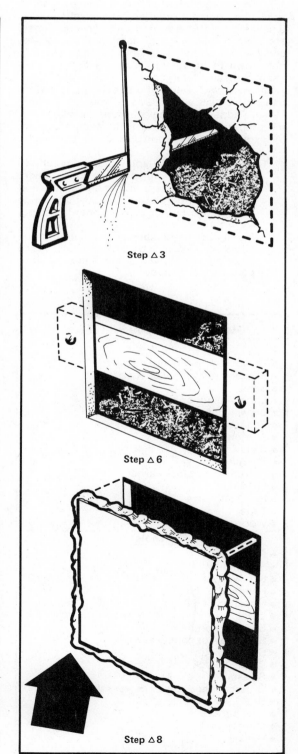

Step △ 3

Step △ 6

Step △ 8

Now, here is how to take care of those bigger patches. Rather than applying many layers of the compound to patch, you should insert a scrap of wallboard into the hole.

△ 1. Cut a scrap piece of wallboard into a square that is slightly larger than the hole.
△ 2. Lay the wallboard over the hole and trace around it.
△ 3. Use a keyhole saw to cut along the pattern you just traced.
△ 4. Now you need backing. Select a board about six inches longer than the widest span of the hole you just cut.
△ 5. Slip the backing board into the hole, and hold it firmly against the inside of the wallboard.
△ 6. Insert countersunk screws through the wall and into the backing on each side of the hole to hold the backing securely against the inside of the wall. Keep turning the screws until the flat heads dig down below the surface.
△ 7. Now butter all four edges of the patch with spackling compound or joint compound, and spread compound over the back of the patch where it will rest against the backing board.
△ 8. Ease the patch into place, and hold it there until the compound starts to set up.
△ 9. When the compound is dry, fill up the slits around the patch. Then cover the entire patch—plus the screw heads—with spackling, using a brush or trowel to make the compound match the texture of the rest of the wall.
△ 10. Let the entire area dry; then prime and repaint.

Drywall Patch In A Kit

You can patch holes up to four inches square in sixty minutes with a kit called Perfect Patch from Mechanical Plastics Corporation. The kit contains the unique Perfect Clips to hold the patch in place, a 4x4-inch patch, a small disposable keyhole saw for cutting the hole to match the patch, spackling compound, a disposable spatula for applying the compound, as well as sandpaper for smoothing the dry surface and feathering the edges. Available in paint and hardware stores, the Perfect Patch Kit works on gypsum board, plasterboard, or wallboard from ⅜ to ⅝ inches thick.

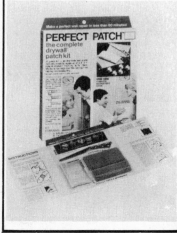

Walls

Paneling a Wall

THE TREMENDOUS selection in wall paneling makes it possible to achieve almost any effect you want in a room. You can purchase actual plywood paneling either finished or unfinished, or you can buy hardboard panels in finishes ranging from barn siding to marble. The plastic-coated finishes on both hardboard and plywood panels are almost impervious to scratches and stains, and they are entirely washable as long as you do not drown them. Just go over the finish with a damp cloth and detergent.

The ease with which the panels go up makes paneling a wall a simple do-it-yourself project. Modern adhesives virtually eliminate nailing, and the preparation and basic installation steps are the same for both plywood panels and hardboard.

1. You could actually apply panels directly to the studs where you have new construction, but since the panels tend to give a little and are far from soundproof, it is best to provide either a plywood or gypsum board backing. Nevertheless, if you decide to apply paneling directly to the studs, make sure that the studs are free of high or low spots. Plane away high spots and attach shims to compensate for low spots.

Here Is What You Will Need

Materials

- Plywood or hardboard paneling
- Plywood or gypsum board backing
- Shims
- Long straight board
- Drywall compound
- Sandpaper
- Furring strips
- Nails
- Shingles
- Polyethylene vapor barrier
- Moldings
- Panel adhesive
- Tape
- Wood putty

Tools

- Plane
- Putty knife
- Screwdriver
- Hammer
- Measuring tape
- Level
- Scribing compass
- Saber saw or coping saw
- Caulking gun
- Padded block
- Scissors
- Crosscut hand saw or power saw
- Drill
- Keyhole saw
- Miter box
- Nailset

2. Remove the molding and trim from existing walls and check for highs and lows by drawing a long straight board across the wall and watching for any gaps as it moves across. Build up the lows with drywall compound, and sand down the high spots. If the walls are badly cracked or extremely uneven, you should install furring strips.

3. Masonry walls must always be furred and waterproofed. Furring strips are actually slats of wood (1x2's or 1x3's) nailed to the wall. Nail the furring horizontally on 16-inch centers, starting at the floor and finishing at the ceiling. Place short vertical strips between the horizontals, spacing them every four feet so that they will come under the joints between the panels. Nail furring strips to the wall with masonry nails, compensating for lows by wedging shingles under the strips. A four mil polyethylene vapor barrier should be placed over the furring of masonry walls and on any other type of walls where moisture might be a problem.

4. Remember that you must compensate for the increased thickness of the wall at electrical switches and wall outlets. Remove the plates and reset the boxes out the necessary distance.

5. Allow the paneling to stabilize to the moisture content of the room before you begin attaching it to the walls. Stack the panels with strips of boards between each one, and then leave them there for at least two days. This step is very important for a successful paneling job.

6. When the panels are ready to go, lean them against the wall as you think they should be placed. This gives you a chance to match the wood graining in the most pleasing manner. When you have them the way you want them, be sure to number the panels.

7. Measure the distance from floor to ceiling at several different points. If the panels have to be cut for height, you can cut all of them the same, provided that there is no more than a quarter inch variance. If there is more variance than a quarter of an inch, you should measure the height for each panel and cut it to fit. If you are not going to use a ceiling molding, each panel must be cut to conform to the ceiling line, but if you do use ceiling moldings—and you should—leave a quarter inch gap at the top. There also needs to be a quarter inch gap at the floor which will be covered by the floor molding.

8. Since very few corners are plumb, place the first panel which is to go in a corner next to the wall and check the plumb with a level. Get the panel plumb and close enough to the corner so that you can span the space with a scribing compass. Then run the compass down the corner, with the point in the corner and the pencil marking a line on the panel. Cut the panel along the line with a saber saw equipped with a fine-toothed blade or with a coping saw.

9. If instead of cementing the panels you plan to nail them, use the nails made by the paneling manufacturer. You can use 2d finishing nails to attach the panels to furring strips, but if you must go through a wall to reach the studs, be sure to use nails long

Match Your Nails To The Paneling

Rather than countersinking and then applying wood putty over the nails that hold your paneling to the wall, you can save yourself some work by using nails that match the panel color. Most paneling manufacturers market such nails, and many fastener makers specialize in colored nails. Panelmatch markets a line of nails for just about every paneling color available. Philstone Nail Corporation, MazeMade, and Wilmod Company, Inc., also offer a wide selection in colored panel nails.

Panel Adhesive Makes Installation Easy

Panel adhesives come in bulk or in cartridges for use with a caulking gun. The latter method makes installation of 4x8-foot panels especially fast and easy. Most panel makers market their own brand of panel adhesive, but there are many other good ones. Goodyear Plio-Nail Panel Adhesive, for example, is quick setting, but not so fast that you don't have time to make adjustments. In addition to almost eliminating the need for nails, Plio-Nail also has the advantage of compensating for slightly uneven surfaces to which the panels are being attached. It can also be used to attach drywall, hardboard, or rigid foam insulation to most wall surfaces.

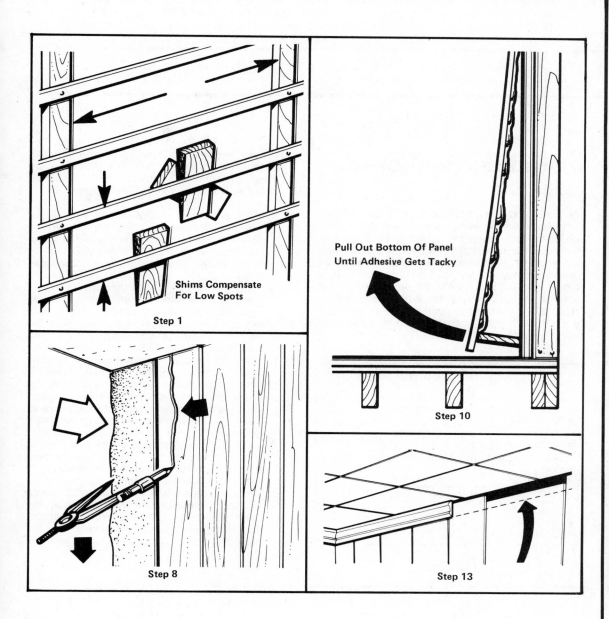

Shims Compensate For Low Spots
Step 1

Pull Out Bottom Of Panel Until Adhesive Gets Tacky
Step 10

Step 8

Step 13

Not All Wall Panels Come In Big Sheets

While most paneling is sold in 4x8-foot sheets, other sizes are available. For example, Decro-Wall markets self-adhesive Tudor-style panels that measure 12x24 inches. The panels—which simulate weathered crossbeams over a stucco wall—are made of a durable vinyl that is washable, grease- and stain-resistant, and can be cleaned of most soil using only a damp cloth or sponge. Decro-Wall panels are fire resistant and do possess some soundproofing and insulating qualities. And since they are equipped with peel-and-stick backings, the paneling project goes quickly.

Masonite Wall Paneling Covers Decorating Spectrum

No matter what your decorating motif, Masonite probably makes an appropriate wall paneling pattern. In addition to finishes that closely resemble woods of all kinds, Masonite also makes paneling that looks like marble, tapestry, and even leather. Masonite also has a line of companion products, including color-matching nails, panel adhesives, moldings and trims, and putty sticks that cover up nail holes and scratches. Other leaders in the paneling field are Georgia-Pacific, Abitibi, U.S Gypsum, Barclay, U.S. Plywood, Conwed, and the private-label brands at Sears, Montgomery Ward, and J.C. Penney.

---

enough to penetrate about an inch into the studs. Drive the nails every six inches along the edges and about every twelve inches through the center. Check frequently to make sure you are hitting the furring strips.

10. If you are using mastic to panel the wall, get the kind that you apply with a caulking gun. Run a ribbon across all furring strips or—if there are no strips—in about the same pattern as if there were furring strips. Place the panel against the wall and nail it in place at the top with a pair of nails. Then pull the bottom of the panel out from the wall and prop it with a scrap block of wood until the adhesive gets tacky. When this happens, remove the block and press the panel against the wall. Then secure the entire surface by pounding the panel with a padded block and hammer.

11. When you come to a door or window, take one of the large pieces of paper that came between the sheets of paneling and use it as a pattern. Tape the paper in place, press it against the door or window frame and then cut it with a scissors. Use this pattern to mark the panel, which you can then cut with a fine-toothed crosscut hand saw or with a power saw equipped with a fine-toothed blade. When using a hand saw or a table saw, cut the panel with the face up. When using a hand power saw, cut with the face down.

12. To make cutouts for electrical outlets or switches, drill pilot holes and then use a keyhole saw.

13. Next comes the finishing touch that will hide any and all of your mistakes—the application of molding. Most panel manufacturers offer prefinished moldings to match. You can get floor moldings, ceiling moldings, inside or outside corner moldings, and just about anything else you need. Use a miter box and a fine-toothed saw to cut the moldings, and be sure to countersink the nails and fill the holes with matching wood putty.

Walls

Jars Hang From Pegboard

Small jars are always handy for storing such items as brads, screws, washers, etc. Now you can get baby-food size unbreakable Handy Dandy Jars that hang from perforated hardboard panels. The colorful red caps of the Handy Dandy Jars fit into either 1/8- or 1/4-inch pegboard, and they stay in place as the jars are removed. Handy Dandy Jars are available from Wickliffe Industries.

Peg-Board Hooks Hold Many Tools

The Masonite Complete Home Workshop Kit contains 40 assorted Peg-Board fixtures plus four hook stabilizers and eight mounting fixtures. The standard metal hooks work just fine for holding these crescent wrenches and pliers. Peg-Board Fixtures —available in more than 75 different styles—include brackets for shelves, clips for brooms, racks for magazines, and even a holder for hats.

Stanley Saw Handle Gives You The Angle

Two panel saws from Stanley Tools feature an unusual handle. By positioning the handle against the work in one way, you can mark the top edge of the saw blade. In off a perfect 45-degree angle on the other position, you can mark a 90-degree angle. This unique handle is made of polypropylene with contoured and textured finger grips. The 26-inch model has eight points to the inch, while the 20-inch blade has 10. The shorter version is best for pegboard cutting. The teeth are cross-filed for faster and more accurate cuts. The saws, packaged in their own protective sleeves with how-to instructions for best use come in handy for many projects.

Installing Pegboard

NO DOUBT you have seen pictures of workshops where every tool hangs neatly from the wall. Chances are the hanging was done with hooks and a perforated hardboard panel commonly called pegboard. Installing pegboard is an easy way to provide wall storage for a multitude of items. You can use it all through the house, not just in a garage or workshop. When painted, pegboard has a pleasing appearance that can blend in with nearly any decor. You can also buy pegboard with prefinished wood tones and patterns. The hanging devices now include special hangers to hold all sorts of items, including dishes, shelves, record albums—even lawn mowers.

Here Is What You Will Need
Materials
• 1/8-inch or 1/4-inch pegboard
• Sandpaper
• Nails, screws, or hardboard adhesive
• Rubber spacers or furring strips
• Expansion or toggle bolts
• Paint
• Moldings
Tools
• Fine-toothed saw
• Hammer
• Screwdriver

1. Most pegboard comes in either 1/8- or 1/4-inch thicknesses. You should require only the 1/8-inch size for home uses, but you may want the 1/4-inch pegboard for especially heavy items like lawn and garden tools.
2. Pegboard comes in 4x8 foot sheets. If you can use a complete sheet, fine; but if not, you will find that pegboard is easy to saw with a fine-toothed blade. A cross-cut is the best handsaw for straight cuts, a coping saw is for making curved cuts, and power saws can provide good results at greater speed. For a smoother cut, saw from the finish side with a handsaw and from the back side with a power saw. For the sake of appearance, avoid cutting through any of the holes. Pegboard edges can be sanded if necessary.
3. Lean the panels against a wall in the room where they are to go, and leave them there for 48 hours to give them time to adjust to existing humidity conditions.
4. You must provide a minimum of 3/8-inch clearance behind each panel to allow for the insertion of most hangers. If you are attaching the pegboard to exposed studs, as is the case in many unfinished garages, you can

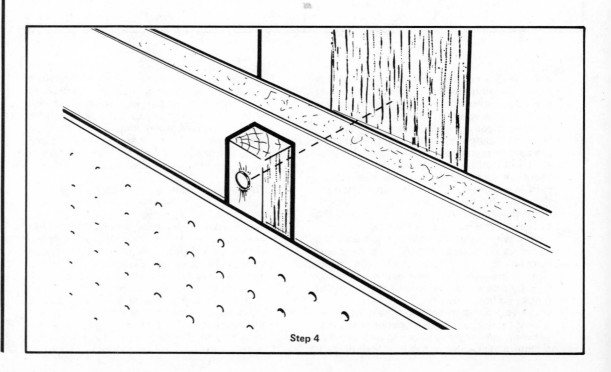

Step 4

Perfix Hooks Are Self-Locking

The Fulton Corporation markets pegboard hooks that are self-locking. The line, which includes a wide variety of pegboard attachments, is gaining distribution in hardware stores and home centers throughout the United States.

A Word About Perforated Hardboard Panels

There seems to be some confusion as to the proper name for perforated hardboard panels. "Peg-Board" is the registered trademark of the Masonite Corporation, but without the hyphen and the capital letters "pegboard"

has become a generic name applying to all perforated hardboard. Of course, not all pegboard is of equal quality. Some is made poorly and damaged easily. But Masonite's Peg-Board, as well as the versions offered by other well-known names in hardboard paneling, can be relied upon to provide years of excellent service.

Trays Fit Into Pegboard Panels

These trays made of tough ABS plastic can all be mounted on perforated hardboard panels. The various designs include compartmentalized trays, trays with no compartments, a tray made specifically to hold small jars, and another to hold small tools like screwdrivers, pliers, chisels, etc. Nice additions to any perforated hardboard wall—be it in the shop, the kitchen, the office, the garage, or sewing room—these inexpensive trays are available from Trophy Products.

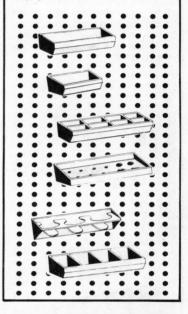

use nails, screws, or hardboard adhesive to attach the panels directly to the studs. Over a solid wall, though, you must bring the pegboard out some distance to allow the hooks to go in the holes. The rubber spacers sold at hardware stores can serve the purpose. Furring strips nailed to the wall will also do the job. Locate the studs behind the wall and then fasten the strips to the studs with nails, screws, or the adhesive. If you plan to attach the panel in between, use expansion bolts (Mollys) to hold the pegboard. For 1/4-inch panels that will hold heavy tools, you might consider using toggle bolts.

5. When attaching more than one panel, avoid butting the panels tightly together. Moderate contact between the two is all you need.
6. If you want to paint the panel, first attach it to the wall and then apply any paint you would use on wood. Just make sure that the panel is clean and dry before you paint it.
7. If you want to finish off the corners, you can attach inside or outside molding with the same adhesive you use for putting the panel on the wall.

Pegboard need not be confined to walls. You can use it as a room divider or place it on the inside of closet or cabinet doors. Just keep two things in mind: (1) Make sure you attach the panel securely, and, (2) be sure to provide space behind the panel for the hooks.

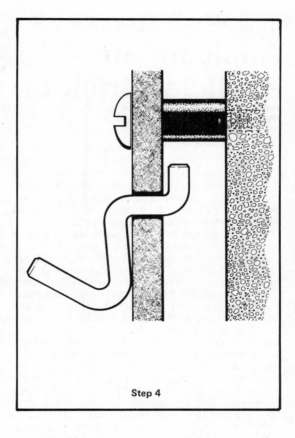

Step 4

Locking Hooks For Perforated Panels

A frequent complaint concerning pegboard panels is that the holes become slightly reamed after considerable use. Then, when you try to take something from its hook, the hook comes out too. That can't happen with Homecraft's Locking Peg Panel Hooks. Once installed in the holes, these hooks lock in place via a lever on the face of the fixture. A distinctive break with the traditional "bent-wire" design in pegboard hooks, Homecraft's Peg Panel Hooks are made of solid cast metal with a durable bright finish. Available in eight styles, they fit either 1/8- or 1/4-inch perforated board.

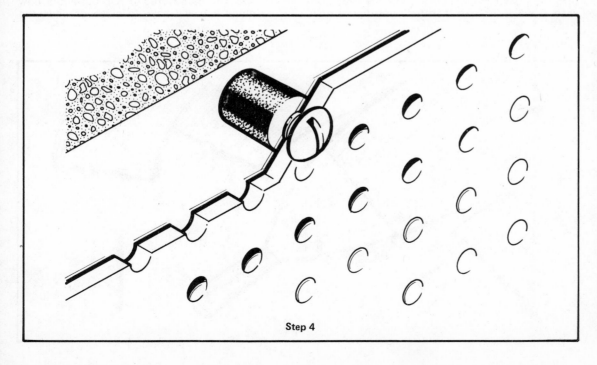

Step 4

Walls

Bric-Mold Is For True Do-It-Yourselfers

Bric-Mold Corporation carries the do-it-yourself brick wall one step further with molds that allow the homeowner to cast his own brick or stone. Casting is done with plaster of Paris, and the bricks are colored either by painting them or by adding limeproof cement coloring to the water before mixing. The latter gives a more authentic look. The reusable molds require no lubricant for the release of the finished product. If this sounds like your kind of project, you'll have to order the molds by mail. Each brick set makes 16 bricks; the stone set renders 12 different sizes and shapes of stone. Complete instructions and some handy tips come with the molds. Order from Bric-Mold Corporation, 70 Jerusalem Avenue, Hicksville, NY 11801.

Masonite's Roxite Bricks Come In Panels

The Heritage Series in the Roxite line from Masonite Corporation consists of mini-panels which render the appearance of authentic brick. Each panel has 12 bricks and is applied either with nails or with adhesive. Roxium brand mortar can be applied with a caulking gun to cover nail heads and give the joints the look of authenticity. Roxite corners come in units four bricks high that fit over outside corners. Made of a mixture of crushed limestone and fiberglass, Roxite brick panels can be used inside or out.

Care Free Bricks Create Beautiful Illusion

Dacor Miracle Bricks, made from high-density polyester, are practically care free. Available in a variety of styles, the bricks look authentic even upon close inspection. The special mastic, moreover, comes in three colors, all of which dry to look like mortar. In addition to the flat-face bricks, Dacor also offers L-shaped corner bricks that add to the illusion of a real brick wall. Miracle Bricks are made by Dacor Manufacturing Company.

Applying an Artificial Brick or Stone Wall

IT USED TO BE that artificial bricks looked extremely artificial, but now there are several manufacturers offering synthetic brick-like materials that are unbelievably authentic in appearance. You can choose from complete lines of brick and stone styles, with most including outside corner pieces. You also have a wide choice of mastic colors, with all resembling actual mortar.

Installation of a real brick wall might compel you to make all sorts of structural changes so that your house could take the additional weight. With the artificial bricks, however, the only preparation you need to make is the surface which you are covering. These bricks can be applied to any surface that is clean, structurally sound, and dry. A wallpapered surface should be stripped of all the wall covering. A porous surface—or any wall not already sealed—must first be painted with an appropriate sealer, and all painted or finished walls should be given a scuff sanding. When cleaning, make sure that you get the surface completely free of all dirt, dust, wax, and grease.

Once you pick out the brick pattern you want, give the dealer the dimensions of the area you wish to cover. He can then help you figure how much mastic—as well as how many flat pieces and corner pieces (if any)—you will need. With the walls prepared and the materials purchased, you are ready to apply your artificial brick wall. Here is all you have to do.

1. If you have decided on a mixed pattern, lay the bricks out on the floor so that you can establish the sequence you want. At the same time, measure the number of bricks per foot, including the spaces for mortar joints. Plot this measurement against the space to be covered to find out about how much you will have to close or open the

Here Is What You Will Need		
Materials		
● Synthetic bricks		
● Mastic		
● Paint		
● Sandpaper		
● Wall cleaning solvent		
● Sealer		
Tools		
● Measuring tape		
● Joint measuring guide		
● Putty knife		
● Line level		
● Paintbrush		

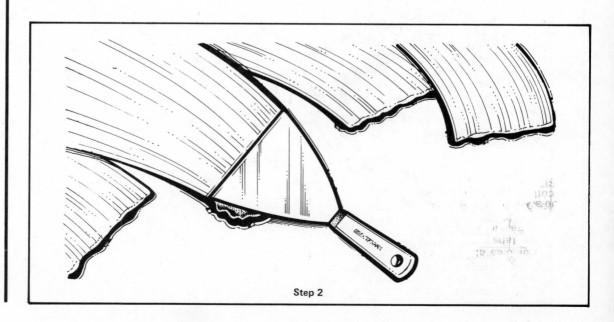

Step 2

Put Up Z-Brick With Z-Ment

Z-Brick comes in a number of brick styles, all of which look very authentic. The material used to form the bricks, vermiculite, is quite durable. With some patterns, Z-Brick offers pre-cut corner kits, but for the most part you will have to miter-cut and fit your own corners. Z-Bricks are easy to cut with a hacksaw, and a few swipes with a rasp smooth any rough edges. Z-Brick and the adhesive Z-Ment are both weatherproof.

Brickettes Mini-Panels Go Up Fast

Modern Methods make the Brickettes Mini-Panel, real fired clay bricks that are just like regular bricks except for the fact that they are only a half inch in thickness. The bricks come factory applied to half-inch insulation board, and you can nail the panels to the studs or to most wall surfaces, or you can glue them to the walls.

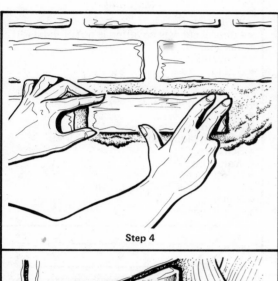

Step 4

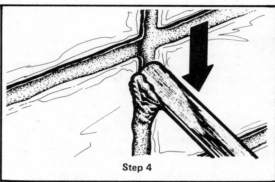

Step 4

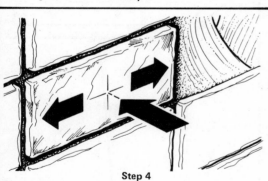

Step 4

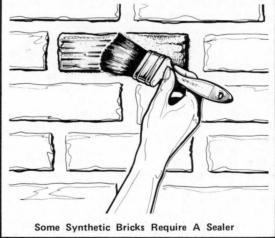

Some Synthetic Bricks Require A Sealer

Here's How To Get Your Wall Stoned

Do-it-yourself decorating can be fun with Dacor Stones from the Dacor Manufacturing Company. To apply, you merely press each stone (previously buttered with adhesive mortar) into position and wiggle it slightly from side to side against the wall to embed it firmly. Mortar lines form automatically in the open space between the stones as the adhesive mortar squeezes out on all sides of each stone. Complete installation instructions come with each carton of Dacor Stones.

Brock Bricks Come Wired

The Brock Company's artificial bricks—called Brick'N'Wire are cast over a steel wire netting that looks much like chicken wire. The result is a 2x4-foot panel of bricks that can be nailed or mortared quickly in place. If the panels are nailed, the spaces between the bricks must be filled with mortar to hide the wire and the nails.

mortar joints to end up with an even course of bricks. Strive for mortar joints that are about 3/8 of an inch wide. A stick cut to the width of the joint makes a handy guide.

2. Use a wide putty knife to spread on a thin coat of the mastic; all you need is enough to cover the old surface. Avoid starting at an outside corner, if possible. Cover an area across the top that is large enough to accommodate two courses (rows). Go down to the floor on the left side, keeping the mastic coat wide enough for only one full brick.

3. Butter the back of each brick with additional mastic.

4. Press each brick firmly into place on the coated surface, and wiggle the brick slightly to set it. Use your stick to measure even mortar joints between bricks.

5. Work all the way across the top with your two rows, and then come back and work down, alternating a full brick with a half brick if that is the pattern you want. This method establishes your horizontal and vertical dimensions. If you discover that you

must make some adjustments to make the rows come out even, do your adjusting now while the bricks will still slide.

6. Spread additional mastic, but cover only about four to six square feet at a time. Work across under your two starter courses, adding three or four courses at a time.

7. Step back often and examine the courses, using the previous course as a guide to getting all of them on straight. If you have long walls to cover, a line level (a string stretched taut across the area with a hook-on level) can come in handy. When the bubble lines up, you know the string is level, and the string should line up with each course of bricks.

8. Check all the mortar joints periodically. If they need any smoothing, fix them with your finger.

That is really all there is to it. Some synthetic brick walls require a sealer after the mastic sets, but most are ready immediately.

Walls

Protect Your New Wallcoverings

Any wallcovering that has been up for a while starts to show dirt, hand marks, cooking grease, etc., but you can protect your wallcoverings with Zynolite's Wallpaper Protector. Clean, odorless protection against grease, crayon, chalk, pencil, and finger marks, it dries almost instantly and wipes clean with a warm damp cloth. Available in a spray can or in

brush-on liquid, Zynolite Wallpaper Protector is recommended for washable as well as non-washable papers.

First-Rate Trimmer Cuts Easily and Accurately

Considered by many to be the best tool of its type, the Hyde Century Trimmer can be positioned instantly alongside the straight-edge. Its super-sharp blade—individually hardened, tempered, and honed—runs true for an accurate cut with no wobble or sway. When the long lasting blade does wear out, you can replace it quickly and without difficulty. Although the Hyde Century Trimmer is an unquestionably excellent tool, it is too expensive to buy for a one-room paperhanging assignment.

Wallpaper Smoother Kit

The Padco Wallpaper Smoother & Applicator is different. Consisting of a resilient nyfoam pad that is bonded to a firm back of expanded polystyrene, the tool's big 2x11½-inch face is covered with thousands of nylon bristles which work with the resilient pad to render remarkable smoothing action. The Padco Wallpaper Smoother—which can also serve as a paste applicator—is particularly useful on metallic and flocked wallcoverings whose surfaces can be damaged by ordinary smoothers. In addition to the Smoother & Applicator, the Padco Wallpaper Kit also includes a plumb line, chalk, a razor blade knife, and two replacement blades.

DIF Makes The Difference In Wallpaper Stripping

DIF Wallpaper Stripper is a two-part formula that combines enzymes with an effective blend of wetting agents. This combination re-wets more thoroughly and breaks down the molecular structure of the paste more completely than other wallpaper strippers. That means less hacking and scraping to remove the paper. DIF may be sprayed or sponged on, after which it should be allowed at least 15 minutes to do its thing. When applying the stripper to waterproof coverings, you must first score the surface so the mixture can penetrate and reach the adhesive. DIF—a creation of William Zinsser & Company, Inc.—is available wherever wallpapering materials and tools are sold.

Papering a Wall

WALL COVERINGS can make a dramatic difference in a room's appearance. Vinyl wall coverings are extremely popular because they are washable, fade resistant, and most are strippable. That last advantage looms large when you have to recover the walls later on. Strippable coverings can be peeled off the wall all in one piece, eliminating messy steaming, soaking, and scraping. Prepasted coverings are also very popular because they are easy to use and less messy than unpasted coverings. Prepastes require the use of a water box, however. You must put the strip in the water box to activate the paste. If you select a covering that is not prepasted, you must be sure to use the prescribed type of paste. If you are applying a vinyl covering, for example, use one of the special vinyl adhesives that are much stronger and mildew resistant than the wheat paste.

Figuring how many rolls to buy is strictly a mathematical exercise, but you have to know the rules. No matter how wide the roll is, any wall covering roll contains approximately 36 square feet. A roll 24 inches wide is 18 feet long, while a roll that is 27 inches wide is only 16 feet long. Because of trim and waste, though, you can never use all 36 square feet on a roll. The actual yield is usually only about 30 square feet. To figure how many rolls you will need, measure the perimeter of the room and multiply that figure by the room's height. That gives you the square footage. Deduct one roll for every two openings—such as doors and windows—and then apply the yield of 30 square feet against the total. The final figure is the number of rolls to order.

Now you are ready to start to work. But the first thing to do is prepare—not paper—the surface.

1. A paper wall covering can be applied over old paper, provided that the old covering is sound. If it is not sound, remove any spots of loose paper and feather the edges. If there are more than two layers of old paper, or if you are applying a vinyl wall covering, you should remove all of the old covering. Removing old paper is no easy job, however. You can rent a steamer from the wallpaper store, but you still have to scrape off most of the covering with a wide putty knife.
2. An unpapered wall that is textured should be sanded to remove all the bumps. You need not sand it as slick as glass, but you must get most of the bumps off. Remove the gloss from any enameled surfaces.
3. Fill all cracks and holes.
4. Apply sizing (a sort of glue) over the wall. Absolutely necessary on new wallboard, unpainted plaster, and other such surfaces that would absorb paste, sizing also works

Here Is What You Will Need

Materials
- Wall covering
- Adhesive (if wall covering is not prepasted)
- Sandpaper
- Spackling
- Sizing

Tools
- Measuring tape
- Steamer
- Putty knife
- Chalked plumb line
- Scissors
- Water tray
- Paintbrush
- Sponge or smoothing brush
- Roller
- Razor blade

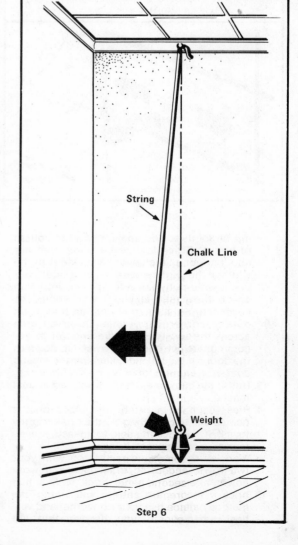

String

Chalk Line

Weight

Step 6

Wallpaper In Squares Is A Neat Idea

If you've ever wrestled with a long piece of wet sticky wallpaper, you'll appreciate Decro-Wall's Wallpaper In Squares. Pre-pasted, each square is easy to place, fit, and match. Squares measure 15¾x15¾ inches and come in packages of 18; there are 20 patterns from which to choose. Each package contains a picture of the overall wall effect as well as application directions.

Hyde Putty Knife Competitive in Price And Quality

Hyde Tools makes about 150 different products, all of which measure up to the competition in terms of quality and price. The Hyde Putty Knife, of course, can be used for many other purposes besides paperhanging, and you should be able to find it in just about any good-sized hardware store.

Supergraphics Leads To Super Wallcoverings

The Supergraphic system of wall decoration consists of strippable wallpaper, a kit that helps you design and draw your own wall-graphics, and various aids to place the pattern on the wall. After the pattern is laid out on the wall and masked, you can paint the design in your selected color scheme. The effect is smashing. The Super-Strippable wallpaper is sold in rolls, and the Super-graphic kit contains the designs and rendering aids. A new product in the United States, the Supergraphic system may not be available at your paint and wallpaper store. If that is the case, contact Wood Davies & Company Ltd., 184 Front Street, East Toronto, Ontario, M5a 1E6.

well on most other surfaces. Talk to your wallpaper dealer; he can tell you which sizing is compatible with the adhesive you are using.

5. Now you are ready for papering. Select the most inconspicuous corner in the room, and measure out along the wall adjacent to that corner a distance one inch less than the width of your roll.

6. Drop a chalked plumb line from that point, and snap it to show the true vertical. A plumb line is nothing more than a string with a weight on one end. Tack the chalk-coated string at the ceiling so that the weight almost touches the floor. When the weight stops moving, the string is vertical. Hold the bottom end tight and snap the string to place a vertical chalk line on the wall.

7. Now you are ready to put up your first strip of paper. Measure the height of the wall, and cut your strip about four inches longer.

8. If you have the prepaste type of wall covering, put the rolled-up strip in the water tray and leave it there for the prescribed amount of time. If you must apply the paste yourself, put the strip face down on a large table and start brushing on the paste at the top. Cover the top half, and then fold the top over—paste against paste—making sure not to crimp or crease the paper. Do the bottom half and fold it over the same way. This technique allows you to carry and work with the strip without getting paste all over you.

9. When you get to the corner, unfold the top half of the paper strip, position the edge next to the chalk line, and be sure it lines up. This step is very important. If the first strip does not line up, the whole room will be out of line. Leave about half of the extra four inches of length sticking out at the ceiling. Start smoothing over toward the corner, using your hand, and work over the entire top half. When you get to the corner, you will find that an extra inch of wall covering remains; take the extra amount around the corner and stick it to the other wall.

10. When the top half is smooth, unfold the bottom half and apply it the same way.

11. Use a sponge or smoothing brush to force out excess paste and air bubbles. Always work toward the edges.

12. Hold the smoothing brush vertically, and actually pound it against the corner to push the paper back in the corner until it sticks.

13. Use the same pounding technique along the baseboard and at the ceiling. Do not trim the top and bottom yet.

14. Now unroll some new paper, and make sure it lines up according to the pattern before you cut the second panel.

15. After you prepare the second panel for hanging, place it right next to the first, and then slide it over to butt against the edge.

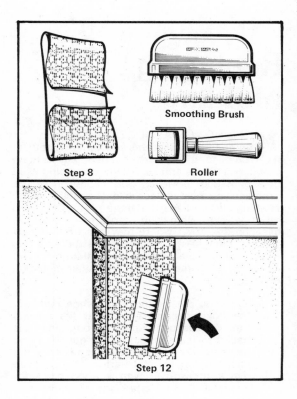

Smoothing Brush

Roller

Step 8

Step 12

16. Roll the seams after you smooth each panel.

17. Wait until after you put up and smooth the next panel before trimming the previous one. Use a sharp razor blade, and change to a new one as soon as you start to notice the blade getting dull.

18. Continue on all the way around the room. Do not skip any areas around doors or windows.

19. When you come to doors and windows, hold the strip over the door and use a hard object to crease an outline of the frame in the wall covering. Then trim the panel to fit, and paste it in place. You can trim it more precisely with a razor blade later.

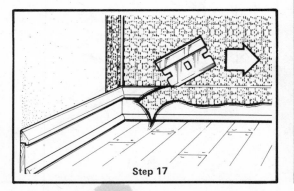

Step 17

Sizing Helps Bond Paper To Walls

Most—if not all—wallpapering jobs turn out better if sizing is applied to the walls prior to papering. Sizing provides a better surface to work on, a longer-lasting bond, and it insures tighter seams too. Adhesium, from the Muralo Company, is one of the most popular brands in sizing. In addition to sealing the wall and strengthening the bond, Adhesium Sizing—when mixed into the paste—also makes it easier to position the wallcovering on the wall. Muralo makes several other Adhesium products to aid the paperhanger.

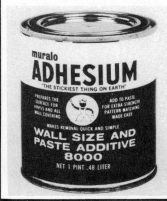

Back Saws Great For Mitering

Due to the stiff spine that goes down its back, the backsaw possesses extra rigidity that prevents it from wavering during the cutting process. The Spearior Back Saw, made by Spear and Jackson, has a chrome-vanadium steel blade expertly sharpened and blocked which is fitted to the heavy brass spine; both blade and spine are screwed securely to the beech handle, which has dowelling for extra strength. Available in 8-, 12-, and 14-inch lengths with either 20 or 15 teeth per inch, the Spearior Back Saw can be relied upon to make the clean smooth cuts needed to mate mitered corners of molding.

Small Pry Bar Can Take Off Molding

A small pry bar like the Omega Utility Bar can do a great job of removing molding without damaging it. Although only six inches long, the Omega Bar's shape makes it very versatile. Quite sturdy, it is able to take much more force than ever would be required for removing molding. The Utility Bar is a product of the Omega Precision Hand Tool Company.

Epoxy Bonds Hammer Head To Fiberglass Handle

Easco's Epoxy Bonding process assures that the heads and handles of Easco hammers remain together permanently. The epoxy fills all openings to provide maximum adhesion, and the polished head is heat treated and tempered for durability and safety. The 16-ounce hammer is big enough to handle most home chores, yet light enough to give you excellent control.

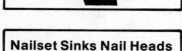

Nailset Sinks Nail Heads

The nails used to install moldings should be hidden, and the tool for driving the nail heads below the surface of the molding is called a nailset. Nailsets come in various sizes, and it is important to match the point of the nail set to the head of the nail; otherwise, you can damage the molding while trying to hide the nail. The Mayhew Nailset, one of the popular square-head variety, is made of high-grade tempered steel and has a knurled body with a polished point. Mayhew Steel Products, Inc., has been in the tool business for about 120 years and enjoys an excellent reputation for producing fine tools.

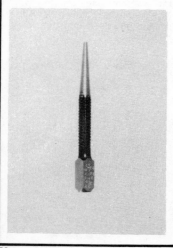

Replacing Molding

MOLDING IS ALMOST a panacea for botched-up wall seams and joints. Of course, it can be decorative as well, but generally its main function is to hide cracks. When the molding itself gets damaged, however, you cannot hide the problem; you must replace at least a section of the molding and perhaps the entire piece. Since the most easily damaged moldings are the baseboards—down where they can be hit by all sorts of things—the following instructions describe how to replace baseboard molding, but you can apply the same technique to other moldings in other places.

Here Is What You Will Need

Materials

- Wooden wedges
- Replacement moldings
- Finishing nails
- Paint

Tools

- Putty knife
- Screwdriver
- Wood block
- Pry bar
- Hammer
- Pliers
- Mitre box
- Backsaw or hacksaw
- Coping saw
- Nailset
- Paintbrush

1. First, you must remove any shoe molding, the quarter-round piece that fits against both the baseboard and the floor. Since it is nailed to the subfloor, apply gentle prying pressure with a putty knife at one end of the shoe molding to get it started. Then you can use a screwdriver with a wood block for leverage. Once started, the shoe molding should come up fairly easily. Try not to be too rough, though, or you can break it, adding to your replacement costs and troubles.
2. Next, pry out the damaged baseboard. Start at one end, inserting a small flat pry bar between the baseboard and the wall. Pry gently, and move further down the line whenever you can, slipping small wooden wedges in the gaps. Work all the way along the baseboard prying and wedging. Then work back between the wedges, tapping the wedges in deeper as the baseboard comes out more. The baseboard soon will come off.
3. Check to see if any nails have been pulled through either the shoe molding or the baseboard, if so, pull out the nails completely.

If the old baseboard came out intact, you can use it as a pattern for cutting the new one. If part is missing or if it is badly damaged, however, you must cut the new moldings to fit without the aid of a pattern. You will need a mitre box to cut the moldings; an inexpensive wooden mitre box will

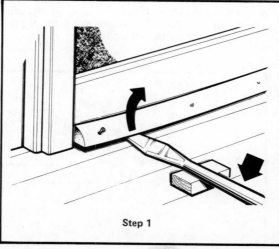

Step 1

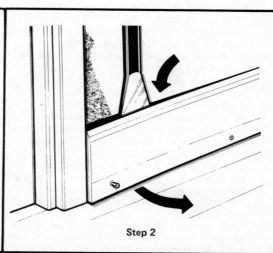

Step 2

Decorative Moldings Reproduce Classics

Those fancy moldings one sees in fine old homes and estates are now available in imitation form from Focal Point, Inc., a company which makes reproductions directly from the wood or plaster originals. The moldings themselves are made of lightweight polymers that can be nailed, drilled, screwed, sanded, sawed,

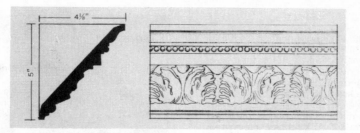

or planed. Focal Point also offers reproductions of ceiling medallions, fireplace mantels, and other accessories.

PVC Moldings Have Advantages Over Wood

Vinyl Shield PVC Moldings from Georgia-Pacific come in seven wood-grain patterns and solid colors. They can be sawed and mitered just like wood, and they can also be nailed in place. But unlike wood they are warp-proof, shrink-proof, resistant to impact damage, and—since they are already finished—they require no painting. Georgia-Pacific Vinyl Shield PVC Moldings (as well as most other brands) are generally used to finish off a paneled wall, but they do nicely as replacements for molding in almost any room. They are usually available wherever paneling is sold.

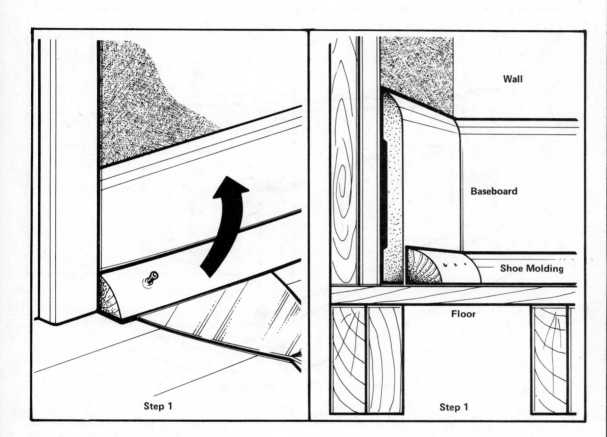

Step 1

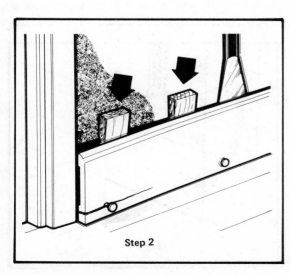

Step 2

be adequate for this work. The slots allow you to cut 45-degree angles, and you should use either a backsaw or a fine blade in a hacksaw. Be sure to place the molding you are about to cut next to the molding against which it will rest in order to make certain that the cut you plan to make is the right one. Then follow these instructions to cut the new molding.

△ 1. Place a scrap of wood in the mitre box.
△ 2. Make sure that the lip of the mitre box presses against the edge of a table or bench so that you can hold it steady.
△ 3. Hold the molding tightly against the side of the mitre box to prevent it from slipping as you saw.
△ 4. After you make the cut, the molding should fit perfectly against the other mitred piece to form a right angle.

If you need an inside right angle, though, you could go crazy trying to get the two angled pieces to fit. The solution to this vexing problem is called a coped joint. Here is how you make such a joint.

○ 1. Cut one piece of baseboard to fit precisely in the space.
○ 2. Lay this piece of baseboard flat on the floor with its backside facing up.

(Continued on next page)

Mitre Box Designed For Home Handyman

Designed and priced just right for the home handyman, Stanley's Mitre Box features pre-set 45- and 90-degree cutting angles, making it ideal for mitering moldings. As simple to use as the mitre boxes used by professional carpenters, this Stanley version is made of lightweight plastic, yet it is rigid in construction. It holds lumber of various types and sizes (up to a standard 2x4) for cutting with a backsaw or cross-cut panel saw. Holes in the Stanley Mitre Box permit it to be fastened to a workbench or to a replaceable bottom board.

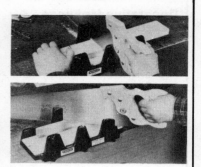

Putty Knife Eases Moldings Loose

Putty knives can be used for many different purposes, but prying is generally not a recommended one. If you are careful, though, you can use a putty knife to great advantage in removing molding. The advantage a putty knife offers is that it can slip into the tiny crack between the wall and the molding without damaging either one as a screwdriver could. Great Neck Saw Manufacturers, Inc., markets a good line of moderately priced tools, including a sturdy putty knife.

16-Ounce Claw Hammer Is All-Round Performer

The all-purpose 16-ounce claw hammer—16 ounces refers to the weight of the head—is available in versions with wooden handles, fiberglass handles, or with steel handles. Like many of the hammers and hand axes from Estwing Manufacturing Company, the 16-ounce claw model features a steel handle and the company's original leather grip. Since it is a top quality hammer, this Estwing hammer should last a lifetime. It also has excellent balance.

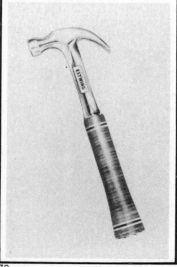

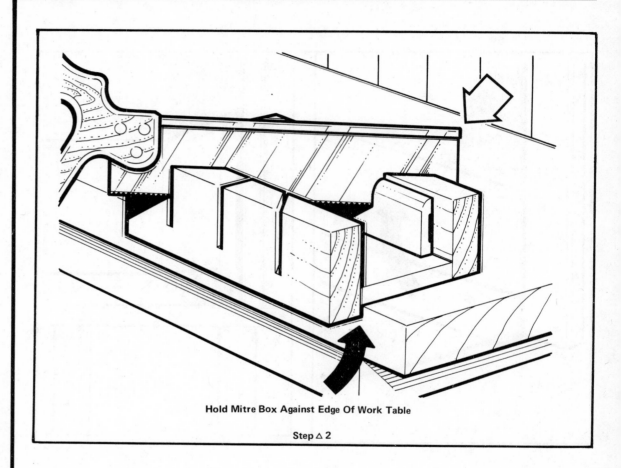

Hold Mitre Box Against Edge Of Work Table

Step △ 2

(Continued from previous page)

○ 3. Place another piece of baseboard molding down against the back of the piece on the floor. The tapered end of the top molding should point to the edge of the bottom piece. If it does not, turn the top piece end for end. Now it is in place.

○ 4. Trace the contour of the top piece onto the bottom piece.

○ 5. Use a coping saw to cut along the pattern.

○ 6. When cut, the two pieces will fit closely together to form a false mitre—referred to as a coped joint—that creates a perfect inside corner.

When you finish all the mitring and coped joints, you are ready to install the new baseboard molding and to reinstall the shoe molding.

□ 1. Fit all the pieces together before nailing to make sure that you cut them correctly.

□ 2. Nail the baseboard in place with finishing nails. Then use a nailset to drive the nail heads below the surface of the molding.

□ 3. Reinstall the shoe molding with finishing nails as well. Remember, shoe molding must be nailed to the floor and not to the baseboard. Drive the nail heads below the surface of the shoe molding with a nailset.

□ 4. Paint all new moldings to match your walls.

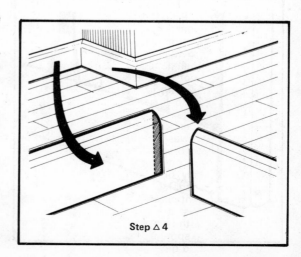

Step △ 4

Special Shears For Paperhangers

The scissors used by the professional paperhangers are longer and skinnier than standard household shears. Warner Tools, a firm that makes just about every paperhanging tool, markets lightweight imported paperhanging shears that are made of forged steel and that measure a full 12 inches long.

Patching Paste Helps Hold Loose Edges

When repairing loose wallpaper edges, you'll find a special product called Paste-Bak to be a big help. Made by Murray-Black, Paste-Bak comes in a tube with a thin flexible plastic tip that slips under loosened edges or slits without tearing the paper. Once the tip is in place, you merely squeeze out as much paste as you need to hold the recalcitrant edges. Paste-Bak is a special formula that sets firm but does not spot the paper.

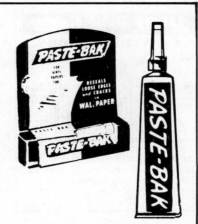

Seam Roller Puts Down Edges And Patches

A good seam roller is quite helpful in getting patches and edges to lie down flat and adhere firmly to the wall. Most seam rollers are pretty much the same: some have plastic rollers, while others have wooden rollers; and some have plastic handles, while others have wooden handles. But there is one seam roller that is truly different: Hyde's two-in-one Side Arm Seam Roller. By altering the axle's position vis-a-vis the handle, the Side Arm Seam Roller can be converted quickly (just a screwdriver is required) to a corner roller. Another unique tool from Hyde is the three-in-one One Arm Paperhanger. At one end of the handle is a seam roller, while at the other end are a rolling knife wheel—called a casing knife—for regular trimming and a corner knife for trimming corners.

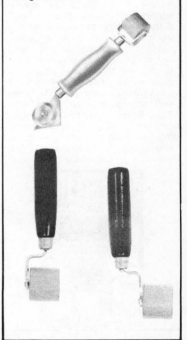

Wallpaper Patching

AFTER A WHILE, you may notice the appearance of some wallpaper problems. If not remedied, a loose seam, a slight tear, or a bubble will surely become a bigger and more unsightly aspect of your walls. When you think back to what you went through in putting the paper up originally, you will certainly prefer to repair than to repaper.

1. You can simply repaste seams that come unstuck. Save a small container of the paste for that purpose, and squirt a bit under the loose flaps or spread it on with a small artist's brush. Then use a seam roller to press the paper back down.
2. If you have overlaps in a vinyl covering that refuse to stay down, buy some of the special paste made for vinyl-to-vinyl adhesion. An application of this special paste will do the job.
3. Just when you think you did the world's smoothest papering job, you see some bubbles! Do not despair. Merely slit them twice to form an "X" across the center of the blister. Then peel back the tips of the slit and squirt paste into the blister. The tips may overlap a little, but such overlapping is seldom noticeable. If you notice the blister shortly after you finish papering—but after the paste has dried—the thick blob under the blister may still be wet paste. Try sticking a pin in the blister and then forcing the paste out. If that trick does not do the job, slit and repaste.
4. Patching a torn section of wallpaper is easy to do—provided you saved the scraps from the original papering job. Select a scrap section that matches the pattern, and tear the patch in an irregular shape so that the edge can be feathered back under the patch. Such a patch blends in much better than if it were cut evenly.
5. When nonwashable paper gets dirty, use a blob of rye bread or a kneaded eraser (available at an art store) to rub away the dirt. Incidentally, nonwashable wallpaper can be made washable with an application of a transparent coating now on the market. Be sure to test the coating on a scrap before covering the entire wall with it, however. You can sponge washable wall coverings with a mild detergent and even scrub some

Here Is What You Will Need
Materials
- Wallpaper paste
- Vinyl-to-vinyl paste
- Pin
- Rye bread or kneaded eraser
- Sponge
- Mild detergent
- Colored ink pens
Tools
- Small artist's brush
- Seam roller
- Razor blades

vinyls, but to find out just how much elbow grease your paper can take, work on a scrap first.
6. If some of the wallpaper's design has rubbed off and you do not have the scraps to patch over it, you might try using colored inks to redraw the design.

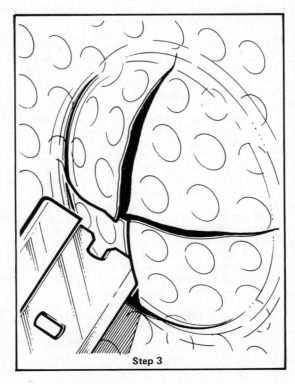
Step 3

Wallpaper Repair Tips

After wallcoverings have been exposed to light and air, their colors change just a bit. The change will never be noticed until you put a patch of the unexposed original material in place; then you'll see the difference. If you plan ahead by allowing some of the unused wallcovering material to weather, you will have properly exposed paper on hand when you need a patch. You can staple several pieces of leftover wallcovering to the inside of a closet door, or you can pin the scraps to the back of a couch or chair that goes right up against a wall. These leftovers will then be exposed to much more light and air than if they were left rolled up in a dark basement corner. One other repair tip: always put any leftover wallpaper paste in an empty, tightly capped plastic squeeze bottle. Wallpaper paste will keep for a long time if stored properly, and then it will always be handy when repairs are needed.

Walls

Plastic Anchors Hold Screws In Wall

Any wall surface that cannot hold a screw can be made to hold a screw with plastic anchors of the Jord-EZE type. Available in sizes ranging from those made for very small screws on up to those made for ⅜-inch lag screws, Jord-EZE Anchors are weatherproof and shrink-proof for use indoors or out. Packaged with or without screws, all Jord-EZE anchors come with instructions regarding the proper size drill bit to use.

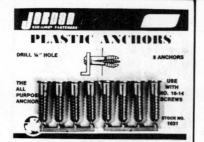

Jordan Industries also makes nylon and lead anchors, as well as many other fine fastening products.

Humble Hook Can Have Class

Homecraft's Futura line consists of a number of fancy hooks to match nearly any decor. From smooth-sculptured contemporary versions to carved classics, each Futura Hook is made of rustproof metal with a quality plated finish. The antique finishes are lacquered for durability, and the painted hooks are coated with chip-resistant baked enamel. Homecraft hooks are made by Gries Reproducer Company.

Stick It With Stik Tabs

You can hang many small objects securely with Stik Tabs. These two-sided pressure-sensitive tabs provide a quick and easy way to mount such items as mirror squares, tie racks, pictures, wall plaques, spice racks, tissue dispensers, and all sorts of other items. They adhere to any clean dry solid surface—whether it be brick, wood, tile, wallboard, or metal—and they eliminate the possibility of creating ugly holes and cracks in your walls. Stik Tabs, which consist of a thin layer of foam with an adhesive backing, are sold in packages of 50 and are quite inexpensive. They are made by Metalco.

Hang Things On Hard Walls Without Drilling

The Moore Push Pin Company —makers of a complete line of wallhanger products—has come up with a plastic hanger that allows you to attach things to a concrete, cinder block, soft brick, or hardboard wall with no drilling, no anchors, and no messy adhesives. All you need is a hammer. Each Moore Hardwall Hanger has four steel pins (they look like the old-fashioned phonograph needles) that you can drive right into the wall. Then you just hang something lightweight (like a picture) on the plastic hook.

Hanging Things on Walls

THE OLD SAYING, "What goes up must come down," need not apply to things you hang on the wall. Most homes today have hollow wall construction, and that means something like sheetrock is nailed to studs within the wall. When you drive a nail into such a wall to hang something, the weight of the hanging will probably pull the nail out of the sheetrock before too long—unless you drive the nail into a stud. Generally, studs are located on 16-inch centers, which means that there are 16 inches from the center of one stud to the center of the next. You can usually locate studs with a magnetic finder, but frequently the studs are not located where you want to hang your pictures, mirrors, etc. Then you must know how to hang things where you want them when there are no studs available.

To hang lightweight pictures, use a picture hanger. All you need do is place the hanger plate flat against the wall and drive the nail through it at an angle. The angled nail and the flat plate will hold most lightweight objects securely. When you drive the nail in, though, be sure to place a tab of cellophane tape over the spot to prevent the surface from crumbling as the nail penetrates.

For hanging lightweight objects like drapery rods, use plastic wall anchors. Buy the anchors made for the size screws you have, and examine the package to find out what size drill bit to use for the holes. Then, to install these anchors, just follow these simple steps.

1. Drill a hole in the wall to accommodate the plastic anchor.
2. Tap the anchor in all the way.
3. Insert the screw through the item it is to hold, and then turn it into the anchor. The screw expands the anchor to make it grip the sides of the hole.

As you get into heavier hangings, such as shelves and mirrors, the best device is the expansion anchor—commonly called the Molly. Mollys come in different sizes to accommodate differences in wall thickness and in the weight of the things they are to hold. Once you get the right Molly, here is how to install it.

△ 1. Consult the package to see what size drill bit to use, and then drill a hole in the wall.
△ 2. Lightly tap the Molly in place with your hammer.
△ 3. Turn the slotted bolt clockwise.

Here Is What You Will Need

Materials
- Picture hangers
- Cellophane tape
- Plastic wall anchors
- Expansion (or Molly) bolts
- Toggle bolts

Tools
- Magnetic stud finder
- Hammer
- Drill
- Screwdriver

△ 4. When you cannot turn it any more, back it out. The Molly is then secure against the inside of the wall, and you are ready to hang your shelves, mirror, etc.
△ 5. Put the bolt through the item or the item's hanger, and reinsert the bolt in the Molly. That is all there is to it. One Molly can support up to five hundred pounds.

For really heavy installations—such as cabinets or a bookshelf unit—use toggle bolts. Available in several sizes, toggle bolts also require that you drill holes in the wall. If you buy the packaged kind, you will find the size of the hole specified on the package. Here is how to install them.

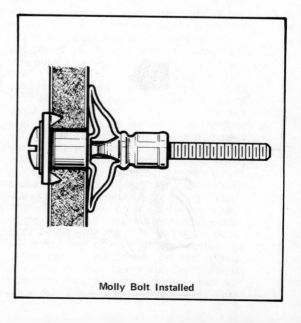

Molly Bolt Installed

Magnetic Stud Finder Ends Hang-Up Woes

Ever try to find a stud in the wall when you need strong support for a heavy mirror or picture? Most people find it a frustrating task and wind up hammering the nail or picture hook into every place but the stud. Fortunately, Stanley Tools has come to the rescue with a special tool for locating wall studs easily. The tool, Stanley's Magnetic Stud Finder, consists of a strong cylindrical magnet in a red sleeve that is housed in clear

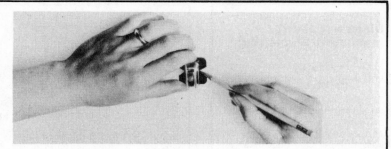

plastic. The blue base of the stud finder is grooved so that you can mark the stud location precisely with a pencil. Although it doesn't

cost very much, the Stanley Magnetic Stud Finder is one of the handiest tools to have around the house.

Drive Fasteners Into Masonry

Most masonry fasteners necessitate some form of drilling—either a masonry bit in an electric drill or a hammer and star drill. With the Ammo DriveTool and special Ammo DrivePins, though, you can drive fasteners into masonry without drilling. The DriveTool concentrates hammer impact on the head of the pin, as it holds the pin straight, secure, and right on the spot where you want it to go. Ideal for attaching wood (such as furring strips or even 2x4s) to masonry, the Ammo DriveTool can also be used for attaching metal brackets. The Ammo DriveTool and DrivePins are products of the USM Corporation.

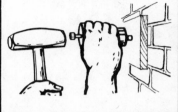

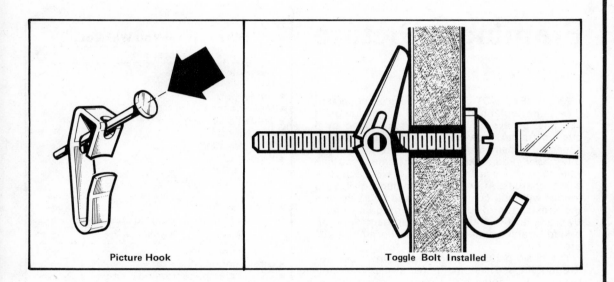

Picture Hook

Toggle Bolt Installed

o 1. Drill the hole.
o 2. Remove the bolt from the flange.
o 3. Put the bolt through the object to be hung or through its hanger before you insert it into the wall. You cannot remove the bolt after the toggle bolt device is in the wall without the flange falling down between the wall. Reinsert the bolt in the flange.
o 4. Crimp the flange with your thumb and forefinger and push it into the hole. Of course, you must hold the object you are hanging

right next to the wall as you insert the toggle bolt. When the flange goes through, pull the bolt back toward you until you feel the flange hit the back of the wall.
o 5. Turn the bolt clockwise until the hanger or the item itself is flat against the wall.

For specialized hanging problems, chances are that you will be able to find an inexpensive anchor of some kind to do the job. Check your local hardware store.

Toggle Bolt Springs Into Action

The Star Snapin Toggle Bolt has a spring within the winged head that causes it to open automatically once the head gets through the hole. Made in a wide range of sizes, Star brand toggle bolts come carded with two bolts to the pack. They also come in three head styles: round, flat, and mushroom. Instructions on the package tell you what size drill bit you need to make the proper size hole. The Star Expansion Company makes a complete line of hang-up devices and tools for all types of walls.

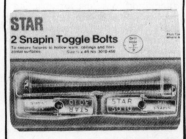

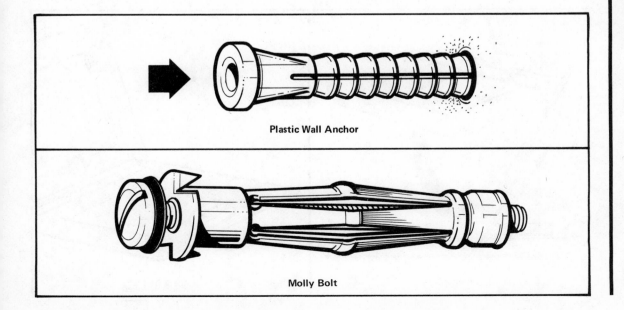

Plastic Wall Anchor

Molly Bolt

Everybody Has Heard Of Molly

The best-known name in hollow wall fasteners is, without a doubt, Molly. In fact, many similar expansion anchors are called Molly bolts, but the genuine Mollys are made only by USM. Manufactured in various sizes for different wallboard thicknesses and for different weights to be held, Mollys even come in a stubby version for attaching things to hollow doors. Regular Molly bolts are inserted in a drilled hole, but there is a version which can be hammered into the wall.

Hobby Knife Grips Blade Tightly For Clean Cuts

A new entry in the hobby field is the line of knives by X-PO. The X-PO hobby knife utilizes a four-jaw chucking method that results in stronger blade-holding power, minimizing rocking motion of the blade. Even the least expensive X-PO knife model, the No. 111, works exceptionally well on picture frame mats. Several types of interchangeable surgically sharp blades are available for use with X-PO knives, which are available at most art and hobby shops.

Disaster Follows Inaccurate Measuring

Many projects, both professional and amateur, have gone astray due to inaccurate measurement. The Exact aluminum rule is truly parallel and accurate. The edges are smooth, square, and straight, and its numbers are large and easy to read. One edge has calibrations in eighths and the other in sixteenths. Exact aluminum rules range in length from 24 to 96 inches.

Mat Cutter Bevels Edges

Professionally framed pictures frequently include mats with beveled edges. Although the amateur can use a knife to bevel, the results are likely to look amateurish. But with the Dexter Mat Cutter, you can make a perfect beveled edge every time. Just set the cutter blade to the angle you desire, lock it into place, and push the cutter along the side of a straightedge. Easy to work with because it fits the hand well, the Dexter Mat Cutter—a product of

the Russell Harrington Cutlery Company—is available at most large art supply stores.

Mitre Frame Clamp Holds Entire Frame At Once

The Hargrave Mitre Frame Clamp, a product of the Warren Group, clamps all four corners of a picture frame at one time. Easy to attach and to adjust for absolute accuracy, the clamp can handle frame sizes up to 14 inches, but you can purchase extension screws that add as much as 12 inches to the basic unit. In fact, you can add as many extension screws as you need to attain the correct frame size. The Hargrave Mitre Frame Clamp is a quality instrument, with aluminum alloy corner blocks and steel screws and adjusting nuts.

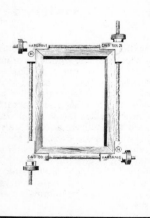

Framing a Picture

YOU NEED NOT own a priceless art collection to have plenty of attractive wall hangings. If you pay to have all your treasures framed by a custom framer, however, you will find yourself spending considerable sums of money. If, on the other hand, you make your own frames, you can save somewhere near 75 percent of what a professional charges. After you get the hang of it, your frames will look custom made and you will have the satisfaction of turning out a product of your own creativity. You can even create "one-of-a-kind" frames suited exactly to the picture you are hanging.

The basic picture frame is made from decorative moldings. These moldings, available at lumberyards and some home centers, are quite inexpensive and they come in many sizes and shapes. Try to find a store where you can select the moldings yourself. That way, you can be assured of getting straight pieces without pockets of sap, knots, warps, and bows. To start, try a two-part frame, consisting of a sub-frame and moldings for the decorative outer frame. Here is how it goes.

Here Is What You Will Need

Materials

- Decorative moldings
- Mat
- Spray glue
- Masking tape
- White polyvinyl glue
- Fasteners
- Finishing nails
- Wood putty
- Sandpaper
- Nonreflective glass
- Brads
- Heavy brown paper
- Picture hanger or wire and screw eyes

Tools

- Artist's knife
- Straightedge
- Corner clamps or framing clamps
- Mitre box and hand saw or table saw
- Nailset
- Hammer
- Scissors

1. You must decide whether the painting or photo needs a mat. In many cases, a mat enhances the picture. After selecting the color and texture of the mat board you want, draw a pattern of the picture on the mat.
2. Use a sharp artist's knife and a straightedge to cut along the line you drew. As you cut,

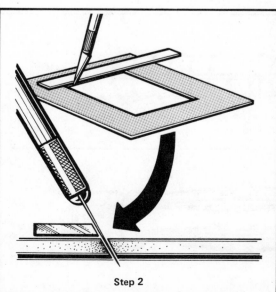

Step 2

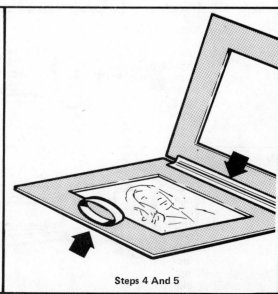

Steps 4 And 5

Mitre Box Can Be A Precision Tool

While an inexpensive wooden or plastic mitre box will do for most molding jobs, you should get a better one if you intend to pursue precision picture frame construction. The Millers Falls Mitre Box consists of a one-piece cast-iron bed and back with steel swinging lever and posts. It can lock in at any desired angle—right or left—and an automatic catch holds the saw up as needed. The Millers Falls Mitre Box comes equipped with a top quality saw.

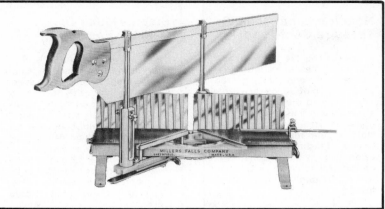

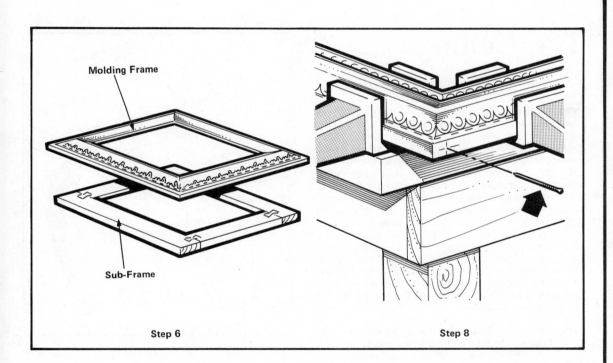

Molding Frame

Sub-Frame

Step 6

Step 8

Save Money With Do-It-Yourself Frame Moldings

Many hardware stores, home centers, and hobby/craft shops carry large selections of unfinished wood picture frame moldings. The Klise Manufacturing Company markets the Accent line, which includes both traditional and contemporary moldings with 11 different styles in all. Klise also offers a how-to leaflet at the Accent Moldings display.

Special Tool Sets Wiggle Nails

If you use corrugated fasteners (commonly nicknamed wiggle nails) to join the corners of your picture frames, you should consider buying the Stanley tool designed specifically for setting these fasteners firmly in place. A metal sleeve on the tool accepts the fastener, and then you insert a flat piece in the sleeve over the fastener before hammering. An inexpensive tool, the Stanley Fastener Holder can save your thumb and forefinger, to say nothing of the frame. It makes an otherwise hit-and-miss task go well every time.

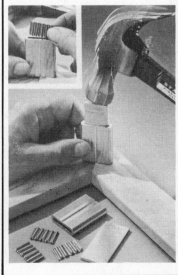

bevel in toward the picture.

3. Next, cut a backing piece to match the mat size. You can use heavy cardboard, but another piece of mat board works best. Mount the picture on the backing with spray glue.

4. Make a hinge out of masking tape by running it along the edges of both the mat and the backing.

5. Form a loop out of masking tape with the sticky side out to hold the other mat in place.

6. Now you are ready to make the sub-frame. The opening of this part must be slightly larger than the mat and mounting. Cut the four pieces and glue them together (white polyvinyl glue works well) in simple butt joints, clamping the corners with inexpensive corner clamps or framing clamps. While the clamp is holding the corner, attach a fastener to secure the joint.

7. The moldings must be wider than the material used in the sub-frame and must overlap toward the center a quarter of an inch to form a rabbet into which the picture will fit. Miter the molding very carefully. A wooden miter box and a hand saw will do, but if you have a table saw, you will be able to set it for a more accurate miter. When all four pieces are cut, check them against the sub-frame before gluing.

8. Glue and clamp the frame moldings, and

while the clamps are on, drive tiny finishing nails into the frame so that they go into the adjoining pieces.

9. Use a nailset to drive the heads below the surface.

10. Fill the holes over the nails and sand.

11. Attach the two frames together with glue and nails.

12. Finish the frame in any manner you like.

13. When the finish is dry, insert a piece of glass cut 1/8 of an inch less than the frame in both width and length to compensate for any irregularities. Nonreflective glass is best for paintings and photos. With the glass in place, insert the mounted picture.

14. Use brads to hold the picture and its backing in the frame. Drive in two brads per side, and make sure that both the picture and glass are as snug against the front of the frame as possible.

15. Next, add the dust cover, which is a piece of heavy brown paper glued to the back of the frame to seal in the picture. After the glue sets, take a damp cloth and rub lightly over the dust cover. The cloth must not be wet enough to soak through, however. When it dries the paper will shrink, creating a tight dust jacket.

16. The frame itself is finished. Now you can add either a hanger or wire in screw eyes and hang your new creation.

Ceilings

Adhesive Quickens Tile Installation

Quick bonding, fast setting ceiling tile adhesive can make tiling a ceiling a painless task. United States Gypsum's Wal-lite Ceiling Tile Adhesive is a resin-based high-strength product that forms an instantaneous bond, freeing the do-it-yourselfer from holding the tile against the ceiling until bonding strength is adequate. The Wal-lite adhesive, however, is formulated to allow ample adjustment time before it holds the tile in its final position. Moisture resistant for use in humid conditions, Wal-lite Ceiling Tile Adhesive cleans up easily with mineral spirits.

Clip-Strip Improves Do-It-Yourself Ceiling Installations

The do-it-yourselfer who wants to install a new tile ceiling no longer needs to staple or nail the tiles in place. The unique Clip-Strip system, available from the Gold Bond Building Products Division of National Gypsum Company, provides a suspended channel that accepts tongue-and-groove ceiling tiles from both sides. The result is a tight-fitted seam that runs the entire length of the new ceiling.

The system, designed exclusively for installation of tongue-and-groove (wide-flange) ½-inch and ⅝-inch 12x12-inch ceiling tiles, is composed of extruded plastic wall molding and lightweight galvanized metal Clip-Strip channels. The two elements provide a raceway for sliding tiles into neat, snug-fitting rows for a smooth, professional looking job with no exposed fasteners.

Aside from providing a fastening channel, the 10-foot plastic molding acts as a coving to eliminate the need for installing any trim. The four-foot metal Clip-Strips can be fastened to furring strips or across joists with staples or nails. Once the tiles are installed, of course, they completely hide both the plastic moldings and the metal strips.

Nondirectional Ceiling Tiles Are Goof-Proof

A new ceiling tile pattern called "Abstract" has been introduced by the Gold Bond Building Products Division of National Gypsum. The easy-to-clean, embossed acousticrylic finish is nondirectional in design, speeding installation and resulting in a continuous finished surface. Gold Bond tiles can be applied with ceiling tile adhesive, staples, or with Gold Bond's Clip-Strip metal furring.

Staples Make Tile Ceilings Easy

One squeeze of Arrow's T-50 heavy-duty all-purpose staple gun drives a staple wherever a nail can be driven—into the hardest of woods and even into light metals. When equipped with a special wire staple called Ceiltile, the gun is ideal for attaching ceiling tiles. A product of the Arrow Fastener Company, the T-50 can also be used for hundreds of do-it-yourself chores with the five other staple sizes it is designed to hold. It even comes in a T-50 MP kit with attachments for screens, wiring, and shades; three boxes of staples (including Ceiltile); and a staple lifter.

Tile Ceilings

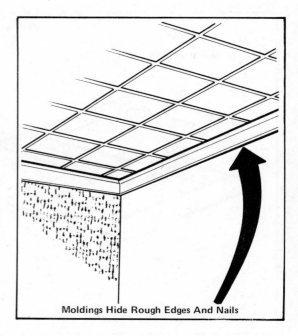

Moldings Hide Rough Edges And Nails

THE EASY WAY to have a new ceiling—as long as the old surface is sound and you do not wish to lower it—is to install ceiling tiles. Some ceiling tiles can absorb a good deal of the noise in the room, but you should realize that not all tiles are acoustical tiles. If your reason for wanting a tile ceiling is noise reduction, then you must do some very careful comparison shopping.

You apply ceiling tiles in one of two ways, either with staples or with adhesive. A sound ceiling of wallboard or plaster takes adhesive well, but if a plaster ceiling is unsound, you must install furring strips and then staple the tiles to the strips. Staples can also be used on wallboard. Different tile manufacturers have different systems for joining tiles together, but the installation principles are all about the same.

1. You must find out how large your border tiles are to be. You do not want to end up with less than half a tile at the borders, and you want the borders at each end to be the same width. Here is what you do. Measure each wall, disregarding the number of feet involved but paying close attention to the number of inches. For example, suppose that one wall measures ten feet three inches. All that counts is the number three. Add twelve to that and then divide by two. The result—7½—is the border tile width for each end. Now if the other wall measures ten feet, eight inches, the borders along the other sides would be ten inches (eight inches plus twelve equals 20 divided by two equals ten).

2. Pick a corner to start in, measure out the width of the border tiles, and snap a chalk line each way. It is also a good idea to snap a chalk line at the center as a guide.

3. If you are going to staple the tiles in place, cut the corner tile first with the staple tabs

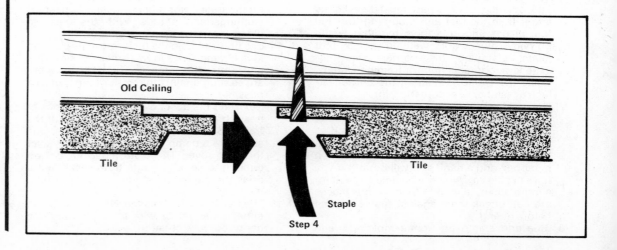

Old Ceiling

Tile

Staple

Tile

Step 4

Special Tiles Just For Kitchen Ceilings

The new Chandelier ceiling by Armstrong-Gourmet is designed especially for the kitchen. Since they are acoustical, these ceiling tiles absorb the noise of appliances working, children playing, and traffic rumbling. In addition, Chandelier ceiling tiles are non-combustible and thus will not feed a fire. Chandelier tiles have no edge bevels to interrupt the surface texture, and since all supporting metal is hidden behind the tiles, the ceiling looks like a one-piece installation.

Easy-To-Install Ceiling Tiles

Wal-lite ceiling tile, manufactured by United States Gypsum, is insulated to protect you from summer's heat and winter's cold. This washable ceiling tile (the pattern shown is Sierra) can be installed with adhesive, with nails into furring strips, or with USG's Wal-lite Series S-1 Suspended Grip System.

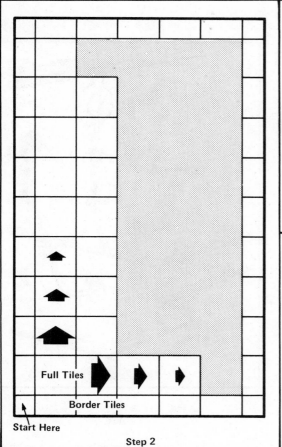

Start Here

Full Tiles

Border Tiles

Step 2

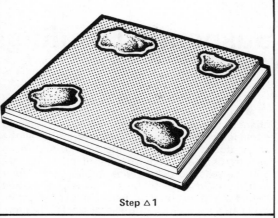

Step △ 1

Here Is What You Will Need
Materials
- Ceiling tiles
- Staples or adhesive
- Furring strips
- Nails

Tools
- Measuring tape
- Chalk line
- Staple gun
- Fiberboard knife or a fine-toothed saw
- Hammer

Decorator Tiles Don't Look Like Tiles

Armstrong's Decorator ceiling tiles fit together so tightly that it is almost impossible to tell where one tile ends and another starts. Several of the patterns are acoustical, and all are fire resistant and immune to variations in temperature and humidity; they will stay in place without warping, buckling, or separating. The use of decorative molding adds a dramatic effect to any ceiling.

Forget About Furring

To eliminate wooden furring strips, Armstrong Cork Company has developed a new system of lightweight steel channels. Designed for attaching the company's Chandelier ceiling tiles to plaster, drywall, or exposed joists, the channels are manufactured in 12-foot lengths.

aimed toward the center. Use a sharp fiberboard knife or a fine-toothed saw for cutting, and cut with the tile turned face up.

4. Staple the corner tile, after placing it carefully against the chalk lines. You can nail the back sides in place because any nails will be covered by molding later on. The staple flange will be covered by the interlock of the next tiles.
5. Now staple a complete course of cut border tiles along one wall, nailing the back sides in place.
6. Run the border tiles along the other wall.
7. Work in rows with the full tiles, stapling them as you go.
8. Border tiles at the other end will have no staple tabs. Nails plus the interlocks will hold them in place.

If you are applying the tile ceiling with adhesive,

then follow these steps.

△ 1. Apply four dabs of adhesive to the back of a tile about an inch and a half in from each corner.
△ 2. Place the tile near either the chalk line or the next tile, and slide it into place.
△ 3. Press the tile with your hand to make sure it adheres firmly against the ceiling. If a tile seems uneven, pull it back down and adjust the amount of adhesive to compensate for any irregularities.

Be sure to cut holes in the tiles for ceiling light fixtures. Remember that since the fixture's plate will cover the opening, the hole you cut need not be a work of art. When you get all the tiles up, place molding in the corners and you will hide all the rough edges as well as the nails. You should have a great looking ceiling!

Ceilings

Tinsnips Cut Grids To Pieces

Some of the segments in a suspended grid system are likely to need cutting, and a good pair of tinsnips—like the Channellock Aviation Snips—can make the job easy. Capable of cutting through 18-gauge cold rolled steel, the Channellock snips possess more than enough cutting action for grids. They feature heavy vinyl cushion grips, a latch, and drop-forged blades of molybdenum alloy tool steel that is heat treated for extra strength, toughness, and durability.

Completely Luminous Ceiling

One way to create a truly dramatic suspended ceiling is to install prismatic panels from Leigh. Available in frost white or clear, these polystyrene panels consist of inverted hexagon prisms that produce uniform light diffusion. All of Leigh's Light Diffusing Panels come in two sizes, 2x2 or 2x4 feet, and all are destaticized to minimize dust attraction. The metal parts in Leigh's Klip-Lock Suspension System come in white or wood-grained finish, and Leigh also markets, of course, non-luminous ceiling panels for installation in the Klip-Lock System.

Certain-Teed Ceilings Do It All

The fiberglass suspended ceilings offered by Certain-Teed Products come in a wide choice of patterns to fit into almost any decor. The Granada texture shown here enhances the Spanish decorating motif that is currently so popular. All Certain-Teed panels offer approximately 75 percent light reflection, 60 to 80 percent (depending on the pattern) noise absorption, and all are flame resistant. Easily installed in an exposed grid system, the panels are so flexible—requiring only a two-inch minimum grid drop—that they even go into tight places without difficulty.

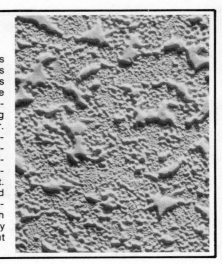

Needlepoint Effect Makes Striking Ceiling

The Bouquet pattern by Wal-lite is an attractive floral design ceiling panel that provides a needlepoint effect. Like many Wal-lite decorative and deep-dimension wood fiber panels, the Bouquet pattern is washable and is available in the two standard sizes, 2x2 and 2x4 feet. Wal-lite products are made by United States Gypsum.

Utility Knife Cuts Ceiling Panels Down To Size

Almost all suspended ceiling panels can be cut easily with a utility knife, and the Gerson Utility Knife shown is typical of the good models available. It has two blade positions, and the blade locks securely in place. The handle is made of indestructible plastic, is contoured for a firm and comfortable grip, and stores up to five extra blades. Even if you never hang a suspended ceiling, the utility knife is a tool you must have around the house; you will find dozens of uses for it.

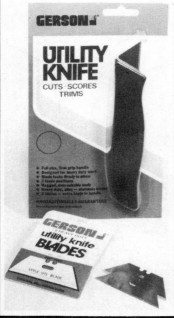

Suspended Ceilings

IF YOU EVER thought about converting a garage or basement into a family room, chances are you were discouraged by what you considered the impossibility of covering up all the wires, ducts, and pipes in the ceiling. And in an already finished room you might have thought that the existing ceiling was in such bad repair that it would have to be completely refinished before the room could be made useful once again. You can surmount all of these obstacles, though, by installing a suspended ceiling.

Suspended ceilings allow you easy access to pipes and ducts when you need to reach them, and special lamp units that you place in the ceiling in place of certain panels make lighting the room a snap. There are several different systems on the market, all claiming to be the easiest to install. Since all work on about the same principles and all go up fairly easily, however, make your choice of suspended ceiling systems based on some other factor than ease of installation. Here is how to install a typical suspended ceiling system.

1. Determine the height you want the ceiling to be, and snap a chalk line around the perimeter of the room. Use a level to make sure that the line does not slant.

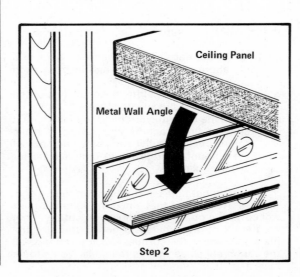

Step 2

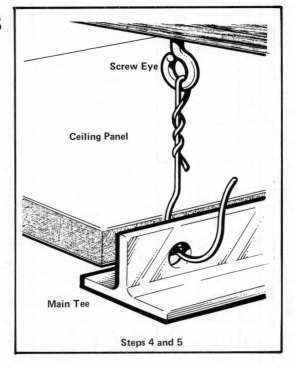

Steps 4 and 5

2. Nail the metal pieces called wall angles all the way around the room at the chalk line.
3. Measure the room to determine the size of the border tiles. Most suspended ceiling panels are 2x4 feet. Decide which way you wish the longer dimension to run, and divide the room length by four and the width by two. What is left over is your border area. Since your borders should be the same size at both ends, divide the remainder by two. Measure out from the wall the proper distance for the border panel, and stretch a string from one wall angle to the other at that point. If the ceiling joists above are exposed, run the string across perpendicular to them.
4. Drive screw eyes or nails into the sides of the joists. If you are installing a suspended ceiling over an existing ceiling, use screw eyes which are long enough to go through the ceiling and into the joists. Attach wires to the screw eyes or nails, and bend the wires at the level of the string.
5. When you finish attaching all of the wires

Ceiling In A Kit

National Gypsum Company had the do-it-yourselfer in mind when it designed the Gold Bond Ceiling Grid Kit. Available in two sizes—100 square feet and 192 square feet—the kit contains all the metal tees, cross tees, wall moldings, and hanger clips that would be needed to install a suspended ceiling that size. On the front of each kit is a chart that shows how much material is required for various room sizes, and the chart also indicates how many 2x4-foot ceiling panels will be needed. All metal parts in the Gold Bond Ceiling Grid Kit are pre-painted with baked-on white enamel.

along that line, install one of the metal pieces called a main tee (available in 12-foot lengths). Place one end of the main tee on the wall angle, and attach the wires through the holes in the tee.

6. Proceed with the other main tees at four-foot intervals all across the room. Cut odd lengths with tin snips, and check the tees regularly with a level.

7. When all of the tees are in place, start installing the cross tees. Cross tees are four-foot sections that fit perpendicular to the main tees and lock in place with a twist. Work your way across the room from wall to wall, installing all the cross tee sections.

8. Cut and snap each end of the cross tee pieces into the main tee.

9. Attach the remaining rows of cross tees every two feet all across the room.

10. When the entire grid system is hooked together, just tilt the panels to fit above the grids and then lower them into place.

11. You can cut the end panels easily with a sharp utility knife.

Here Is What You Will Need

Materials

- Wall angles
- Nails
- Ceiling panels
- String
- Screw eyes
- Wire
- Main tees
- Cross tees
- Light fixture ceiling panels

Tools

- Measuring tape
- Chalk line
- Level
- Hammer
- Tin snips
- Utility knife

12. Attach light fixtures to the joists above or—if you have the kind equipped with special brackets—attach them to the grid system. A special translucent panel lets the light through to the room.

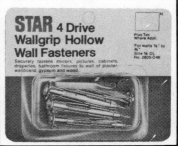

Who Hid The Grid?

Armstrong's Integrid Suspended Ceiling System is easy to install and goes up fast, but the best part is that the Integrid panels butt tightly together to form what appears to be a continuous unbroken surface. Each panel or tile has a slot into which the grids slip, and when adjoining tiles are put in place the metal parts are concealed. The Integrid System can be used in full suspension, attached directly to the exposed wood joists, or even attached to an existing suspended system of the conventional type. Armstrong Integrid tiles measure 1x4 feet and come in several surface designs; recessed fluorescent fixtures are also available for the Integrid System.

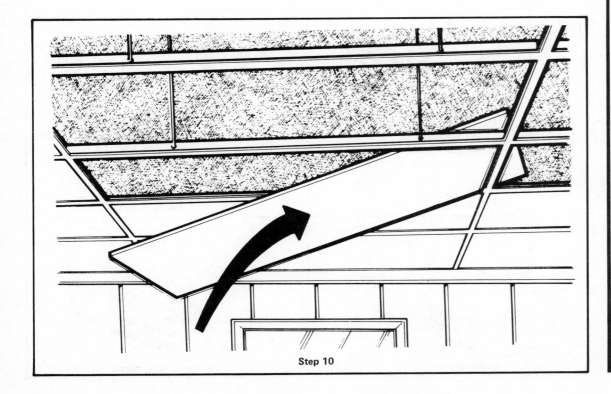

Step 10

Ceilings

Beams In Longer Lengths Mean Fewer Seams

Since they come in lengths up to 18 feet, Decorator Beams by Emco can span most ceiling and wall applications without seams. Made of polyurethane, these beams look like hand-hewn beams centuries old. The Emco Decorator line also includes such accessories as a junction box, corbels, and a jointer strap. Emco markets an adhesive and a touch-up stain that exactly matches the color of the beams, which, incidentally, are channeled so that wiring can run concealed behind them. Along with the Emco display, you'll find a free brochure containing additional ideas on the use of artificial beams on walls and ceilings.

Panel Adhesive Bonds Beams To Ceilings

While most manufacturers of artificial beams also market their own brands of beam adhesive, a tube of quality panel adhesive and a caulking gun will do the job. Mister Thinzit Panel Adhesive MC-98 is a rubber-based panel adhesive that can handle most fake beam installations. When applied according to directions, this black adhesive creates a permanent bond between artificial beams and most ceiling surfaces. A product of the Michlin Chemical Corporation, Mister Thinzit MC-98 cleans up with any ordinary paint thinner.

You Don't Have To Fake It

If you want honest-to-goodness hand-hewn wood beams for your ceiling, find a lumber dealer who handles Barclay Industries World of Wood line. Barclay hand-distressed beams come in eight-foot lengths and in four- or six-inch widths. They each have a three-inch hollow to fit over, and they can be secured to three-inch furring with finishing nails. Barclay also offers shelving and trim accessories to go along with the beams.

Installing Artificial Beams

MANY ROOMS can achieve real character with the addition of a rough hewn beamed ceiling. Not long ago such a project would have been impossible for the average homeowner, but today it is an easy do-it-yourself task. In fact, you will not even need an assistant to help carry the beams.

The change is due to the advent of synthetic beams made of a rigid polyurethane foam. Although available in wood finishes, some beams are obtainable unfinished and ready to take any oil-based paint or stain. You buy the fake beams in sections or in kits, and you attach them to any sound, dry surface with adhesive. All you have to do is select a design, figure the number of beams you will need, and follow these steps to install a beamed ceiling.

1. Make sure that the surface is sound, dry, and clean. If the surface is glossy, apply a deglosser.
2. Measure the length the beams are to span, and cut them to fit. You can cut the beams with a handsaw.
3. Mark the position of all beams with light pencil marks on the ceiling.
4. Hold each beam in place to make sure that they fit.
5. If you plan to install corner beams, attach

Here Is What You Will Need

Materials
- Polyurethane foam beams
- Deglosser
- Panel adhesive

Tools
- Measuring tape
- Handsaw

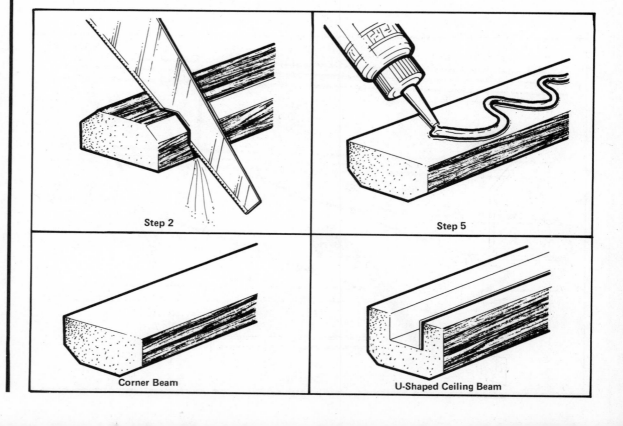

Step 2

Step 5

Corner Beam

U-Shaped Ceiling Beam

Hand-Hewn Beams The Easy Way

Ever consider making your own hand hewn beams from real wood? If so, you should know that there is an easier way than whacking at the wood with your axe. A tool called Hew-Do-It (a mailorder only item from Ironworks Hill, Box 191, Brookfield, Conn. 06804) consists of a set of eccentric wheels and a special curved blade that you add to your regular plane. The wheels make the plane bob up and down, scooping a cut of wood on each down stroke.

Saw Or Knife Cuts Beams

Artificial beams can be cut so easily that you can even do the job with a sharp kitchen knife. But a truly inexpensive hand saw like the Trophy 8-position keyhole model is worth having for this and dozens of other household tasks. Packaged with three interchangeable blades, the Trophy keyhole saw has a turret head that adjusts for eight different cutting angles. The three blades include a 5-inch wood-cutting blade, a 10-inch wood-cutting blade, and a 7½-inch metal-cutting blade. The metal-cutting blade, with its 13 teeth per inch, is a bit smoother in cutting artificial beams, but the other two work satisfactorily as well. Although the eight different cutting angles are not needed for sizing fake beams, the Trophy keyhole saw is very handy for shaping end pieces that must fit against irregular surfaces.

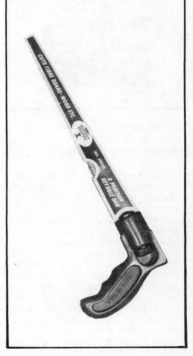

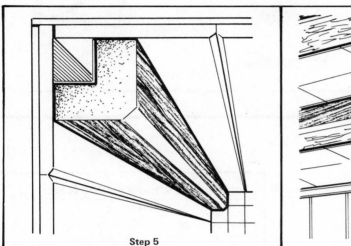 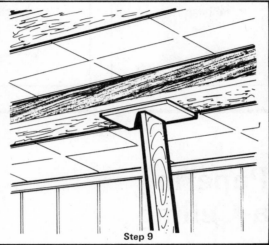

Step 5

Step 9

them first. Corner beams are half the size of the regular U-shaped ceiling beams. To install them, run a 1/8-inch bead of adhesive in a wiggly line along the back of the beam. Some manufacturers suggest running an additional bead on the ceiling or wall. If you have the beams with adhesive already on them, you just peel the coating paper off and stick the beams to the ceiling.
6. After you apply the adhesive, press the beam against the ceiling in line with the pencil marks. Push firmly to flatten the adhesive.
7. Remove the beam to allow the adhesive to cure.
8. When the adhesive starts to get tacky, replace the beam and press it firmly in place.
9. Apply some sort of temporary support until you are sure that the adhesive has set up completely.
10. Next, put up the center pieces. If you are installing an odd number of beams, put the middle beam up and then work to each side. Before you know it, you will have a beautiful beamed ceiling.

Unusual Federal Style Beams From Archcraft

Fake beams are generally much the same, but there are a few unusual designs like Archcraft's Federal style beams. The simulated carved wood moldings and trim create a striking effect, especially when set off by such additional components as the junction box in the center of the ceiling, the bracket where the beams meet the walls, and the cove molding panels around the top of the walls. Made of lightweight and fire retardant urethane foam, the Archcraft beams can be attached to wall and ceiling surfaces with either wall panel or contact adhesive. Archcraft beams, manufactured by Williams Products, Inc., are also available in English Renaissance versions (including pilaster capitals and columns) as well as in an Early American simulated hand-hewn style.

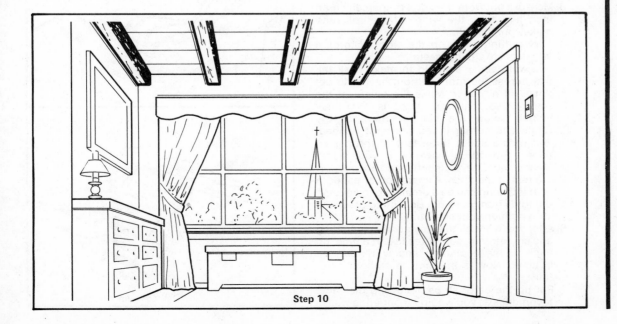

Step 10

Ceilings

Wallpaper Removal Can Get You All Steamed Up

Murray-Black's Electromatic wallpaper remover furnishes plenty of steam under pressure, but it does so easily and safely. Highly portable, the machine merely needs to be filled with either hot or cold water and plugged into a standard wall outlet. Then you just press the lever as you apply the steamer section to the wall or ceiling. This kind of positive control results in no loss of steam when the unit is not actually being used. Moreover, the Electromatic's automatic pressure control, safety plug, and automatic low-water shutoff make it a safe machine to operate. Of course, there are no fumes, no odors, no chemicals, and no special ventilation problems to worry about when working with the Electromatic.

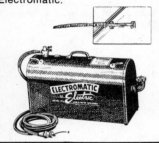

Additive Aids In Removing Old Paper

Among the several liquids available that aid in removing old wallpaper, there is a fast-acting non-caustic super concentrate called Room Groom. The contents of one can, when mixed with three gallons of water, should be sufficient to remove all the paper from an average sized room. Room Groom acts as a wetting agent, penetrating the paper rapidly to release the adhesive. The wallpaper then peels off easily and quickly. Papers that resist water, however, must have their surfaces scored as much as possible before the remover is applied. Room Groom is a product of Mantrose-Haeuser.

Match The Adhesive To The Covering

Using the wrong kind of adhesive for the wallcovering can result in disaster. The strips can fall off or curl up at the seams, while the paste can mildew underneath and smell up the entire house. Henkel makes several different pastes and adhesives, each one with a specific purpose. Just be sure to use the one made for your type of covering. If you are not certain regarding which type of adhesive to apply, be sure to ask your wallcoverings dealer when you buy your paper.

Papering a Ceiling

MOST PEOPLE like the contrast of a painted ceiling and a papered wall, especially when they find out that papering a ceiling is rather difficult. Nevertheless, if you plan to repaper a room—including both walls and ceiling—you should know how to do the job right. Always do the ceiling first, and follow these steps.

1. Do the same preparation work you would for papering walls.
2. Hang the strips crossways rather than lengthwise. One of the major difficulties in papering a ceiling is handling those long strips.
3. Measure out from the edge of the ceiling an inch less than the width of the roll, and make your chalk line.
4. After putting paste on the strip, accordion fold it, paste against paste.
5. You will need a scaffold to make it all the way across the room without having to get down off a ladder. Make the height of the scaffold so that your head is about six inches below the ceiling. Start at the right-hand corner if you are right handed, and unfold about three feet of the pasted paper. Smooth it down with your hand. Meanwhile, use your left hand to support the rest of the folds. A spare roll of paper in your left hand can be a great help in keeping the folds from sagging. Be sure to place the strip right on your chalk line.
6. After you work all the way across, unfolding and smoothing about three feet at a time, go back to the beginning and work out the bubbles. Now is the time to smooth carefully.
7. Put up the other strips, following the same techniques as you would for papering walls.

Tool Kit Has Basics For The Paperhanger

Two kits from Warner Tools furnish all the tools needed to paper a room. The components of each kit are about the same, but the smoothing brush in the kit made for standard wallcoverings is somewhat different than the brush in the kit for vinyl wallcoverings. In addition to the smoothing brush, each kit contains a paste brush, a trimmer, extra blades, a trim guide, a seam roller, a chalk line, and an instruction booklet. Unless you plan to go into professional wallpapering as a vocation, these Warner kits, available at many paint and wallpaper dealers, should fill all your paperhanging needs.

Here Is What You Will Need

Materials

- Wall covering
- Sizing
- Adhesive (if wall covering is not prepasted)
- Sandpaper
- Spackling

Tools

- Scaffold
- Chalk line
- Measuring tape
- Steamer
- Putty knife
- Sponge or smoothing brush
- Scissors
- Water tray
- Paintbrush
- Roller
- Razor blade

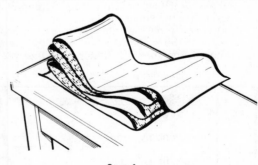

Step 4

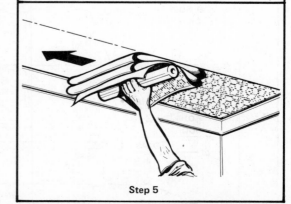

Step 5

Plumb Hammer Has Unbreakable Handle

The 16-ounce nail hammer from Fayette R. Plumb, Inc., has a nonbreakable fiberglass handle. The polished steel head is at-tached to the handle through the Plumb Permabond assembly method, and the fiberglass handle gives the hammer a well-balanced and solid feel. Plumb Tools, from the Ames Division of the McDonough Company, are widely distributed.

Spray Lube Keeps Windows Moving

Sil-Glyde is a spray silicone lubricant that is ideal for windows. Made by American Grease Stick Company, Sil-Glyde is a clear lubricant with high-film strength. American Grease Stick Company also manufactures Door-Ease stick lubricant, Lith-Ease white lithium grease, and Lock-Ease liquid graphite for locks.

Unsticking Windows

DO YOU HAVE a window that refuses to budge? Have you checked to make sure that the window's lock is unfastened? The next most common cause of sticking is that windows often mistake a paint job for a glue job. The simple steps for getting your stuck window moving again are as follows.

1. Examine all around the frame to see where the paint has sealed the sash to the stop. Usually the seal is complete all the way around.
2. Insert a sharp knife—a medium wide putty knife is good—in where the crack should be. If you cannot get the knife in the crack, tap the knife's handle with a hammer. If the window was painted both inside and out, cut the seals on both sides.
3. With the seal cut all around and the window still not moving, check the tracks above. If the paint is too thick in the track—preventing the window from sliding—remove the excess with a sanding stick, rasp, chisel, or a hobby-size power tool.
4. Lubricate the track. Rub a candle or a bar of soap along the track, or shoot some silicone spray on it.
5. If the window still refuses to budge, use a small flat pry bar on it. Pry from the outside if possible, and place a scrap block of wood under the bar.
6. Next, tap the frame away from window with a hammer and a 2x4. Even the slightest movement may be enough to free the sash.
7. If at first you fail, pry, pry again.

When you finally get it open, give some thought as to how you can paint it the next time without gluing it shut. Here is one easy way to prevent future window misery.

△ 1. Raise the window about four inches.
△ 2. Paint.
△ 3. When you finish painting—but before the paint hardens—move the window up and down. The seal will not form, the window will not stick, and your temper will not flare.

Here Is What You Will Need

Materials

- A candle, bar of soap, or silicone spray
- A block of wood

Tools

• Putty knife	• Sanding stick, rasp,
• Hammer	chisel, or hobby-size
• Pry bar	power tool

Step 1

Step 2

Pry Bar

Step 5

Pry Bar Raises Window

The Enderes Pry Bar is made for heavier work than unsticking windows, but some windows require heavy-duty tools. Just be sure not to damage wood on or around the window any more than is absolutely necessary. Made of drop-forged high carbon tool steel that is scientifically heat treated, the Enderes Pry Bar is a product of the Enderes Tool Company, Inc.

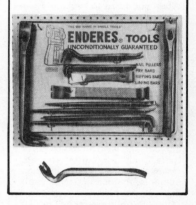

Unstick Painted Windows With Windo-Zipper

Probably 90 percent of all stuck windows become that way due to a careless paint job. But you can combat such paint sealings with a special tool called the Windo-Zipper from Red Devil, Inc. The stainless steel blade has serrated edges that cut right through the paint which is causing the window to bind. The sharp points on the tip penetrate the seal, allowing the Windo-Zipper to be inserted between the frame and the sash. Then you work the tool along the edges to break the seal holding the window.

Windows

Power-Driven Wire Brush Removes Putty Particles Fast

With a wire brush attachment in your electric drill, you can get out all the old putty particles in a hurry. Howard Hardware Products, Inc., markets a cup type wire brush that fits right into the chuck of the drill. Howard also makes wire wheels for use with a power drill. The cup brushes are available in two-inch and three-inch diameters, while the wheels come in 2½-inch, 3-inch, and 4-inch diameters. Both types—cups and brushes—are made in coarse and fine versions, and all have a ¼-inch shank.

Zip Strip Putty Knives Are Tough

The Zip-Strip brand is associated primarily with furniture refinishing compounds, but the line also includes some tools, including a pair of fine putty knives. These knives feature carbon steel blades —in your choice of stiff or flexible—that have been heat treated and lacquer dipped. The handles are made of tough polypropylene

plastic, and the tangs of the blades extend all the way through the handles. You'll find these tools, products of the Star Bronze Company, wherever other Zip-Strip items are sold.

Safety Glazing

When you need to replace a window, why not replace it with a break-resistant acrylic sheeting that is clearer than glass and stays that way. There are a number of acrylic sheet brands on the market, and probably the best known in the glazing category is Plexiglas. But Swedglaze from Swedlow, Inc., is another good name to consider. Swedlow offers a how-to booklet on measuring, cutting, and installing Swedglaze SG acrylic, and also markets acrylic tools such as cutters, scratch removers, polishing kits, cleaners, cements, applicators, and caulking compounds. The company's "Don't Scrap the Scraps" booklet even tells you how to use remainders to make decorative things for the home.

The toughness is there. You just can't see it.

Replacing a Broken Pane

NO MATTER what time of the year it is, all across the country kids are trying to break either Hank Aaron's home run record or Joe Namath's passing feats. Usually, however, the only breaking that results is what occurs when a stray ball heads toward your windows. At that point, rather than calling for the help of a professional glazier, why not replace the pane yourself? It is a simple job, even if you want to cut the replacement glass to size yourself. Since any hardware store or lumberyard that sells you the glass will cut it to size, however, you can fix the broken pane without ever concerning yourself with the techniques of glass cutting. Here, then, are the basic procedures for painless pane replacement.

Step 4

1. Remove all the old glass. Wear gloves and be careful as you wiggle the pieces back and forth until you free them. If there are pieces which are too firmly imbedded in the putty to come loose with wiggling, take a hammer and knock them out.
2. When the glass is all out, scrape away all the old putty from the frame. You can soften dried putty with heat from a propane torch, or—if you do not have a torch—you can brush the puttied areas with linseed oil and let it soak in. The linseed oil should soften the putty sufficiently to allow you to scrape it away. As you remove the old putty, be on the lookout for little metal tabs (in a wooden frame) or spring clips (in a metal frame). The tabs (called glazier's points) and clips are important later on when installing the new pane.
3. Use a wire brush to remove the last traces of putty, and coat the wooden area where the putty was with linseed oil. Just brush it on.
4. Measure the frame across both directions,

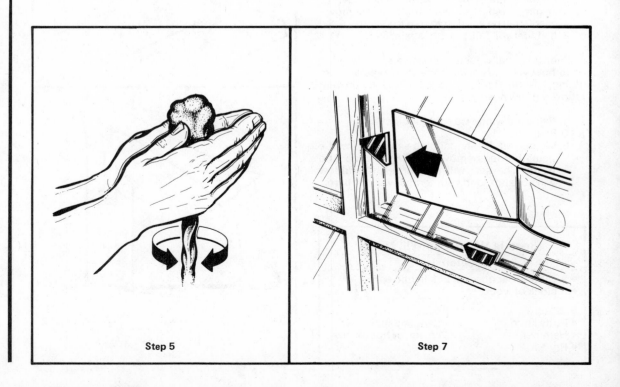

Step 5

Step 7

Plexiglas Scraper Won't Scratch Glass

After you paint the putty around a new pane, you'll undoubtedly see paint specks on the glass. What you need is the Saf-T-Scrape from the S/V Tool Company. It has a Plexiglas blade that will not scratch the glass. The unique blade design can be rotated to expose any one of its four scraper edges, and after all four become

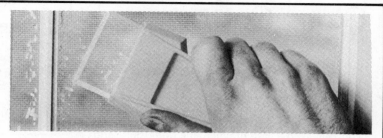

dull, you can resharpen the blade with sandpaper. The lightweight

plastic handle is shaped for comfort.

Push Points Mean Fewer Broken Windows

Those little triangles called glazier's points have accounted for more than a few broken windows. Many people try to install the points with a few hammer taps, but one misplaced tap and there goes the new pane. Push Points from Warner Tools are different. Since they have a projection that lets you push them into place with the end of your putty knife, no hammer blows are needed and no glass breakage is likely to occur. No matter what type of points you are using, however, keep in mind that they do not have to go into the frame very far.

and subtract 1/16 of an inch from each measurement to compensate for the fact that most frames are not perfect rectangles and for the expansion and contraction of the glass that will occur later on. In fact, if there is a wide lip on the frame, subtract as much as 1/8 of an inch from both the vertical and horizontal measurements.

5. Roll either glazier's compound or glazing putty (the compound is preferable) between your hands to form a string about as big around as a pencil. Press this string against the outside of the frame where the glass is to fit.

6. When the putty completely covers the lip of the frame, press the glass in place against the putty. Press firmly, and pay no attention to the fact that some of the putty is pushed out around the frame.

7. With the pane pressed firmly in position, insert the glazier's points or spring clips to hold the glass in place. The clips snap in holes, while the points must be pushed into the wood. Use your putty knife to push them in; they need not be pushed in very far. The points should go in about every six to eight inches around the frame.

8. Now you are ready to finish off the job by putting putty around the outside of the glass. The object here is to make your new bed of putty look like the others on windows around it. The best way to go about it is to place blobs of putty all around the glass

Here Is What You Will Need

Materials
- Linseed oil
- Glazier's compound or putty
- Replacement pane
- Paint

Tools
● Work gloves	● Wire brush
● Hammer	● Paintbrush
● Chisel	● Putty knife
● Propane torch	● Glaziers points
● Measuring rule	

against the frame, and then use your putty knife to smooth them out. If the putty knife seems to stick to the putty, pulling it away from the glass and frame, dip the knife in linseed oil (or even water) to stop it from doing so.

9. Remove the excess putty from both inside and outside the frame, and put the putty back in the can.

10. Allow the putty to cure for three days, and then paint it. Paint all the way from the frame up to the glass, letting a little paint get over on the glass to seal the putty completely.

Glazing Compound Instead Of Putty

Although putty is still around, glazing compound usually works better. It is easier and less messy to work with, and generally outlasts regular putty. DAP '33' Glazing Compound, for example, works equally well on wood and metal window frames and can even be used on unprimed wood, although a coating of linseed oil over bare wood is recommended. Most importantly, DAP '33' does not dry out and harden as putty does, and it takes paint with good results. DAP products are in wide distribution.

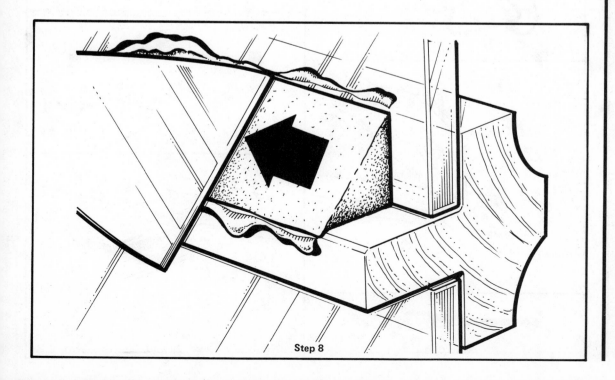

Step 8

Linseed Oil Makes Glazing Easier

By brushing the frames of windows where the bed of putty will lie with boiled linseed oil, you can prevent the wood from drinking oils from the putty. Raw linseed oil, moreover, is great for making old and dry putty workable again. Just add a few drops of raw linseed oil to the unused putty, and then knead it until it is again soft and pliable. Raw linseed oil can even help in the removal of dried and hardened putty on the frame; brush the raw linseed oil over the surface and let it soak in before attempting to chop it out with your chisel.

Picking Up Pane Of Glass Can Be A Pain

After you cut the glass and it is lying there flat on the table, how do you pick it up? The easy answer is with a vacuum cup made expressly for this purpose. Red Devil makes a single cup version consisting of a thick rubber disc and channel-type vacuum levers. The base is cast aluminum. When properly seated, the cup will hold the glass until the vacuum is broken with the vacuum lever. Red Devil also makes double and triple cup models with four-, five-, and six-inch cups. The vacuum cup can come in very handy when installing window panes, as it gives you a surer hold on the glass and eliminates the danger of cutting your hand on the sharp edges.

Straightedge A Must For Glass Cutting

Since most window glass cutting consists of straight cuts, you must have a straightedge. Some pros prefer the wood type because they have a wider edge to follow and do not slip as easily. Others prefer a metal rule. The stainless steel model made by T.A. Altender and Sons (in the rule business for more than 120 years) should last forever. Altender also makes quality T-squares.

Glass Cutters Are Inexpensive Tools

Although there are fancy glass cutters on the market, the inexpensive versions work just as well if they are well made and if you keep them in good shape. The Gold Tip cutters from Fletcher-Terry Company should service all your glass cutting needs. Just make sure to oil the wheel at the time you cut and also when you put the cutter into storage. In addition, protect the cutter wheel against nicks at all times. A nicked wheel means a worthless cutter; toss the tool away and get a new one. Fletcher-Terry also markets a well-made cutting instrument for use on acrylic sheet goods.

Glass Cutting

ANY HARDWARE store that sells glass will cut it to your exact specifications, but if you do a great deal of glazing or if you do your own picture framing, you can save money by doing the cutting yourself. With a little practice, the right tools, and proper instructions, you can be cutting glass to size in no time. Just follow these steps.

1. Select a flat surface on which your piece of glass will fit.
2. Clean the surface of the glass.
3. Lubricate the tiny wheel on the glass cutter with machine oil or kerosene. You should also brush a film of the lubricant along the line you intend to cut.
4. Hold the glass cutter between your index and middle fingers, with your index finger resting against the flat area on the handle. Your thumb should be on the handle's bottom side. Grip the cutter firmly but not too tightly.
5. Place a straightedge along the line to be cut, and hold it firmly in place.
6. Position the cutter so that it is almost at a right angle to the glass.
7. Start your cut about 1/8 of an inch (or less) from the edge farthest from you. The stroke must be an even flowing motion toward you that continues until the cutter goes off the near edge. The idea is not to cut through the glass, but merely to score it. Experiment with scrap pieces of glass to discover how much pressure you must apply to attain an even scoring. Never let up on the cutter and never go back over the line.
8. As soon as you score the glass, make the break. Glass heals, and if you wait too long it will not snap along the line. The idea in snapping is to provide a raised area under the scored line. Some people position the glass so that the cut is along the edge of the table, and then they snap the glass along the table edge. Others slip a pencil under the glass and center it on the line, while still others place finishing nails at each end of the scored line.
9. To make the snap, press down on the glass firmly on both sides of the line.
10. Smooth the newly cut edge with fine wet-dry sandpaper.

Keep the wheel of the glass cutter well lubricated between uses, and protect the wheel from anything that might nick or dull it.

Here Is What You Will Need
Materials
● Machine oil or kerosene
● Finishing nails
● Fine wet-dry sandpaper
Tools
● Glass cutter   ● Straightedge

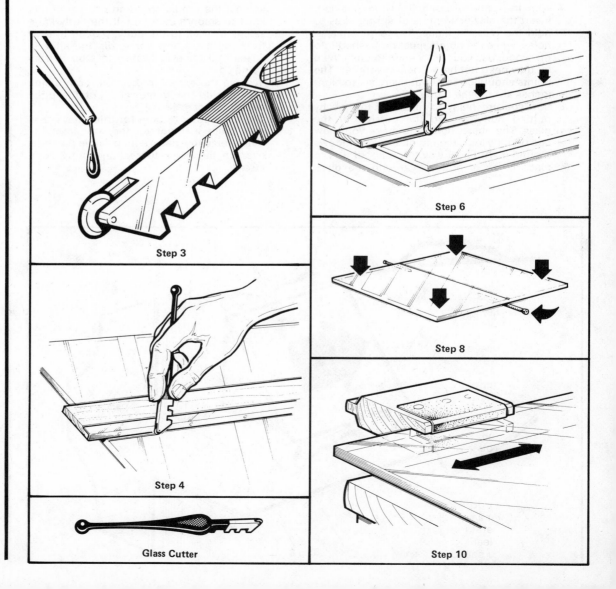

Step 3

Step 4

Glass Cutter

Step 6

Step 8

Step 10

Scaffold In A Ladder

Windows always seem to be just a little higher than you can reach, and most ladders are a bother because you must move them so frequently. The Multi-Position Ladder from the Goldblatt Tool Company, however, is different. It can perform exactly like any typical straight ladder, but it can also be shaped into a sturdy scaffold or A-shaped ladder. The Multi-Position Ladder is available in either 12- or 16-foot lengths from the Goldblatt Tool Company, makers of a full line of quality tools.

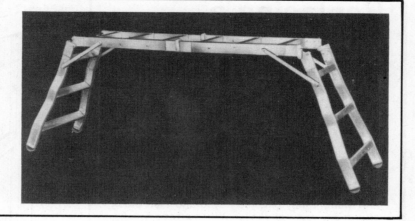

Arrow Hits The Mark

Of the innumerable window cleaning tools on the market, most are fairly flimsy. For a good sturdy tool, though, look at the Arrow Combination Window Cleaner. It has a large, soft, pliable poly sponge on one side and a squeegee on the other side. Made with either an eight- or 10-inch blade and with a wood or metal handle, the Arrow Combination Window Cleaner is a product of the Greenview Manufacturing Company, makers of many other fine squeegee and scraper products.

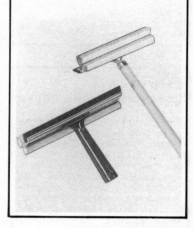

Cleaning Windows

Here Is What You Will Need

Materials
- Window cleaner
- Household ammonia
- Hot water
- Newspapers

Tools
- Rubber gloves
- Sponge
- Squeegee
- Rag
- Hose with sprayer

HOW OFTEN YOU need to do your windows depends on whether you live in an area where there is much air pollution and whether your lifestyle inside the house creates grease and grime that will leave a film on the windows. If they get dirty faster either outside or inside, both sides do not have to be cleaned every time. For a complete cleaning, here is a good procedure to follow.

1. Try to work with a co-cleaner so that you can clean both sides at once. If that is not possible, work on one side with horizontal strokes and the other with vertical strokes so that streaks and missed spots are easier to track down.
2. Apply the window cleaner. If you use store-bought products for this purpose, follow their directions. Here is a mixture that will save money and do a fine job. Add a tablespoon of household ammonia to a quart of hot water. Although this is a very diluted solution, wear rubber gloves to prevent any skin irritation.
3. Sponge it on.
4. Squeegee it dry. Wipe the squeegee blade often.
5. Polish windows to a shine using crumpled up wads of newspaper. These not only give a high shine, but they also seem to leave a film that resists dirt to a certain extent.
6. For outside windows that are not easily reached, use a sprayer on the end of a garden hose to which you add automatic dishwasher detergent. Turn on the water full blast and shoot the spray right through the screens. This will not do as good a job as you could do by hand cleaning, but it is better than nothing.
7. If you use the regular method of hand cleaning, and you have the screens off, use a strong blast from the hose to clean them too.

That is how to do windows without too much trouble. Shoot for a time of day when you will miss the hottest temperatures and direct sunlight. This will allow the cleaning solution to stay on the window until you squeegee it away. If it dries on

the window, it may leave dirt. For in-between touch ups, mix a small amount of our solution and put it in a spray bottle. Be sure to identify the new contents.

Step 1

Clean Paint Off Window, But Leave Seal

In painting over the putty around a window, painters should allow a tiny bit of the paint to come over onto the glass in order to make certain that the putty or glaziers compound is sealed in properly. If that excess paint is removed carelessly, the seal can be broken. Fortunately, Stanley has developed a paint scraper for windows that is designed to leave a small space between the window and the blade. Thus, you can clean unwanted paint off the glass without endangering the seal. A good little tool that does not cost much and is available at hardware and paint stores, the Stanley Scraper stores replacement blades safely when not in use.

Windows

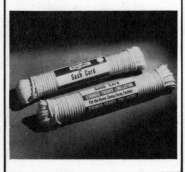
Replacing a Sash Cord

MOST WOOD WINDOWS are operated by a system of ropes, pulleys, and weights hidden inside the wall. The ropes are attached to the sash—a fancy name for a frame that moves up and down—and then go along the tracks in which the window moves, finally extending up to a pulley at the top of the track. The rope passes over the pulley and then is tied to the weight, which acts as a counterbalance so that the window stays at the level to which you raise it. Ropes being what they are, though, they become frayed and then break after many years of service. When a rope breaks, of course, the weight falls down to the bottom inside the window frame. It also means that the window no longer stays where you want it to. Here is the step-by-step cure.

1. Remove the stop molding from the side where the broken cord is, but do it carefully or the molding might break. If there is a paint seal along the molding strip, cut it with a sharp razor blade. Then use a wide putty knife blade or a flat bar to pry the stop molding out.
2. With the stop strip out of the way, angle the sash out of the frame to expose the pocket in which the rope is knotted.
3. Untie the knot and remove the rope from the sash frame.
4. Ease the sash out of its track on the other side, and untie the rope there. Knot this rope to prevent it from disappearing inside the wall.
5. Set the entire sash out of the way.
6. Look for the access plate. You should be able to locate it in the lower part of the track, but it may have been painted over several times. If it is hidden by the paint, tap the track with a hammer until you reveal the outline. Then cut along the line with a sharp razor blade. Once you locate the access plate, find the screws holding it in place and remove them. (Some older windows do not have access plates; if that is what you find, you must pry the entire frame out to get at the weight inside.)
7. With the access plate removed, you will see the weight. Lift it out.
8. Untie the old cord and use the two broken pieces to measure the replacement cord.
9. Weight the new cord with something small enough to be fed in over the pulley, and feed the cord in.
10. When the cord reaches the access plate

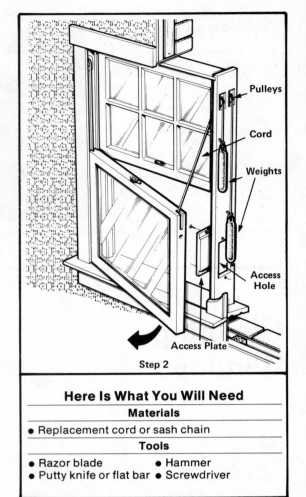

Step 2

Here Is What You Will Need

Materials

- Replacement cord or sash chain

Tools

- Razor blade
- Hammer
- Putty knife or flat bar
- Screwdriver

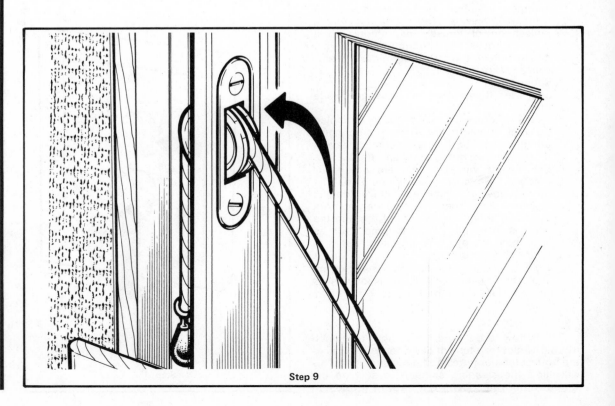

Step 9

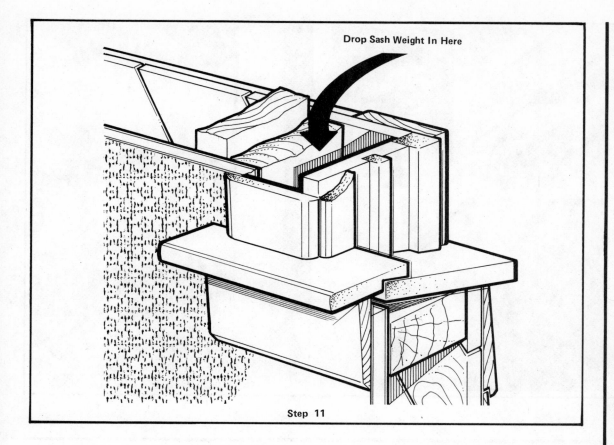

Drop Sash Weight In Here

Step 11

If you experience more than your share of trouble with the window balance system or if your windows rattle and are drafty, consider installing new channels. Quaker's CBW Window Channels are made for double-hung windows with standard wood sashes 1⅜ inches thick. The replacement channels have their own system that allows for easy raising and lowering and keeps the window in place where you want it. Easily installed by the do-it-yourselfer and relatively inexpensive, Quaker CBW Window Channels are sold through lumberyards, home centers, and hardware stores.

opening, pull the cord through the opening.

11. Remove the small weight you had put on earlier, and knot the cord to the regular window weight. Put the weight back into the access hole.
12. Tie the cord opposite the one you have been working with to the sash, and reinsert the sash in the track.
13. Tie the new cord to the sash, and then hold the sash against the parting strip as you raise it to the top.
14. Inspect the weight at the access hole. It should be about three inches above the sill as you hold the sash at the top. If it is not, adjust the rope at the sash.

15. When you get the weight properly adjusted, replace the access plate and the stop strip.

If the broken cord is in the upper sash of a double hung window, you follow the same procedure except that you must remove the parting strip after removing the lower sash in order to be able to get at the upper sash.

That is all there is to it. As long as you are replacing the cord, though, you should think about replacing it with a sash chain that will not wear out or break or stretch as rope does. The chain comes with a hook that you fasten to the weight and with a spring that you attach to the sash.

Replacement Sash Balance System

A device called a Sash Balance, made by the Caldwell Manufacturing Company fits into the cavity formerly occupied by the pulley and permits the window unit to go up or down with ease and holds it securely in place. These units are sold through lumberyards and hardware stores, but if you cannot locate one, write to Caldwell Manufacturing Company, Box 444, Rochester, NY 14602.

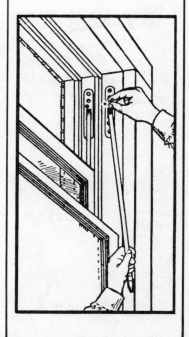

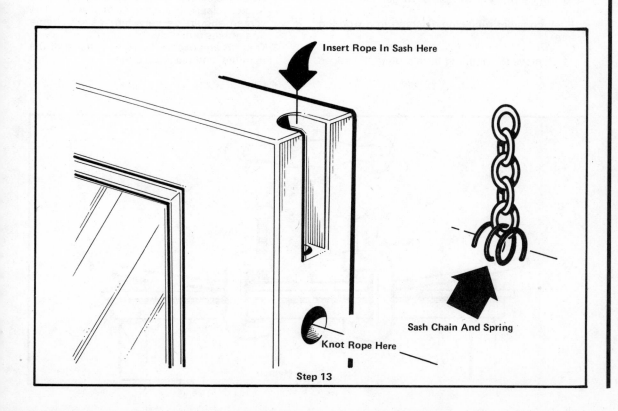

Insert Rope In Sash Here

Sash Chain And Spring

Knot Rope Here

Step 13

Windows

Replacing The Screen In A Sliding Patio Door Can Be Easy

An easily installed screen replacement for a sliding patio door has been developed by Jim Walter Window Components. Available in building supply stores and home centers, the replacement screen door can be installed in four simple steps. First the screws holding the nylon rollers are loosened to free the rollers at the four corners of the screen door. Then the door is lifted into place on the existing tracks. The adjustable plates at the top and bottom of the screen door are positioned equally to fit the door opening, and then they are screwed tight. Finally, the bug strip (marked for easy tearing) is pressed onto the door's leading edge. The Jim Walter sliding screen door, called Xplora, is available in three-, four-, and five-foot widths and in bronze, white, and silver. The frame is adjustable from 78½ inches to 81½ inches and can be mounted for either left- or right-hand opening.

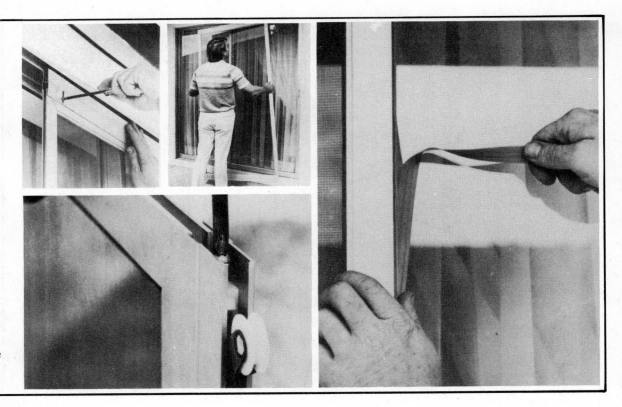

Fix Up Aluminum Screens With New Spline And Splining Tool

You could use a screwdriver to push the spline into an aluminum frame, but a splining tool makes the job much easier. An inexpensive device, the splining tool consists of two wheels with a handle in between. One of the rollers is used to push the screen down into the track of the frame, while the other wheel inserts the spline which holds the screen in the groove. If the spline in your aluminum screen frames is worn or damaged, replace it with spline of the correct diameter. Frost King's spline and splining tool, products of Thermwell, Inc., can take care of most aluminum screen problems.

Screen Replacement

WHEN YOU SPOT a hole in your screen door or window screen that is too large to patch, you should start thinking about replacing the entire screen. In most cases you can buy screen cut to the proper width for standard doors or windows, and the actual installation of the new screen is not difficult—provided, of course, that the frame is still in good shape. The secret to any good re-screening job is knowing how to get the screen taut.

First, consider replacing a screen in a wooden frame.

1. Remove the molding from around the edges of the screen, but be sure to pry carefully so as not to damage the molding. Leave the brads in the molding.
2. Remove the old screen which is either tacked or stapled in place. Be sure to remove all the old tacks or staples.
3. Now you need to bow or arch the frame. Use either the weighted method or the clamp method.
4. With the frame arched, use a staple gun to attach the screen at each end; stapling is much quicker than tacking. Staple every two or three inches all along the top and bottom of the frame.
5. When the screen is fastened securely to the frame, release the weights or clamps. The screen should be very taut as the frame straightens out.
6. Trim off any excess screening, reinstall the molding, and the job is done.

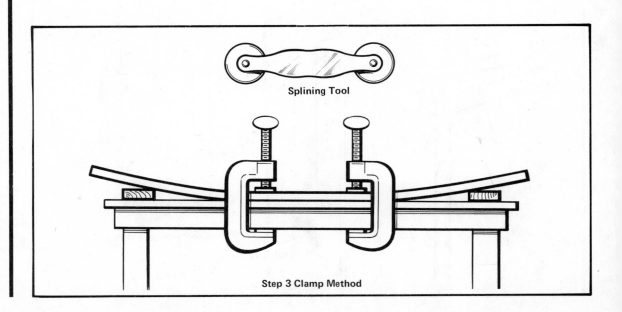

Splining Tool

Step 3 Clamp Method

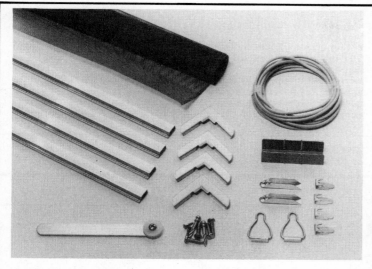

Complete Screen Replacement Kits

Three screen replacement kits for either aluminum or wood window frames are available from Jim Walter Window Components. Designed for the do-it-yourselfer, the kits come complete with metal framing, fiberglass screening, spline, splining tool, corner angles, hangers for aluminum and wood frames, and a mitre box. Kits are made in three sizes: 3x3 feet, 4x4 feet, and 5x5 feet. Easy-to-follow directions are included in each kit.

Little Giant Is Much More Than A Sawhorse

With a pair of Little Giant Workhorses, you can go from sawhorse to workbench to scaffold in a matter of seconds. They're ideal for working on window screens. The versatile tubular steel pedestal legs combined with the adjustable vise arms result in a cleverly engineered device. Even the height is adjustable. After the job is done, the Little Giant folds to hang flat against the shop wall.

Electric Staple Gun Is Now Available For Do-It-Yourselfers

While the electric staple gun has had industrial uses for many years, its cost has kept it out of the hands of home handypersons. But recently the Duo-Fast Corporation introduced an electric staple gun for consumers. Able to handle the six most popular size staples, the Duo-Fast gun features pushbutton operation that can staple a new screen in place in no time. It can do every chore that a standard staple gun does.

Screens Can Help Save Energy

In addition to keeping the bugs out of your house, aluminum Sun Screens from Phifer Wire Products Company can also block out the sun without depriving you of the view. Sun Screens can block out up to almost 70 percent of the sun's rays—as well as most reflected rays from the ground—resulting in a much cooler home during the summer. Available in all the standard widths in rolls up to 50 feet long, all Sun Screen packages contain complete installation instructions. Phifer's special flat weaving process reduces the possibility of a do-it-yourselfer damaging a Sun Screen during the replacement process.

With aluminum frames, you must examine the spline to see that it is still in good shape. The spline is a sort of rubber rope that holds the screening in the track all around the frame.

△ 1. Remove the old screen and spline.

△ 2. Position the new screen (about as wide as the entire frame) over the frame, aligning one end and one side of the screen with the corresponding edges of the frame.

△ 3. For best results, you should have a splining wheel to insert the new screen in the frame. Use the end with the convex roller to push the screening down into the groove, working on the end and side you just aligned with the frame. Then do the remaining two sides. The screen should be quite taut.

△ 4. Now you are ready to reinstall the spline. Use the other end of the tool—the concave wheel—to work the spline into the track all the way around the frame.

△ 5. Trim off any excess screening, and your aluminum screen is as good as new.

Here Is What You Will Need
Materials
● Replacement screening
● Staples
Tools
● Putty knife
● Pliers
● C-clamps or metal weight
● 2x4
● Work table or sawhorses
● Staple gun
● Scissors or wire cutters
● Splining tool

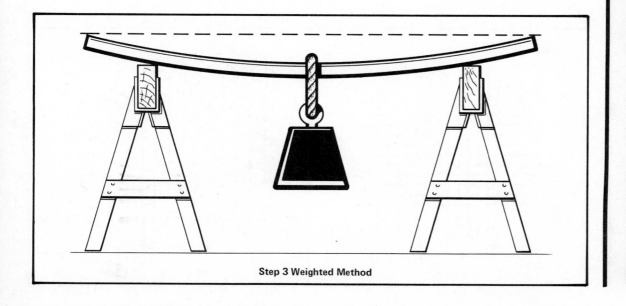

Step 3 Weighted Method

Windows

Awl's Well That Ends Well

You need a sharp pointed tool for many screen repairs. General Hardware Manufacturing Company offers a trio of Scratch Awls, all with blades of hardened and grounded tool steel. Awls of this quality, of course, can serve many more purposes than just screen repairs. They can be used to create starter holes for screws in soft wood and for lining up and marking screw and bolt holes.

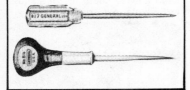

Don't Let Your Screen Door Get Out Of Line

Because it swings so much, a screen door frame has a tendency to get out of line. Usually the best way to repair it is to attach a wire that will make the screen door stronger and pull it back square. Rather than trying to stretch a wire taut, however, you will find it much simpler to add a turnbuckle in the middle of the wire for tightening purposes. The Jordan Turnbuckle works well and comes in various sizes for various types of installations. Jordan makes a complete line of good quality anchors and fasteners.

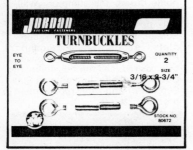

Paint Can Prolong Screen Life

Some screen materials require painting from time to time. Unless you have attempted this task you might consider spraying or brushing, but neither technique works particularly well. Fortunately, Red Devil offers an inexpensive tool called the Speed Demon Screen Painter that spreads paint quickly and evenly without clogging the screen mesh. Its small size (3⅛x4½ inches) makes it easy to handle, yet it provides fast coverage.

Screen Patches Snap In Place

The Screen Patch Company markets inexpensive small patches that are all set for installation. Called Snap-Patches, they consist of regular screening in 2x2-inch segments, but the ends of the wires have tiny hooks that snap into place over the hole in the existing screen. Once the Snap-Patch is in place, it is almost invisible. Sold in packages of five, Snap-Patches come in either aluminum or galvanized screening. Most hardware stores carry them or quite similar patch kits.

Screen Repairs

SCREENS ARE GREAT when they let in air and light and keep out the bugs, but they always seem to develop holes. You then discover that even the tiniest hole lets all the flies in the neighborhood come into your home. Patching is the way to cure most small holes in screens.

1. For a tiny hole, use an ice pick (or any pointed object) to move as many strands as possible back toward the hole. If none of the wire strands are torn, you can close the hole back up and make the screen as good as new.
2. Unfortunately, there generally are a few torn strands. If that is the case, you can close up the hole by painting over it with either clear nail polish or shellac. Brush on a coat and let it dry; then keep applying more coats until the hole is sealed over.
3. If the hole is a long rip, you may need to stitch it back together. Once again, close the gap with your sharp pointed tool, and then use a strand of wire or a strong nylon thread to bind up the wound. A needle will make the sewing go quicker, and a few coats of clear polish or shellac will prevent the stitching from unravelling.
4. For a bigger hole, cut a square—at least two inches bigger than the hole all the way around—from a separate piece of screening.
5. Pick away at the strands of wire on all four sides to leave about a half inch of unwoven strands sticking out.
6. Fold the unwoven edges forward, and insert these wires into the screen over the hole.
7. Fold the unwoven strands toward the center of the patch on the other side, and stitch around the patch with a needle and nylon thread. Once again, a few coats of polish or shellac will seal the patch and stitching in place.
8. Repair fiberglass screening by laying a patch of the material over the hole and running a hot iron around the edges. The heat melts and fuses the patch in place. Be sure to place a scrap of foil over the screen itself to prevent the iron from touching it.

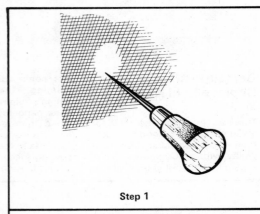

Step 1

Here Is What You Will Need

Materials

- Clear nail polish or shellac
- Strand of wire or strong nylon thread
- Needle
- Screening material
- Fiberglass patch
- Aluminum foil

Tools

- Ice pick (or any pointed tool)
- Small brush
- Scissors
- Electric iron

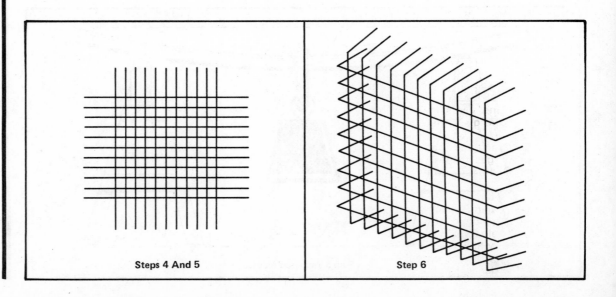

Steps 4 And 5

Step 6

Windows

Stained Glass By Mail Order

Good sources of stained glass are relatively rare. If you cannot find what you want locally, you may be faced with ordering through the mail. Pendleton Studios is one mail-order firm to consider. In addition to a good supply of glass, Pendleton also offers top-quality supplies and tools for stained glass work. Everything Pendleton sells is selected by working stained glass artisans. For a catalog, write Pendleton Studios, 2708 Boll Street, Dallas, Texas 75204.

Old Timer Is The Knife You Need

Although there are special knives made for cutting lead, a quality pocketknife like an Old Timer is all you really need for most stained glass work. Old Timer, made by Schrade Cutlery, is truly a quality knife; it will probably outlive anyone who takes proper care of it. Each Old Timer is subjected to more than 100 quality-control inspections before leaving the factory.

Stained Glass Work

RECENTLY, THERE HAS been a resurgence of interest in working with stained glass. Tiffany-type lamps are very popular, and stained glass windows have come to be regarded as a great addition to almost any style home. The techniques have remained largely unchanged from the methods of hundreds of years ago, although much of the glass is now machine made, with only the truly dedicated artisans using old world hand-blown techniques.

One big advantage you have over the old masters is in the tools that are available to you. An electric soldering iron with a thermostat to control temperature makes stained glass work much easier. Glass cutters are far superior to what old world craftsmen were forced to use.

The pieces of glass are joined together with metal channels called came. U-shaped channels are used around edges and for ornaments, while H-shaped channels are used for connecting pieces together. Lead is more popular than other metals, but came is also available in zinc and brass for small ornamental work. Copper foil tape, which allows for better joints with smaller and more delicate lead lines, comes in rolls. Double-faced tape helps hold your pattern against the glass while you're marking it for cutting.

Follow these basic instructions for any stained glass project you are considering.

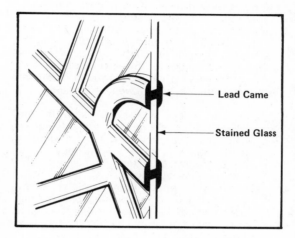

Lead Came

Stained Glass

1. Draw the design with colored pencils to help you decide what colors of stained glass look best.
2. Trace the design onto the glass. A quick-drying felt marker works well for this purpose.
3. Use a glass cutter on the smooth side of the glass to score a line around the marked pattern. Angle the cutter about 45 degrees and push down with both hands. Always follow the inside edge of the line you marked.
4. Grip the glass with breaking pliers, and snap along the scored lines. Always make the break as soon as possible after scoring, since the scored line "heals" quickly and will not snap cleanly if left alone for a while.
5. Use grozing pliers to nibble away at any parts of the glass that did not break away smoothly. A grinding wheel with a silicone carbide wheel will enable you to make really smooth edges on intricate designs, but hobby-type motorized hand tools do almost as well.
6. Assemble the pieces in the proper order. If you are making a lamp or anything else that is not flat, obtain one of the mold forms made to help form the curves.
7. When everything is set from a design standpoint, foil wrap the edges. Foil is used because solder will not adhere to the glass,

and copper foil generally works best. Cut the strips to fit, and then trim the width before removing the backing paper. As you stick the trimmed foil in place, use a pointed hardwood dowel to make the foil tape adhere where you want it.
8. Cut the lead channels to fit around the pieces.
9. Solder the channels (properly called came) inside and out. Use 60 percent tin/40 percent lead solder that is solid (no core). For flux, you should use either an oleic acid type for lead or a universal type, either paste or liquid, which is right for all metals.

After your project is finished, you will probably want the lead and solder to look weathered and all be the same shade. There are products made specifically for these purposes, but the bluing used for guns is as good as anything. You can find such bluing at any sporting goods store.

Choice Of Soldering Iron Is Important

An excellent choice among the many soldering irons that can be used for stained glass work would be the Weller Model W-60. Featuring a control that keeps the tip temperature constant, the 60-watt Weller W-60 is perfect for working with lead. Just the right size, it has nearly everything the hobbyist needs to do his best work. Weller soldering irons constitute some of the products in the Cooper Group.

Forms Make Tiffany Lamp Creation Easy

The Worden forms, very popular with stained glass artisans, allow you to put together repeat designs in separate sections that will be later joined to form the complete shade. Since the form has the design imprinted right on it, you work directly on the form, soldering as you go. There is also a flat paper pattern to use in cutting the various pieces, and there are blank forms for those who wish to create their own designs. Available in a wide variety of shapes and designs, Worden forms lay flat on a table when you work on them. The packaged molds, equipped with instruction guides, can generally be found at shops selling stained glass supplies.

Here Is What You Will Need
Materials
- Stained glass
- Came
- Copper foil tape
- Double-faced tape
- Solder
- Oleic acid or universal flux
- Bluing

Tools
- Glass cutter
- Glass-breaking pliers
- Grozing pliers
- Soldering iron
- Felt marker
- Colored pencils
- Mold form
- Pointed hardwood dowel
- Grinding wheel or hobby tool
- Pocketknife

Windows

Foam-Filled Vinyl Seals Windows

A permanent type weatherstripping that works well for windows is the foam-filled tubular vinyl that is attached to a vinyl nailing strip or to an aluminum channel. A good version of the latter type is Deflect-O's Energy Seal Rigid Vinyl weatherstripping. Packaged in 17½-foot segments with an ample supply of nails, Energy Seal Rigid Vinyl weatherstripping is installed with the window closed; the vinyl tubing is pushed firmly into place before it is nailed through the aluminum channel. The channel can be cut to fit with a hacksaw.

Springy Metal Strips Last For Years

Wood windows can be weatherstripped with M-D's Numetal Weatherstrip, a springy metal strip that is nailed to the window sash channels and to the bottom of the sash rail. Available in bronze, stainless steel, copper, and aluminum, the strips come packaged with the appropriate type of nails. Moreover, all M-D brand weatherstripping—whether metal, foam, or vinyl—comes with excellent installation instructions for the do-it-yourself homeowner. A product of the Macklanburg-Duncan Company, Numetal Weatherstripping enjoys good distribution.

Transparent Tape Seals Window Cracks

Hardly visible but able to seal out the winter wind around drafty windows, Mortell's Transparent Weatherstrip Tape is a heavy-duty poly tape that requires no more than fingertip pressure to apply to any clean, dry surface. Best of all, when you wish to remove the tape and open the windows during mild weather, you will see that Mortell's Transparent Weatherstrip Tape leaves no adhesive residue. Mortell also makes an effective closed-cell vinyl foam tape for doors and windows, as well as many other fine weatherstripping products.

Weatherstripping

IF YOUR WINDOWS are letting cold air in during the winter and cold air out during the summer, you are losing a great deal of money to the utility companies. It will pay you to check your windows' weatherstripping for air tightness. If you can reach the windows from the outside, direct the air flow from a hand-held hair dryer all around the frame as someone inside follows your movements and marks the bad spots.

If your windows have no weatherstripping at all, you can install it without much trouble. You can use the spring metal type or the pressure sensitive adhesive-backed type or the vinyl tubular type. All are easy to install. The following instructions are for the vinyl tubular type of weatherstripping.

1. Measure all cracks that could allow the passage of air to determine how much material you need. If you have a number of windows, it is often less expensive to buy weatherstripping in bulk than to buy individual rolls for each window.
2. Since you attach vinyl tubular weatherstripping from the outside of each window, you can save yourself several trips up and down the ladder by cutting the strips before you start climbing.
3. Nail the strips in place with brads placed about every two inches.
4. Install the vertical strips first, attaching them to the parting strips of the lower sash. The tubular portion should press lightly against the sash.
5. Next, attach a strip to the outside of the lower sash bottom rail in such a way that the tubular portion will rest snugly against the outside sill when the window is down.
6. Attach the strip for the upper sash bottom rail with the tubular part facing in toward the lower sash and positioned so that it will press lightly against the lower sash when it is down.
7. If the upper sash is movable, you must attach strips to the blind stop and a strip across the top of the yoke.

Vinyl tubular weatherstripping is very easy to install if the windows are easily accessible from the outside. It is also very effective when installed properly, and it will last a long time. The big disadvantage to such weatherstripping is the fact that it cannot be painted; paint often makes vinyl tubular weatherstripping stiff and reduces its effectiveness. In addition, the vinyl tubular type is probably the least attractive kind of weatherstripping.

Here Is What You Will Need

Materials
● Vinyl tubular weatherstripping
● Brads

Tools
● Hand-held hair dryer
● Ladder
● Hammer

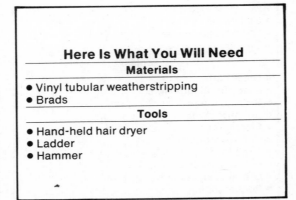

Step 3
Tubular Vinyl Nailed In Place

Steps 4 - 7
This Type Fits Outside Windows

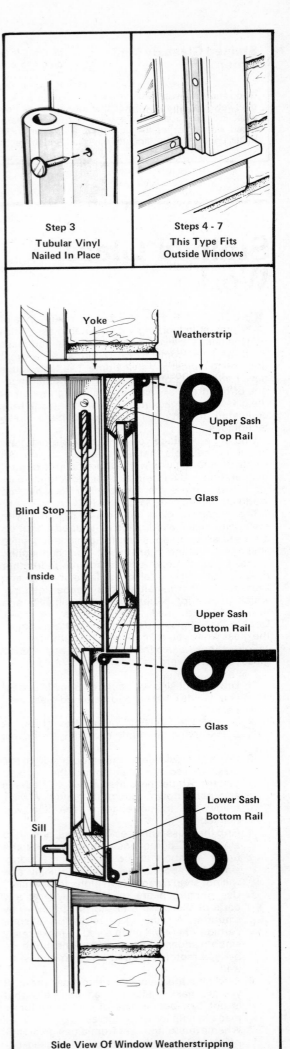

Side View Of Window Weatherstripping

Shades Are Never Misfits

Magic Fit Window Shades are adjustable window shades that you size at home. Since there is no in-store cutting, there is little likelihood of a misfit. You merely slide the adjustable roller into the window shade brackets, and then strip the shade to size in seconds. You need no tools or straight-edge. Just peel the appropriate trim tab, and the excess shade material strips off like magic, leaving a perfectly straight edge. Made in five basic sizes that fit all windows, Magic Fit Window Shades are also available in translucent and room-darkening styles. Newell Window Products—the manufacturer of Magic Fit Window Shades—also makes Magic Fit accessories.

Make Decorator Shades Yourself

Stauffer Chemical Company has put out a pamphlet that tells you how to measure your windows for shades and how to cut shade material. By following four easy steps and using Stauffer Tontine brand Tri-Lam and Tran-Lam window shade cloth, you can laminate fabric to the shade, attach it to the roller, and install the shade in your window frame. The brochure is available at shops which carry Stauffer Tontine materials.

Window Shades

ANY SHADE THAT refuses to go up and down and stay up or down the way you want it is a pain in the neck. Some shades are so wound up that they could almost lift you off the ground, while others are so slack that they fail to go up at all. In most cases, the remedy is just a matter of adjustment; but in order to know how to adjust a shade properly, you should understand how one works.

Look at the deceptively simple looking wooden roller. One end of the roller is hollow, with a concealed coil spring in it. There is a pin at either end of the roller; the one at the spring end is flat and rotates, winding or unwinding the spring. When you pull the shade down, the spring winds tight. When you stop pulling, a little lever—called a pawl—falls in place against a ratchet at the spring end of the roller. The pawl prevents the spring from winding the shade back up. When you wish to raise the shade, you tug down slightly on the shade, moving the pawl away from the ratchet and allowing the spring to carry the shade back up. Now that you know how a shade works, you should have no problem in figuring out what you have to do to adjust it.

1. The shade that refuses to go back up as far as you would like obviously lacks sufficient spring tension. To increase the tension, first pull the shade down about two revolutions, and then remove the flat pin from its bracket. Now roll the shade back up by hand. When you get it all the way up, put the pin back in its bracket and test the tension. If the shade still will not go up far enough, repeat this procedure until the spring tension is just right.
2. If the shade wants to pull you up with it, you must decrease the spring tension. To do so, take the flat pin out of its bracket while the shade is up, and unroll it by hand about two revolutions; then return the pin to its bracket and see whether you have tamed your shade's spring tension sufficiently.
3. If the shade fails to stay down, you know that for some reason the pawls are not catching. Remove the metal cap from the flat-pin end of the roller; then clean the pawl and ratchet mechanism.
4. A shade that wobbles when it goes up or down usually has a bent pin. Apply gentle pressure with a pair of pliers to straighten the pin.
5. When a shade falls out of its brackets, you must move the brackets closer together. If the brackets are mounted inside the window casing, you must add a shim behind the brackets. Usually, a cardboard shim will do. If the brackets are mounted outside the window casing, you can either reposition them or bend them slightly toward each other.
6. The shade that binds is the victim of brackets which are too close together. You can move outside brackets farther apart, but you must resort to other techniques for those mounted inside the window casing. First, try to tap the brackets lightly with a hammer. If that does not move them enough, take the metal cap and fixed round pin off the roller, and sand down the wood a bit.

Here Is What You Will Need

Materials
- Graphite or dry lubricant
- Cardboard shim
- Sandpaper

Tools
- Pliers
- Screwdriver
- Hammer

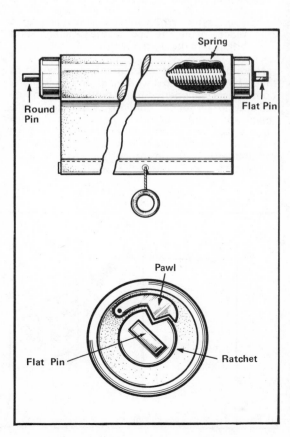

Spring

Round Pin

Flat Pin

Pawl

Flat Pin

Ratchet

Woven Wood Shades Need Little Care

The same principle used to produce bamboo shades twenty years ago has been updated and refined to produce today's woven wood shades. The Del Mar Woven Wood Company spins and dyes the yarns, mills and finishes the wood, weaves the fabric, and then cuts and assembles the finished product. Available in four different installation styles—Roman, spring-roller, cord and pulley, and double-fold—these shades improve room acoustics and heat and light control, while requiring only an occasional vacuuming. They are made to fit any type of window—double-hung, sliding glass, angle, cathedral, etc.,—of any size.

Black-Out Shades Take On Color

It used to be that black-out shades were about as ugly as you could imagine. Now, however, room-darkening shades are made to be decorative. For example, J.C. Penney offers a textured shade with a sheen that gives it the look of delicate silk. Available in colors as well as black and white, the shade is made of cotton with a vinyl coating that makes cleaning with a damp cloth easy. The room side of the shade has the color while the outside is white. Best of all, not only do these room-darkening shades really shield out light, but they also provide a measure of insulation, reducing energy costs when installed and used properly.

Accent Fold Stacks Draw Draperies

Marshall-McMurray's Accent Fold System consists of plastic tabs that cause the drapes to fold in a unique flat-stacking system that looks attractive from outside as well as in. After the tabs are sewn onto the drapes, they can be attached to Marshall-McMurray's Aluma Track draw drape hardware.

Power Tape Works Well For Drapery Hardware

The Lufkin Mezurlock Power Tape is handy for all sorts of measuring chores, including the installation of drapery hardware. Just pull the tape out 18 inches or more, and it locks in place for accurate measuring. A click of the toggle switch, and the blade glides back into the case. The Mezurlock features easy-to-read black on yellow markings that are protected with a clear tough epoxy coating. Lufkin measuring tapes, products of the Cooper Group, are available with either inch/foot designations or with metric calibrations.

You Can't Get Stung With A Yellow Jacket

A new, low cost plastic anchor called the Yellow Jacket, is designed to hold drapery hardware in hollow wall spaces or in studs. No longer need you worry that the hole may go into a stud, often prohibiting use of the anchor. The Yellow Jacket, a product of the U.S. Expansion Bolt Company, comes in attractive red, white, and blue packs, and the displays contain a selection of masonry drill bits for special problems.

Drapery Hardware

ALL TOO OFTEN, when you try to hang curtain or drapery rods yourself, they wind up sagging at one end. Then, if you fail to remedy the situation, the whole unit falls off when you open the drapes. This sad scene need not occur, though, if you learn how to hang drapery rods properly.

1. If you plan to attach the rods to a wooden window frame, use the frame as a guide for getting the curtain rods up straight. You can position the end brackets at the outside corners of the frame and install a center brace (if needed) at the frame's center. Make sure that the screws you use to hang your drapery or curtain rods are at least 3/4 of an inch long.
2. If there is no window frame to use as a guide or if you want the drapes out away from the actual opening, you must measure out laterally from the top of the opening and up toward the ceiling from the corners of the window opening. Make a cardboard template that fits against the corner of the window opening to indicate where the bracket goes. Place the bracket over the cardboard, make dots where the screws will go, and punch out the holes where you marked the dots. Then just reverse the template and you are all set to mark the holes on the other side of the window.
3. Drill pilot holes at the spots you marked on the wall. If you have hollow wall construction, use either plastic wall anchors or expansion bolts. If there are studs where you want to hang the brackets, use screws that are long enough to go through the sheetrock and into the studs.
4. Attach as many center support brackets as are needed to prevent the rods from ever sagging.
5. Adjust the end brackets and center supports so that they are as far out from the wall as you desire. When all the brackets are in place, place the rod in the brackets and adjust it to the proper length.

Naturally, you want to rig up the traverse rod so that when you hang the drapes and pull them, both panels will open at the same time and go all the way to the ends. Similarly, when you close them, you want the rod to carry both drapery panels back to the center and not leave a six-inch gap in the middle. Here is how to adjust a traverse rod to draw your drapes properly.

Here Is What You Will Need

Materials
- Drapery or curtain rods
- Cardboard
- Plastic wall anchors or expansion bolts

Tools
- Screwdriver
- Measuring tape
- Drill

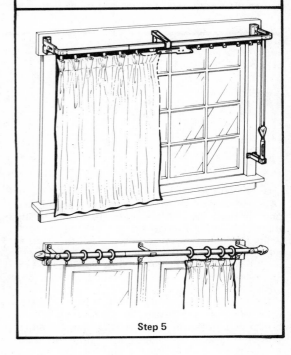

Step 5

△ 1. Lift the rod out of the brackets and lay it on the floor face down.
△ 2. Pull the outer cord at the side to bring the master slide on that side all the way over as far as it will go toward the cord.
△ 3. While holding the cord tight, manually slide the other master slide over as far as it will go.
△ 4. On this second slide you will notice a loop of cord running through two holes. Lift up the loop and hook it over the lug just below it.
△ 5. Now replace the rod back in the brackets and lock it in place. Insert drapery hooks through the plastic slides, and remove any extra slides at the end gate.
△ 6. When you pull the drapes open and closed, you will see both sides moving at the same time and at the same rate and hanging from drapery rods that are not going to fall down.

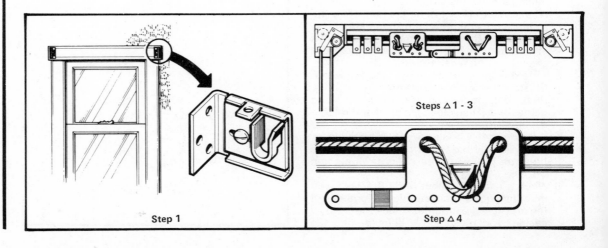

Step 1

Steps △ 1 - 3

Step △ 4

Venetian Blinds

EVEN IF YOU have trouble adjusting Venetian blinds, you will be pleasantly surprised to find that repairing them is a relatively simple task. The two major Venetian blind problems involve the webbing and cords getting broken or frayed. Since replacements are readily available at hardware stores and are easy to install, most Venetian blind problems are really not major ones at all.

First, consider the cords. As you can see, there are two sets of cords. One set, called the "lift cord system," raises and lowers the blinds. The other, called the "tilt cord system," changes the amount of light coming in by altering the angle at which the blinds tilt. Most replacement kits come with both sets of cords, and it is a good idea to change both cord sets.

1. Make a sketch of your own Venetian blinds to help you get the cords back in their proper places.
2. Open the blinds.
3. Start with the lift cord, and examine the knots under the tape at the bottom of the bottom rail. The tape may be stapled on, or—if the rail is metal—it may be held in place by a clamp. Untie the knots and remove the cord by pulling on the loop as if you were going to raise the blinds.
4. Now, starting at the side next to the tilt cord, feed the new cord through from the bottom up through the openings in the slats. Be sure that the cord goes on alternate sides of the ladder tapes (webbing) as you feed it in.
5. Go up to and over the pulley at the top.
6. Then, run the cord along the top until you reach the mechanism at the other side. Thread the cord under the first and over the second pulley.
7. Bring the cord down through the lift cord locking device.
8. Now, go back and knot the other end, and then pull the cord until the knot is nearly against the bottom rail.
9. Feed the unknotted end back into the top rail, over the other pulley (or pulleys), and down through the slats in the same manner as you did on the other side.
10. When you get the cord all the way through, adjust it to set the size of the loop. Then snip off the excess from the unknotted end before tying the knot.
11. Install the equalizer and adjust it.
12. Now you are ready to replace the tilt cord. Just run it over the pulley and back down. When you get it positioned, add the pulls and knot the cord.

To replace the ladder tapes (webbing), just follow these steps.

△ 1. Remove the blinds from the window and move them to the floor or a large table.
△ 2. Remove the bottom rail clamp (or staples) to expose the knots on the two ends of cord under each tape.
△ 3. Untie the knots and pull the cords up through the slots all the way up to the top of the blinds.
△ 4. The slats will now come out of the tapes. Remove them.
△ 5. Unhook the top of the tape from the tilt tube by removing the hook.
△ 6. Hook in the new tape at the tilt tube.
△ 7. Insert the slats in the new tapes.
△ 8. Weave the cord back down through the slots, making sure that the cord goes on alternate sides of the ladder tapes.
△ 9. Knot the cord under the bottom rail.

Here Is What You Will Need

Materials
- Replacement webbing
- Replacement cord
- Silicone spray

Tools
- Scissors
- Pliers

△ 10. Reattach either the clamp or staples.

About the only other thing that you can do to Venetian blinds is keep the gears and pulleys—which can pick up lint and fail to work as they should—clean and well lubricated. If you think that the gears and pulleys need lubrication, apply a silicone spray.

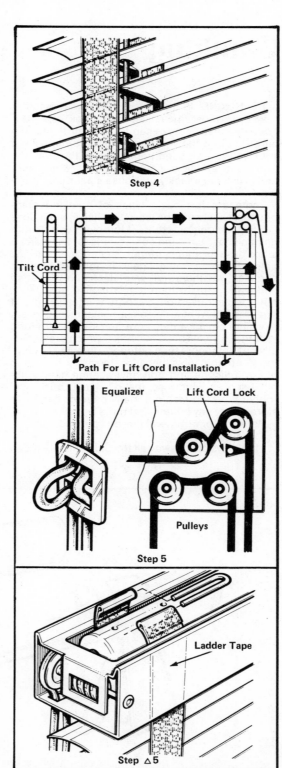

Step 4

Path For Lift Cord Installation

Step 5

Step △ 5

Quick Mend For Loose Ladders

One common malady to afflict blinds involves the crosspieces between the ladder tapes that support the slates pulling loose from the tapes. Since access to the problem is often quite limited, sewing the crosspieces and tapes back together again can be tricky. What you really need to make such repairs is a transparent, flexible, and waterproof liquid fabric glue that you can apply without having to remove the blinds. Fortunately, the Magic American Chemical Corporation offers just such a product: Magic Liquid Stitch. Able to hold any fabric, Liquid Stitch can be laundered, dry cleaned, ironed, or even boiled.

Cords Come In Nylon Or Cotton

You have a choice between nylon or cotton in replacement cords for your blinds. Take your pick; either will do the job. The Gold Metal Brand braided cotton cord from the Indian Head Yarn and Thread Company is a good one, as is Puritan's Gold Braid Nylon Cord from Wellington Puritan Mills.

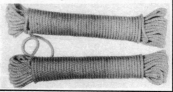

If Blind Repairs Leave You In The Dark, Get A Kit

The Venetian Blind Renew Kit from Globe will handle just about any problem that can strike your blinds. Consisting of 11 feet of plastic tape with cross-slat holders, 27 feet of cord, a pair of plastic pulls, and a metal equalizer, the kit allows you to renew anything on any blind up to 64 inches long. On the back of the kit are complete instructions covering disassembly of the blinds, removal of the old tape and cord, and the subsequent reassembly. No special tools are required. A pair of scissors can take care of everything, unless the new tape must be stapled to the bottom rail.

Windows

Darworth Caulks Are Among The Best

Seamseal Acrylic Rubber Caulk, from the Darworth Company, is a fine general purpose caulk created for exterior joints that are subject to above average movement and extreme weathering, such as around basement windows. A caulk that remains flexible indefinitely and bonds well to glass and other materials, Seamseal is also an ideal glazing caulk. The caulk bead can be painted after curing and will not bleed through any paint. It is water soluble before it cures. Another Darworth product, Polyseamseal, resists mildew and contains no oil. It, too, will not bleed through any type of paint and excels at sealing out cold drafts in winter and sticky heat in the summer. Polyseamseal comes in a squeeze tube or a cartridge.

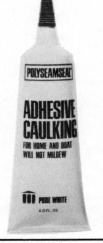

Caulk That's Guaranteed For 20 Years

Super Caulk, from the Macco Adhesives Division of Glidden Coatings and Resins (part of SCM), is an acrylic latex caulk for both exterior and interior use. Easy to work with, Super Caulk cleans up with soap and water, providing you start cleaning hands and tools before the caulk sets. You can paint Super Caulk with latex or oil-base paint a half hour after you apply it.

Caulking Gun Is Tool Of Many Uses

Since there are dozens of do-it-yourself repair compounds being packaged in cartridges, the caulking gun can handle many jobs in addition to injecting caulk into cracks. The Michlin Chemical Corporation makes a popular model, and the company's ThinZit compounds in cartridges comprise a good example of the many chores the gun can handle. These products include concrete crack fix, roofing compound, and—naturally—a variety of caulks.

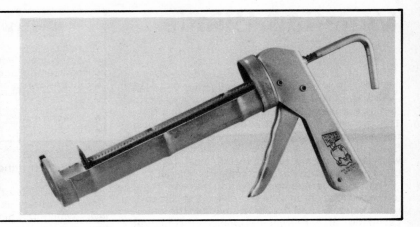

Caulking

CAULKING IS important for three reasons. First, most uncaulked areas look bad. Second, uncaulked cracks can let cold air in and hot air out during the winter and just the opposite if your house is air conditioned during the summer. And third, a lack of caulking allows water, dirt, and insects to attack your house's paint and framing.

There are five basic types of caulking compounds. Oil base is the least expensive, but it does not last as long as others. Moreover, you cannot paint oil base caulking compounds for 24 hours. A latex base is much longer lasting and can be painted almost immediately. It adheres to most surfaces, weathers well, and cleans up with soap and water. Butyl rubber caulk is also long lived, but it is best used on masonry to metal joints. It requires a solvent for clean up. Silicone caulks are excellent because they cure quickly and are long lasting. Polyvinyl acetate caulks, which are generally better indoors than outdoors, lack the flexibility of other caulks because they dry hard and brittle. Silicone and polyvinyl acetate caulks are not used as widely as the oil, latex, and butyl rubber types. In fact, not many paint or hardware stores carry any but the first three types.

Here are some general tips on caulking.

1. Always clean away all the old caulking. It can

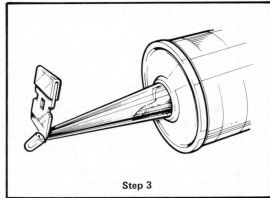

Step 3

Here Is What You Will Need

Materials
- Oil-, latex-, butyl rubber-, silicone-, or polyvinyl acetate-type caulk
- Cleaning solvent

Tools
- Knife
- Caulk gun

be scraped, peeled, gouged, and pulled away. Once you get rid of all of it, clean the area to be caulked with a solvent. You want the area to be as free of dirt, oil, wax, and dust as possible.

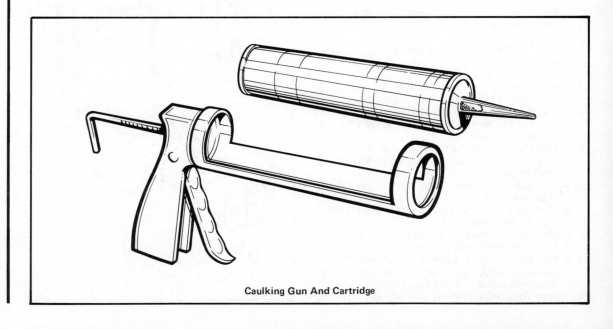

Caulking Gun And Cartridge

Elmer Is In The Caulk Market Too

Elmer's Acrylic Latex Caulk is a versatile indoor/outdoor caulk. It can handle just about any sealing job around the house, and it can be painted over in thirty minutes with latex or oil-base paints. Elmer's Acrylic Latex Caulk cleans up with soap and water—so long as the clean up is initiated before it cures.

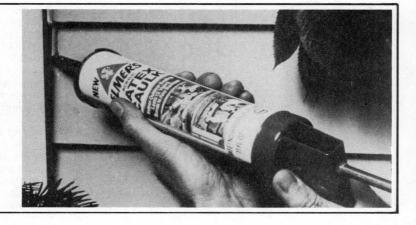

Wringer Gets All Caulk Out Of Tube

While most caulking is not expensive, you still want to get your money's worth out of every tube you buy. The Tube Wringer, a product of the Gill Mechanical Company, is an ingenious little device that gets just about everything out of either metal or plastic tubes. The Tube Wringer also seals ruptures as it passes over them, and it even works on toothpaste tubes.

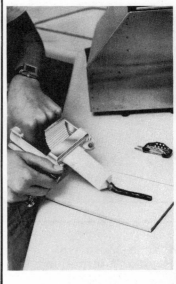

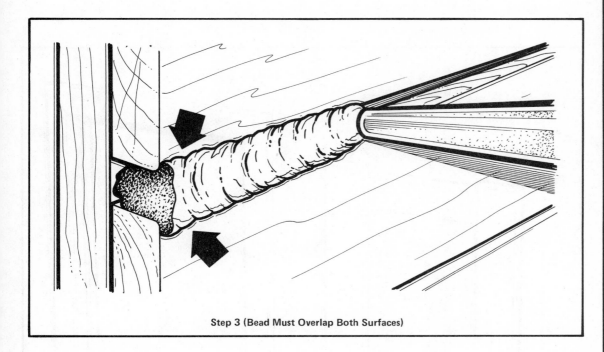

Step 3 (Bead Must Overlap Both Surfaces)

2. Try to do your caulking work in warm weather. If that is not possible, warm the caulking tube itself before you apply its contents. In extremely hot weather, the caulking can get too runny; try placing the tube in the refrigerator for a brief period to slow down the caulk.
3. Cut the spout at a place that will give you the proper size bead for the job. The bead should overlap onto both surfaces. Make your spout cut at an angle.
4. Hold the gun at a 45-degree angle in the direction of your movement.
5. When you have to stop, twist the L-shaped plunger rod until it disengages in order to stop the caulk from oozing out.

Where should you caulk? As a rule of thumb, any place that has two different parts that come together with a crack in between should be caulked. Think particularly in terms of places where two different materials come together. Here is a sample list of caulking spots:

△ 1. Around doors and windows where the frame and the side of the house come together.
△ 2. At the point where the side of the house and the foundation meet.
△ 3. In the joint where steps or porches and the main body of the house meet.
△ 4. Where the chimney meets the roof, around the flashing, and the gap in the seam between flashing and shingles.
△ 5. Where plumbing goes through walls to enter the house.
△ 6. Along the seam formed at corners where siding meets.
△ 7. Around the exhaust vent for the clothes dryer.
△ 8. In the spaces between air conditioner window units and window frames.

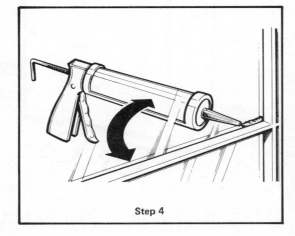

Step 4

Three From U.S.G.

Three new Durabond Caulking Compounds from United States Gypsum Company provide protection for your home, indoors and out, all year round. Durabond Acrylic Caulk is a fast-drying, premium-grade caulking compound that remains flexible despite the fact that its surface forms a tough film to resist cracking. The Utility Caulk adheres to wood, metal, brick, and stone, but allows for expansion, contraction, and vibration to protect joints and openings. Butyl Caulk is designed for use where temperature extremes are expected. All three compounds can be applied with a caulking gun on surfaces that are clean and free of old caulk, paint chips, and mortar. While the Acrylic and Utility Caulks can be applied to damp surfaces, the surface must be dry for applications of the Butyl Caulk.

Doors

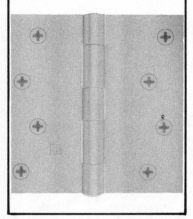

Hanging Various Types of Doors

DOORS PLAY an important role in storage projects. They are essential parts of closets and cabinets, and their selection and installation are not the open-and-shut matters you might think.

If you were to draw up the basic requirements for closet doors in general, you would certainly include the following:

1. The door must not waste space in the closet when opened or closed.
2. It should take up as little space as possible in the room when opened.
3. It should provide maximum access to all corners of the closet.
4. The door must operate easily and require little maintenance.
5. It should be attractive.

No single type of closet door meets all of these requirements, but some come closer than others.

When hanging a hinged door, the door should be $\frac{3}{32}$ to $\frac{1}{16}$ of an inch narrower than the finished door opening and 115 of an inch shorter at the top.

△ 1. Lay the door across a pair of sawhorses and cut off the protruding lugs at the top.
△ 2. Cut off enough of the door's bottom to provide clearance at the top and any additional clearance for the carpet.
△ 3. Pencil a line parallel to the latch edge of the door to show how much must be trimmed off.
△ 4. Set the door on the floor, hinge-edge down, and clamp it to your workbench; it must be

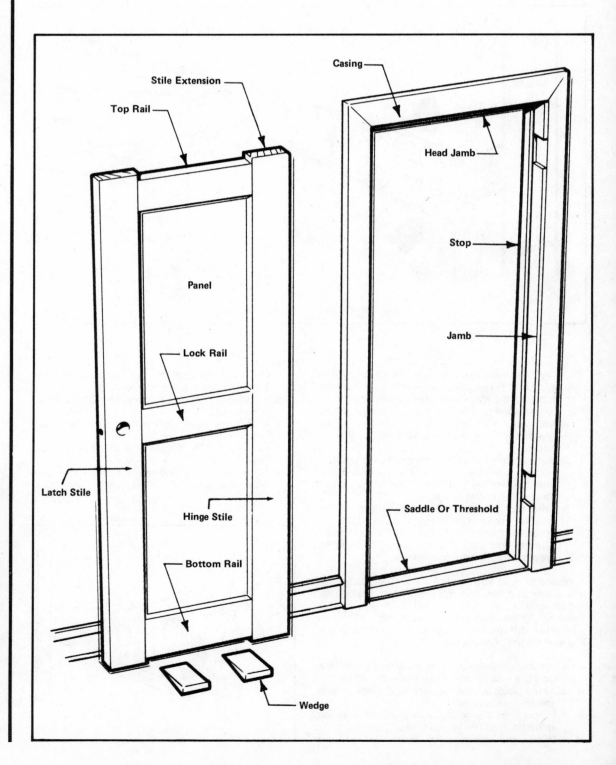

held perfectly straight up and down.

△ 5. Plane the latch edge almost to the pencil line. Before you reach the line, however, hold the door in the door opening to make certain that the planed edge is parallel to the jamb.

△ 6. If the jamb is a little out of plumb, mark the edge of the door accordingly and finish planing.

△ 7. When you fashion the door to the correct size, bevel the latch edge backward very slightly to allow it to clear the jamb as it swings open and shut.

△ 8. Round off all of the door's corner edges slightly to prevent them from splintering, and sand all surfaces smooth.

△ 9. Set the door in the opening and force it tight against the hinged jamb by driving a wedge into the gap on the latch side.

△10. Lay a 6d nail across the top of the door and drive a wedge under the door until the nail is snug against the top jamb. This procedure provides the proper amount of space between the top of the door and the jamb.

△11. Mark the positions for the top and bottom hinges on both the door and the hinge jamb. The hinge should be 3½-inch butts with loose pins. The tops of the pins must, of course, point directly upward.

△12. With a sharp pencil, draw the outlines of the hinges on the edge of the door and on the jamb. The hinges should be set in from the face of the door and from the front edge of the jamb 1⅛ inches. To simplify this operation and the next one, buy a butt marker for a 3½-inch hinge. This device marks the position and outline of a hinge; then, when you hit it with a hammer, it cuts the outline into the wood to the proper depth.

△13. If you lack a butt marker, use a chisel or knife to cut the outlines of the hinges in the door edge. Then, carefully chisel out the wood within the outlines to make the mortises for the hinge leaves. To do this properly, make a series of closely spaced cuts across the wood with the chisel and rake out the chips.

△14. Smooth the bottom of the mortise and set the hinge leaf into it. The top of the leaf should be flush with the surrounding wood; continue chiseling out wood and testing the depth until the leaf is flush.

△15. After you complete the four mortises, take the hinges apart and screw the leaves firmly into the door edge. Screw the other leaves into the jamb but drive in only one screw per leaf. Do not make the holes for the other screws yet.

△16. Set the door into the opening and fit the hinge leaves together. If they fail to fit, loosen the jamb leaves a little and try again. If you still cannot make them fit, adjust the jamb leaves up or down in the jamb as necessary.

△17. When you get the right fit, slip the pins into the hinges. Then finish driving the remaining screws into the jamb.

△18. If the door strikes the latch jamb when you push it closed or if there is too much of a gap between the door and the latch jamb, loosen the screws in the jamb and insert narrow shims of cardboard under the leaves. A shim placed under the inner edge of a hinge forces the door away from the latch jamb; placed under the outer edge (pin edge), the shim forces the door toward the latch jamb. The thicker the shims, of course, the greater the movement of the door.

△19. Step into the closet and pull the door shut. Draw pencil lines on the jambs around the sides and top of the door.

△20. Cut stops (flat moldings) to fit around the door, position them along the pencil lines, and nail them to the jambs.

Step △ 7

Step △ 7

If all of this sounds like too much trouble to go through to hang a hinged door, you can buy a prehung door unit—consisting of a door frame and hinged door already installed—at your local lumberyard or building supply dealer. In some cases, the latchset is also in place, and the whole unit is prefinished. To install the unit, you simply set it into the rough door opening, plumb it, wedge it, nail it, and apply the trim on one side.

Exactly how you install a bi-fold door depends on the hardware you use. You must, therefore, follow the directions which the manufacturer of the hardware (or of the doors) supplies. Generally, you can save yourself some work if you purchase bi-fold doors that are already hinged together and equipped with the pivots on which they swing. It takes longer to assemble a pair of doors or a set of four doors from scratch, but you can choose from a much wider selection of door styles and sizes when you are willing to do all the work yourself.

For the most part, you install bi-fold doors as follows:

○ 1. The height of the finished door opening equals the height of the door, plus approximately ½ inch for clearance at the floor plus approximately ¾ of an inch for the track to be mounted on the head jamb. The width of the opening for a two-panel door equals twice the width of a single panel, plus approximately ½ inch to allow for a slight crack between the hinge edges of the two panels plus clearance at the jambs. For a four-panel door, add ¼ of an inch.

○ 2. Establish the position of the door in the frame. Normally, it is installed flush with the front edges of the jambs, but you may center it in the frame between the front and back edges if you want.

○ 3. Trim the doors as necessary to fit the opening and hinge them together with three butts mortised into the door edges. These are the only hinges used in an installation.

○ 4. Install one of the pivots on which the bi-fold swings in the top edge of the door, close to one corner. Install a metal guide in the edge at the opposite corner and then install a second pivot in the bottom of the door directly below the top pivot. Use a plumb line to align the pivots.

(Continued on following page)

Don't Replace A Door Just Because It's Ugly

If you think that you have to replace a door because it happens to be ugly or just plain, you should know about Photodoor from Scandecor, Inc. Photodoors are full-color pre-pasted decorative panels that are big enough to cover most standard doors; they may be trimmed to fit smaller doors. To apply a Photodoor, you need only dip the roll into a water tray for a half minute, and then hang and smooth it on the door as you would a wallpaper panel. The design selection is so varied as to topics and colors that you should encounter no difficulty in finding one to fit your decorating scheme. A Photodoor could very well save you the time, trouble, and expense of hanging a new door.

Sliding Glass Doors Are Installed Easily

Since sliding glass doors can take up an entire wall, installation would seem to be a huge undertaking. It can be, but units like the Sunliners, from Reynolds Metal Company, install square with only hammer and nails and screwdriver. In fact, a simple turn of a screwdriver is all that's needed to adjust the Reynold's Sunliner doors up or down. Be sure to follow the caulking and weatherstripping instructions carefully for a weatherproof installation. Reynold's Climate Guard line comes with double-pane insulated glass as well as insulation throughout the frame.

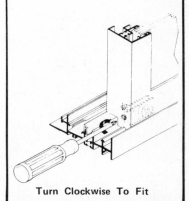

Turn Clockwise To Fit

Doors

(Continued from Previous page)

Pivot Bi-Fold Hardware A "Snap" To Install

Stanley's bi-fold hardware features a unique ramp-type track socket which literally makes bi-fold door installation a snap. The bottom pivot, attached to the bottom of the door, is placed in the jamb bracket, leaving the pivot to support the weight of the door. Since the door's weight is on the bracket, the installer is freed from supporting its weight. The top pivot and guide roller are then guided in the track towards the jamb, where the top pivot snaps into the unique ramp-type track socket. With the door in place, plumb adjustment can be made quickly at the top and/or bottom with the wrench provided. This Stanley bi-fold hardware comes in a choice of steel or aluminum track; the steel track provides a smoother operating surface at a lower cost. Stanley's locking snubber is a nice feature in that it prevents the popping effect—one side popping open as the other side is closed—on a four-door set.

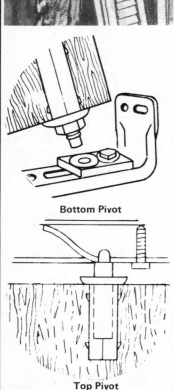

Bottom Pivot

Top Pivot

5. Screw the sockets for the pivots to the head jamb and floor and then screw the U-shaped metal track which guides the door to the head jamb. If the track is flush with the head jamb, you should lower the head vasing to conceal it; many people, though, simply paint the track to match the trim.

6. Set the door into the opening and insert the pivots in the sockets and the metal guide in the track.

7. Test the door to make certain it works smoothly and then screw knobs to the panels on both sides of the hinge joint.

8. In a four-panel installation, metal aligners are attached to the doors at the bottom so that the doors will butt together in a smooth line when closed.

When hanging a folding door, determine the height and width of the door opening by obtaining all the specifications for the particular folding door you are buying. In other words, if the door measures 80 inches from the bottom to the top of the track in which it slides, you must make the door opening 80½ inches high to allow for clearance at the floor. If the door is designed for a four-foot wide opening, however, your opening can be a trifle less since the door expands and contracts like a coiled spring. You can buy a folding door (or pairs of doors) with all the necessary hardware included. Here are some important steps to take when hanging a folding door.

1. Check to make sure that the door you buy is the right height by inserting the hangers on the top edge in the track, pulling tight, and measuring the distance from the top of the track to the top of the door. If necessary, cut off the bottom of the door with a fine-toothed crosscut saw.

2. Position the door in the opening so that, when open, the sharp front edges of the folds align with the front edges of the jambs.

3. Mark the position of the U-shaped metal track on the head jamb.

4. With the door hangers inserted in the track, set the door in the opening; position the track on the head jamb; and screw it tight.

5. Screw the stationary end of the door to the appropriate jamb.

6. Install the catch on the other jamb and door edge.

Conventional bypass sliding doors are usually 1⅜ inches thick, but ¾-inch doors are available. The hardware depends on the thickness of the door, and the installation depends not only on the design of the hardware but also on the brand.

1. The finished door opening for a two-panel door should be twice the width of a single panel, minus one inch to allow for the overlap at the center when both doors are closed.

2. The height of the door opening should equal the height of the door, plus approximately 1⅜ inches to allow for the hanger hardware plus ½ inch clearance at the floor.

3. Position the doors so that the front panel is 1¼ inches back from the front edges of the jambs.

4. Cut the metal track (from which the doors hang) to the length of the head jamb, and screw it into place.

5. Screw two hangers (rollers) to the back of each door panel within about two inches of the corners along the top edges.

6. Hang the panels in the tracks by slanting them outward at the bottom until the rollers slip easily into the track.

7. Go inside the closet, push one door against the side jamb, and adjust the hangers until the door lies parallel to the jamb. Adjust the other door in the same way. On the best bypass doors, you make these adjustments by turning knobs on the hangers.

8. Screw a slotted guide to the floor directly under the doors in the center of the opening to keep the doors from swaying back and forth.

9. Cut a board to the length of the head jamb. It should be just wide enough to conceal the top edges of the doors when mounted on the head jamb.

10. Nail it to the jamb, parallel with and ¼ of an inch out from the front door panel.

If a sliding door consists of three panels, the standard practice is to hang one panel in the front track and two panels in the back track. Since this arrangement permits you to reach into only one-third of the closet at any time, however, you might prefer to add a third track and hang each door in its own track. With a four-panel door, you hang two panels in each of the two tracks.

Here Is What You Will Need

Materials

- Door
- Wedge
- Nails
- Hinges
- Cardboard shims
- Flat molding
- Latchset
- Door knobs
- Metal track for bi-fold doors
- Hardware for doors

Tools

- Sawhorses
- Saw
- Tape measure
- Pencil
- Clamps
- Plane
- Sandpaper
- Hammer
- Chisel
- Screwdriver
- Plumb line

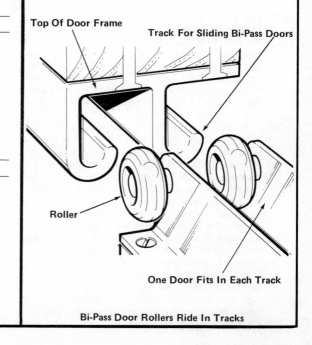

Top Of Door Frame

Track For Sliding Bi-Pass Doors

Roller

One Door Fits In Each Track

Bi-Pass Door Rollers Ride In Tracks

Lubricate Track Rollers And Pulleys With Spray

The easiest way to lubricate garage door components is with a spray, and getting the door running smoothly before you hook up the automatic opener is a must. LPS has sprays for all parts of your garage door. LPS 1 cleans out caked and hardened grease from the track, LPS 3 provides proper track lubrication, and pulleys and rollers need LPS 2 on their moving contact parts. Available in bulk as well as in aerosol spray cans, LPS products are made for just about every lubrication application.

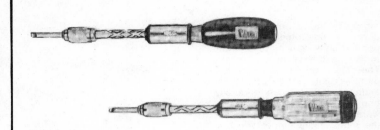

Ratchet Screwdriver Does Double Duty As Drill

The handy ratchet screwdriver drives screws or removes them with a simple pumping action on the handle. It can also be used as a drill, and different size drill bits—as well as various screwdriver styles—are interchangeable in the ratchet handle; extra bits and screwdriver tips are held in a compartment in the handle. The Vaco ratchet screwdriver comes with three drill bits, a slotted screwdriver blade, and a Phillips screwdriver tip. It is a good tool that will undoubtedly find dozens of uses around your home.

Installing an Automatic Garage Door Opener

CONVENIENCE AND safety are the two major reasons for having an automatic opener on your garage door. If you have decided to get one, you can save up to $50 by installing it yourself. Before you buy your opener unit, though, make certain that it will be adequate for the size and type of garage door you have. Then check to make sure that there is adequate clearance between the arc of the door and the garage ceiling to accommodate the unit. Once you have the right unit, here is what to do.

1. Oil the garage door's rollers and pulleys—if any—and grease the tracks. Also make certain that the current mechanism is adjusted and working properly.
2. Remove the present lock or make it inoperable.
3. Find the exact center of the door and of the header beam above the door.
4. Attach the header bracket to the header beam, centering the bracket exactly. These parts may be called something else in your unit; use the unit's parts list and diagram to identify them.
5. Install hanger straps (some units may have two sets of hanger straps) in the ceiling with lag screws. If your garage does not have exposed beams, locate the beams behind the ceiling, and then use additional lag screws to attach a 2x4 centered on the door and about three-quarters of the way back to where the motor unit will go.
6. Now you are ready to attach the track assembly to the header bracket and the hanger strap. In most cases the track and motor unit will be attached, but if not, you must fasten them together. You will need help in holding the parts together while you attach them.
7. Next, put the connector arm plate on the garage door. Position it right at the top and in the exact center of the door.

8. Attach the connecting arm to this plate, and then to the carrier in the track. Move the carrier all the way toward the door by hand-turning the unit.
9. Hook up the wires from the push button unit and from the automatic reversing control to the opener, and then plug the opener into a convenient outlet. Some units must be wired into a junction box.
10. Install batteries in the transmitter, a light bulb in the socket, and put the housing in place over the opener unit.

Now try it out, but take it easy if the opener fails to work just right. Most units must be adjusted. There is a plate attached to the unit itself telling you how to adjust the opener. All adjustments are simple; just turn a nut to change the unit's opening or closing. To adjust the automatic reverse, merely turn a nut at the header bracket.

Here Is What You Will Need

Materials

- Automatic opener unit
- Oil and grease
- Lag screws

Tools

- Screwdriver
- Measuring tape
- Adjustable wrench

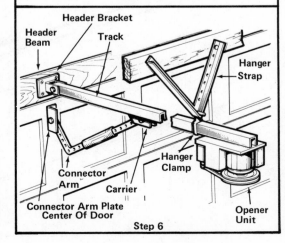

Step 6

Socket To It

A ratchet socket wrench makes adjusting the tracks and installing the new opener go much faster. Of course, you would not buy an elaborate set for a single project, but a socket wrench is a handy tool to own, and a good one—like the 24-piece Classic MPI—lasts forever. MPI stands for molded plastic insert, and it makes keeping track of all the components easy. You can select the socket you need quickly, and tell at a glance when a part is missing. The size of each socket is imprinted on the tray under the socket's nesting place, and the metal case serves as a tool box for the set. Classic tools are made by Indestro.

What About Security?

Digital controls for garage door openers allow you to vary the electronic signal that activates your unit. Since you can set hundreds of different codes, such a control provides against someone being able to open your garage door with a standard control module. Codes are set by using a pencil to flip any combination of switches inside the wall-mounted receiver. Then the corresponding switches are set in the car transmitter in the same manner. Digital controls are available with Sears top-of-the-line garage door openers.

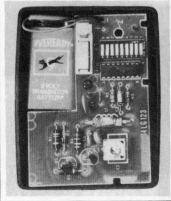

Doors

Not All Open Upward

Although the overhead garage door is undoubtedly the most popular style, you may have another type that is in need of repair. The hinged doors have very few parts—usually just hinges, locks, and braces. You can generally find most of these parts at hardware stores; just make sure that the replacement hinges you buy are heavy enough to support the doors. Sliding door hardware is a little more complex, but Montgomery Ward offers good by-pass sliding garage door hardware.

Different Door Hinges

At first glance, you might conclude that the various hinges at the different joints or sections of a folding garage door are all the same. Close observation, however, will reveal that two or three different types of hinges are probably involved. If you have a hinge problem, therefore, you would be wise to remove the bad hinge and take it with you when buying a replacement. Several companies make replacement hinges, and most package the units with all necessary hardware and installation instructions.

Garage Doors Can Be Decorative

Think about it; your garage door accounts for a fairly large portion of your home's exterior. If it is unattractive, it detracts from the appearance of the rest of the house. Fortunately, you can replace an ugly door with a truly handsome one. The Overhead Door Corporation offers a wide variety of styles, including the rough-sawn flush door Series 125. The texture of wood grain is embossed into exterior grade hardboard that will not crack or splinter, and the surface can be stained, painted, or antiqued.

Replace Worn Lift Cables And Pulleys

The replacement cables and pulleys from Clopay's Overhead Door Division are especially easy to install because each part is packaged with easy-to-follow directions. Many garage door parts are identical no matter who the maker of the door might be, but Clopay also supplies specific parts for particular models. Clopay also makes a complete line of insulated overhead garage doors in fiberglass, aluminum, steel, and wood.

Garage Doors

MOST GARAGES built during the past twenty years have overhead doors. There are two basic types of overhead garage doors, the roll-up and the swing-up. Both types rely on a heavy spring (or springs) for their ease of operation. When the door slows down or becomes difficult to raise or lower, most people try to remedy the problem by adjusting the spring. In most cases, however, the spring is not the culprit. Here are the steps to a smoother upswing in your garage door.

1. Check the vertical tracks with a level to be sure they are plumb. If they are not, adjust the tracks by loosening the brackets which hold the tracks to the wall, and then tap them back in alignment.
2. Check all tracks for any crimps. If you find any, straighten them out.
3. Be sure the tracks are positioned so that the rollers do not bind in the track.
4. Inspect the tracks for dirt. Old grease can collect dust and dirt, and you might need to swab out the track with a solvent to dissolve the old grease and remove the dirt.
5. Lubricate the track, the rollers, and the pulleys (if any). Use machine oil or spray lubricant on the rollers and pulleys; use grease in the tracks.
6. Look for any loose hardware such as hinges, tracks, or brackets. Any of these can cause balky operation when they loosen.
7. After you have checked everything else, you can go to work on the spring. If you have the type of roll-up door with a spring on either side, try shortening the spring cable while the door is up. This cable is held in a hole in

Here Is What You Will Need

Materials
- Cleaning solvent
- Machine oil or spray lubricant
- Grease
- Paint

Tools
- Carpenter's level
- Adjustable wrench
- Hammer
- Screwdriver

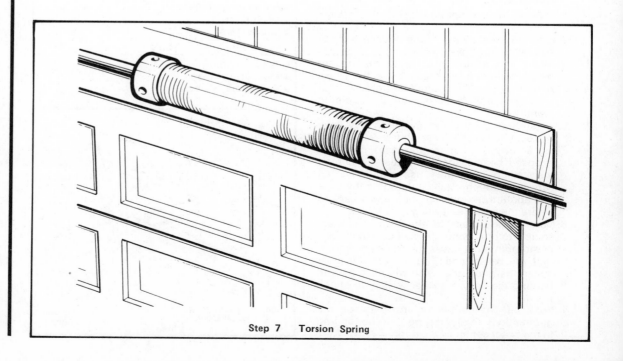

Step 7   Torsion Spring

Garage Doors Need Weatherstripping Too

While top-quality garage doors come equipped with weatherstripping along both top and bottom, there are plenty of doors that could use some help in fighting off the winter wind. Mortell's Garage Door Weatherstrip Cushion (made in lengths for single or double garage doors) can be easily installed to the bottom of any wooden garage door. Just nail it in place with the nails that come with the weatherstrip. Mortell's

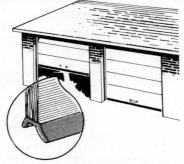 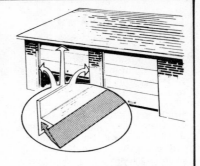

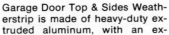
Garage Door Top & Sides Weatherstrip is made of heavy-duty extruded aluminum, with an ex-

tra-wide, long-wearing vinyl seal that is set on an angle and self-adjusts to any door warpage.

Garage Door Lock Should Be A Good One

Garages afford an easy way to gain entry to your home. If the burglar can get into your garage, he can usually move on into the house without being seen. Therefore, make sure the lock on your garage door is a good one, and replace a faulty lock immediately. Replacement locks are easy to install. The Torch Side Lock (from the Torch Products Company) attaches to the existing key cylinder or to a new one.

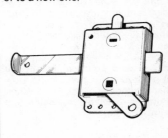

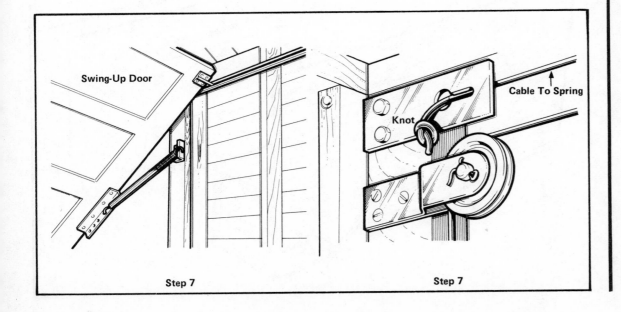

Step 3   Rollers Ride in Metal Track

a plate above the door. To shorten the cable, move the knot (or stay) inward. The other type of roll-up door has a torsion spring in the center. If you have this type, seek the help of a pro who has the proper tools and experience; the torsion is so great that you could easily be hurt. The swing-up type doors have springs that hook into holes or notches; you can adjust them by moving the

spring hook from one hole or notch to another.

8. Another reason for doors not working properly is that they become too heavy. A wooden door can absorb a great deal of moisture. You can prevent serious moisture problems by painting the garage door; just make sure to paint both sides and to seal the top, bottom, and sides.

Swing-Up Door

Knot   Cable To Spring

Step 7   Step 7

Garage Door Parts Purveyors

There are many firms offering quality replacement garage door parts. Chances are, a hardware store or home center that enjoys a good reputation will carry a line of good quality parts. If you are in doubt, though, look for one of the following brands: Clopay, Door Products, Frantz, Lawrence Bros., Overhead Door, Richards-Wilcox, and Stanley Hardware.

Hints On Replacing Garage Door Parts

Until you are sure that you know what you are doing, never remove more than one part of your garage door at a time. Novices often become confused when they start dismantling several garage door components at once. Then, when you go shopping for replacement parts, take the old parts with you. That way the dealer can make sure you get exactly the parts you need. As you might expect, extension springs (those on both sides), cables, and pulleys are much easier to replace when the garage door is open. You can use a 2x4 to prop the door open, or you can attach clamps to prevent it from closing.

Garage Door Rollers Can Go Bad

If the tracks on your garage door are not straight or if you fail to lubricate the rollers regularly, you may discover that one or more of the rollers is in need of replacement. There are several types of rollers, and Door Products Company packages most of them as well as other universal garage door parts. You can find them at lumberyards, home centers, and hardware stores.

Doors

Patch Around New Mortises With Rock Hard Putty

For patching wood, you can hardly do better than Durham's Rock Hard Water Putty. It comes in powder form that you mix with latex paint instead of water; it dries fast; and it sticks to many types of surfaces—i.e., plaster walls, concrete, stone composition, etc. Although you can slow down the setting time by adding a little vinegar to powder/paint mixture, Durham's Rock Hard Water Putty sets so quickly that you should mix only as much as you can work with in a short time. After it sets, you can saw, chisel, sand, polish, mold, or paint it. A product of the Donald Durham Company, Rock Hard Water Putty is available at paint and hardware stores.

Easydriver Makes Driving Easy

A significant improvement in the screwdriver has been achieved. Called the Easydriver, it's a ratchet tool with a handle about the size of a tennis ball which gives the user a much better grip than any conventional screwdriver handle. Equipped with two Phillips heads and two slotted tips—plus the standard 5½-inch shaft—the Easydriver's interchangeable accessories include a short (1¾ inch) shaft, a long (9½ inch) shaft, additional screwdriver tips, a socket set, and an extra-leverage handle for the ball. A bench stand holder for all the accessories is also available. Easydriver is manufactured by Creative Tools Inc.

C-Clamps Are Always Handy

Holding a door for planing is just one of hundreds of ways to use a C-Clamp. The three-inch Clamp-It, just one of many different types of clamps and vises made by the Brink and Cotton Manufacturing Company, is a good clamp that features a swivel no-mar button. You can store C-clamps easily by clamping them to the edge of a shelf or to exposed studs in a

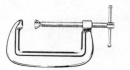

shop or garage, but be sure to lubricate the clamps well if storage will expose them to moist conditions.

Vaughan Hammer Has Hollow-Core Handle

Vaughan feels that a hollow-core fiberglass handle provides better balance and absorbs more shock—all of which makes a hammer less tiring to use. The head is drop-forged, precision-machined, quality steel with a handsome polished finish. Vaughan hammers, products of the Vaughan & Bushnell Manufacturing Company, come in all styles and sizes.

Unsticking a Door

FEW THINGS ARE more annoying than a sticking door. When you finally do get it open, you cannot get it closed again. Unfortunately, most homeowners grab a plane and start shaving away some wood. Although frequently there is no alternative, planing down your door should be a measure of last resort. The first thing to do is to inspect the door to see what is causing it to stick. Here are the steps to follow.

1. Close the door, if possible, and examine the edge opposite the sticking place. If you see a large gap there, the problem may well be in the hinges.
2. If there are no gaps—or very few—anywhere around the door, then the wood probably is swollen with moisture.
3. Open the door and place a square against the frame to see whether it is out of line. If that is what you find, then the house has probably settled and forced the frame out of shape.

If your diagnosis is a hinge problem, here are the steps you should follow.

△ 1. Check all the screws in the hinges to see that

they are tight. If any continue to turn, it means that the screw holes have become enlarged. Insert pieces of toothpick into the hole, reinsert the screw, and you should find that the screw bites securely.

△ 2. If the hinges are not loose, they may need to be shimmed up or recessed to relieve the sticking problem. Look at the door to see where it is rubbing. A door that sticks toward the top of the latch side and down at the bottom against the floor is a door that is tilted out at the top. Bring the bottom hinge

Here Is What You Will Need

Materials

- Wooden toothpicks
- Shim (shirtboard)
- Chalk
- Penetrating oil
- Large wooden box
- Paint
- Padded 2x4

Tools

• Plane	• Carpenter's
• Hammer	square
• C-clamp	• Screwdriver

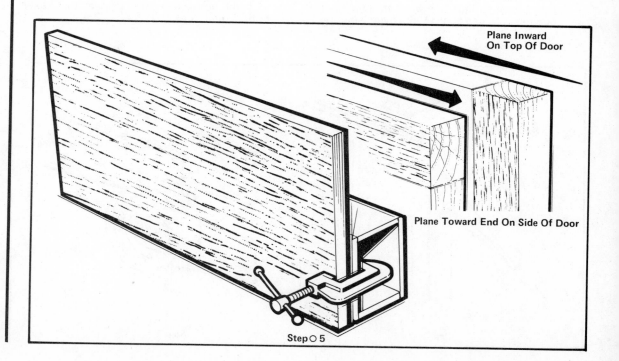

Plane Inward On Top Of Door

Plane Toward End On Side Of Door

Step ○ 5

Shaving Down A Sticking Door Is Plane Simple

If you are certain that the only way to make your door fit its frame is by shaving off some of the wood, consider using Arco's 3-Way Plane to do the job. The handle adjusts to three positions, and the multi-bite ten-inch blade has a thousand sharp cutting teeth. In addition to door work, the Arco 3-Way Plane removes paint, bevels, rounds corners, and does

smoothing work on wood, wallboard, plastic, and even soft metal. It really cuts fast, and yet leaves a smooth finish.

Surform Tool Does Plane's Work

While a good plane is usually required for heavy-duty wood removal tasks, the Surform Tool from Stanley is great when you just need to shave a little bit off a door to stop it from snagging. Non-clogging, the Surform Tool makes quick work of surface removal. Moreover, there is no need to set the blade because the hundreds of tiny hardened and

ground cutting teeth (replaceable) are ready to tackle any wood removal task.

---

out a bit, and you may solve the problem. Try cutting a piece of shirtboard to fit between the bottom hinge and the door jamb; then slot the cardboard so that you only have to loosen the screws to insert the shim. Retighten and see if the shim cures the problem. If it helps but does not eliminate the problem, add another thickness of shim. Naturally, if the door sticks toward the bottom of the latch side, you should shim out the top hinge. If the door sticks along the latch side and there is no gap along the hinge side, you can sometimes cut a deeper mortice in the jamb to set the hinge deeper and move the door away from the frame on the latch side. Similarly, if the door sticks at the top and there is more than 1/4-inch space at the bottom, you could consider moving the hinges down a bit.

When you determine that the door is swollen with excess moisture and is just too big for the frame, then you have to remove some of the wood. Here is how to go about planing down your door.

○ 1. Mark the sticking places with a piece of chalk.

○ 2. If the door binds along the top, you can plane without first removing the door from its hinges. Just make sure that when planing the top (or bottom) you cut from the edge toward the center; otherwise, the plane could catch the side rail and rip off a piece of the door.

○ 3. If the door sticks along the side, remove the door by tapping out the hinge pins. Always remove the bottom pin first. Place the tip of a screwdriver under the pin, and tap the screwdriver handle with a hammer. If the pin refuses to budge, insert a nail into the bottom of the hinge and tap upward. Penetrating oil can also help loosen stubborn pins.

○ 4. Once the pins are out, the door is free.

○ 5. Anchor the door to a large wooden box with a C-clamp to help keep the door upright during planing.

○ 6. When planing the side, always cut toward the edges. Keep in mind that the latch side is slightly beveled to prevent the edge from striking the frame when you close the door. Therefore, try to plane the hinge side instead; but if you must plane the latch side, make sure your planing retains this bevel.

○ 7. After you plane all the chalked spots, put the door back on the hinges and give it a trial run. If it still sticks, plane off some more wood.

○ 8. Once you get the door to open and close easily, paint the newly planed areas and any other bare wood to prevent future moisture problems.

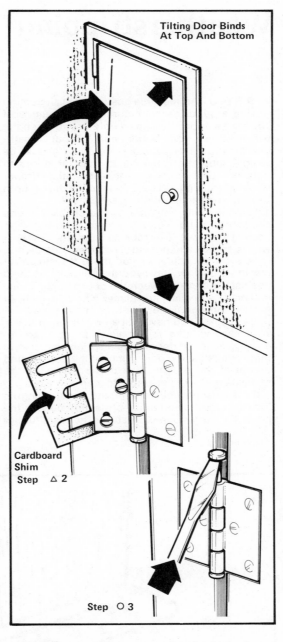

Tilting Door Binds At Top And Bottom

Cardboard Shim
Step △ 2

Step ○ 3

If the door frame is out of line from the house having settled, there is little you can do. Try placing a padded 2x4 against the frame, and then hitting the padded board several times with a hammer. Sometimes you can reset the frame just enough to allow the door to pass without sticking. If that does not work, try moving the hinges or planing off enough wood to make the door fit the misaligned frame.

A Good Chisel Makes Mortising Go Faster

The Mayhew Steel Products Company developed the Ambertuf Butt Chisel to provide the qualities that craftsmen seek in a chisel. Made of highly polished alloy steel, the Ambertuf Butt Chisel is precision balanced and boasts a razor-sharp edge. Well known as a manufacturer of fine steel hand tools, Mayhew packages six Ambertuf chisels in a set which should accommodate any mortising task around the home.

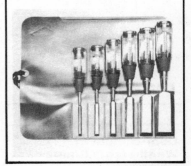

Trimmatool Makes Filing Almost Fun

Although it looks like a plane, the Trimmatool (from the Aven Division of Firth Brown Tools, Ltd., in Sheffield, England) is actually a combination file and plane. The single blade is two faced—one face coarse and the other fine. The larger handle of the two handles folds back for filing, and there is a tension nut that allows you to use the tool on either flat or curved surfaces. The blade is a curved milled tooth file that resists clogging even when used on soft metals like aluminum.

Doors

Easco Makes Quality Screwdrivers

Screwdrivers are among the tools most commonly picked up at the bargain bin, but in most cases the bargain screwdriver should be left in its bin. Buy good screwdrivers and take care of them; they'll provide a lifetime of good service. Easco makes a quality screwdriver. The cross-ground chrome-vanadium blade is strong and durable due to the high-strength steel alloy used. It is machine ground and rust-proofed, the tip is ground accurately, and the plastic handle is big enough and shaped properly for good gripping. The four-sided handle even offers a thumb pad to give you extra gripping power. Easco tools are tough enough for the pros but economical enough for do-it-yourselfers.

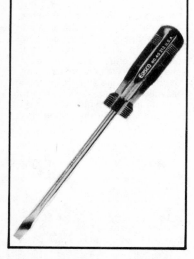

Threshold Can Stop Drafts

A worn or inadequate threshold should be replaced, and the aluminum thresholds with heavy-duty vinyl inserts are hard to beat. The vinyl is pressed down when the door closes over it, providing a good seal against drafts. Such thresholds are easy to install, as the only tools needed are a screwdriver and hacksaw. Installation screws come with the threshold. M-D thresholds—products of the Macklanburg-Duncan Company—

are fine units and come in three different heights to accommodate different floor covering types and thicknesses.

Normark Scissors Cut Many Weatherstripping Materials

Many weatherstripping materials can be cut with a good pair of household scissors like Fiskars from Normark. Fiskars feature lightweight molded handles, but they do a heavy-duty job. South-paws will be happy to know that the comfortable Fiskars come in left-handed versions, too.

Door-Bottom Weatherstrip Clears Carpeting

If an entry door lacks proper weatherstripping along its bottom due to a rug or carpet that gets in the way, Mortell's Automatic Door Bottom may be just the solution. The Mortell unit lowers snugly against the floor when the door is closed, but then rises automatically to clear the floor covering when the door opens. Consisting of a durable and flexible sealing strip set in a sturdy aluminum frame, the Mortell Automatic Door Bottom can be installed on the outside of the door in a matter of minutes. Although it comes in a 36-inch length, it can be cut to fit easily with a hacksaw.

Weatherstripping

IF YOU CAN feel little gusts of cold air coming in around the door during the winter, or if you have a door that hums a note or two when the wind blows, you better check your weatherstripping. All of your outside doors should be airtight, and the same holds true for doors to unheated basements, garages, and attics. Proper weatherstripping will save you money during both heating and air conditioning seasons.

There is really only one way to check a door's weatherstripping. You must direct a strong wind against it to see if air comes through. The best way is to use a handheld hair dryer outside and have a helper inside. As you move the stream of air along the door, have your helper hold his hand against the crack between the door and the frame and mark with chalk any places where he feels air coming through. Take your time and make a thorough check. If you have just a few minor air leaks, you may be able to fix your present weatherstripping. Most doors have a springy metal strip that fits against the door jamb all the way around except at the bottom. See if you can bend the metal flange out a little more to stop any leaks.

If the existing weatherstripping is not doing its job, you can add additional protection outside the jamb. The easiest type to install is the foam rubber strip that has a pressure sensitive adhesive backing.

1. Unroll enough of the stripping to go around the top and both sides of the door.
2. Cut the strip into pieces to fit each of these three sections.
3. Open the door and clean the face of the jamb.
4. Let the wood dry.
5. Peel the backing off of the strip and apply the foam rubber to the face of the jamb so that the door closes against it.

Here Is What You Will Need

Materials

- Chalk
- Foam rubber weatherstripping
- Cleaning solvent
- Nails
- Replacement threshold
- Metal strip weatherstripping
- Brads

Tools

● Handheld hair dryer	● Screwdriver
● Scissors	● Hacksaw
● Hammer	● Tin snips

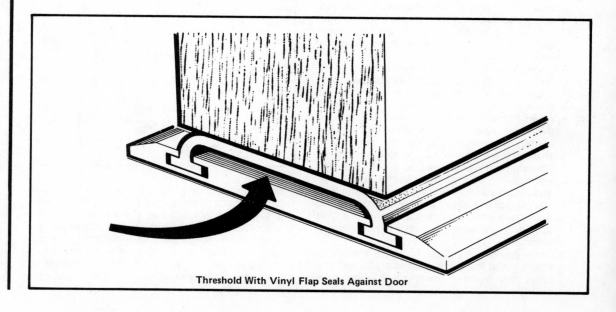

Threshold With Vinyl Flap Seals Against Door

Miniature Hacksaw Handles Hard-To-Reach Cutting

While any kind of hacksaw can cut aluminum weatherstripping and thresholds, Estwing's Mini-Saw reaches places that the frame of a regular hacksaw cannot fit into. The Mini-Saw uses regular hacksaw blades—it can even use broken parts of a blade—and it starts cuts easily, cuts flush, and can even saw curves. Featuring all-steel construction, except for the comfortable, nonslip vinyl

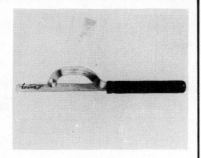

handle, the Estwing Mini-Saw can be adjusted easily with its handy locking screw.

Anchor Tapes Down Weatherstripping Problems

Anchor Continental, Inc., markets an assortment of tapes to solve weatherstripping problems. The assortment includes a regular foam tape, a double-sided foam tape, a clear poly tape, and an aluminum foil tape. All have strong adhesives designed for use indoors or out that can withstand all sorts of weather conditions and temperature extremes.

Apply Deflecto Weatherstripping Wherever You Need It

Deflecto weatherstripping, called Energy Seal, is a complete line that includes self-sticking closed-cell foam, door bottom sweeps, door jamb crack covering, garage door weatherstripping, and other types as well. Energy Seal does the job and is easy to apply.

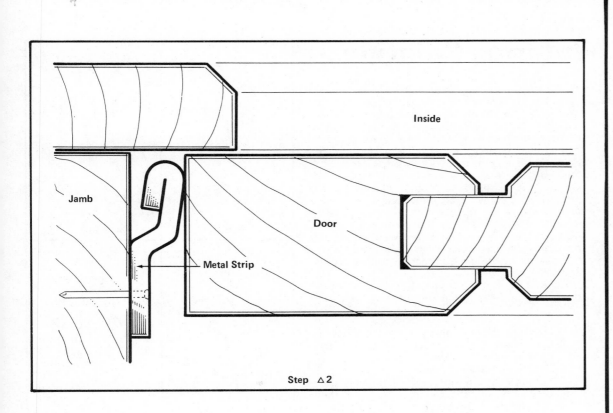

Step △2

Old-Fashioned Felt Weatherstripping Hangs In There

The first weatherstripping material to become popular was felt, and felt weatherstripping products still constitute a major share of the market. Felt possesses excellent resiliency, as well as fine wearing qualities. Moreover, when notched, flexible aluminum material is wrapped around the felt, an extremely secure and long-lasting weatherstripping results. Frost King's Serrated Metal And Felt Weatherstrip Kit exemplifies this type. The kit includes a 17-foot roll of the stripping plus the nails needed to attach it. Frost King materials are made by Thermwell Products Company, Inc.

Stronghold Nails Are Independent

Independent Nail markets the Stronghold line, which includes many nail types and sizes. The Stronghold brand appears on regular wire nails, bronze nails for marine use, colored nails, pallet nails, spiral nails, and many other special varieties. Independent also markets nails under the Screw-Tite and Kolorpin brands.

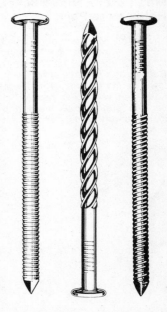

6. Recheck the door for leaks.

If the leak is at the bottom of the door, you may need a new threshold. If the threshold is the problem, you can put a new one in easily.

Aluminum thresholds with vinyl flaps that seal against the door come packed with all the screws and instructions. You can cut the aluminum to size with a hacksaw.

There are also strips of both wood and metal that you attach to the jamb with nails. You fit these strips so that they will be snug against the closed door, and then you nail them in place.

△ 1. Unroll enough of the thin metal weatherstripping for the hinge side of the door. Use tin snips to cut the strip to the exact size required.
△ 2. Place the strip against the jamb so that the springy part that flares out faces to the outside and is almost against the stop.
△ 3. Nail the strip in place by driving tiny brads in about every two inches. Tack the strip at top and bottom first to make sure that it goes on straight.
△ 4. For the latch side, attach the folded strip that comes with the roll right next to the striker plate. If there is no such strip with the roll, you can purchase one separately.

△ 5. Cut the strips to fit above and below, and nail them in place.
△ 6. Cut the strip for the top, miter it at each end, and then nail it in place.

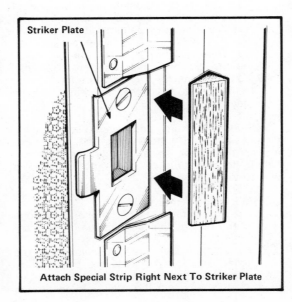

Attach Special Strip Right Next To Striker Plate

Painting

Bucket Tray Combo

E-Z Paintr offers a unique painter's tray that sits atop a reservoir which holds a substantial amount of paint. To replenish the paint supply in the tray, you merely tip the unit. Equipped with a bracket that fits over a ladder step and locks in place, the E-Z Paintr Tray is designed for use with pad applicators—a complete line of which is available from E-Z Paintr.

Exploded Tip Process For Synthetic Brushes

The Wooster Brush Company has developed a process called Exploded Tip for its synthetic brushes. The process bursts each filament into multi-flags, leaving each filament with from nine to 17 flags. What this means to the do-it-yourselfer is that a Wooster MagiKoter Brush with synthetic bristles (either polyester or nylon) will pick up more paint with each dip and flow it more evenly onto the surface.

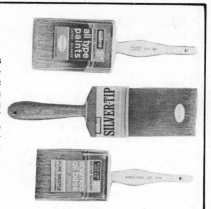

Eliminate The Mess In Pouring Paint

Among the pouring aids available to the do-it-yourself painter is Pour-Ezee, which fits over any standard one-gallon paint can and provides a drip-proof spout that lets you control and regulate the flow. When you are finished pouring, the plastic cap seals the spout airtight. And since the cap is an integral part of the one-piece Pour-Ezee unit, it can never get lost. A real mess saver, the Pour-Ezee spout can be used over and over because it is made of a special type of plastic to which paint cannot adhere.

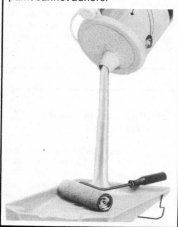

MagiKoter Handy Bucket Holds More Paint

The sturdy six-quart plastic pail from the Wooster Brush Company is called the MagiKoter Handy Bucket. Its extra capacity means fewer refills for you. The MagiKoter Handy Bucket has a flat back, a pour spout, measuring marks, and it comes with a grid screen.

Interior Painting

DO YOU HAVE interior walls that need repainting? Few do-it-yourself projects can make such a dramatic improvement in the appearance of your home and few can save you so much money over having the job done professionally. Painting can be fun, and it is easy to do well if you follow the rules. Even if you have never painted before, you can produce professional results by just following some simple directions.

Always buy top quality paint. In most cases, latex paint is your best bet. It goes on easily, dries fast, and cleans up with soap and water. After the paint dries fully, you can wash the surfaces without fear of damaging the appearance of your walls and ceilings.

The first key to a good paint job is preparation. Here are the basic steps for interior wall and ceiling preparation.

1. Inspect walls and ceilings for any protruding nails. If you find any, drive them back in and cover them with spackling paste.
2. Patch any cracks or holes.
3. Scrape away any loose or flaking paint.
4. Clean the wall and ceiling surfaces. If they are merely dusty, brushing may be all that you need to do. If there are grease spots or other dirt, however, wash your walls and ceilings.
5. Degloss any shiny surface. You can buy liquid deglossing preparations at a paint store.
6. Move all furniture, pictures, drapes, and rugs out of the room if possible. Protect everything that must stay in the room with drop cloths or newspapers.
7. Mask all trim which is adjacent to wall areas that you will paint.
8. Remove wall outlet plates and switch plates.
9. Loosen light fixtures and let them hang down. Then wrap the fixtures in plastic bags.

With the preparation completed, you are ready to start painting. Do the ceilings first, walls next, and woodwork last. Use a roller with an extension handle for painting ceilings, and follow this procedure.

△ 1. Mix the paint thoroughly.
△ 2. Use a brush to paint a border along the edge of the ceiling. This technique is called "cutting in."
△ 3. Fill up the roller tray with paint, load the roller, and roll it across the tray grid to remove excess paint.
△ 4. Start painting with the roller right next to the

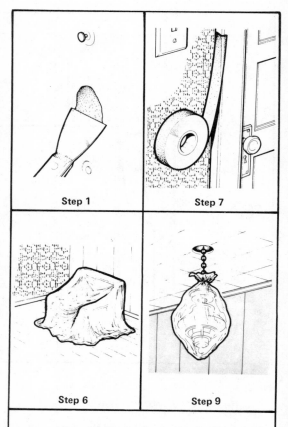

Step 1

Step 7

Step 6

Step 9

Here Is What You Will Need

Materials

- Spackling paste
- Wall cleaner
- Liquid deglosser
- Drop cloths and newspapers
- Masking tape or shirtboard
- Plastic bags
- Latex interior paint
- Latex enamel

Tools

- Hammer
- Putty knife
- Paint scraper
- Screwdriver
- Measuring tape
- Mixing stick
- Roller with extension handle
- Roller tray
- Paintbrushes
- Rag
- Sandpaper

Sash Brush Is Angled

The sash brush, angled to make it easier to get down along the baseboards, has nylon bristles for use with Benjamin Moore's Regal Aquaglo Latex Satin Finish Enamel. Note that the painter is using a shirtboard as a moving masker to prevent paint from spotting the flooring.

No More Paint Spatters

If you've ever painted with a paint roller, you know how easy it is to end up with paint specks all over you. A lightweight accessory called the Spatter Shield can keep you clean. The reusable plastic shield snaps in place on all types of standard roller frames, and is easy to clean after use. A product of the Kagil Corporation, Spatter Shield is available at many paint stores.

Corner Paint Pad

Cutting in is the process of painting strips where a wall meets a ceiling, another wall, a door, or a window frame. You can do your cutting in with a small brush, but Padco's Corner Paint Pad is a real time saver. Angled to paint both surfaces in a corner simultaneously, the Padco Corner Paint Pad can also be used for trim work or any other single-surface painting.

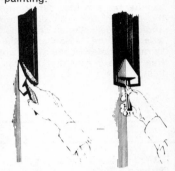

cut-in strip. Use slow steady strokes, working back and forth over the width of the ceiling. Fast strokes spin the roller and can sling paint. Use cross strokes to smooth the paint on the ceiling.

△ 5. Keep working in strips across, always working against the wet edge of previously painted strips. If you allow a strip of paint to dry, you may leave streaks when you paint over it. Therefore, be sure to paint the entire ceiling without stopping.

For wall painting, follow the same procedure just described for painting ceilings.

○ 1. Cut in along corners and around doors and windows.
○ 2. Start in the left-hand corner if you are right handed. Begin at the top and work up and down all the way, moving across as you finish each strip. Again, use cross strokes to smooth; always work against the wet edge; and avoid having to stop in the middle of a wall.
○ 3. Roll horizontally to paint the narrow strips over doors and windows.
○ 4. If you did not mask the woodwork with tape, use a shirtboard as a moving masker. Should you happen to get some wall paint on the trim, use a rag to wipe it off as you go.

When you finish all the wall, you are ready to go to work on the woodwork. You should use an enamel on the trim, and it should have some gloss to it. A glossy enamel is easier to clean than a flat paint.

□ 1. Clean all trim surfaces and remove the gloss by sanding or by applying a surface preparation chemical available at the paint store. These chemicals degloss and also leave a tacky surface which makes the new paint adhere better. Be sure to follow the directions on the label.
□ 2. Mix the enamel paint thoroughly.
□ 3. Although you can use rollers or foam pads to paint large flat areas, appropriately sized brushes are better for painting most woodwork.
□ 4. Start with the baseboards and use a moving masker as you paint.
□ 5. Do the windows next, but be sure to mask the panes of glass and to open the sash about three or four inches before you start painting. Then, after you paint but before the paint starts to set, move the sash up or down to prevent window from sticking.
□ 6. Do the doors and door frames last. Remove all hardware before painting the doors, and make sure that the enamel is dry before reinstalling the hardware.

Step △ 5

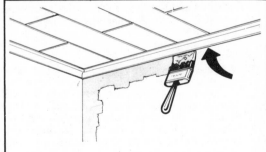

Step ○ 4

Paint Pads Are Popular Applicators

Paint pads are catching up quickly on rollers as the most popular means of applying paint. The pad applicators, which fit on regular extension handles, come in widths of up to nine inches and in various textures for different surfaces. Replacement pads are available, although the pads are reusable in most cases.

Patch Before You Paint

You must patch cracks and holes before you begin painting. Muralo's Spackle is a vinyl patch that comes in ready-to-use paste form and in powder form to be mixed with water. Tools used to apply Spackle vinyl patch clean up easily with soap and warm water. Muralo also manufactures Exterior Spackle for use outside.

Painting

Latex Stains Made For The Do-It-Yourselfer

The paint division of the United States Gypsum Company has expanded its specialty product line with the introduction of Durabond Latex Rustic Stains. Geared for do-it-yourself application, these stains offer easy application, quick (10 to 30 minutes) drying, and simple clean-up. These stains resist fading, chalking, and weathering, and they can form a flat durable finish on both new and previously stained or painted wood surfaces. Nonflammable, Durabond Latex Rustic Stains are free of lead, mercury, and asbestos.

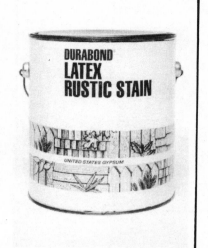

This Paint Bucket Is A Box

More convenient than a tray or a bucket is the new Paint Box Bucket from Padco, Inc. A rigid plastic unit that either hangs from a rung of your straight ladder or stands by itself, the box holds a gallon of paint and comes with a plastic grid. It is designed primarily for use with paint pad applicators, but it can also be used with brushes or rollers. The Paint Box Bucket can also serve as a handy tool tray.

Big Roller Handles Big Jobs In Big Hurry

Some paint jobs, such as covering exterior masonry walls, seem to take forever. But the Big Job Paint Kit, manufactured by Adams Products Company, Inc., is made to cut your work time on such projects to the bare minimum. The kit includes a 12-inch roller frame, a 12-inch roller cover with ½-inch nap, and a 44-inch extension handle.

Latex Works Well Outside Too

In most cases, you can use latex exterior paint with excellent results. Most of the failures of any paint job are due to lack of proper preparation rather than any intrinsic deficiency on the part of the paint. Devoe's Vinyl Acrylic Latex provides excellent results on exterior wood. It is fast drying, becoming dry to the touch in a half hour and ready for another coat—if necessary—after three hours. Highly resistant to chalking, blistering, and cracking, it also withstands damage from sun, fumes, and salty air. Of course, its chief advantage becomes apparent after the painting is finished, as soap and water make clean-up a quick and easy task.

Thick Paint Glides On

Glidden Spred Gel-Flo exterior alkyd paint is so thick you can scoop it up, yet it glides on with a roller or brush. The extra-thick consistency hides hairline cracks, pits, and other minor flaws, and generally requires only one coat to cover most colors. Spred Gel-Flo comes in several white and off-white shades, as well as in many ready-to-use trim colors.

Exterior Painting

THE SAME TRICKS of the trade for interior painting apply to exterior painting as well. Preparation is again a big part of a successful paint job. Here are the steps to follow to prepare exterior walls for a fresh coat of paint.

1. Caulk around all doors and windows and any other joints that might let in moisture or air.
2. Repair or replace any damaged wood or other exterior siding material.
3. Remove all loose paint with either a scraper or a wire brush. Feather any chipped edges by sanding away the sharp edges of the remaining paint.
4. Reset any loose nails.
5. Prime all bare spots with a primer suggested for use with the paint you have selected. Latex exterior paint offers the same ease of application and cleaning as latex interior paint, and—when used properly—it provides long lasting coverage. Nevertheless, some people still prefer oil-based paint for exterior use.
6. Be sure to remove any mildew on exterior surfaces. Add a mildewcide to the paint if mildew has been a problem, but do not expect the mildewcide to kill the existing fungus. You must do that before you paint.
7. Make sure that all surfaces you intend to paint are clean. Hose off any loose dirt.
8. Wait until the surfaces are dry before starting to paint.
9. Cover walks, drives, patios, and shrubs with tarps. Plastic suit bags from the dry cleaners are very handy for wrapping shrubbery.

You will get the best results if you paint the outside of your house when the temperature is mild, the humidity is low to moderate, and when no rain is forecast. Naturally, you must take the proper safety precautions. If you are going to rely on a ladder, make sure that it is sturdy and that it is tall enough for you to reach all areas without stretching. Although buying scaffolding for a job you do only once every few years makes no sense, renting scaffolding does. Most rental outfits can provide the scaffolding you need at very reasonable rates.

With all the preparation completed, you are ready to start painting your house. Follow these simple steps for professional results.

△ 1. Mix the paint well.
△ 2. Try not to paint in the hot sun.
△ 3. Start at the top, completing all broad main areas first. Work in a band across the width, painting a swath of about three to four feet wide, and continue painting such bands all the way down.
△ 4. When you finish the main part of the house, go back and paint the trim. Pad the ends of a straight ladder that must rest against the newly painted areas in order not to mar the new paint job.
△ 5. Wait to apply a second coat until the first one is fully dry.

Step 1

Nylon Brushes Are Tops For Latex Paint

H&G's Tynex (a DuPont product) nylon filament brushes are Dulshene-treated, an exclusive process by which the nylon filaments are given tiny barbs all along their lengths throughout the entire stock of the brush. Already flagged, tipped, and blended, the filaments are then put together to form a brush that will pick up and lay on an exceptional amount of paint. H&G Industries also make orel brushes that can be used for latex and oil-based paints, though most often used for latex.

Latex Stain Makes Exterior Beauty Easy

Some wood surfaces look better stained then painted, but many do-it-yourselfers would never think of staining exterior siding or trim because they recall the messy staining jobs of years ago. But the new latex stains, like DuPont's Lucite Exterior Stain, are a different story. Lucite stains come in eight solid colors that resist chalking, fading, cracking, blistering, and peeling. They can be thinned with water for a semi-transparent effect that lets the wood grain show through, and they dry in about an hour. Best of all, though, Lucite Latex Exterior Stain cleans up like latex paint, requiring nothing more than soap and water.

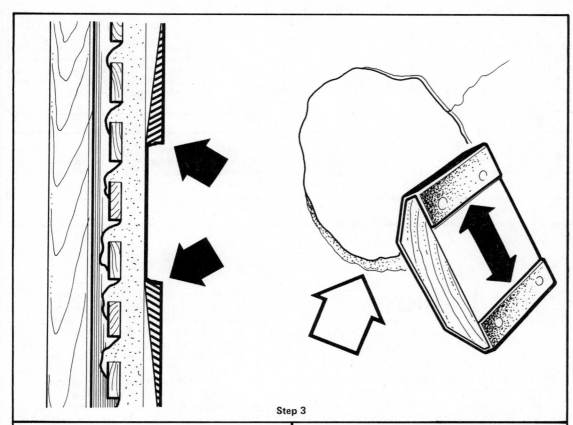

Step 3

Paint Conditioner Solves Chalk Removal Problem

Flood Company markets a product called E-B that, when mixed with latex paint, forms a bonding agent that does away with the need to remove chalking. If the old paint is sound, E-B (Emulsa-Bond) actually bonds the chalk, converting it to an undercoat. E-B contains Penetrol, a Flood non-evaporative paint conditioner that extends the drying time of latex paint, making it easier for the slower painter to do a professional job.

Here Is What You Will Need
Materials
- Caulk
- Sandpaper
- Primer
- Tarps and plastic bags
- Latex or oil-based exterior paint

Tools
- Caulking gun
- Paint scraper or wire brush
- Hammer
- Garden hose
- Ladder or scaffolding
- Mixing stick
- Paintbrushes

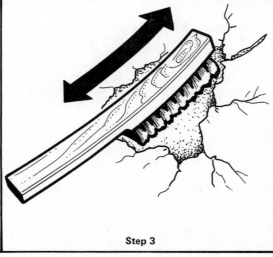

Step 3

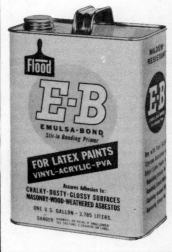

Painting

Wire Brush Removes Paint Quickly

The wire brush from Wright Bernet Company is a sturdy paint remover that comes with a handy scraper on the back. In addition to helping out in painting chores, the wire brush is a useful tool for rust removal, brick and masonry cleaning, and many other household tasks.

Feather Edges With Sanding Block

After you remove all the loose paint, it is imperative that you feather the sharp edges where paint meets bare surface. The Bear Sanding Block is versatile because it has a little resiliency to adapt to mild contours, but still is solid enough to do an effective job on flat surfaces. The Bear Sander, called Speed-Grit, holds an entire roll of abrasive to prevent your running out in the middle of the job. It loads much like a camera. Bear products are made by the Coated Abrasives Division of the Norton Company.

Wire Brush Drill Attachment Removes Loose Paint

Although the wire brush can be particularly helpful in removing paint and rust from metal objects before painting, it is not always easy to reach all the spots on grill work or metal lawn furniture with the traditional wire brush. But Arco's End Brush can get into many tight spots. Available in coarse or fine wire grades and made to fit any electric drill, the Arco End Brush will take much of the elbow grease out of the paint removal chores that befall you.

Wonder Brushes Do The Job For Budget-Minded Handymen

When you need an inexpensive paintbrush, look for the Wonder Brush display at hardware and paint stores. Available in two sizes—larger brushes are in the Big Job display, while the smaller ones are in the Little Job rack—all Wonder Brushes feature bristles of 100 percent golden nylon epoxy set in plastic handles. The brushes are imported and marketed by Wonder Color, Inc.

Surface Preparation Foils Failures

One of the major causes of paint failing to adhere properly on woodwork can be traced to the old paint's glossy finish. You must remove that finish before you paint. One of the really good surface preparation compounds is Paso made by Charles Paint Research, Inc. Paso not only deglosses, but it also leaves the surface tacky, allowing the new paint to adhere even better. Especially good when you want to apply latex paint over an oil-based finish, Paso is easy to use as long as you follow the directions carefully.

Remove All Wax And Grease Before Painting

One major cause of paint failure is a surface that was not properly cleaned of wax and grease. Special wax removers can be costly, but the best wax and grease remover for many surfaces is plain, inexpensive paint thinner. Sunnyside Specs Paint Thinner is low in odor, and you can apply it with a rag and then wipe it off. When working with any paint thinner, however, you must observe all caution notices.

Mildewcide Can Be Added To Paint

You can fight against mildew attacking your paint job by using a mildew-resistant paint. If your paint does not come with a mildew inhibitor, you can purchase a mildewcide additive for mixing with the paint. In fact, your paint dealer can mix the mildewcide additive at the same time he mixes the color into your paint.

Paint Failures

SOMETIMES PAINT problems lie within the paint itself, but most times, it is the fault of the painter. Usually, the preparation by the painter is not enough. Here are some common failures and what causes them.

1. Peeling—paint curls away from surfaces, usually because of moisture in the wood. You have to find out where the moisture is coming from and stop it before you can expect a good paint job. Often, the cause is painting over wet wood. It can also be from moisture within the house pushing its way out. If you cannot control the moisture, try latex primer coat and latex paint. Latex will allow some moisture to pass right through the paint. The other usual cause for peeling is that the paint was applied over a dirty surface or a glossy surface. To undo the damage, all the loose paint flakes must be scraped off with a wire brush and the surface sanded to feather any sharp edges. Bare spots must be primed before the new top coat is applied.
2. Alligatoring—paint crawls into islands; this problem looks just like its name implies and results from the top coat not adhering to the paint below. It can be caused when a paint not compatible with the paint below is used, or it can be caused when the second coat is applied before the first one is fully dry.
3. Blistering—paint rises from the surface forming hollow blisters. Same causes as peeling; moisture in the wood.
4. Wrinkling—paint forms uneven surface, caused when the paint you are using is too thick and the surface starts to dry before the bottom of the layer does. This will cause wrinkles. It can also happen if you paint in cold weather; the cold surface slows drying underneath. To recoat, make sure the new paint is the proper consistency and be sure to brush it out as you apply. Before doing this, you will have to sand the wrinkled area smooth, and in some cases, remove the paint altogether.
5. Chalking—paint has dusty surface. Oil-based exterior paint is generally made to chalk. This means that a very fine powdery layer is removed when it rains, acting as a self-cleaning system for the surface. In most cases, this is desirable; however, it is not desirable if the chalking runs down over the brick below. In that situation, you will need a non-chalking exterior paint. Excessive chalking is not desirable and indicates that you will be repainting much sooner than you

Boxing Is Best Way To Mix Paint

All paint should be mixed thoroughly before it is used and then stirred regularly during use. The initial mixing is best done by a process called "boxing." Pour off about two thirds of the paint into another container. Use a paint paddle, available free at most paint stores, to stir the remaining paint, making sure to explore the bottom of the can with the paddle to lift any settled pigment. Add the paint you previously poured off, stirring it in as you pour. Finally, pour the paint back and forth between the two containers for complete mixing. You should perform this boxing process just before you are ready to paint—even if the paint was machine mixed at the store.

Aid Makes Latex Painting Smoother

If you experience difficulty in getting a smooth finish with latex paints because they start drying too fast, try Smooth-Aid, a product which, when stirred into either latex enamel or flat wall paints (interior or exterior), slows down the drying process. Problems of brush and roller marks, lapping, skips, and streaks are quickly eliminated. Smooth-Aid also cuts down on drag, since the paint goes on easier and smoother.

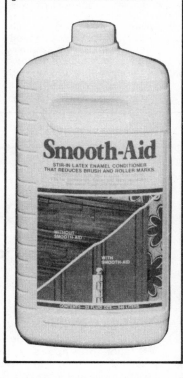

Straining Kit Purifies Paint

Using leftover paint can make good sense in terms of your home repair budget . . . unless lumps and/or impurities leave you with a bad paint job. As a preventive measure, you should always strain old paint. An inexpensive kit from Gerson will do the job. The kit, which comes with a paint can opener and a stirring paddle, has six strainers in assorted meshes to remove flakes, lumps, and impurities.

Peeling Paint Must Be Removed

You cannot paint over chipped or peeling paint and expect good results; all the loose paint must be removed. There are many ways to remove the old paint, but probably the fastest method involves scraping it off with a quality paint scraper. The Red Devil flip-over model has two blades, making it suitable for fine or coarse scraping. The blades are of high carbon steel and can either be resharpened with a file or replaced. After removing the paint chips, feather the edges to provide a smooth surface for your paint.

Here Is What You Will Need

Materials
- Latex paint and primer
- Laundry bleach
- Laundry detergent
- Mildew remover

Tools
- Wire brush
- Sandpaper
- Paintbrush
- Garden hose
- Stiff broom

should. Too much chalking is caused by a chemical imbalance. This can be caused by an inferior paint that never had a proper chemical balance. It can also be caused from a previous coat of paint that was too thin or was placed over a porous surface that absorbed too much of the paint's binders. To repaint over a chalking surface, you should hose down the surface with a strong spray, then use a stiff broom to remove the powder. If this does not remove all the chalking, after it dries try this solution: mix a quart of laundry bleach, a tablespoon of laundry detergent, and enough warm water to make a two gallon mixture. Scrub with this solution and then hose off with a strong spray.

6. Mildew—painted surface has moldy growth on it. This is not a paint failure. However, if you paint over a mildewed surface, the mildew will come through the new paint film. The mildew problem will have to be solved before you can repaint. Use a commercial mildew preparation according to the directions of the manufacturer.

7. Running sags—paint has wavy, irregular surface. The probable cause is poor brushing technique in which you failed to brush out the paint to a consistent coat. To correct it after the paint is dry, you will just have to sand and repaint.

8. Paint that will not dry—paint surface remains tacky. This is a sign of inferior, low-quality paint. If you apply the paint too thickly or during too humid a period, a poor paint will be slow to dry. However, a good paint will dry. If you have a poor paint, removing it and repainting is the only answer.

This sounds like there are lots of ways for your paint job to go wrong, but if you prepare the surface properly, use a quality paint of the proper type, and apply it according to the manufacturer's directions under the right weather conditions, it will turn out just the way you hoped it would.

Painting

Paint Spreaders Handle Shutters With Ease

Painting the louvers in shutters with a brush is not easy — even for professional painters. But the small, flexible, and disposable Paint Spreaders from Padco are great for getting into louvers and other nooks and crannies as well. The nylon bristled applicator pad, measuring 2⅛x2 inches, is bonded to a fiberboard backing that features lift-up finger grips to make painting especially easy. Morever, since the Padco Paint Spreaders are quite inexpensive, you merely toss them away when the job is done.

Scrape Paint-Spotted Windows Clean With Child-Safe Unit

Among the multitude of razor blade holders around to rid splattered paint from your window panes, there is one that is designed to prevent children from accidentally opening the blade. Gerson's Child-Safe Razor Blade Scraper features a patented safety button that locks the blade into the handle; the spare blade compartment also locks. Like competitive units, the Gerson Child-Safe Razor Blade Scraper (a product of Louis M. Gerson Company Inc.,) does a good job of scraping windows clean of splattered paint.

Latex Is The Big Favorite Inside

Due to the ease with which it can be both applied and cleaned up, latex paint is by far the favorite of do-it-yourself painters. A flat latex paint like Pratt and Lambert Vapex is a good choice for interior walls. Vapex is washable, as is its companion for woodwork, Pratt and Lambert Aqua-Satin Latex Enamel. Both Vapex and Aqua-Satin offer good covering qualities and go on smoothly with a brush, pad, or roller.

A Masking Tape That Goes Down And Comes Up Faster

Since there are so many brands of masking tape available, it can be difficult to choose one over the others. If you want to try something different, though, buy a roll of Easy-Mask, a product of Daubert Chemical Company. Easy-Mask, pressure sensitive along only one edge of its 3¾-inch width, both goes down and comes up faster. Its extra width masks more than conventional tapes, and you can slip the edge of newspaper under the non-sticky edge for additional coverage. Most paint stores carry Easy-Mask.

Painting Doors, Windows, and Shutters

WHEN IT COMES to putting a coat of paint on doors or windows, you will get much better results if you follow the prescribed sequence of professional painters. You may have been lucky and had good results before without even knowing that there was such a sequence, but by following these guidelines you can be certain that your doors and windows will come out looking professionally painted.

First, consider painting a paneled door.

1. Arrange to have the time to finish the door completely without stopping.
2. Start with the inset panels at the top, painting all the panels and the molding around them.
3. Next, paint across the top rail.
4. Work on down to cover other horizontal rails.
5. Finish the door by painting the side rails.
6. If both sides of the door need painting, follow the same sequence before painting the edges.
7. Now, paint the top edge, followed by the hinge and latch edges.

Here is the step-by-step procedure for painting double-hung windows.

△ 1. Raise the bottom sash more than half way up, and then lower the upper sash until the bottom rail of the upper sash is several inches below the lower sash.
△ 2. Paint the lower rail of the upper sash and on up the sides (stiles) as far as you can go.
△ 3. Next, paint the outside and inside channels as far as you can go above the lower sash.
△ 4. Paint across the head jamb.
△ 5. Now lower both windows, and paint the out-

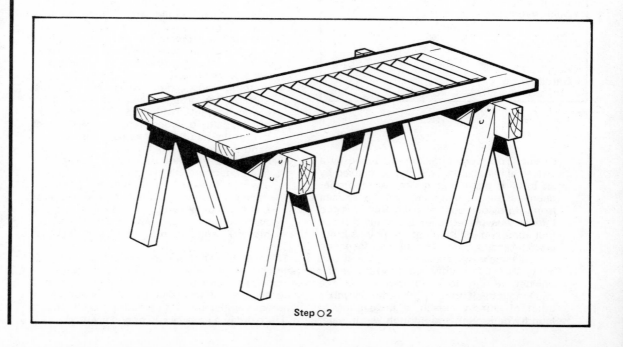

Step ○ 2

Trim Guard Does Away With Masking

An odd looking plastic gadget called the Dual Trim Guard features a short section for use when painting windows and hard-to-reach corners of all sorts. The longer edge is an ideal moving masker for baseboards and other large areas. A product of Red Devil, Inc., the Dual Trim Guard is made of a plastic that can be cleaned easily after every use.

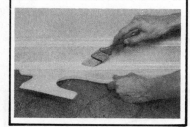

Masking Goes Quicker With Wrist-Mount Dispenser

The Quicker Sticker is a novel tool. A wrist-mounted tape dispenser, it makes masking and other taping chores go much faster and easier. The plastic wheel holds any of the most commonly used widths of masking tape, and the plastic band straps the tape and wheel to your wrist. You always know where the masking tape is, and thus you never lose painting time trying to locate the roll. The dispenser itself is lightweight and comfortable; the only weight factor is the tape, but if you use narrow rolls you'll hardly notice that the Quicker Sticker is strapped to your wrist.

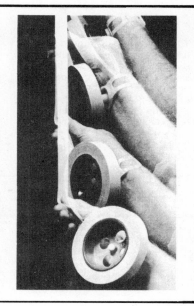

Heavy-Duty Plastic Drop Cloths

Stop rummaging through your supply of old sheets to protect floors and furniture during a paint job and invest in a package of 9x12-foot plastic drop cloths. Red Devil, Inc., offers heavy-duty reusable plastic tarps that cover everything and that clean up nicely with a damp cloth.

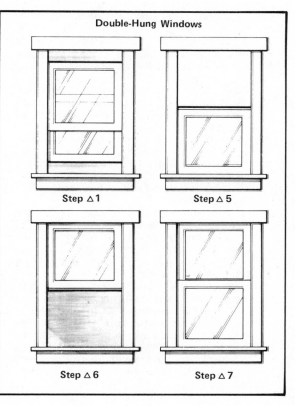

Panel Door

Double-Hung Windows

Step 7 · Step 3 · Step 2 · Step 5 · Step 4

Step △1 · Step △5 · Step △6 · Step △7

Deglosser Makes Things Tacky

Any of the several liquid deglossers on the market can save you a substantial amount of elbow grease over the old method of preparing a painted surface with sandpaper. D. I. Y. Deglosser from Red Devil, Inc., takes away all the gloss of the previous paint, and, at the same time, removes grease, wax, and dirt from the surface. It also creates a temporary tacky surface, creating a stronger bond between the surface and the new finish. It is, of course, extremely important that you read and follow the directions for best results and observe the caution notices.

side and then inside channels on both sides.
△ 6. Raise both windows and paint the remainder of the two channels.
△ 7. Lower the bottom sash and finish the stiles and top rails of the upper sash.

Here Is What You Will Need
Materials
● Latex paint
Tools
● Paintbrushes

△ 8. Raise the lower sash a few inches and paint it.
△ 9. Be sure to move both the upper and lower sash before the paint can dry, sealing the sash and causing the windows to stick.

Shutters seldom require much of a sequence, but they usually turn out much better if you remove them from the wall before painting.

○ 1. Examine the shutters to see how they are attached. Decorative shutters are often nailed in place (even to brick walls).
○ 2. Do whatever you must to remove the shutters, and then lay them on a flat surface.
○ 3. Use a narrow brush to paint the louvers first, the frame second, and the edges last.

Painting

Breathe New Life Into Dead Brushes

Brushes that were not properly cleaned and even those that have been allowed to harden in paint can often be revived. Select a prepared brush cleaner, and then follow all the manufacturer's suggestions. Sunnyside's water rinsable Liquid Brush Cleaner does a good job of restoring dried, hardened brushes. Most brush cleaners carry some caution notices; heed them.

A Bonanza Of Brush Care Tips

You can learn a bundle of tips about brush care and cleaning in the *Super Handyman's Encyclopedia Of Home Repair Hints*. In addition to brush and paint information, this book is a one volume A to Z encyclopedia of handy hints covering every phase of home repair. Written by syndicated columnist Al Carrell and published by Prentice-Hall, Inc., the book is available in both hardbound and paperback editions.

Comb Your Brush

To get dried paint from a brush, use brush cleaner to soften the paint and then comb the bristles. Red Devil's Brush Comb and Roller Cleaning Tool has strong, chrome-plated steel teeth to break up and comb out any paint left in the brush. The half circle on the other side of the solvent-resistant plastic handle is designed to squeeze paint out from a roller.

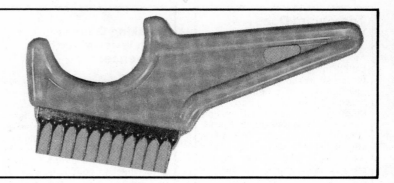

Paintbrush Care

ALMOST EVERY so-called painting expert recommends buying only top quality brushes. You would be wise to follow the experts' advice. If you fail to take proper care of your brushes, though, even the best ones might not last beyond the first paint job. On the other hand, a good paintbrush can give you years of service when you take proper care of it. Here are some rules to follow to extend the life of your brushes.

Step △ 6

1. Never use your brush to stir paint. To do so could cause it to become floppy. Instead, use those wooden mixing paddles available free at the paint store.
2. Never dip your brush into the paint bucket more than half way up the bristles. You should try to prevent paint from getting into the heel.
3. Never paint with the side of your brush. That causes curling.
4. To remove excess paint, tap the brush against the inside of the can instead of drawing the brush across the edge of the can. The latter method can cause the bristles to finger, which means that they separate into clumps.
5. Never leave the brush in the bucket. Its own weight will bend the bristles against the bottom of the can and cause them to curl.
6. If you stop painting for a short period of time while applying a latex paint, wrap the brush in a damp paper towel or insert it in a plastic sandwich bag. Latex paint dries quickly, and partially dried paint in a brush can stiffen the bristles.

7. Pick the right brush for the job. For example, use only nylon brushes for latex paint. No brush is capable of doing all your painting, and forcing a brush to do things it is not shaped or sized to do will damage the brush.

The best way to get the most mileage out of a brush is to clean it immediately after each use. Here are the basics of brush cleaning.

△ 1. The solution in which you clean your brush can make a big difference. For latex paints, use soap or detergent and warm water; avoid putting nylon brushes in solvents. For oil-based paints, use paint thinner or turpentine. For shellac, use wood alcohol. For lacquer, use lacquer thinner. For varnish, use paint thinner or turpentine.
△ 2. Let the brush soak for a few minutes to saturate the bristles completely. Make sure to use enough cleaner to cover all of the bristles. Suspend the brush in such a way that the bristles do not rest on the bottom of the container.
△ 3. Work the brush against the side of the container for several minutes to get the paint out.
△ 4. Squeeze the bristles with your hands. Start at the heel of the brush and work to the tip.
△ 5. Work the brush against a section of newspaper to remove excess solvent and to check whether all the paint is gone. If there is still some paint present, repeat the cleaning process.
△ 6. With latex paint, you can just rinse the brush out by holding it under a faucet.
△ 7. When the brush is clean, shake out the excess solvent or water and comb out the bristles.
△ 8. Wash solvent-cleaned brushes in warm, soapy water, and comb them again to separate the inner bristles and to allow the brushes to dry straight.

Here Is What You Will Need

Materials

- Soap or detergent
- Paint thinner or turpentine
- Wood alcohol
- Lacquer thinner
- Aluminum foil
- Linseed oil
- Brush cleaner
- Newspapers

Tools

- Wooden mixing paddles
- Comb
- Wire brush or putty knife
- Bucket and rod

A Brush-Soaking Tip

An empty coffee can with a plastic lid makes an ideal brush soaker because the brush can be suspended without the bristles touching the bottom and because the lid seals the can to prevent solvent loss through evaporation. Make two slits in the center of the plastic lid to form an X, push the brush handle through the X, and put the lid in place.

Save Money With A Turpentine Substitute

Nu-Turp, a substitute for turpentine, looks like and even smells like turpentine and it does all the same basic tasks as turpentine, but it does them at a much smaller cost. Nu-Turp is made by T&R Chemicals, Inc., and is packaged in pints, quarts, one- and five-gallon cans, as well as in 55-gallon drums for industrial use. Of course, you won't notice much of a savings when you just clean a few brushes, but if you find yourself going through a substantial amount of turpentine when you work around the house, you'll appreciate the economy as well as the performance of Nu-Turp turpentine substitute.

Enjoy Convenience Of Brush Cleaner In Small Pouch

Red Devil's D.I.Y. Sav-A-Brush comes in a three-ounce pouch of powder which mixes with water to make one quart of brush cleaner. A quart is usually an ample amount for most do-it-yourself brush clean-up tasks. Not only does Sav-A-Brush restore old, paint-hardened brushes, but it also can remove paint from clothes and other places paint should not be. It works well on all types of paint.

Step △2

Step △7

Even a clean brush must be stored correctly or it will go bad before you need to use it again. Here are some storage hints.

O 1. Always let brushes dry by suspending them with the bristles down.
O 2. Wrap natural bristle brushes in aluminum foil after they have dried. Wrap carefully to hold the brush in its proper shape during storage, and pour in a little linseed oil before crimping the foil around the handle.

If you neglected your brushes and now they are hard with caked paint, here are some steps you can take to restore them to usefulness.

☐ 1. Go to the paint store and buy a commercial brush cleaner. Some are liquid, while others are dry and must be mixed with water.

☐ 2. Let the brush soak in the cleaner. If there is dried paint up under the metal ferrule, make sure that the brush gets into the cleaner that deep.
☐ 3. When the cleaner has softened the paint sufficiently, use a wire brush or putty knife to scrape the residue away. Work from the ferrule downward.
☐ 4. Rinse the brush in the cleaner. If you still can see caked paint, soak the brush some more and repeat the cleaning steps.
☐ 5. Now follow all the steps as if you had just finished painting with the brush.

You will not be able to reclaim all your old brushes caked with paint, but it is worth a try because brush cleaner costs much less than new brushes. If you treat your paintbrushes properly from the start, of course, you need never worry about getting in such a fix again.

Savogran Makes Non-Solvent And Solvent Brush Cleaners

Just mix with water and Savogran's powdered TSP brush cleaner is ready to go to work on tough brush cleaning jobs. Unlike solvent cleaners, though, TSP is non-flammable. Savogran's TSP is an ammoniated heavy-duty cleaner that can handle smoke and soot stains; concrete, rust, and grease stains; and other tough cleaning chores. Savogran also makes a solvent-type brush cleaner called Kwikeeze.

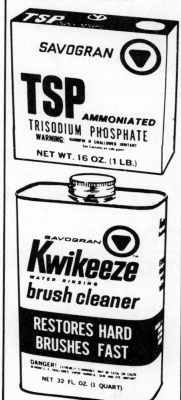

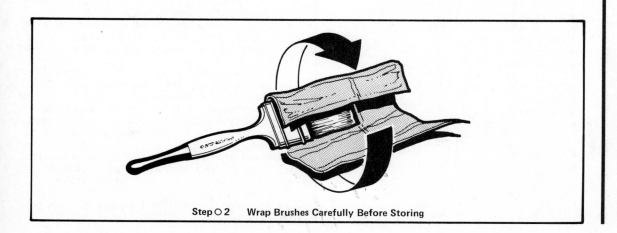

Step O2   Wrap Brushes Carefully Before Storing

Painting

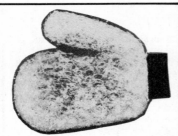

Mitt Can Make Painting Metal Easier

A painter's mitt can give you a hand. Made of material much like that found on a paint roller, a mitt like the Spee-Dee Mitt from Eller

Manufacturing Company, Inc., comes in handy for painting grille work, railings, round columns, and many other metal objects. Merely dip the mitt into the paint and then apply to the metal surface.

Make Your Own Spray Paint

With the Preval Spraymaker aerosol power unit, you can make any paint into spray paint. The unit, which contains three ounces of propellant, has a molded collar that attaches to a six-ounce graduated container. A pushbutton on top activates the sprayer. For best results, you should thin paint to the same consistency as recommended for conventional spray equipment. The Preval Spraymaker is a product of the Precision Valve Corporation.

Rust Stopper Paints, Primers

Rust-Oleum paints and primers are especially formulated to prevent rust from attacking metal surfaces. Speedy Dry, a fast-drying Rust-Oleum aerosol paint, becomes dry to the touch in half an hour and comes in many colors. Rust-Oleum also makes brush-on paints, and the company's primer—769 Damp-Proof Red—soaks right through rust down to the bare metal to drive out air and moisture, preventing future rust from forming.

Little Job Can Be A Big Helper

Little Job, a Derusto product from DAP, is a small can of spray enamel that comes in a large number of colors. The ideal size for all sorts of small metal-painting tasks or touch-ups, Little Job is very quick drying. As with all sprays, shake Little Job well before using, and remember that several light coats are usually much better than a single heavy one.

Painting Metal

PROBLEMS IN painting metal—like problems in painting all other materials—usually emanate from faulty preparation. If you prepare the surface properly, the work involved in actually applying the coating should go quite rapidly, and the results should be attractive and long lasting.

Here are the steps to follow in painting bare metal that has never been painted before and that does not have a galvanized coating.

1. Remove all rust with an abrasive, a wire brush, a chemical remover, or a combination of these items. A power sander can be a big help in rust removal.
2. Clean the surface. A quick application of a solvent will remove any oils, grease, or dirt.
3. Always use a primer or a paint containing a rust preventive. Your selection of a primer should be governed by the nature of the top coat you plan to apply. The label on the paint can tells you which primer to use; follow that recommendation.
4. Be sure to allow sufficient time for the primer to dry completely.
5. Apply the top coat, either by brushing it on or by spraying it on. If you spray, make

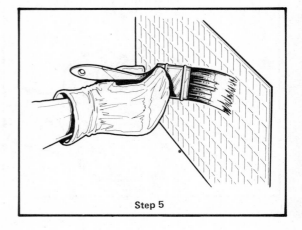

Step 5

certain that you protect nearby items from the overspray. If a second coat is needed, make sure that the first coat is fully dry before applying the second.

New metal requires some special preparation. Here are the keys to paint metal fresh from the mill.

△ 1. New metal is covered with an oily film that must be removed. Any mineral spirit paint thinner can remove the film.
△ 2. Galvanized metal should not be painted until it weathers from six months to a year. If for some reason you cannot wait for it to weather, bathe the entire surface with pure white vinegar to remove most of the new-metal film. Rinse the vinegar away and let the metal dry before painting.
△ 3. Be sure to use a primer—like a zinc-chromate based primer—that is made especially for galvanized metal.
△ 4. New aluminum should be given a scuff sanding with steel wool to etch the surface and allow the paint to take a better bite.

When painting previously painted surfaces that are still sound, you need only clean away all the dirt, dust, wax, oil, or grease. If the existing paint has a gloss, degloss it. Then you're ready to paint. If the surface shows chipped or rusted places, remove the rust, feather the edges, and spot prime.

Metal that is constantly exposed to salt-laden moist air must be cleaned to get rid of all traces of salt. Warm water and detergent followed by rinsing with a hose will get rid of the salt, but always make certain that the surface is dry before painting.

Here Is What You Will Need
Materials

- Abrasive or chemical rust remover
- Cleaning solvent
- Primer with rust preventive
- Paint with rust preventive
- Paint thinner
- White vinegar
- Zinc-chromate primer
- Steel wool
- Deglosser
- Sandpaper
- Detergent

Tools

- Wire brush
- Power sander
- Paintbrushes
- Paint sprayer
- Hose

Destroy Rust And Tarnish With Magic

Rid 'O' Rust, a product of the Magic American Chemical Corporation, is a special cleaner for removing rust, dirt, and tarnish from all types of metal as well as from sinks and tubs. Easy to use, Rid 'O' Rust comes in tubes and it polishes while it cleans. Then, after all the rust or tarnish is gone, a thin film of Rid 'O' Rust remains to protect the metal from future corrosion.

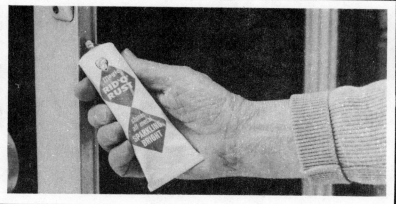

Naval Jelly Makes No Jokes About Rust

Although Duro's Naval Jelly sounds like a funny product, it is really a serious way to fight rust. Very simple to use, you just brush Naval Jelly on the metal surface, let it do its thing, and then wash it off. The rust disappears; you can forget all about onerous tasks of sanding, wire brushing, and scraping. Duro Naval Jelly is a product of the Woodhill Chemical Sales Corporation.

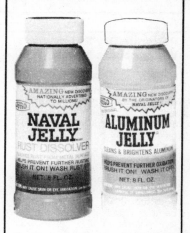

Cleaning Metal

DIFFERENT METALS develop different types of tarnish and, therefore, require different cleansing treatments. The two biggest problems are oxidation and rust. Oxidation occurs on bronze, copper, brass, aluminum, and other metals, while rust generally attacks iron and steel. All metals, of course, can get dirty and grimy, depending on what they are used for and to what they are exposed. There are commercial compounds made for cleaning specific metals, and there are some home remedies that can frequently do a good job. Just make sure that you apply the appropriate treatment to the type of metal that needs cleaning.

1. Oxidized bronze, brass, and copper will usually come clean with a salt and lemon juice treatment. Mix the juice of one lemon with a tablespoonful of salt and apply with very fine (0000) steel wool. If the brass or bronze pieces are covered with a clear coat of lacquer (put on to prevent tarnish), this must be removed before any type of polish or cleaner can be effective. Use lacquer thinner to remove the protective coating. For removing very light tarnish on bronze, brass, and copper, rubbing the metal with white vinegar will often do the job.
2. Aluminum often oxidizes and starts to pit. Remove the oxidation as soon as you see it by rubbing the aluminum with 0000 steel wool, either dry or with a metal cleaner. After the corrosion comes off, apply a coating of wax or, better still, lacquer to retard future oxidation. Sometimes rubbing a slightly tarnished aluminum surface with crumpled aluminum foil will clean it.
3. Painted, plated, or coated metals can usually be cleaned with warm water and detergent.

Here Is What You Will Need
Materials

- Salt
- Lemon juice
- 0000 steel wool
- Lacquer thinner
- White vinegar
- Metal cleaner
- Wax
- Lacquer
- Aluminum foil
- Detergent
- Chrome cleaner
- Kerosene
- Protective lubricant
- Clear plastic spray

Tools

- Brush
- Nylon net

Never use anything abrasive enough to scratch the finish. Stubborn spots can be scrubbed with nylon net or a brush, usually without any surface scratching. To remove tar from the chrome parts of an automobile, use one of the solvents (available at auto supply outlets) made especially for this purpose. Kerosene will also dissolve tar and road dirt, but remember that kerosene is flammable and must be used with caution.

The best way to fight metal corrosion is with preventive maintenance. Keep the surfaces clean and free from excessive moisture. If metals must be exposed to high humidity, coat them with a protective lubricant, and where possible and practical, spray bare metals with a coat of lacquer or clear plastic spray.

Aluminum Jelly Fights Oxidation

Dirt, grime, and oxidation can now be removed quickly and easily from aluminum surfaces with Duro Aluminum Jelly. Manufactured by Woodhill Chemical Sales Corporation, Duro Aluminum Jelly cleans and brightens aluminum and helps prevent further oxidation on the surface. Simply brush it on the surface, allow it to stand until corrosion, dirt, and grime dissolve, and then wash it off.

Art Restoration Specialist Creates Exceptional Metal Polish

Rubin-Brite, a metal polish used in museums, is truly exceptional. Developed by art specialist and restorer David Rubin, Rubin-Brite cleans, polishes, and shines, and then leaves a protective coating that seals against future tarnish. Unfortunately, Rubin-Brite is available only by mail order. Contact David Rubin, Art Specialist and Restorer, 42 Somerset Street, Springfield, Massachusetts 01108.

Step 1

Painting

Roller Selection Is Key To Successful Masonry Painting

The roller you choose for any type of painting exerts a controlling influence on the results you will achieve, and that is especially true for masonry painting. Select a quality roller; if you are unsure about a particular brand, ask your dealer. E-Z Paintr, a name you can rely on, offers three long-nap rollers for painting masonry. Generally, the rougher the surface you

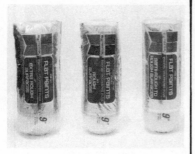

plan to paint, the longer the roller nap you need.

Masonry Paints

While many general household paints claim that they can be used on masonry, paints specifically made for masonry or concrete are more effective. If, for example, you want a really tough finish over unpainted concrete or previously epoxied finishes, try Sears Epoxy Concrete Enamel. A two-component epoxy-based paint that resists wear, scuffing, stains, water, and weather, Sears Epoxy Concrete Enamel can be applied above or below grade and dries

overnight. For really good bonding, etch the surface with muriatic acid or another type of etching compound before painting.

Poxymix Dry Paint Waterproofs Masonry

Paint Master Industries offers a dry paint for exterior or interior use. Poxymix Dry Paint, fortified with epoxy-silicone-vinyl, is guaranteed to waterproof porous surfaces. It can be used above or below grade; achieves excellent results on concrete block, cinder block, concrete foundations, poured concrete, brick, or stucco; and it provides a thorough surface coating even over previously painted surfaces. Available in gallon cans (one gallon covers from 40 to 80 square feet, depending on the texture and porosity of the surface), Poxymix Dry Paint is easy to prepare; just add water and Poxymix is ready to use.

Special Masonry Brush Takes On Tough Jobs

The Ruff-Rider, a product of H&G Industries, Inc., is a brush made for rough cleaning jobs like masonry, brick, cinder blocks, shakes, and shingles. Made of 100 percent custom-processed nylon, the Ruff-Rider lets you work fast while still getting full coverage, and its Groove-Edge is very helpful in reaching those hard-to-get-at places. The Ruff-Rider carries a lifetime guarantee against defects.

Painting Masonry

GENERALLY, MASONRY painting is more difficult for the average homeowner and less satisfying in terms of results than the painting of other types of surfaces. Moisture is a major cause of masonry painting problems. Most masonry is porous, and water that comes through it pushes at the paint, causing small particles to come off. In addition, the alkalinity in most masonry affects the adhesiveness of some paints and attacks the pigments in others. Of course, paint that goes on masonry surfaces designed for rough treatment—floors, patios, walks, drives, etc.—must be tough to withstand the punishment. Paint selection, therefore, is of crucial importance, and preparation must be thorough and complete.

There are a number of latex-based masonry paints, all of which offer the advantages of easy cleaning and easy application; in addition, they can be used in damp conditions without adhesion problems. Cement-based paints, those with actual portland cement in them, are frequently used on previously unpainted concrete where very low pressure moisture is a problem. Epoxy paints are often applied where a hard finish that resists moisture and chemicals is needed. Just make sure that the paint you use is compatible with the existing paint (if any) and with the type of masonry you are covering. If you tell the paint salesman the particulars of your painting plans, you stand a better chance of leaving the store with the best paint for your purposes.

The first phase of any masonry painting task is preparation. To do the job right, follow these steps carefully.

1. Repair and patch all cracks and holes. Then allow the patching compounds to cure fully.
2. Remove efflorescence, the whitish bloom that appears in spots on brick and concrete, with a mixture of four parts water to one part muriatic acid. Scrub the surface with the mixture, let it stay for four hours, and then flush it away. Be sure to exercise caution whenever you work with muriatic acid.
3. Clean the surface, removing any loose or chalking paint. Driveways and garage floors must be free of grease and oil. To clean such surfaces, try a solution of TSP and hot water or a prepared concrete de-greaser.
4. Vacuum the surface just before painting.
5. Very rough and porous masonry surfaces should be coated with a block filler, a fairly thick mixture available at the paint store. Be sure the type you get is compatible with the paint you are planning to apply. You can try rolling the block filler, but if the roller fails to

get into the pores of the masonry surface, use a brush to apply the block filler.
6. Be sure to read all the directions on the paint can label. Various paints require special preparation procedures.

Painting masonry is usually best done with a long-napped roller, although on very rough surfaces you may need a brush. Allow the paint to dry thoroughly before walking on the surface. When painting a swimming pool, be sure to wait the full time specified on the paint before you fill the pool.

Many people decide on the spur of the moment to paint the exterior brick of their homes. While painted brick can be attractive, in many instances, just keep in mind that once painted, brick cannot easily be restored to its original appearance. Moreover, unpainted brick requires no periodic touching up as does painted brick.

Here Is What You Will Need

Materials

- Latex-, cement-, or epoxy-based masonry paint
- Primer
- Patching compound
- Muriatic acid
- Block filler
- TSP or prepared concrete degreaser

Tools

- Putty knife
- Scrub brush
- Paint scraper
- Vacuum cleaner
- Paintbrushes
- Long-napped paint rollers

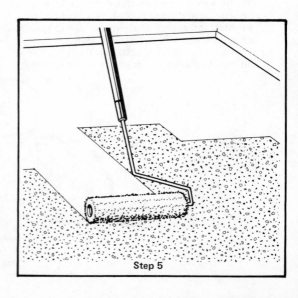

Step 5

Chair-Loc Locks Loose Chair Rungs

A special product made just for loose chair rungs uses a chemical process to swell the fibers of the wood, thereby tightening the joint. The process takes only a few minutes and requires no clamping or bracing. The product is called Chair-Loc, and it works well on any kind of loose furniture joints. Some people even put it on the wooden handles of new hammers, picks, axes, etc., to provide additional security against the head flying off. The plastic squeeze container makes it easy to get Chair-Loc precisely to the place where it's needed. Available at hardware or furniture repair supply stores, Chair-Loc is a product of the Chair-Loc Company.

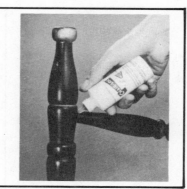

Elmer's Special Wood Glue Fixes Furniture

Elmer's Professional Carpenter's Wood Glue is fine for fixing furniture because it grabs fast on initial contact and yet allows repositioning for the final clamping. Since it dries quickly, it won't tie up your clamps, and it has high heat and water resistance. Sandable and paintable, Elmer's Professional Carpenter's Wood Glue comes in plastic squeeze bottles like the white glue, but the contents have a yellow look. It can also be purchased in large quantities—up to 55-gallon drums—if you are really into furniture repairs.

Loose Chair Rungs

Here Is What You Will Need

Materials
- Vinegar
- White polyvinyl glue
- Rope
- Wooden stick

Tools
- Pry lever
- Pocketknife
- Web or belt clamp

DID YOU EVER sit down in a chair and start rocking back and forth—and then suddenly realize you are not in a rocking chair? The problem is probably no more than a loose rung, but one loose rung usually leads to every joint in the chair coming loose. Before you do more damage to the chair, take a few minutes to fix it.

1. Remove each loose rung from the dowel hole. You can often use a homemade pry lever, but in severe cases you may have to disassemble the chair completely.
2. Remove all glue from both the rung and the dowel hole. Hot vinegar will dissolve some glues, but other types require that you scrape them away with a pocketknife.
3. Now you are ready to reglue. A white polyvinyl (like Elmer's) glue is fine. Just be sure that the wood is free of dust before you apply the glue.
4. With the glue applied to both the dowel and the hole, insert the dowel and make sure it goes fully into the hole.
5. Now you need clamping pressure. A web or belt clamp is the proper thing to use, but lacking such a device, loop a rope around the legs and use a stick to create a tourniquet. Tighten the tourniquet around the legs to provide good clamping pressure.
6. Push the stick up until it rests against either the bottom of the seat or another rung; that way, it cannot unwind.
7. Leave the tourniquet in place for 24 hours to give the glue a chance to set up. Now remove the rope, and—if everything went right—you should find no more rocking the next time you sit down.

Be Kind To Your Chair When Taking It Apart

If you use a regular hammer to remove the rungs and legs from a chair that needs regluing, you will probably end up with a chair that is in worse shape than the one you started with. A soft mallet of some sort is much kinder to the wood, while providing enough power to get the job done. A rubber mallet like the Bonney Rubber Tire Mallet works well on furniture, although it is designed primarily for automotive applications. The head consists of a special tough resilient rubber that is molded onto the handle. Bonney is a brand name for products made by the Utica Tool Company, a subsidiary of the Triangle Corporation.

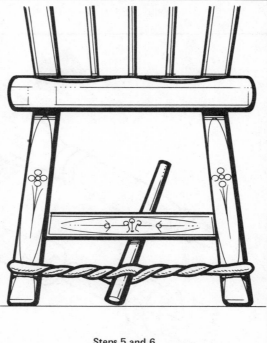

Pry Lever

Step 1

Steps 5 and 6

Furniture

Double Insulation Spells Safety

Double-insulated tools provide an extra margin of safety in that they isolate metal parts from internal electrical components. The ⅜-inch variable-speed reversible drill from Wen is double insulated, and it features a die-cast metal superstructure inside to hold all the interior components. A squeeze trigger adjusts the speed from zero to 1200 rpm, and a control button lets you pre-select a particular speed for a particular job. Available with or without a kit that includes a compact carrying case, bits, rubber disc backing

pad, sanding discs, and a chuck key, the ⅜-inch drill is one of several fine drills made by Wen Products, Inc.

Clamps Are The Key To Proper Gluing

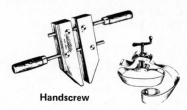

Handscrew

Band Clamp

Anytime you use glue to repair furniture parts, you must have the proper clamp for the job. The Adjustable Clamp Company—manufacturer of Jorgensen and Pony brand clamps—makes just about every type of clamp you would ever need. The Jorgensen Handscrew is a must. Its treated hardwood jaws will not mar wood, and they hold tight over a broad area with even distribution of pressure. Every woodworker needs at least a pair. The Jorgensen Band Clamp solves many problems where round or irregular shapes require uniform pressure at several points simultaneously. It is ideal for chair rung replacement. The Pony Clamp fastens onto an ordinary pipe to make a bar clamp of any length, handy when gluing parts of a table-top back together. Most well-stocked hardware dealers carry Jorgensen and Pony clamps from the Adjustable Clamp Company.

Chisel Accessory For Electric Drill Speeds Furniture Repairs

You can make all of the various cuts used in furniture joining with your electric drill and the Stanley Electrichisel. The Electrichisel does the work of a hand chisel, but does it faster and easier. Consisting of a hollow cylinder of high quality alloy steel with multiple cutting edges machined into the working end, the tool can cut a mortise and tenon joint, a rabbet joint, and make dado cuts. The Stanley Electrichisel comes in ½- and ¾-inch sizes to fit any ¼-inch electric drill.

Woodworker's Vise Is Different

If you plan to do much furniture work, plan on getting a woodworker's vise. A woodworker's vise enables you to work with long wood either vertically or horizontally. The Columbian Woodworker's Vise features a "power-slide" mechanism which can be a big help. Turn the handle clockwise and the vise provides unrestricted holding power. Turn the handle counterclockwise and the hold is released; the jaws open with a sliding action for fast adjustments. All Columbian Woodworker's vises—made by the Warren Tool Group—come with a template and instructions for proper mounting on your workbench.

Broken Parts

RIGHT NOW, in attics and cellars across the country, there are perfectly good tables and chairs that have been stored away because they have a few broken parts. Probably the most common fracture is a broken rung or broken leg, but if it is a clean split along the grain and the parts fit back together, you can put your sick furniture back on its feet again in no time.

1. Use a resin glue for a split; apply it to both pieces.
2. Attach a C-clamp to exert clamping pressure on the pieces, but be sure to protect the wood with pads.
3. Wait the full drying time prescribed by the glue maker before removing the clamp.
4. If slivers of wood are missing, fill in the break with plastic wood after the gluing is done. Your alternative to using plastic wood is to

use a casein glue for the whole job. Casein glue fills in voids better than the resin glue.

If the break is straight across, there is little chance you can merely fit it back together. Your best bet is to follow these steps.

Here Is What You Will Need

Materials
- Resin glue or casein glue
- Plastic wood
- Dowel
- Thread
- Mending plates
- Strong thread

Tools
- C-clamp
- Drill
- Belt or web clamp or rope
- Bar clamps
- Dowel centers

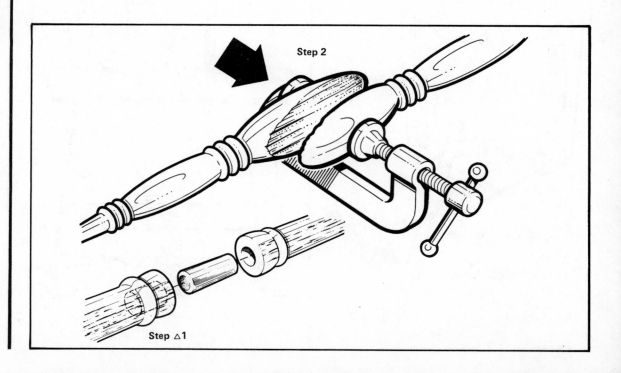

Step 2

Step △1

Furniture Refinishing Can Be Fun

If you would like to get into furniture refinishing more deeply, pick up a copy of *The Super Handyman's Fix and Finish Furniture Guide*. Written by syndicated columnist Al Carrell, the book covers the basics of refinishing in easy to understand language and has plenty of illustrations to help you comprehend just what you are supposed to do. Published by Prentice-Hall, Carrell's book will convince you that furniture refinishing has much to offer as a fun hobby.

All-Purpose Power Tool Does Everything Well

Usually, the term "all-purpose" refers to something that can function in a great many capacities, but do nothing very well. The Shopsmith, however, is a different story. In a matter of seconds, it converts from a 10-inch circular table saw to a 12-inch disc sander to a 34-inch lathe to a horizontal or to a vertical drill press. One heavy-duty motor is dial-adjustable to speeds from 700 rpm up to 5200 rpm. An extremely accurate tool, Shopsmith is certainly a money saver when you consider how much it would cost to buy all five of these basic tools; it is also quite a space saver for those who lack sufficient space for a full-sized workshop. The Shopsmith is a product of Shopsmith, Inc.

Centers Match Dowel Holes To Dowels

Generally, you can solve furniture repair problems easily if you know about and have the proper tools. To make dowels match their holes, for example, all you need are Arco Dowel Centers. Arco's package of dowel centers contains two each of ½-, ⅜-, ⁵⁄₁₆-, and ¼-inch centers. When you want to join two pieces of wood with dowels, just drill a hole in one and place the appropriate size center in the hole. Fit the other piece against the center and tap or push it so that the center leaves a punch mark to indicate the exact center of the hole to be drilled. An inexpensive solution to the dowel matching problem, Arco Dowel Centers are made by the Arco Products Corporation.

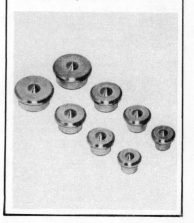

△ 1. Drill a hole in both pieces to accommodate a dowel.
△ 2. Cut the dowel to fit, and then check the fit before applying the glue.
△ 3. Apply glue to all surfaces involved, and then clamp the pieces together. You can use a belt or web clamp (or a rope) to form a tourniquet.

Large flat surfaces such as a chair seat, table top, or dresser top sometimes develop splits. There are several steps that you can take to repair such a split, the easiest of which is to glue the two pieces back together. With a chair, however, where the split is subjected to strain each time someone sits on it, gluing may not work. It is worth a try, though. Follow this procedure.

○ 1. If it is only a partial split, consider splitting the piece all the way to make it easier to clean the surfaces, apply the glue, and line up the parts for clamping. In any case, clean off all dirt, dust, wax, and any other foreign matter.
○ 2. Put the pieces back together and clamp without any glue to be sure the parts line up.
○ 3. Apply resin glue to both sides of the split. If it is still a partial split, use a length of strong thread to help get the glue all the way back into the end of the split.
○ 4. Install bar clamps for pressure.
○ 5. Wipe away any glue that gets squeezed out by the clamping pressure.
○ 6. Leave the clamps in place until the glue has cured completely. Read the glue label to find out exactly how long that is.

For a more secure joining, install dowels along the split. Remember, though, that the dowel holes must line up precisely or else the two pieces will be out of alignment. You should have a set of dowel centers, which are little buttons that fit into the dowel holes. When the pieces are lined up, the dowel centers in one piece make a starter hole in the other to indicate exactly where to drill. Another way to strengthen such a split is to attach mending plates underneath.

Of course, sometimes a part breaks off completely, or it gets lost and must be replaced. Unless you are very proficient in wood working, this is probably a job for a pro. Sometimes, though, you can scrounge parts from a similar piece that is too far gone for repairs. If you decide to make parts, try to obtain the same kind of wood, and—if possible—use wood from furniture that is as old as your broken piece.

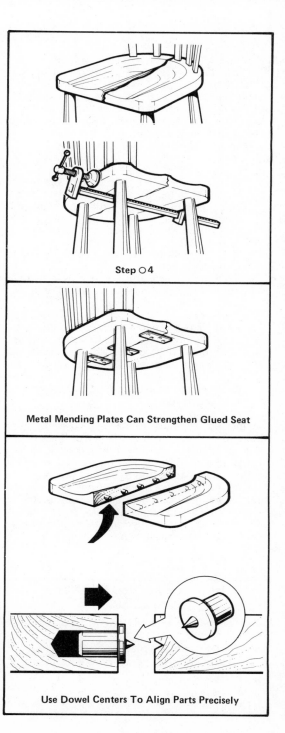

Step ○ 4

Metal Mending Plates Can Strengthen Glued Seat

Use Dowel Centers To Align Parts Precisely

Grooved Dowels Hold Better

A dowel that is exactly the size of the hole it fits into can push much of the glue to the bottom of the hole and not hold as well as it should. But a dowel with a groove or two distributes and holds the glue along its surface for a more secure bond. A versatile hobby tool called the Dremel Moto-Tool can create grooves in dowels as well as handle scores of other home repair needs. Precision engineered to be a fine tool, it saws, grinds, routs, shapes, sands, carves, forms, and polishes. The Dremel Variable Speed Moto-Tool kit includes over 30 accessories plus its own carrying case. Dremel also makes a compact scroll saw called the Moto-Shop and the new Moto-Lathe. Dremel Tools are found in hobby shops as well as in hardware stores and home centers.

Furniture

Replacement Legs End Wobble Woes

When table legs are the source of your table's problem, you may find the best solution is to replace all four legs. Packaged unfinished legs come in several styles and are available at hardware, paint, and lumber retailers. Gerber Wrought Iron Products Company makes such wooden legs. Most come with a threaded hanger bolt, which is screwed into a metal clinch plate on the table top. If the table does not have such a clinch plate, Gerber also makes legs that fasten with wood screws. When buying replacement legs, try to select a wood—legs are made in both pine and hardwoods—that will match your table after you apply the finish.

Waterproof Resin Glue Holds Wood Tight

Just mix the plastic resin powder with cold tap water and Craftsman's Plastic Resin Glue is ready for immediate use. Excellent for all sorts of furniture work including joints and veneers, it provides a strong and long-lasting bond. Craftsman Wood Service is a mail order house carrying products of interest to the wood hobbyist.

Special Fastener Pulls Table-Top Joints Together

The Tite-Joint Fastener creates a firm and solid joint without gluing. A product of Knape & Vogt Manufacturing Company, the Tite-Joint Fastener eliminates the tendency of a joint to twist or buckle. To install, drill holes and install the sleeves; then insert a rod into the holes in the ball to tighten. Not only is the Tite-Joint Fastener great for wobbly or loose table tops, but it also provides a handy way to repair broken chair seats and bar or counter tops.

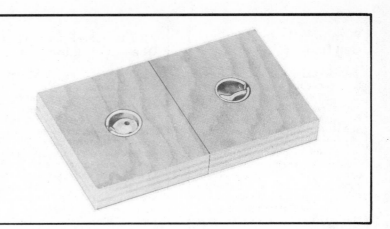

Wobbly Table Legs

WHILE MOST chair rungs are glued in position, table legs are generally held on with bolts. Often as not, all the wobbly table leg needs is a little first aid in the form of your tightening the nut. In that case, your repair is as simple as step 1. If you have to proceed to steps 2 or 3 or beyond, however, it is worth the effort. A wobble today can develop into a collapse tomorrow. Here are the steps for successfully stabilizing your table.

1. Check the nuts under the table to see whether the loose leg is caused by a loose bolt. If so, tighten the nut with an adjustable wrench.
2. As long as you are under the table, tighten all four bolts.
3. If the leg still wobbles, flip the table over and remove the bolt.
4. Examine the bracket; sometimes it can slip out of its slots. Reset the bracket and reinstall the bolt.
5. If the bracket is not at fault, examine the hole to see if it has become enlarged. If that is the case, either fill the hole with wood putty and start a new hole, or dip wooden toothpicks into wood glue and wedge them into the hole. Break the toothpicks off at the hole's surface, and reinstall the bolt when the glue starts to set up.

If the leg is glued in place, follow the same gluing ideas found in the chapter on loose chair parts. In addition, you can strengthen glued legs by adding glue blocks. Just make sure to redrill the holes if you are going to use screws as well as glue for holding the blocks. Other methods for strengthening glued legs include: countersinking screws in the apron adjacent to the legs; adding a bracket; or using L-shaped metal mending plates to hold the legs or the apron to the top.

Here Is What You Will Need
Materials
● Wood putty or wooden toothpicks and glue
● Glue blocks
● L-shaped mending plates
Tools
● Adjustable wrench
● Screwdriver
● Drill

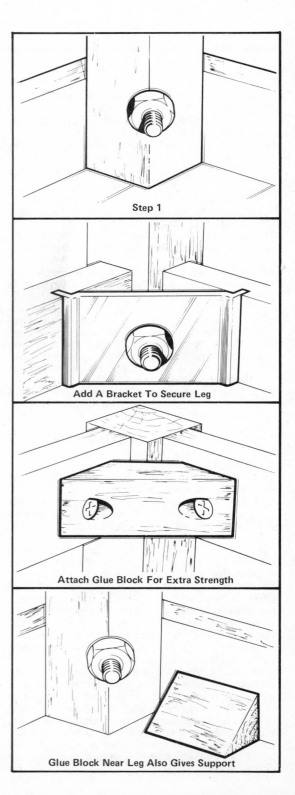

Step 1

Add A Bracket To Secure Leg

Attach Glue Block For Extra Strength

Glue Block Near Leg Also Gives Support

Casters

CASTERS DO a number of good things for furniture. In addition to making pieces easier to move about, these gadgets can stabilize wobbly furniture by compensating for a low place in the floor or for a leg that is shorter than the others. There are three basic types of casters: the stem type, the plate type, and spring adapter type. These designations refer to the methods for installing the casters. Within each type there are several different designs and sizes. The particular style you select depends on the weight it must support, the type of flooring under it, and how often you plan to move the furniture. Generally, you should install the largest caster that will look well on a particular piece of furniture.

Here is how to install a stem-type caster:

1. If the present height of the furniture is what you want it to be, you must saw off some of the legs to compensate for the height of the casters. Measure the caster from the bottom of the wheel to the top of the socket base, and remove that much from the legs.
2. Find the center of the bottom of each leg. On a square leg, draw two diagonal lines from corner to corner; the point at which the lines cross is the center of the leg. On a round leg, cut out a paper circle to match the circumference of the leg. Fold the paper twice to form a quarter circle. The point thus formed is the center of the circle and, therefore, the center of the leg.
3. Drill a hole of the correct size to accommodate the socket. Insert the socket in the hole.
4. Insert the stem of the caster into the socket until it snaps into a locked position. If the stem fails to lock, tap the caster with a

Here Is What You Will Need

Materials
- Stem-, plate-, or spring adapter-type casters
- Large-head nail
- Screws

Tools
- Saw
- Measuring tape
- Drill
- Hammer
- Screwdriver
- Vise grip pliers
- Wood block
- Paper

hammer until it does so.

Plate type casters are held by screws driven into the leg through a flat metal plate. Here is how to attach such casters to your furniture.

△ 1. Place the plate against the leg bottom to make sure that there is enough space for the screws to go into solid wood.
△ 2. Mark the screw holes on the bottom of the leg.
△ 3. Drill pilot holes in the wood to make for easier installation and to avoid splitting the leg.
△ 4. Drive the screws into the leg, fastening the plate-type caster to the furniture.

The spring type caster, used for tubular metal legs, is held in place against the inside of the leg by a spring device. You must order spring-type casters to match the size of the tube.

If you are replacing a caster, pry out the old one with a screwdriver. Then, if the old socket will not accommodate the new stem, drive a nail into the socket head first. Use a nail with a head that is large enough to force open the head of the socket. Once the head goes through, clamp vise grip pliers to the nail and—using a block of wood to give you leverage—pry out the old socket.

Nail-On Glides

Any angled leg needs a swivel glide. Chason's nail-on swivel glides are easy to install and feature a non-marring plastic base. Chason also offers light-duty ball casters called Wheelees. Available in six mod decorator colors, Wheelees are made for either stem or plate fastening. Chason Industries, a division of Waxman Industries, Inc., offers all sorts of casters, glides, cups, and tips.

Locking-Grip Pliers Are Versatile

Among the several companies making locking-grip type pliers, the best-known name is probably Vise-Grip. A versatile tool, Vise-Grip pliers can function as a clamp, a vise, a pliers, or a wrench. Once clamped around the work, it locks easily and holds almost any shaped item. Then it releases quickly with a flick of the quick-release lever. Vise-Grip pliers, products of the Peterson Manufacturing Company, Inc., come in several different sizes.

Hard-Surface Casters

Hard-surfaced floors are just as susceptible to damage from furniture as are carpeted floors. Fortunately, you can protect your vinyl, tile, hardwood, ceramic, terrazzo, linoleum, and other hard-surfaced floors with Shepherd Saturn Casters. Long-wearing rubber treads that won't mar your floors are permanently bonded to the metal wheels. Smooth-rolling casters with self-lubricating bearings, the three-inch Shepherd Saturn Casters come in either plate-fastening or grip-neck styles. A smaller 2¼ inch version is called the Nova. Shepherd Products US, Inc., manufacturers a wide variety of casters, glides, and cups.

Step 1

Step 4

Step 2

Step △ 4

Vise Grip Pliers

Old Socket

Wood Block

Nail Head

Drive Nail Into Old Socket Head First To Pull Out For Replacement

Furniture

Shellac Seals Drawer Bottoms Against Moisture Problems

Once you have the drawer working properly, seal it against future swelling due to moisture. There is no easier way than with a spray shellac like the one packaged by New York Bronze Powder Company. If you elect to go with a brush-on treatment, thin down the shellac considerably since you're only using it as a sealer. With either the spray or liquid, one coat of shellac should be sufficient.

Sandpaper Assortment Packs Cover Many Sanding Needs

Howard Hardware Products, Inc., packages sandpaper in quarter-sheet packs of assorted grits. The economy pack contains 26 assorted sheets. Howard manufactures another type of abrasive just for rough shaping and paint removal; it's a non-clogging steel sandpaper called Sand Shark. Howard also offers an aluminum oxide assortment and an emery pack.

Paraffin Solves Some Drawer Problems

By rubbing paraffin on the edges of a drawer, you apply a clear lubricant that can often take care of a sticking problem. Gulfwax, made by the Gulf Oil Company, is a popular paraffin that can be found in hobby shops and in stores handling canning supplies. Paraffin actually serves a host of purposes. Screws and nails go into wood easier when rubbed in paraffin. Matches can be water-proofed by dipping them in

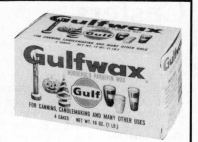

paraffin. It is also a good lubricant for tracks and other flat surfaces.

Drawer Slides Make It Easy To Have Pull

Any homeowner who installs Accuride Drawer Slides can expect precision drawer operation every time. The Accuride ball bearing center drawer slide is a snap to install on either a new piece of furniture or on an existing drawer. Available in six different sizes to accommodate just about every drawer, these heavy-duty cadmium-plated slides can handle up to 35 pounds. The ball bearing action is self polishing, which means it actually improves with age. Accuride is a well-distributed brand from Belwith International, Ltd., a subsidiary of Keeler Brass Company.

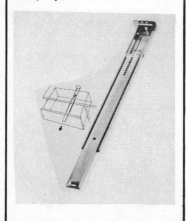

Unsticking Drawers

ALMOST EVERY home has one or more drawers in either a cabinet or a dresser that are totally wasted space because they are next to impossible to get open. This problem is caused by either something in the drawer that is sticking up too high or the drawer itself has swollen and cannot be moved.

The first problem can usually be solved by inserting something flat into the slit at the top of the drawer. A metal kitchen spatula will usually work. Sometimes a larger item is needed, and careful use of a saw blade may be the answer. The idea is to get the flat piece in the slit and use it to move the items that stick up so they no longer hinder movement of the drawer. Once you get the drawer open, transfer some of the items to another place.

The swollen wood in a drawer represents another problem. If you can work the drawer back and forth a little and get it open, you can follow our ABC's to insure it never sticks again. However, if it is stuck solid and will not move, here are some things to try:

1. Remove a drawer above the stuck drawer, if there is one, and see if you can use a hammer and padded block to drive the drawer out.
2. Remove a drawer next to the offender, if there is one, and try to pry the stuck drawer out.
3. With all adjacent drawers removed for more working space, dismantle the stuck drawer from inside.
4. If you can get the drawer open even a few inches, place an electric light bulb and socket into the drawer and turn it on. The lighted bulb should dry out the wood and cause it to shrink, allowing you to remove the drawer. Place a piece of aluminum foil under the bulb so the heat does not scorch the wood.

After you have removed the drawer by one means or another, you can make sure this problem never happens again by taking the following steps:

△ 1. Examine the tops, bottoms and sides of the drawer to determine where it is sticking. Also check the cabinet for places where binding occurs.
△ 2. Sand down all surfaces that bind on both the drawer and the cabinet. For really big jobs, use a plane to remove the bulk of the wood,

Move Obstructing Objects With Spatula   Step 4

Drawer Slides Mount On The Side

Knape & Vogt makes sturdy side-mount drawer slides of the wraparound variety that will work for either flush or overlap type drawers. The slides allow you to lift the drawers out easily, while built-in stops prevent the drawers from being pulled out accidentally. Knape & Vogt packages these nylon-roller slides—rated for 50-pound loads—in pairs with all the necessary screws and illustrated installation instructions.

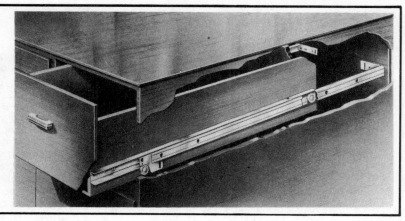

When The Candle And Bar Soap Fail...

When drawers refuse to work smoothly, many people use the old trick of rubbing a candle or a bar of soap on the wood contact points. While the candle or soap can often solve the problem, a better way to lubricate is with a prepared spray like Elmer's Slide-All. A dry spray with a Teflon base, Slide-All can be used on metal, rubber, and even painted surfaces as well as on wooden drawers.

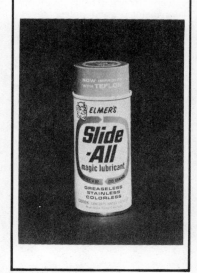

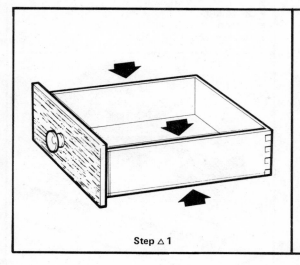

Here Is What You Will Need

Materials

- Aluminum foil
- Shellac, varnish or lacquer
- Silicone lubricating spray
- Candle

Tools

- Metal spatula or saw blade
- Hammer
- Padded wood block
- Light bulb and socket
- Sandpaper
- Plane

Step △ 1

and then sand. Make all surfaces as smooth as possible. Test the fit after sanding, and if it is still tight, keep working at it until the drawer slides easy again.

△ 3. Now you must coat the wood to prevent its absorption of moisture in the future. Shellac, varnish or lacquer will do this. The easiest way is to use an aerosol spray. A light coat is all you will need.

△ 4. When the sealer is completely dry, lubricate all contact points on both the drawer and the cabinet. Use either a silicone spray or rub the surfaces with a candle.

Drawers that occasionally become stubborn, usually do so when the humidity is high. When the air in your home dries out, so does the wood. Why not make sure you never have a real problem by giving them the above treatment now before you need something from a drawer in a hurry.

The Little Shaver Is A Big Cut-Up

Great Neck's Little Shaver Plane measures only 3½ inches long and an inch wide, but it does a great job on drawers and other cabinet sticking problems. Ideal for taking off just enough to let the drawers move in and out again, the Little Shaver has a cast-iron body with an enameled finish. Small as it is, the Little Shaver offers most of the features of a big plane. Its adjustable alloy steel blade is sharp and true, and it has been properly hardened and tempered.

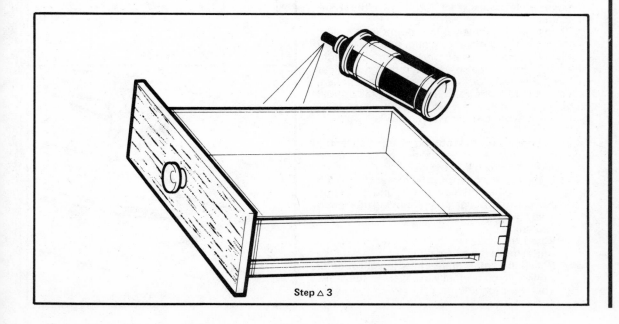

Step △ 3

Furniture

Paint Thinner Can Clean Furniture Too

Even though it obviously is not marketed for cleaning furniture, a good paint thinner like NanKee ST-100 can remove wax, grease, and dirt from tables, chairs, etc. Since ST-100 is a blend of solvents, it is markedly superior to plain mineral spirits or even turpentine. If you read and follow the caution notices on the container, paint thinner is not dangerous to store or use around the house. NanKee Company, Inc., markets a full line of solvents, caulks, aluminum paints, wood preservatives, Paco denatured alcohol, and the Triumph brand polyurethane finishes.

Steel Wool Smooths The Way

Steel wool can be particularly helpful in curing minor furniture faults. The 4/0 (0000) grade is extremely fine, and when wet with oil or wax, will not scratch your furniture's finish. SunRay steel wool, made by the Williams Company Division of James H. Rhodes & Company, comes in 0000 as well as in all other grades.

First Aid For Scratches Comes In A Bottle

Furniture scratches, nicks, and mars can be hidden quickly with Scratch Magic, a product of the Magic American Chemical Corporation. Just use the handy brush in the cap to dab along the scratch. Scratch Magic dries fast to a durable finish that blends in with the wood shade. Available in six shades—Oak, Maple, Light Walnut, Cherry-Fruitwood, Dark Walnut, and Red Mahogany—Scratch Magic can also be used on paneling.

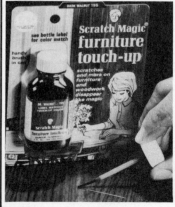

First Aid

YOU OFTEN SEE a piece of furniture that looks so bad you think that only complete refinishing will help it. Although that may be the case, you should do everything you can to avoid the considerable time, money, and mess involved in a complete refinishing job. Before you go the whole route, try some furniture first aid.

1. Clean furniture that is suffering from a severe wax build-up by rubbing it with a cloth dampened with paint thinner. Paint thinner is a great wax remover.
2. Get rid of cracking and checking in the finish by going over your furniture with four ought (0000) steel wool and lemon oil. Be careful not to rub so hard as to allow the steel wool to cut into the finish, and always rub with the grain.
3. You can often cover scratches. If they are surface scratches (just in the finish and not into the wood), furniture polish usually hides them. If they are down into the stain, you must replace the color. The best way is to apply some stain with a toothpick or a tiny artist's brush. You can also try liquid shoe polish, a crayon, or iodine diluted with denatured alcohol to match the color of the stain.
4. Candle wax on a table can look awful and seem impossible to remove, but a little furniture first aid should do the job. The two best approaches are: (1) Put a blotter over the drippings, and then press the blotter with a hot iron; just make sure that you move the blotter frequently so that a clean and absorbent spot is over the wax drippings at all times. (2) Hold an ice cube against the wax to make it more brittle; then just pry the drippings off.

There are all sorts of ways to create white rings and spots on your furniture. Setting an iced drink glass down without a coaster under it is one good way. The condensation on the glass drips down, and if left on the furniture long enough, a white ring will form. A hot dish left on a table without a trivet will leave a hazy spot, and spilled hot coffee, alcoholic drinks, and perfume can also cause white or hazy spots. If you thought that there was no alternative but to refinish the whole table top, you have some good news in store. With an abrasive, rubbing oil, and a little elbow grease, you can remove white spots from furniture without refinishing.

Choose a mild abrasive; four ought (0000) steel wool will do. It is extremely fine, and unless you really bear down or use it dry, it will not cut into the finish. You can also use such things as cigar ashes, table salt, tooth powder, or silver polish; each is a mild abrasive. Pure lemon oil is a great rubbing oil, but you can also use petroleum jelly, salad oil, mayonnaise, or even paste wax.

△ 1. Put enough of the rubbing oil on to cover the white spot. If you are using a powdery abrasive, sprinkle it into the oil.
△ 2. Using a soft cloth or the 0000 steel wool, rub in a circular fashion all around the spot. Keep it up, occasionally moving the goop away with your rag to see how well the spot is coming off.
△ 3. When the spot is gone, take a clean cloth and remove the oily residue.
△ 4. Polish the entire table top with your regular polish. If you normally use wax on the table, you will probably have to rewax the entire surface.

Here Is What You Will Need

Materials

- Fine steel wool (0000) or other mild abrasive
- Lemon oil, petroleum jelly, or other rubbing oil
- Soft cloths
- Furniture wax
- Household ammonia
- Stick shellac
- Alcohol flame
- Clear fingernail polish
- Nail polish remover
- Paint thinner
- Furniture polish
- Wood stain or liquid shoe polish
- Crayons or iodine diluted with denatured alcohol
- Ice cubes
- Blotter

Tools

- Dull rounded knife
- Clean knife
- Toothpicks or artist's brush
- Electric iron

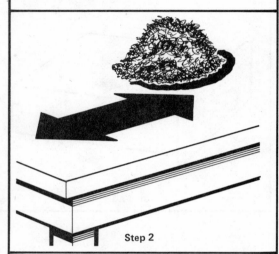

Step 2

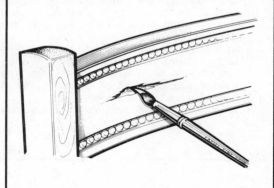

Step 3

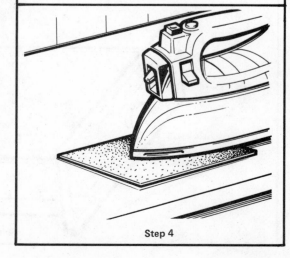

Step 4

Step △ 2

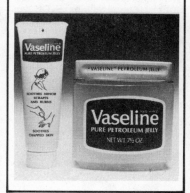

If you can work on alcohol stains right away, you can lift them with a small amount of household ammonia on a soft rag. Squeeze the rag as dry as possible, and then brush it over the stained spot lightly.

It seems that after every party you discover that someone inadvertently put a cigarette down on the edge of a table and then forgot it until the table acquired an ugly burned mark. No matter who is to blame, it is up to you to fix the damage. Here are some tricks that you can use to hide the burns in your furniture.

○ 1. The first step is to scrap away the black char. Use a dull rounded knife, and be sure to get all of the black off—even going into the wood.
○ 2. If you go down into the wood on a piece that was stained, you must replace the stain. Your paint dealer should be able to help you match the color. Remember, though, that different stains react differently to various woods. One stain might give five distinctive shades when placed on five different woods.
○ 3. With the stain back in, you are ready to fill in the gouge. Try to make it level with the rest of the table. One way is to fill the low spot with stick shellac. Stick shellac, however, is a little tricky to work with and requires some practice. You put it on by heating a knife over an alcohol flame, touching the hot knife to the stick shellac, and flowing the shellac into the indentation. You should use an alcohol flame because it does not leave sooty deposits on the knife that would mix with the shellac on your table. Flow in enough shellac to make the burned spot higher than the rest of the table. Then use a very fine abrasive (0000 steel wool) and lemon oil to cut it down even with the surface.

If you want to avoid the hassle of using stick shellac, here is another technique. Though not quite as professional in its results, it will do the job. Mix clear fingernail polish and nail polish remover about half and half, and swipe the mixture across the gouge with the polish brush. This will leave a thin coat that dries very fast. As soon as it dries, put on another coat, and keep adding coats until you build up the gouge to a point where it is level with the rest of the table. While the spot may still look a little different from the rest of the table, it will not be as unattractively different as the ugly burn was.

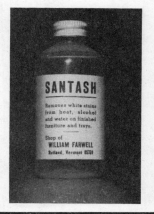

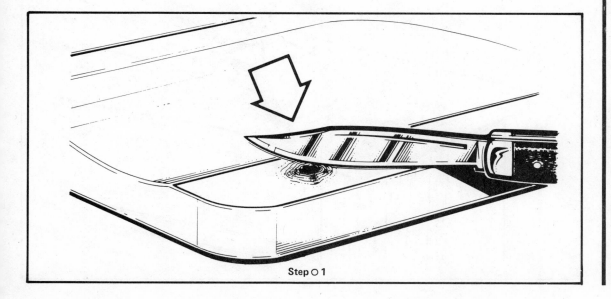

Step ○ 1

Hose Away Old Paint

With H₂Off paint remover, you can wash away old paint. After you apply the remover and let it do its thing, you hit the furniture with a strong blast of water from your garden hose and take away the paint with a putty knife. Of course, this means that you must be situated in a place where water and chemicals can run off without damaging anything. And since water is a natural enemy of wood, you must make sure to follow all the suggestions on the label. But, for many removal jobs, H₂Off can provide a very quick and easy way to get around an onerous task. H₂Off is one of several paint and varnish removal products from The Savogran Company, makers of Kutzit and Strypeeze.

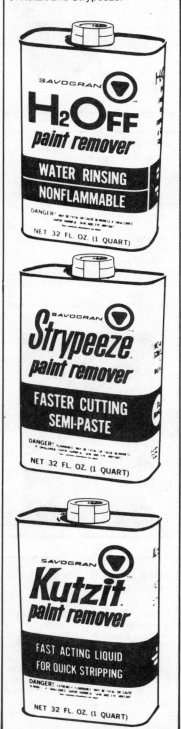

Remover Even Strips Epoxy Paint

Tough as they are, epoxy paints can be removed with RAP (Removes All Paint) Paint and Varnish Remover. Made by RAP Products, Inc., it also removes polyurethanes as well as conventional paints and varnishes. Non-flammable and water washable RAP Paint and Varnish Remover is heavy enough to remain on vertical surfaces without running off. Since it stays wet longer than many other removers, it therefore works longer, but it will not stain or harm even the finest furniture woods.

Stripping

WHEN THERE IS nothing that can be done to revive the finish on an old piece of furniture and when no amount of first aid can make it look nice again, you are faced with having to remove the old finish. There are several ways to strip furniture. Sanding and/or scraping is a sure way to get the old finish off, but it is also a slow and sure way to get a backache. The easier way is to apply a paint and varnish remover that you can buy at the hardware or paint store.

Here are some things to consider in selecting the stripper. If the piece can be turned over — permitting you to work on a horizontal surface at all times — you can get by with a liquid finish remover. The liquid costs a little less than other types. If you have to work on quite a bit of vertical surface, however, get a paste finish remover. And if the piece has veneer on it, avoid any remover that requires you to use water from a garden hose to remove the loosened paint.

Although you must be sure to follow the directions on the label, here are some general pointers on stripping.

1. Find a spot to work in that can handle the mess. If you have the kind of stripper that requires flushing with water, do the work outside on a day the weather permits. Check the label for caution notices. It may tell you that you need good ventilation, and it may tell you to wear rubber gloves.

2. If you work inside, place plenty of newspaper underneath the furniture.

3. Select older brushes for applying the stripper; even dime store brushes will do.

4. If you are working with a piece of furniture that has legs, set the leg bottoms in flat containers such as those aluminum pans that come with frozen pies. The pans catch any runoff, and you can dip your brush into the pan and use the excess stripper again. Even if you are using a paste stripper, there will always be a little runoff.

5. Brush over an area once only and brush in just one direction. Going back over what you covered will break the thin film that forms, allowing solvents to evaporate sooner and thus lessen their softening qualities.

6. The label will inform you as to when the remover will start softening the finish underneath it. At about that time, use a putty knife or scraper to check whether the layers of finish are softened all the way down to the bare wood. Incidentally, the best scraper is a flexible putty knife with the sharp corners filed off. Sharper scrapers will probably damage the wood.

7. When the finish is softened down to the

Step 6

When It Comes To Steel Wool, Think American

American Steel Wool Manufacturing Company Inc., is the oldest steel wool maker in the country. American produces steel wool in all grades and sells it in poly bags, assortment packs, and Flex-Fold pads. Many people who are just starting out in furniture refinishing shy away from using steel wool because the only experience they've had with this abrasive has been with the coarse grade made for scrubbing kitchen pots. Proper use of the finer grades of steel wool won't scratch fine furniture. The well-stocked home workshop always contains several grades of steel wool.

Jack The Stripper Cuts Away Paint In Seconds

A solid black block of foam called Jack The Stripper lets you rub away any paint finish amazingly fast. Unlike sanding, which takes forever, gentle rubbing with Jack The Stripper cuts right down to the bare wood in seconds; with a little practice you will never leave even the slightest scratch on the wood underneath. The noticeable odor it creates during use is no cause for concern; it goes away soon after you finish rubbing. In limited retail distribution, Jack The Stripper can be ordered from its Canadian manufacturer. Contact Jack The Stripper, 1373 Freeport Drive, Mississauga, Ontario, Canada.

Here Is What You Will Need

Materials
- Liquid or paste finish remover
- Aluminum pans
- Coarse steel wool or burlap rag
- Heavy string or twisted burlap
- Cleaning solvent
- Sandpaper

Tools
- Garden hose
- Rubber gloves
- Inexpensive paintbrushes
- Putty knife or scraper

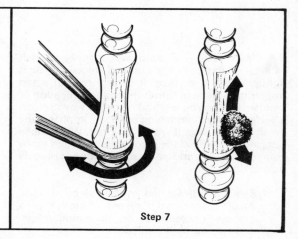

Step 7

Refinish Without Stripping

Any varnish, shellac, or lacquer finish can be cleaned and dissolved without stripping. Without going into details, the basic procedure is to rub the surface with 0000 (super fine) steel wool dipped into Formby's Refinisher. The old finish dissolves in seconds. Do small areas until the entire surface is stripped, and then go back over—this time with the grain. All dirt, wax, and grime comes off, but a thin protective layer of the old finish remains. You are then ready to apply a finish; Formby suggests either lemon oil or tung oil. Formby Refinishing Products are available in the housewares sections of fine department stores as well as in paint and hardware stores.

wood, scrape the mess away. For rounded areas where the putty knife is of little value, use coarse steel wool to cut through the sludge; just be careful not to scratch the wood. You can substitute for the steel wool by using a burlap rag to mop the residue away. In narrow places, try a piece of heavy string or a twisted strip of burlap.

8. If the directions tell you to clean the stripped furniture with a solvent, do not skip this step just because the piece looks clean. The solvent is recommended to remove all traces of an invisible wax put in the remover to retard evaporation.

In some cases, you must go over parts of the furniture for a second time with the finish remover. You may also find that there are small spots which you can remove more easily by sanding than by stripping.

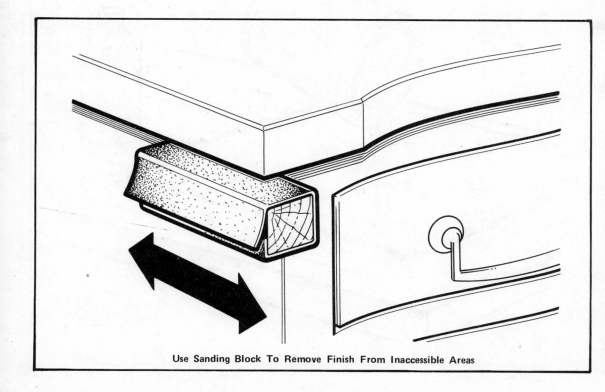

Use Sanding Block To Remove Finish From Inaccessible Areas

Furniture

Tack Rags

A TACK RAG is a cloth with a tacky varnish touch that removes dust and lint as you run it lightly across a surface. It is very helpful when preparing a piece of furniture for an application of varnish. In fact, you will find no better way to clean a surface before varnishing or before applying any finish than to wipe it with a tack rag. While these rags are available at the paint store, you can make your own easily and save some money. Here is how to do it.

1. Select a well-washed lint-free piece of cloth. An old diaper, part of an oxford cloth shirt, a piece of cheesecloth, an old handkerchief, or anything similar will do.
2. Dip the cloth in warm water.
3. Wring it out as completely as possible.
4. Now soak it with turpentine.
5. Wring it out again.
6. Lay the cloth on a flat clean surface.
7. Drip varnish over the surface until the cloth has small dots of varnish about two inches apart all over it.
8. Fold the cloth over, and then roll it up and wring it out to distribute the varnish. Keep doing this until the cloth—when unfolded—is uniformly coated with varnish. It should feel tacky, but not leave any varnish on your hand.
9. Between uses, store the tack rag in a sealed jar.
10. From time to time, sprinkle small amounts of turpentine and water on the rag to restore its tackiness.

Here Is What You Will Need

Materials

- Lint-free cloth
- Turpentine
- Varnish
- Sealed jar

Tools

- None

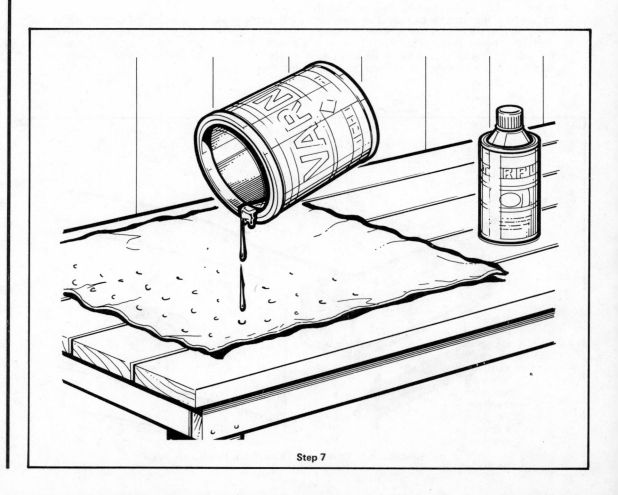

Step 7

Spray Stains Handle Hard-To-Reach Areas

A chest with louvered doors might take a while to stain if you had to brush the stain onto each louver. A spray-on stain like Behr Spray Stain and Sealer handles such tasks easily, getting into all the nooks and crannies and drying to the touch in five minutes. It comes in a variety of the most popular decorator shades. Behr also makes a wiping stain in the same colors, and if you lean toward wiping stains, you will find the spray handy for hard-to-reach places and for future touch-ups. For touch-ups and very small jobs, Behr also offers four-ounce cans of stain called Behr Cubs. Behr stains are the products of the Behr Process Corporation.

Stain And Finish In One Step

For staining inexpensive bare woods, you would be hard pressed to find an easier product to use than DuPont One Step Polyurethane Stain and Finish. One Step can be used over old finishes with good results; and if one application is not dark enough, you can add a second coat. It is smooth flowing and leaves a low-luster satin sheen, resulting in a durable finish that is resistant to wear, water, stains, heat, and alcohol. One Step dries to the touch in about three hours and can be recoated in about six hours.

Staining

Y OU CAN FIND many good reasons for staining furniture. Sometimes you want a darker shade of wood, while in other cases you think that the natural wood lacks an interesting grain pattern. If you do not know whether to stain or not because you do not know exactly how the bare wood will look after you put on the finish, you can get a good idea with what is called the "wet test." Dampen a cloth with turpentine and rub it over the surface. While it is still wet, the wood resembles what it will look like after you apply the finish. The wetness brings out the grain and shows the contrasts. If you do not like what you see, then you should not stain the furniture.

There are a number of types of stains on the market. The neophyte in furniture staining should stick with a pigmented wiping stain. It is the easiest to use and yields the best results. It is also preferable because wiping stain allows you to correct most of your mistakes. Here are the simple steps to follow for getting good results with wiping stain.

1. Be sure you have a smooth surface for the stain. If the furniture has any blemishes, the stain will bring them out and make them more pronounced.
2. If the piece has just been stripped, make sure it is completely dry.
3. If the grain was raised in the stripping process, sand it down.
4. Make sure the surface is clean and free of wax.
5. Test the stain on an obscure part of the piece to see what it will look like. Make sure that you also check an end grain, because the end grain absorbs stain at a different rate than the rest of the surface. If the end grain looks much different than the rest of the piece, you may wish to use a thin wash coat of sanding sealer on it.
6. Stir the stain well before you start, and then stir it frequently as you go. Otherwise, the pigment will settle.
7. Brush the stain on. You need not concern yourself about going with the grain or getting a smooth coat. Just cover all of the surface.
8. When the surface starts to lose the wettish

Here Is What You Will Need

Materials

- Rags
- Turpentine
- Pigmented wiping stain
- Sandpaper
- Sanding sealer
- Paint thinner

Tools

- Paintbrush

look and begins to dull, wipe with an absorbent cloth. Try to wipe all the stain off. In other words, put some muscle behind your wiping. Turn the rag over frequently to expose a clean part as the other section gets loaded.

9. If you do not like the results, you can start over. Paint thinner on a rag will remove nearly all of the stain. You must rub hard, though. If the problem is just that the piece is not dark enough, you need not remove the stain. Put on another coat and let it stay on a little longer before wiping. You can, of course, always try adding a darker stain to the original mix.
10. When you achieve the right color tone, wipe down the furniture with a clean rag to remove any more surface matter. Then let it sit for at least 24 hours before you apply the finish.

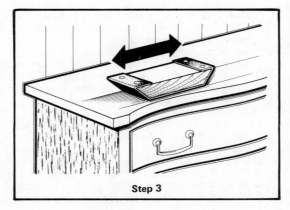

Step 3

Wiping Stains Are Easier To Control

The easiest furniture stain to control insofar as the shade is concerned is a wiping stain. Just wipe or brush the stain on, and then wipe off the excess. If what you see is too dark, wipe harder. If you rub off too much, apply more stain. With a little practice on a scrap beforehand, you can probably get it right the first time. Beverlee's Satin Stain is a product of the United Gilsonite Laboratories.

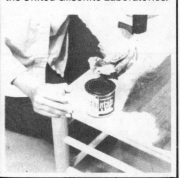

Latex Stains Make Clean-Up Easy

Just like latex paints, latex stains can be cleaned with soap and water. Rez makes a latex wiping stain that is odorless and quick drying. It works best on bare wood. Just brush or wipe the stain on; wait until it soaks in, and then wipe off the excess. Always wipe with the grain. Rez Latex Stain, a product of PPG Industries, comes in many wood tones.

Rottenstone Is A Bad Name For A Good Product

A perfectly good abrasive has a name that sounds like something that should be left outside. But Rottenstone from the Synkoloid Company is not rotten at all. Rather, it is a very fine limestone abrasive, finer even than pumice, for use on furniture.

Furniture

Shellac Still Wins At The Finish

It is fairly easy to get a good finish with shellac. It dries fast, leaving little time for dust to collect; it is easy to brush on; and it levels out by itself. Shellac cleans up with alcohol or with ammonia and warm water. Bulls Eye Shellac, from the William Zinsser Company, comes in gallon cans and in a spray version for small or hard-to-reach areas. Always check the date stamped on the can; all shellacs have a short shelf life, and shellac that is more than six months old may not be good. By the same token, never buy more shellac than you can use within a relatively short period of time.

The Wax Finish

Many furniture experts claim that wax is no finish at all, but you can use wax to add a good protective coating over your furniture. Minwax Finishing Wax comes in both paste and liquid, the paste variety providing a richer appearance and offering more protection than the liquid. Regular Minwax Finishing Wax is made for close-grain and light woods; a special version is formulated for open-grain and/or dark woods. The Minwax Company, Inc., also produces polyurethane finishes and an antique oil finish.

Bring Out The Best In Wood

It used to be that a hand-rubbed finish demanded true devotion from someone willing to rub the surface seemingly forever. Watco Danish Oil Finish, however, has made the job much simpler. Just apply, and then allow it to penetrate the wood. When you wipe the furniture dry, the result is a beautiful natural finish that makes the wood up to 25 percent harder and more resistant to stains and scratches. Watco Danish Oil Finish—available in Natural, Medium, Dark, and Black Walnut—offers one major advantage in that it is spot repairable. Watco Teak Oil Finish, another product of the Watco-Dennis Corporation, is made especially for exotic woods like teak, rosewood, and other tropical species.

The Original Hand-Rubbed Oil Finish

Linseed oil is regarded as the original hand-rubbed oil finish, but if you plan to apply it, be prepared to do plenty of rubbing. First mix a solution of two parts boiled linseed oil—Sunnyside is one good brand—to one part turpentine. You do not boil the linseed oil; that is merely the name of the product. Since the mixture works best when warm, put a container of the linseed oil/turpentine in a pan of hot water removed from the stove. Never heat the mixture over a flame or electric coil! Then, when it is sufficiently warm, rub the mixture on until the wood can no longer absorb the oil. Then wipe off the excess and polish with a cloth for about 15 minutes. Repeat the process each day until you achieve the depth of finish you desire.

Finishing

THE FINISH ON a piece of furniture is put there to protect the wood and also to make the piece look its best. Although there are many types of finishes, the three basic surface finishes are shellac, lacquer, and varnish. Learn the advantages and disadvantages and how to apply each, and then you can make up your mind about which finish to use on your furniture.

Shellac is the easiest finish to apply and provides a very high degree of shine. The big disadvantage is that shellac offers little resistance to water and alcohol. That means you would not want to use shellac in a kitchen, on a coffee table, or on a bar top. If you do have furniture you want to finish with shellac, though, here is how to do it.

1. Make sure that the shellac is fresh. Most makers stamp the date of manufacture on the lid. Never buy any shellac that is more than four months old, and never buy more than you need because you cannot keep it long.
2. Stir the shellac, but avoid making waves. Never shake shellac to mix it because shaking causes bubbles.
3. Use a very thin shellac for the first coat. Shellac is thinned with wood alcohol, also called denatured alcohol.
4. Apply the shellac with a well-loaded, soft-bristled, and fairly wide brush. You want to put the shellac on fairly rapidly. Use as few strokes as possible, but do not stroke fast. Overlap each stroke against the wet edge. Lap marks will tend to even out.
5. After the first coat dries (in an hour or so), sand with an open coated 220-grit sandpaper.
6. Clean the furniture and apply the second coat. Put on another thin coat; several thin coats are much better than one thick coat.
7. When dry—the second coat usually takes a little longer than the first to dry—sand with a 240-grit paper.
8. Keep adding coats to suit your taste. Some people stop at two, while others go to five or six. For all subsequent coats, use 4/0 (0000) steel wool instead of sandpaper for smoothing.
9. If you plan to wax the furniture, wait at least 24 hours after the last coat.

Lacquer has an advantage that is often a disadvantage: it is very fast drying. To a pro, fast drying is an advantage, but to an amateur, this can spell disaster. Lacquer can be sprayed or brushed, but spray equipment is expensive and it is not something you use without experience. Although aerosol cans of lacquer work well and are easy to use, they are far too expensive for finishing a large piece of furniture. If you plan to brush on the lacquer, be sure to ask for brushing lacquer. The type used in a spray rig would be dry before you could move the brush from the can to the furniture. Buy as much thinner as you buy lacquer; you will need to keep the lacquer thin and free flowing. Here is how to apply it.

△ 1. Select a clean, wide brush for faster coverage.
△ 2. Flow the lacquer on with the grain. Work fast and always against a wet edge.
△ 3. Although lacquer dries to the touch in a few minutes, consult the label to find out how long to wait between coats. Sanding is unnecessary because each subsequent coat dissolves the covering layer of the previous coat and fuses them together. Therefore, sand only for smoothing, not adhesion.
△ 4. After the last coat, apply a very fine abrasive such as pumice and rubbing oil to provide a high polish.

Varnish is the most popular finish of the three basic types. Available in glossy or satin finishes to suit your taste, varnish is tough, water resistant, and heat resistant. The biggest disadvantage with varnish is that it is very slow to dry. A long drying time means that varnish has longer to gather lint—and it does. It is more difficult to apply than

Synthetic Finish Dries Quickly

Among the synthetic finishes that have appeared in recent years, one of the most popular is Varathane, a product of the Flecto Company, Inc. A quick-drying plastic that you can brush on, Varathane flows on smoothly and is self leveling. Right there are two big advantages Varathane enjoys over varnish, which can be stubborn in application and leaves brush marks when it dries. Since Varathane is formulated from polyurethane resins, it dries very hard and creates a surface that resists marring, chipping, or peeling. It dries to the touch in about a half hour—another advantage over varnish—and can be recoated as little as six hours after the initial application. Varnish remains wet much longer, almost inviting dust particles to settle and ruin your finish. Varathane Clear Liquid Plastic comes in both gloss and satin finishes.

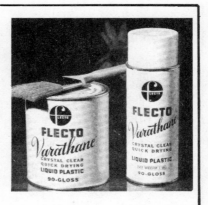

Complete Finishing Kit

Providing everything you need to finish about 100 square feet of furniture, the 1-2-3 Beautiful Wood Finishing Kit from General Finishes can convert plain pine pieces to living room furniture quickly and easily. The kit includes two pints of #1 Sealacell, a pint of Varnowax, and a pint of Royal Finish. All three are applied with a rag which, incidentally, is included as well. The kit also contains dusting and application cloths, 12 sheets of garnet finishing paper in medium-fine and fine grits, three pads of steel wool, an instruction booklet, and even two drop cloths.

Rez Skirts The Skips

Naturally, a water-based varnish is much easier to clean up than a regular varnish, but Rez Water Based Varnish offers more important advantages. Since it has a milky color when you flow it on, you can spot and repair any skips in the coating while the varnish is still wet. Moreover, it dries to a clear semi-gloss finish in an hour and can be recoated in four hours, a big time-saving factor over conventional varnishes. Rez Products are made by the Coatings and Resins Division of PPG Industries.

the other two, and if not done right, a varnish finish ends up with bubbles and brush marks. The new synthetic varnishes are much faster drying and easier to apply, with the most popular type for furniture seeming to be the polyurethane. Here is how to do the best possible job with varnish.

- 1. Try to eliminate the dust problem as much as possible before you start to apply the varnish. Pick a dust-free room with no drafts (including no heat vents), but make sure that the room has some ventilation. Vacuum the room, and then wait a couple of hours for the dust to settle.
- 2. Wear synthetic, lint-free clothes.
- 3. Work your brush against your hand before you start to make sure there are no loose bristles.
- 4. Go over the entire piece of furniture with a tack rag right before you start. A tack rag can pick up minute particles of dust and lint.
- 5. Work opposite a light source so that you will not skip any spots as you apply the varnish.
- 6. Learn how much varnish to get from each dip of the brush in the can. You want to avoid having to rake the brush across the can to remove the excess because raking creates bubbles. Flow the varnish on in long, slow strokes, using as few strokes as possible. Work against the wet edge at all times, and brush with the grain.
- 7. Pick up the brush at the exact moment you reach the edge. If you pause, you will leave a ridge of excess varnish along the edge.
- 8. Be sure to let each coat dry completely before even thinking about a second coat. Test by pushing your thumbnail into the finish on an obscure part of the piece. If your nail leaves any indentation, wait some more.
- 9. Fine sanding between coats will take off the gloss and give better adhesion. Use a 4/0 (0000) steel wool for sanding.
- 10. Before applying the next coat, go over the piece with your tack rag.

Two or three coats of varnish are recommended. Although it takes time and care, varnishing usually yields a fine finish in the end.

Step 4

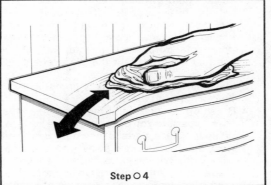

Step 4

Here Is What You Will Need

Materials
- Shellac, lacquer, or varnish
- Denatured alcohol
- Sandpaper: 220 and 240 grit
- Steel wool: 4/0 (0000)
- Lacquer thinner
- Pumice and rubbing oil

Tools
- Paintbrush
- Tack rag

Tung Oil Is Tough

Although people have known about tung oil for hundreds of years, not until recently has it become popular as a tough finish for fine furniture. Better than linseed oil finishes in that it does not get gummy or mildew in humid climates, tung oil is also easier to apply; it provides that hand-rubbed effect with much less rubbing than linseed oil finishes demand. It is an excellent sealer, resisting just about everything that could attack wooden furniture. Be sure to follow all the directions on the label; since tung oil is more expensive than many finishes, you should use it wisely.

No More Brush Marks With Wipe-On Varnish

A product of United Gilsonite Laboratories, Wipe-On Zar is an unbelievably fast finish which leaves a durable semi-gloss covering that resists rings, scratches, and alcohol spots. Since you use a lint-free rag instead of a brush to apply it, Wipe-On Zar can leave no brush marks. Zar is made for interior use only, and, though it creates a tough finish, it is not designed for floor applications.

Furniture

Make Your Own Glaze

A tube of artists paint and a small amount of clear varnish are all you need to make your own glaze. Most glazes come in earth tones like burnt sienna or raw umber, and even if you plan to shoot for a colored tone in the glaze, it is often wise to start with an earthy look. Cook Varnish, from the Cook Paint & Varnish Company, is fine for antiquing purposes or for general furniture finishing.

Highlights Produce Subtle Antiquing Effect

You can add touches of lustrous color to your antiquing projects with just the touch of your finger . . . and a tube of Rub 'n Buff. Just squeeze a tiny bit of Rub 'n Buff decorator finish on your finger, and then rub it into the wood where you want highlighting. Then buff with a soft cloth. Once the accents are just what you want, spray a clear protective finish over the surface. Available in 18 colors including gold and silver and bronze metallic finishes, Rub 'n Buff is available at hobby shops as well as paint stores. It is a product of the American Art Clay Company, Inc.

Latex Paint Kits Make Antiquing Simple

Antiquing kits have always been convenient, but the ones that contain latex paint are even more so. The Martin-Senour kit, for example, comes with a latex-base coat in a choice of 12 decorator colors, glaze of the water clean-up type, a brush, and an instruction booklet. Martin-Senour also offers a color glazing kit that can provide beautiful antiquing effects over enamels.

Make Your Own Kit

If you want to be more creative than the people who put together antiquing kits, you can make your own merely by purchasing semi-gloss enamel for the base coat and a glaze. And if none of the prepared glazes is exactly the shade you desire, remember that you can mix most glazes to produce almost any shade or color. You can even add powdered metal to some glazes for a gold or bronze effect. Creative antiquing usually doesn't cost very much,

Antiquing

THE TECHNIQUE of furniture refinishing called antiquing first started when paint companies brought out antiquing kits a few years ago. While kits are still available, you can save money and be much more creative by purchasing the required materials separately. As far as the paint is concerned, any semi-gloss enamel will do. The antiqued effect results from a glaze applied over the paint. You can buy different kinds of glazes in many shades and colors. In addition, you can make your own glaze by mixing thinned artists' oil colors into a varnish or other clear sealer that will take oils. The entire antiquing process is simple if you follow these directions.

1. Apply the base coat as you would for any other paint job. You need not remove the old paint as long as it is sound, but you should make sure that the finish is smooth. Moreover, as with any paint job, you will obtain better adhesion if you degloss the surface before painting it.
2. Let the base coat dry. If the coverage is incomplete, put on a second coat. Paint a scrap the same color to use for experimental purposes. The scrap will let you see just how to attain the glaze effect you want.
3. Make sure that the paint is completely dry before applying the glaze.
4. Brush on the glaze, but take no pains other than to be sure you cover the entire surface.
5. When the glaze starts to look dull, wipe it off. How much you wipe away and what you wipe with determine the furniture's final appearance. A soft cloth removes more glaze than a coarse one, and very coarse material—like burlap or a carpet scrap—will leave streaks.
6. As you wipe the glaze away, take more off in the center than in the corners to give the finish an aged look.
7. For a simulated wood grain finish, drag a dry brush or a carpet scrap across the piece (going with the grain) after you wipe the glaze. This technique takes practice before you can expect professional results.
8. Another popular treatment is called spatter-dashing, which means leaving little dark dots over the surface. Dip a toothbrush into dark (almost black) paint and hold the brush close to the surface with the bristles pointed upward. When you draw a stick across the

Here Is What You Will Need

Materials

- Antiquing kit or latex semi-gloss enamel and glaze
- Deglosser
- Wiping cloths
- Dark paint
- Carpet scrap

Tools

- Paintbrushes
- Toothbrush

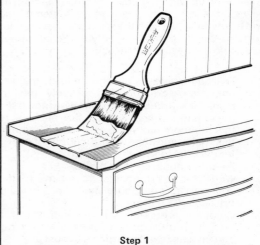

Step 1

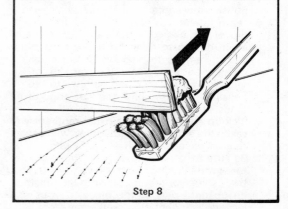

Step 8

bristles toward you, you will cause the paint to spatter on the furniture. Since spatter-dashing is usually done after the base coat and before the glazing, you must make certain that the glaze you buy will not dissolve your dots.

Three-Dimensional Finish Goes On In One Coat

Perhaps you've seen table tops that look as though the finish is an inch deep and wondered how many coats of varnish were required to achieve that effect. Chances are, the deep-down finish you saw resulted from a product called Build 50 from the Behr Process Company. A two-component pour-on finish, Build 50 must be used on a horizontal surface only, and since the finish is self leveling, you must make the surface as level as possible before applying. The finish is made for interior use, but you can make it stand up to outside elements through regular applications of carnuba wax. To decorate furniture with Build 50, just follow Behr's instructions for placing coins, seeds, documents, or clippings on the table top. When coated with Build 50, these objects will produce a very personalized table that will be a real conversation piece. Build 50 can be found at most paint stores and hobby shops.

Decoupage To Decorate Furniture

Decoupage is a popular way to decorate many home furnishings, but few people think of applying this ancient craft to pieces of furniture. The basic procedure involves gluing pictures to a piece of stained or painted wood. Decotiques from "Heirloom" Crafts—a division of Lok-Box, Inc.—consist of rub-on decals that adhere instantly to bureaus, cabinets, chairs, hope chests, etc. The surface is then sealed with something like Deft Interior Clear Wood Finish, which dries in about 30 minutes.

Decorating Furniture

THIS IS A very broad heading, and we will just touch on some of the ways you can decorate furniture rather than present a step-by-step procedure for each method.

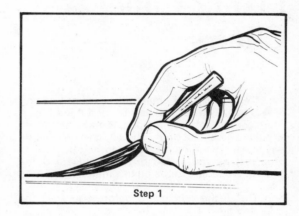
Step 1

1. Striping is the technique of putting a thin accent stripe about an inch from the edge of a table top or around a cabinet door front. It can be added to a piece of furniture long after it has been finished. It is best to buy a special striping brush and do the striping free hand. Even if you can not draw a straight line, with a little practice you will be able to make a stripe straight enough to accent the furniture. The surface must be completely clear of wax. Use a highly-thinned oil base enamel—a tablespoon of thinner to a half cup of paint should be enough. To get the straight line effect, the middle finger should act as a guide along the edge of the furniture. Practice a lot before you try the furniture.

2. Stencils give a pleasant look to furniture. An art store will have stencil paper and maybe even already precut stencil patterns or a book on stencil cutting with designs to copy. Separate stencils are required for each color. Test the design on shellacked poster board. Use a stencil brush, also from the art store, and blot away excess paint before dabbing at the cutout in the stencil. Often you have to wait for each color to dry or you will smear previous colors.

3. Decals are fine for painted children's furniture because the decoration can be changed as the child ages. They come in all sorts of themes and sizes and are available at art and paint stores. Removing a decal can be done by compressing warm vinegar over the decal to soften it.

4. Decoupage can add to a piece of furniture. Arts and crafts stores have all the supplies and give classes or instructions on this craft.

5. Gold leaf treatments can be a very effective decoration for a piece of furniture. It can be done the easy way with bronzing powders or bronzing liquids. Bronzing liquids, however, are little better than gold paint. The bronzing done with powders is done by dusting the powders over a tacky glue coat called final size. The dusting is done with a scrap of velvet, and it takes practice to get the right amount of coverage. The other way is the true gilding treatment involving the use of gold leaf. This requires lots of work, patience and practice.

This just touches the surface on what you can do to decorate furniture. Almost every month there is an article in one of the good home magazines about a new way to decorate. You can even create ways of your own. Whatever you do, if it is not to your liking, or if you get tired of it, you can strip off your handiwork and start all over again.

Here Is What You Will Need
Materials
- Oil base enamel paint
- Paint thinner
- Stencil paper
- Decals
- Vinegar
- Decoupage kits
- Bronzing powders on liquids
- Shellacked poster board

Tools
- Striping brush
- Stencil brush
- Piece of scrap velvet

Plant-Ons Create Carved Furniture Instantly

Plain furniture can be made to look carved with the addition of pieces of pressed wood or plastic known as plant-ons. Some plant-ons are actually made of wood, machine cut to look as though they were hand carved, but any kind of plant-on—even the plastic pieces—can be stained and finished to look like wood. Bendix Mouldings, Inc., a subsidiary of Lightron Corporation, makes plant-ons, coordinating decorating moldings, and a complete line of carved decorator knobs.

Decorative Stenciling Can Enhance Furniture

With the aid of a stenciling kit like one made by Duro Art Supply, you can add your own touch of style to painted furniture. The Duro stencil kit has everything you need to get started in stenciling, and numerous stencil books are available at art stores to provide even more stencil designs. One of the keys to successful stenciling is to make sure that what you are stenciling over is completely dry. The Duro kit and the various stencil books offer a multitude of tips to make your work go faster and easier.

Furniture

Shellac Your Cane Bottoms

Most people find that applying a protective coating to cane bottoms makes them easier to keep clean and more durable. A spray coating like fast-drying Zynolyte Clear Spray Shellac works well on cane bottoms. Be sure to mask around the seat so that the spray doesn't get on the wood finish, and use several thin coats instead of one thick one. Zynolyte Clear Spray Shellac is made by the Zynolyte Products Company.

Paper-Cane Makes Attractive Alternative

Paper-Cane, offered by the Minnesota Woodworker's Supply Company, is sold by the lineal foot in 54-inch widths. Very inexpensive, Paper-Cane is made of extremely durable kraft paper. Impervious to damp or humid conditions, it can be stained, painted, or varnished. It is recommended primarily for chair backs and other non-stress areas such as cabinet doors or speaker covers. Paper-Cane can be applied by splining, or it can be stapled or tacked.

Cane Bottoms From Kits

If you have never touched a cane chair except to sit in it, you might want to consider getting a Newell Caning Kit rather than starting from scratch. The kit contains all the items you need: the awl, the pegs, the sponge, the instruction booklet, and a chair-lot of cane. A chair-lot covers about one square foot, which is enough for the average chair. The kit also has binder cane for finishing the perimeter of the caned area. You can order the Newell Caning Kit through the mail from the Newell Workshop, 19 Blaine Avenue, Hinsdale, Illinois 60521.

Pre-Woven Cane Saves Time

If you lack the patience to weave cane, you can buy pre-woven mesh by the lineal foot. Held in place with splines, the cane comes in a variety of weaves and in widths from 12 to 36 inches. The Cane and Basket Supply Company (1283 Cochran Avenue, Los Angeles, California 90019) carries a wide selection of pre-woven cane patterns as well as kits and supplies for those who wish to weave for themselves.

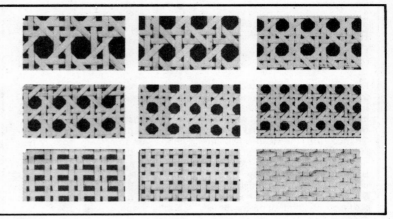

Fixing Cane Chairs

A CANE BOTTOM chair with worn-out caning is usually a bargain as a second hand buy. If you have the bottom replaced, it may not end up as such a steal, but do it yourself, and you will be way ahead of the game. You can buy pre-woven cane just as you would buy fabric. Here is the general procedure for using this material:

1. Do all the refinishing before you start the caning.
2. Carefully measure the opening. Order enough material to cover the opening; go down into the groove underneath and still have about 2 inches extra all around. (The groove is there to accept stiff splines that hold the cane in place. If the chair does not follow this method, you can still use the material by sewing it in place using the holes for the previously woven seat. You can order binder to hide the sewing and holes.)
3. Make a pattern to follow before cutting the material.
4. After it is cut, soak it in warm water to make it pliable. (This would not apply to some fake cane material, as they are already pliable.)
5. Tape the material in place over the opening.
6. Cut some inch-long blocks the width of the groove. Tap the blocks part way into the groove to hold the cane. Work your way around the chair, removing the tape as you go.
7. When you have blocks all the way around, use a sharp bladed utility knife to trim off excess material.
8. Squeeze white glue into the groove.
9. Replace the spline by tapping it down into the groove, removing the blocks as you go. Do not tap it down tight until you have gone all the way around; then tap it down all the way. This will pull the caning tight, and, as it dries out completely, it will tighten even more.

If you wish to actually reweave a chair bottom, there is an easy way to do this too. There are kits available that supply everything for this project including step-by-step instructions. This takes a little longer, and requires a certain amount of patience, but after you have done one chair using the kit, you should be able to buy the supplies separately instead of needing additional kits. The kits are inexpensive, and if there is a furniture repair supplier that carries caning materials, he should also have the kits.

Here Is What You Will Need

Materials
- Pre-woven cane material
- Tape
- White glue
- Wood blocks

Tools
- Tape measure
- Scissors
- Saw
- Hammer
- Utility knife

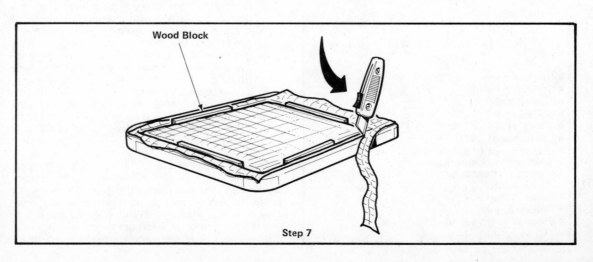

Wood Block

Step 7

Artificial Marble Has Do-It-Yourself Applications

If you would like to install your own marble counter tops, vanities, or table tops, consider the advantages offered by Corian, an artificial marble produced by Du-Pont. Corian patterns possess the same delicate veining found in real marble, but the stone-like material can be sawn, drilled, and even routed like wood with ordinary home power tools. Tough and resistant to impact damage, it is non-porous and therefore easy to keep clean. Corian is available in sheets and in some pre-molded vanity and counter-top units.

Marble Requires Special Polishes

Mar-Glo is a widely distributed marble polish that has enjoyed a long reputation for quality. It cleans and polishes and leaves a fine protective coating that repels stains from spills, even liquor spills. On the market since 1908, Mar-Glo is a product of the Golden Star Polish Manufacturing Company.

Spray Cleaner For Marble

Marble Magic is a non-abrasive aerosol foam cleaner formulated especially for marble. Just spray it on and wipe it off. It does a fine job of removing most spots and stains, and it polishes as it cleans. Although it contains no wax, Marble Magic leaves a protective coating and enhances the natural veining in marble. Marble Magic is made by the Magic American Chemical Corporation and can be found in most hardware and paint stores.

Care Of Marble

STONES ARE thought of as being hard and, therefore, able to take all measure of abuse. Marble is certainly hard if you happen to bump into it; however, it is soft when it comes to resisting stains and other maladies. Here are some steps in the care of your marble furniture tops:

1. Keep all marble surfaces properly sealed, and this will prevent most stains from getting to the marble. Marble sealers are available where marble cleaning and polishing products are sold. If you have trouble finding a sealer, go to your local tombstone cutter.
2. Mop up all spills immediately with a damp cloth.
3. If that does not work, use a mild detergent solution. Regular use of some household detergents tend to yellow the marble. If you are sloppy and have to clean the top often, buy a marble cleaner.
4. Never use home remedies such as lemon juice or vinegar solutions. These remove stains, but they also can etch the surface.
5. Vacuum the surface before you clean as grit can scratch the surface.
6. Stains that will not wash away can often be removed with hydrogen peroxide. The solution you buy already bottled usually is not strong enough, so ask your druggist for a 35% solution. Make a pad from a folded-over rag, soak it in the peroxide and place it over the spot. Now pour several drops of household ammonia onto the rag. When it stops bubbling, remove it and wipe the area with a damp cloth.
7. Tiny scratches are buffed out with a wet chamois and tin oxide. You will have to go to a marble dealer for this product unless you find a housewares department that carries a marble polishing kit. The kit will have abrasive stones, coated abrasives, and abrasive powders. Deep scratches are best removed in a marble shop with a marble polishing machine.
8. Broken marble can be repaired with epoxy cement following the directions for the particular brand you use.

Here Is What You Will Need

Materials

- Marble sealer
- Mild detergent solution
- Marble cleaner or marble polishing kit
- Hydrogen peroxide
- Household ammonia
- Tin oxide
- Epoxy cement

Tools

- Damp cloth
- Vacuum cleaner
- Chamois
- Rag

Special Stain Remover Made For Marble

The trick to removing stains from marble is to avoid damaging the marble surface, veining, or color. Goddard Marble Stain Remover and Polish removes such stains as milk, coffee, and mayonnaise and does so without harming the surface. Produced by J. Goddard & Sons, Ltd., of Surrey England, Marble Stain Remover and Polish is distributed in the United States by Johnson Wax.

Security

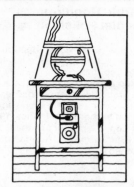

Timers Help Fool Burglars

By setting an inexpensive timer to turn on various lights and radios at logical times, you can create the illusion that your house is occupied when actually no one is home. The GE Home Sentry Timer plugs directly into the wall outlet, and the light or radio then plugs into the outlet on the front of the timer. Set the dial to the correct time, and then set the trip levers to the time you wish the apparatus to go on and off. You can also use the GE Home Sentry Timer to turn outside security lights on and off at the proper times.

Lock Plate Makes "Loiding" Less Likely

Spring-latch locks can be opened easily with nothing more than a plastic credit card. In the burglary trade, opening such locks is known as "loiding," and a good thief can open a spring-latch lock faster than you can with your key. There are several products on the market that thwart this type of entry. One is the Lock Plate made by Belwith International, Ltd. The teeth on the Lock Plate prevent any tool or credit card from reaching the latch bolt. Although not as effective in keeping out intruders as a deadbolt, the Belwith Lock Plate is an inexpensive accessory that takes little time or effort to install. Belwith International Ltd., is a subsidiary of Keeler Brass Company.

Dial Your Home's Security

Dialoc is a combination door lock that you operate by dialing four numbers on a dial much like that on a telephone. Since the lock has no tumblers, the combination can't be detected by sound, sensitivity, or X ray, and the latch is a dead-locking plunger. The dial is covered by a hinged plate that bears a handsome bronze liberty bell medallion. Made by Dialoc Corporation of America, Dialoc can be opened easily from inside by turning a knob in either direction.

Security Tips

A RESIDENTIAL burglary occurs somewhere in the United States every thirteen seconds. By making your home more secure, you might cause the local thief to try another house down the block. While there is no way to make your home absolutely burglar-proof, you can make it somewhat less vulnerable. Here are some steps you can take to deter a burglar from your home.

1. Install a deadbolt lock on every outside door. Many doors have the convenient spring-latch locks, but these locks are also convenient for the burglar. Anyone can open a spring-latch lock with nothing more than a plastic credit card. Your lock dealer will be happy to show you how to install deadbolts, and the job itself is usually a snap.
2. Install a wide-angle viewer on each outside door to permit members of your family to

Here Is What You Will Need
Materials
- Deadbolt locks
- Wide-angle viewer
- Nails
- Rods or pipes
- Extra window locks
- Exterior lighting
- Screws

Tools
- Screwdriver
- Hammer
- Drill

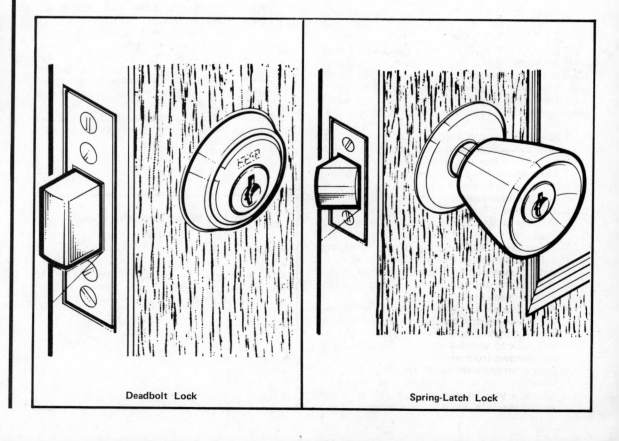

Deadbolt Lock   Spring-Latch Lock

144

Yale Padlock Is Made To Be Sturdy

The Yale name is one of the oldest in the lock business, yet Yale locks constantly emerge with new design features and improved operation. The Yale 7200 is an attractive and sturdy padlock which features a case of high-density rust-resistant alloy with a clear coated finish. The pin tumbler mechanism is far superior to warded type padlocks, and the shackle is of hardened steel with heavy plating and a clear chrome finish. Available in several different sizes, this Yale padlock also comes in a solid brass case. Yale is a division of the Eaton Corporation.

Stop Alarm Combines Stopper And Siren

The Sunbeam Stop Alarm fits over the bottom edge of a door that opens inward. When the door is closed, the unit's arm is folded down against the floor and the arm's rubber tip is angled against the floor surface to prevent the door from opening. In addition, any pressure against the arm sets off a loud piercing alarm. The inexpensive Sunbeam Stop Alarm, available at hardware stores, can be carried easily for use on hotel and motel doors.

Katy-Bar The Door

If you have a sliding glass door, you need a Katy-Bar to prevent the door from being jimmied. The Katy-Bar attaches to the door frame on the stationary side with self-tapping screws. When you wish to lock the door, the Katy-Bar folds down and telescopes out to push against the sliding panel; it can be locked in place with a twist. Able to fit any size sliding door, the Katy-Bar also makes it possible to leave the door open just a crack for ventilation without endangering your home's security. When not needed, the Katy-Bar folds up against the frame. The aluminum tubing cannot rust, and the plastic tip on the end of the tube protects against any marring of the door frame. The Katy-Bar is a product of the Dalton Manufacturing Company.

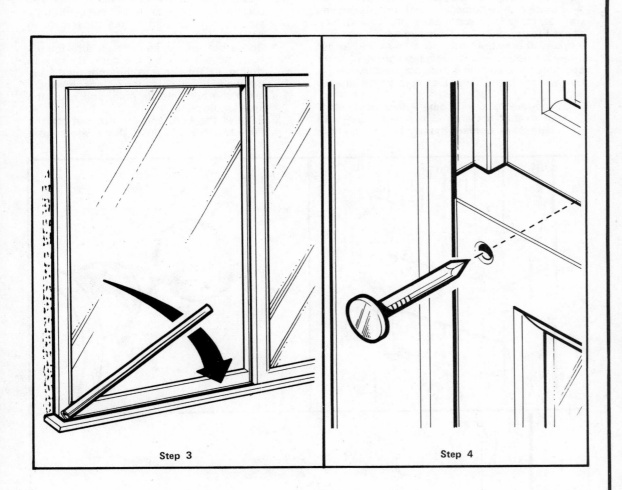

Step 3

Step 4

see who is calling without opening the door.

3. Prepare a rod or pipe to fit in the track of every sliding glass door. In addition, if the sliding door is of the type that can be lifted out of its track for repair, install three sheet metal screws in the track above the door at its closed position. If you should ever need to lift the door out, slide it open and remove the screws.

4. Provide an auxiliary lock or pin on windows so that no one can merely break the glass, reach in, and open the window.

5. Check to see if shrubbery hides doors and windows from view. Such shrubs might allow an intruder to break in without being seen.

6. When you leave—even for just a few moments—lock up.

7. Always keep your garage locked.

8. Avoid leaving tools and ladders outside where a burglar could use them to his advantage.

9. When you are outside doing yard work, keep all doors locked.

10. Keep all gates to your yard locked.

11. Provide good lighting all around your home, and keep it on all night long. Burglars seldom like to be seen on the job.

12. Check the Crime Prevention Department of your local police department and ask about a property identification program. This program enables you to borrow an electric engraver to mark your valuables. You should, of course, always maintain a record of the serial numbers from your appliances, guns, TV sets, and stereos.

Security

Schlage Double-Locking Unit Provides Double Security

The locks in the Schlage "G" series possess many unusual features for extra security. Basically, they have two different locking systems. The upper lock is a deadbolt controlled by a key outside and a thumbturn inside. The inside lock button on the lower doorknob locks the mechanism, but a turn of either the knob or the thumbturn retracts both bolts. It is not possible to break the lock by applying wrenching force to the outside knob because the knob spins freely whenever the inside locking button is pressed. The key cylinder outside is recessed to prevent tampering, and the deadbolt has a hardened steel roller inside to resist sawing. Underneath the decorative outer cover (called the Meteor design and available in a choice of several finishes) the vital lock mechanism is protected by armor plate. The Schlage line of attractive locks, locksets, and door handles enjoys a fine reputation for quality and durability.

Jig Cuts Lock Installation Time

Many lock retailers will rent or loan you a handy tool called a jig when you purchase a new lock. Although too expensive to buy for a one time lock installation, the jig simplifies your work and produces professional results. When on the door, the correct locations for all holes—both through the door and on the edge—are automatically set. If your lock retailer does not have a jig, check with local tool rental outfits. Make sure, though, that you get the jig that matches your new lockset; there are variations. Kwikset makes all sorts of security devices.

Installing a Lock

MANY PEOPLE are upgrading the locks around their homes. One of the best moves you can make is to put a deadbolt cylinder lock above the present knob. This additional lock may increase the amount of time it takes you to get into your house, but it provides important extra protection. Installation is not complicated. Here is how you can put in a new lock in very little time.

1. The new lock will come with a paper template that fits around the door's edge to permit you to mark the two holes. One hole goes through the side of the door for the cylinder, while the other goes into the edge of the door for the bolt.

2. Use a hand brace and an expansion bit or a power drill with a hole saw attachment to drill a hole of the size specified for your lock. Be careful not to damage the veneer on the opposite side of the door. When you see the point of the drill coming through, stop and go around to the other side to finish the hole.

3. Drill a hole of the appropriate size for the bolt into the edge of the door. Be sure to drill at a right angle to the door, and keep drilling until you reach the cylinder hole.

4. Insert the bolt into its hole, and mark the area for the plate.

5. Remove the bolt, and mortice out for the plate to make it fit flush. Use a wood chisel

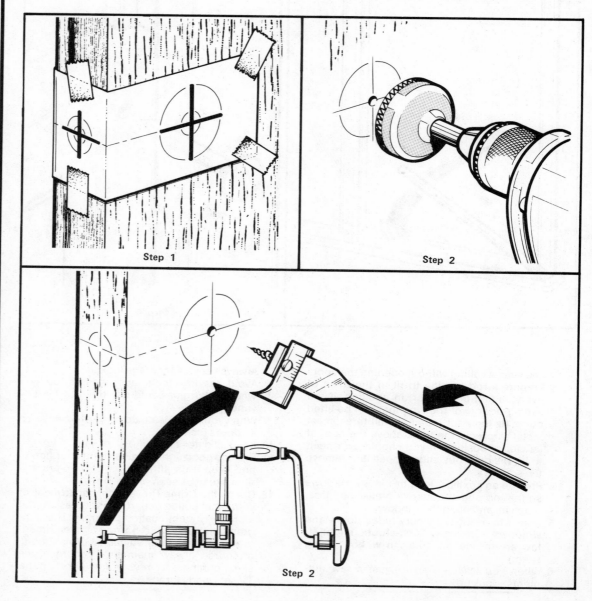

Step 1

Step 2

Step 2

Auxiliary Locks Add Deadbolt Security

It makes sense to add a lock above or below the old spring-latch lockset. A deadbolt installed as an auxiliary lock not only provides extra security but also saves you the trouble of covering the holes left by an old lock when

replaced with a new one. Either a rim lock or a bored auxiliary lock is what you want, and Yale makes both types. The bored lock has a deadbolt with a one-inch throw, and an armor pin through the bolt makes this Yale lock highly resistant to any type of sawing. The Yale rim lock possesses two hardened steel, interlocking, vertical bolts. Both locks are available in a

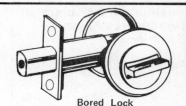

Rim Lock

Bored Lock

version that requires key operation from inside and outside, as

well as in a version with a knob inside.

to cut the mortice.

6. Insert the plate in the mortice, and drill pilot holes for the screws.
7. Install the screws to secure the bolt in place.
8. Insert the outside cylinder so that the stems or the connecting bar fits into the bolt assembly.
9. Attach the interior cylinder and secure it with screws.
10. Locate the proper spot for the strike plate on the jamb.
11. Drill the required size hole.
12. Use the plate as a pattern, mark the jamb for morticing, and cut the mortice.
13. Install the plate with screws so that it fits flush with the jamb.

If you just want to replace an existing lock with a better one, look for a new lock that will fit in the

Here Is What You Will Need
Materials
- New lock
- Large escutcheon plate
- Screws

Tools
- Drill
- Wood chisel
- Screwdriver
- Hand brace
- Expansion bit

existing holes. Sometimes you will not be able to cover the old holes with the new lock, but you can generally cover them with a large decorative escutcheon plate. If need be, you can usually enlarge mortices and holes to accommodate the new lock.

Pushbutton Lock Is Your Key To Security

Keys always present a security problem. There are several ways crooks can get hold of your keys and make duplicates. With pushbutton locks, however, you can change the number quickly anytime you suspect that someone knows the combination who should not know it. Simplex Security Systems, Inc., makes a pushbutton deadbolt system designed to be installed above the regular lockset on either left- or right-handed doors. The lock can be set to use as many of the five buttons as you desire, and it only opens when the right ones are pushed in precisely the right order. While there are only five buttons, two numbers pushed simultaneously register differently than if the same two numbers were pushed in either sequence. The Simplex Pushbutton Security System is popular for industrial purposes and could be the answer for your home or apartment.

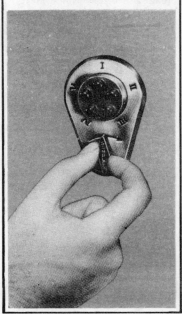

Step 3

Step 4

Step 5

Steps 8 and 9

Step 13

Security

Pushbutton Combination Deactivates Alarm System

Bowmar Security System Products markets a digital combination entrance control that allows you to turn off the system by pressing five numbers in the proper sequence. When you punch in the correct sequence of numbers, a green light comes on to let you know that your intrusion alarm is deactivated. The chance of accidentally finding the right combination by pressing random numbers is about one in 30,000 and you can change the combination anytime you wish. Part of a solid state system that includes a fire alarm as well as the intruder alarm, the Bowmar deactivation unit has a standby battery to take over, should the power go out. Bowmar also makes the Trap Mat, a security device that goes under carpets and rugs and which sets off the alarm when stepped upon.

Battery-Powered Alarm Attaches Without Nails Or Screws

The Guardian I Pre-Entry Door Alarm operates on long-life alkaline batteries; no wiring is involved. Designed to work on a variety of doors and windows—including sliding types—Guardian units are mounted with a double-faced pressure-sensitive tape. Products of Guardian Service Security Systems, a division of Presto, the Guardian line includes neighborhood alert units, heat sensors, and early warning smoke detectors.

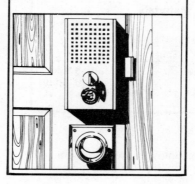

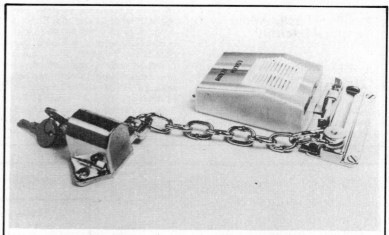

Electronic Door Chain Fools And Frightens Intruders

The Loxem Manufacturing Corporation markets a door chain with something extra. First, its locking system allows you to put the chain on when you leave your home or apartment. Since a hooked chain is always a sign that someone is at home, the intruder who succeeds in opening your door may well assume that he should go no further. Second, the Loxem door chain has a battery-powered alarm that sounds when entry is forced, hopefully scaring the intruder away. An ideal addition for an apartment dweller, the Loxem door chain can be installed easily; it comes with tamper-resistant mounting screws. Loxem makes door and window locks, viewers, and other home protection products.

There's An Alarm In Your Mailbox

One mail-order source for almost anything connected with electronic security is the Mountain West Alarm Supply Company. The Mountain West catalog offers more than 500 professional quality security products, including complete systems as well as components with which you can create and install your own system. If you have trouble finding what you want in local stores, write to the Mountain West Alarm Supply Company (4215 N. 16th Street, Phoenix, AZ 85016) for a free catalog.

Electronic Systems

WHILE ELECTRONIC security has been around for a long time, the real home security market is in its infancy. It is growing like crazy, and new systems or improvements of old ones are cropping up every day. Basically, there are three types in popular use. They are: 1. self-contained units covering a single door or window; 2. motion sensing units that cover a single room; and 3. the perimeter system which has a central unit connected to every entry.

Self-contained alarms can be very inexpensive

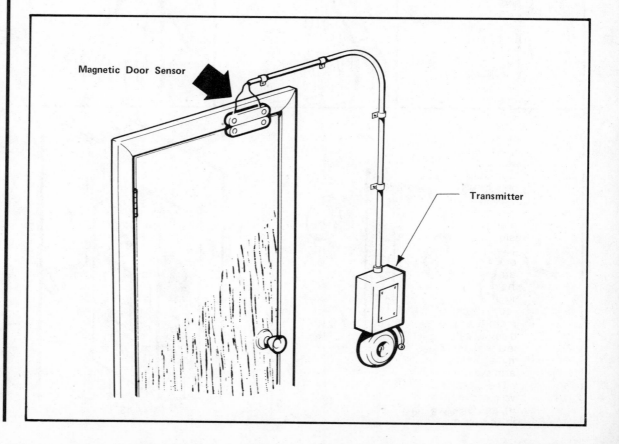

Magnetic Door Sensor

Transmitter

Signals Through House Current . . . Easy Homeowner Installation

J.C. Penney sells an easy-to-install radar system that operates through the current in your house wiring. The transmitters plug into regular wall outlets, and the only wiring is from the magnetic switches—installed at each point of entry—to the transmitters. Each transmitter can handle up to five magnetic switches. Installation is simple and safe because it is done with the transmitter unplugged. The basic kit—called Gard-Site Security System—consists of the control center, two transmitters, 50 feet of installation wire, four magnetic switches, 40 mounting clips, the indoor alarm, and installation instructions. You can add extra transmitters and switches and such accessories as an outside alarm, extra indoor alarms, or a panic button. When adding components, however, be sure to get only those which are set for the channel on which your basic system operates. The Gard-Site Security System is available at larger J.C. Penney stores.

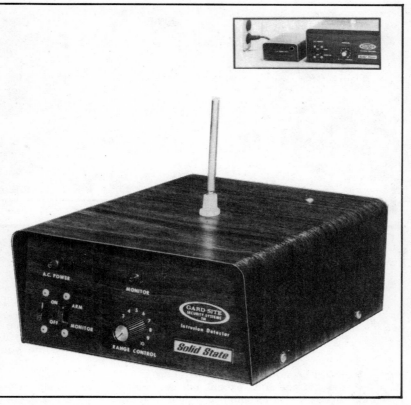

Know The Tricks Of The Burglar's Trade

Enterprising crooks like to avoid electronic alarm systems, and one way they have of finding out whether you have such a setup is by calling you and posing as sales people for a new security system. They are generally glib, and, of course, knowledgeable about burglar alarms. Just answer that you have a system—whether you do or not—and that you're happy with it. If you wish to have a system installed, you be the one to make the contact and call a reputable firm.

Screen Out A Thief

A unique way to wire a perimeter system is with Imperial Alarm Screens. These fiberglass screens have a woven grid system that results in crisscrossed wires every four inches. It is almost impossible to cut the screen without setting off the alarm. The screen also sets off the alarm if someone tries to remove it from the window. Wired in with a simple plug and socket connector, the screen is also good at keeping out insects. Imperial Alarm Screens are products of the Imperial Screen Company, Inc.

Outside Bell Has Shut-Off Timer

The Kwikset exterior alarm bell rings for five minutes and then shuts off automatically to prevent disturbing the neighborhood after the burglar runs away. The eight-inch diameter bell is extremely loud and is designed to withstand a great deal of weather abuse. Kwikset also makes alarm kits, locksets, and all sorts of components for electronic security systems; in fact, moderately priced Kwikset electronic security systems can be found in a great many hardware stores and home centers.

and are easy to install. This type is mostly battery operated and is attached to the inside of a door or window. Others are of the lock and alarm type and are set when you lock up. The problem is that they really do not make a lot of noise, usually only enough to alert you if you are at home. The alarm, be it bell, horn, or siren, will not let the neighborhood know that someone is trying to gain entry to your home. Since the unit is right there where the burglar is, he should know that you are not there. He then steps inside and cuts off the alarm. Another disadvantage is that if you have a big house with lots of doors and windows, it becomes a more costly project.

Motion detection devices are also usually self-contained. Usually you set them in the corner of the room and plug them into the house current. This system operates by sending ultrasonic waves across the room. Anything that disturbs the waves is sensed by the unit, and the alarm goes off. The big disadvantage is that the units are not cheap, and if you need to rig more than one room, it rapidly runs up the cost. Also, nothing happens until the intruder has already entered your home. If you have pets or walk in your sleep, forget this alarm because any movement will set it off. (Sometimes a curtain blowing in the breeze causes the alarm to go off.) This type is better used in a business situation where one particular area needs security while other areas do not. It would be good for a homeowner to use it for securing a garage workshop or tool storage shed.

Probably the best bet for the homeowner can be found among the several perimeter alarm systems. These sophisticated systems do more than just monitor entries. The central alarm can be connected to sensors for smoke, fire, or just about whatever else a sensor could work on.

For security against entry, installation of the perimeter alarm system can easily be done by the homeowner. The units at each entry will usually consist of two parts, one on the moveable object (like the door) and one on a fixed object (like the frame). When the entry is closed, the two parts

make contact. Open it, and the circuit is broken which sends a signal to the central control to set off the alarm. How the signal travels depends on the type of system. Most use a separate wiring system. Some, called carrier systems, utilize your house wiring. Others send radio signals and are wireless. These are the easiest to install and are called radio frequency or R.F. systems. Those using their own wiring system are often equipped with a battery backup in case of a power failure.

One advantage to the perimeter system is the ease in activating it. In most cases, you go to the central box, push one button, and it is on. With a delayed action mechanism, you will have time to get out of the house before the alarm goes off. Others will have a shunt lock outside where you can activate or deactivate the alarm.

Many systems have extra alarms besides the one at the central control. An outside alarm to alert the neighbors is good, but it should be up out of the reach of a potential intruder. The addition of a flashing light outside will alert the neighbors as to which house is sounding the alarm. If you add other watching chores for your system, it is good to have a different sounding alarm for fire, illegal entry or whatever else.

Physical evidence that you have electronic security is often a deterrent. Most manufacturers furnish decals or stickers. Post these where they will be seen. Outside bells and shunt locks are also something crooks look for. Metallic tape over glass in windows and doors indicates that you are wired against entry.

Many extra features can be worked into your electronic systems. Dialers can be added to some units that dial the police or fire department and play a taped message. A reciprocal arrangement can be worked out with neighbors so alarms go off in another house when a burglary occurs.

Whether you put in your own alarm system, or have one installed, it will not work unless you activate it when you want it on. Also, if it uses batteries, have spares and check the system regularly to be sure it is in working order.

Storage

Iron-On Edge Veneer

A standard household iron is all you need to apply plywood edging if you have Edgemate strips from the Westvaco Corporation. Real wood veneer that is pre-glued with a heat-activated adhesive, Edgemate eliminates the need for clamping or waiting for glue to set up. Edgemate comes in eight-foot rolls of walnut, oak, and birch veneers; the instant-adhering strips are $^{13}/_{16}$ of an inch wide.

Modular Systems Yield Fine Storage Walls

Some of the modular wall systems are truly pieces of fine furniture. The Design-A-Wall from Rutt Custom Kitchens, Inc., is such a system. Rutt has long been known for making quality kitchen cabinetry, and the Rutt line of modular wall components for other rooms of the house are made to the same high standards. The line includes shelves, side panels, drawer cabinets, desk sections, and even decorative components such as valances and spool rails. The only limit is your imagination . . . and your budget.

Screw Ball Is A Handy Ratchet Screwdriver

The S-V Tool Company, Inc., has come up with a space-age screwdriver that really does a better job. The Screw Ball is a ratchet driver that can be set so the ratchet works forward or backward; the ratchet mechanism can also be locked. The large two-inch diameter handle has a good feel and delivers more turning power than ordinary screwdriver handles. A heavy-duty magnet holds the interchangeable tips in place, and it magnetizes the tip to prevent screws from dropping. Extra tips can be stored in slots in the handle. The Screw Ball certainly has a place in every home.

Storage Walls

BUILDING A storage wall is a major project. No other storage unit—except a closet of equal proportions—yields as much diversified storage space. Although not difficult to construct, the storage wall does take time due to its size. Furthermore, because a storage wall is so prominent a feature of your home's furnishings, it must be constructed and finished with extra care.

You can build the storage wall against a room wall or place it as a divider in a large room. One of the most popular locations is between the living and dining areas of a room serving both functions. The storage wall can be any length, any depth from about 12 to 30 inches, and any height from six feet all the way up to the ceiling. It can be compartmented in any way that suits your needs, and in a free-standing divider the compartments can open to either or to both sides.

There is no problem in anchoring a storage wall which is built against a room wall. All you have to do is drive nails into the studs diagonally through the back edges of the unit's sides and intermediate uprights, or attach angle irons. A free-standing storage wall used as a room divider, though, is something else again. When filled, it tends to be top-heavy, and it can fall over without much provocation. The two best ways to prevent such an accident are: (1) to place one end of the wall against a room wall and nail it securely to the studs, or (2) to extend the wall to the ceiling and

nail it to the joists. The following procedure will tell you how you can build a storage wall.

1. Since the unit's top, bottom, ends, intermediate uprights, and shelves are the same depth, you can cut them all at once. Make the base of two long boards held together by two or three cross-braces cut from the same lumber.
2. Install the braces like the rungs of a ladder between the long boards so that they help to bear the weight of the structure above.
3. Anchor the base to the floor with right-angle mending plates, and nail the plywood bottom on top.
4. Nail the end panels of the storage wall over the ends of the base and top.
5. Install the intermediate uprights between the top and bottom, and nail the shelves between them.
6. To reinforce shelves which will bear very heavy loads (such as a television set or a multi-volume encyclopedia), install 1x2-inch wood cleats under the shelves and enclose the space in which the cleats are installed. The alternative is to support the shelf on right-angle mending plates mortised into the uprights to make them more or less invisible.
7. If you want to close in a space between shelves for use as a cabinet or chest of drawers, install the back panel within the space framed by the shelves and uprights. In other words, do not apply the back over the edges of the shelves and uprights so that it protrudes beyond the main plane of the storage wall.
8. In the event that you want two adjacent spaces—one above the other—enclosed, you can either install separate back panels over each space or apply a single big panel over the two.
9. If you opt for the single panel, you must trim the back edge of the shelf between the spaces so that the back panel will lie flat. Never apply a single panel over two shelf spaces which are side by side, however; for appearance's sake, the edges of the uprights should not be concealed.
10. You can install drawers easily in a storage wall with exposed edges as long as the drawers are mounted on metal drawer slides. Cut the front of the drawer to fit snugly within the shelves and uprights surrounding the space. The drawer itself should be approximately one inch (depending on the thickness of the drawer slides) narrower than the space.
11. Take a slide apart and screw one section to one side of the drawer, midway between the top and bottom edges; screw the other sec-

Here Is What You Will Need

Materials

- ¾-inch plywood
- 1x2-inch wood cleats
- Metal drawer slides
- Wrap-around hinges
- Nails
- Right-angle mending plates
- Metal lid supports
- Paint
- Piano hinge
- Paste filler
- Wood tape

Tools

- Saw
- Tape measure
- Hammer
- Screwdriver
- Sandpaper
- Paintbrush

Hand Sander Holds Belt

The Flex-Face Hand Sander is something different. A product of the Universal Metal Division of Reflect-O-Lite Corporation, it uses standard 3x21-inch sanding belts. The belts can be changed or rotated easily and are held tight by spring loading. The Flex-Face Hand Sander offers a hard face on one side and a flexible face on the other.

Wedge Screwdriver Provides Sure Grip

The Quick-Wedge screwdriver from Kedman Company is truly ingenious. The double split blade forms a powerful wedge that provides a very positive grip inside the screw slot. You control the wedging action by moving a sleeve up and down via a plastic button. Push it forward, and the split blade flares out to wedge; pull it back, and the wedge releases its grip.

Stanley Shaver Rescues Botched Wood Cuts

If you strayed a bit when sawing some of the wood for your storage wall, you can often make quick corrections with a Surform Shaver from Stanley. A compact tool that measures only 7½ inches long, the Surform Shaver features a lightweight plastic handle and edge-cutting teeth that get into curves, corners, and other tight places. The handy device shaves, trims, or scrapes with an easy pulling action, and works on wood, plaster, plastics, aluminum, and even painted surfaces. The blades are non-clogging and can be changed in a matter of seconds.

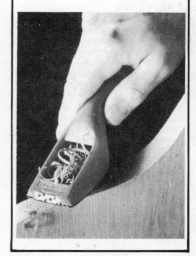

tion to the adjacent upright in the wall.

12. Repeat the process on the other side of the drawer, and then slide the drawer into the wall just as you slide a drawer into a kitchen cabinet.
13. To turn a shelf space into a cabinet, cut a pair of flush doors to fit between the shelves and uprights.
14. Hang each with a pair of wrap-around hinges.
15. A tilt-out front for a desk or bar counter is installed in much the same way. Cut the front to fit within the shelves and uprights—the face must be flush with the edges of the surrounding frame—and attach the front to the bottom shelf with a piano hinge.
16. Mortice one hinge leaf into the top of the shelf along the front edge, and screw the other leaf to the bottom edge of the tilt-out front. To hold the front in a horizontal position when it is open, attach metal lid supports (such as Stanley No. 432 or No. 430) at both sides.
17. If you wish to paint the storage wall, sand the exposed edges of the plywood carefully and brush on paste filler to fill the pores. Several applications of filler may be necessary. Then apply semi-gloss or gloss alkyd enamel. For a storage wall with a natural finish, merely cover the plywood edges with wood tape.

Edging Clamp Gets A Hold On Trim Problems

Brink & Cotton's Edging Clamp looks like a poorly designed C-clamp, but, in fact, it is a most practical tool. Ideal for holding trim to the edges on cabinets, furniture, or countertops, it can also handle more unusual clamping problems with ease. The strong frame is nickel plated; the steel screws have V threads; and all of the buttons swivel. The clamp opens 2½ inches and has a depth of two inches.

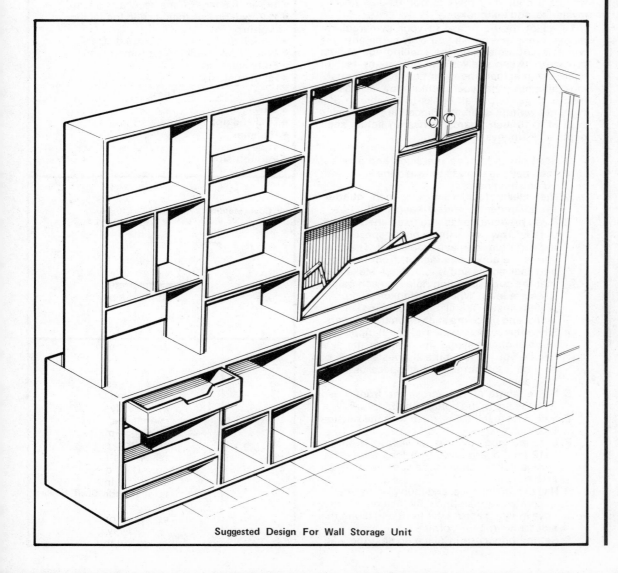

Suggested Design For Wall Storage Unit

Storage

Trim Square Can Often Do Chores of Mitre Box

A handy and lightweight tool called the Estwing Trim Square should find plenty of uses in your carpentry efforts. Placed down on your work, it provides a guide for sawing mitered corners or for cutting straight right angles. Though not designed for the precision mitering needed in making a picture frame, the Trim Square is exact enough for sawing trim and molding. Since it is made of a tough alloy aluminum, it cannot rust or corrode.

Boltmaster Brings Steel Parts Close To Home

With the do-it-yourselfer in mind, Boltmaster Corporation is marketing its threaded rods, plain rods, angle irons, slotted angles, flats, and couplers in a Steel Center rack that you can find at many hardware stores, home centers, and lumberyards. With material like this and a few nuts and bolts, you can build some very substantial shelving for garage and shop storage or for shelves inside a closet, attic, or basement.

Plywood Blades Cut Plywood Smoother

Your power saw will do a smoother job on plywood if you equip it with a blade made specifically for plywood. For example, if you own a circular saw, consider the Skokie Chieftain Plywood blade. A high quality, brightly polished, heat-treated blade, its teeth are filed and precision set for cutting plywood, paneling, and plastics. Skokie also makes a budget-priced plywood blade in the Black Chief line.

Wire Brads Are Tiny Fasteners

When you need a tiny nail either to apply trim or molding or to hold two things together while glue sets up, reach for the wire brads. Tower markets a complete line of nails, including wire brads. The only difficulty you will probably encounter in working with brads is that since they are so small, you can hit your finger with the hammer while trying to get them started. A pair of needle-nose pliers can really be helpful in such instances. By holding the brad with the pliers, you are able to see everything perfectly while keeping your fingers well away from the danger zone.

Bookcase

THERE CAN BE no question about it: houses are no longer built for book lovers. Fortunately, the problem is easy to correct.

The bookcase described here is a small one which can be placed in the middle of a wall, in a corner or recess, or used as a free-standing divider — if you add a plywood or hardboard back. It is designed to hold many oversized volumes as well as a couple of rows of normal-size novels, mysteries, and textbooks.

To adapt the bookcase to your own requirements, group the books you own by height; this will help you determine the spacing you should provide between shelves and how many feet of shelves you actually need. In figuring shelf spacing, remember that you should allow at least ½ inch of space above all books to be able to pull them out without difficulty. Since the bookcase is built of 1x10-inch boards, it has an actual shelf depth of 9¾ inches.

1. Start out by cutting the sides and shelves; then nail the shelves between the sides with 8d finishing nails.
2. Nail cleats (cut from a ⅝-inch quarter-round) under the ends of each shelf.
3. If you prefer adjustable to fixed shelves, drill parallel rows of ¼-inch holes spaced one inch apart inside each side panel. The rows should be about one inch in from the front and back edges and ½ inch deep. Make sure that the corresponding holes in each pair of rows are level. When the bookcase is completed, insert metal shelf hangers in the holes, and place the shelves on the hangers.
4. Since the vertical plates of the hanger protrude slightly beyond the faces of the side panels, you must cut the shelves about ¼ of an inch less than the actual space between the panels.
5. Nail a length of 1x4 across the front, flush with the top of the bottom shelf.
6. Nail 1x2's to the sides, flush with the outside faces.
7. Cut the top of the bookcase from a 1x12-inch board, making it long enough to overhang both ends of the case by about an inch.
8. Nail the top in place, and then give its edge a decorative appearance by nailing ¾-inch cove molding across the front and along the sides, mitering the corners.
9. Set the bookcase in place against the wall,

and secure it with finishing nails driven diagonally through the top into the wall studs.
10. Paint the bookcase with semi-gloss or gloss alkyd enamel; or stain it and then finish it with a coat of shellac and two coats of varnish.

Here Is What You Will Need
Materials

- 1x10-inch boards for the sides and shelves
- 1x12-inch board for the top
- 1x4-inch board for the base facing strip
- 1x2-inch boards for side and top facing strips
- ⅝-inch quarter-round for shelf cleats
- ¾-inch cove molding for trimming top
- Finishing nails
- Paint or stain

Tools

- Saw
- Drill and drill bit
- Hammer
- Tape measure
- Paintbrush

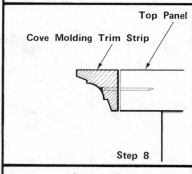

Top Panel
Cove Molding Trim Strip
Step 8

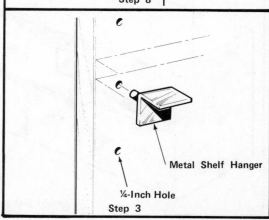

Metal Shelf Hanger
¼-Inch Hole
Step 3

Urethane Level Is Warp-Proof

It may look like it is made of wood, but the new Pro Ultimate Level is actually constructed primarily of warp-proof urethane. The core is an aluminum I-beam, the top and bottom of which are exposed to form the level's edges. Urethane forms the body of the level. The Pro Ultimate Level comes in 24-, 42-, and 48-inch models; the two longer versions have a pair of hand holes, while the 24-inch model has recessed hand grips.

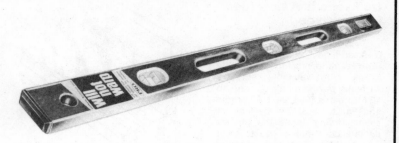

All have six vials—four for level and two for plumb. Shock-absorbing plastic caps protect the ends of the Pro Ultimate Level, an extremely accurate tool from Pro Products, Inc.

Build Adjustable Shelves Into Your Bookcase

By installing metal standards similar to those used in hanging shelving systems, you can equip your bookcase or other cabinet with adjustable shelves. Knape and Vogt makes both steel and aluminum standards in a choice of natural metal, bronze, gold, or walnut finishes. Once the standards are fastened to the side walls inside the bookcase, clips can be inserted in the standards; the shelves then rest atop the clips, which are adjustable on 1½ inch centers. Padded clips prevent shelves from slipping and are also good for supporting glass shelves.

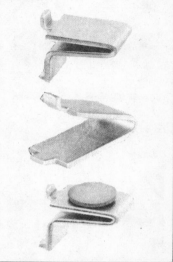

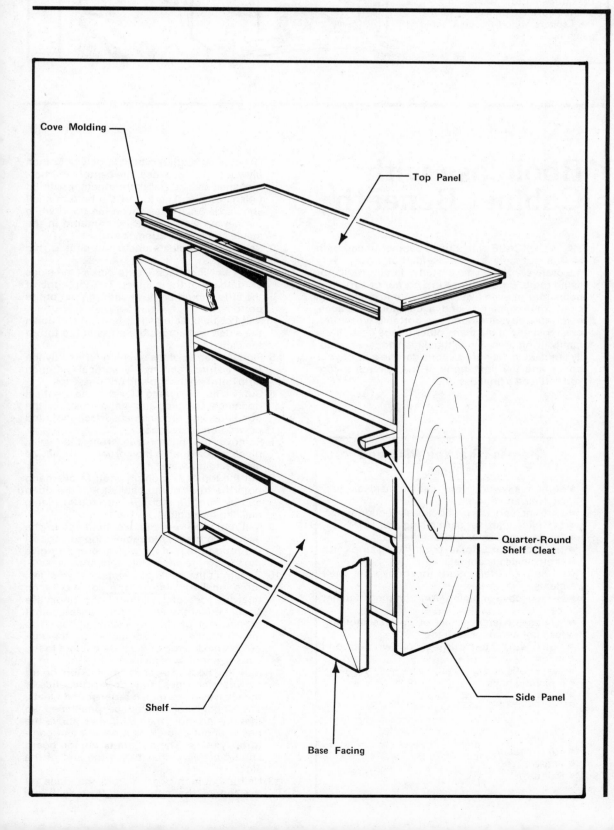

Cove Molding

Top Panel

Quarter-Round Shelf Cleat

Side Panel

Shelf

Base Facing

Assortment Pack Provides Wood Screws For Most Purposes

For the person who is so new to the home fix-it field that he or she does not know what sizes or types of wood screws to buy, the Wood Screw Assortment Fix-It Kit from U-Fasten-It may be just what is needed. The kit provides enough wood screws to handle most fix-it chores, as well as a few construction projects. U-Fasten-It also markets similar Fix-It Kits of sheet metal screws, nuts and bolts, nails, and a nail/tack assortment. All are housed in handy compartmentalized plastic snap-lid boxes. Kits are far from the least expensive way to buy these fasteners but they are handy.

Pocket Tape Measures Up Storage Projects

A retractable measuring tape that you can carry in your pocket is generally sufficient for constructing smaller storage projects. Evans Thin Tapes fit the bill. Made by the Evans Rule Company, Thin Tapes come in watch-thin lightweight cases, and you can choose among all-English markings, all-metric designations, or combined English-metric measurements.

Storage

Forged Cabinet Hardware Adds Decorative Touch

The Hager Hinge Company offers several styles of forged metal cabinet hinges, pulls, and knobs in either flat black or old copper finishes. All visible screws are of the pyramid head variety. By choosing attractive cabinet hardware, you can make a plain piece of storage furniture blend nicely with other components of a particular decorating motif.

Dial-A-Dado

There are many ways to use dado cuts in woodworking, and Arco's Dial-A-Dado Saw Washers allow you to make dados in 40 different widths with your regular saw blade. Once the Dial-A-Dado is in place (it fits any bench saw or radial arm saw with a ½- or ⅝-inch arbor), you just dial the desired width; the blade is then angled to make the correct cut in one pass. Arco also makes a regular Dado Set with blades and chippers.

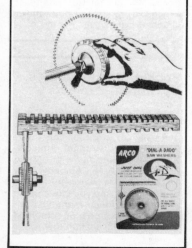

Quiksand Is A New Idea In Abrasives

Quiksand, a product imported from England, is a firm yet flexible block with reusable abrasive surfaces permanently bonded to all four sides. The square corners and flat surfaces are perfect for even sanding, while the block's flexible core allows you to sand curved areas. Quiksand comes in two grits—a medium-coarse and a medium-fine. When the abrasive surfaces become clogged, just rinse Quiksand under the faucet and let it dry. A product of Plasplugs, Ltd., Quiksand is distributed in the United States by the Landers Import-Export Company, Inc.

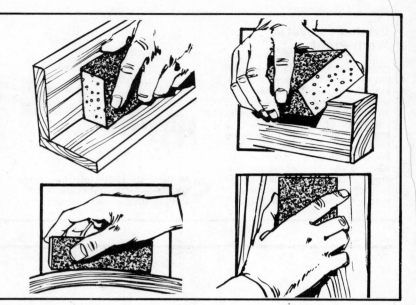

Bookcase with Cabinet Beneath

A BOOKCASE with a deep cabinet underneath is not only a very useful but also a very decorative addition to a study, family room, or living room. Best installed in a corner of a room, it holds four or even five shelves of books; an open shelf for magazines; and a cabinet for games, card table covers, hobbies, a portable typewriter, or almost any of the many other things used in the family living area. Since the dimensions are readily adjustable, be sure to consider the size of your books and the limitations of the shelves before you settle on a final design.

Here Is What You Will Need
Materials

- ¾-inch plywood for cabinet sides, top, shelves, and doors
- 1x10-inch boards for bookcase section
- 1x4-inch board for base facing strip
- 1x6-inch board for top facing strip
- 1x2-inch boards for all other facing strips and shelf cleats in cabinets
- ⅝-inch quarter-round for bookcase shelf cleats
- ⅝-inch cove molding for trimming cabinet top
- ⅝-inch (or larger) cove or cornice molding for trimming bookcase top
- Four surface-mounted or wrap-around hinges
- Two knobs and catches
- Finishing nails
- Paint

Tools

- Saw
- Hammer
- Tape measure
- Screwdriver
- Paintbrush

1. The cabinet section is built largely of ¾-inch plywood. Cut the sides, the center, and bottom shelves, and put them together with 8d finishing nails. The top of the bottom shelf should be 3⅝ inches above the floor, while the center shelf should be centered in the space above the bottom shelf.
2. Nail 1x2-inch cleats under the ends of the shelves.
3. Nail a 1x4-inch facing strip across the sides at the base of the cabinet. The top edge of the strip should be flush with the top of the bottom shelf.
4. Nail 1x2-inch facing strips both up and down the sides and across the sides at the top of the cabinet.
5. Find the center of the opening formed by the facing strips, and nail a vertical 1x2-inch strip between the top and bottom strips.
6. Cut two flush doors to fit within the identical openings created, and hang them in the openings with ornamental surface-mounted or wrap-around hinges.
7. Remove the baseboards from the walls, place the cabinet in the corner, and nail the cabinet to the walls.
8. Cut the top of ¾-inch plywood to overhang both the front of the cabinet and the open end by ⅞ of an inch. Set the top in place; nail it to the cabinet.
9. Nail and glue ⅝-inch cove moldings to the exposed edges of the cabinet top to conceal the rough grain of the plywood and to give the top a more decorative appearance.
10. Construct the bookcase section—two sides, three shelves, and a top—of 1x10-inch boards. The total width of the bookcase should equal the width of the base cabinet proper, not of the base cabinet top. The length of the sides should equal the distance from the top of the base cabinet to the ceiling, minus ¼ of an inch.
11. Nail the bookcase shelves and top board between the sides, and support the ends of the shelves on ⅝-inch quarter-round cleats. The upper shelf should be positioned so that it is no more than 80 inches above the floor—about as high as a person can comfortably reach. The bottom of the top board should be 5⅝ inches below the end of the sides.
12. Nail a 1x6-inch board across the sides (at the top of the bookcase), flush with the

Fins Make Sliding Cabinet Doors Easy To Install

A system of plastic fins makes the installation of sliding cabinet doors an easy and efficient proposition. Called the Rudy-Door-Guide, the system consists of a plastic fin on the bottom of the door and a spring-loaded fin at the top. Once you attach the Rudy-Door-Guide system to the door, you need only a piece of stiff cardboard to depress the spring in the top fin for installation or removal. Packaged with four top fins and four bottom fins, (enough for two doors), the Rudy-Door-Guide system is a product of Rudolph Industries.

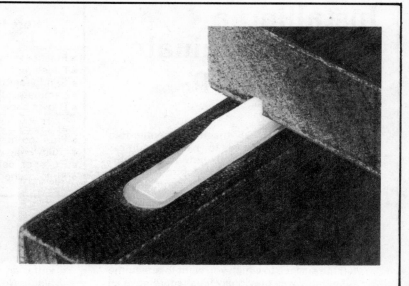

Level Your Shelves

Few people install shelves that slant noticeably, but even shelves that are only slightly unlevel can lead to problems. Minor vibration can cause items to walk off an unlevel shelf. Fortunately, it is a very simple matter to install shelves that are perfectly level. Stanley's 18-inch lightweight level has two large acrylic vials, one for level and the other for plumb.

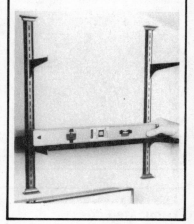

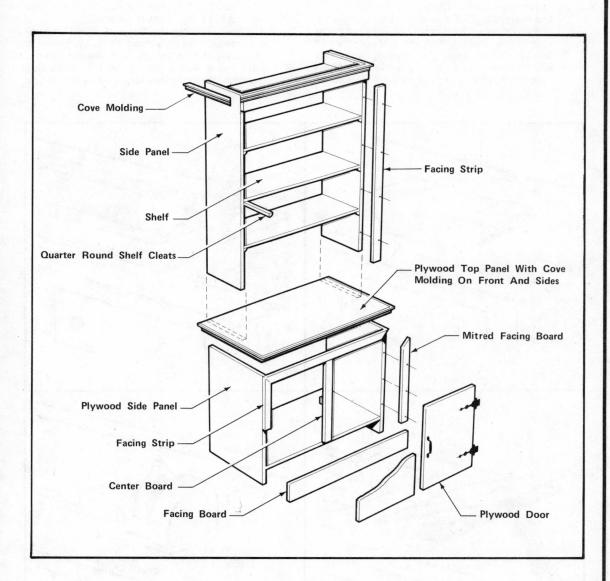

Cove Molding

Side Panel

Shelf

Quarter Round Shelf Cleats

Facing Strip

Plywood Top Panel With Cove Molding On Front And Sides

Mitred Facing Board

Plywood Side Panel

Facing Strip

Center Board

Facing Board

Plywood Door

Carved Cabinet Doors Make Storage Unit Distinctive

When you build a storage unit that you intend to be seen, you can add to its beauty and character by attaching carved doors and drawer fronts. Carved wood is terribly expensive, but you can achieve the carved wood look with Norwood polyurethane molded foam doors and drawer fronts from Urethane Arts, Inc. Norwood reproductions are relatively inexpensive, easy to install, and come in four styles and 190 different sizes. Colors include dark walnut, fruitwood, and antiques of green, blue, or white. Easy to clean with warm soapy water, Norwood doors and drawer fronts do not need refinishing, although a finishing kit is available to make the framework around the doors and drawer fronts match the color and style of the reproductions.

Push Drill Comes In Handy For Hinges And Hardware

The ratchet action of the Stanley Automatic Return Push Drill makes drilling pilot holes for hinges and small hardware effortless. With each push of the handle, the bit turns and the handle comes back up for another stroke. The drill can accommodate a number of different drill bit sizes, and the handle is large enough to provide an effective yet comfortable grip. Due to its small size (only 10½ inches long with a bit in the chuck), the Stanley Automatic Return Push Drill gets into places where a power drill could not fit.

bottom edge of the top board, and then nail 1x2-inch facing strips up and down the sides.
13. Set the bookcase on the base cabinet, scribe it to the wall if necessary, and nail it to the wall and to the cabinet.
14. Nail a cove or cornice molding around the very top of the bookcase to cover the joint between it and the ceiling.
15. Install knobs and catches on the cabinet doors.
16. Finish the entire storage unit with semi-gloss or gloss alkyd enamel to match the surrounding decor.

Get A Good Roller For Proper Bonding

If you lack a good laminate roller, your bonding projects are probably not going to work out. The Jay Roller from Minnesota Woodworkers Supply Company is a good but inexpensive three-inch wide, solid, non-marking roller that lets you exert 20 to 25 pounds of pressure per inch. The no-axle end permits you to roll flush against walls without marring them. On the higher side of the price scale is the Rollo Press from Niemi Enterprises.

File Finishes Laminate Edges

Hand filing is still a popular finishing method, and it can render good results if you use a fine-toothed mill file like the one from the Skokie Saw and Tool Company. If you decide to hand file your counter top, get some scraps of plastic laminate from your dealer and practice until you can finish and bevel with ease. Always move the file into the face of the decorative surface, and never cut on the back stroke; otherwise, slight chipping may occur. Skokie files are all made from high-carbon steel.

Laminates Must Be Cut Carefully

The wrong cutting tool can chip or crack your plastic laminate. Therefore, get a good one like the BernzCutter from BernzO-Matic with an interchangeable blade designed specifically for cutting laminates. The tool features a Spring-Bak Blade for faster and easier cutting, and since the BernzCutter lets you work from underneath, the tool does not impair your view of the cutting line. The BernzCutter also cuts lightweight metal, screening, roofing, hardboard, and various other materials.

Installing a Plastic Laminate Counter Top

CERTAINLY ONE OF the most trouble-free and attractive materials for kitchen counters is plastic laminate. Although putting in a new counter top used to be a project restricted to specialists, modern materials and adhesives are so easy to work with that the job is well within the capabilities of an inexperienced—but handy—homeowner. After you select the plastic laminate in the thickness and the pattern and the color you want, here is what to do to install it.

1. If the surface to which you want to attach the laminate was previously finished, remove all the paint or varnish right down to the bare wood. The surface must be sanded smooth, and it must be clean. Never try to cover over badly dented surfaces; the dents will show through the counter top before long.
2. Cut the laminate to fit the counter top. To cut the material, hold a fine-toothed hand saw at a low angle, and always cut with the good side of the laminate facing up. If you plan to use a power saw, be sure to insert a fine-toothed blade and to position the laminate so that the teeth cut into the good side for less chipping. You can also score and then break plastic laminate with a utility knife equipped with a special laminate blade. No matter how you cut, though, always leave a tiny margin that you can trim later, and be sure to support the sheet as you cut it.
3. Scuff the surfaces lightly with sandpaper, and then apply a contact cement made for laminates to both the surface of the counter and to the back of the laminate.
4. Let both surfaces dry the prescribed amount of time or until they become tacky. Examine the area of counter top to make sure that it still has a glossy look to it. If it does not, some of the adhesive has soaked in and you

Here Is What You Will Need

Materials
- Plastic laminate
- Finish remover
- Sandpaper
- Laminate adhesive
- Brown paper

Tools
- Fine-toothed hand saw or power saw
- Utility knife with laminate blade
- Roller or mallet and wood block
- Fine-toothed file

Step 1

Step 2

Step 2

Step 2

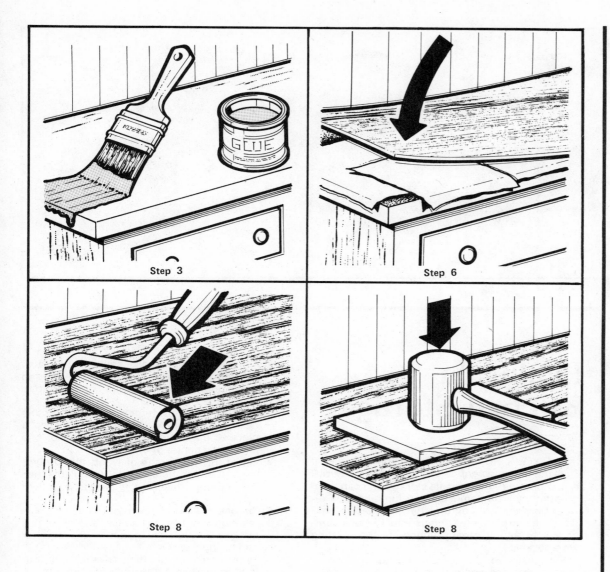

Step 3

Step 6

Step 8

Step 8

should put another coat over that area.

5. Now comes the tricky part. As soon as the two cemented surfaces touch, they will be stuck together permanently. Since you only get one chance, you must make sure that the laminate goes on the counter at the exact spot that it should go. The key to doing the job right is to place large sheets of brown paper on the counter to prevent the laminate's adhesive from coming in contact with the counter's adhesive until you get everything lined up. The paper will not stick.

6. After you line up the two surfaces, lift up one edge of the laminate and pull the first sheet of paper out, making sure not to move any more of the laminate than you must.

7. Press that end of the laminate down into the adhesive. Then continue to pull out the sheets of paper until the entire sheet of laminate is in place.

8. Use a roller or a mallet and wood block over the entire area to eliminate any air pockets and to attach the plastic laminate securely.

9. Use a fine-toothed file to remove the excess plastic laminate around the edges.

10. Apply adhesive to the edges.

11. Cut strips of laminate to fit the edges, and coat the backs of the strips with the adhesive.

12. When the mastic gets tacky, put the edge strip in place carefully. Make the first contact at the center of the strip for better control.

13. Roll the edge strip to press it firmly in place.

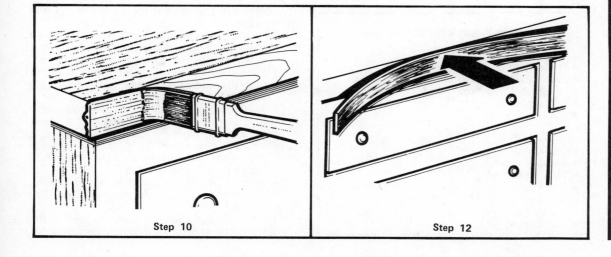

Step 10

Step 12

Moldings Hide The Rough Edges

Any cabinet or woodworking project may leave you with a few rough edges, but you can often hide these blemishes with molding. Even if the edges are clean, molding often lends a more finished look to a piece of do-it-yourself furniture. Craftwood markets a large line of unfinished moldings; any of the 54 patterns can be used for interior trim. Craftwood also markets a line of color-coded dowels that allow you to find the right diameter quickly by matching the color on a chart with the color on the dowel.

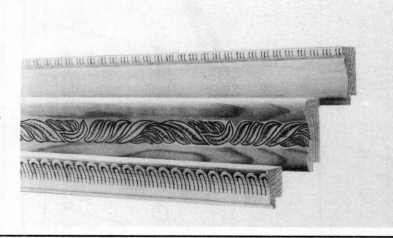

Rockford Wood Screws Are Color-Coded For Convenience

Anyone can track down the right screw to use from the Rockford display, despite the fact that the display contains 176 different items. The Post-R-Pack has a large picture of the type of screw it contains, and the screw size is plainly marked on each pack. The back of the pack contains information as to the drill bit size required for pilot holes, and it even has a rule along one edge. The Rockford name also appears on a complete line of 116 bolts; all are from the Packaged Fastener Division of Rockford Products Corporation.

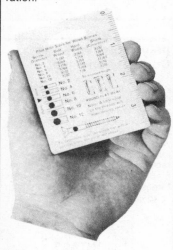

R 22 Pcs. 7167

8 × 1 Flat Wood Screws

ROCKFORD PRODUCTS CORPORATION, ROCKFORD IL 61105

Peninsula Kitchen Storage

IF YOUR KITCHEN is large enough—and if the arrangement of sink, range, and refrigerator permits—a peninsula storage unit can be of great utility. The peninsula can function as a divider between working areas; it can help to control traffic through the kitchen; it increases counter space; and it greatly augments the existing storage space.

For maximum utility, the peninsula should include both base and wall cabinets, and all cabinets used in the peninsula should be designed specifically for that purpose—with doors opening to both the front and back. You can, however, use ordinary base cabinets and cover the backs with a single sheet of plywood or hardboard. Since base cabinets cannot be screwed to a wall, you must anchor them to the floor.

The wall cabinets in a peninsula are harder to install. Buy prefabricated cabinets and a filler (if necessary) to make a row equal in length to the row of base cabinets.

1. Support the wall cabinets on two posts formed by 2x4's—or by a post at one end and an existing wall at the other, depending on the orientation of the peninsula in the room.

Here Is What You Will Need

Materials

- Wall cabinets
- Select 2x4's for cabinet supports
- Rough 2x4's for cross-blocks
- Screws, nails
- Glue

Tools

- Drill and drill bit
- Keyhole saw
- Tape measure
- Saw
- Hammer
- Plumb line
- Screwdriver

2. After you get the base cabinets in place, determine the center of the free end, and notch out the overhang of the countertop to accept the 2x4 vertical.
3. Directly above the notch, cut through the ceiling between two joists, and remove a piece of the ceiling from the center of one joist to the center of the other.
4. Select the best grade of wood the lumberyard offers for the uprights. If available, use B and Better white pine; it takes an excellent finish.
5. Cut one 2x4 to the height of the ceiling plus the height of the joist space, and place this upright through the notch in the counter and the hole in the ceiling.
6. Plumb carefully, and then drive three or four long screws into the upright through the side of the end cabinet in the base peninsula.
7. Secure the top of the upright to the ceiling joists. If the upright happens to touch one of the joists, simply nail it to the joist with three 10d common nails.
8. If there is a slight gap between the upright and a joist, wedge a board between them, and then nail the upright to the joist with 20d or 40d nails.
9. If the upright comes up more or less in the middle of the joist space, you must nail a couple of 2x4 cross-blocks across the space on either side of the upright; then you nail the upright to the cross-blocks.
10. Cut a rectangular notch across the upright on the peninsula side. The notch should be 1⅝ inches high by ⅝ of an inch deep, 18 inches above the counter.
11. Make a large hole in the wall 18 inches above the counter at the closed end of the peninsula.
12. Nail a 2x4 cross-block across the stud space, making sure that the top of the block is 16⅜ inches above the counter.
13. Cut the other piece of select grade 2x4 to fit from the back edge of the cross-block to the back of the notch in the upright.
14. Set it into the hole on top of the cross-block, fit it into the notch, and then nail or screw it to the cross-block.
15. Use glue and a couple of 10d finishing nails driven through the face of the upright to fasten the 2x4 to the notch.
16. Starting at the open end of the peninsula, center the cabinets on the horizontal 2x4 support.
17. Drive three screws through the end of the first cabinet into the upright, and then set

A Cutting Board That Takes No Counter Space

When you construct kitchen cabinets from modular components, you can opt for some rather unique accessory pieces. For example, consider the pull-out Athena cutting board from Yorktowne, a division of the Wickes Corporation. The well-constructed board is made of sturdy edge-grain maple and measures 24 inches wide. Yorktowne cabinets for islands, base, and wall installations come in seven different hand-rubbed finishes, and the workmanship is of good quality.

Keyhole Saw Features A Rotating Blade

The Rotater from Trophy Products is an inexpensive keyhole saw with a fully hardened and tempered 10-inch blade of polished steel. The teeth are precision set with eight points per inch, but the Rotater's chief distinction is its turret head which allows the blade to be rotated into eight different positions. Ideal for cutting into drywall or any of the other cutting chores that an ordinary keyhole saw would do, the Rotater has a very comfortable plastic pistol-grip handle. Blades are replaceable and lock securely into the chuck.

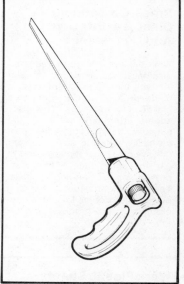

the middle cabinet on the support and screw or bolt it to the side of the first cabinet.

18. Set the last cabinet on the support, scribe the filler (if needed) to the wall, and fasten it to the cabinet.
19. Attach the last cabinet to the side of the middle cabinet.
20. Make sure that the entire row of cabinets is still centered on the support, and drive screws through the third cabinet into the wall. You will need very long screws for this procedure—especially if a filler is involved—in order to achieve a firm grip in the studs.

21. If the cabinets happen to be centered over a stud space, making screws ineffective, use spring-wing toggle bolts.
22. Now screw all the cabinets to the horizontal support.
23. Patch the holes in the ceiling and wall with gypsum board, and finish the support and upright to suit your decorative scheme. By installing the wall cabinets in this way, you make them appear almost to be floating in air because the spaces above and below them are open. This not only imparts an open feeling to the entire kitchen, but also permits you to use the entire counter from either side of the peninsula.

Chalk Line Plumb Bob Is Easy To Hold, Easy To Reel

The Chalk-Mor plumb bob and chalk line carries its own supply of chalk in its enameled die-cast case. The ball-shaped case is made for easier holding, and the Chalk-Mor has a long offset handle to let your fingers clear the case as you reel in the line; the winding handle locks quickly and easily. The screw-type filler cap makes refilling the leak-proof case easy, and the line is on a "pop-in" reel for instant replacement. The Evans Rule Company, makers of Chalk-Mor, also markets refill chalk in dark blue, dark red, white, and yellow. Chalk-Mor is available with either a 50-foot or 100-foot line.

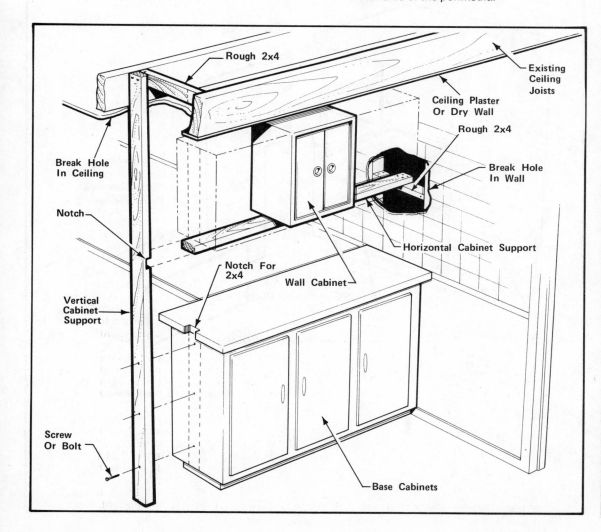

Labels: Rough 2x4 · Existing Ceiling Joists · Ceiling Plaster Or Dry Wall · Rough 2x4 · Break Hole In Ceiling · Break Hole In Wall · Notch · Horizontal Cabinet Support · Notch For 2x4 · Wall Cabinet · Vertical Cabinet Support · Screw Or Bolt · Base Cabinets

Storage

Fruit and Vegetable Cabinet

VERY FEW cabinet manufacturers make special bins or compartments for fresh produce. Unless a homemaker has a very large kitchen, she usually winds up keeping such food under the kitchen sink, in the basement, or in bowls on a counter. Although the storage conditions in this cabinet are no better than those under the kitchen sink or in a bowl atop the refrigerator, the cabinet at least provides a specific and attractive place to keep fruits and vegetables.

Probably the best way to build this cabinet is to buy a cabinet that matches the others in your kitchen and rebuild it. The ready-made unit saves work and maintains the consistency of your cabinet lineup. If you prefer to build an entirely new cabinet, however, you can do so quite easily with plywood. The cabinet in our example is a prefabricated kitchen wall cabinet 30 inches high and 24 inches wide, turned upside down and set on toeboards to bring it up to the standard 34½-inch base cabinet height.

1. The first step in adapting the prefabricated cabinet is to remove the shelves and doors. Whether you can reuse the shelves depends on how they are constructed. You will need three shelves for this project.
2. If you must make new ones, cut them out of ½-inch plywood or particleboard to the full interior width of the cabinet, and to the full depth measured from the back to the front edge of the facing strips around the door opening.
3. Notch the corners to fit around the facing strips.
4. Out of the same material, cut the vertical dividers that separate the cabinet into right- and left-hand compartments. These dividers should be the same depth as the shelves and about nine inches high; their actual

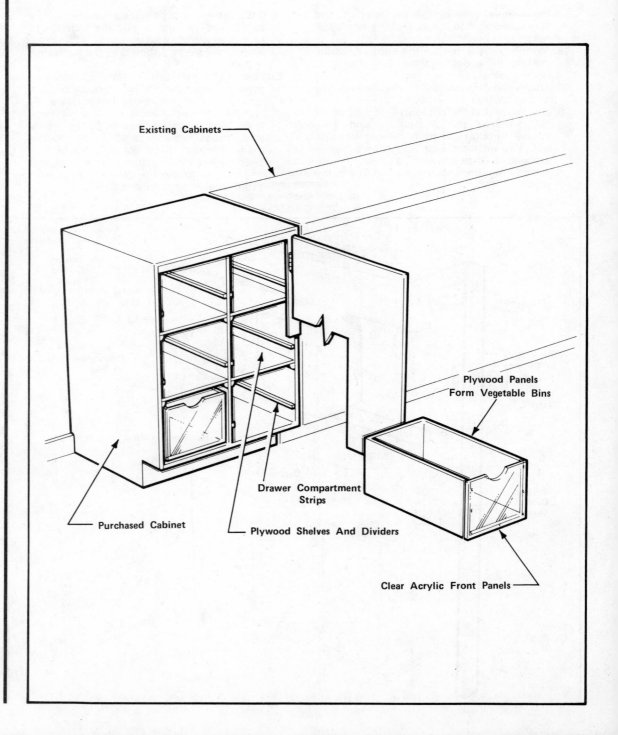

Existing Cabinets

Plywood Panels Form Vegetable Bins

Drawer Compartment Strips

Purchased Cabinet

Plywood Shelves And Dividers

Clear Acrylic Front Panels

height depends on the height of the door opening.

5. Although the cabinet already has a bottom (formerly the top), you probably will have to lay a shelf over it to provide a smooth base on which the vegetable drawers can slide in and out.

6. After setting the shelf, glue a divider to its top.

7. Install the next shelf. Support the ends on ⅝-inch quarter-rounds, and fasten the shelf to the divider below with glue and 1½-inch brads.

8. Glue a divider to the top, and install the last shelf and top divider in the same way. The last divider should be nailed to the framework in the top of the cabinet.

9. Now drive brads through the back of the cabinet into the three dividers.

10. The final step in preparing the cabinet is to install strips of wood on the outer walls of each drawer compartment.

11. Measure the distance which the facing strips project from the walls, and make the drawer compartment strips the same thickness. They should extend from the back of the facing strips to the back panel of the cabinet.

12. Install one in each compartment about three inches above the bottom of the compartment. The purpose of the strips (or guide rails) is to keep the drawers straight when you slide them in and out of the cabinet.

13. The drawers should be ⅛ of an inch narrower and shorter than the compartments, but the same depth. Build the bottom, sides, and back of ½-inch particleboard or plywood.

14. Cut the bottom the same depth as the sides (shelf depth minus ¼ of an inch), and glue and nail the bottom between the sides ¼ of an inch up from the bottom edges.

15. Then fit the back into the "U" formed by the sides and bottom.

16. Make the drawer fronts of ¼-inch clear acrylic, and install them over the edges of the side panels and bottom.

17. Then cut semicircular handholds in the top edges.

18. To do this, first find the middle of the top edge.

19. Then open a compass to four inches, place a carpenter's square perpendicular to the middle of the plastic, and set the compass point two inches out from the middle point.

20. Draw a semicircle on the plastic, and cut along this line with a coping saw. Use a blade with at least 14 teeth per inch and go slowly.

21. When you complete all the cutting, finish the edges of the acrylic.

22. Fasten the acrylic fronts to the drawers with ¾-inch round-head chromium-plated or brass screws. Use two in each side and two in the bottom.

23. Before driving the screws in, drill holes through the acrylic ¼ of an inch in from the edges. The diameter should be about 1⅓ times larger than the smooth sides of the screw shanks to allow for thermal movement. The corresponding holes in the particleboard or plywood should be smaller than the threaded portions of the shanks.

24. Paint the drawers with gloss enamel or—for a clear finish—with stain, shellac, and varnish.

25. Do the exposed edges of the shelves and dividers at the same time. Use a paste filler; otherwise, you may need three or four coats of paint to get a smooth finish on the edges of the wood.

26. When the paint is thoroughly dry, screw the acrylic fronts to the drawers. Drive the screws in tight—but not overly tight—and

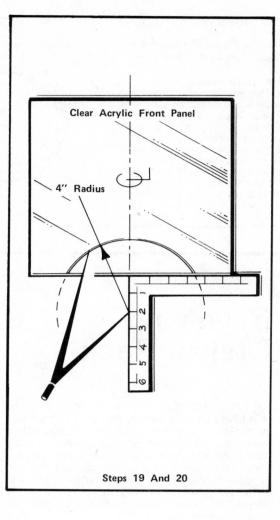

Clear Acrylic Front Panel

4" Radius

Steps 19 And 20

then back them off a quarter turn to allow for thermal movement.

27. Test the drawers in the cabinet to make sure that they slide easily.

28. Sand down the runners (the bottom edges of the sides) as necessary, and then replace the cabinet doors, if you want them. The vegetables and fruits will actually keep better, though, if you leave the doors off so that fresh air can get in. The cabinet is also more interesting looking without doors.

Here Is What You Will Need
Materials
- 1½-inch brads
- Paste filler
- ½-inch plywood or particleboard for shelves, dividers, and drawers
- Approximately 1x1-inch wood strips for guide rails
- ⅝-inch quarter-rounds for shelf cleats
- ¼-inch acrylic sheet
- Glue, nails, round-head screws
- Paint, stain, shellac or varnish

Tools
- Hammer
- Saw
- Tape measure
- Compass
- Carpenter's square
- Coping saw
- Sandpaper
- Screwdriver
- Drill and drill bits
- Paintbrush
- Sandpaper

Make Your Drill Stop At Just The Right Depth

When drilling pilot holes for screws, you could really use a device that would make the drill stop at precisely the depth you need. Fortunately, an easy-to-install device that does just that is available from the Century Drill & Tool Company, called Drill Stop. It is a hard plastic collar that slips over the bit and locks in place at the desired depth. Drill-Stop can fit drill bit sizes from 1/16 up to ½ inch.

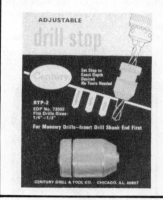

Urea Resin Bonds Stronger Than Wood

National Casein of California offers "DR" powdered resin glue, which dries very strong on either hardwoods or softwoods and can be used for all wood working, including veneering. The powder must be mixed with water for about a minute, but then is workable for at least four hours at 75 degrees. "DR" does require good clamping pressure, which must be maintained for six to eight hours or even longer. Thus, it is not the glue for people in a hurry. But used properly, "DR" glue can create joints that are stronger than the wood itself.

Careful Measuring Is Key To Success

Sloppy measuring can ruin any building project, and a good rule is a must. Ridgid's Fiberglass Folding Rules are precision made of durable heavy-duty fiberglass, with easy-to-read bold-faced figures and graduations. All rules are ⅝ of an inch wide and six feet long, and some are available in a combination English-Metric version.

Milwaukee Saws Handle Heavy-Duty Chores

If you do a great deal of building and need a rugged saw, consider buying the brand that many builders own. The Milwaukee Contractors Saw is a heavy-duty circular saw that weighs only 10½ pounds. It offers a two-position switch control along with quick and accurate miter adjustments.

Here's The Replacement For Broken Coping Saw Blade

No matter how careful you are, you are going to break a few coping saw blades. The wise woodworker, therefore, always has a good supply of replacement blades on hand. Trojan Coping and Jig Saw Blades are sharp, durable, and fast cutting. Available in pin end or lock loop ends, Trojan blades range from coarse to extra fine. Look for the rack with carded Trojan blades from Parker Manufacturing Company. You will find saber saw and hacksaw blades there as well.

Fuller Backs Screwdrivers With Full Replacement Guarantee

An unconditional replacement guarantee on tools is hard to come by these days, but that is exactly what you get when you buy Fuller Super Quality Screwdrivers. Consisting of extra-large unbreakable amber handles attached to hot drop forged chrome vanadium tempered steel blades, these screwdrivers feature a lacquered mirror-sheen finish with precision ground flats, edges, and tips. If any Super Quality Screwdriver ever displays defects in workmanship or materials, Fuller Tool Company will replace it.

Utensil Rack Revolves In Plastic Pole Sockets

Plastic pole sockets are what allow the utensil rack to revolve. Ferum brand plastic pole sockets will do the job, as will any quality sockets available at your local hardware dealer. Made of white durable plastic, Ferum pole sockets are designed, of course, to support a closet pole up to 1⅜ inches in diameter. Ferum offers a wide variety of cabinet and door hardware.

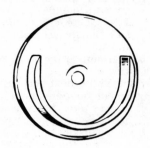

Revolving Utensil Rack

A UNIQUE storage unit for the housewife who likes to hang pots and pans on a kitchen wall but lacks enough wall space to do it, this attractive revolving pegboard rack can be mounted anywhere. Installed vertically between the top of a kitchen counter and the ceiling, the rack takes up no more than a 9x9-inch space, while it provides an actual storage area 36 inches wide by 42 inches high. Here is how you can build your own revolving utensil rack.

1. Build the rack of four 9x42-inch pieces of ⅛-inch pegboard. Cut four 40-inch lengths of ¾-inch quarter-round, and fasten two of the lengths to each of two pieces of pegboard with glue and ¾-inch brads. The edges of the quarter-rounds should be flush with the edges of the pegboard pieces, and the quarter-rounds' ends should be one inch in from the pegboards' ends.
2. When the glue is dry, attach the other two pieces of pegboard to the quarter-rounds to form a tall square.
3. Instead of overlapping the edges of the pegboard at the corners, however, cover the corners with ¾-inch outside cornerbeads 42 inches long.
4. The top and bottom of the rack are nine-inch squares of one-inch board. Find the exact center of each piece, and drill a 1⅜-inch hole through it. Then fasten the squares into the ends of the rack with glue and brads.
5. The axle on which the rack revolves is a 1⅜-inch wood round (usually sold for use as a closet rod). Cut the wood round ⅜ of an inch less than the distance from the countertop to the ceiling, insert it through the holes in the ends of the rack, and center it. It should extend approximately nine inches beyond both ends of the rack.
6. Apply glue to the joints between the axle and rack, and work it in by sliding the axle back and forth slightly. After the glue sets, drive two or three 6d finishing nails diagonally through the ends of the rack into the axle.
7. Plastic sockets—ordinarily used for hanging closet rods—hold the axle and allow it to turn. Anchor one socket to the countertop by applying a little epoxy or silicone-rubber adhesive to the base, and then driving a screw through the screw hole in the center.
8. Set the bottom end of the axle in the socket,

and fit a second socket on the top end. Swing the rack into a true perpendicular, and mark the position of the socket on the ceiling.
9. Spread adhesive on the back of the socket, reposition it on the ceiling, and press it tight.
10. Drill three screw holes through the flange of the socket, and drive long round-head screws through the holes into the ceiling.
11. Paint the entire rack with gloss alkyd enamel, and—after it dries—hang your utensils with pegboard hangers.

Here Is What You Will Need

Materials

- ⅛-inch pegboard
- ¾-inch quarter-rounds for corner blocks
- ¾-inch outside cornerbeads
- 1x10-inch board for ends of rack
- 1⅜-inch closet rod
- Two plastic closet rod sockets
- Glue, brads, screws
- Paint

Tools

- Saw
- Tape measure
- Hammer
- Drill
- Screwdriver
- Paintbrush

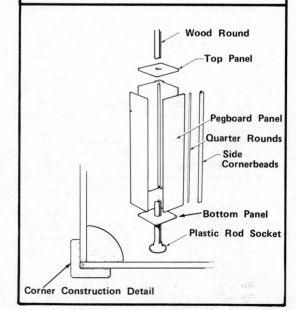

Wood Round
Top Panel
Pegboard Panel
Quarter Rounds
Side Cornerbeads
Bottom Panel
Plastic Rod Socket

Corner Construction Detail

Measure Your Success In Two Ways

The push-pull pocket rule from Roe International is a combination metric-English tape measure. The attractive case is made of tough, durable ABS Cycolac, and the hook on the end of the tape is self-adjusting for accurate inside and outside measuring. Available in both six- and twelve-foot versions, the Roe blade is printed in two colors for easy reading and epoxy coated for long life. If you want your project to measure up to expectations, be sure to have an accurate measuring device like the Roe Push-Pull Pocket Tape.

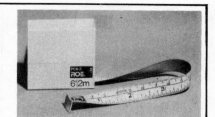

Filigree Hardboard Makes Unusual Cabinet Doors

You can attain some striking decorative effects with filigree hardboard from Barclay Industries, Inc. Made in four patterns, filigree hardboard panels would have to be set in with hinges, catches, and knobs in order to serve as a door. Filigree can also be used as a plant-on when glued to the surface of a door or other part of a cabinet. Barclay filigrees, available in a walnut finish, are sold at many building supply stores.

Kitchen Storage Above Cabinets

Here Is What You Will Need

Materials
- Hardboard for doors and cabinet end panel
- 1x1-inch boards for facing strips and cleats
- 1x2-inch boards for facing strips
- Sliding door tracks
- Finishing nails, brads, screws
- Paint

Tools
- Hammer
- Tape measure
- Pencil
- Saw
- Sandpaper
- Drill
- Paintbrush

YOU MAY GLANCE around your kitchen and think that not even an inch of storage space remains, but you are probably overlooking a very valuable place. If your kitchen wall cabinets are hung a foot or more below the ceiling, there is a great deal of space above them for storing such seldom-used items as punch bowls, fondue sets, canning equipment, Mason jars, polyethylene freezer boxes, Christmas tree ornaments, waffle irons, etc. In many houses this space is already enclosed with boards or other panels, but you can remove such enclosures easily and without fear that the cabinets will fall down or be damaged. Here is how you can make the best use of such space.

1. Mark lines on the ceiling that are parallel with the front and side edges of the cabinets.
2. Nail a 1x1-inch wood facing strip to the ceiling flush with the front line, and attach another facing strip to the tops of the cabinets flush with the cabinet fronts.
3. If the cabinets have overlay doors, you must use a wider strip (such as a 1x2) to be able to fasten it to the cabinets and at the same time have it project out flush with the door fronts. It may also be necessary to raise the strip off the cabinets with ⅛-inch hardboard in order to provide clearance over the doors.
4. Install short lengths of 1x2 vertically between the horizontal strips at both ends of the row of cabinets.
5. At the open end of the cabinet row, nail 1x1-inch cleats ⅛ of an inch back from the ceiling pencil line, from the edge of the cabinet, and from the corner 1x2.
6. Cut a piece of hardboard for the end of the

new cabinet, and fasten it to the cleats with brads.
7. Install sliding door tracks right behind the horizontal front facing strips. Mount the shallow track on the cabinet, the deep track on the ceiling.
8. Measure the space from the bottom of the bottom track to ⅛ of an inch above the lower edge of the top track, and cut pieces of hardboard to this measurement for the doors. The doors can be from 24 to 30 inches wide, but all should be the same width and overlap one another by one inch.
9. Sand the edges smooth, and then drill a ¾-inch hole through each door near the left- or right-hand bottom corner to serve as door pulls. Then slip the doors into the tracks and test them.
10. You can decorate the new cabinet to match or to contrast with the wall cabinets. Use semi-gloss or gloss alkyd enamel, a clear finish, or wallpaper. If you want a natural-wood effect, make the sliding doors from hardboard that has been finished to resemble wood.

Cup Pulls Are Attractive And Functional

Handles of any sort can get in the way of sliding doors. That's where cup pulls come in handy. National Manufacturing Company offers cup pulls in two different sizes with a bright brass finish. An oblong device called a flush pull serves the same purpose, and National offers flush pulls in brass, bronze, and chrome finishes.

Cup Pull

A Dustless Orbital Sander

Black & Decker's Finishing Sander can be equipped with a special attachment that connects the sander to a vacuum cleaner. The result? You quickly achieve dustless sanding and go a long way towards having a clean workshop. The B&D Finishing Sander operates at a fast 10,000 orbits per minute on wood, plastic, and metal. It provides fast, smooth sanding, and its double-insulated construction is a positive safety factor.

Facing Strip   Sliding Door Track

Hardboard Sliding Door

Verticle End Piece

Storage

Spice Rack Can Even Mount Vertically

One of the cleverest spice racks is the Blisscraft Every Room Organizer. Each rack holds six wide-mouth jars with snap-tight lids, and comes with labels and mounting screws. The rack can be mounted horizontally to the underside of a shelf or to a smooth wall, or it can be mounted verti-

cally to walls or doors. Blisscraft is a brand name of the Williamhouse Regency Company.

Dish Drainer In A Cabinet

If you don't like the idea of a dish drainer exposed on the drainboard in your kitchen, you'll love the idea of a drainrack that moves in and out of a cabinet over the sink. Sparkledry, a product of Double J Systems, Inc. is pulled down out of the cabinet and loaded with dishes as they are washed; then it goes back up into the cabinet with its load of wet dishes. The entire rack hides behind the cabinet doors, but water from the wet dishes drips down into the sink. Sparkledry comes in several widths.

Under-Cabinet Drawers Utilize Wasted Space

Rubbermaid's Spacemaker drawers come in two styles—utility drawers and bread drawers—that attach underneath kitchen wall cabinets with only two fasteners. The utility drawers are four inches high, 15 inches wide, and 12 inches deep; the bread drawer and the dispenser unit are the same except for their 5½-inch height. Available in any of three different front panels, Spacemaker drawers come complete with all the necessary installation hardware.

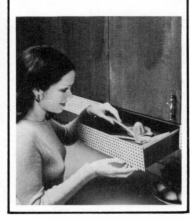

Revolving Shelf Keeps Stored Items Accessible

Scheirich, makers of fine cabinetry for the kitchen, offers a cabinet lazy susan called the Revolving Shelf Pantry-Pak. It allows for easy access to all items, in contrast to most deep cabinets in which items at the rear are almost impossible to reach. There are also free-standing revolving storage units that you merely place in the cabinet. The H.J. Scheirich Company markets "furniture for the kitchen" primarily through builders.

Convert A Closet Door To A Sizable Pantry

The back of a typical kitchen closet door can hold a large number of the cans and bottles that would otherwise take up space in a cabinet when equipped with a Dor-Wall Unit from the Schulte Corporation. Dor-Wall holds over 50 cans and bottles on its eight shelves, and it comes in 12-, 18-, and 24-inch widths for 18-, 24-, and 30-inch door widths. Made to cover a regular 70-inch door height, each Dor-Wall is 4¾ inches deep. The unit is made of welded steel rods coated with an epoxy plastic that is fused on for long life and rough wear. Dor-Walls are available in brown or white finish.

Extra Kitchen Shelf

EVERY HOMEMAKER needs another kitchen shelf; and what better place is there for such a shelf than immediately under the wall cabinets? Almost without exception, the wall space underneath the cabinets goes unused, despite the fact that it is within easy reach at all times. Since there is no better place for storing salt, pepper, seasonings, spices, and such frequently used foodstuffs as spaghetti and peanut butter, you should build the extra kitchen shelf without delay.

1. Cut a 1x4-inch board to fit under the selected cabinets, and then cut two ends for the shelf from the same board. The length of the ends should be 4¾ inches, plus any additional distance between the bottom edges of the wall cabinets and the actual cabinet bottoms.
2. In most kitchen cabinets, the bottom is suspended within the cabinet frame—not flush with the frame's bottom edges. If necessary, cut notches in the end pieces to fit around the bottom back edges of the cabinets.
3. Nail the shelf between the ends, and install the ends up under the cabinets, screwing them to the sides of the cabinets. Use bolts instead of screws if the cabinets are made of steel.
4. The back edge of the shelf should be tight against the wall, and—if you measured the end pieces correctly—the shelf should be four inches below the wall cabinets.
5. For a shelf that is only four feet long, no further support is required. For a longer

shelf, however, nail a ⅜-inch quarter-round to the wall under the back edge of the shelf to provide additional support.
6. Paint the shelf and hangers with gloss or semi-gloss alkyd enamel, or finish it with shellac and varnish.

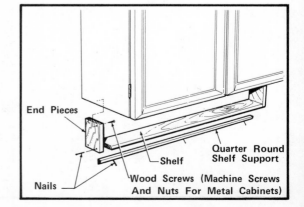

End Pieces / Nails / Shelf / Quarter Round Shelf Support / Wood Screws (Machine Screws And Nuts For Metal Cabinets)

Hanging Overhead Utensil Rack

U TENSIL RACKS suspended from the kitchen ceiling above an island or peninsula are usually fixed in position, forcing the cook to walk around them when something is needed from the opposite side. The turn-around rack, on the other hand, brings the utensils to the cook. Although it measures just two feet square, it can hold three good-sized utensils (not just forks and spoons) on each side.

Make the overhead utensil rack of a beautiful hardwood such as black walnut, cherry, or even teak. Since you need so little, select the best 1x4-inch boards available. Here is how to make it.

1. Cut the board into four two-foot lengths, miter the ends, and fasten them together with glue and finishing nails.
2. After the glue in the corner joints dries, fasten four small screweyes to the top of the rack.
3. Center them carefully in the corners, attach four lightweight chains or wires (about three feet long) to the eyes, and—once you determine the proper height for the rack—fasten the four together to a swivel at the top.
4. Hook the swivel, in turn, into a large screweye fastened through the ceiling into a joist.

5. The height at which you hang the rack depends on the height of the cook and the proportions of the room. Start at six feet, and go up or down from there, but remember that the utensils should clear the counter or range beneath by at least two feet.
6. Finish the rack with a coat of shellac, followed by a coat of varnish.
7. To hang your utensils, screw one-inch shoulder hooks into the wooden sides of the rack one inch from the bottom edge. Use three hooks per side, and space them carefully so that the utensils and rack stay balanced.

Here Is What You Will Need

Materials

- 1x4-inch boards
- Four small screweyes
- Large screweye
- Lightweight chain or wire
- Swivel
- Twelve shoulder hooks
- Shellac and varnish

Tools

- Saw
- Tape measure
- Hammer
- Pliers
- Paintbrush

Shoulder Hooks Have Many Uses

The shoulder hooks from which you hang kitchen utensils are also called L-type screw hooks. They come in different sizes, and most manufacturers put them up in carded packages like those from Jordan Industries. Jordan's shoulder hooks are made of steel and are plated with zinc chromate.

Chain Can Be Both Strong And Decorative

The chain you buy for the hanging utensil holder need not be a plain metallic type. Consider, instead, the lightweight plastic chain available from Mr. Chain. It comes in packages or rolls of black, white, gold, yellow, green, red, and blue chain with matching "S" hooks. Offering many uses both indoor and out, Mr. Chain's plastic chain never needs repainting and does not suffer from rust or corrosion. Mr. Chain, a division of M-R Products, Inc., also makes decorative posts to use in chaining off a drive, walk, or flower bed.

Connector Links Swivel To Screw Eye

If you think that locating a swivel is difficult, you will be pleased to discover that swivel snaps—like the one from Great Neck—are stocked at most hardware stores. To connect the swivel to the screw eye in the ceiling after the chains have been hooked to the snap, however, you need some sort of chain connector link. The gadget to look for is called a Quick-Link, a chain connector link made by the E.A. Karay Company.

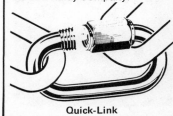

Quick-Link

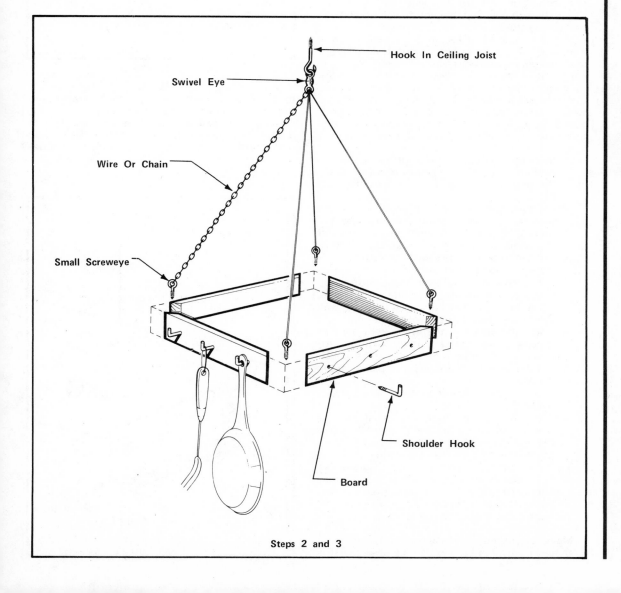

Hook In Ceiling Joist

Swivel Eye

Wire Or Chain

Small Screweye

Shoulder Hook

Board

Steps 2 and 3

Storage

Spindle Systems Create Free-Standing Storage Furniture The Easy Way

With do-it-yourself spindle furniture, you can make anything from a foot high shelf to a 12-foot wide storage wall. Emco Specialties markets a line of spindles with modular shelves and cabinets that let you design whatever you need. The spindles come in five styles and in 12- or 15-inch lengths; the accessories include connectors, finials, spacers, and shelf plugs. Since the shelves and cabinet parts have predrilled holes for the connectors, you can put together just about any design without using any tools whatsoever. Then attach some cabinet hardware and finish the unit to suit your taste. Emco modular furniture components are available in hardware stores, lumber dealers, and home centers.

Shelving Standards Need Not Be Standard

Easy-to-install wall-mounted shelf units don't all have to look alike. Cranmere shelving by Kirsch consists of wood-grain vinyl (there are two finishes available, Walnut or Southern Pecan) that resists many of the spills that would normally stain wood. Shelves are 10 inches wide by 24, 40, and 56 inches long. When mounted on studs with standard 16-inch centers, Cranmere shelves all line up evenly with a four-inch overhang on every shelf. Specialty shelves are also available, like the 18x36-inch shelf for holding a stereo, as well as the 10x10-inch pedestal shelf. The Cranmere system from Kirsch, makers of drapery hardware, includes three different bracket styles.

Plastic Shelf Supports Are Handy

There is something new from Plasplugs Limited: plastic shelf supports. To install, you insert plastic sockets into predrilled holes and then slip the support pieces into the sockets. The shelf rests on the supports, but can easily be lifted off. In case you wish to change shelf height, each support comes with an extra socket. The supports themselves come in either white or brown, with four supports and eight sockets per package. The U.S. representative for Plasplugs Limited is Landers Import-Export Company, Inc.

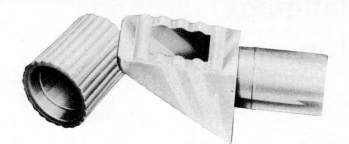

Adding Shelves

MANY HOMES seem to have less than adequate shelf space when actually there is room in the dwelling for many additional shelves. Where you find this additional space for shelves is a matter of putting on the old thinking cap and using a little imagination. How you erect the shelves is our concern. We will try to give you some clues that will enable you to put up shelves that will be sturdy, and even look good.

The materials used for shelving can be solid boards, plywood, or particle board. Naturally, the load the shelf will bear should enter into your selection of materials. Plywood and lumber are much stronger than particle board. If the shelves are to be extra wide, or if they need to be tailored to fit width-wise, particle board and plywood are easier to work with and less expensive. Here is how to install a fixed shelf in a closet or cabinet.

1. Mark the position of the shelf on the inside wall. In a closet with sheetrock walls, locate the studs for proper attachment of the bracing.
2. Cleats at each end of the shelf provide an easy means of installation. You can use 1x2 inch boards. Cut the cleats to the width of the shelf, or longer if additional length is needed to secure the cleat to the studs.
3. Mark the position of the cleat on one side, and then use a line level or measure to be sure the cleat on the other side will give you a level shelf. A chalk line along the back wall can be checked with a level to be sure.
4. Install the cleats in the studs with nails or wood screws. If stud spacing is not appropriate, use a wall anchor to attach the cleats.
5. Cut the shelf to fit and lay it in place on the cleats.
6. Use nails or screws (countersunk) to attach the shelf to the cleats.
7. If the shelves are long and must carry a heavy load, place braces at intervals along the span. The braces should be positioned on the studs if possible. Metal shelf brackets are inexpensive and effective. If studs are not properly situated, you may add a cross support and attach brackets to that. For very heavy loads, a bracket on every stud (16 inches apart) is recommended.

Movable shelves are easily added to closets or cabinets, or even to bare walls. The easiest way is

Here Is What You Will Need
Materials

- Solid, plywood, or particle boards
- 1x2-inch boards for shelf cleats
- Common nails
- Wood screws
- Wall anchors
- Metal shelf brackets
- Shelving tracks and brackets

Tools

- Tape measure
- Saw
- Level
- Hammer
- Screwdriver
- Hacksaw

to purchase commercially produced tracks and brackets. The tracks attach to the wall either in the studs or into wall anchors. The brackets fit into the track in slots at the desired height. Be sure to place tracks with brackets no more than 32 inches

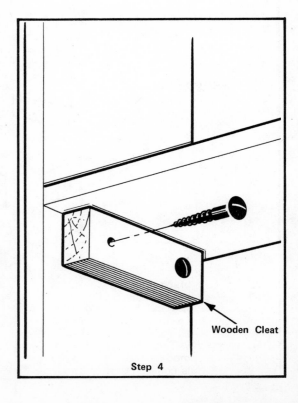

Wooden Cleat

Step 4

Tempered Glass Shelves Eliminate Breakage Woes

Most glass shelves suffer from one big disadvantage. They can break. But Cal-Tuf glass shelves are made of super-strong tempered glass. Moreover, since they come in standard widths of 4, 6, 8, 10, and 12 inches, Cal-Tuf shelves fit on standard wall brackets. They are available in lengths of 24, 36, and 48 inches. Look for Cal-Tuf shelves—made by the Cal-Tuf Glass Corporation—at hardware stores and home centers.

Wall-Mounted Heavy-Duty Shelf Units Are Easy To Hang

When you assemble and hang the Quaker Wall Storage Unit, you have a sturdy yet attractive three-shelf unit that really carries its load. The all-steel shelves are 16 inches deep; overall the unit measures 30 inches high and 36 inches wide. W-posts, steel bracing on the back and sides, double wall ribbed shelves, and nut and bolt fastening give the Quaker Wall Storage Unit its super strength. Two hanging braces that fit either 16-inch or 24-inch stud spacing are included, and no special tools are needed for assembling or hanging. The Quaker Wall Storage Unit—a product of Quaker Industries, Inc.—can be positioned nearly anywhere you need extra shelves.

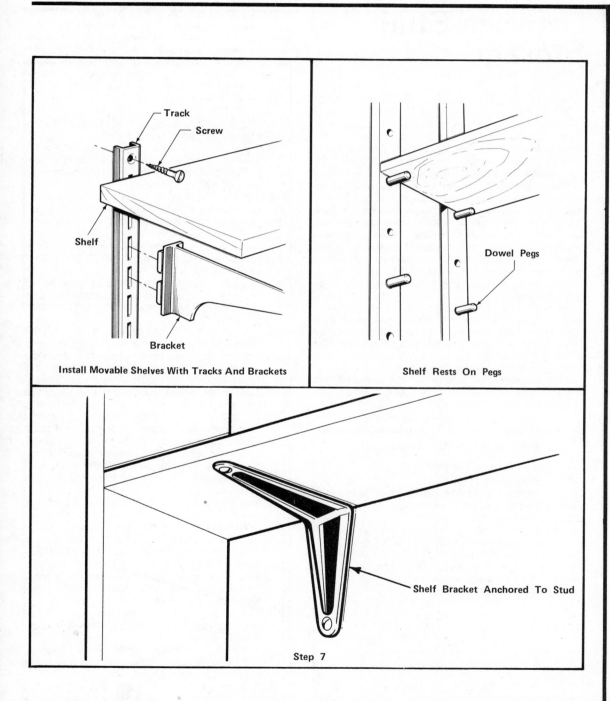

Install Movable Shelves With Tracks And Brackets

Shelf Rests On Pegs

Shelf Bracket Anchored To Stud

Step 7

Turn Do-Nothing Walls Into Organized Storage Walls

Probably the biggest name in do-it-yourself shelving is the Knape & Vogt Manufacturing Company. K-V markets standards and brackets for standard factory-made shelves as well as for shelves that you fashion, and—like many competitive shelving systems—K-V shelf units can be attached either to solid wall surfaces or to drywall. If you plan a drywall installation, however, be sure to use an adequate wall anchor or toggle bolt to insure that the shelving will be able to stand up under heavy loads.

apart for proper bracing.

The tracks come in many lengths, so you can put up one set of tracks and position shelves all up and down it. If a standard length is not suitable for your purposes, the tracks are easily cut to fit using a hacksaw. The brackets come in several lengths to accomodate the desired shelf width, and the materials come in several attractive fin-

ishes and colors. There are also prefinished shelves of various widths and lengths available.

Another way to provide adjustable shelves is to drill holes in the side of the cabinet or in wooden pieces that attach vertically to the wall. The holes accommodate dowels that support the shelf, and can be moved to different holes to change the height.

Storage

In-Wall Pantry Fits Between Studs

Called the Handy-Can Cupboard, an in-the-wall plastic cabinet that stands 5½ feet high with adjustable shelves is available from National Recessed Cabinets, Inc. The Handy-Can Cupboard is sized to fit between the studs, but other NRC models are available for surface mounting. All cabinets have magnetic catches and concealed hinges and are available with wood-grain vinyl doors, unfinished for wallpapering, or primed ready for painting. NRC also makes a smaller version of the Handy-Can Cupboard for bathrooms; it's called the Versa Cabinet.

Unique Butterfly Hinge Decorates Storage Project

The latest addition to Acorn Manufacturing Company's line of colonial hardware is the Butterfly hinge. The design, taken from an old form of English origin used on 16th century chests, is available in black, antique copper, pewter, and old English finishes. The Butterfly hinge can be mounted anywhere there is an inch or more of outside frame.

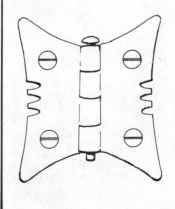

Versatile Drill Does Many Things Well

The power drill has always been a versatile tool due to all the attachments you can get for it. But the J.C. Penney Triple Action Drill takes versatility one step further. In addition to providing the rotary action needed for drilling, it offers impact action that turns the drill into a power wood chisel; the speed of the impact action is controlled by your finger pressure on the trigger. The drill even has a combination setting which creates rotary impact action for drilling concrete and masonry. The regular rotary drill action, of course, is variable in speed and reversible in direction.

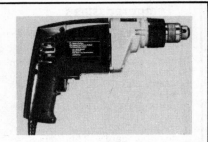

Between-Stud Storage

FEW PEOPLE are aware of the vast amount of storage space that goes unused in nearly every house. Inside the hollow walls is plenty of space for storing canned and packaged foods, jars of nails, packages of screws, fishing rods, ironing boards, and children's toys—anything, in fact, which is less than 3½ inches deep.

Building cabinets into the voids between studs is a simple undertaking, yields plenty of convenient storage space without sacrificing valuable floor space, and detracts little from your home's decor. Although between-stud cabinets are particularly useful in kitchens, bathrooms, and utility rooms, they serve many purposes elsewhere. If you paint or stain the doors and trim, moreover, the installation can be just as handsome as a large storage wall.

Water pipes and electric cables in the stud spaces should cause no difficulties, although they may reduce the storage area slightly. Even large drain pipes are not necessarily objectionable. The only things which must be avoided are wall switches, outlets, and light fixtures.

In a conventional house, all the cabinets will have an inside width of about 14⅜ inches. The height depends on the height of the stud space and/or your own needs. You can extend the cabinets from the floor to the ceiling or to any point between. In a kitchen or laundry, you can squeeze the stud-space cabinets in between the tops of the counters and the bottoms of the regular wall cabinets. Follow this procedure to build a between-stud storage area.

1. First locate the edges of the studs, and then outline the cabinet on the wall.
2. If the wall is surfaced with gypsum board, bore large holes in the four corners of the outline, and cut out the board from hole to hole with a keyhole saw.
3. If the wall is plaster, cut along the penciled lines with a chisel. Take your time, and do not pound too hard lest you crack the plaster outside the outline.
4. When you reach the lath, cut it out with a saw or—if it is steel mesh—with a hacksaw or tin snips.
5. Smooth the cut edges of the gypsum board or plaster with a rasp, pocketknife, and sandpaper. The edges should be flush with the studs.
6. If a cabinet extends only part way to the ceiling or part way to the floor, cut a 2x4 into lengths to fit tightly between the studs on either side of the opening. These are cross-blocks.
7. Toenail the cross-blocks to the studs at the top and bottom of the opening. Naturally, cross-blocks are unnecessary if a cabinet runs from floor to ceiling; the sill and plate are all you need.
8. Line the opening with strips of ⅛-inch hardboard equal to the depth of the studs and cross-blocks, plus the thickness of the wall surface.
9. Nail these strips to the four sides of the cavity with brads.
10. If the back wall of the stud space is plaster applied to wood or steel lath, it will have a rough and unattractive surface which reduces the depth of the cabinet slightly. Knock off the worst of the protruding plaster lumps, and paint the surface with latex paint, or cover the entire rough surface with ⅛-inch hardboard. In the latter case, install the hardboard before putting in the liners on the sides.
11. Make the shelves of one-inch boards, mounted on cleats from 1x1-inch boards or ¾-inch quarter-rounds.
12. Nail the cleats to the studs, set the shelves across them, and nail the shelves with a single long finishing nail angled through each end into the studs.
13. For adjustable shelves, drill two vertical rows of ¼-inch holes in each side of the cabinet, space the holes one or two inches apart, and insert steel shelf hangers.

The interior arrangement of the cabinet can, of

Here Is What You Will Need

Materials

- ⅛-inch hardboard for liners
- ¾-inch plywood or particleboard for door
- 1x6-inch boards for shelves
- 1x2-inch boards for trim
- 1x1-inch wood strips or ¾-inch quarter-rounds for shelf cleats
- 2x4 for cross-blocks
- Shelf hangers for adjustable shelves
- Two or three wrap-around hinges
- Magnetic or spring catch
- Knob
- Nails, brads
- Paint

Tools

- Pencil
- Tape measure
- Drill and drill bit
- Keyhole saw
- Chisel
- Hammer
- Hacksaw or tin snips
- Rasp or sandpaper
- Saw
- Screwdriver
- Paintbrush

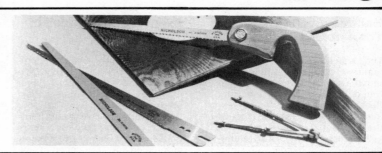

Nest Of Saws Is Three In One

Both keyhole and compass saws are useful in building storage projects, and you can get both—with a metal-cutting blade as a bonus—with the Nicholson Nest of Saws. The interchangeable 10-inch keyhole, 12-inch compass, and 12-inch metal-cutting blades fit securely into a hardwood handle and can be assembled quickly with a stud, washer, and wing nut. The professional quality silver steel blades allow you to cut any wood (including plywood and particle board) plus plaster board, plastic, and soft metals.

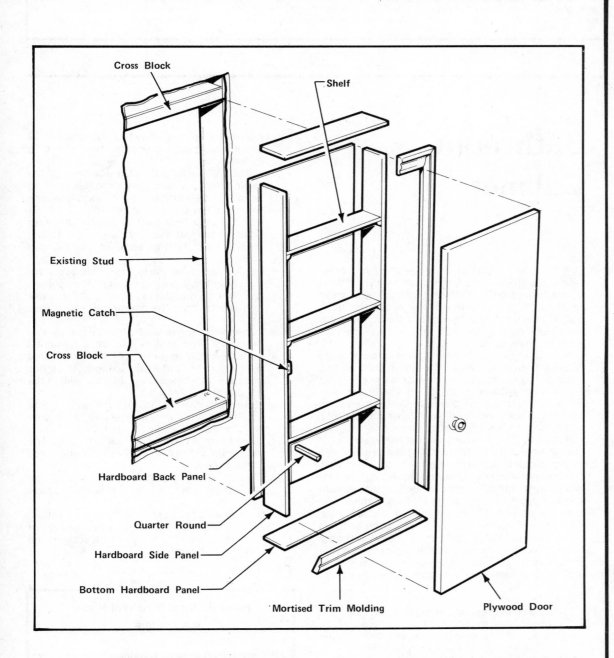

Cross Block
Shelf
Existing Stud
Magnetic Catch
Cross Block
Hardboard Back Panel
Quarter Round
Hardboard Side Panel
Bottom Hardboard Panel
Mortised Trim Molding
Plywood Door

You Can Buy Drawer Units Made To Fit Between Studs

Drawermaster drawer units are designed to fit between standard 16-inch stud spacing. Of course, Drawermaster units cannot go in a plain wall because of their depth, but they can be ideal when you wish to add drawers under a stairway, in an attic knee-wall, or in any situation where the space behind the wall can be devoted to drawer space. Installation and assembly are very easy. The front frame attaches to the studs, and the Drawermaster unit is engineered to make the front frame the only support needed. You can stack units to provide as many drawers as desired, and you have a choice of three drawer fronts. The frame has a lip to cover any rough edges created when you cut the hole in the wall. Drawermaster is made by Freedman Artcraft Engineering Corporation.

Concealed Cabinet Blends Into Wall

When you do not need a mirrored medicine cabinet, consider installing the Zenith Model 96 unit from Zenith Metal Products Corporation. It can be papered over or painted to match the surrounding walls. Designed to fit between studs, the cabinet has two adjustable glass shelves and a magnetic catch, and it can be installed for right or left door swing.

course, be designed to fit whatever you are storing. Instead of shelves, you can divide the cabinet into vertical compartments for skis, guns, fishing rods, etc. You might omit all shelves and dividers for storing an ironing board, or you might put in a combination of shelves and vertical dividers.

14. Trim the door opening with 1x2-inch (or wider) boards or with casing moldings. The inside edges of the boards should be flush with the faces of the liner strips.
15. Make the door of ¾-inch plywood or particleboard. Cut it to the size of the trimmed opening, minus ⅛ of an inch for clearance at the sides and another ⅛ of an inch for clearance at top and bottom.
16. Install the door with wrap-around hinges mortised into the edge of the door and the edge of the trim, or use ornamental surface-mounted hinges. Use two hinges on a door less than four feet high, but put three on a larger door. Install the top hinge about six inches from the top of the door, the bottom hinge the same distance from the door bottom, and the third hinge—if needed—centered between them.
17. Install a magnetic or spring catch and a knob, and your between-stud storage cabinet is ready to stock.

Storage

Handy Saw Cuts Through Sheetrock

The Master Saw from Allway Tools features blades that snap-lock into the handle, and then adjust to four different positions for making flush cuts at any angle. A very inexpensive tool—as are most of the products in the Allway line—the Master Saw has an aluminum pistol-grip handle with simulated leather inserts.

Make A Storage Wall In The Bathroom

By assembling cabinet components from the Long-Bell Division of the International Paper Company, you can create a most attractive storage wall in your bathroom. Long-Bell makes hardwood cabinets for the entire house, all of which are completely assembled and prefinished in several different colors to coordinate with a variety of interior decors. Easy to install, Long-Bell cabinets go right from the carton to the wall, but you must carefully measure the area and work closely with your dealer to get precisely the components you need. Filler pieces are available to finish out a boxed-in area.

Increase Bathroom Storage With A Stor-Wall

A quick way to expand your bathroom storage area is to install a Stor-Wall unit from the Schulte Corporation. The one-piece unit has four shelves that will hold a multitude of items. Of welded construction and coated with an epoxy plastic that is fused to the steel frame, Stor-Wall never rusts and never needs repainting. Available in white or brown and in 18-inch or 24-inch widths, it comes with hanging hardware as well as easy instructions for the do-it-yourselfer.

Bathroom Cabinet

BECAUSE THEIR storage facilities are often inadequate, bathrooms often lack the things which should be kept there. Bath towels, wash cloths, and other bathroom linens are the most typical examples, but there are others: toilet paper, soaps, heat lamps, hair dryers, cleaning supplies, cosmetics, etc.

What is required, obviously, is a large storage cabinet. It need not be elaborate; in fact, all you need is a kitchen wall cabinet or pantry cabinet with a substantial amount of unobstructed storage space. It should be deep enough to hold such things as diaper pails and extra-large bath towels, and it should have ample shelf space.

Here is an easy-to-build cabinet that meets all of the requirements. Although designed to stand in a corner, it can be set in the middle of a wall as well. The cabinet extends from floor to ceiling, is 12½ inches deep and 27¼ inches wide (outside dimensions), has space for a large clothes hamper and five shelves with 10 square feet of surface area. You can, of course, redesign the cabinet to fit your own situation, but try to stay with the 12½-inch depth. You can make the cabinet wider or narrower, and you can reduce the height or rearrange the shelves to suit your needs and desires.

1. Build the toespace first. Nail boards four inches wide together to form a rectangle. To make the job easier, assemble the cabinet on the floor first, and then lift it into place.
2. In order to fit the unit neatly between ceiling and toespace, you should build it about ¼ of an inch shorter than the wall height.
3. Make the walls and shelves of 1x12-inch boards. Nail the top, bottom, and sides together; then set the frame upright on the toespace and fit it to the wall, scribing any serious irregularities. Generally, you can cover a bad joint between the side and wall with a small quarter-round or cove molding.
4. Return the frame to the floor, and install the shelves with 8d finishing nails driven through the sides.
5. Suit the spacing between shelves to your needs, but if you are uncertain of your needs, try spacing three of the shelves 12 inches apart and the other two about 15 inches apart.
6. Leave a 20-inch space at the bottom of the cabinet to accommodate a clothes hamper or other tall articles such as plumber's friends, toilet-bowl brushes, etc.
7. Nail 1x2-inch facing strips around the four sides of the cabinet, followed by a facing strip across the top edge of the hamper section.
8. Use ¾-inch plywood to cut flush doors for the upper and lower sections of the cabinet; both doors should be ⅛ of an inch narrower and shorter than the opening in which they fit.
9. Place three hinges on the large door, two on the small. The hinges can be ornamental surface-mounted units or semi-concealed wrap-arounds, but avoid using butt hinges because the screws may not hold well in the edge grain of plywood.
10. Mount the cabinet against the wall before you hang the doors. Nail the unit to the side wall, toeboards, and ceiling joists.
11. Drive finishing nails diagonally through the back edge of the side to fasten the open side to the back wall.
12. Conceal the gap between the top of the cabinet and the ceiling with a small cove molding.
13. Hang the doors; install catches and knobs; and finish the cabinet with gloss or semi-gloss alkyd enamel or with stain, white shellac, and varnish.

Here Is What You Will Need

Materials

- 1x12-inch boards
- 1x4-inch boards for toespace
- 1x2-inch boards for facing strips
- ¾-inch plywood for doors
- ⅝-inch- or larger cove molding
- Surface-mounted or wrap-around hinges
- Catches, knobs
- Finishing nails
- Paint or stain

Tools

- Hammer
- Saw
- Tape measure
- Screwdriver
- Paintbrush

Increase Bathroom Storage With A Vanity Cabinet

Why not buy a complete vanity and replace that old lavatory? The units from Commodore Vanity Company are quite inexpensive, come fully assembled, and are available in several styles and sizes. The bowl, counter top, and backsplash consist of one-piece cultured marble. Available with or without drawers, all Commodore vanities are ready for you to install with new or old plumbing fixtures. The Commodore Vanity Company is a division of G.J. Industries.

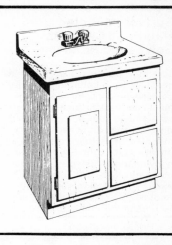

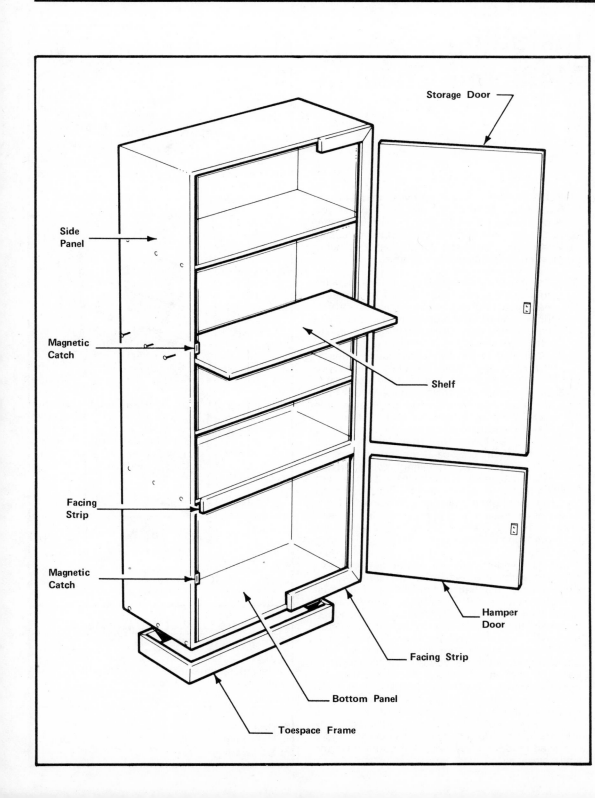

Storage Door

Side Panel

Magnetic Catch

Shelf

Facing Strip

Magnetic Catch

Hamper Door

Facing Strip

Bottom Panel

Toespace Frame

Hide The Pipes And Add More Storage Space

A neat cover-up for exposed lavatory pipes is available from the Hide-A-Pipe Company. Hide-A-Pipe's Vanitique not only conceals the trap, but also provides extra storage space for bathroom supplies. The molded styrene unit—which comes in a choice of white, black, yellow, pink, or blue—is installed with just six screws. It measures 16x18x20 inches and fits under most wall-hung lavatories.

Safe Hinges For Cabinets

Safe is a brand name found on many quality hinges and other types of cabinet hardware. Safe makes solid brass hinges that come in a red and white View-Pac with brass screws for mounting. The Safe bullet catch, which can be used in many cabinet door installations, is also marketed in the View-Pac package. When the catch is closed, the spring-held, door-mounted bullet pushes against the receiver well that is positioned in the cabinet base below the catch. The bullet catch is strong enough to hold the door shut securely, but it requires only a slight pressure to release. Safe also makes many hinges in brass-plated steel.

Colored Ceramic Knobs Add Life To Storage Cabinet

Called Accents, the brightly colored ceramic knobs and pulls for bathroom cabinets are made by the Weiser Company, a division of Norris Industries.

Storage

Surface-Mounted Bathroom Cabinets Solve Stud Problems

You may well discover that the studs in your bathroom are not situated properly for mounting a medicine chest. In such instances, you should consider installing one of the attractive surface-mounted units that merely hang on the wall. Auth Electric Company markets inexpensive wall-mounted chests with integral light fixtures and sliding mirror doors. Another advantage of the surface-mounted unit is that its size

is not restricted by the distance between the studs. Auth Electric Company is a division of Sta-Rite Industries, Inc.

Medicine Chest Provides Three-Way Viewing

Williams Division of Leigh Products markets two medicine chests that offer three-way viewing. The Trio model, which offers three square feet of mirror space, achieves its three-way effect with outer wings that are hinged to open toward the center. The center mirror door also opens, permitting full use of the storage space in the big chest. Due to its size, the Trio unit must be surface mounted, but that can be accomplished easily with four screws.

Lighting for the Trio is an optional feature. The other model, called the Mini Trio, is 24 inches high and comes in either 30- or 36-inch widths.

Triangular Cabinets Fit In Corners

Corner Vista Cabinets from Nu-Tone can provide three-way viewing plus cabinet space in a small area. Just install two Corner Vista Cabinets, one on each side of a recessed medicine chest or surface-mounted mirror, and you immediately create a flexible three-way viewing system. Corner-Vista units come in two heights, and they are reversible for right- or left-hand openings.

Who Says Medicine Chests Must Be Square?

While the cabinet is still rectangular, the mirror on the Crown Oval medicine chest from General Bathroom Products Corporation certainly is no square. Mounted just like any other between-the-studs model, the medicine chest itself is hidden with an oval mirror framed in your choice of antique gold, antique silver, or a gold and white combination. General Bathroom Products Corporation markets medicine chests, vanity tops, vanity bases, faucets, and bathroom accessories in a wide variety of styles.

Installing a Medicine Chest

MOST HOME construction over the past thirty years has been of the dry wall type. If you have dry wall type walls and if your bathroom lacks a medicine chest, you can install one easily. Recessed medicine chests come sized to fit inside the 16-inch spaces between wall studs.

1. You must first find the studs. An inexpensive tool called a stud finder utilizes a magnet to help you find the hidden nails. Once you find a line of nails, you know that there is a stud behind the wall to which these nails are attached.
2. When you locate two consecutive studs in the right area, hold the chest where you want it to go and draw an outline around it.
3. Drill a hole inside the outline and saw from the hole toward either stud, using a keyhole saw. When you reach one of the studs, cut along the outline you drew.
4. Cut a pair of 2x4s into 16-inch lengths, and toenail them in place at the top and bottom of the opening. Toenailing means driving nails at an angle. Position these crossbraces so that they are behind the surface of the wall but right at the edge of the hole.
5. Set the cabinet unit in the hole, and drive in screws on all four sides to hold the new medicine chest securely.

Cabinets wider than the space between two adjacent studs are available, but they require some special installation procedures. You must saw out sections of the studs that interfere with the cabinet, and then nail in crosspieces (headers) to regain the support lost by the missing stud sections. If you discover plumbing or wiring behind the wall at the spot where you want your medicine cabinet to be, you should forego a recessed model and install a surface-mounted unit instead. Unfortunately, the selection of surface units is not nearly as large as the choice of recessed cabinets. If you cannot find a suitable surface-mounted medicine chest, you should look into the kits that let you install a sleeve around a recessed model so that you can mount it on the wall's surface.

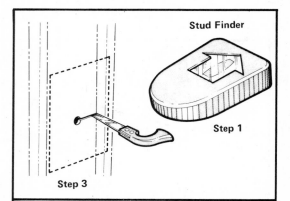

Stud Finder

Step 1

Step 3

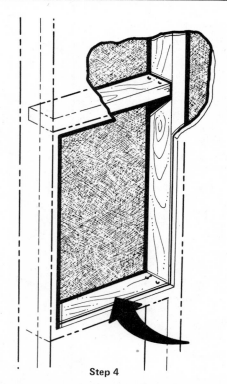

Step 4

Here Is What You Will Need

Materials

- 2x4s
- New medicine chest
- Screws
- Nails

Tools

- Stud finder
- Drill
- Keyhole saw
- Screwdriver

Saber Saw Offers Variable Speed Control

Rockwell's Variable Speed Jig Saw offers a wide-ranging speed control from zero to 330 strokes per minute. The tool tilts 45 degrees left or right for bevel cuts, and offers a two-inch depth of cut. Like most of the portable power tools in the Rockwell line, moreover, this one is double insulated for safety. While Rockwell tools provide all the features and performance that the home handyperson normally requires, they sell at very competitive prices. Rockwell also markets single-speed and two-speed saber saws.

Space Builder Increases Closet Storage

Closet Maid Corporation manufactures vinyl-coated steel rod shelving that makes it easy to get the most out of a closet. Space Builder units can be used in both new and old closets to maximize the amount of storage space available. You can also use Space Builder shelves in a utility room, in a pantry, in a garage, or in a workshop. The system includes shelves, spacers, floor and wall supports, special racks, and other components that you can fit together the way you want. The ver-

satile Space Builder system can create almost immediate storage space on any spare wall.

U-Shaped Closet Shelf

Here Is What You Will Need

Materials

- 1x12-inch boards for shelves
- 1x4-inch board or shelf moldings for shelf supports
- Nails, glue, brads
- Paint
- Sandpaper

Tools

- Hammer
- Saw
- Tape measure
- Pencil
- Straight edge
- Vise
- Paintbrush

HOW DO YOU handle the shelving in a large, deep closet? One of the best solutions is to build U-shaped shelves that provide a wide expanse of storage area without blocking you out of the closet as regular shelves would. Here is how it is done.

1. Nail shelf supports to the walls on all sides of the closet. In a clothes closet, the supports are usually made of 1x4-inch boards to which coat hooks can be attached. In linen closets—or any others with tiers of shelves from floor to ceiling—use standard shelf moldings which are rabbeted along the upper edge to receive the shelves.

2. To make each U-shaped shelf, cut a 1x12-inch board into three pieces. The board in the base of the U should be cut to the width of the closet, while the two side arms should equal the space between the front and back walls of the closet minus 11 inches.

3. Cut a 45-degree bevel in one end of each side arm.

4. Measure ¾ of an inch from the end of each board, and draw a line across the board.

5. Place the board on edge in a vise, angle a cross-cut saw from the pencil line to the opposite corner, and carefully cut a triangular piece off the end of the board. Sand until smooth.

6. Cut corresponding bevels in the front edge of the third board at both ends.

7. Measure in 11¾ inches from both ends, and draw lines perpendicular to the front edge.

8. Measure in ¾ of an inch from the front edge, and draw lines parallel to it.

9. Place the board in the vise, and saw a sloping notch first in one end and then the other.

10. Set the long board across the back of the closet on the shelf supports.

11. Set the side arms in with the beveled ends overlapping the bevels in the long board. If they fit satisfactorily, toenail the three boards to the shelf supports, and fasten the beveled joints with glue and brads or with corrugated fasteners.

12. Painting the shelf will complete this project.

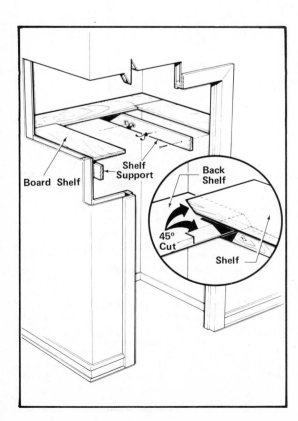

Board Shelf — Shelf Support — Back Shelf — 45° Cut — Shelf

Adjustable Metal Closet Shelves Install In Minutes

Leigh adjustable steel closet shelves come ready to be installed. All hardware is included, and in most cases all you need is a screwdriver to complete the installation. Available with or without the hanger rod and in 12- or 16-inch depths, the Leigh shelves come in lengths from 20½ inches on up to 108½ inches. Sturdy and durable, these steel shelves will never sag or warp, and their white baked-on enamel finish is protected with a scuff coat.

Closet Accessories Eliminate Crowding

The Over-the-Rod hanging shoe rack holds 30 pairs of shoes up off the floor, with the soles facing the wall so they cannot come in contact with clothes. Although best used with sliding door type closets, the Over-the-Rod shoe rack works in almost any closet, and since it merely hangs over the rod, no installation is required. The Slack Pole is another useful closet accessory. It holds eight pairs of slacks in little more space than one pair normally consumes. The slip-proof arms rotate a full 360 degrees, and the unit reaches from floor to rod. Both of these space savers are available via mail-order from United States Purchasing Exchange, 5260 Vineland Avenue, North Hollywood, California 91601.

Storage

Spring And Roller Catch Works Well, Costs Little

The spring and roller catch is a simple mechanism consisting of a spring which keeps two rollers pulled toward each other and, of course, the striker. The mechanism is mounted inside the cabinet; then the striker is mounted to the door and positioned to hit between the two rollers when the door is closed. The catch functions when the striker separates the rollers enough to squeeze through, and then the spring pulls the rollers snug to keep the door closed. Jiffy Enterprises, Inc., makes a good spring and roller catch as well as many other types of cabinet door catches.

Fold-N-Store Legs Can Be Cut To Size

Because they can be sawed easily to any height under 29½ inches, Fold-N-Store legs from Quality Steel Products, Inc., are great for any woodworking project that calls for the installation of folding legs. Made of one-inch steel tubing with a zinc-chromate plated finish, Fold-N-Store legs possess positive locking hinges made of heavy-gauge steel. The legs are packaged in sets of four, with an equal number of non-marring tips included.

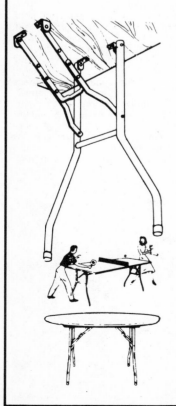

Si-Clone Blades Slash Through Wood

Simonds Si-Clone line includes four different types of circular saw blades: Chrome Plated, Teflon Coated, Carbide Tipped, and Abrasive Cut-Off. Various models within these four categories cover all of the major cutting chores the homeowner is likely to encounter. Available in all sizes and for all types of saws, Si-Clone blades possess excellent edge holding qualities, and they are accurately ground.

Sewing Door

MOST HOMEMAKERS who take up sewing seriously are badly cramped for working space. This sewing door is a possible solution for their dilemma. In one compact unit (which is completely hidden in a closet when not in use), the sewing door provides a sizable table for the working surface; a cabinet for the machine; and an additional cabinet for storage of spools, yarns, fabrics, and the many other supplies and accessories a good seamstress needs.

Since this unit is quite heavy, it cannot be hung on the back of a hollow-core flush door; it must be hung on either a traditional paneled door or a solid-core flush door. Regardless of which type it is, take the door down and install a third butt hinge midway between the existing top and bottom hinges before you start building the sewing storage unit.

The dimensions of the cabinet and sewing table can be adjusted to suit the size of your sewing machine. Although you should make the unit no larger than necessary, remember that a sewing machine is no small item; make the cabinet big enough to allow you to take the machine out and put it back in without difficulty.

1. Build the box-like sewing machine compartment first. Cut the bottom and top from a 1x10-inch board or from ¾-inch plywood; cut the sides and door from ½-inch plywood.
2. Nail and glue the bottom between the three sides.
3. Screw three eight-inch shelf brackets to the closet door so that the top of the completed compartment will be 29¼ inches above the floor.
4. Set the partially assembled cabinet on the brackets (make sure that the door in the end faces toward the latch edge of the closet door), and screw it to the closet door with three screws driven near the top of the compartment.
5. Drive screws up through the brackets into the bottom of the compartment to make certain that the unit is supported and anchored securely to the closet door.
6. Nail and glue the top of the sewing machine compartment across the tops of the three side panels; and then to complete the compartment, cut a flush door to fit within the door opening.

Here Is What You Will Need

Materials

- ¾-inch plywood for table top, table leg, and top and bottom of sewing machine compartment; or one-inch boards for the top and bottom of the compartment
- ½-inch plywood for sides of sewing machine compartment and for supplies compartment and shelves in the compartment
- ⅛-inch tempered hardboard for top of table, back of supplies compartment, and lips on shelves in the compartment
- Two wrap-around hinges
- Two 2x2-inch butt hinges
- One butt hinge for closet door to match existing hinges
- 1½x20-inch piano hinge
- Two table leg braces
- Two five-inch hooks and eyes
- Three eight-inch shelf brackets
- Door pull
- Spring catch
- Nails, brads, screws, glue
- Paint

Tools

- Saw
- Tape measure
- Hammer
- Screwdriver
- Paintbrush

7. Hang the door with a pair of wrap-around hinges, and install a spring catch and pull.
8. Make the table top of ¾-inch plywood, to which you can glue ⅛-inch tempered hardboard on the upper side to provide a smooth work surface. The width of the top should equal that of the sewing machine compartment; the length is 42 inches.
9. Attach a leg to the underside of the table top by cutting ¾-inch plywood to the width of the table and 29¼ inches high, and installing it with a pair of 2x2-inch butt hinges.
10. Screw one leaf to the back of the leg, and the other to the underside of the table (mortises are not required).
11. Set the leg back eight inches from the open end of the top, and—to make sure that the leg stays upright when you use the table—screw a pair of table leg braces to the edges of the leg and top.
12. Before you install the table top, build the supplies compartment that hangs on the closet door above the sewing machine compartment. The supplies compartment

A Tool For The Home Chiseler

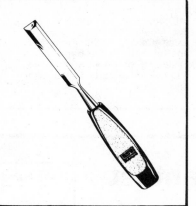

The well-known Fish & Hook brand chisel, made by the Sandvik Steel Company, is designed for the professional but priced for the amateur handyperson. The top quality Swedish steel blade should provide years of dependable service, and the plastic compressed handle is well designed to be comfortable and efficient. Sandvik Steel Company, primarily noted for its line of quality saws, offers its Fish & Hook chisels in the most popular sizes.

Inexpensive Friction Catch Does The Job

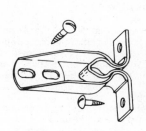

One of the most popular catches for cabinet doors is the friction catch. Jiffy Enterprises, Inc., makes a good friction catch with clips so flexible that the striker is easily engaged and released. In addition, elongated holes on the unit permit quick installation and adjustment. Just loosen the screws slightly to move the catch up or back. Many companies make good friction catches at reasonable prices.

Steel Hammer Features Built-In Shock Absorber

The Tru-Test Supreme Hammer is a 16-ounce solid steel hammer. Of course, a solid steel hammer should supply some means of shock absorption or else you would feel each blow all the way up your arm. The Tru-Test Supreme Hammer, therefore, is equipped with a hickory insert in the head to serve as a shock absorber. In addition, the handle's permanently bonded rubber grip has built-in air pockets to enhance the user's comfort. If you plan to own just a single all-purpose hammer, get a good 16-ounce model; it's big enough to be effective. The Tru-Test Supreme Hammer is available at any of the 5400 True Value hardware stores across the country.

should be the same width as the sewing machine compartment, but its height should equal the distance from the top of the sewing machine compartment to the top of the door, minus three inches for clearance at the top of the door and an additional six inches for clearance above the sewing machine compartment. The depth should be four inches.
13. Cut the four sides from ½-inch plywood and nail ⅛-inch hardboard to them to form the back.
14. The shelves, made of ½-inch plywood, should be fastened between the sides with glue and 1¼-inch brads and spaced about six inches apart. Slant the upper shelves downward toward the front of the compartment at an angle of about 30 degrees, and use these shelves for storing spools of thread.
15. Install the lower shelves flat, and use them for needles, scissors, hanks of yarn, etc.
16. Nail a one-inch lip of hardboard to the front

edges of all shelves, but take care that the lip does not project beyond the sides of the compartment.
17. Attach the compartment to the closet door with four screws driven through the back, and attach the table top to the top of the sewing machine compartment with a 1½-inch piano hinge. Screw one leaf to the back edge of the table, the other to the top of the compartment. The knuckle of the hinge should be five inches from the closet door face.
18. Drive a pair of screweyes into the edges of the table top, and mount five-inch hooks on the closet door. The eyes and hooks will hold the table top upright against the closet door when you are not using it.
19. Paint the entire cabinet (except the hardboard table top) with gloss or semi-gloss alkyd enamel. If you wish, you can glue a sheet of bulletin board cork to the front of the table leg with linoleum cement to serve as a pin-up board for patterns.

Drill Holes For Wood Screws The Three-In-One Way

Sometimes, you discover that you must drill a pilot hole, a shank hole, and then still another hole for a countersunk screw. With the Trojan Wood Screw Countersink Bit Set, though, you can perform all three drilling operations at once. The bits fit any electric drill and make it easy to drill as many holes as you need exactly the same size. Equally important, the Trojan bits cancel all concern about depth because they provide the correct depth every time. The set includes four bits plus an automatic Depth-A-Dapter that stops the drill at any of three drilling depths. The standard bits in the kit should answer your drilling needs, but if not, you can buy individual bits in any of 12 sizes.

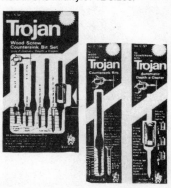

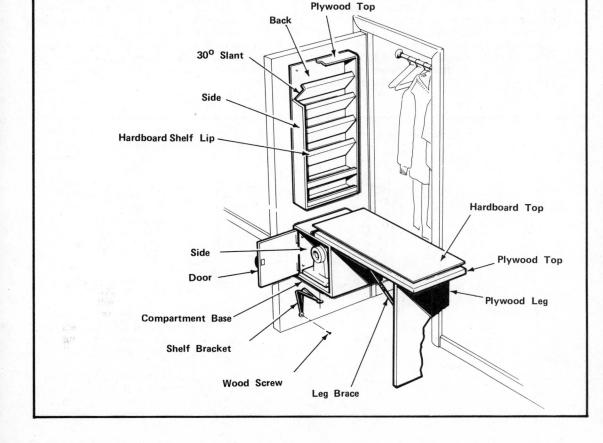

Storage

Synthetic Wood Compound Takes Stains Well

FI:X Wood Patch from Darworth, Inc., comes in all of the most popular wood colors, which means that you stand a good chance of avoiding any staining chores when you repair gouges. Wood Patch will, however, take stains, although care must be exercised since the wood around the compound may accept the stain to a different degree than the patch itself. In addition, you must take care not to get Wood Patch on the surrounding wood because the synthetic compound contains solvents that could damage the finish on the undamaged portions.

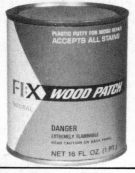

Packaged Screws Provide Convenience

While the cost per unit is undoubtedly higher, buying wood screws by the package for small jobs is a real convenience. Just make certain that the package contains all the wood screws you need. The wood screws from the Sharon Bolt and Screw Company are packaged so that you can see plainly what you're getting.

Something New In Nails

Unless you spend a great deal of time in hardware stores, lumberyards, or building supply houses, you may not know about the Scotch nails from Bethlehem Steel Corporation. They are square shanked nails with angled serrations all along the length of the shank. The serrations create a nail that resists loosening while reducing the possibility of splitting the wood. Since Scotch nails are lightweight, you get more nails per pound, and they are available in just about all of the most popular sizes and styles.

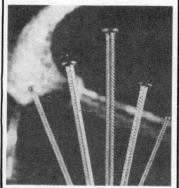

Toggle Bolts In Assortment Pack

Jordan Industries offers an assortment of toggle bolts called the Handyman's Fastening Kit that contains the most popular sizes for home use. The wings on Jordan toggle bolts have a patented locking prong called Prong-Eze, and the bolts in the Handyman's Fastening Kit are all round headed. The kit is carded in a clear blister pack.

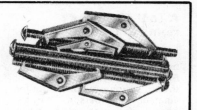

Stairway Cabinet

WHEN YOU THINK that every nook and cranny in your house that can be used for storage is already filled, there is probably still one place you are overlooking: atop the balustrade enclosing the stairwell in the second-floor hall. It is surprisingly easy to build a cabinet here without detracting from the appearance or open feeling of the hall and stairway, and without posing a threat to people climbing or descending the stairs.

1. To test the effect, nail a cleat to the wall parallel with the side of the balustrade and level with the top of the railing. Lay a couple of boards across the cleat and railing, and set a huge cardboard carton on top. Are you satisfied? If so, then replace the cleat with a good 1x4-inch board or decorative casing molding cut to the depth of the cabinet (24 inches or less), minus the width of the railing.
2. Nail it securely into the studs with 10d finishing nails; if you hit only one stud, use a couple of toggle bolts in addition.
3. Construct the cabinet of ½-inch standard plywood if you plan to paint it, or of ¼-inch decorative hardboard or hardwood plywood glued to a backing of ¼-inch standard plywood if you like a natural finish.
4. The cabinet should be wide enough to rest securely on the railing and cleat. If the railing is flat on top, the side of the cabinet can be flush with the side of the railing. If the railing is round or has a beveled top, on the other hand, the cabinet should extend only about ½ inch beyond the very top of the railing. Otherwise, there will be an unattractive wedge-shaped gap between the bottom of the cabinet and the railing on the hall side.
5. Cut the bottom and top of the cabinet to butt against the sides and back (that is, to fit within the sides and back) so that the edge grain is concealed.
6. Fasten the pieces together with glue and 3d finishing nails.
7. Nail 1x2-inch facing strips around the front of the cabinet, and rest a plywood shelf (or shelves) on cleats in the cabinet.
8. Cut a pair of flush plywood doors to fit in the door openings. Hang the doors with surface-mounted or butt hinges, and install magnetic catches and pulls.
9. Set the cabinet across the railing and cleat (you may need a helper), screw it into the studs in the wall, and nail it to the railing and cleat.

Here Is What You Will Need

Materials

- ½-inch standard plywood or ¼-inch hardwood plywood or decorative hardboard and ¼-inch standard plywood
- 1x2-inch board for facing strips
- 1x4-inch board for cleat
- ⅝-inch quarter-round for shelf cleats
- Four surface-mounted or butt hinges
- Magnetic catches, pulls
- Finishing nails, glue, toggle bolts, screws

Tools

- Hammer
- Saw
- Tape measure
- Drill
- Screwdriver

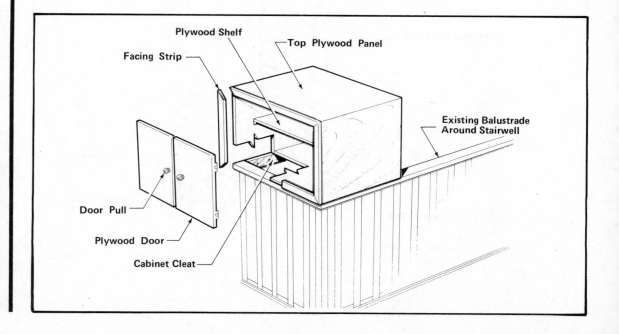

Plywood Shelf

Facing Strip

Top Plywood Panel

Existing Balustrade Around Stairwell

Door Pull

Plywood Door

Cabinet Cleat

Building a Cedar Closet

THE TIME TO build a cedar closet, of course, is before you have a moth problem. The cedar aroma does not kill moths, but it does repel them. Just make sure that your clothes are moth free before you put them in the closet.

The cedar closet is an exceptionally easy project now because there are companies that package cedar planks in bundles. Each bundle contains 40 board feet of aromatic red cedar, which covers 30 square feet. The planks come in random lengths from two to eight feet, and in widths from two to four inches. All the strips are ⅜ of an inch thick.

This project involves the creation of a new closet; if you have an existing closet that you want to line with cedar, skip over steps 1 through 3, and start with the lining of the closet. By selecting a spot in which you can use existing wall, you will save quite a bit of framing. The following instructions are for doing it the hard way; building a complete closet out in the middle of the floor in either a basement or an attic. Here is how it goes.

1. Build a framework for the closet—the size will depend on the available space—out of 2x4s. Frame it as you would a house, with the studs and floor braces on 16-inch centers. Make sure that the frame is structurally sound and that it is tall enough so that any family member can walk into it without ducking.
2. Add floor, sides, and ceiling. Three-quarter inch plywood will do, but if the closet is to be in a basement or garage where moisture could be a problem, you should use exterior grade plywood.
3. For doors, you can either use more plywood or pick up used hollow-core doors at a wrecking yard. Frame around the doors for as tight a fit as possible.
4. Now you are ready to start installing the cedar strips. As mentioned before, the bundles contain boards of random lengths, and you should apply the strips in a random pattern. Start at the floor and work up, installing the strips horizontally. Start the tongue-and-grooved strips with a grooved edge down. Start in any corner, use 4d finishing nails, and drive the nails below the

surface with a nailset. Work all the way across, and cut end pieces to fit.
5. When you get the first course all the way across, work on up, doing one course at a time. The next course will interlock, tongue in groove, with just a light tapping. You need just a minimal number of nails because of the locking properties of the boards.
6. When one wall is completely lined with cedar, do the others in the same way. Then line the door(s).
7. Next, line the floor and ceiling in the same manner.
8. Install cedar molding at corners and where floor and ceiling meet walls.
9. Weatherstrip the door(s) to contain the cedar aroma.
10. Make shelves of cedar too.
11. Install a hanger bar; a length of pipe will do nicely. Use cedar for the brackets to hold the bar, drilling a hole in one bracket and cutting a slot in the other one.
12. Paint the outside of the closet if you wish, but never put anything on the cedar that would seal in the aroma.

Although you may need to adapt this plan to suit your needs and space, the general procedures for building the cedar closet will be the same. Incidentally, if the cedar aroma starts to fade after several years, you can restore it by lightly sanding all the cedar surfaces. In addition, keep the walls dust free so that the pores in the wood stay open.

Here Is What You Will Need

Materials

- 2x4s
- ¾-inch plywood
- Nails
- Hollow-core door(s)
- Cedar strips, moldings, shelves, brackets
- Finishing nails
- Weatherstripping
- Pipe
- Sandpaper   • Paint

Tools

- Hammer
- Tape measure
- Saw
- Nailset
- Drill
- Paintbrush

Add Skil To Your Sawing

Most of the storage-construction projects require some sawing, and one of the basic power tools to consider owning for such work is a circular saw. Skil makes a 7¼-inch model that has a powerful two-horsepower motor for tough cutting jobs. It is double insulated and has a safety switch, safety guard lift, and, safety guard stop. Both height and bevel adjustments can be made easily. All in all, the Skil 7¼-inch circular saw is an accurate and safe cutting machine for the home handyman.

Cedar Panels Complete Closet Quickly

Flakeboard (also called particle board and pressed wood) panels made from 100 percent Tennessee aromatic red cedar come in 4x8-foot sheets from Giles & Kendall. They make creation of a cedar closet very fast work. Able to be mounted with either nails or panel adhesive just like any wall paneling, the G&K cedar panels can be cut to size with a plywood blade.

Door · Cedar Strips · Wall · Frame

Steps 1-4

Tongue-and-Groove Cedar Strips

Cedar Brackets · Hanger Bar

Step 11

Storage

Plywood Edges Can Look Finished

Plywood edges normally reveal the layers of laminated wood, but there are rolls of wood trim available to match all the different species of plywood. A good example is Weldwood's Flexible Wood-Trim, available in either one- or two-inch wide rolls. The trim material is made of genuine wood. To apply, you simply peel off the backing paper — exposing the pre-coated pressure-sensitive adhesive — and then press and clamp the Flexible Wood-Trim in place.

flexible Wood-trim

Rasp Is Crucial To Any Woodworking Project

Most carpenters consider the rasp a must tool for smoothing or removing wood. Available in different shapes and with different teeth, the all-purpose rasp and file should fill every need around the house. Nicholson's — available in 8- and 10-inch versions — is flat on one side and half round on the other. Each side has a rasp at one end and a file at the other, and each of the four sections has a different coarseness. Nicholson is part of the Cooper Group of tool manufacturers.

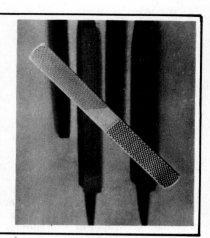

Ruff'N Ready Shelving Includes Small Wine Rack

Ruff'N Ready Shelving from Northland Wood Products Company consists of shelves, standards, and brackets that have a rustic carved appearance. Among the unique specialty products that can be added to the Ruff'N Ready Shelving is a small seven-bottle wine rack. If you want greater capacity, you can always put two or more racks against each other for a longer wine storage unit. Ruff'N Ready shelving and specialty items come in either forest brown or misty white.

The Wine Vault

You need not be a connoisseur to appreciate the Wine Vault marketed by the Viking Sauna Company. Models range from small vaults that hold up to 156 bottles up to enormous wine storage units. All of them keep wine at just the right temperature and humidity. Installation requires no plumbing, drains, or flues, and the Wine Vault operates on regular house current. You can put a Wine Vault in the kitchen or basement, behind a bar, under a stairway, or build one into an existing wall.

Wine Racks

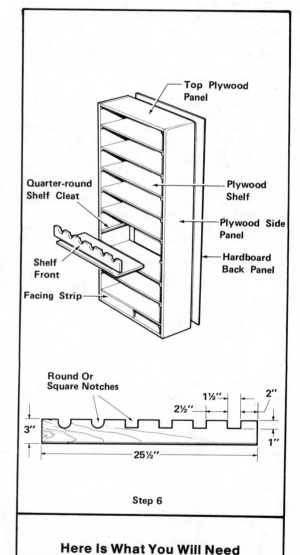

A FAVORITE hobby of wine lovers who also enjoy cabinetmaking is designing and building attractive small racks for wine bottle storage. This rack is for the person who buys and stores his favorite vintages in quantity; it is strictly utilitarian — to be kept in a corner of the basement where the temperature is cool and reasonably constant. Like all good wine racks, however, this one is strong enough to support a great deal of weight, and it is made to store the bottles on their sides to keep the corks wet and tight.

Build the rack as tall as you like, but stick to the following basic dimensions: inside width — 24 inches; outside width — 25½ inches; inside depth — nine inches; outside depth — 9⅞ inches. The distance between each pair of shelves should be six inches.

1. Build the sides, top, and bottom of ¾-inch plywood cut nine inches wide.
2. Nail the top and bottom across the ends of the sides, and then cover the back of the frame with ⅛-inch tempered hardboard.
3. Cut the 9x24-inch shelves from ¾-inch plywood, and nail them between the sides.
4. Nail cleats of ⅝-inch quarter-rounds or 1x2-inch boards under the ends, and fasten the hardboard back to each of the shelves with three or four 2d common nails.
5. The shelf fronts are the only parts of the rack which take some time to construct. Make the shelf fronts of 1x3-inch board cut 25½ inches long.
6. Cut six rectangular (or if you prefer, circular) notches 1½ inches wide by one inch deep in the top edge of each shelf to accommodate the six bottles every shelf can hold. Space the first and sixth notches two inches in from the ends of the boards, and allow 2½ inches between adjacent notches.
7. Nail the shelf front boards to the edges of the shelves.
8. Once you anchor the entire rack to the wall against which it is placed — or to the ceiling joists — you can simply lay your wine bottles on the shelves with the necks projecting through the notches in the shelf fronts. If the bottles tend to roll around a little, spread a piece of thin rug cushion (preferably of foam rubber or urethane) on the shelves to help steady them.

Here Is What You Will Need

Materials

- ¾-inch plywood
- ⅛-inch tempered hardboard
- 1x3-inch boards for shelf fronts
- ⅝-inch quarter-rounds or 1x2-inch board for shelf cleats
- Nails

Tools

- Saw
- Tape measure
- Hammer

A Bracing Bit Of Information

The hand brace can drill just about anything, and many people prefer to use it over power drills. The Fuller Ratchet Bit Brace features a 12-point ratchet and reverses easily for working in close quarters. The alligator chuck can grip round or tapered shank bits, and can even accommodate a screwdriver blade. The head and center grip handle are made of hardwood.

Cleaning Closet

VACUUM CLEANERS, brooms, mops, dust pans, dust rags, and the dozens of other cleaning supplies in nearly every home are difficult to store efficiently. What you need, therefore, is a special cleaning closet designed to bring as much order out of the chaos as possible.

This closet will accommodate most types of vacuum cleaners, the largest item to be stored in the closet. Before starting construction, however, make sure that your vacuum cleaner will fit inside. If it is exceptionally large, increase the closet depth accordingly. The length should remain constant, however, since there is extra space provided at the end of the vacuum — even a long tank model — for other supplies.

1. The first step is to attach 1x2-inch cleats to the ceiling. The sides of the closet will bear against these cleats. Use nails for this procedure only if the cleats cross or are directly beneath ceiling joists; otherwise, use toggle bolts.
2. Install a cleat between the front ends of the side cleats. The space from the front edge of the front cleat to the back wall is 11¾ inches, while that between the outside edges of the side cleats is 36 inches. These are the inside dimensions of the closet; the outside dimensions are 12½x37½ inches.
3. Drop a plumb line from the side cleats, and nail corresponding cleats to the floor below.
4. The sides of the closet are made of 1x12-inch boards, 96 inches (or whatever is the actual height of the ceiling) long. Fit the back edges to the wall, and then nail the boards to the cleats at top and bottom.
5. Nail 1x2-inch facing strips to the sides and to the cleat across the front of the closet.
6. Cut three shelves 36 inches long from a 1x12-inch board, and bore a row of five or six one-inch ventilating holes parallel to, and one inch back from, the front edges.
7. Install the shelves in the closet with the ends resting on cleats cut from ⅝-inch quarter-rounds or 1x2-inch boards. The top of the bottom shelf should be 60 inches above the floor, and the next shelf should be 14 inches above the bottom one to accommodate those super-size boxes of detergents. Install the third shelf eight inches above the second one.
8. Cut a shallow shelf from a 1x4-inch board, install it a foot below the bottom shelf, and nail another 1x4-inch board to the front edge to keep articles from falling off.
9. Cleats are unnecessary; simply drive nails through the sides of the closet into the shelf ends. You can add more shelves of the same kind below if there is no vacuum cleaner hose to hang on the back wall.
10. Cut two long, narrow flush doors from ¾-inch plywood or particleboard to fit within the door opening.
11. Drill rows of four or five one-inch ventilating holes three inches from the bottom and top, and then hang each door with three wrap-around or surface-mounted hinges.
12. Attach spring catches on the backs of the doors and on the underside of the lowest 12-inch shelf; then attach door pulls.

Store brooms and mops on the backs of the doors and on the sides of the closet below the shelves, using spring clips made for the purpose. To store a vacuum cleaner hose (which because of its stiffness has an annoying tendency to slide off a single hanger unless perfectly balanced), screw a pair of coat hooks to the back of the closet about one foot apart and level. Use cup hooks to hang dust cloths, dust pans, small brushes, etc.

Finish your new cleaning closet inside and out so that it goes well with the decorating motif of its surroundings.

Here Is What You Will Need
Materials
- 1x12-inch boards for sides and shelves
- ¾-inch plywood or ¾-inch particleboard for doors
- 1x4-inch board for shallow shelf
- 1x2-inch boards for facing strips and cleats
- ⅝-inch quarter-round (or 1x2-inch boards) for shelf cleats
- Six wrap-around or surface-mounted hinges
- Two spring catches and pulls
- Clips, coat hooks, cup hooks
- Nails, toggle bolts
- Paint or stain

Tools
- Hammer
- Saw
- Tape measure
- Plumb line
- Drill
- Screwdriver
- Paintbrush

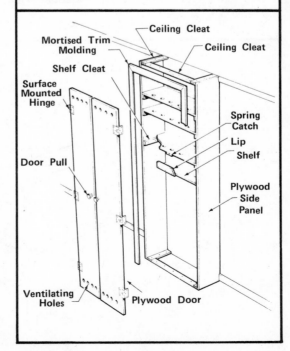

Ceiling Cleat
Mortised Trim Molding
Ceiling Cleat
Shelf Cleat
Surface Mounted Hinge
Spring Catch
Lip
Shelf
Door Pull
Plywood Side Panel
Ventilating Holes
Plywood Door

Gibson Gripper Is Handle Holder

Any good cleaning closet should include several broom clips, and the Gibson Gripper is among the better broom clips available. Made of flexible sheet steel that has been oil tempered and brightly finished, the Gibson Gripper (a product of Gibson Good Tools, Inc.) has no sharp edges. Blister packed with two large and two small clips or with all large or all small clips, the Gripper can be installed with just one screw.

Adjustable Clips Enhance Cleaning Closet Usefulness

The Finger Grip Adjustable Clip from Arthur I. Platt Company can be set to hold light or heavy tools with just a turn of the holding screw. After the clip is installed properly, you can adjust its holding power, making the fingers pull closer together for heavier tools and loosening them for lighter items. Once properly adjusted, the Finger Grip Adjustable Clip holds items securely, yet permits easy removal and replacement. Made in three different sizes, the Finger Grip Clip can also serve a multitude of purposes in the shop or garage.

Auger Bits Made For Drilling Wood With A Hand Brace

Auger bits, such as those made by the Irwin Auger Bit Company, are used strictly for drilling wood with a hand brace. Irwin manufactures top quality products, including excellent bits for power drills. The company packages its auger bits in sets and small assortments, as well as by individual units. Although the Irwin 13-bit assortment, which comes housed in a Borchest (a finished wooden chest with steel clips to hold the bits), provides more bits than the homeowner can probably use, it is a handsome set, deserving the attention of anyone who drills with a hand brace.

Storage

Unique C-Clamp Takes Versatility Honors

Made by the same people who make the Vise-Grip Pliers, the Vise-Grip C-Clamp clamps easier and faster than a regular C-clamp and has many more uses. You merely adjust the C-clamp's opening to the size you need, and then squeeze to lock the clamp in place. The jaws can spread up to 3¾ inches wide, but they can perform efficiently with minute openings, too. To remove the clamp, all you do is touch the easy-release lever. Very effective in spreading its gripping pressure, the Vise-Grip C-Clamp can handle sizable wood strips with good results.

British Backsaw Is Made Of Sheffield Steel

The Tenon Saw from W.H. Clay, Ltd., of Sheffield, England, is a very fine tool indeed. The blade and rigid spine are made of the finest Sheffield cast steel, and the beechwood handle is quite comfortable. The Clay Tenon Saw, which is available in 8-, 10-, and 12-inch blade lengths, is part of Clay's complete line of carpenters and joiners tools. The Clay line enjoys wide distribution through Anglo-American Distribution, Ltd.

Spray Paint Finishes Your Project Quickly

For painting a small woodworking project, there is no faster method than applying a spray enamel. Tru-Test Supreme comes in scores of colors, dries quickly, and leaves a beautiful high gloss finish. Available at all True Value hardware stores, Tru-Test Supreme paints constitute one segment of a highly regarded line of paint products.

Take The Pain Out Of Pounding Wire Brads

Wire brads are actually tiny nails that come in many sizes and are usually sold in small cardboard boxes or plastic containers. Tower Wire Brads are easy to spot in their red and yellow window boxes at most hardware stores. The problem in working with wire brads is that due to their size you stand a good chance of missing the brad and hitting your finger with the hammer. A gadget from Raylor Company, though, can save your fingers. It holds the brad in its slotted plastic jaws until the brad is well started. The tool also provides a nail penny gauge and is a handy four-inch ruler.

Hot Melt Glue Gun Renders Quick Stick

The electric glue gun provides an easy and effective way of handling many gluing chores. Thermogrip's Electric Glue Gun feeds hot melt glue that can be used on wood, fabric, leather, many plastics, ceramics, and other materials. After the gun is heated, thumb pressure against the glue stick applies the hot glue, which then reaches 90 percent of its bonding strength within 60 seconds. Thermogrip also offers a more convenient trigger-fed model. Thermogrip Electric Glue Guns and Hot Melt Glue Sticks and Hot Melt Sealer-Caulker are all made by the Consumer Products Division of U.S.M. Corporation.

Lift-Out Tray

ONE OF THE best ways to increase the capacity and efficiency of drawer space is to install a sliding lift-out tray. You can fill the tray with all sorts of small items that you frequently use, and then fill the drawer space beneath the tray with articles you seldom need. On the few occasions when you need to reach the things in the drawer space below, all you have to do is slide the tray backward or forward, or lift it out of the drawer entirely. Use the following procedure to build this helpful tray.

1. Attach two rails to the inner sides of a drawer with glue and brads. If possible, make the rails of a hardwood such as maple, cutting them from ½x½-inch strips to the length (inside dimension) of the drawer. If hardwood is not available, use ⅜-inch quarter-rounds.
2. You can make the tray to fit either the full size of the drawer or only half. The full-size tray obviously holds more, but you must lift it out for access to the bottom. The half-size tray is therefore generally preferred.
3. The width of the tray should be about ⅛ of an inch less than the width of the drawer; the height should equal the distance from the rail to the top edge of the drawer, minus ¼ of an inch.
4. For the bottom of the tray, use ⅛-inch tempered hardwood—preferably of the type that is smooth-finished on both sides.
5. For the sides and divider (if any), use ⅜-inch boards.
6. Fit the sides and divider together with glue and brads, then glue on the bottom.
7. Finish the wood with a couple of coats of white shellac to protect it from moisture and prevent it from swelling.

Here Is What You Will Need
Materials
• ½x½-inch hardwood strips or ⅜-inch softwood quarter-rounds for rails
• ⅛-inch tempered hardboard for tray bottom
• ⅜-inch boards for tray sides and divider
• Glue, brads
• Shellac
Tools
• Hammer
• Saw
• Tape measure
• Paintbrush

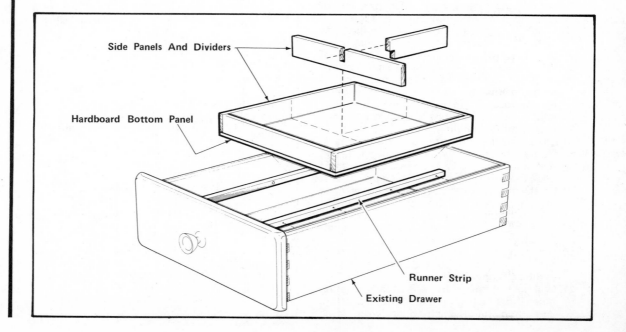

Side Panels And Dividers

Hardboard Bottom Panel

Runner Strip

Existing Drawer

Big C-Clamp Is A Lightweight

The Exact Level & Tool Manufacturing Company markets heavy-duty C-clamps that are very light in weight. Made of special triple-strength aluminum alloy, these clamps possess more than 28,000 pounds of tensile strength. Of course, the aluminum frame is rust-proof. The threaded screw, however, is made of steel, as are the sliding bar handle and the ball ends. The end pad is a securely

fastened swivel action. The sturdy heavy-duty models come in four-, five-, and six-inch sizes. Exact also makes light-duty aluminum clamps.

Teflon-Coated Saw Blades Cut Smoother

The application of Teflon coating on handsaws proved so successful that the treatment is being given to many other tools, including circular saw blades and saber saw blades. The Teflon coating results in less friction and therefore smoother cutting with less drain on the motor. The Disston Teflon-Coated Circular Saw Blade is part of the Satin Slide series which covers almost every cutting

function for every size circular saw.

Tilt-Out Wall Bin

BINS THAT TILT out of a wall or base cabinet have various uses: storing potatoes, onions, and other vegetables not requiring refrigeration; children's blocks and toys; the family's soiled clothes; etc. Since bins must be fairly deep to hold very much, they are more often installed in cabinets than in walls; but this project involves the installation of a tilt-out bin in a standard interior partition framed with 2x4's. Nevertheless, all of the construction and installation information is applicable to a cabinet installation as well.

In this particular case, the bin is installed just above the baseboard in a kitchen wall which backs on to the basement stairway. In this location, the bin can be loaded or emptied from either side of the wall. Here is how to build a tilt-out wall bin.

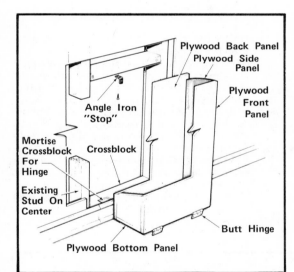

Plywood Back Panel
Plywood Side Panel
Plywood Front Panel
Angle Iron "Stop"
Mortise Crossblock For Hinge
Crossblock
Existing Stud On Center
Butt Hinge
Plywood Bottom Panel

Here Is What You Will Need

Materials

- 2x4's for cross-blocks
- ½-inch plywood
- Casings
- Two 2½x2½-inch butt hinges
- 1-inch angle iron
- Nails, glue
- Paint

Tools

- Saw
- Drill and drill bits
- Key hole saw
- Hammer
- Sand paper
- Compass
- Tape measure
- Screwdriver
- Paintbrush

1. The first step is to cut a hole in both sides of the wall between a pair of studs.
2. Smooth the edges of the gypsum board or plaster.
3. Then nail 2x4-inch cross-blocks into the wall, flush with the top and bottom edges of the hole.
4. Make the bin of ½-inch plywood. Cut the front panel to fit within the wall opening and to have 1/16 of an inch clearance on all sides. The side panels should be six or seven inches deep, depending on how far they can project into the basement stairway without getting in the way of people going up or down. The height should be similar to the height of the front panel, minus ¼ of an inch.
5. After you cut rectangles for the side panels, place the point of a compass on the bottom front corner of each panel. Open the compass until the pencil touches the top front corner, and then sweep the pencil across the top of the panel to make a curve.
6. Cut the panels along the curved lines. Make the back panel the same width as the front panel and one inch higher than the back edges of the side panels.
7. Glue and nail the side panels between the front and back panels.
8. Cut a plywood bottom to fit within the four panels, and glue and nail it into place.
9. Mortise a pair of 2½x2½-inch butt hinges into both the bottom of the bin's front edge and into the bottom cross-block so that the front of the bin is flush with the kitchen wall.
10. Glue a sliver of wood (the same thickness as the hinges) to the cross-block at the back edge to assure that the top edge of the bin is also flush with the wall when the bin is closed.
11. Screw a one-inch angle iron to the top cross-block about two inches back from the face of the kitchen wall. The purpose of the iron is to engage the projecting edge of the bin's back panel and prevent the bin from tipping all the way out into the room when you open it.
12. Nail casings to the kitchen wall around the bin.
13. Paint the bin with semi-gloss or gloss alkyd enamel to match the kitchen wall.

Heavy-Duty Screwdriver

One heavy-duty screwdriver that can stand up to just about any screwdriving or removal task is available from the Rosco Tool Company. If you encounter a particularly difficult screw to remove, be sure to apply penetrating oil and allow it time to do its work. Then use a screwdriver of the correct size to avoid stripping the slot in the screwhead. Of course, you should never use a good screwdriver like one from Rosco for tasks other than working with screws. You can ruin even the finest and toughest screwdriver by using it as a prybar, chisel, or can opener.

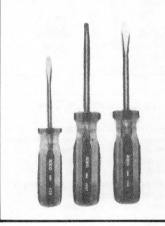

Treasure Chest Of Decorative Hardware

Hardware provides the crucial finishing touch to any carpentry or cabinet making project. Stanley Hardware's Classic Brassware adds beauty and dignity to whatever it is applied. The solid brass hinges, handles, knobs, hasp and hook sets, corner braces, brass corners, and other decorator units are reasonably priced and well distributed through hardware, building supply, and home center outlets.

Storage

Screws Provide Greater Fastening Security

Although the screen and storm window rack you put together with nails should prove strong and durable, wood screws are the fasteners to use if you need a sturdier rack for a large number of heavy windows. Though not as quick to put together, the screw-fastened rack will also not be as quick to come apart. Sharon Bolt and Screw Company markets quality stainless steel wood screws, although in most cases it is more important to get the right size and type of screw than to seek out a specific brand name.

Add Storage Space To Your Screen And Storm Window Rack

By simply adding chicken wire to the bottom of your screen and storm window rack, you can create a see-through shelf for storing many lightweight items. Gilbert & Bennett Manufacturing Company's Hex Netting—available at farm stores, lumberyards, and hardware stores—can be cut to fit and stapled in place easily. You can also staple Hex Netting across wall studs in a garage to make a utility tool holder.

Protect Your Storage Rack From Moisture

Even though a screen and storm window rack is not exactly a fine piece of furniture, it deserves the protection of a coat of paint. The easiest paint to apply comes in an aerosol spray can, and you will probably find just the color you want in the Plasti-Kote selection.

Five Ladders In One

You need a stepladder to work on the garage ceiling, and Montgomery Ward offers an interesting and versatile model. It can be a stepladder, an extension ladder, two separate straight ladders, a two-man stepladder, or an uneven ladder for use on stairs. Quite sturdy in any of its five forms, it converts in seconds without any tools. It also has a big pail shelf with slots for tools and rags. Made in six-, seven-, and eight-foot stepladder heights (each is twice that high as an extension ladder), the five-in-one ladder is available at larger Ward stores or can be ordered by mail from the Ward catalog.

Overhead Screen and Storm Window Rack

STORING WINDOW screens and storm sash on the basement or garage floor wastes floor space and may cause your screens and sash to rot or warp. A far better solution to this storage problem is to construct an overhead rack. You can put one together in about 15 minutes, using standard framing lumber. Here's how:

1. Measure the screens first, group them according to size, and then build separate racks for each group of six to nine screens. The racks could handle more, but they would have to be built so deep that they would hang dangerously far beneath the basement or garage ceiling.
2. Cut a 2x4 into four lengths equal to the depth of the joists (usually 8 or 10 inches), plus the thickness of the stack of screens to be stored, plus about six inches for maneuvering room.
3. Install one pair of 2x4s perpendicular to the joists, nailing the pair to the joists with three or four large common nails. The space between the 2x4s should be slightly greater than the screen width.
4. Nail the other pair of 2x4s to the same joists, with the space between the first and second pairs 18 to 24 inches less than the length of the screens.
5. Nail 1x4-inch boards flat to the bottom edges of each pair of 2x4s (for a slightly more finished look, you can notch the 2x4s for the boards). In any case, use large nails; and if the boards are cut from yellow pine or another hardwood, drill holes for the nails to prevent splitting.
6. Then just lay the screens (or storm sash) flat across the two racks.

Here Is What You Will Need

Materials
- 2x4s
- 1x4-inch boards
- Common nails

Tools
- Tape measure
- Saw
- Hammer
- Drill

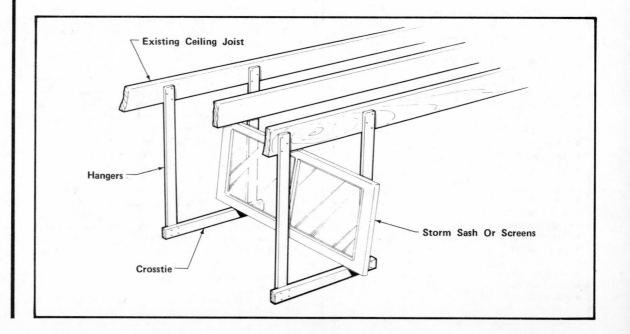

Existing Ceiling Joist

Hangers

Crosstie

Storm Sash Or Screens

Wall Storage For Storm Windows And Screens

Spacemaster Home Products offers accessory cross bars for the Superwall unit that can be attached to create tip-proof racks for screens or storm windows. The Superwall system involves heavy-duty steel standards mounted on a garage or basement wall to which hooks, brackets, and shelves can be added easily. Superwall can contain just about all your clutter.

Bracket Puts Teeth Into Shelving

Couple-It is a bracket that features steel teeth where the shelf rests grab the shelf and hold it in place. In addition, part of the one-piece Couple-It bracket extends over the back edge of the shelf, providing further locking power. Shelves held by Couple-It brackets cannot be moved to either side or outward, but they can be lifted up. Couple-It comes in two styles, for flat wall mounting

or for attaching to the side of an exposed stud in a shop or garage. Couple-It is made by the William Shine Design Company, Inc.

Overhead Closet in Garage

ONE WAY to increase storage space in the garage or carport is to build a large cabinet—with shelves at either end—for installation on the wall above your car's front bumper. The cabinet is built almost entirely of ¾-inch plywood. The top and bottom measure 20x64 inches; the back 54x64 inches; the two sides 20x52½ inches; the two front panels 13½x54 inches; and the two doors 18⅜x50⅝ inches.

The reason that you build the cabinet 64 inches wide is so that you can fasten it to four wall studs; since a large storage unit such as this becomes very heavy when loaded with tools and other items, it must be anchored securely. Although you can alter the depth of the cabinet somewhat, do not change the height at which you hang it; it should be 3½ feet above the floor. Although high enough for any car to nose in underneath, the cabinet is also low enough to allow you to reach all the shelves easily. Follow these steps to build an overhead storage cabinet.

1. Place the side panels 11¾ inches from the ends of the cabinet, and nail them between the top and bottom with 8d common nails. Then attach the back.
2. Before you add further to its weight, however, you should fasten the cabinet to the garage wall. Have a helper hold it in position, while you drive in three 2½-inch round-head screws per stud.
3. Position the front panels at the ends of the cabinet, and nail them to the top, bottom, and sides.

Here Is What You Will Need
Materials
- ¾-inch plywood
- 1x12-inch boards
- 1x2-inch boards for facing strips and cabinet shelf cleats
- Surface-mounted hinges
- Spring catches, pulls
- Common nails (galvanized if the garage is damp)
- Screws

Tools
- Tape measure
- Saw
- Hammer
- Screwdriver

4. Cut two 1x2-inch boards to fit between the front panels, and nail one to the top and one to the bottom of the cabinet to frame the door opening. Toenail the boards to the front panels at the ends.
5. Cut cleats from 1x2-inch boards to support the shelves in the central closed section of the cabinet, and fasten the cleats to the sides with screws.
6. Cut shelves from the plywood, and nail them in place on the cleats.
7. Hang the flush doors in the door opening with surface-mounted hinges, and then install spring catches and pulls.
8. The only task remaining is to cut shelves for the open ends of the cabinet from 1x12-inch boards. Nail the shelves between the back and front panels with 6d nails. Since the shelves for the open ends are short, no cleats are necessary.

Free-Standing Steel Shelves Offer Stable Storage

Three, four, and five-shelf steel units constitute Fort Steuben's answer to heavyweight storage problems in the shop, basement, attic, or garage. The corner posts are ribbed for extra rigidity and have holes every 1½ inches to permit the shelves to be set at nearly any desired position. All Fort Steuben units have sway braces for added strength and stability. Each corner post is equipped with a plastic floor protector, and all shelves have safety edges. Assembly is simple; all parts—including nuts and bolts—are included in the package.

Ready-Made Rack Hangs In There

If you can install four screw hooks four feet apart in a square, you can have a new 4x4-foot rack hanging from the ceiling of your garage or basement. The Stow Rack is a sturdy storage unit—all metal with an attractive galvanized finish—designed to hold up to 175 pounds of clutter. Ideal for over the hood of the car, Stow Rack hangs down 3½ feet from the ceiling. Stow Rack is a product of Garco Manufacturing Company.

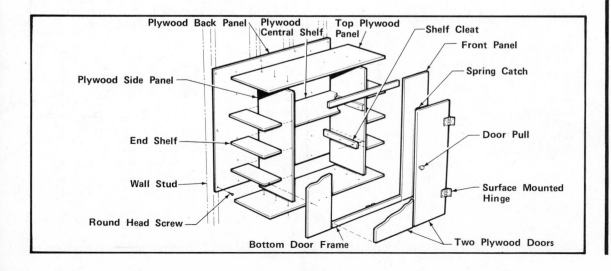

Storage

Pick The Right Nails For Your Purpose

Grip-Tite is the brand name for nails made by Wire Products Company, producers of a wide variety of nails, most of which come packaged in boxes. There are many good brands of nails on the market. Just make sure that you pick the right size and type of nails for the project you are doing. Safety is also a vital consideration. Always use proper nailing techniques and wear safety goggles at all times.

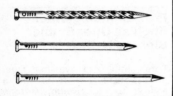

Ventwood Good Indoors Or Out

Ventwood's plant shelving system can be used indoors or out. Since the open design of the shelves allows for water drainage and air circulation, it can be used on the patio as a plant stand. The modular system can be tailored in size and number of shelves to your needs, and assembly is easy, requiring only a screwdriver. The unfinished pieces of Western Highland Hemlock take stains quite well, but they can also be left natural or painted. You will find it easier, though, to do all the staining, painting, or other finishing before you assemble the Ventwood System. Ventwood is a product of Howard Manufacturing Company, makers of more traditional wall shelving.

Lid Supports Hold Fold-Out Shelf

The simple house plant center with a fold-out desk/shelf calls for lid supports. Brainerd Manufacturing Company offers two different models, one curved and one straight, although both are made of brass and come packaged with brass screws for installation. Both can be adjusted easily, are fairly sturdy, and are of the friction catch type. Brainerd also makes solid brass hinges, brackets, corners, pulls, handles, and other decorative cabinet hardware.

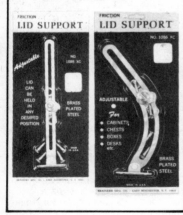

Stainless Steel Saw Cuts Swiftly

Often a handsaw is much more convenient for small cutting jobs than the large power saw. The Great Neck Stainless Steel handsaw cuts with ease. A 26-inch crosscut saw, it is available with either a laminated hardwood handle or with a plastic handle; both offer comfortable grips. Great Neck, which scientifically treats stainless steel to give it longer lasting qualities, makes saws in all price ranges and for all purposes.

House Plant Center

EVEN IF you do not care much for house plants, you can probably use this storage unit. For instance, you can use it for storing wrapping materials, cookbooks, or hobby supplies.

The house plant center, nonetheless, is getting to be an increasingly important item in many homes. More and more families are growing plants indoors, and almost all of them need space to store pots, potting soil, fertilizer, insecticide, fungicide, tools, syringes, watering cans, etc. Most of these gardeners would also appreciate a place where they can prune or repot plants without messing up the kitchen counters.

Whatever you use it for, the cabinet is surprisingly easy to build to any dimensions. The dimensions in this example are 30 inches wide, 24 inches high and 6½ inches deep (all outside measurements).

1. Cut the frame and shelves from 1x6-inch boards.
2. Nail and glue the top and bottom between the sides; then nail in the shelves, spaced to suit the articles you will store.
3. Cut the back from ⅛-inch tempered hardboard, and nail it over the frame and to the shelves with one-inch brads.
4. Hang the cabinet on a wall with four three-inch round-head screws driven through the back into the studs; the height you hang it depends on whether you will work at the unit standing up or sitting down. If you stand, the bottom of the tilt-down front should be a little below elbow height; if you sit, the bottom of the tilt-down front should be 30 inches above the floor.
5. Cut the tilt-down front from ¾-inch plywood or particleboard so that it will overlay the edges of the cabinet frame, and fasten it to the frame with a piano hinge.
6. Screw one leaf to the back face of the plywood, the other to the front edge of the bottom member of the frame.
7. To support the front when it is open, use metal lid supports or support chains.
8. Install a magnetic catch in the top of the cabinet to hold the front closed.
9. Finish the house plant center with semigloss or gloss alkyd enamel, or with stain, shellac, and varnish. You can further protect the shelves and work surface by covering them with self-stick vinyl fabric.

Here Is What You Will Need

Materials
- 1x6-inch boards for cabinet
- ¾-inch plywood or particleboard for front
- ⅛-inch tempered hardboard for back
- Self-stick vinyl fabric
- Two lid supports
- Magnetic catch
- Pull
- Nails, glue, screws, brads
- Paint or stain

Tools
- Saw
- Hammer
- Screwdriver
- Tape measure
- Paintbrush

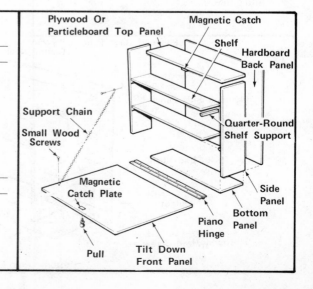

Mildew Vanishes Before Your Eyes

There are several good products on the market that make mildew disappear so fast you'll hardly believe it. Max-44 is such a product. It comes packaged with a trigger spray, and all you do is shoot the Max-44 on the mildew. That's all you do. The mildew vanishes, and you don't even have to wash away any residue. A product of Chemik, Inc., Max-44 can be used outside.

Prevent Mildew With Moisture Remover

Since the Valley Dehumidifier soaks up moisture from the air, it is the ideal thing to have in a bathroom. Just remove the lid and place the plastic jar on the floor or on a shelf. It absorbs about 250 cubic feet of moisture at 75 percent humidity. The Valley Dehumidifier is a mail-order item; write to Lillian Vernon, 510 South Fulton Ave., Mt. Vernon, N.Y. 10550.

Kill Mildew Outside And Inside

Tested and proved in the most humid areas, Jomax Mold and Mildew Remover is a concentrate that you apply with a standard garden sprayer or with a sprayer that fits on the end of a garden hose. Mix the concentrate with water in a ratio of one quart Jomax to make five gallons of the mixture. Spray it over all of the exterior and then hose it off. Jomax removes mold and mildew in seconds. A homeowner could rid an average size house of a big mildew problem in less than two hours. Jomax is a product of the Chempro Corporation, makers of Mil-X, a mildew remover for interior use that comes in a trigger spray bottle.

Mildew

EVEN THE NICEST homes can have mildew, an ugly looking mess that can also produce an unpleasant odor. Mildew is a fungus that floats in the air until it finds the right conditions to start growing on the wall. What are those right conditions? Mildew spores must have moisture and dirt to feed on; soap scum is one of mildew's choice dishes. The bathroom walls, of course, are among the most common places for mildew to settle, but you can get rid of the fungus easily if you follow these simple steps.

1. Cover all the mildew spots you can see with household bleach. Since most of the fungus will be along the grout lines between tiles or in corners, a good way to apply the bleach is with a plastic squeeze bottle (such as a shampoo or dish detergent bottle). Be sure to observe all of the caution notices on the bleach bottle regarding dangers to your skin and respiratory system.
2. Most of the mildew spots will disappear in a few minutes, but stubborn spots may need additional bleach and perhaps a light scrubbing. An old toothbrush is ideal for scrubbing between tiles and in the corners.
3. When all the mildew is gone, rinse all the bleach away with water.
4. When you are sure that none of the bleach remains on the walls, wash the walls with household ammonia. **REMEMBER: YOU MUST NEVER MIX BLEACH AND AMMONIA.** The combination releases potentially fatal chlorine gas. The ammonia will kill the spores of the fungus, preventing the mildew from making a speedy return.

Of course, new mildew can get started unless you eliminate the conditions that allow it to thrive. Find out what is causing the excess moisture. If the mildew occurs in a bath, kitchen, or laundry room, you know where the moisture comes from, and your problem then is to discover a way to exhaust the excess moisture. A dehumidifier or an exhaust fan may be the answer, or regular airing of the room may do the job. If the moisture comes from a leak under the house or bad drainage, you must correct the problem to eliminate your mildew problem for good. Naturally, it is always a good idea to keep walls free of dirt, grease and soap scum.

Mildew also forms outside. Many people think that they can kill the fungus when they paint their homes with a mildew-retardant paint. Usually, however, they see the mildew growing back through the paint in a matter of weeks. No paint can kill mildew; you must kill mildew before painting. Here is how to get rid of fungus from exterior walls. Mix 2/3 cup TSP (trisodium phosphate—available at most paint stores), 1/3 cup powdered detergent, and one quart liquid household bleach. Add enough warm water to make one gallon of solution, and scrub the affected areas with a stiff brush or broom; then hose them off. Be sure to trim back trees and bushes that prevent air and sunlight from reaching mildew-prone areas.

Here Is What You Will Need

Materials
- Household bleach
- Plastic squeeze bottle
- Household ammonia
- Dehumidifier or exhaust fan
- Trisodium phosphate
- Powdered detergent

Tools
- Toothbrush
- Stiff brush or broom
- Garden hose

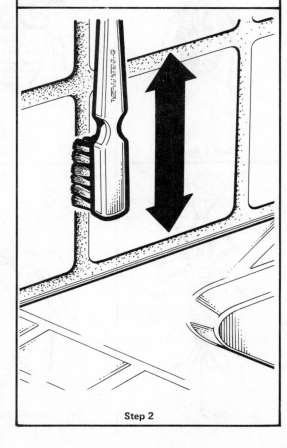

Step 2

Humidity Control Controls Mildew

Excess moisture is one of the prime ingredients in making a mildew problem. If you are unable to install an exhaust fan or a dehumidifier, try one of the chemical dehumidifiers; they can take a sizable amount of moisture out of the air. De-Moist comes in a bag that you hang in closets, basements, or other damp areas. It not only soaks up the moisture, but it also acts as an air freshener, and best of all, the De-Moist bag can be used over and over again. There is also a De-Moist Mildew Spray that protects clothing, rugs, furniture, and camping gear against mildew and musty odors. Both bag and spray are made by Coughlan Products, Inc.

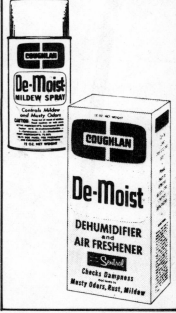

Pesky Problems

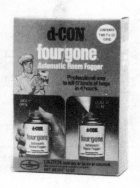

Insect Control

DO BUGS BUG you? If you have them, in one way or another they will bother you. Maybe they are just a nuisance, maybe they bite, or maybe they repulse you. In any case, we can help you get rid of them.

Insects can invade any home. Controlling them is a matter of choosing the right weapon. There are many different types of pesticides that vary by formula, by form, and by type. Selection of the right insecticide is one of the keys. The wrong formulation may or may not zap a particular bug. Even the right one today may not be the right one at some date in the future because the little devils develop immunities. The other key is taking measures to keep them out once you have killed the ones that are in the house.

We cannot include all the bugs in the world, but will comment on just those that seem to bother most homes. If we miss one that is bugging you, call your county agent. He will know what to suggest. When using insecticides, be sure to read the label on the container and follow all directions. Here are the suggestions we recommend.

1. Ants. Use dust, spray, or liquid that is residual to interrupt ant trails at their entry. Look for one of these ingredients—diazinon, lindane, or malathion. The dust should be used outside. Ant traps with kepone as the base are effective for many varieties.

Here Is What You Will Need

Materials

- Diazinon
- Lindane
- Malathion
- Kepone
- Pyrethrum
- Baygon
- Ronnel
- Methoxychlor
- Contact spray
- Residual moth spray
- Pest strips
- Moth crystals, flakes, or balls

Tools

- Sprayer

2. Bedbugs. Strip the bed and spray the mattress with either pyrethrum or malathion or lindane-based formula. Be sure to get all the crevices on both sides as well as under the straps. Also spray the floor, baseboards, walls, under rugs and any furniture around the bed. Pay particular attention to papered walls and spray all seams and cracks. Do this in the morning and leave the bed unmade until evening.

3. Bees. It is all right to spray a bee that has entered your house, but do not try to eradicate the hive. If they are in your yard or in between the walls of your house, a beekeeper would probably like to have the en-

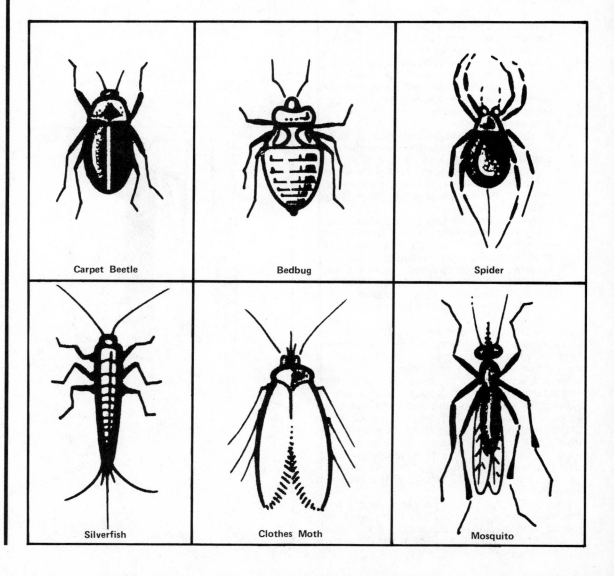

Carpet Beetle

Bedbug

Spider

Silverfish

Clothes Moth

Mosquito

tire hive. Bees are good for the ecology, so try every way possible not to destroy them. After the swarm has been removed, patch up the entry so that a new swarm will not be back next year.

4. Cockroaches. These bugs are tough to get rid of because they develop immunities to insecticides. Before chlordane fell into ill favor, it worked great against roaches for a while. Now, cockroaches are becoming immune to it. Use a residual spray with diazinon, lindane, baygon, malathion, or ronnel. Clear out all the cabinets and spray all the cracks and crevices.

5. Crickets. Many people are superstitious about killing crickets. You will not feel like that after they chew up your drapes or clothes. Use a contact spray and get them as you see them. Also use a residual moth spray to control those you cannot see.

6. Fleas. Use a malathion household spray on all carpets. Be sure to stop them on pets, also.

7. Flies. Pest strips help control flies. Use only as directed. Also use pyrethrum, ronnel, or malathion. The preventatives to follow are most important with these pests.

8. Mosquitoes. Indoors, use a flying insect spray with pyrethrum, malathion, or methoxychlor. Close the room and spray well. Leave it closed for an hour. Go after the outside mosquitoes with foggers. Removal of standing water will also help.

9. Moths. Remove all clothes from the infested closet and spray with moth spray or methoxychlor based aerosol. Launder or dry clean all clothes before putting them back in the closet. Moth crystals, flakes, or balls should be added to clothes in storage. Cedar closets help.

10. Scorpions. A diazinon-based spray controls scorpions. Use any contact spray when you see them. Get into dark places and move stacks of newspapers, magazines, and clothes. Strip off bedclothes and cushions and spray there.

11. Silverfish. Use malathion or pyrethrum and spray in dark, damp places. Also spray in the bottoms of drawers and trunks and in cracks.

12. Spiders. Use a contact spray on those you can see. Remove webs and spray the area with malathion.

13. Ticks. Control ticks on pets before they bring them into the house, and get rid of those in the house with a diazinon or malathion spray on carpets.

14. Wasps. Zap any wasp in the house with a contact spray for flying insects. Eradicate nests by spraying at night with diazinon or malathion.

15. Weevils. Remove all foods, clean the cabinets, and spray malathion or lindane over the shelves. Throw away any infected cereals, flour, etc. Keep future supplies in glass jars. Drop a bay leaf into containers as a weevil repellent.

The other phase of fighting insects is in the area of preventive maintenance. Here are some steps you should take.

△ 1. Make sure all screens are in good repair and that they fit snugly.
△ 2. Close up all the holes and cracks around doors, windows, pipes, and any other place where the bugs can get in. Put self closers or springs on outside doors so they are not left open.
△ 3. Caulk outside to keep bugs from getting inside the walls. If they get that far, they are liable to make it all the way.
△ 4. Keep a clean house. Do not leave food scraps out. Keep garbage in sealed, sanitary containers.
△ 5. Do not leave stacks of papers or magazines around.
△ 6. Remove pet waste outdoors as this is a breeding place for flies.
△ 7. Do not allow water to stand in gutters or pots outside as this is a breeding place for mosquitoes.
△ 8. Control ticks and fleas on pets so they will not bring them in the house.
△ 9. Launder or dry clean all clothing before storing.

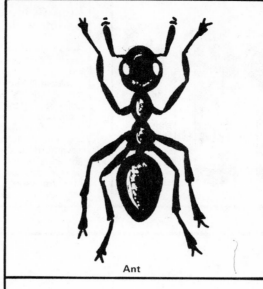
Ant

Housefly

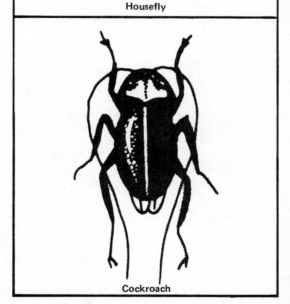
Cockroach

Dial Hose Sprayer Mixes Water Precisely

For a more accurate mixture of water going through a hose end sprayer, try the Air-O-Matic Golden Supreme Sprayer from the Gilmour Manufacturing Company. The unit has a dial you can set to mix the ratio of water to chemical. It has an all-brass metering head, while the container is a nonbreakable polyethylene. The instructions for setting the dial to proper ratio are printed on the container.

Moth Protection Comes In Many Forms

You can buy protection against moths in many forms—crystal, balls, flakes, and bricks—and Excell Chemical makes them all. The two basic ingredients in most popular household moth products are napthalene and paradichlorobenzene, and you'll find one or the other of these chemicals as the active ingredient in each Excell product. Since these products do evaporate, though, be sure to replace the supply before it's all gone. Used properly, the Excell chemicals will protect your clothes against the ravages of hungry moths.

Pesky Problems

Shell Spray Insecticides Feature Child-Safe Tops

The Child Protector Top is an added safety feature on all Shell household spray insecticides. The top is no excuse for carelessness, and you still must treat all insecticides with caution, but the safety top has proven effective in preventing small children from abusing these chemicals. Shell insecticides include Ant and Roach Spray, House and Garden Spray, Flying Insect Spray, and Outdoor Fogger.

Ciba-Geigy's Spectracide Does It All

Best known for lawn and garden chemicals, Spectracide also markets a Professional Home Pest Control package that can be used safely indoors with no unpleasant odors. The half gallon can, equipped with a trigger sprayer and a hose, has a handle to make the unit easily portable; you will have no difficulty applying the insecticide right where you need it. Spectracide can control all common household pests, including roaches, ants, and flies. Spectracide products are produced by the Ciba-Geigy Corporation.

Sevin Is Safe And Effective

Sevin is a broad-spectrum insect control that is widely recognized as one of the safest synthetic insecticides in the all-purpose category. Effective on many types of insects, Sevin is used in several insecticide formulas. Hopkins Sevin Insect Bait and Sevin Dust-5, for example, may be used on fruit trees and vegetables as well as on lawns. Used properly, Sevin requires only a one-day restriction on the harvest of most edibles, but be sure to read the instructions and the caution notices on this and any other insecticide you use. Hopkins insecticides are products of the Hopkins Agricultural Chemical Company.

Fog Dispenser Disposes Of Insects

If you find that you can no longer sit on the patio, work in the yard, or even carry out the garbage without being bothered by flies and mosquitoes, you're a candidate for a BernzOmatic Thermo Fogger. With this lightweight, cordless, propane-powered fogger, you can knock out flying insects such as mosquitoes, flies, wasps, bees, gnats, ants, and ticks easily and completely. The non-staining BernzOmatic insecticide (which is registered with the Environmental Protection Agency) is discharged from the Thermo Fogger in a completely dry cloud, penetrating deep under leaves and bushes. The fog is non-toxic to people, pets, birds, and all warm-blooded animals, and one filling is enough to handle half an acre. The Thermo Fogger, Jet Fog insecticide, and propane cylinders are available in home centers, hardware, garden supply, and camping equipment stores.

A Word About Insecticides

THE USE OF insecticides should be done with safety foremost in your mind. While many formulas are relatively harmless to humans and pets, all should be used with caution. Also, because the Environmental Protection Agency is constantly checking insecticides for safety reasons, be sure that you are not using one that has been pulled off the market. Here are some rules to keep in mind:

1. Read the label. If there is a folder with the insecticide, read that too. Be sure that you understand what you have read and follow the directions.
2. Make sure the product you are using is specified for the pest you are after.
3. Avoid contact with any insecticide. Wash all exposed skin surfaces after its use.
4. Be sure not to inhale any spray or fumes.
5. Take care to keep the spray away from foodstuffs.
6. Avoid using spray on counters where food will be prepared.
7. If you smoke, do not do it while using insecticides, and be sure to wash your hands before handling cigarettes.
8. Remove pet dishes before applying insecticides.
9. Use only the amount needed to do the job. Overkill is wasteful and can be dangerous.
10. If mixing is required, do it in a well-ventilated place.
11. Do not spray near a flame, pilot light, or furnace.
12. When using a space spray, leave the room and close the door as soon as you are through.
13. Avoid residual insecticides where children play. Prevent their touching such areas.
14. Do not use pest strips in a nursery, sick room, or where food is prepared.
15. Do not use your mouth to clear nozzles used as sprayers.
16. Do not reuse containers used for insecticides. Rinse and dispose of them.
17. If you have leftovers, leave them in the original containers.
18. Store all insecticides in a safe place away from heat and out of the reach of children.
19. Immediately change clothes after spraying, or if you should spill any insecticide on your clothes.
20. If you get any insecticide in your eyes, flush them completely with water and have someone get you to an emergency room.
21. If you accidentally take any insecticide internally, read the label for the antidote. Have someone call a doctor immediately and read him or her the active ingredients listed on the label.
22. If you feel any ill effects after using an insecticide, contact a doctor and read the label telling him the active ingredients.

Step 1

Build A Better Mousetrap, And . . .

If the old adage has any validity, the world will beat a path to the McGill Metal Products Company.

McGill's mousetrap is better—it's called the Best—because it doesn't have to be baited. The trap's plastic trigger is impregnated with an irresistible (to mice) scent that eliminates the bother of baiting. In addition to the Best trap, McGill also makes Can't Miss mouse and rat traps and All Steel mouse traps.

Rodents

NOBODY LIKES to talk about rodents, and yet they are a very dangerous menace. They do damage, carry diseases, can bite children, and scare the daylights out of most people. Controlling these pests comes in two phases. Phase one is to rid the premises of the rats and mice already inside, and phase two is to prevent future entry. Both phases are difficult and require persistance if there are very many of the creatures around.

The two ways used to rid your house of rats and mice are with poisons and with traps.

1. Poisons are the most effective weapons, yet they pose a real danger to children and pets. If you can use poisons under the house, in the attic or in other areas where only the rats and mice can get them, use them. Although rats are beginning to develop immunities and dislikes for some poisons, there are many poisons on the market, and by trying several different kinds, you will hit on one that does the job effectively. There are some poisons that are less harmful to humans than others. Warfarin is one of these and is probably the most widely used. If you try one brand with warfarin in it, and it does not attract the rodents, be sure the next brand is made with a different base. Some poisons attack the intestines and make the animal want lots of water. These are ideal if you do not have a supply of water for them in the house. They will then go out in search of water and die elsewhere.
2. Traps can catch rats and mice, but if you have a large number of pests, they may reproduce faster than you can catch them. Buy traps made for the type of rodent you have. Bait mouse traps with cheese, peanut butter, or raw bacon. Bait rat traps with raw or cooked meat, fish, bread, or strong smelling cheese. All of these baits can be further enhanced by adding a few drops of fish oil.

The second phase, keeping rats and mice from getting in, is most important, too, because even if you kill off an entire colony, others can still get in. Here is what you should do:

△ 1. Start by looking inside the house for entry possibilities. Mice can enter around pipes with even a tiny opening.
△ 2. Look for separations between floors and walls, cracks around cabinets, outside doors without weatherstripping, and, of course, any holes in walls and floors. If you wonder how the holes got there, you should know that rats and mice can eat through wood and many other solids.
△ 3. All of these possible entries should be sealed. Put poison in there before you seal them up. Poke steel wool into cracks before plastering or spackling. Add molding or nail strips of wood to cover cracks.

Here Is What You Will Need

Materials

- Poison
- Traps, bait, and fish oil
- Steel wool
- Molding or 1x2 strips of wood
- Nails
- Mothballs or moth flakes

Tools

- Hammer

△ 4. Next, examine the outside of the house. Rat entries can be high as well as low. Here again, put poison into the holes or cracks before you seal them up.
△ 5. After you have sealed up all holes inside and out, check them again in a few days. The rodents may have come back through the same way. To prevent this, use metal wherever it can be used. Pay particular attention to garages and basements in your search.

One reason that the rats or mice found your home attractive is because you probably made it so by providing food and water. Do not leave food around, and do not forget that any pet food left scattered around is a great dessert for rodents. If you feed your pet dry food, transfer it from the sack into a covered metal or plastic container so the mice and rats cannot get to it.

Also considered in the rodent category are such animals as squirrels, gophers, chipmunks, and bats. All of these animals are repelled with mothballs or moth flakes, but you must use several pounds. For example, to drive bats out of the attic, you should scatter the moth repellent throughout the attic. There are also commercial repellents on the market. Except for bats, traps can be used to catch the animals. After you have gotten rid of them, you must then plug up all their entries so they will not come back.

If you are ever bitten by a wild animal, catch it if you can, so it can be examined for rabies. Always consult your doctor.

The fight to rid your premises of rodents takes time, but it is well worth the effort.

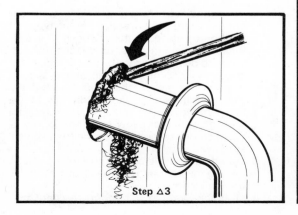

Step △3

Metal Mouse Trap Is Easy To Set

The Woodstream Easy-Set Metal Mouse Trap is different in appearance, but very effective in catching mice. First you bait the bait pedal, and then you press the trap as you would a large paper clamp. Once the trap engages, it is all set to catch mice. To dispose of the captured mouse, you need merely press the clamp again and the mouse drops out. The Victor Easy-Set Metal Mouse Trap is about as clean and simple to use as a trap can be. Victor also makes a line of conventional rat and mouse traps as well as traps for larger varmints.

Outsmart Those Rats

A new rat and mouse killer called Pest-Rid from Crown Chemicals encapsulates each crystalline warfarin particle with a coated material. Warfarin is an anticoagulant used in many rodent killers, but apparently rats have learned to detect its taste and odor and they refuse to eat it. The Pest-Rid coating hides the warfarin's taste and odor, making it much more effective. Be sure to read and observe all caution notices on any rodent killer you use.

This Killer Always Gets Its Rat (Or Mouse)

Although not available for sale to the public until recently (though used by professionals for some time), RoZol is an easy-to-use and safe-to-handle paraffinized pellet that can be used in wet or dry areas, indoors or out. Even rats who have developed high resistance to warfarin will die from RoZol. Used properly, one dose of RoZol—a product of the Chempar Chemical Company, Inc.—wipes out all the rats and mice in a typical home. Be sure to read and observe all caution notices.

Pesky Problems

A New Twist In Caulking Needs No Gun

With Space Age Caulk, made by GX International, you don't need a gun. The cartridge is made so all you have to do is twist the cap on the bottom to force caulk out the spout. Space Age packages a latex and acrylic caulk as well as tub caulk and panel adhesive in the same type of self-dispensing tube. It's really a new twist in caulking.

Whispertone Gobbles Up Noise

Install a new ceiling of Johns-Manville Whispertone fiberglass panels, and you will notice that your house is distinctly quieter as well as more attractive. The 2x4-foot panels, which consist of a pressed fiberglass base covered with an embossed vinyl surface, absorb up to 70 percent of the sound that reaches them. They not only tone down the noise in the room in which they are installed, but they also make adjoining rooms quieter. Installed with a grid system and requiring a three-inch clearance, the Johns-Manville Whispertone panels are available in eight different textured patterns to blend with nearly any room decor.

Floret.
A Whispertone fiber glass panel.

USG Helpers Quiet Down New Construction

Easy-to-install Thermafiber Sound Attenuation Blankets from USG are made for use inside walls and ceilings. For wall installations, the blankets are cut with a serrated blade knife and stapled in place. No fastening is needed for ceiling applications; just lay the USG Thermafiber Sound Attenuation Blankets on the ceiling's top surface. USG Acoustical Sealant is also used primarily in new construction of office buildings, apartments, and homes.

Noise and Sound Dampening

IF NOISES bother you, we do not have to remind you of the effects it can have on you. But there are many people who are subjected to noise pollution and do not know that this may be causing fatigue, loss of sleep, and general bad nature or bad temper. If you are planning to build or remodel your house, there are several very effective steps you can take to build noise resistant walls and to control noise transmission. Walls can be made more sound resistant by doing any or all of the following things:

1. Use double studs instead of single studs. This allows for weaving acoustical blankets between the studs. It also prevents the transmission of sound directly through the stud, which is one of the ways sound travels through a wall.
2. Use sound deadening materials for wall coverings. There are several different types of wallboards made for this purpose. One system calls for ¼-inch sound deadening wallboard to be attached to the studs, and a wall covering of ½-inch gypsum board applied over this. However, this works best if the wall covering is not applied directly to the first surface, but is attached to horizontal furring strips that allow for a sound dampening air pocket space between the two wall surfaces.
3. Sound dampening batts and blankets can be used between any new walls to halt noise transmission.
4. All cracks around the sound resistant wall

should be sealed. This includes seams, joints, and spaces under doors and around windows.

Planning during the building process can also help to control noise problems. Here are some things to keep in mind:

1. Separate activity rooms from bedrooms if possible.
2. Put bedrooms toward the back or quiet areas of the house.
3. Avoid long, straight hallways and stairways. They act as sound tunnels and do a beautiful job of carrying sound which travels best in a straight line.
4. Use solid core doors to bedrooms and activity rooms to block sound.
5. Position closets as buffers between bedrooms and sources of noise.
6. Carpet as many rooms as possible.

There are many other steps that can be built in, and you should talk with your builder and architect about them. If they know you want every sound control advantage, they will be thinking along those lines.

But what about the existing house that is noisy? That is something that affects far more people than those building or remodeling. There are many things you can do to help bring the noise level down to a slight roar. We realize you will not be able to do all of these things, but if you can do any of them, it will help. The more things you do, if they are applicable, the better off your eardrums and nerves will be. One of the first things to do is to try to track down the source of noises. Are they outside noises coming in or inside noises that are coming back to haunt you? First, let us go after the outside noises:

1. Storm windows and doors will cut out many sounds that come in through the windows

Water Pipe Noise Can Be Heard 'Round The House

Many plumbing systems make noise as the pipes expand and contract, and some do so just as water passes through. Whatever the cause, Teledyne Mono-Thane easy-to-install Foamedge Pipe and Tubing Cover will absorb most of the noise. The quarter-inch foam covers, which must be slit in order to slip over the pipe, also stop loss of heat from hot water pipes and condensation dripping from cold water pipes.

Digital Measure Goes Tapeless

Rotarul is a precision measuring device that calculates distances without using a tape. A wheel rolls over the surface to be measured —up to 1000 feet—and a magnified dial gives you a digital reading. Its 32-inch telescoping handle lets you roll it over walls, ceilings, floors, and even curved surfaces. Not just a gimmick, Rotarul is a well-made measuring instrument from MTI's Digital Instruments Division.

Tapered Saw Helps

The general-purpose saw from Eclipse has some unique and useful features. The replaceable 14¾-inch blade is made to cut both wood and metal, and it is coated with a low-friction substance called Xylan that makes sawing easier. A lock nut allows you to fasten the handle to the blade at any of nine blade angles, and the tapered blade is most welcome when you must do your cutting in confined areas. Eclipse saws, made by James Neill Tools, are available at hardware stores.

Insulation Batts Create Noise Barrier

Owens-Corning calls its 2½- and 3½-inch thick Fiberglas batts "Noise Barrier Batts." Ideal for use in inside walls and ceilings where you don't need a higher R-value for insulation purposes, they reduce sound transmission through framed walls and impact noise in floor/ceiling situations. Since the Noise Barrier batts require, of course, that you have access to the inner wall spaces for installation, plan to put them in when constructing a new home or when remodeling or converting an attic, basement, or garage to living space. The Owens-Corning batts fit tightly between studs without adhesives, staples, or other support methods.

Here Is What You Will Need

Materials
- ¼-inch sound deadening wallboard
- ½-inch gypsum board
- Furring strips
- Sound deadening batts and blankets
- Caulking
- Weatherstripping
- Lubricating oil
- Nails
- Acoustical tiles

Tools
- Tape measure
- Saw
- Hammer
- Caulking gun

and doors. They are expensive, but with fuel savings they may pay for themselves, and the noise control will be a bonus.

2. Caulk around doors and windows. Sound can come in through small cracks as well as open windows.
3. Hang lined drapes on noisy walls.
4. Weatherstrip around doors and windows.
5. Add a second wall covering using horizontal furring strips in between. The air pocket between the walls helps as does the added sound resistant material.
6. Trees and shrubs help to absorb sound before it hits your house. This may not help today, but it will in the future.
7. High, solid, wood fences, if permissible, will also block off sounds.

The sounds within the house can also be tamed by taking some of these steps:

1. Quiet as many plumbing noises as possible. Wrap pipes. Fix noisy faucets by changing washers. Stop pipe movement and water hammer.
2. Oil squeaky things such as doors and motors.
3. Put washing machines, dryers, and other large appliances that vibrate on pads.
4. Replace noisy casters with quieter models.
5. Use door closers or anti-slam devices.
6. Put carpets or rugs down on noisy floors.
7. Add acoustical tile ceilings to absorb sounds. Most people do not think of it, but halls are excellent places for acoustical ceilings if the hall is a noise corridor.
8. Replace hollow core doors with solid core doors.
9. Weatherstrip interior doors. Sealing around the door will often make a big difference. The sound you think is coming through the door may be coming under or around it.
10. Put acoustical tiles on doors to basement playrooms to help absorb noise.
11. Position the TV so it backs up to an outside wall.
12. With the current off, remove the wall outlets and wall switches and put insulating material around them. Caulk around them too.
13. Remove moldings at the floor and ceilings and caulk with acoustical sealant along the floor and ceiling seams.
14. If you have back-to-back bathrooms, remove the medicine chests and put insulating material around them.
15. Use acoustical material as lining on closets housing central heating and air conditioning units.
16. Insulate around heat ducts since uninsulated metal carries more sound.

Hopefully, some of these ideas will be enough for you to start enjoying some peace and especially quiet.

Children and Pets

Protect Your Upholstered Furniture

Scotchgard, the same formulation that waterproofs sports clothing and camping equipment, can also childproof your upholstered furniture. Just follow the directions and spray Scotchgard Fabric Protector on your furniture. It creates a protective film, and soils and stains wipe off easily with a damp cloth. A 3M product, Scotchgard cannot protect your upholstery from rips and abrasions, but it can go a long way toward making the fabric stain and soil resistant.

Keep-Stakes Keep Kids Safe

If you have play equipment in your yard, make sure it's securely anchored down. Keep-Stakes Anchors, products of A.B. Chance Company, will do the job. They really hold; even kids on swings can't budge Keep-Stakes. Available in several sizes, Keep-Stakes can be used for supporting trees, anchoring down outbuildings and fences and even television antenna towers. The auger end makes them go into the ground with relative ease, yet holds them there with childproof tenacity.

Doorway Gates Keep Tots Corralled

If you have small toddlers and a two- or three-story home, you should certainly install folding gates at the top and the bottom of all stairways. The E-Z-Tach gate from C.J. Johnson Company is easy to install, and it allows you to go about your business without worrying. Once the kids outgrow the gate stage, keep it around to corral your pet(s). If the pet is small enough to crawl through the gate openings, extend the gate and staple nylon netting over it. The netting prevents the pet from getting through, but it does not prevent you from folding the gate whenever you wish. The Johnson E-Z-Tach gate is sold through hardware, department, and infant stores.

Latches Can Prevent The Unthinkable

No parent likes to think about what would happen if a small child were to start playing with the typical household chemicals stored under a sink. But you can keep your inquisitive child away from harmful substances, cutlery, and valuable breakables easily by installing Kindergard Latches on cabinets and drawers. The 100-percent nylon latches mount inside, are totally invisible when the cabinets and/or drawers are closed, and lock automatically. They release with finger pressure, but even a toddler who sees how

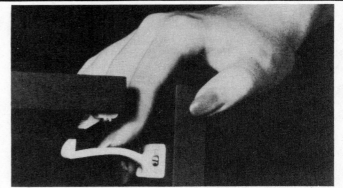

to open the latch cannot exert the force that is necessary to separate the two parts of the latch. Installed within minutes in either metal or wood, Kindergard Latches—a creation of the Kindergard Corporation—are available at hardware, department, and children's stores.

Childproofing Your House

IF YOU HAVE children, you want your house to be a home for them. You want it to be a place they can live in, play in, and enjoy without being constantly afraid that they will do something to throw their parents into a trauma. Your children should not have to worry about such things as the mess they make or the things they could break, but you especially do not want them to be exposed to danger. Let us see what steps you can take at different ages to give you peace of mind instead of a mind that goes to pieces.

1. Before the new baby arrives, make sure that the nursery or room where the baby will sleep has no lead-based paint. There are none being made now, but if you picked up a second hand bassinet for refinishing, or if the woodwork has many layers of paint on it, a bottom layer on either could contain lead. If there is any doubt, strip down to the bare wood and repaint. Also, do not use any old leftover paint that could contain lead.
2. As soon as the baby starts getting around, you should put baby gates at the top of stairs and at doors when you want to keep a child in or out of a room.
3. Put plastic safety caps over reachable electrical wall outlets.
4. Move all those kitchen chemicals out from under the sink or lock the cabinets. Many everyday items are dangerous if swallowed.
5. Eliminate electric cords that hang down from an appliance and could be pulled down by the child.
6. Provide play areas where it is okay to make a mess (within reason).
7. Provide a chalkboard or a wall with strip-pable and washable wallpaper squares that will take pencil and felt marker ink. As the child gets older, add a bulletin board.
8. If you do not have children's furniture, get second hand pieces and saw table and chair legs off to make them child size.
9. Put slip covers over good furniture.
10. Keep tools for lawn work and for the shop under lock and key. Arrange for big power tools to be on a separate circuit that allows you to throw a switch so they cannot be

turned on. Do not let children watch or play in the shop until they are old enough to start to learn about using tools safely.
11. If you have a choice, use resilient tile floors in the child's room and play area. They are easier to keep clean.
12. Install wainscotting along hallways to take the fingerprints and knocks.
13. Keep good furniture out of the normal pathway through the house.
14. Add a secondary hand rail to stairs that will be the right height for a child. It can be taken down later, and any holes used for brackets can be filled in.

These are mostly common sense ideas, but if we reminded you of one step you did not think of, it will be good for your child and for you.

Here Is What You Will Need

Materials

- Non-lead paint
- Baby gates
- Electrical outlet safety caps
- Cabinet locks
- Furniture slip covers
- Resilient tile
- Wainscotting for walls
- Hand rail for stairs
- Chalkboard

Tools

- Screwdriver
- Saw

Store Dangerous Chemicals In A Locked Cabinet

Paint Enlivens Closet

By applying a bright paint job to your newly constructed child's closet, you not only protect the surfaces but you also may make the unit interesting enough that your child will actually want to hang up his or her clothes. Du-Kwik Acrylic Latex Enamels are just the ticket. Most of the colors are bright and light, and they come in handy half-pint see-through containers. Du-Kwik Latex Enamels dry in 30 minutes and clean up with water. Du-Kwik is a product of Armstrong Paint Co.

Hook Kids On Neatness

You can create a great deal of extra storage space on the inside of a closet door by installing two rows of clothes hooks, one down low for the child to use and another up high for you to use. You'll entice your children into actually using the hooks if you make every other hook a Magic Mount with Mickey Mouse on it. Magic Mounts can be attached to any surface by just peeling off the backing and pressing in place. Products of Miller Studio, Magic Mounts are made for all sorts of hanger and hook applications.

Get A New Angle On Your Project

Not a square and not an angle, the Squangle from Mayes Brothers Tool Manufacturing Company includes all the features found in a framing square, a combination square, and a T-square. Its thumbscrew adjustment allows you to set any angle from 45 to 90 degrees. The Squangle also features a level bubble vial, a rafter scale, and protractor settings. Handy for many projects, the Squangle is the ideal tool for measuring consistent slot angles in a child's closet.

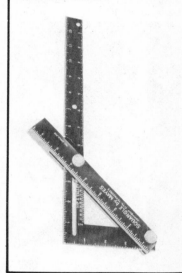

Child's Closet

ONE OF THE problems involved in designing and constructing children's clothes closets is that the child soon outgrows the unit. A four-year-old soon becomes a six-year-old, then a ten-year-old—and you find that you must rebuild the closet again. There is a way, nonetheless, to make a closet that keeps pace with your child's changing measurements. Here is how to do it.

1. Remove the rod, shelf, and shelf supports from an existing closet.
2. Cut a 1x6-inch board into two four-foot lengths, and cut a series of slots in the edge of each piece from top to bottom. The slots, which extend to within about two inches of the opposite edge, should be spaced about four inches apart and should be 1/8 of an inch wider than the diameter of the closet rod. Slant the slots downward at an angle of about 45 degrees, and round the ends for better appearance.
3. Nail the boards to the sides of the closet, with the tops six feet above the floor and the back edges nine inches out from the back wall. Face the slotted edges backward, and make certain that the corresponding slots in the boards are level.
4. Slip the rod into—what are for the present—the proper slots, and then move the rod a notch higher as your child grows.
5. Make the closet shelf adjustable too. Attach two four-foot slotted metal standards to the back wall, and then cantilever the shelf from them on metal brackets.

Here Is What You Will Need

Materials

- 1x6-inch board
- Two four-foot slotted metal standards and shelf brackets
- Nails

Tools

- Saw
- Sandpaper or round file
- Hammer
- Tape measure

Your Child's Closet Can Hold Twice As Much

Since children's clothes are short, much of the space in a full-length closet is wasted. But you can double the storage capacity of a child's closet with U.S. Gypsum's adjustable shelving system. The all-steel components feature a smooth, mar-resistant coating that won't crack, chip, or rust. Available in seven basic sizes, the components expand to take care of almost any closet situation; no cutting, sawing or painting is required. These shelves are made for clothing, with an adjustable hanger rod, but U.S. Gypsum also markets other types of storage shelves.

Nail

Clothes Rod

Slotted Board

Children and Pets

Invisible Hinges Add A Professional Touch

Soss Invisible Hinges look complicated at first, but they are actually simple and easy to install. Installed properly on a door, the hinge disappears completely when the door is closed. Applicable almost anywhere that ordinary hinges would work, the Soss Invisible Hinges can be used on metal as well as on wood. Since Soss makes about 20 different versions, there is sure to be one in the size and style you are seeking. Soss Invisible Hinges are widely distributed, and you should be able to find them wherever cabinet hardware is sold.

Dovetail Joints Make Strong Drawers

The sturdiest drawers that are easy to make are those with dovetail joints. The old-fashioned furniture makers used to make them with hand tools, but you can do the job rapidly with a dovetail bit in an electric router. Montgomery Ward's Powr Kraft ⅔-horsepower Router is double insulated against electrical hazards and can produce 25,000 revolutions per minute. It has a hard, phenolic sub-base that will not mar or scuff wood, and it has very comfortable pistol-grip handles, with the switch in the right-hand handle for easy and safe operation. The Powr Kraft Router is available at larger Ward retail stores or through the catalog.

Vaco Tool Has A Screw Up Its Sleeve

The Vaco Screw Holding Driver is an ingenious tool. The tip, manipulated by an adjusting sleeve, wedges into the screw slot to hold the screw firmly while turning it. Great for holding screws in hard to reach places, the Vaco Screw Holding Driver also has a great gripping power, a definite aid in preventing slips when trying to remove stubborn screws. In driving screws, you maintain the tool's grip until the screw is well started,

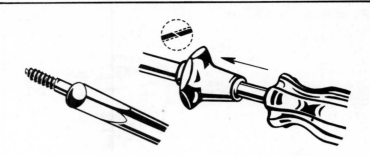

and then you release the adjusting sleeve and use the Vaco tool as a conventional screwdriver. Constructed of quality materials, the Vaco Screw Holding Driver is available in six popular sizes.

Teenager's Desk and Storage Wall

DOES YOUR teenager lack the desk and bookshelves he or she needs? If so, then this project might well be the solution to the problem. Although the desk and storage wall take up only a little more than five square feet of floor space along one wall, they provide more than enough space for books, papers, hobbies, and knickknacks. The desk has work space for two people, and the unit itself lends a decorative touch to the entire room. Use the following procedure to build a teenager's desk and storage wall.

1. Remove the baseboard from the wall against which the unit is to be placed. Since the major part of the unit is constructed of 1x12-inch boards, you can cut most of the pieces required all at once.
2. Cut the boards for the sides 80 inches long, the top and bottom 63⅜ inches, the vertical divider 75¼ inches, and the nine shelves 31 ⁵⁄₁₆ inches.
3. Assemble the storage unit on the floor first, before tilting it up against the wall. Nail the top and bottom between the sides with 8d finishing nails; the upperside of the bottom should be four inches above the floor.
4. Next, nail the divider between the top and bottom at midpoint, and nail a 3¼-inch board or block under the bottom to bear the weight of the divider when the shelves are filled.
5. Install the shelves on either side of the divider, using ⅝-inch quarter-round cleats to support the ends.
6. Position the upper side of the fourth shelf from the top 29¼ inches above the floor.
7. Allow a 12-inch space between the top and bottom of all shelves above that one.
8. On the right side of the divider, place the fifth shelf from the top 12 inches below the fourth.
9. Cut a sheet of ⅛-inch hardboard to cover the back of the storage unit, and nail it to the sides and shelves with 2d common nails.
10. Turn the unit over, nail a four-inch facing strip across the bottom of the frame, and nail 1x2-inch facing strips to the front edges of the sides, top, and divider (center the facing strip on the divider).
11. Also nail a 1x2-inch strip across the edge of the bottom shelf in the left compartment,

making sure that the top edge is flush with the top of the shelf.
12. Now, tilt the unit against the wall, level it, and secure it with finishing nails driven diagonally through the sides into the studs.
13. Drive a few screws through the hardboard back into the studs.

Ideally, you should purchase a desk top made of ¾-inch plywood with laminated plastic bonded to the surface and to the three exposed edges. Such a desk top is a very smooth, decorative surface which is highly resistant to dents and stains. You can, however, make the top yourself of ¾-inch plywood or of ⅛-inch tempered hardboard glued to ⅝-inch plywood.

14. Make the desk support of ¾-inch plywood, 22 inches wide by 29¼ inches high.
15. Fasten the support to the desk top, six inches from the open end, with a pair of 2x2-inch butt hinges.
16. Screw the hinges directly to the underside of the top and to the reverse side of the support (without mortises) so that when you lift

Here Is What You Will Need

Materials

- 1x12-inch boards for sides, shelves, etc.
- 1x6-inch board for the four-inch facing strip
- 1x2-inch board for facing strips
- ⅝-inch quarter-rounds for shelf cleats
- ⅛-inch hardboard for back of cabinet
- Desk top
- ¾-inch plywood for desk support
- 2x2s to brace desk top
- ⅜-inch plywood for drawer sides and bottoms
- Drawer slides
- Drawer pulls
- Two 2x2-inch butt hinges
- 1½x30-inch hinge
- Two table leg braces
- Transom catch
- Nails
- Piano hinge
- Bulletin board cork and linoleum cement
- Paint or stain and varnish

Tools

- Hammer
- Screwdriver
- Saw
- Tape measure
- Level
- Paintbrush

Cork Tiles Are Easy To Apply

The use of cork to cover a portion of the teen desk is a great idea. If you get cork tiles like the Deco-Cork brand from Decocraft, consider adding a miniature bulletin board on the wall behind the desk. You can mount individual squares wherever you want them or create an entire corked wall for both decorative and functional purposes. Any number of adhesives can hold cork tiles; contact cement works quite well.

How To Make A Soft Drink Can Talk

Don't throw away that empty 12-ounce beer or soft drink can. Instead, convert it to an extension speaker with the Tim-Can kit from Innovative Audio Systems, Inc. Available at retail stores throughout the United States, the Tim-Can Speaker Kit contains everything you need to build a loudspeaker except the beverage can itself. It's a real conversation piece for your teenager's desk and storage wall.

Drawer Slides Make The Difference

Any woodworking project calling for drawers will turn out more professionally if the drawers ride on drawer slides. The Tri-Roller Drawer Slide unit from Amerock Corporation is a good one that makes use of two side rollers and a center roller. The center roller, fastened to the back of the drawer, operates in a track mounted below the drawer. The metal is Perma-Bright zinc-finished steel, and the rollers are poly. Easy to install and relatively trouble free, the Amerock Tri-Roller Drawer Slide can support up to 50 pounds.

---

the top into the cabinet, the support folds down over it.

17. Attach a pair of table leg braces to the edges of the support.
18. To strengthen the top, screw and glue a pair of 2x2s to the underside. The 2x2s should extend to within six inches of both ends, and they should be parallel to the desk support. Allow just enough space between the 2x2s and the edges of the support to accommodate the table leg braces when folded.
19. Screw the other end of the braces to the inside edges of the 2x2s.
20. Attach the desk top to the cabinet with a 30-inch piano hinge screwed to the back edge of the top and to the top edge of the facing strip on the bottom shelf in the left compartment.
21. Work the desk top up and down several times to make sure that it fits and operates well.
22. Install a transom catch on the upper end to lock the top into the cabinet when no one is using it.
23. Cover the front of the desk support with a sheet of bulletin board cork, applying linoleum cement to hold the cork in place.
24. You can make the three drawers below the desk top in the left compartment of equal or of different depths. Make the fronts from one-inch boards, the rest of ⅜-inch plywood. The fronts should be one inch wider than the sides.
25. To install the drawers, nail vertical blocks of wood into the front and back corners of the cabinet; the blocks should project from the sides of the cabinet the same distance as the facing strips.
26. Screw metal drawer slides to the blocks and to the sides of the drawers.
27. Drawer construction, however, is not a simple task. If you wish to bypass it, simply cut a ¾-inch plywood door to fit flush within the opening, and hang the door with a couple of wrap-around hinges. Your teenager can use the space behind the door to store games, hobby kits, and other big, flat articles.
28. When you complete the unit, paint it with semi-gloss or gloss alkyd enamel; or give it a natural finish with stain and varnish.

Old Company Offers New Nail Line

Masonite Corporation, long a leader in the hardboard field, has introduced a new line of prepackaged common and finishing nails, representing the company's initial offering of basic hardware accessories. The nails include five sizes of common nails from 1½ to 3½ inches, six sizes of finishing nails from 1¼ to 3½ inches, and a 1¼ inch underlayment nail. Masonite thus can provide all the nails you need as well as the hardboard cabinet backing for your teenager's desk and storage wall.

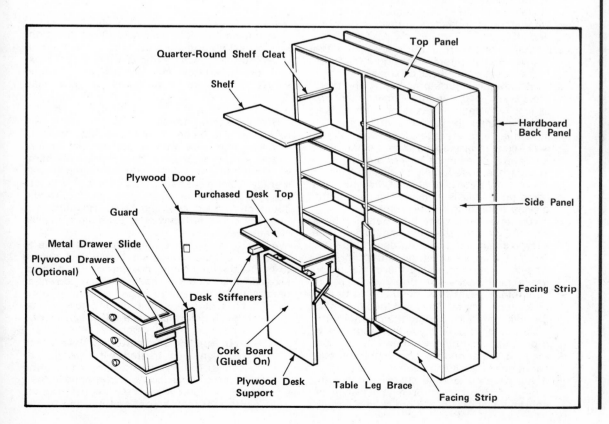

Quarter-Round Shelf Cleat
Shelf
Top Panel
Hardboard Back Panel
Plywood Door
Purchased Desk Top
Guard
Metal Drawer Slide
Plywood Drawers (Optional)
Desk Stiffeners
Cork Board (Glued On)
Plywood Desk Support
Table Leg Brace
Side Panel
Facing Strip
Facing Strip

Continuous Hinges Come In Many Sizes

The piano or continuous hinge is a simple butt hinge with leaves in one continuous piece. Available with or without holes for mounting screws, these hinges come in several widths, lengths, and finishes; brass plate is the most popular finish. Some of the quality brands in hinges include Spartan, Hager, Macklanburg-Duncan, National, Taco, Braun, and Lustre-Line.

Children and Pets

Park Your Bike On The Wall

Storing a bike from the ceiling is a bother for active cyclists because it takes time to get the machine down and back up. But with the Bike Keeper from Continental Marketing, you can park your bike in an upright position against the wall. To park, you need only roll the front wheel up the wall until the Bike Keeper can grip it and hold the bike securely. All you need is a screwdriver to attach the Bike Keeper to a garage wall, an apartment balcony, or nearly anywhere else you care to park your bike.

Double-Locking Cable Secures Bikes From Thieves

The Mark II Cable from Helistrand, Inc., has three loops so that you can lock your bike in two places instead of one. Wrap the cable around both front and back wheels, and then lock the cable to a post. The Mark II Cable weighs only nine ounces, has a tough vinyl covering, and is self coiling for more convenient storage under the bike seat. It is available at many leading bicycle shops.

Family-Sized Bike Rack

You can store as many as four bikes in a rack available from Montgomery Ward. It can be used free-standing, but you would be smart to anchor it permanently to the garage floor or other secure area. To park a bike—the rack holds all sizes—just put the front wheel in; the rack supports the front hub. The wire-like brackets are zinc plated, and the base is vinyl coated. Look for the rack at Ward retail stores or in the Montgomery Ward catalog.

Bicycle and Tricycle Storage

THERE IS NOTHING more frustrating to non-bike-riding members of the family than having to wade through, trip over or move bicycles. Having a place where bikes are stored out of the way will eliminate this aggravation. It also protects the bike from damage and theft.

During periods when the weather prevents bike riding, it often makes sense to have still another more out of the way place to store them. Rather than give you a specific plan for making one bike storage rack, we have come up with several suggestions on the problem, any one of which may help you. Maybe you will wish to incorporate several of them.

1. Store your bike in a garage, storage shed, or in the house so that the building can be locked. Until CB radios came along, bikes were among the leaders in items being ripped off.
2. If you have to bring the bike inside the house, clean it before you bring it in. Try to find a closet where it can be stored.
3. If the garage is your storage area, and there are several bikes in the family, mark off spaces with paint on the floor so that bikes are never left in the path of a car.
4. Individual bike storage along one garage wall takes up less space than a single rack for several bikes to be parked side by side. This can be done simply by using a belt or strap to hold the bike against the wall. This takes up a little less space than when the bicycle is standing on the ground.
5. If you have to park the bike outside, make sure the machine is always kept locked. Use a large chain and a case hardened lock. Try to arrange so the chain goes through both wheels as well as around the frame. If you use a rack, make sure the rack is set in concrete. Thieves have been known to take bikes, rack, and all. They just load the entire grouping into a truck, and then work on the locks at their leisure. If you lock your bike to a post or something anchored, make sure that it is tall enough so the chain and bike cannot be lifted over the top.
6. If you have no storage space in either the garage or the house, or if you live in an apartment where you do not have a garage,

Here Is What You Will Need

Materials

- Primer
- Paint
- Bicycle chain and lock
- Bicycle hooks and hangers
- ⅝-inch exterior plywood
- 2x4s
- ¾-inch board for gas pump sign
- Asphalt roll roofing and roofing cement
- Wood preservative
- ½-inch hose
- Galvanized nails
- Silicone caulking

Tools

- Paintbrush
- Tape measure
- Saw
- Miter box
- Hammer
- Plane
- Clamp
- Caulking gun

maybe this idea will help. Take the front wheel off and store the bike in the trunk of your car. Usually, this is wasted space except when traveling. At that time, you could park the bike in the middle of your living room.

Bike hooks and hangers are certainly the easy way to go. If you cannot find just what you want, however, improvise with something similar. For example, there are many screw hooks at the hardware store that could be used for ceiling or wall storage. To prevent bare metal from touching and possibly scratching your rims, plastic tubing could be slipped over the hook. Regular shelf brackets could be converted to make a bicycle storage rack.

A good way to store children's tricycles is to build this unique garage-service station, geared to house the equivalent of a pair of tricycles for six-year-olds. You can scale it up or down as necessary. No matter how large you make it, however, such a storage unit is bound to clear up some of the clutter from the garage or basement.

△ 1. Start by building a framework of 2x4s which have been well treated with wood preservative. The framework consists of three sills, three plates, and four corner posts.
△ 2. Miter the plates where they meet at the back corners of the garage, and nail the frame-

Hooks Hang Bike From Rafters

SMC's No. 16 Utility Storage Hangers are heavy-duty, steel, screw hooks that make great bike hangers. Their tough, plastic cushion coating prevents them from ever scratching the bike. They come packed in pairs, and you can use them to hang either one or two bikes. If you use both for one bike, position the hooks in the ceiling so that the bike hangs upside down with the hooks holding each tire.

Limited Garage Space Need Be No Barrier To Bike Storage

Often the garage is the only place for bike storage, and when the garage must house two bikes plus the family car, space may become critical. The Bike Bin by Spacemaster is designed to solve this problem. It holds two bicycles upright in the least possible space. The Bike Bin's front wheel retainer prevents leaning, thereby keeping the handlebars clear of one another and at the same time preventing the bikes from falling. Made of heavy-duty steel, the Bike Bin can be assembled so that the bikes face in opposite directions. Additional units can be joined to the first one—either side by side or facing each other—to accommodate more than two bicycles.

work together with 10d galvanized common nails.

△ 3. Cut the sides, back, and roof panels of ⅝-inch exterior plywood, and treat them with wood preservative.

△ 4. Miter the top edges of the roof panels with a plane, and then nail the roof panels to the framework with 6d galvanized common nails.

△ 5. Bevel a length of 2x4 to match the angle of the roof peak, clamp it in place beneath one of the roof pieces, and nail the plywood to the 2x4.

△ 6. Position the other roof piece, nail it to the 2x4, and run a bead of silicone caulk along the joint.

△ 7. The false front of the garage is a rectangular piece of ⅝-inch plywood cut to reach from the edge of one roof overhang to the other, and from the bottom of the plate to two inches above the roof ridge.

△ 8. Apply wood preservative, and nail the plywood to the framework and to the end of the

ridgepole.

△ 9. Build the gas pump of ⅝-inch plywood treated with preservative. It should measure about 10 inches across the front, eight inches deep, and 30 inches high.

△10. Nail the back to one end of the garage so that it overlaps the corner post. Then assemble the other sides around it.

△11. Cut the sign for the pump from a ¾-inch board, and nail it to the underside of the pump top before nailing the top on the four sides.

△12. Attach a length of ½-inch (or smaller) hose to the side of the pump.

△13. Cover the roof with two strips of asphalt roll roofing stretched over the ridge from eave to eave, and glue it to the roof with asphalt roofing cement.

△14. At the eaves, drive roofing nails through the roofing into the top plates.

△15. Paint the garage with a coat of special latex primer, followed by two coats of latex house paint.

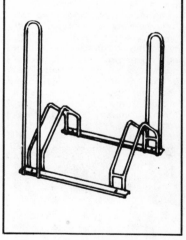

Asphalt Roll Covering

Ridgepole Planed To Match Roof Angle

Plywood Roof

Plane To Match Roof Angle

Miter Corner

JOHN'S GARAGE

Framework

Plywood Front, Sides and Back

Painted Air Pump

Rubber Hose

Plywood Gas Pump

Give Your Bikes A Lift

Get your bike storage plans off the ground with Sears bike storage lift. A 26-inch lift bar, four pulleys, and nylon rope (capable of holding up to 750 pounds) do the job. All of the hardware needed to make the easy installation is provided, including a cleat on which to anchor the rope when raising the bicycles. If your garage is tall enough, you can actually store bikes above the car, but in most cases, plan on positioning the bikes over the car's hood. The storage lift is available at Sears larger retail stores and through the catalog.

Children and Pets

Providing for Pets

ALTHOUGH MAN'S best friend can do tricks, and cats are considered independent, they still must rely on you in many ways. If you do not make provisions for them in all areas of their lives, you and your pet will never have the ideal relationship.

Food and water must be provided for your pets. Of course, when you are home, you can take care of these needs. However, if you work, you must arrange to have water supplied while you are gone. After you establish how much water your pet drinks, find a container that will accommodate the required amount. If your pet has a habit of knocking over the water dish, an angel food cake pan can come to your rescue. A sturdy stake in the ground will hold the angel food cake pan in place when you fit the pan over the stake.

You can also purchase an automatic watering system that hooks up to a water outlet and lets in fresh water when the supply gets below a certain level. There is also a gadget that screws on to the faucet. With the water turned on, when the pet licks the side of the gadget, the valve opens, and water trickles out. Believe it or not, most dogs learn the trick in very short order, and you never have to worry about running out of fresh water for your pet. The gadget is easily removed when you need the water outlet for other reasons.

Getting up in the middle of the night to let your dog or cat out, can be a problem. You can either attempt to regulate them to a schedule which calls for going out only when you wish, or you can provide them with their own entryway. For cats, the best plan seems to be a cutout with a hinged door in a window screen. Use a window that has easy access to inside. Outside, provide a ledge or shelf so the animal has a place to land before coming in. You will also find this to be a favorite spot for sunning. Here is how to make the entry:

1. Make the cutout in a lower corner of the screen, just large enough for the cat. Keep in mind that even after the cat is mature enough to roam outside, he may still grow larger.
2. Make a cut along the bottom of the entry and on the two sides.
3. Bind all the edges with tape, and then outline the door with thin strips of wood lath.
4. The screen will be a natural hinge in most cases. However, if it does not work as smoothly as you or the cat would like, cut off the top and run loops of wire through the door and the screen above, adjusting the screen size until it opens freely each way.
5. If the cutout allows too much air in, block off all but the portion needed for entry with a piece of hardboard cut to fit. This is best attached to the screen so that the window can be lowered from inside when necessary. Also, you might want to put up some sort of wind screen outside.

The advantage of this raised entry is preventing a dog or some other animals from following your cat inside. It is also easier to cut into a screen than into a door, and usually, there is a window partially covered by shrubbery that will be less obtrusive. If you have a fenced backyard, and there is not a window that suits your purpose, a door entry like the one for dogs will do.

There are several good doorway entry units on the market. These units will work well, are fairly easy to install, and, in many instances, will look much neater than a homemade job. However, if you keep your dog in the garage or an outbuilding

and still want him to be able to go out into the yard at will, you can make your own door.

△ 1. Cut out an opening just big enough for your dog. The cutout should be made near the bottom, but should leave enough of the door to maintain its strength. The same is true of the strength along the sides. In most cases, centering the door between the side edges will be best.

△ 2. Outside doors are usually solid core. If not, put in solid pieces within the door all around the cutout.

△ 3. Make the door from either hardboard, sheet aluminum, or plywood, keeping in mind that it must be lightweight so the dog can move it and so it will not slam down and hurt him.

△ 4. Use hinges that allow the door to swing both ways. Fit the door and mount it before finishing it in case you have to cut it again for a better fit. It can be mounted inside or outside, depending on what locking arrangement you wish to make and whether you need a hanging burlap piece for insects.

△ 5. Burlap is used to brush off flies as the dog enters. In some areas, this is not necessary. If it is, attach the burlap to the outside with staples and mount the door from the inside. The curtain should be in two pieces with a vertical opening in the center. You do not have to use burlap, but it is coarse enough and heavy enough to do the job. Make sure whatever you use is heavy enough to hang down without fouling. Add weights to the bottom if necessary.

△ 6. If the entry door is mounted on the inside, arrange for a locking device. It could be a sliding bolt or an actual hasp and lock. If the entry door is mounted outside, provide a sliding piece that can be put in place and locked from the inside.

△ 7. Finish all the edges with molding. The molding on the pet entry door should match the molding on the main door.

A dog that stays outside needs a doghouse. They can be elaborate or simple. Ours is simple but has the features that should be included for the dog's best interest. These features include a wind baffle, easy cleaning and airing, and warmth. We suggest using ⅜ inch or thicker outside or

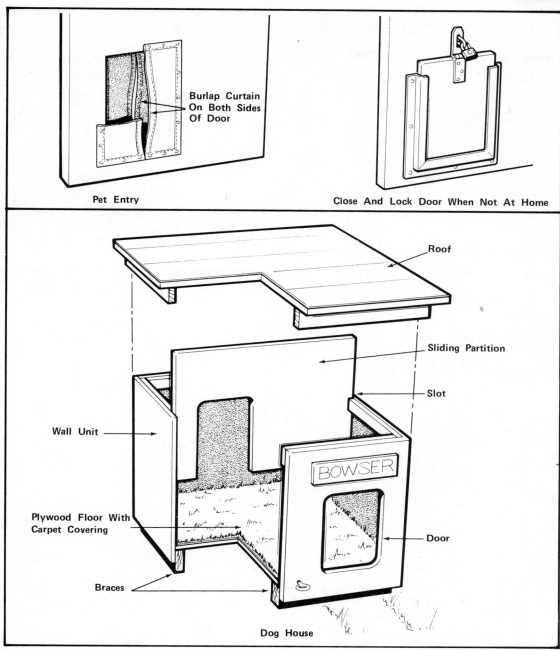

Burlap Curtain On Both Sides Of Door

Pet Entry

Close And Lock Door When Not At Home

Roof

Sliding Partition

Slot

Wall Unit

BOWSER

Plywood Floor With Carpet Covering

Door

Braces

Dog House

marine plywood, good on one side. (Marine plywood may not be available, and it does cost more.) The size of the house will depend on the size of the dog.

o 1. Draw a plan after you decide on the size. Then sketch out an actual sized floor plan with chalk on a concrete surface and test the size with the dog. Keep in mind that the dog must be able to turn around to get back out.

o 2. Construct the framework for the house as if you were building a box. Use 2x2s. If water could be a problem, make sure the floor will be up off the ground.

o 3. Cut out the sides, floor, roof, and the piece for the wind baffle partition. Nail or screw the sides and the floor to the frame.

o 4. Staple 2-inch thick insulating batts to the sides and under the floor.

o 5. Cover the insulation with hardboard or thin plywood. If the floor insulation will be against the ground, it must also be covered.

o 6. Build a track of either wood or metal for the partition to slide into. The partition is important because while a dog can stand cold temperatures, he cannot tolerate drafts in most instances.

o 7. Make the roof larger than the box so there

will be an overhang. Also staple insulation to the underside and cover it. In framing the ceiling to cover the insulation, build it so the roof has at least a slight slant. Hinge the roof at the back. This allows for easier cleaning, and also lets you prop up the roof piece to air out the doghouse.

o 8. Add a burlap covering over the door opening. This will be an additional wind baffle and keeps insects from coming in with the dog.

o 9. The house can be painted or stained. It should definitely be protected from moisture with some coating. Provide a warm bed in the back. Cotton seed, if available in your area, makes a warm base for a cloth bed. Carpet scraps make a good floor covering for the entire house. Some people also add carpeting to the walls for a snugger home.

o 10. Be sure that there are no protruding sharp things that could harm the dog.

If you have questions about your pet, your vet may be a good source of information, although some are getting as hard to talk with as your doctor. The local Humane Society may be able to help. There are also books you can read. There is a volume for nearly every breed of dog and cat as well as for other pets.

Automatic Leash Gives Dog Freedom

If you tether your dog in the yard, both you and your dog will like the freedom afforded by Cordomatic's Dog Tenda. A leash in a reel, the Dog Tenda, extends and retracts as the dog moves. Its feather-like tension is responsive to the dog's movements without ever being dangerously restrictive. The vinyl-covered flexible steel cable is 15 feet long, providing 30 feet of running room and a roving area of approximately 700 square feet. Quickly and easily installed, the Dog Tenda keeps the dog safely in tow, but allows plenty of freedom. Dog Tenda is the brainstorm of Cordomatic Reels.

Your Dog Can Have His Own Septic Tank

If disposing of dog waste presents problems for you, consider installing a Doggie Dooley which works like a miniature septic tank, utilizing bacterial action to reduce waste matter to a liquid that can be absorbed into the ground. Consisting of a level plastic lid with a foot lever and a below-ground moisture-holding tray, the Doggie Dooley works well for one to three small dogs or a single medium-size dog, but it could not handle a large dog like a Great Dane satisfactorily. Installation requires digging a hole three feet deep for the moisture-holding tray. Doggie Dooley, from Huron Products Company, can be found at most pet stores. It comes with a plastic scoop and a supply of Enzyo Digester.

Magnetic Pet Door Stays Shut

The Dog Dor, a product of the Dog Dor Company, uses magnets to keep it closed and silent against wind. Simple to install, the Dog Dor consists of two plates that fit over the hole you cut and four nuts and bolts which hold the plates together. Dog Dor only comes in two sizes and cannot accommodate all sizes of dogs, but it will take care of most. It comes with a gray enamel finish, but you can paint it to match the door. It has a hook lock on the inside.

Children and Pets

Spray Glue Is Convenient

Just a push of a button and USM's Bostik Spray Glue quickly and neatly bonds paper, cardboard, fabrics, styrofoam, plastics, fiberglass, glass, and metal. This non-flammable, waterproof adhesive has dozens of uses around the home and on the job. It is washable, colorless and will not stain, wrinkle, or curl. It can be used for permanent or temporary bonding. Valuable to the home handyman, homemaker, decorator, artist, craftsman and mechanic, USM Bostik Spray Glue is pressure sensitive and fast drying for jobs where neatness counts.

Masking Tape Makes Chalkboard Painting Neat

If you plan to convert just part of a surface into a chalkboard, you'll want a straight line between the painted board and the rest of the surface. Masking tape is the best answer, and Super-Stik from Superior Insulating Tape is a good masking tape. Remember to remove all masking tape as soon as you finish painting. If you let it sit on the surface for a week or so, you may well find either that the tape won't come off cleanly, or that it leaves behind a gooey residue.

Spray Paint Your Chalkboard

You can convert any smooth, non-porous surface into a chalkboard with Chalk Board Finish Spray Paint. Able to adhere to wood, metal, glass, plastic, or hardboard, this paint contains fine particles of slate-like abrasive material that creates an ideal chalkboard surface and can stand up to years of continuous service. Chalk Board Finish Spray Paint, available in green and black, is a product of Illinois Bronze Powder & Paint Company.

These Frame Fasteners Are Unique

If you elect to put a frame around your chalkboard, consider using Skotch Fasteners at the joints. Ideal for butt joints, Skotch Fasteners send four points into each member and have a metal tie spanning the joint. Skotch Fasteners are easy to install because they stay in place by themselves and require only a steadying hand with the first hammer tap. The Superior Fastener Corporation makes these handy fasteners in four sizes.

Making a Blackboard

NOTHING YOU provide for children will keep them totally entertained, and many things are good only at certain ages. One provision that stems the age tide fairly well and can keep little minds and hands busy for more than a few minutes, is a chalkboard. It also has other values. It helps children learn to write, print, and spell. It helps them learn to draw. Later on, it can be used as a message center, and it may also keep them from writing on the walls.

This should be an easy project for you to do. The first thing to decide is where the chalkboard will go. It can be made part of an existing surface, or it can be hung on a door in the child's room or even on the inside of a closet door. Very smooth wall surfaces can be converted. If you do not have a suitable surface, make a chalkboard to your liking using the following general steps. Vary it to suit your circumstances.

1. Use a hardboard surface such as Masonite. Cut the board to the size you wish.
2. Get chalkboard paint. It comes in either

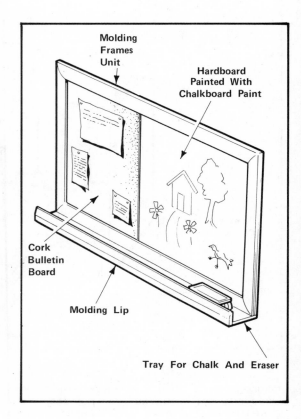

Molding Frames Unit

Hardboard Painted With Chalkboard Paint

Cork Bulletin Board

Molding Lip

Tray For Chalk And Eraser

Here Is What You Will Need
Materials

- Masonite or other hardboard
- Chalkboard paint
- Masking tape
- Cork squares
- Glue
- Molly bolts
- Molding
- Nails

Tools

- Saw
- Tape measure
- Paintbrush
- Drill
- Screwdriver
- Hammer

spray or brush-on and in either green or black.
3. Mask off parts of the hardboard that you do not want as chalkboard. For example, it is a good idea to also have a bulletin board as part of the unit. This can easily be done by gluing cork squares over a section of the surface.
4. The board can be attached directly to the wall or door with Molly bolts or similar anchors. However, for growing children, keep in mind that you may want to raise it as the children grow older. In that case, it could be hung like a large picture using wire. However, this is not as sturdy as the other method.
5. Use molding to go around the edges to frame the unit. This gives it a more finished look.
6. Add a ledge or a rack to hold chalk and erasers.

Hard Hat Covers Not So Hard Heads

One safety aid that is not used as often as it should be is the hard hat or hard cap. The American Optical Corporation markets several hard hats; all are lightweight, comfortable, and inexpensive. They also have cap liners to keep you warm while working outside during the winter. American Optical's safety products, all bearing the Safeline name, include goggles, shields, respirators, and noise protectors.

Gloves Protect Hands From Shop Compounds

Many workshop chemicals are not dangerous, but they can be rough on hands. For this reason, you should wear rubber or plastic gloves. The Pioneer Rubber Company makes a number of different brands of household rubber gloves. Frequently considered a woman's product, rubber gloves come in sizes for just about every size hand. Pioneer's Bluettes are cotton lined with a neoprene outer coating, but Pioneer also markets industrial type rubber and plastic gloves for heavy-duty work. Tight-fitting rubber and plastic gloves have one big drawback in that they are difficult to pull on. By putting talcum powder both on your hands and in the gloves, however, you can make them go on much easier. The talc

also makes the gloves feel more comfortable and reduces sweating.

Let There Be Light In The Shop

A workshop without adequate lighting can be a dangerous place. The best lighting for most shops is fluorescent. You don't need a fancy fixture—just a hood to reflect the light down on the work. The Dayton two-tube fixture holds 40 watt lamps and is designed to be suspended by chains from the ceiling or to be rigid mounted. No electrical installation is involved because the fixture comes with a six-foot cord that you plug into a regular wall outlet. This rapid-start unit measures a big 48-inches long. Dayton Electric specializes in lights, motors, and tools.

Workshop Safety

THE WORKSHOP can be a source of great pleasure to the do-it-yourselfer who gets involved with this fascinating hobby. It can also be a place to save money by doing repairs and building things yourself. But this same place can turn into a source of pain instead of pleasure, of medical expenses instead of money in the bank if you fail to adhere to common-sense safety rules. Here are some general safety rules for your shop.

Here Is What You Will Need
Materials

- Power tools owner's manuals
- Goggles, gloves, ear protectors
- Face mask
- Electrical cutoff switch
- First aid kit

Step 10

1. Know your tools. Know what each tool is capable of and don't demand more of it than it can handle. When you buy power tools, read over the owner's manual before you ever operate the tool, and then keep the manual for reference.
2. Keep all tools in proper operating condition. This means sharp, clean, and lubricated.
3. Wear safety gear whenever such equipment might possibly be needed. Goggles, gloves, and ear protectors can save you from injury.
4. Never wear a necktie, jewelry, long hair, or loose clothing that could get caught in the moving parts of a power tool.
5. Be sure all your power tools are properly grounded.
6. Make certain that the circuits in your shop are adequate to carry the load your tools require.
7. Never work with power tools on a damp or wet shop floor.
8. When a toxic chemical or sawdust is in the air, be sure to have adequate ventilation. Wearing an appropriate face mask is always a good idea when working with such substances.
9. No shop is a safe shop unless there is adequate lighting in every work area.
10. Keep children out of the shop. Your workshop should never become a play area. Lock up all power tools whenever you're away, and it's even a good idea to install a master switch that cuts all electricity in the shop except what is necessary for lighting.
11. Make certain that you don't have to reach across hazardous areas to turn power tools on and off.
12. Keep visitors at a safe distance from your work, and don't try to converse with them while working. Always concentrate on what you're doing.
13. Never start working on a job that could be dangerous without first thinking out exactly what you want to do. If you have any doubts, clear them up before you begin.
14. Don't tackle tough or dangerous projects when you're tired or otherwise not at your best.
15. Keep a first aid kit handy.

Always put safety first, and you'll derive the work and savings satisfaction that only a home workshop can provide.

Watch What You Breathe

Paint spray vapors, insecticide dust and sprays, and certain other chemicals commonly used around the house are highly dangerous. Always wear a protective mask when working with these substances. The Agri-Tox mask from Willson Products uses dust filters as well as activated carbon cartridges to filter out airborne impurities. Both filters and cartridges are replaceable. Willson Products, a division of ESB Inc., markets a complete line of home safety products.

Don't Ignore Noise Hazards

Noise-induced hearing loss is the most common nonfatal occupational hazard today. Industry is taking steps to reduce the hazard, but the home handyperson often tends to ignore it. That is foolish. Why not invest in a simple set of ear plugs like the Shoplyne Ear Plugs from the Fibre-Metal Products Company? Attached to each other by a molded cord that is worn around the neck, the plugs can be kept in their own plastic container when not in use. Plug them in your ears any time you use a power tool in the shop or on the lawn and when you use a striking tool in a confined area.

Workshop

Avoid The Frills And Buy Good Power Tools For Less Money

If the efficiency and accuracy of a tool is more important to you than exterior appearance, then you should look into AMT power tools. AMT (American Machine and Tool Company) devotes everything to the workings and nothing to colored knobs, chrome, or other unnecessary frills. If it doesn't help the tool work better, AMT does not include it. AMT provides a 10-year guarantee on every part except motors (all are either GE or Westinghouse) which carry a one-year guarantee. All AMT sales are via mail order. If you wish more information and prices, write to American Machine and Tool Company, Inc., 4th and Spring Streets, Royersford, Pennsylvania 19468.

Radial Arm Saw Is Many Tools In One

The DeWalt Deluxe Power Shop is a radial arm saw that converts to several other power tools. With attachments, it becomes a disc, belt, or drum sander; a router; a drill; a jointer; and a grinding or buffing wheel. The radial arm saw, which can handle all sorts of cutting and dado operations, cuts when the blade is pulled through the work, in contrast to a table saw's stationary blade that cuts when the work is pushed through it. A shop should have a radial arm saw or a table saw if much woodwork is to be done. Each has its advantages, and before you buy one or the other, you should examine both to see which better suits your needs. If you opt for the radial arm saw, the DeWalt Deluxe Power Shop—part of the Black & Decker line—certainly merits your consideration.

Bandsaw Cuts Quickly And Smoothly

The bandsaw's name derives from the fact that its blade is a continuous band revolving on two wheels. It can make intricate curved cuts rapidly and quite smoothly. The Rockwell 14-inch wood cutting bandsaw has upper and lower guides that adjust independently to micrometer accuracy. The table tilts a full 45 degrees for mitering and is grooved for the addition of a miter gauge and machined for a rip fence. Rockwell makes a full line of heavy-duty tools for the home workshop.

A Phone In Your Shop

If you hate to run from your shop to take a phone call, why not rig an extension? Tel Products sells just about everything you need—plugs, jacks, extension cords, phone wire, and a reconditioned phone—to install an extension unit in your shop. Rigging a phone is an easy and safe do-it-yourself project, but some phone companies object strenuously and you should check out that aspect before you proceed. If you would like to see just how easy and inexpensive it is to have a shop phone, however, look for the Tel Products display.

Should You Buy A Complete Tool Set?

One way to get most of the basic tools you need in a workshop all at once is to buy a complete tool set. While you may end up with some items that you may seldom use, you'll also own just about every important tool. Is it a good deal? Perhaps. You must be careful about sets from manufacturers whose names are unfamiliar to you; some are good quality, and some are not. If you buy a set from a quality source, however, it can turn out to be a good investment. The 70-piece BernzOmatic tool set is a good one, as are those available at Sears and Montgomery Ward stores.

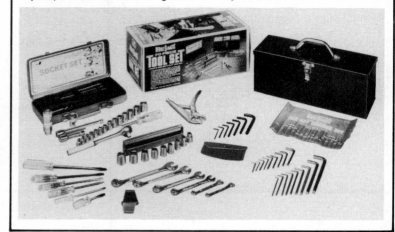

Planning a Workshop

A WELL-PLANNED workshop pays off in years of working pleasure, efficiency, and safety. Since every home presents different circumstances, no two workshops will be the same. Your first consideration is where to put the shop. A point to consider in selecting a "where" is just how deeply you plan to get into home repairs and other shop uses. You don't need much space if all you plan to do is cope with emergencies until the repairman arrives. Thus, your workshop can be as small as a closet or a section of a garage wall, or it may be an entire basement. In selecting the best place for your shop, keep these factors in mind:

1. Allow enough space to work comfortably. Keep in mind that you may eventually embark on a project using full 4x8-foot sheets of plywood; make sure you have room to work with such materials.
2. Plan as much counterspace as possible. In a closet shop you may have to settle for a fold-out workbench, but try to maximize counterspace even if you must shortchange other areas.
3. Seek out a well-ventilated spot if possible. Many of the compounds you will be using require good ventilation for health and safety factors. In addition, any woodworking you do will create large amounts of sawdust. If the area you intend to convert into a workshop lacks proper ventilation, you should plan to install an exhaust fan. A fan is a wise addition even in a shop with plenty of natural ventilation.
4. Adequate electrical wiring is a must. You should have (or add) ample wall outlets in your workshop. Keep in mind, too, that you may need outlets on circuits capable of handling more than the 15 amps normally available in house wiring. For example, if you plan to install large-motor power tools, you may need to have considerable rewiring done in your workshop. Be sure every modification you make is done according to the local electrical code.
5. Consider the noise factor, too. Try to locate the shop so that you will not disturb other members of the family who may be trying to sleep, watch TV, or just relax. Some shop tools are very loud.
6. Remember that you have to bring materials (some of which are large) into the shop, and you have to get the completed project (as well as the trash) out. Think about access in and out as you plan your workshop.
7. Inaccessibility is also important—inaccessibility to your children and to thieves. Your shop should be located where it can be locked to prevent children from getting in and possibly getting hurt. It should also be secured from burglars, who make a practice of taking expensive tools and components.

Here Is What You Will Need

Materials

- Exhaust fan
- Lighting units
- Locks
- Heating and/or cooling units
- Shelving and drawers
- Workbench
- Floor tiles
- Carpet strip
- Stool
- Extension telephone
- Intercom
- Radio
- Sink

Drill Press Drills Precisely Through All Materials

If you want a drill press in your shop, consider a radial arm type, preferred by many due to its ability to perform any number of drilling operations without requiring you to reposition the work. The Shopmaster 24-inch Radial Arm Drill Press is a heavy-duty tool, providing a full 4½-inch thrust and four operating speeds. It drills horizontally, vertically, and any angle in between. This is a big industrial size drill, and you might want to look at a smaller unit for occasional workshop drilling chores. Shopmaster makes other quality workshop tools.

Craftsman Table Saw Belongs In Your Shop

The Craftsman 10-inch table saw outfit is designed and priced for the average home workshop. It does all the things you expect of a table saw, and it offers many built-in safety features. The pull-on switch prevents the saw from being turned on by an accidental bump, and its removable locking key prevents children from using it. Additional safety features include a transparent blade guard and pawls to prevent wood from jumping back. The unit's induction-run motor is quieter than the universal motors used in many other bench saws. Craftsman tools, made for and sold at Sears stores and through the Sears Catalog, are made to high standards and backed by a strong Sears guarantee.

Handymen Need Not Have Handyman Hands

If you've spent time in a workshop doing your own repairs, you know all about getting your hands dirty. Fortunately, there are hand cleaners for the shop that remove dirt and grime without removing your skin. Quickee is a lanolin enriched waterless hand cleaner that dissolves paint, grease, tar, and other shop grime. Available in a 14-ounce jar and a three-ounce tube (ideal for keeping in the car in case of problems out on the road), Quickee Waterless Cream Hand Cleaner can be found in hardware, paint, and auto supply stores. It's made by Quickee, Inc.

Keep Jack Frost Out Of The Shop

All the fun goes out of having a shop when you try to work with frozen fingers. Among the heaters designed for use in workshops is the Reddy Heater Model M-30. Capable of providing fast heat in any workshop or garage, the heater burns kerosene or no. 1 fuel oil and requires no installation. The blower fan operates on house current and just needs to be plugged in to deliver 30,000 BTU's per hour. A lightweight unit that can be moved easily, the Reddy Heater Model M-30 has good built-in safety features, but you should use it only where ventilation is adequate. Available at hardware, building supply, and lumber retailers, Reddy Heater is made by the Atomaster Division of Koehring Company.

8. Heat and humidity are factors you certainly must consider. Not only must you be warm in winter and cool in summer, but also your tools must be protected from excess humidity. Plan to add heating and/or cooling units to comfort-condition your shop.

You may decide that it's best to sacrifice some space for the sake of other considerations. All things being equal, a garage workshop usually offers better access, easier cleaning, and is generally equipped with good locks. After you have decided on the place for your shop, here are some other factors to include in your planning.

△ 1. Draw a floor plan showing all the stationary power tools you plan to have. Make scale cutouts of each one and move them around the floor plan until you determine the best workshop layout. Keep in mind that you must allow room for yourself and for the materials around each power tool and do not forget to include the workbench in your floor plan.

△ 2. The workbench is the single most important item in the majority of home workshops. Plan its location for the greatest convenience possible. If you cannot have a stationary workbench, consider building or buying one that can be rolled into a larger work area.

△ 3. Be sure to provide for plenty of storage space. Keep in mind that you will need to store long materials like lumber and pipes. Plan to install more shelves and drawers than you think you will ever need.

△ 4. Plan adequate lighting, which means a fixture over each power tool and each work area. Consider movable fixtures like track lighting.

△ 5. Proper tool storage is crucial. You are certain to build up a collection of expensive tools after a while, and you must protect them from theft, from damage, and from rust and corrosion. You also want them to be easy to reach when needed, of course.

△ 6. Consider the floor surface. A concrete floor is probably the easiest to keep clean, but most inexpensive floor tiles are easy to maintain as well. For comfort, you may want to install a strip of carpet in front of the bench or in other areas where you'll be standing for long periods.

△ 7. Since many shop tasks can be done while sitting, get yourself a comfortable stool to sit on when safety doesn't require your standing.

The planning you put into your shop now, before you drive the first nail, will reap benefits well into the future. And planning covers more than just the absolute necessities. Think how convenient an extension telephone or an intercom system would be. A radio can be a welcome source of diversion as you work, and a sink can make cleanup much faster and easier. If you plan to get really involved in your shop, make it as safe, as convenient, and as comfortable as possible. Planning ahead helps on all counts.

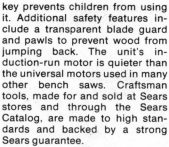

Step △ 4

A Well-Equipped Shop Has Plenty Of Saws

There are specific saws for specific purposes, and a good shop should possess a number of different types. The crosscut saw is used for cutting across the grain of wood, but it can also do a pretty fair job of ripping (cutting with the grain). There are, however, rip saws that do that job better. The rip saw should never be used for crosscutting. The hacksaw is primarily for cutting metal, while the coping saw is for cutting curves and circles. The compass and keyhole saws cut less intricate curves in heavier wood than the coping saw. The Nicholson Division of the Cooper Group makes a wide variety of quality saws.

Workshop

Height-Adjustable Sawhorse Offers Convenience

One man's ideal working height is another's backache, and a standard workbench is often wrong for both. Recently, height-adjustable folding sawhorses became available for do-it-yourselfers. With any convenient board or sheet of plywood, a pair of Handy Horses can create a level bench or a table adjustable from a low of 23 inches to a high of 39 inches; the width is 35¾ inches. Calibrated to make leveling easy, Handy Horses are equipped with convenient built-in lock stops, and they fold flat in seconds. All hardware is treated to resist rust, and the rubber feet prevent slipping. Sold complete with wall hanger, Handy Horses are available by mail-order from Croton Craft, 2 Memory Lane, Croton-On-Hudson, NY 10520.

Super-Horse Wins The Derby Of Workshop Helpers

If space is a problem and you want a sturdy sawhorse, get a Super-Horse. Super-Horse legs clamp onto a 2x6; then, the spreader arms lock the unit in place. The rugged steel legs have durable, non-skid plastic feet to prevent scratching floors or slippage. The 2x6 (instead of the 2x4 found in most sawhorses) gives you a much wider and more stable work area. In fact, two Super-Horses create a larger work surface for wallpapering or the basis for a quick picnic or ping-pong table. Super-Horse, which comes with either rigid or adjustable legs, is made by Bestop Manufacturing Company, Inc.

Metal Legs Make Quick But Durable Workbench

In less than an hour, you can create a sturdy and attractive workbench out of a 4x8-foot sheet of ¾-inch plywood and a set of Steel City Work Bench Legs. The Steel City legs are made of 16-gauge steel, have a baked-on enamel finish, and contain knockouts for double plug electrical outlets. Steel City Corporation also makes the Steel City Tool Rack, a wall-mounted unit that can hold up to 34 small tools.

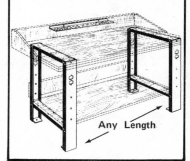

Any Length

You Too Can Own An Old World Craftsman's Bench

The Danish Folding Bench is one of several European models sold by Garrett Wade Company. So beautiful that you might be reluctant to ever use it, the Danish Folding Bench is as sturdy and rugged as any bench you can find. The top itself weighs 53 pounds and is held to the heavy folding base by steel pins. The wood, Danish beech impregnated with linseed oil, is sealed with two coats of lacquer. The end vise has steel dogs that fit into the slots running the length of the bench. The tools tray may be positioned on the side or fastened to the end. If the idea of a special bench of high quality appeals to you, write to the Garrett Wade Company, Inc., 302 Fifth Avenue, New York, N Y 10001 and ask about the Danish Folding or other Old World benches.

Building a Workbench

NO MATTER HOW many exotic power tools you have, the most important item in your workshop is the workbench. It is the center of most shop activity.

Your choice of a bench depends on many factors. The amount of room you have is of prime consideration. With plenty of space available, you may opt for an island in the middle of the shop; that gives you access to the work surface from all four sides. Many people, though, don't like the island type because they want easy access to tools, which are generally stored on a wall. A variation of the island is the peninsula workbench that sticks out into the middle of the shop but still has one end butting up to a wall.

Most shops, of course, contain a workbench that is located right against a wall, and where space is at a premium, a fold-out bench is often employed. The following plans are for a sturdy and serviceable workbench that you can build in about two hours. Here is how to build a basic inexpensive workbench for your shop.

1. Cut all the pieces for the frame. The standard height is 32 to 34 inches, but you should tailor the bench to your height so that you end up with the most comfortable and convenient working surface. Use 2x4s for the framing.
2. Each end requires two crosspieces 24 inches long. Use 2x4s for the crosspieces.
3. Assemble the two ends, using lag screws for fastening. Be sure to drill the proper sized pilot holes before installing the screws. You can provide additional bracing by installing angle braces, but such bracing generally is not required.
4. Next, cut three crosspieces 50 inches long from 2x4 stock to support the 60-inch bench top. The ends can stick out five or six inches on each end, but if your bench top is to be longer, lengthen the crosspieces accordingly. If your bench is to be exceptionally long, you should strengthen it with two bottom crosspieces instead of the one in the center.
5. Attach the bench-top crosspieces with lag screws.
6. Now cut the pieces for the top. Three 60-inch lengths of 2x10-inch stock provide an adequate work surface.
7. Attach the top pieces to the frame with heavy countersunk wood screws. Again, drill pilot holes before attempting to drive the screws.
8. Cut a backplate from 1x6-inch lumber, and attach it to the top with wood screws.
9. Cut either a 1x10-inch or a 1x12-inch board to create a bottom shelf. If you wish, you could make a full shelf by attaching two bottom crosspieces. The shelf is valuable not only for its storage capability, but also for the extra stability it gives your workbench.

There's the basic bench. You can modify it greatly to suit your personal taste. Here are some ideas for enhancing the simple workbench. Cover the bench top with a large carpet scrap or

Here Is What You Will Need

Materials

- 2x4-inch lumber
- Lag screws
- Angle braces
- 2x10-inch lumber
- Countersunk wood screws
- 1x6-inch lumber
- 1x10- or 1x12-inch lumber
- Carpet scrap, hardboard, or plastic laminate
- Drawer unit
- Screen door hooks

Tools

- Saw
- Drill
- Screwdriver

Have A Workbench Even Without A Workshop

Many people lack the room to have a workshop, but they still want to handle household repairs. Black & Decker's WorkMate may be just what they need. A workbench with enough surface to accommodate many tools and mate-rials, it doubles as a sawhorse, a giant vise, and can accomplish many clamping jobs. Though lightweight, WorkMate is so well balanced that it never wobbles. Best of all, when you're through working, just fold up WorkMate and put it away. Even if you have all the workshop room in the world, WorkMate can be a great addition.

Make Sawhorses The Easy Way

With a set of Dalton Sawhorse Brackets you can convert scrap pieces of 2x4s into a very sturdy sawhorse. All Dalton Sawhorse Brackets are made of steel with a rust-resistant finish. The less expensive Thrif-T brackets are secured to the 2x4s with nails driven through predrilled holes; the holes are flanged to allow quick removal when the sawhorse needs to be put away. The more expensive Dalton brackets, Model 100, feature a system that requires only a twist of a wingnut to lock the legs and the cross rail securely in place. Dalton also markets sets of metal legs that convert a single 2x4 into an extra strong sawhorse without nails or screws. Dalton Sawhorse Brackets are products of the Dalton Manufacturing Company.

Thrif-T

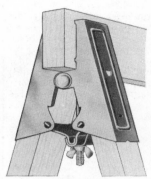

Model 100

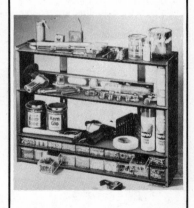

Backstop

Top

Frame

Shelf

Brace

Leg

Shop Organizer Mounts On Wall Or Sits On Bench

The Akro-Mils Bench-Mate has steel shelves and 20 see-through drawers for storing workshop tools and supplies. The shelves are seven inches deep and 28½-inches long, while the drawers come in two different sizes for housing a host of small items. Akro-Mils also makes a 36-drawer unit, called the Quik-Pik, with a handle that allows it to be taken wherever the parts are needed. Useful in every shop, the Akro-Mils storage organizers can be found in hardware stores and home centers.

with a piece of hardboard. You can attach either to the basic top with countersunk screws. Plastic laminate can also serve as a bench top covering, but it is far more difficult to replace than the carpet or hardboard.

Add drawers to the bench. There are factory-made drawer units designed to be suspended under such a top. Whatever type you decide to install, make sure the drawers have sturdy stops. Most shop drawers are usually heavy, and without good stops a drawer could easily be pulled out too far and come smashing down on your foot.

You may want to attach the bench to the wall. Many projects create so much vibration that they can even cause a heavy bench to start walking. If you do decide to attach your bench to the wall, do so in such a way that you can detach and move it easily for cleaning. Large screen door hooks work well for holding the bench to the wall, while also allowing easy removal.

Workshop

Magnetic Tool Rack Holds Big Hand Tools

Magnetic bars are popular for storing tools on a shop wall, but the magnetic bars made for kitchen utensils cannot hold heavy hand tools. What you need is the bar from Dowling Miner Magnetics Corporation. It has permanent ceramic magnets that will never lose their power and that are strong enough to hold a 20-inch pipe wrench. With its rugged aluminum support brackets, the bar can be mounted to any wall surface with screws or molly bolts. Not yet available in stores, the magnetic tool rack (made in four lengths, 12, 18, 24, and 36 inches) can be ordered from Dowling Miner Magnetics Corporation, 124 Paul Drive, San Rafael, California 94903.

Modular Shelf Helps Organize Tools

Rubbermaid, well-known for its kitchen organizers, also makes a handy shelf system that can help organize any workshop. The gridwork shelf holds several screwdrivers, awls, brushes, drill bits, and other tools. Each unit measures six inches high, and shelves —which measure 12¼x6½-inches—interlock at all four corners for stacking. Available in housewares departments, the Rubbermaid tool organizer can be assembled instantly with no tools. It won't chip, dent, or corrode and is easy to clean with a damp cloth and soap or detergent.

Tote Your Drill In A Tool Tote

The Akro-Mils Drill-Mate holds the drill itself, either a ¼-inch or ⅜-inch model, plus 25 drill bits in an indexed section. Another section holds the disc attachment and its accessories. There are also two small spill-proof drawers for small items, and the retractable handle allows for easy access to the drill. Akro-Mils also makes the Saw-Mate/Sander-Mate as well as other tool totes, all of which are made of high-impact lightweight polystyrene.

Saw-Mate/Sander-Mate

Drill-Mate

Tool Storage and Protection

PROPER STORAGE of tools is important. Tool storage has to be planned so that it affords protection from theft, damage to the tool because of contact with other tools, rust, and from injury to children too young to handle tools. You will also want to store tools so they are easy to get at, and so you always know where they are. Much of this is accomplished by planning for your workshop ahead of time. Here are some ideas that will help you accomplish these aims:

1. Be sure all tools are locked up. If they are stored in a workshop hanging from the wall, make certain that the lock to the shop is adequate. If they are kept in a cabinet or closet in a garage or basement, have locks on the storage unit. Discourage children from using any tools for playthings.

2. Tools with points, teeth or cutting edges should be protected to prevent damage to and from these sharp surfaces. A saw can be protected with a slit piece of garden hose

Here Is What You Will Need
Materials

- Cabinet locks
- Piece of garden hose
- Tool racks
- Household oil
- Saran wrap
- Aluminum foil
- Cone of carpenter's chalk
- Paint

Tools

- Paintbrush
- Electric engraver
- Knife

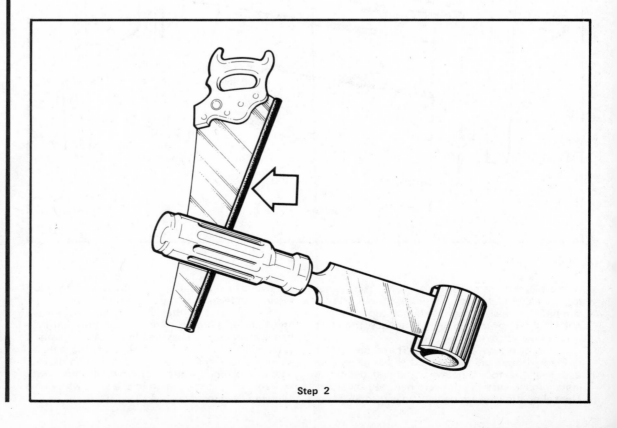

Step 2

Identification Protects Tools From Thieves

If you engrave identification on all your tools, you stand a better chance of getting them back if they are borrowed or stolen. In addition, burglars are reluctant to take tools that can be identified because they are not easy to fence. The Dremel Electric Engraver allows you to write an identifying name or number on steel (as well as softer metals), plastic, or wood. The calibrated stroke adjustment regulates the depth of engraving for marking different

materials, and the solid carbide engraving point is virtually wear-proof. The Dremel Electric Engraver even has a built-in hanger ring for on-the-wall storage.

Tool Boxes Are Portable Workshops

A tool box can be anything from a plastic fishing tackle box to an elaborate roll-around metal chest. The Park Manufacturing Company makes a wide range of tool boxes, chests, and cabinets, all of which are top quality. The Park carpenter's tool box is quite long, measuring 32-inches, in order to hold the hand saws which most tool boxes cannot accommodate. It has slotted rests for saws, clips to hold a level, and even a knockout for a carpenter's

square. Designed for a working carpenter, this Park tool box could also serve a home handy-person well.

slipped over the teeth. Screwdrivers and chisels can be housed in racks that let them hang out of the way. Drill bits should be housed in cases.

3. Tools must be stored where they will not be subjected to moisture. This can be accomplished by keeping a thin coating of oil over the metal parts. Tools can also be kept in Saran wrap, wrapped in foil or stored in their own special cases. Keep a cone of carpenters chalk in a tool box. It will absorb moisture.

4. To always know where certain tools are, have a definite place for each tool, and

make sure it gets put back in the right place when you are finished with it. If you use pegboard walls to hang tools from, outline each tool with paint using an artist's brush. You will know where each tool goes and you can also see at a glance when a tool has not been put back.

5. As theft protection, in addition to locking up, etch an identification mark on your tools with an electric engraver.

6. Paint tool handles a bright color so that they will be easily seen if left out, and so that a borrower will immediately know that they are yours.

Case Stores And Protects Drill Bits

The drill bit case from General Hardware Manufacturing Company not only stores bits, it also indexes them. Just open the case, tilt the cover, and all the bits are at your fingertips. The index is easy to see and easy to read, and the case protects your bits from being damaged by other tools.

Tool Rental Makes Sense

Renting tools makes sense in many cases, but only if the tools have been properly maintained. They must be in good operating order, or they can be dangerous as well as ineffective. When renting tools, look for the symbol of the ARA, American Rental Association, an association of independent rental companies. While not all the good rental companies belong to this association, member firms generally do pride themselves on offering quality tools that are well maintained. ARA members are knowledgeable in the use of tools and are happy to tell you how to operate them efficiently and safely. Never rent a tool that you know nothing about without first finding out exactly how it works.

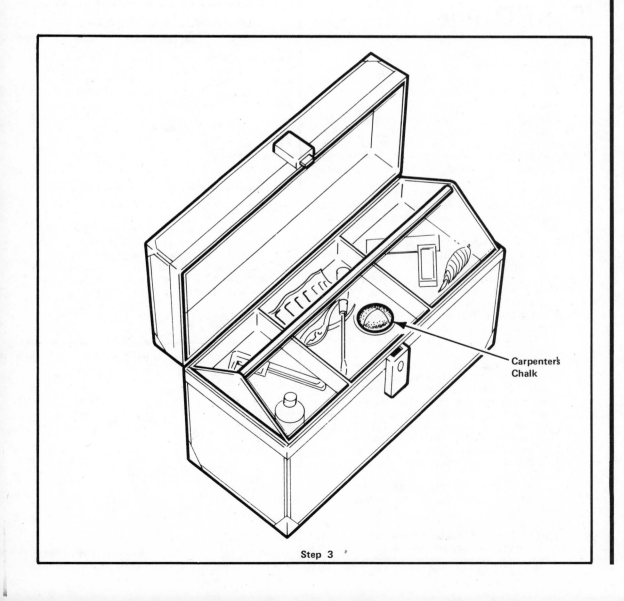

Carpenter's Chalk

Step 3

Workshop

With Six You Get A Tool Rack

Buy the six-piece set of Stanley Thrifty screwdrivers and you get a handy rack for your workshop. Each screwdriver features a full-sized black and yellow plastic handle and a forged steel blade. The convenient, molded-plastic rack holds one four-inch and one six-inch standard tip screwdriver, one three-inch and one six-inch cabinet tip screwdriver, as well as a No. 1 and a No. 2 Phillips tip driver.

Big John Racks 'Em Up

One of the best metal tool racks around is called Big John. A full yard long, it has a unique two-tier design to hold a double row of hand tools and a drill index that holds and identifies 14 bit sizes. Big John, made of sturdy heavy-gauge steel with a neutral gray enamel finish, can easily be mounted on a workbench or shop wall—even on pegboard. The ends are die-cut square and clean

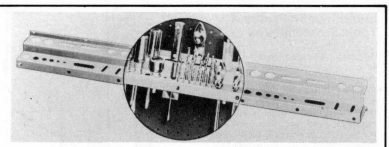

so that additional racks can be butted together to appear as one.

Big John is made by Dalton Manufacturing Company.

Plastic Level Is Rugged And Light

The eight-inch plastic Torpedo level from Trophy Products is inexpensive and lightweight but practically indestructible. Available in two- and three-vial versions, the three-vial Torpedo level measures level, plumb, and 45 degrees. Trophy also makes a wide range of aluminum levels in all sizes up to 36-inches long. These aluminum levels are easily adjustable for maximum accuracy.

Reversible-Blade Screwdriver Performs Double Duty

The reversible-blade screwdriver, from Vaco Products Company, is not just another gimmick tool.

Once you snap the Phillips or slotted blade end into the handle, you find yourself working with a top quality screwdriver. Vaco offers seven different double-ended blades to snap into the tough plastic handles.

Fasten Your Tool Rack To A Cinder Block Wall

Many workshops are in basements or garages where the walls are cinder block. An easy way to fasten tool racks to such walls is with the Do-It-Yourself Remington Fastening System. The system fires fasteners into the concrete like a gun. There are four load levels and several different-sized fasteners to handle various fastening problems. The Remington fastening tool is too expensive for just occasional use but it could be a money-saver if you plan a remodeling project. It can attach framing to a concrete floor; furring strips to cinder block walls; anchor iron railings to steps, walks, and patios; mount awnings and shutters to brick walls; and, of course, mount shelf brackets and your tool holder to the shop wall. The Remington Fastening System is made by the Power Products Division of DESA Industries.

Guide Wheels Make Sawing Safer

A new tool accessory called Safe-T-Guide can be attached to a radial arm saw, a band saw, a table saw, a shaper, or a jointer. When in place, the guide wheels revolve on an inclined spring-loaded axis, forcing the material toward and against the rip fence. Safe-T-Guide improves accuracy while at the same time reducing kick backs. Capable of handling material up to two-inches thick and of any width, Safe-T-Guide just about does away with the need for a helper when ripping. A new tool, Safe-T-Guide may not be available at local stores. For prices and details, write to Quadmatic Industries, Inc., P.O. Box 337, Dorchester, Wisconsin 54425.

Tool Rack

IF YOU ARE short of wall space on which to hang your workshop tools, a pegboard rack with wings will allow you to store almost everything you own in a space no more than four feet wide. The rack can range from two to eight feet high.

1. To make the 4x4-foot rack, buy a 4x8-foot sheet of ⅛-inch pegboard, and cut it in half crosswise.
2. Cut four four-foot lengths from 1x1-inch wood strips, miter the ends, and nail them together into a frame.
3. Screw one of the pieces of pegboard to this frame with ⅝-inch round-head screws spaced a foot apart.
4. Place a 1x3-inch board 46¼ inches long up and down the center of the frame between the 1x1-inch strips, and fasten the pegboard to it with brads.
5. Nail the completed wall panel to the wall, centering the 1x3-inch strip over a stud.
6. Cut a four-foot length of 2x4, center it over the hidden 1x3, and spike it to the stud with five 60d common nails. If you install your tool rack on a masonry wall, you must put it up with screws driven into lead anchors.
7. Saw the remaining pieces of pegboard into two pieces 22⅛ inches wide by 48 inches long.
8. Screw them to frames made of 1x1-inch wood strips. These panels are the wings of the rack.
9. Hang each wing on the 2x4 with a pair of butt hinges that measure three inches high and two inches wide (when open).
10. It is not necessary to make mortises for the

Here Is What You Will Need

Materials

- 4x8-foot sheet of ⅛-inch pegboard
- 2x4-inch board
- 1x1-inch wood strips
- 1x3-inch board
- Four butt hinges
- Nails, screws, brads
- Pegboard hangers
- Lead anchors

Tools

- Saw
- Screwdriver
- Hammer

hinge leaves; simply screw one leaf in each hinge to the face of the 2x4 at the edge, and screw the other leaf to the edge of the wing.

11. Hang your tools on the front and back of the wings—and on the front of the wall panel—with standard pegboard hangers.

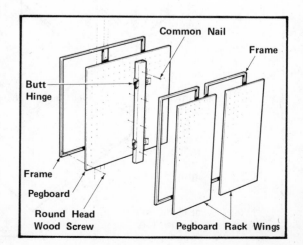

Tool Safety

MANY ACCIDENTS happen because of something beyond your control. If you have an accident with hand tools, however, it is because you did it to yourself. There is really no reason for most of these accidents. Very few are from lack of knowledge about the tool. Most are from carelessness, either in the use of the tool or in its care.

According to safety experts, hand tool accidents happen more often percentage-wise to professionals or competent handypersons than to the rank novice. There are probably several reasons for this, among which is the fact that the person who has used a hand tool often may get careless. Also, the newcomer has a fear that makes him cautious, while the "expert" may be blase. Here are some rules for everyone who uses a hand tool:

1. Examine each tool before you use it.
2. Make sure cutting tools are sharp. Sharp tools are less dangerous than dull tools. With a dull tool, you will be straining more and have less control.
3. See that handles are whole and securely attached. A loose handle is always a threat to safety.
4. Clean oil and grease off tool handles, otherwise you cannot get a firm grip on the tool.
5. Examine wooden handles for splinters, and metal handles for burrs.
6. Use tools only for the purpose that they were made for. Using a makeshift tool can be dangerous as well as not being very effective.
7. Never carry sharp tools in your pocket. When walking with them, make certain the point is aimed down and away from you.
8. Avoid glancing blows when using a striking tool, and never hit the face of one striking tool against the face of another.
9. Wear safety goggles when using a striking tool.
10. When using saws, chisels or pointed tools, be sure the cutting edge is aimed away from you and that the force you exert carries the tool away from you.
11. When you encounter a stubborn screw or bolt, use penetrating oil rather than take a chance on having to use too much force and slipping.
12. When using a wrench in a resistant situation, pull it toward you or push it with the palm of your hand, in the open position, so you do not slip and smash your knuckles.
13. Use clamps to hold work if there is any danger that it might slip.
14. Always be alert to the fact that there is danger in using any tool if you get careless.

Any homeowner who tackles very much in the way of repairs, maintenance or improvements will end up with some power tools. They make things go faster and easier, and in most cases, make projects turn out with a professional look.

Today's modern power tools do things in seconds that used to take hours. A creative handyperson must cultivate thorough respect for his new, more complicated power tools before using them.

The areas most deserving of attention are electrical and operating safety. Of course, the most important rule of all is to first read the owner's manual thoroughly. Here are some good tips to follow.

△ 1. Ground all tools unless they are double insulated. If the tool is equipped with a three-pronged plug, it should be plugged into a three-hole grounded receptacle. If an adapter ("pigtail") is used to accommodate a two-pronged receptacle, the adapter wire must be attached to a known ground. Never remove the third prong from a plug. Double insulated tools require only a two-prong outlet or cord.
△ 2. Do not abuse the cord. Never carry a tool by its cord or yank on it to disconnect it from a receptacle. Keep the cord away from heat, oil and sharp edges.
△ 3. Keep the work area clean and dry. Do not use a power tool in damp or wet locations.
△ 4. Perform regular maintenance on your power tool if required. Consult the owner's manual for proper tool care. If it is not operating properly, repair it or take it to a service shop.
△ 5. Store tools when not in use. Tools should be stored in dry, high, or locked-up places out of the reach of children.
△ 6. Always keep guards in place and in perfect working order.
△ 7. Wear proper apparel—loose clothing, ties, and jewelry can become entangled in moving parts. Rubber gloves and footwear are recommended especially when working outdoors. Safety goggles, face shields, and ear plugs should be worn when needed.
△ 8. Be sure to have good lighting conditions.
△ 9. Secure work by using clamps or a vise to hold it. It is much safer than using your hand, and it frees both hands to operate the tool.
△10. Never overreach. Keep proper footing and balance at all times.
△11. If outdoors, position equipment on a flat land surface.
△12. Disconnect tools when not in use; before servicing; and when changing accessories such as blades, bits, cutters, etc.
△13. Be sure the switch is "off" before you plug a tool into the outlet.
△14. Remove adjusting keys and wrenches. Form the habit of checking to see that keys and wrenches are removed from the tool before turning it on. Also, never carry a plugged-in tool with your finger on trigger or switch.
△15. Keep children and visitors away from the work area.

Here Is What You Will Need

Materials

● Penetrating oil

Tools

● Sharpening file
● Holding clamps

Step △5

Step △7

Step △3   Step △7

Know What Your Tools Can Do

One key to power tool safety is knowing the capabilities of each power tool. When you purchase a new tool, read the owner's manual carefully. Find out exactly how it operates. After the job is finished, clean the tool and (if necessary) lubricate it. Then store the tool properly to keep it at its best. If you have a tool without an owner's manual, contact a power tool retailer and ask for a copy; if none is available, write to the manufacturer of the tool and request that an owner's manual be sent to you.

A Good Grip Is Crucial To Safe Tool Use

Skinned knuckles, strained or sore hands, and a bad disposition can often result from slipping when using a tool. Now, though, you can find tools with grips that reduce the possibility of slips. Many Crescent Company tools are now equipped with Cushion Grip handles made of a fiber-impregnated plastisol (PVC) with a textured surface. Baked onto the handles of the Crescent tools, Cushion Grip renders a sure and comfortable grip even under greasy or damp working conditions. Crescent is a member of the Cooper Group.

Avoid Seeing Stars When Using A Star Drill

Smashed fingers and injured eyes are ever-present hazards when using a star drill to bore holes in masonry. To create a handle that will keep your hand away from the drill, try Vise-Grip locking pliers. Lock the pliers to the shaft of the drill, and you will find that you can turn the star drill easily while keeping your hand out of danger. The Star Expansion Company, well-known for all those gadgets that anchor things to walls and floors, makes a quality star drill. Vaughan & Bushnell make the Value Brand drilling hammer as well as safety goggles that fit over regular glasses. The Vaughan goggles—very important whenever you chip away at masonry—are quite comfortable as the frame is flexible and conforms to facial contours.

Workshop

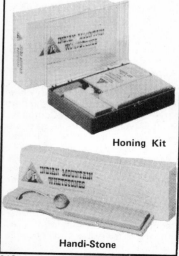
Keeping Tools Sharp

ALTHOUGH IT MAY seem hard to believe, a sharp tool is actually much safer than a dull one. A dull tool forces you to use more muscle, which means that you have less control over it. A sharp tool is not only safer, of course, but it also allows you to do better work. Sharpening is not a difficult task, and the tools required are not expensive.

The basic implements needed for sharpening are files, stones, and grinding wheels. A grinding wheel is basically a shaping tool. It does not give you a razor sharp edge. After you shape the edge, you add the sharpness with a stone. The whetstone is the basic sharpening stone. You hold it stationary as you sharpen by drawing the tool over the stone's surface. Slip stones, on the other hand, are moved along the edge of the tool's blade. Files can be used for both shaping and sharpening when a bevel is all that is needed for cutting. If you do not know the specific degree of bevel that is best suited for a particular cutting edge, just try to recapture the shape of the original cutting edge put there by the manufacturer. Unless the edge is severely nicked and worn, you should be able to spot sections that have retained their original shape.

1. The most basic cutting tool, the pocket knife, is one of those blades that can overheat if you grind it. Instead, use your whetstone to hone it regularly. Set the blade at about a 30-degree angle to the stone with the cutting edge turned away from you, and move the cutting edge into the stone. Draw the blade in a diagonal direction beginning at the heel and ending at the point. At the end of each stroke, flip the blade and hone the other side the same way but with the

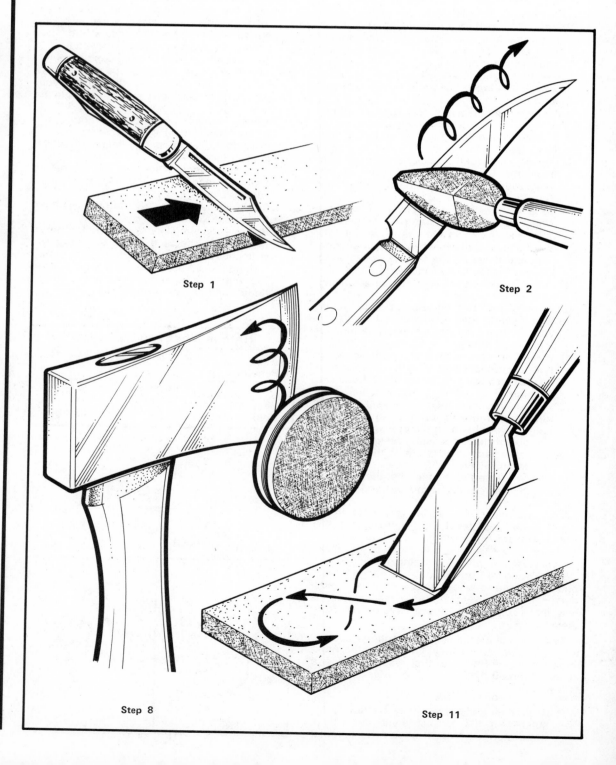

Step 1

Step 2

Step 8

Step 11

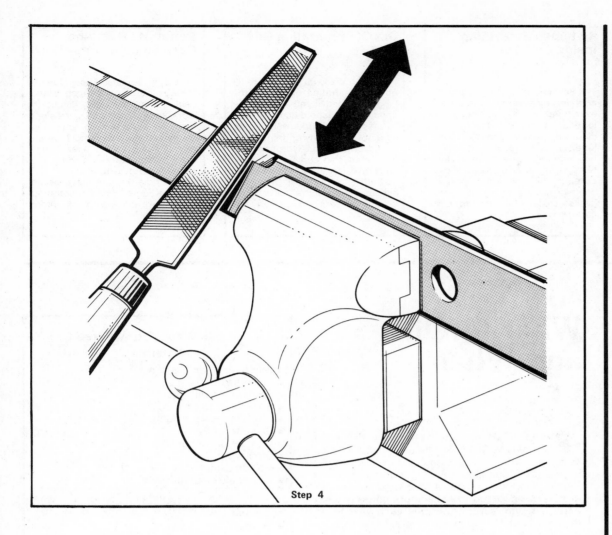

Step 4

Bench Grinder Belongs In A Sharp Shop

The bench grinder is great for tool sharpening, and every well-equipped shop should have one. The Wen Six-Inch Bench Grinder No. 1800 is the world's first double-insulated bench grinder, and it has a ½-horsepower universal motor instead of the more typical shaded-pole motor. The unit has a removable water tray and a built-in small parts and tool tray. There are adjustable eye shields over both wheels, adjustable spark arrestors, and a non-mar, non-glare finish on the unbreakable housing. The Model 1800 Bench Grinder has rubber shock mounting feet, and it features Wen's exclusive dynamic brake for fast stops. Wen makes many good tools for the home handyperson.

blade moving toward you.

2. For sharpening kitchen knives, purchase the special teardrop shaped stone with a handle called a kitchen sharpener. Hold the kitchen sharpener at about a 30-degree angle against the cutting edge, and stroke the stone against the knife edge in small circular motions going from the heel to the tip of the blade. Now reverse the blade and repeat the same motions on the other side.

3. To sharpen carving knives, use a long bar called a sharpening steel. Place the heel of the blade on the tip of the bar at about a 30-degree angle, and then swing the blade down to the hilt of the bar, using a light curving stroke in order to hone the entire length of the blade. Alternate sides of the bar with each stroke to sharpen both sides of the knife.

4. To restore the cutting edge on the blade of your rotary lawn mower, remove the blade

and put it in a vise. Then use a file to remove any nicks and to reestablish the original bevel.

5. Stroke scissors on a whetstone with the bevel flat against the stone. Always move the blades away from you into the stone.

6. Clippers and shears are not supposed to be extremely sharp. They are just beveled, which you maintain by filing. Stroke forward, starting at the heel and going all the way to the tip.

7. Ice picks, awls, and other sharply pointed tools can best be sharpened by rotating the point against the side of the whetstone.

8. Sharpen an axe or hatchet with a special round stone called a combination axe stone. The combination axe stone has a coarse side and a fine side. Move the stone across the blade in a circular fashion, starting with the coarse side and finishing with the fine side.

9. To sharpen drill bits properly, use a jig that adjusts to the bit size and also positions the bit for exact grinding. There is also an electric tool for sharpening drill bits that works much like an automatic pencil sharpener.

10. Saw blade sharpening also requires special tools. Each tooth must be sharpened with a file. There is a tool designed to set the file at the precise angle you need, and there is another tool (called a saw set) to bend the teeth to the correct angle after filing.

11. Chisels must be held at the proper angle and sharpened on a whetstone. There are jigs designed to hold the chisel at this angle and roll with the chisel as you move it back and forth in a sort of figure-eight pattern over the stone.

12. Gouges—or any tool with a curved cutting surface—must be sharpened with slip stones that have curved or tapered surfaces.

Here Is What You Will Need

Materials
● None

Tools
● Grinding wheel
● Whetstone
● Slip stones
● Files
● Kitchen sharpener
● Sharpening steel
● Vise
● Combination axe stone
● Drill jig
● Saw set

Using The Right Sharpening Stone Gives You The Edge

Many different types of stones are used to sharpen different tools. The Carborundum Company makes a variety of sharpening stones. The No. 196 Woodman's Stone has a different grit on each side. You use the coarse side first, and then the fine side. The No. 15 Gouge Stone is made especially for sharpening wood gouges, while the No. 46 Gardener's Stone keeps many gardening tools at their best. In addition to these stones, the Carborundum Company makes just about everything you need for home sharpening.

No. 15 Gouge Stone

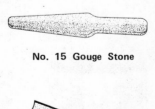

No. 46 Gardener's Stone

No. 196 Woodman's Stone

Workshop

Spray Away Frozen Parts

Excellent for disposing of heavy rust problems, Permatex also works well on corrosion, paint, scale, and gummy deposits that normally freeze parts together. A popular spray-on penetrator, Permatex also comes in liquid form in spout-top cans.

Kit Lubes Everything Inside And Out

The Seymour of Sycamore lube kit contains nine spray cans, about everything you'll ever need for lubrication chores. The kit includes an aerosol can of silicone lube, penetrating oil, belt dressing, ignition sealer, battery and terminal cleaner-protector, carburetor cleaner, white grease, open gear and chain lube, and gasket sealer. All the products perform well.

Out Of Penetrating Oil?

When you discover that you're all out of penetrating oil just at the time you need it most, try these common household items as substitutes. Iodine works well, but be sure not to get any on things that would be stained. Hydrogen peroxide can also serve to cut rust and corrosion, as can lemon juice, but not as effectively. Of all the substitutes for actual penetrating oil, though, kerosene is clearly the best.

Penetrate Rust And Corrosion The Easy Way

Probably the best known penetrating oil is Liquid Wrench. When using it, you must give it time to work through rust and corrosion; many people squirt it on and then try immediately to remove whatever is stuck. Liquid Wrench has many competitors, including the spray penetrators which can reach spots that are inaccessible with the liquid. Liquid penetrating oils, however, are much more economical.

Banana-Scented Penetrating Oil Has Appeal

No joke. There really is a new penetrating oil-lubricant called Monkey Wrench that is scented with the aroma of banana. Despite the gimmick, Monkey Wrench is a good product for preventing rust and lubricating all sorts of things. Like all the new spray lubes, it's handy for getting down into places you couldn't reach easily with a regular oiler. Monkey Wrench is a product of Industrial Petrolic Corporation.

Here's A Silicone-Free All-Purpose Lube

WD-40 is probably the most popular spray lube around. It certainly enjoys excellent distribution throughout the United States. WD-40 is certainly a fine product. Silicone free, its moisture-displacing capability allows WD-40 to repair electrical shorts caused by moisture. It also works well, of course, as a penetrating oil.

What to Oil and When

EVERY HOME has dozens of things that need lubrication. Many people just wait until they hear squeaking and groaning before even thinking about lubrication, but by lubricating on a regular basis you will never hear such squeaks or groans or be forced to replace prematurely worn parts. Why not set up one time each year to go through your house to oil or grease everything that might need it?

You can assemble a small lube kit for just a few dollars. An empty soft drink carton can tote about all the items you will need, including machine oil, penetrating oil, powdered graphite, an all-purpose spray lube (such as LPS or WD-40), an aerosol can of silicone spray, and a wax candle. If you have special oiling instructions for a particular appliance or motor, place the proper lube in your carton as well.

1. Start with door hinges. Remove the hinge pins and rub them with steel wool to remove any rust. Buff until the pin is shiny, and then coat with powdered graphite or silicone spray.
2. Send a shot of graphite powder into each keyhole, and run the key in and out a few times to distribute the lubrication.
3. Small motors often come with a tag or booklet telling you what kind of oil to use. You can generally apply machine oil or a spray lube, however, if you cannot find the recommended type. It is always a good idea, though, to save the owner's manual that comes with any new appliance. This manual will tell you exactly what lubricant to use, when to lubricate, and where the lubricant should go.
4. Any belt-driven appliance needs a shot of belt dressing from time to time. Each time you spray be sure to check the belt's tension.
5. Wooden drawers often need help even when they do not give you trouble. Rub the edges and tracks with wax or bar soap, or apply a silicone spray.
6. Windows can become balky unless you lubricate the tracks. Rub wax into the track of a wooden window, and move the window up and down. A silicone spray will do the job for either a wooden or a metal window.
7. Spray the tracks of sliding doors with silicone spray.
8. Kitchen appliances that need lubrication can be a problem because you do not want the lubricant to come in contact with your food. Some people use vegetable oil in such cases, while others use a drop or two of glycerin. Neither poses any health hazard, and neither will alter the taste of food.

Here Is What You Will Need

Materials

- Empty soft drink carton
- Machine oil
- Penetrating oil
- Powdered graphite
- All-purpose spray lube
- Silicone spray
- Wax candle or bar soap
- Steel wool
- Belt dressing
- Vegetable oil or glycerin

Tools

- Hammer
- Screwdriver

Assemble Your Own Lube Kit For Just A Few Dollars

Minimum Maintenance Landscaping

NO YARD IS going to get by without some maintenance. Even if you cover the whole surface with concrete and paint it green, you will still have to paint it every so often and patch up the cracks. However, by planning ahead, you can make your yardwork less of a hassle, and still have a good looking yard.

First, you must analyze where most of the work comes from. Mowing and edging come in for a big part of the maintenance routine while watering runs a close second. Weeds are not only time consuming, but they take away from the beauty of the yard. Insects are an ever possible problem. And raking leaves in the fall is not at all that much fun either.

There are other things required of the homeowner who has a yard, but these seem to be universal problems. Taking them one at a time, here are some ways to combat the problem, do away with it all together, or make it easier to cope with.

1. Mowing and edging. Mowing in itself is no problem unless there are slopes or other tough-to-mow areas. If there are steep slopes, we suggest a ground cover, terracing with rocks or stones or changing the slope. There are no easy solutions, but after they are done, the mowing problem is licked. Speaking of ground cover, there are people who eliminate all mowing by using a ground cover instead of grass. There are growing ground covers such as ivy, ajuga, sedum and other such plants and inert ground covers such as pebbles, bark, or gravel. The next mowing-edging problem is with the places where the grass ends. You can install mowing strips where the lawn meets a flower bed, or where the lawn runs right up to a wall. Mowing strips are strips flush with the lawn and wide enough for the mower wheels to ride on. Make these from bricks, concrete blocks, or railroad crossties. Be sure to put a good bed of sand and/or gravel under the mowing strip so it does not sink. If flower beds are not a big part of the yard, corrugated edging strips will prevent grass from getting into the beds.
2. Watering. Of course, the best answer to watering problems is to install an underground sprinkler system and fully automate it. Short of that, be selective in the sprinkler you get. Moving sprinklers are better than a steady spray. Let the shape and size of your yard guide you in selecting a sprinkler. Get one that will adjust to odd shapes without too much waste, but also get one that will cover as much territory as possible without your having to move it. To accomplish this, you

Here Is What You Will Need

Materials
- Mulch or inert ground cover
- Insecticide
- Bricks, concrete blocks or railroad crossties

Tools
- Shovel
- Sprayer
- Sprinkler

may need to have more than one sprinkler. Water only when there is a need to. Overwatering or everyday shallow watering is not as good as deep watering when needed.
3. Weeds. Some people fight weeds and never win. In flower beds, cover the empty spaces with mulch or inert ground cover. Mulch does other good things for the beds like retain moisture. For the lawn, there are herbicides that will kill weeds. They will also kill other plants including the grass unless you are careful and use the right type for your lawn. One of the most effective ways to control weeds is to feed your lawn, give it plenty of water and mow regularly. A healthy lawn will kill weeds, and keeping them cut down will not allow them to seed. Add some hand pulling to that, and you should get rid of them altogether.
4. Insects. The biggest problem here is defining the insect, choosing the proper insecticide, and using it at the time that will be the most effective. The use of combination fertilizer-insecticides will usually do a good preventive job, although you will need specific formulations for some bugs.
5. Leaves. There is not much you can do about leaves if you have trees that shed their leaves each fall. If you are going to plant new trees, find out what trees are native to your area that will serve your purpose, but with less of a leaf problem. Some trees, such as mimosas, not only drop leaves, but shed beans, flowers, and sap at different times of the year. If you have a big leaf problem, get a power lawn vacuum.

With the five biggest problems already discussed, here are some more things to consider in cutting down on maintenance time:

△ 1. Do not cut the lawn area into separate sections.
△ 2. Do not try to grow grass where it will not grow as in areas with no sun.
△ 3. Find out which type of grass grows best in your area.
△ 4. The same goes for trees. Plant trees that are native to the area. You might be able to get others to grow, but it might require a lot more time and effort.
△ 5. Plan for the future. Remember that trees will spread. Do not plant them too close to the house or to each other as they might cause damage.

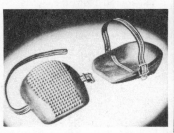

Outdoors

Quality Seed Can Make A Big Difference

Some grasses, of course, do better in a particular climate than others. You can obtain the relevant information from your local nursery or the county agent. No matter what the variety, however, always get a quality brand of seed. Scott seeds are carefully selected and blended to match different lawn needs. The Picture blend would make a fine lawn in many climes. Shady Area is for those trouble spots where too little sun prevents a healthy lawn. Play is a

mixture for badminton courts and other high traffic recreational areas. Scott also packages seeds

for bare spots in a shaker type container that lets you sprinkle the seeds only where they are

needed. All these blends are part of O.M. Scott & Sons line of lawn products.

Get A Good Rake

If you're just starting your lawn, you may not see much need for buying a garden rake, but you'll need one before long. When you do buy a rake, get a good one. True Temper makes a quality rake that is 14¾ inches wide with a 5½-foot handle. Each of its 14 slim tapered teeth measures 2¾ inches long. A good all-purpose rake, this True Temper tool is made to last for years to come.

Here's A Real Sod Buster

There are several good tillers on the market, and the five-horsepower Toro Tiller is one of the best. Available with bolo tines for general soil tilling or with slasher tines to cut through roots as it loosens the dirt, the Toro Tiller has two speeds—high for sod busting and hard-packed earth, and low for blending soil and cultivating. This well-made tiller possesses valuable safety features, and it performs well. Able to till a swath 26 inches wide, the Toro Tiller can be adjusted for depth from one to eight inches.

Planting a Lawn

HAVING A GREEN lawn does much more than just make your home look attractive. A good lawn fights air pollution, prevents soil erosion, helps to dampen sounds, and manufactures oxygen. Of course, most people who have nice lawns work at them primarily for the beauty only a well-manicured lawn can provide. It is a pretty way to set off any style house.

The type of grass that does best in your area varies with the climate, moisture, and soil. You can and should talk with experts, but the best way is to pick out several healthy looking lawns in the neighborhood and ask the owners what they did to achieve such great results. Find out what specie of grass is most successful and how much trouble it is to keep up. The owners will be flattered, and you will learn a great deal.

After you select which type of grass you want, learn which time of year is the best for planting. Here are some general steps to follow when putting in a new lawn.

1. If the grading has not been done yet, you should have it done or do it yourself. The ground should slope gradually away from the house in all directions.
2. After grading, check for low places by turning on a sprinkler and looking for spots where water collects.
3. Next, check the soil; it should have the proper pH. The only way to find out about the soil's pH is to test it. Most county agents and many seed stores will test your soil at no or very little cost to you. Lime is added to soil that is too acid, and gypsum is added to soil that is too alkaline. The soil should also be crumbly. Squeeze a handful tightly in your fist and release it. If the blob falls apart, the soil is too sandy. If it looks like a mud ball, the soil contains too much clay. In either case, three to four inches of peat moss will correct the soil situation.
4. Make whatever soil additions are indicated by the tests, and then till the soil. You can rent a tiller if you do not wish to buy one. When tilling, avoid making the soil too fine. Marble-sized lumps are better than fine dirt.
5. Wet the soil to pack it down and then wait 24 hours.
6. Spread the seed at the rate recommended for the specific variety of seed you are planting. Do not spread the seed too thickly; if

Here Is What You Will Need

Materials

- Lime or gypsum
- Peat moss
- Grass seed
- Fertilizer
- Chemical weed killer

Tools

- Tiller
- Spreader
- Rake
- Roller
- Sprinkler
- Mower

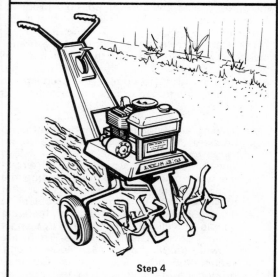

Step 4

Step 6

Any Lawn Needs Regular Watering

If you decide not to install an underground sprinkler system, you're going to have to make arrangements for watering. There are dozens of good sprinklers on the market. One that does an excellent job of distributing water evenly is the Burgess Fluidic. Infinite settings allow the Fluidic to sprinkle such different areas as a yard 3500 feet square or just a narrow strip of lawn. The oscillating mechanism does away with gears, cams, and linkages

—all of which can cause trouble. While the Fluidic is more expensive than many sprinklers, it is a quality product that performs

well. Burgess Vibrocrafters also markets sprinklers on the other end of the price scale; the Shower Stick is quite inexpensive.

Good Spreader Helps Grow A Healthy Lawn

The Cyclone broadcast spreader is—despite its utilitarian appearance—extremely well made and well designed. It has a stainless steel hopper as well as other stainless parts, and it holds up to 40 pounds of fertilizer, seed, granular pesticides, or other dry ingredients. The micro dial insures good coverage, and the tapered feathered edge spread prevents stripes and streaks. A comprehensive spreading chart is included with every Cyclone spreader.

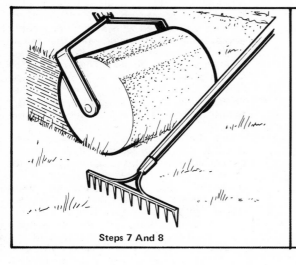

Steps 7 And 8

Step 9

Bluing Beats The Birds

Often, when you scatter grass seed, it turns out that you do nothing more than supply a feast for the birds. If you mix blue cake coloring into the seeds, spread them out to dry, and then scatter the blue seeds, the birds won't eat them. For some reason, birds can't see blue, thus making the seeds invisible. The bluing in no way disturbs the germination of the seeds.

you do, the young seedlings will compete for nutrients and most will die.

7. Rake the ground lightly to cover the seeds partially with soil.

8. Go over the ground once with a roller to press the seeds into the soil. Do not try to bury them.

9. Feed the lawn as soon as you finish the seeding. Use the fertilizer recommended for your variety of grass and follow the directions on the bag.

10. Water as soon as you finish fertilizing. During the next two weeks, water two or three times a day, keeping the top layer of soil damp at all times. When the seedlings are up, cut back to regular morning waterings.

11. Wait until the sprigs are two inches tall and then mow. Mowing will help to spread the root system and make the lawn thicker.

12. Mow weekly until you note the proper thickness; then mow as needed.

13. Never use a weed killer on new lawns. Pull the bigger weeds and mow the rest. As your lawn thickens, many of the weeds will be choked out. You can use a weed killer the second year your lawn is in.

The maintenance of your lawn depends on the specie of grass you planted, the soil condition, and the climate. A lawn specialist or the county agent can tell you what type of fertilizer you should have and how often you should apply it, as well as how much water you should be using.

If your existing lawn is shot, try to renovate it. If there is at least 50 percent of the area still covered with grass, plant new grass in the bad spots. Here are the steps to follow.

△ 1. Get rid of all weeds. Apply a chemical weed killer according to directions.

△ 2. Mow the existing grass very close.

△ 3. Rake the yard to remove all clippings and leaves and, also, to loosen the surface of the soil. Test the soil as described earlier.

△ 4. Follow the same steps (6 through 13) suggested for a new lawn in order to seed the bare spots.

One thing many people fail to realize is that grass cannot grow in total shade. You may have had a good stand of grass several years ago, but now it is all dead around the trees. Years ago the trees probably were not as thick; now they keep the sun out completely. You can thin out the branches to let more sunlight through, and you can try one of the species of seed that grows well in partial shade. Those steps should put you on the way to a greener and more beautiful lawn.

Gypsum Is For Gardeners Who Don't Dig Digging

Gypsum loosens tight soil, thereby letting air and water penetrate. For the new lawn, United States Gypsum's Sof'n-Soil should be spread at a rate of 10 pounds per 100 square feet of lawn. In high clay soils, put it on at 20 to 40 pounds per 100. For an established yard, the 50-pound bag covers about 1000 square feet. After mixing the gypsum well into the soil, water thoroughly.

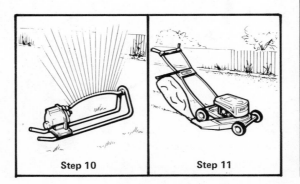

Step 10   Step 11

Outdoors

Convert Your Mower Into A Power Rake

By substituting the Rake-O-Matic for the regular blade on your mower, you can have your own power rake and thatcher. The changeover takes but a few minutes to do, and the Rake-O-Matic will loosen and remove dead grass that would otherwise eventually choke out your lawn. It mulches leaves and aerates your lawn so that new seeds can grow. If you have a single-blade mower—either electric or gas powered—check to see whether the Rake-O-Matic will fit it.

Tune-Up Kit Gets Mower Purring Again

If your mower is not giving you the power and performance you expect from it, it probably needs a tune up. Look for a Prestolite Tune-Up Kit for your mower model. The kit features their new mini-plug, especially designed for your mower. There are seven different kits to take care of just about every mower, snowmobile, garden tractor, and chain saw. You can find Prestolite Tune-Up Kits wherever mower parts are sold.

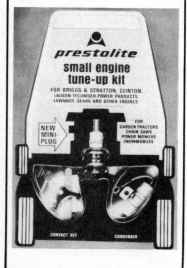

Power Mowers (Gasoline)

THE POWER MOWER was once a luxury. Today anybody who has a few square feet of grass owns a power mower. Many people with small lawns even have a riding-type mower.

Power mowers are simple, hard-working machines that will usually last for years if properly maintained. If you maintain your lawn mower regularly, chances are, nothing will ever go wrong with it, and your mower will be better in every way. Here is what to do: (Warning: Always disconnect the spark plug wire and tape it back out of the way to avoid accidental starting.)

1. Tilt the mower up so the blade can be inspected. If it is not sharp, remove the blade and sharpen it. To remove the blade, you must block the blade so it will not turn with your wrench pressure. A block of wood and a c-clamp should work. Usually you will need to put penetrating oil on the nut to loosen it. Dress the cutting edges with a file. Do not worry about nicks in the blade. Before the blade is replaced, it must be balanced. This can be done by filing more off the heavy side. Rest the blade on a pencil to check its balance.
2. Clean the housing underneath. Clippings can be caked on and will have to be scraped away.
3. Clean the fins that are sticking out on the engine. If these are not clean, the mower can run hot. A stiff brush will usually do the job.
4. Clean the air filter. Most filters are foam sponge. They can usually be cleaned with warm water and detergent. After it is clean, squeeze it out and coat it with lightweight oil. Squeeze out excess oil. Be sure the filter is secure in its housing. The dry type cleaners can be cleaned with a vacuum cleaner and by brushing. However, when they refuse to come clean, replace them. Some mowers have an oil-bath type filter. They are cleaned with a solvent. Be sure it is a safe type solvent such as kerosene. (Never use gasoline as a solvent. It is too dangerous.) Air dry the parts of the filter, reassemble and put in new oil.
5. Check the spark plug. To remove it, you need a spark plug wrench. If you have a socket set, you can buy a special socket for spark plugs. If not, you can get an inexpensive wrench made just for spark plugs. Inspect the electrodes. If the electrodes are just dirty, they can be cleaned. Use a knife or wire brush to scrape away the residue. Blow away all the traces. If the electrodes are pitted or burned away, or if the porcelain shell of the plug is cracked, get a new one. Be sure to get the proper size.

Here Is What You Will Need

Materials

- Penetrating oil
- Lightweight motor oil
- Cleaning solvent
- Spray lubricant

Tools

- Sharpening file
- Block of wood and c-clamp
- Adjustable wrench
- Stiff brush
- Vacuum cleaner
- Spark plug wrench and socket
- Spark plug gapper
- Screwdriver

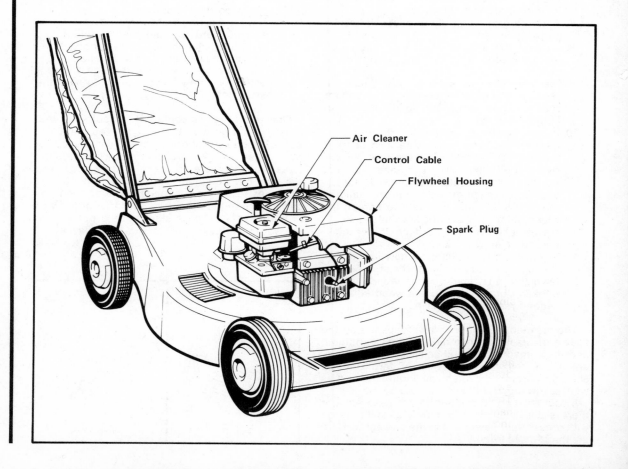

Air Cleaner
Control Cable
Flywheel Housing
Spark Plug

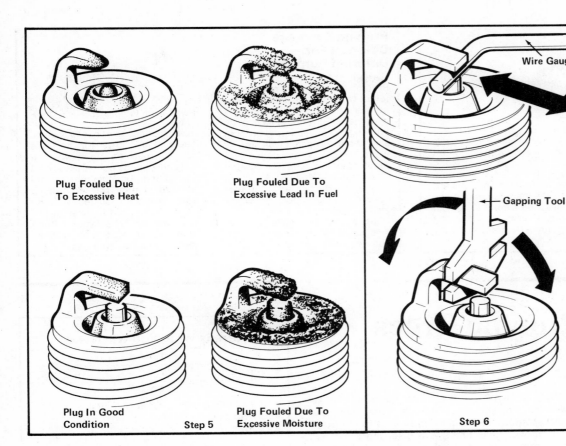

Plug Fouled Due To Excessive Heat

Plug Fouled Due To Excessive Lead In Fuel

Plug In Good Condition — Step 5

Plug Fouled Due To Excessive Moisture

Wire Gauge

Gapping Tool

Step 6

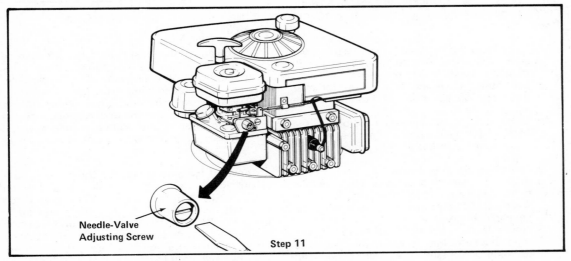

Needle-Valve Adjusting Screw

Step 11

End Grass Cling Under The Mower Housing

The way to end the problem of grass clinging to and caking up under the housing of your rotary lawn mower is to spray the housing with Slip Plate No. 3, a graphite-based lube that goes on dry and can't be washed off. Able to withstand high and low temperatures (from -50 to 800 degrees) Slip Plate No. 3 can be used on plastic, wood, and rubber as well as on metal. It is also available as a brush-on liquid under the name Slip Plate No. 1. When working under the housing or near the blade of your power mower, always be sure to disconnect the spark plug wire and move it out of the way to prevent an accidental start. Slip Plate is manufactured by the Superior Graphite Co.

Spark Plug Changing Requires Socket Tool

There is no need to take your power mower to a mechanic every time a spark plug must be replaced. You can save time and money if you have the Bernz-Omatic five-piece Spark Plug Socket Set. The set contains a flex head ratchet, 5/8-inch and 13/16-inch spark plug sockets, and 1¾-inch and 3-inch extensions and of course, can be used for automobile, boat, and other internal combustion engines. Made of drop-forged, triple chrome plated alloy steel, the BernzOmatic Spark Plug Socket Set is sold in blister packs through auto supply, hardware, and discount stores.

6. Set the gap on the plug. Use an inexpensive wire gauge made for this purpose. Your owner's manual is the best guide. If you do not know the correct gap, .030 of an inch will get you by. The exact gap will do better, however. When putting the plug back in, be sure the threads are clean. Oil them. Hand tighten the plug and then give it about a third of a turn with the wrench. Do not over tighten.

7. Inspect the spark plug wire. If it is frayed, replace it. Some are not easily replaced since doing so requires the removal of the flywheel, and to do this, you will need a special puller. Be sure that this connection is tight. If it fits loosely on the plug, squeeze it gently with a pliers.

8. Check the oil level. If the oil is dirty, change it. It will drain more completely when hot.

9. Lubricate all the moving parts on top of the mower. There will be oiler points indicated in your manual. Also use a spray lube on the throttle and cable.

10. Check to see if the choke is properly adjusted. To do this, remove the air cleaner unit, and look into the carburetor. There will be a round plate. With the control set to "choke," this plate should move down to close the opening. If not, loosen the screw and clamp that hold the cable in place. Move the cable forward until the plate closes. Tighten the cable and check again. Replace the air cleaner.

11. With the engine running and warmed up, you can now adjust the carburetor. Turn the needle-valve adjusting screw clockwise 1/8th turn. Wait a few seconds, then make another 1/8th turn. Do this until the engine slows. Now turn counter-clockwise in 1/8th turns counting the eighths. When the engine falters, stop. Divide the number of eighths by two and turn back (clockwise) that number of eighths. That sets the needle-valve to its best setting. To set proper idle, turn the throttle to its top speed and then back to its slowest speed. Turn the idle speed adjustment screw until the engine sounds as if it is running at about half the maximum speed .

No Need To Climb To Trim

A pruning tool that utilizes a long handle to give you maximum leverage makes it possible for you to prune your trees without risking your own limbs. The Snap-Cut Tree Pruner and Saw features "Multi-Power" cutting action to increase your leverage. The saw is a 16-inch blade with needle point teeth to cut through green wood and large limbs; it can prune limbs up to 1⅛ inch in diameter. The lightweight aluminum alloy poles telescope from 6 to 12 feet with a simple twist. The Snap-Cut line of garden shears is made by Seymour Smith & Son, Inc.

Pruning Saws Are Different For Different Purposes

Full-Length Pruning Saw

Pruning saws come in several different types. The Disston Division of the H. K. Porter Company makes several pruning saws. The full-length conventional pruning saw has a 24-inch blade and is made for cutting big limbs and tough branches. It has the Disston Champion teeth pattern for quick clean cuts. The two-edged pruner does double duty for the homeowner. The coarse side has the Champion pattern, while the other side has an eight-pointed edge for cutting smaller branches. The Disston folding saw has a curved blade that allows for accurate reach-in cuts on green wood; it cuts only on the pull stroke, and it folds into the handle for compact storage. All three Disston pruning saw blades are coated with du Pont's Teflon self-lubricating finish, which means faster cutting with less effort, lifetime rust protection, and easy cleaning.

Two-Hand Lopping Pruner Handles Heavy Pruning

The Bartlett Two-Hand Pruner is typical of the heavy-duty limb loppers that every tree pruner needs. Rugged and made for heavy pruning, it features drop-forged tool steel blades and white ash handles. For easier cutting, place the blade next to the main limb or the trunk of the tree with the hook handles in your left hand. This locks the tool in place so that all the power of the right hand can be devoted to cutting instead of steadying. The Bartlett Manufacturing Company markets other tree pruning equipment as well as garden shears.

Anvil Pruner Clears The Brush

The True Temper anvil pruner, called the Rocket, features a pointed and angled head for easier and more natural operation. The wide-opening blade, which works with a draw-cut slicing action to prune more effectively with an easier squeeze, is coated with a rust-resistant finish. The plastisol grips on the handles are shaped for comfort, and the slide-action thumb catch is convenient. Both the blade and the aluminum anvil are replaceable. True Temper markets a full line of quality lawn and garden tools.

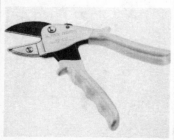

Pruning Trees

YOU SHOULD PRUNE trees for several reasons. Pruning gives trees a more desirable shape, strengthens them by improving their structure, removes dead limbs and diseased portions, and increases the production of foliage, flowers, and fruit. Here are the basic steps for pruning your trees.

1. All pruning tools should be as sharp as possible. Dull tools lead to ragged cuts, and ragged cuts can lead to problems.
2. Use the right size and type of tool for your trees. Too large or too small a tool can make ragged cuts.
3. Make all cuts as close as possible to the base of the piece being removed without damaging the larger limb to which it is attached.
4. Seal all cuts with tree paint.
5. Because their root systems have usually been greatly reduced, newly transplanted trees should be pruned no matter what the season of the year.
6. Winter is the best time for pruning most trees because that is when the trees are dormant. Naturally, trees that exude sap during the winter should not be pruned until the following spring.
7. You can prune most trees lightly for shaping during the spring.
8. Remove broken limbs anytime of the year, but prune dead limbs in the fall.
9. When heavy pruning (the removal of as much as a third of the tree) is needed, do not perform all of the pruning during a single season. Do it, instead, in stages over a two- or three-year period.

Above all, try to do as much of the pruning work as possible while standing on the ground. When you must work from a ladder, never try to reach very far; move the ladder frequently and make certain that it is always on solid ground. Position yourself and your ladder so that the limbs you prune fall free and nowhere near you. If you are cutting away large limbs, make certain that there is no chance of them falling against power lines.

Here Is What You Will Need

Materials

- Tree paint

Tools

- Sharpened pruning tools
- Paintbrush
- Ladder

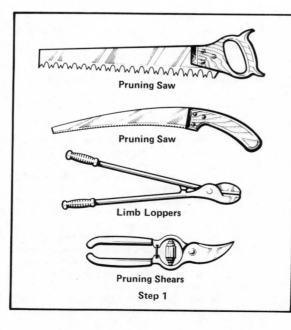

Pruning Saw

Pruning Saw

Limb Loppers

Pruning Shears

Step 1

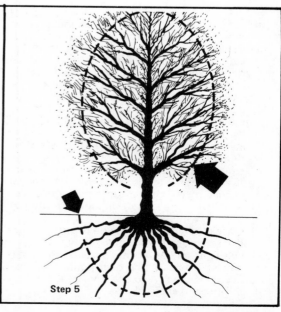

Step 5

Garbage Can Enclosures and Racks

A GARBAGE CAN enclosure serves two essential purposes. First, it conceals one of the home's most unsightly necessities; and second, the garbage can enclosure keeps out rodents, as well as the neighborhood dogs who often tip the cans over in search of thrown-out morsels. Here is how to build one.

1. If you have no reason to worry about rats and mice, build the enclosure with four corner posts sunk into the ground about six inches, and with the sides and doors about two inches off the ground.
2. If rats are a problem, however, build the unit up from a concrete or asphalt base laid next to the foundation walls of the house. The top of the base should be an inch or two above grade, and should slope slightly away from the house for easy cleaning.
3. The dimensions of your enclosure depend on the size and number of your garbage cans. To simplify removal of the cans, make the floor space about four inches wider and deeper than each can.
4. Allow a two-inch clearance at the top of the cans; but if your house wall is covered with beveled siding, you can reduce the clearance slightly or increase it substantially to make the lid of the enclosure come just below the butts of the siding.
5. Cut a 2x4 into two long and two short pieces to form the sills for the enclosure, saturate them with wood preservative, and fasten them to the base with long screws driven into lead anchors.
6. Make the corner posts from 2x4s as well, cutting the back posts three inches longer than those in front.
7. Apply wood preservative, and toenail them to the sills with 10d galvanized common nails. The wide sides of the 2x4s should parallel the ends of the enclosure.
8. Cut the top plates from 2x2s, and nail them to the tops of the posts and to one another.
9. Nail the back plate to the house wall.
10. Use ¾-inch exterior plywood for the end panels, but before cutting them to fit over the posts, sills, and plates, scribe the sheet of plywood to the house wall to eliminate any wide cracks that a rat or mouse could possibly get through.
11. Brush wood preservative on the bottom parts of the panels before nailing them in place.
12. Cut a pair of flush doors out of ¾-inch plywood to fit between the posts, sill, and top plate at the front of the enclosure.
13. Hang the doors, using galvanized T-hinges with four-inch straps.
14. Screw the rectangular pads to the inside edges of the posts to conceal them, and screw the triangular straps to the faces of the doors.
15. Nail a stop to the sill just behind the doors, install spring catches at the tops of the doors, and attach the pulls.
16. The top of the enclosure consists of a 1x6-inch board and a piece of ¾-inch plywood. Cut the board and plywood to overhang both ends and the front of the enclosure by two inches.
17. Scribe the board (if necessary) to the house wall, and nail it to the back plate and upper ends of the side plates.
18. Attach the plywood with four-inch galvanized strap hinges screwed to the top surfaces. Use two hinges on lids up to four feet long, three on longer lids.

Here Is What You Will Need

Materials
- 2x4s for posts and sills
- 2x2s for top plates
- ¾-inch plywood for ends, doors, and lid
- 1x6-inch board for lid
- Stop molding
- Wood preservative
- Four galvanized T-hinges with four-inch straps
- Two or three galvanized strap hinges with four-inch straps
- Two spring catches and pulls
- Galvanized nails, screws, lead anchors

Tools
- Tape measure
- Saw
- Screwdriver
- Hammer
- Paintbrush

A Rolling Rack May Suit Your Needs

If you don't want to build your own rack, you can buy one that rolls the loaded cans out for pick-up. The Trash Kan Kart is both rack and cart. It holds two regular sized cans, although the upper arms of the frame can be pulled out to accommodate larger cans. The frame is made of heavy steel tubing, on which are mounted a pair of six-inch solid rubber tires (front) and a handle (rear). The Trash Kan Kart is a product of Specialty Manufacturing Co.

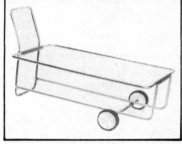

It's In The Bag Easier

Tired of the hassle to keep those plastic grass bags open while you get the clippings or leaves inside? Try the Yard N' Garden Cart from Specialty Manufacturing Company. It has a plastic bag holder rim that adjusts up or down depending on the bag size. An elastic strip around the rim holds the bag up and open. When the bag is full, you merely wheel the Yard N' Garden Cart to the garbage pick-up point and release the plastic bag. Since the rim is removable, you can use the cart as a regular dolly for carting a loaded garbage can. Specialty Manufacturing Company also makes a wall-mounted and a free-standing Bag Butler, utilizing the same bag-holding principle of the Yard N' Garden Cart.

Swedish Saws Saw Swiftly

For a fast-cutting hand saw, look for one carrying the Bushman brand. Bushman saws come in every size and style for every purpose, and each saw comes with its own protective blade sleeve. The blades are made of top quality Swedish steel, well-balanced and properly sharpened and set. Available with wooden or plastic handles, Bushman saws are made by SBI, Inc.

Plywood Hinged Cover · Hinge · Board · Top Plate · Corner Post (Long) · Corner Post (Short) · Siding · Plywood Doors · Sill · Hinge · Plywood Side Panel · Cement Slab

Tablets And Flakes Aid Composting Action

Microorganisms are what give Compost Maker the ability to cause rapid decomposition of leaves, grass clippings, foodstuffs, and other waste. This microorganic action "chews up" huge quantities of waste vegetation in weeks instead of months, shrinking it into plant supporting compost. Compost Maker, available in tablets and flakes, eliminates all odors from composting. Compost Maker is made by the Ringer Corporation.

Fork Turns Composting Matter

A spading fork is an ideal tool for the composter. It enables you to move the top layers down to where the action is. A Craftsman spading fork from Sears Roebuck will do this job, as well as heavy-duty work. Featuring a 30-inch Northern Ash handle with a reinforced "D" grip, the Sears spading fork has four 11-inch tines of forged steel. Craftsman Garden Tools are unconditionally guaranteed.

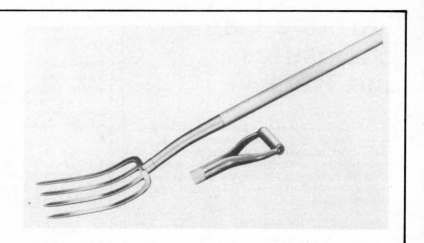

The British Are Com(post)ing!

From England comes a prefabricated Accelerator Compost Bin made of rigid green PVC interlocking and sliding panels that fit together to form a circular bin topped with a matching green snap-on inflatable cover. Since ventilation is so important to composting, each of the panels has three holes in it. There are two Accelerator units for use on dirt, and one model for use on concrete. When the compost is ready, the Accelerator panels slide up to allow for easy removal. Write to Rotocrop U.S.A. Inc., 58 Buttonwood Street, New Hope, Pennsylvania 18938 for the nearest dealer or for information and prices should you wish to order by mail.

Compost Heap

MANY HOMEOWNERS have started small vegetable gardens recently. Even a very small plot in the corner of your yard can yield some delicious vegetables and save you some money. If your garden is going to feed you, though, you have to feed the garden. Rather than spend money on plant food, why not start your own compost heap? It utilizes plenty of the things that you have trouble disposing of anyway, requires very little room, and takes practically no time at all. Here is the easy way to start composting.

1. Select an out-of-the-way corner in the shade. Although you do not need a bin, a bin is much neater than an open heap. You can either build a bin from scratch or buy a kit that is easy to fit together. The requirements for the bin are: (1) it must be able to keep the ingredients together; (2) it must allow ventilation; (3) it should be at least four feet square and four feet tall; (4) it should have an opening which gives you easy access to get at and work the compost; and, (5) it should be fairly attractive.
2. Start with about a six-inch layer of coarse organic material such as leaves, stalks, or weeds. This allows better bottom ventilation.
3. Cover the coarse layer with a thin layer of barnyard manure or a commercial fertilizer with good nitrogen content. If you use the commercial fertilizer, put on about two cups per each twenty square feet of area.
4. Dampen the manure or fertilizer layer, but do not drown it.
5. Add about a two-inch layer of dirt.
6. Now build up a series of six-inch layers composed of any of the following: grass clippings, sawdust, leaves, coffee grounds, egg shells, vegetable peels, ashes, and any other organic matter that will decompose rapidly. Avoid grease, meat, bones, and large tree limbs that would be slow to decompose. Meat scraps also attract rodents. Paper is organic, but unless you render it into shreads, it decomposes too slowly. Top each layer with fertilizer, wet it down, and add a two-inch layer of soil.
7. After at least four layers—the more the better—shape the top layer so that it slants toward the center. Slanting the top layer keeps the moisture working toward the center.
8. Keep the heap moist at all times.
9. Turn the pile with a pitchfork every week or so.
10. When the compost reaches the consistency of peat moss, it is ready to be mixed in with the top soil of your garden or flower beds.

Compost Bin Comes In A Kit

If you want to compost without having to build anything, get the Compost Bin Kit from the Ringer Corp., containing indestructible gridding that can be shaped to fit almost any space. Six twist lock fasteners permit easy loading of raw matter and removal of finished compost. The kit comes with a supply of Compost Maker Tablets and a handy booklet titled "Guide to Scientific Composting" which explains the system in detail. The only thing not furnished in the Compost Bin Kit is the material for decomposition.

Here Is What You Will Need
Materials
- Bin kit or boards (treated lumber scraps), chicken wire, wood support beams, and hook and eye
- Coarse organic material
- Barnyard manure or commercial fertilizer
- Organic matter that decomposes rapidly
- Soil

Tools
- Shovel
- Pitchfork
- Garden hose

Chicken Wire Or Scrap Lumber May Be Used For Bin Walls

Hangers Store Tools Better

After you build the garden tool storage unit, you should try to hang as many tools as possible in order to conserve floor space for things that cannot be hung. Among the many hangers and brackets on the market are two good ones from the Dalton Manufacturing Company. Dalton's Thrif-T is for wide tools—such as shovels, rakes, hoes, and brooms which can rest on the extension arms. Hang-it-All consists of a pair of heavy-duty brackets that can hold a six-inch wide shelf in addition to providing tool-hanging hooks.

Tool Hangers Mount On Support Studs

If your fence storage unit utilizes 2x4s as braces on the inside, you'll like the ease with which sturdy SMC Hang-It-Up hangers can be installed. Made to fasten on each side of a stud, the hangers have loops through which nails are driven for attachment purposes. The weight of the hanger and what it is holding then rests against the stud. SMC hangers, made of steel but cushion coated so that they do not scar or mar the tools, can hold a variety of garden tools.

Garden Tool Storage in a Fence

MORE AND more homeowners are surrounding their properties with six- and eight-foot fences to provide some privacy from neighbors and the surrounding world. If you plan to follow this trend, why not use part of your new fence as a storage place for garden tools and outdoor game equipment?

How much of the fence you devote to storage depends on how many things you have to store in space only four to six inches deep. You must then decide whether the storage section of the fence should look like the rest of the fence or be entirely different.

Since you want the fence for privacy as well as for storage, you must make it either of closely spaced boards or of large sheets of plywood, hardboard, or asbestos-cement board. One of the best ways to build the fence is in eight-foot sections framed by 3x6-inch posts and 2x6-inch rails to which you attach vertical boards. In the first section of the fence, the boards are on your side of the framework; in the next section, they are on your neighbor's side; then your side; and so forth. This gives the entire fence diversity and texture, and makes it impossible for the neighbor to complain that you gave him the ugly side of the fence. Equally important, it allows you to insert the storage unit (which is closed on both sides) without materially altering the appearance of the fence.

1. Space the posts for each fence section eight feet apart center to center. The space between the top and bottom rail should be at least five feet to allow for storage of rakes and other long-handled tools.
2. Cover the back of the storage section (and two adjacent fence sections) with boards.
3. Staple asphalt building paper to the inner surface to keep out moisture.
4. At the center of the storage section, nail a 3x6-inch divider between the top and bottom rails.

Here Is What You Will Need
Materials
- 3x6's for posts and divider
- 2x6's for rails
- 1x6-, 1x8-, or 1x10-inch boards or sheet materials for fence panels and doors
- 1x6-inch boards for cleats
- Asphalt building paper
- Four galvanized butt hinges
- Four galvanized wrap-around hinges
- Four spring catches
- Four pulls
- Clips and hooks for hanging garden tools
- Galvanized nails
- Screws

Tools
- Hammer
- Staple gun
- Saw
- Screwdriver

5. Make two pairs of doors out of the same lumber you use for the rest of the fence.
6. After covering the backs with building paper, fasten the doors together with 1x6-inch cleats installed in a "Z" pattern. Set the ends of the cleats in far enough from the hinge edges of the doors so that they will clear the 3x6's. Fasten the cleats to the doors with screws.
7. The doors overlay the top and bottom rails; those at opposite ends of the storage section completely overlay the posts. Hang them on the posts with butt hinges screwed to the backs of the doors and to the faces of the posts.
8. The two center doors overlay the 3x6 divider to half its width. Hang them with wrap-around hinges, and in order to minimize the crack between the doors, install the hinges for one door slightly higher than those for the other door.
9. Attach spring catches and pulls on the four doors.
10. If you plan to hang garden tools, screw hooks and clips to the back of the unit.

Rack Up Garden Tools

A new garden tool organizer called Rack-A-Tool can put an end to your crowded garage obstacle course. A sturdy 22-gauge steel rack with strong braces and holes for nine tools, Rack-A-Tool can hold rakes, hoes, mops, brooms, and other long-handled tools. To rack up the tools, all you do is poke the handle into the hole; a heavy-duty flexible tool gripper with an "X" in the middle holds the tool in place until you pull it out. Rack-A-Tool is from the Cliff Granberry Corporation.

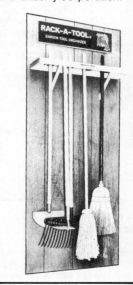

Garden Tote Aids The Green Thumber

Rubbermaid's Garden Carry Caddy is a very handy carryall for small garden tools and supplies. Three compartments keep the various tools and supplies separate. This lightweight plastic caddy comes in a choice of avocado or gold colors, it features an easy-grip carrying handle, and measures 15½ inches long by 10 inches wide by 5¼ inches deep. The Rubbermaid tote would also be helpful in carrying household cleaners and supplies.

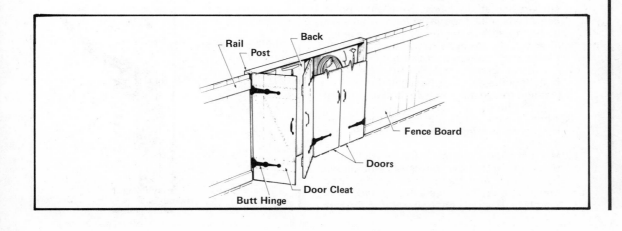

Rail
Post
Back
Fence Board
Doors
Door Cleat
Butt Hinge

Outdoors

Set Posts The No-Strain Way

If the idea of mixing and hauling concrete to set fence posts doesn't grab you, you may wish to do the job the Post Hold way. With Post Hold, you need only dig a small diameter hole, and in one box that you can carry home from your building supply or hardware store, you get enough Post Hold to set up to 20 fence posts. A two-component formulation that mixes in a special plastic mixing

bag and expands to 16 times its liquid volume, Post Hold can be prepared in less than a minute. Poured immediately around the post, it starts its expansion and setting process rapidly and solidifies in a matter of minutes, reaching 90 percent of its strength in the first hour. Post Hold protects the wood from mildew, rot, and insects, and it can be used to set wood or metal posts. Post Hold, made by Post Hold, Inc., also comes in packages for two, four, and 10 posts.

Earth Mount Digs Its Own Post Hole

By using only a jack handle, you can install Ajax Earth Mounts. At the bottom of the Earth Mount are auger teeth that carry it into the ground at the rate of about an inch per revolution, and a special floating stabilizer fin arrangement provides support in all types of soil. Once they are secured in the ground, Ajax Earth Mounts can support metal fence posts. Earth Mounts come in a variety of sizes to accept different metal posts; one unit is designed to hold a

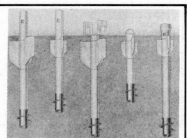

4x4-inch wooden post. In addition to fence posts, these clever anchors can be used to hold mail boxes, flag poles, bird house poles, net supports for games, signs, and many other things.

Aluminum Nails Make Fence Sense

Although they cost more, aluminum nails make good sense for fence building because they never rust or corrode and thus cannot streak the fence. Actually, from a cost standpoint, there is no tremendous difference because relatively few nails are involved. The main problem you'll encounter with aluminum nails is that they take a little getting used to insofar as driving them is concerned. At first, you'll probably bend quite a few, but with a little practice you'll drive them as well as you do steel nails. Hy-Tensil brand aluminum nails are made by Nichols-Homeshield.

Preservative Gives Fence Longer Life

No matter what type of fence wood you select—including those with natural resistance to decay, moisture, and insect damage—you can give it even longer life by treating it with a preservative. Cuprinol Wood Preservative is effective, containing a base of copper or zinc naphthenate to repel moisture and prevent mildew and rot. Cuprinol can be applied easily by either brushing, dipping, or spraying. Cuprinol, a product of the Darworth Company, is available in three formulations: one is recommended for wood in constant contact with soil; another is for use around greenhouses because it does not harm plants; and the third type is clear for use on decks, outdoor furniture, and the upper parts of fences.

green no. 10*

CUPRINOL WOOD PRESERVATIVE

Building a Fence

THERE ARE hundreds of ways to design a fence and dozens of different materials to use. Some fences are for protection, some for privacy, some for appearance, and, of course, some accomplish all three purposes. Before you decide on a specific fence design, check the local building code. It may restrict you to a certain height, style, materials, and positioning in relation to property lines. No matter what kind of fence you decide to put up, though, the key to durability is the proper installation of the posts. Here are some hints for installing fence posts the right way.

1. Stake out your fence. Tap short sharp sticks into the ground, and then run strings from one stick to the next.
2. Using the strings as a guide, drive additional stakes to indicate where each post goes. The spacing depends on the type of fence, the terrain, and the purpose of the fence. As a rule of thumb, posts should range from six to eight feet apart.
3. Select wooden posts of a rot resistant wood like redwood, cedar, or cyprus. If you choose any other kind of wood, be sure to treat the posts with a preservative. Even the rot resistant woods benefit from a preservative treatment. Coat metal posts with asphalt paint to prevent rusting.
4. Dig the holes with a post-hole digger. If you have many holes to dig, look into the possibility of renting a gasoline powered post-hole digger. Dig only the corner posts at first.
5. Try to have about a third of the total length of the post underground, particularly at the corners and at any gates. In-between posts can still be solid, though, as long as they are in the ground to a depth of at least two feet.
6. After you dig the hole to the proper depth, flare it at the bottom with a straight shovel.
7. Put about an inch or two of gravel in the bottom of the hole for drainage purposes.
8. Position the post in the hole, and use a level to get it plumb.
9. When you get it straight and at the proper height, rig outrigger braces to hold the post in place.
10. Mix just enough concrete for this one post. Use a mix of one part portland cement, two parts sand, and three parts medium-size gravel. A wheelbarrow makes a handy mixing place. Use only enough water in the mix

Here Is What You Will Need
Materials

- Short sharp sticks
- String
- Fence posts
- Wood preservative
- Asphalt paint
- Gravel
- Portland cement
- Sand
- Fence sections
- Outrigger braces

Tools

- Measuring tape
- Paint brushes
- Post-hole digger
- Shovel
- Level
- Wheelbarrow

Step 4

Outrigger Braces

Level

Step 9

Pre-Cut Posts Take Pain Out Of Fence Building

Putting up a rustic fence made of pre-cut members from the Koppers Company means that your biggest concern is just digging the post holes. The southern pine is treated to be resistant to attack by decay, moisture, and insects. The treatment involves penta being forced into the wood under pressure. The 6½-foot posts are factory drilled to be either line, corner, or end posts in either two- or three-rail arrangements. The horizontals are eight feet long and

have machined ends. Kopper's fences are available where building materials or lawn and garden supplies are sold.

Drive Metal Posts Three Times Faster

By means of a spring device, the Rancher's Fence Post Driver reduces your time and effort in driving metal posts into the earth. The spring inside the cylinder that fits over the post imparts double impact every time you slam the Rancher down. The first impact derives from the force of your blow, and the second comes from the spring. At the same time the spring provides extra impact, moreover, it lifts the tool back up for your next stroke. The twin handles are smooth and reasonably comfortable. Available in two models, the smaller Rancher's Fence Post Driver develops about 125 pounds additional force per stroke, while the larger model (used on farms and ranches) develops up to 700 pounds of extra force per stroke.

Hercules Helps Dig Post Holes

The Hercules Post Hole Digger is designed for use in hard soil. Its blades are nine inches long, 6¼ inches wide, and feature a point spread (how wide the mouth opens at the points) of 6¼ inches. The tough high-carbon steel blades are riveted to steel frames, and the hardwood handle is smoothed for comfort. Seymour Manufacturing Company, maker of the Hercules unit, markets a full line of post hole diggers.

Step 12

to coat the sand and gravel with cement.

11. Shovel the concrete into the hole around the post, poking the mixture to eliminate any air bubbles.

12. Add enough concrete to fill the hole slightly above the ground, and then slope the concrete away from the post for drainage.

13. Set the other corner posts the same way, and stretch taut cords between them. Now you can line up all the other posts that come between the corners.

14. Let the concrete cure fully before building the rest of the fence. If you wait six days, you can then build whatever fence you want with the assurance that it will last for quite some time.

Stain Your Fence

Some fence woods weather naturally after a while to produce a pleasing rustic look; but many people like the appearance of a stained fence. Cabot's Decking and Fence Stains, available in nine different colors plus black and white, are heavy-duty coatings that stand up to weather; thrive on foot traffic; and resist cracking, peeling, and blistering. They will not rub off. For a weathered look, treat your fence with Cabot's Bleaching Oil. Cabot's Decking and Fence Stains are available in quarts and gallons at paint stores and lumberyards.

Safe-T-Tip Ends Threat Of Chain Saw Kickback

A hardened steel protective device called Safe-T-Tip has been developed by the Homelite Division of Textron Inc., to eliminate the danger of chain saw kickback. Safe-T-Tip, which weighs just one ounce, fits over the nose section of the guide bar, covering the sensitive area of the bar and chain where kickback reaction is generated. Attached with a high tensile strength mounting screw, Safe-T-Tip can be installed or removed in a few seconds. It is offered at no extra charge on all Homelite consumer chain saws and can be purchased as an accessory for most others.

New Goof-Proof Chain Saw File Guide

Nicholson, makers of saws and files for more than 100 years, offers a chain saw file guide that is so simple to use that anyone can sharpen a chain saw like an expert and save money at the same time. The guide features both a filing angle indicator and a flat guide edge that positions the angle and depth of each file stroke. It's practically goof-proof! Lightweight, corrosion-resistant and extremely durable, the Nicholson chain saw file guide (it comes complete with file) is made of nylon to insure free-gliding strokes. You can choose between two sizes: a six-inch guide for ³⁄₁₆-inch and ⁵⁄₃₂-inch chain saw files, and an eight-inch guide for 316-inch and ¼-inch files. Nicholson chain saws are available at home centers and hardware stores.

Chain Saws

THE MOST IMPORTANT key to maintaining your chain saw is to carefully read the owner's manual, understand it, and then practice what it preaches. Different chain saws have different features, and you should know all about yours. There are also safety suggestions that must be followed. Here are some suggestions for keeping your chain saw operating at its best:

1. Constant chain oiling. Most manufacturers recommend that manually-operated chain oiling be done about every five seconds. Those with automatic oilers do this, but it is still a good idea to get into the habit of pushing the manual oiler button periodically, too.

2. Keep the chain tension adjusted properly. It should be checked often. A chain that is too loose wears out faster and can damage other parts of the saw. To adjust, loosen the chain bar adjusting nut, and then turn the tension adjusting screw clockwise to tighten. It should fit snug to the bottom of the bar with the nose of the bar up, but should still move freely with just a slight resistance. When it is set correctly, tighten the nut. Check it again after it is tight.

3. The chain should be kept in a sharpened condition. A dull chain puts too much strain on the engine and on the operator. Sharpening it yourself is something you should learn to do because it may need sharpening in the middle of a job. Use the correct size file and a guide that sets the file at the correct angle. It is important to file all the teeth evenly. Count the strokes and give each blade the same number. File them at the same point on the bar. Do all those on one side first. Then do those on the other side. Read the owner's manual for specific sharpening instructions. With an electric chain saw, always unplug it before sharpening. After sharpening, pull the chain through while pumping the oiler. This will clean it.

4. Miscellaneous things that should be done periodically. Clean the air filter. Check the gap on the spark plug and clean or replace when necessary. Clean the exhaust stack when carbon deposits collect. Adjust the carburetor according to the manual. Clean the housing often. Clean the chain when it gets too dirty. For this, remove it and soak it in solvent. Always give it an oil bath before reinstalling it. Use the same oil used in the chain oiler system.

Here are some general safety tips for chain saw use:

△ 1. Read the owner's manual so you know how the chain saw operates and what it is capable of. Do not push it beyond its limits.

△ 2. Always wear gloves when handling the chain for maintenance.

Here Is What You Will Need
Materials
• Cleaning solvent
• Lubricating oil
Tools
• Adjustable wrench
• Screwdriver
• Sharpening file
• Spark plug gapper

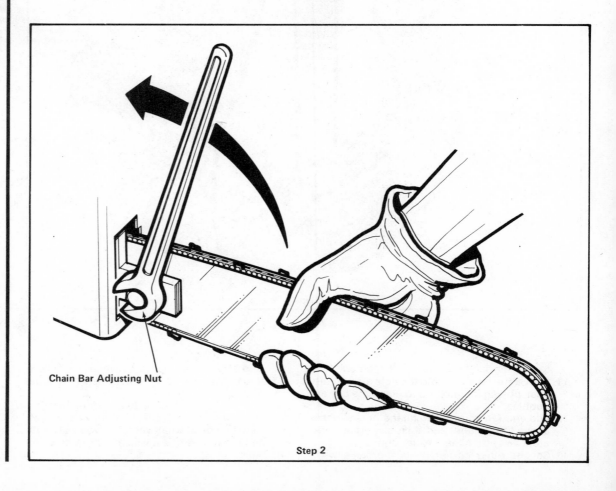

Chain Bar Adjusting Nut

Step 2

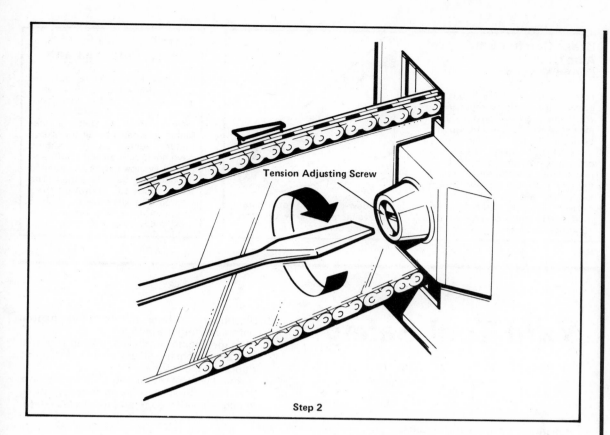

Tension Adjusting Screw

Step 2

△ 3. If your saw is electric, unplug it for maintenance.
△ 4. Wear protective gear for cutting. Always wear safety goggles, gloves, hard hat, and non-slip boots. Hearing protection is also a good idea. Wear close fitting clothes so nothing can get caught in the chain.
△ 5. Be sure the saw is firmly under control for starting.
△ 6. Do not start where you refueled. Move at least a few feet away.
△ 7. Let the saw cool before refueling and never refuel while it is running.
△ 8. Keep other away while you are cutting.
△ 9. Do not use an electric chain saw on wet ground or when barefooted even though it may be double insulated.
△ 10. Always use both hands when cutting and watch for solid objects that would cause kickback.

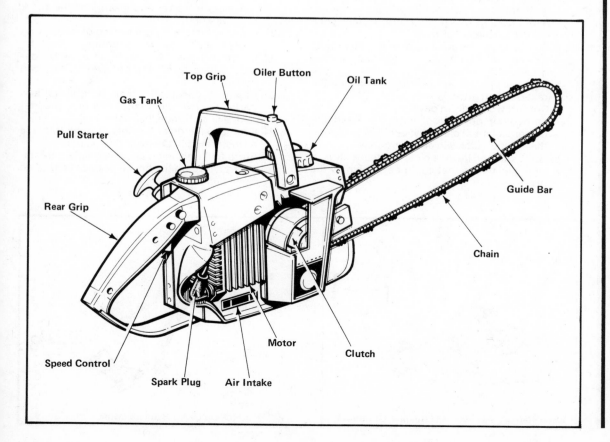

Top Grip
Oiler Button
Oil Tank
Gas Tank
Pull Starter
Rear Grip
Guide Bar
Chain
Speed Control
Motor
Clutch
Spark Plug
Air Intake

Switch From Gas To Electric

If maintaining a gasoline-powered chain saw is too much for you or if you can't stand fumes, check out the lightweight electric chain saw from Sears. Its one-horsepower motor drives the chain over an eight-inch laminated steel bar. Double insulated for safety, the Sears chain saw weighs only nine pounds—ideal for pruning, trimming, firewood, and many other light-duty household uses. You'll find it at most Sears stores and in the Sears catalog.

Gloves Are A Must For Chain Saw Work

Work gloves are advisable for many household chores, but they are a must anytime you pick up a chain saw. Boss horsehide gloves are quality products, as are the other leather work gloves from Boss. Attach a clothespin to the shop wall to hold the gloves when you're not wearing them.

Chain Saw Chains Are Easy To Replace

A chain saw chain is easy to replace. Sabre Saw Chain, Inc., markets 21 of the most popular chain saw chain sizes, and the company's display makes it a snap to get the right replacement. Just find your make and model on the chart, and then pick out the chain indicated. Complete installation instructions are on the back of the replacement chain package. On the same Sabre Saw Chain rack you'll also find a great many chain saw accessories: files, depth gauges, chain breakers, etc.

Outdoors

Flying Debris Poses Big Danger

Objects resting on the grass when you mow can be picked up by the mower and thrown out with great force. If you have a rotary mower, you might want to consider installing a replacement blade called the Safe-T-Disc. It completely covers the underside of the mower housing and features suction cups opposite each blade. These cups capture all the grass (or anything else the blade picks up) and suck it above the disc; from there, the only place the grass and debris can go is into the grass bag. The Safe-T-Disc is also designed to keep your feet from coming into contact with the blade. If your mower or lawn tool dealer does not carry the Safe-T-Disc, contact the M-P Corporation, 6466 Chene Street, Detroit, Michigan 48211.

Cleanliness Means Safety

Police your yard before you mow to ensure that no rocks, toys, cans, bones, or other solid litter that could be thrown out to hurt someone are present. This is especially necessary before the first mowing in the spring. A grass rake makes the job easy because the fingers are so loose that the rake doesn't miss much. The McGuire Bamboo Lawn rake is well made, with bamboo fingers supported by a metal clip and metal spiral. The grip distributes the pressure equally so that each tooth or finger meets the ground without strain; the spiral lets the teeth operate over uneven ground without breakage. McGuire rakes, made by the George W. McGuire Company, Inc., are available in several sizes.

Grass Catcher Bags Also Catch Flying Missiles

Even if you don't care about cut grass flying back over the lawn, you should always operate your mower with the grass bag in place because it also catches dangerous flying objects. If your old grass bag has worn out, get a replacement. Arnold replacement bags fit just about every mower made, and are made to meet or exceed all safety standards. Arnold bags, made of heavy-duty, 16-ounce polyester material that

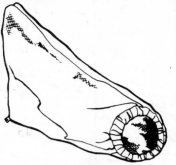

is mildew-proof and rot-resistant, are available at hardware stores and home centers.

Yard Tool Safety

EVERY YEAR many needless accidents are caused by yard tools. Most of these accidents are caused by power tools such as lawn mowers and trimmers. While we will stress the safety rules for power equipment, remember that any tool can do damage if improperly or carelessly used. As with tools for the shop, keep in mind that a dull tool is more dangerous than a properly sharpened tool. Here are some general operating practices that will help you make it safely through the yard.

1. Visually inspect all tools and equipment for defects.
2. Wear safe clothes. Do not wear loose fitting clothes that could get caught in moving parts. Protect arms and legs. Wear heavy leather shoes. Wear safety goggles.
3. Avoid getting overheated and protect your head from the hot sun.
4. Do not allow any adult to operate the mower without your instruction. Never allow children to operate a mower.
5. Never use a plug-in electric mower in the rain or when grass is wet.
6. Do yard work only in daylight.
7. Know your power tool controls. Read the owner's manual carefully. Learn how to stop the engine quickly in an emergency.
8. Make sure the lawn is clear of sticks, stones, wire, and debris that could be thrown by the blade.

Store Gasoline In Special-Purpose Can

It is very important that gasoline for your power mower be stored in a gasoline can, not in some container that you just happen to have around. The Delphos one-gallon gas can has all the safety features such a container should have, including a bright red paint job with yellow letters proclaiming its contents as "Gasoline." The New Delphos Manufacturing Company makes other galvanized products, including larger gasoline cans and metal funnels.

9. Disengage clutches and shift into neutral before starting the motor.
10. Start the engine carefully and keep your feet well away from the blades when starting and operating the machine.
11. Never leave a starter in the cocked position. This refers to starters using a heavy spring which is crank wound and then released for starting.
12. Do not race the engine or alter governor settings. Excessive speed is dangerous and shortens mower life.
13. Never add gasoline to a running engine.
14. Do not add gasoline to a hot machine.
15. Keep children, pets, and others a good, safe distance away.
16. Stop the engine whenever you leave a power tool, even for a moment.
17. Stop the engine before pushing a mower across drives, walks, or roads.
18. On slopes or wet grass, be extra careful of your footing.
19. Never cut grass by pulling the mower towards you.
20. If any cutting tool strikes a solid object, check the blade for damage. If it is a power tool, cut the power and disengage the spark plug wire first.
21. Never adjust the height setting of the cutting blade while the mower is running.
22. Do not work on the engine in a closed garage where carbon monoxide fumes can collect.
23. Regularly check all fasteners, guards, and parts. Follow the manufacturer's maintenance and storage instructions.
24. Keep all shields and safety devices in place as instructed in the owner's manual.
25. Store fuel only in an approved safe container, and never in the house or near heat or an open flame.

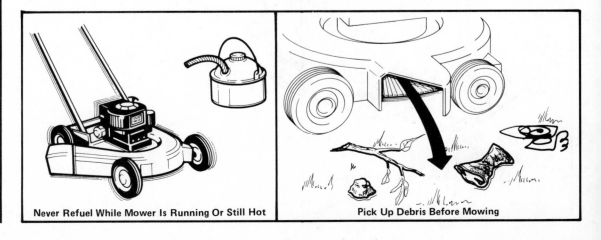

Never Refuel While Mower Is Running Or Still Hot   Pick Up Debris Before Mowing

Build Your Own Redwood Greenhouse Dome

The most popular type of outbuilding is the greenhouse, and complete kits are now available that let you build your own. The Redwood Dome certainly is an economical and functional greenhouse. Redwood is a very durable wood that resists rot, mildew, and insects. The kit from Redwood Domes comes with all parts pre-cut to precision tolerances.

Each wooden member is color coded to prevent construction errors, and the frame can be covered with fiberglass, polyvinyl, or polyethylene according to your choice. All Redwood Domes are ready for assembly with only a few household tools. The complete kit—available in a number of sizes—includes frame, door frame, door, vents, all hardware, covering, heavy ground-level sill, and illustrated instructions. For more information, write to Redwood Domes, P.O. Box 666, Aptos, California 95003.

Cluster Sheds Can Be Outbuildings Or Home Additions

Cluster Shed, Inc., offers a unique way to put up a separate building or to add onto your home. The company's frame package includes basic framing of 6x6-foot timbers that are mortised and tenoned and dovetailed; the framing is held together with oak pegs. The rafters and collar ties are 4x6s. The rafters are secured with 10-inch spikes, and wedges are furnished to tighten the joints. Roofing and siding packages —which include insulation— are also available, but you can buy everything you need in one complete kit as well. The idea of the separate kits is that you can construct your outbuilding or addition in segments as your budget permits. Cluster Sheds are available in four sizes and make ideal poolside cabanas, workshops, garden tool houses, or finished rooms. Easy and fun to put up (you only need one helper), the Cluster Shed frame can be erected in less than a day. If you cannot locate a dealer, write to Cluster Shed, Inc., Hartland, Vermont 05048.

Have A Greenhouse In Your Yard In Less Than One Hour

The incredible walk-in mini-greenhouse, called the Casa Mini, can be assembled in about 50 minutes without a single tool, bolt, screw, nut, or nail required. The tubular plastic frame snaps together, as does the vinyl covering. Four redwood slat tables are included with the Casa Mini. A larger modular version is available; you can keep adding to it to make your greenhouse as long as you wish. If your hardware or garden dealer doesn't carry these products, contact Casaplanta, 16129 Cohasset Street, Van Nuys, California 91406.

Outbuildings

THERE WAS A time when the term "outbuildings" referred to the barn, the chicken house, or the outhouse. Gradually, the need for such outbuildings disappeared for urban and suburban homeowners, but recently these additional structures have enjoyed a resurgence of popularity. The new breed of outbuildings—greenhouses, cabanas, tool sheds, workshops, studios, etc.—is more oriented to leisure and hobby activities than to the purely functional purposes of the barn, chicken house, and outhouse.

Whatever your needs in an outbuilding, here are some things to consider in buying or building one.

1. Consider whether you want to build the outbuilding yourself, have someone else build it, or whether you wish to buy one already built or in kit form.
2. No matter what you decide about building or buying, be sure to check the local building code. There may be all sorts of restrictions as to height, purpose, position with relation to property line, and even regarding the building materials and construction techniques you may employ. It would be a shame to have to raze a building soon after you finish it.
3. Even a small tool shed must be planned. Whether you draw up the plans or have them drawn, you need to know exactly what the finished structure will look like and whether it will accommodate all that you wish to place inside. Check out the space by creating scale versions of all the furnishings that will go in the building.
4. Make a complete list of all the materials you will need. Even if you are buying a building in kit form, you may need to supply your own foundation, bracing, wiring, or other parts and materials.
5. Make sure that you have the tools, time, talent, and helpers necessary to do the job before you begin.

Next comes a most important decision: selection of the site. Keep these factors in mind when deciding where to erect your new outbuilding.

△1. The site you choose must comply with the local building code.
△2. Never position a new outbuilding in the middle of a depression where water drains away from the house. Pick a rise, instead. You don't want to wake up one morning to discover that your outbuilding has floated back even farther behind your house.
△3. Pick a spot that gives you easy access into the building. Can you get inside without having to vault a hedge or ruin a flower bed? If your outbuilding is intended primarily for storage, will you be able to move its contents in and out easily?
△4. If you must excavate for a foundation, are you certain that there are no pipes or utility lines underground that could be damaged? In addition, think about the roots of valuable trees that could be torn up by your digging.
△5. Evaluate how easy and economical it will be to run power and plumbing lines to the new buildings. Sometimes, the proper choice of location can save you hundreds of dollars in utility expenditures.
△6. Ask yourself whether the outbuilding will be attractive enough that you won't mind looking at it from inside the house. A utility shed is probably best placed in a corner, well out of view.

The planning you do before you install an outbuilding in your backyard will pay off in years of enjoyment after the new greenhouse, tool shed, workshop, etc., becomes a reality.

Put A Barn In Your Back Yard

Need more storage space? Want to enliven your back yard? You can accomplish both in short order with the Jer 'Lil' Red Barn. Available in a kit and ready to be assembled without requiring any special tools or skills, the barn-in-a-carton comes with precision-cut frame and trim pieces all numbered to match simple step-by-step building instructions. Door hardware is included. The building supplies dealer who delivers your kit adds exactly the quantities and sizes of all finishing materials needed; this would include plywood siding, roofing shingles, and nails according to your specifications. All you supply is the hammer, saw, screwdriver, metal snips, paint, and brush—and some of your time and energy.

Outdoors

Indoor/Outdoor Carpet Beautifies Concrete Patio

By adding indoor/outdoor carpet you make your patio seem more like an outdoor room than just a concrete slab. Fix the carpet in place with a waterproof adhesive like Durabond Exterior Carpet Adhesive from United States Gypsum. Very fast setting, Durabond Adhesive takes only 15 to 25 minutes to set, even in very humid weather. It can also be applied in temperatures of from 40 to 100

degrees with good results. Use Durabond Exterior Carpet Adhesive when installing any outdoor carpet over concrete, asphalt, or wood.

Patio Windbreak Cures Wind Or Sun Problems

If you have a patio that suffers from either a wind or sun problem, a roll-around windbreak may solve it. A colorful striped canvas windbreak can be fashioned by attaching the material to an aluminum frame. Flaps and locking casters help keep the windbreak in place. The American Canvas Institute offers complete information on using canvas to solve summer heat problems.

Drive Concrete Screws Without Drilling

You can fasten anything to concrete with Helyx Concrete Screws. No drilling is required; they can be driven just like nails, but they hold like screws. Use Helyx Concrete Screws where you would previously have thought about some sort of expansion bolt or anchor, but be sure to observe the proper safety precautions when installing these fasteners in concrete. Helyx Concrete Screws are made by the Hillwood Manufacturing Company, makers of all sorts of nail and tack products.

Anchor Patio Posts And Railings With Wej-Its

There are several methods of anchoring posts or railings to your new concrete patio. Perhaps the easiest way is with Wej-Its, expansion bolts that require but three installation steps. With the fixture in place, you drill a hole the same diameter and length as the bolt. Then you tap in the Wej-It. Finally, you turn the bolt head with a wrench, causing the Wej-It anchoring mechanism to lock both it and the fixture firmly to the concrete. Wej-Its come in 12 sizes to take care of any and all anchoring problems. They are the creation of Wej-It Corporation, a subsidiary of Allied Products Corporation.

A Placer Does It Faster

The Concrete Placer, a big 19½x4-inch tool from the Goldblatt Tool Company, does a faster job than either a shovel or rake for grading, smoothing, spreading, or placing concrete. Made of 14-gauge steel, its all-welded construction means there are no rivets to come loose. It makes quick work of those big concrete placement projects.

Pouring a Patio

THERE IS NOTHING you can do to your back yard other than adding a pool that will give the family as much satisfaction as a patio. However, if you have priced a patio installation job recently, then you know that it is not cheap. Maybe you think it is a little too much of a project to undertake on your own. After all, a 15 x 18-foot patio represents a lot of mixing, spreading and finishing, and if you happen to run into a snag that slows you down, who is going to slow down the hardening of the concrete?

If you only had to mix, pour, and finish a 3-foot square patio, that would be much easier. What we have in mind is a 15 x 18-foot patio that is poured and finished 3 square feet at a time. This way, you can do one square and quit for the day or do as many as you feel like. This patio is even going to have some advantages over a concrete slab poured all in one piece. Here is how it goes:

1. Lay out your patio. Use boards or a garden hose or something to outline it to see if the shape and size are what you have in mind. A garden hose is great if you plan any curved edges. Another good idea is to gather all the patio furniture, the grill, and as many neighbors as you can muster up into the patio area to be sure that the size will accommodate all the equipment and people the first time you have a party.
2. Once the size and shape are decided upon, excavate. Dig down deep enough for the slab if you want it even with the ground, plus about a 4-inch bed of compacted sand and/or gravel. In most cases, omitting the bed can result in shifting, which causes cracks. The thickness of the patio should be about 4 inches. Also, the patio should slope away from the house at a rate of about ⅛-inch per foot.
3. When the excavation is done, smooth away any clods and compact the ground with a tamper. Next, put in the bed of sand or aggregate. If you use aggregate, it can be gravel, crushed stone, or a mixture of sand and gravel. It must be tamped down thoroughly.
4. If you use sand, wet the sand with a mist from your garden hose and tamp it some more. The more compacted the base is, the better your patio will stand up.

Here Is What You Will Need

Materials

- Sand or gravel
- Reinforcing steel
- Redwood or cedar lumber for inside forms
- 2x4s for outside forms
- Nails
- Cement
- Container for cement

Tools

- Level
- Shovel
- Tape measure
- Tamper
- Garden hose
- Saw
- Hammer
- Cement edger

5. You are now ready to put down the reinforcing steel. For this type of patio, you can use welded wire fabric which can be bought in rolls. Many patios are poured with no reinforcing steel, and with this type of patio, you could get by without it. However, your patio will last longer with it.
6. Now you are ready to build your forms. The idea is for the forms to create three foot squares over the entire surface. The wood within the body of the patio stays in place. The outside forms will be removed. The inside forms should be of redwood, cedar or treated lumber that will resist decay. The outside forms can be whatever you have around; 2x4s work best. This means your concrete will actually be the 3⅝-inch thickness of the forms. For the members that will stay in place, they should be notched where they cross. They should also be nailed at each joint. Use lumber that will extend the length of the patio so these pieces will be whole. Nails sticking out in between the joints help keep the concrete and divider strips always level.
7. Once the frame is in place, together and fastened to the outside forms, check to be sure that the slope has been maintained.
8. The patio is now ready for the concrete. Each square should take about 63 pounds of cement (two-thirds of a bag), about 2½ times as much sand and 3½ times as much gravel. Measure the cement in a container and mark it. Then use the marked container to measure out the desired quantity of the

Plan A Weekend Project With Weekender Tools

Weekender brand concrete finishing tools answer the problem of finding professional tools at do-it-yourself prices. The Weekender Cement Trowel and the Weekender Concrete Edger, tools you might use in a patio project, are both made of tempered steel with the feel and features found in professional models. Look for Weekender tools wherever do-it-yourself concrete supplies are sold.

Mix In Some Color

If you want color in your concrete, mix in Far-Go Cement Colors from Dry Mix Concrete Company. These fine powders are added to the mix along with the other ingredients; they can also be used with pre-mixes. Be sure to follow coloring directions carefully because it's difficult to tell what the final color or tone will be until after the concrete is cured. Mixing with white portland cement results in brighter colors.

Another dry color process is called the dry-shake method. The powder is sprinkled over the wet surface, and a float carries the color into the slab. Colorundum Dry-Shake Colors are made by the A.C. Horn division of the Dewey & Almy Chemical Company.

Step 3

Bed Of Sand
Patio
Wire Mesh

Step 5

Step 6

Steps 6 and 7

Aluminum Patio Roof Throws Heat Back

The all-aluminum patio roof, part of Alcan Aluminum Corporation's Leisure Room Line, is available in various sizes and with a choice of baked enamel colors. Alcan Leisure rooms are designed for adding on later. Start with the cover, and add glass or screen wall components later to make a closed room.

Patio Fountain Is A Special Addition

Rain Jet's Shower of Diamonds fountain creates jewel-like patterns of rotating water droplets. The unusual hanging fountain, an ideal patio wall addition, is lighted by its own underwater spotlight and has a built-in recirculating pump. If you wish to create your own fountain setting, Rain Jet Fountain Heads are available for you to hook up to your own pump.

other ingredients. Mix only enough for a square at a time. Be sure to run an edger around both the outside edges and along the forms to be left in. Do as few or as many squares as you like, but be sure that you let each square have its complete curing time.

The wooden dividers have helped make this an easier chore by letting you do a little at a time. They will also make the patio look better, and more importantly, they will act as expansion joints to keep the squares from cracking when temperatures cause expansion.

Outdoors

Fiberglass Patio Roofs Come Striped

Corrugated fiberglass panels represent a popular way to roof patios. Now, Filon has taken fiberglass roofing panels one step further with colorful stripes in both ribbed and corrugated configurations. The light-diffusing color stripes produce a light and airy effect. Filon fiberglass panels can be installed easily by any do-it-yourselfer. A free folder with planning ideas and how-to instructions is available at Filon dealers. Filon is a division of Vistron Corporation.

Enhance Your Patio With Petrified Forest Stepping Stones

Enjoy the natural charm and beauty of wood along with the permanence of stone. Coronado's Petrified Forest Stepping Stones are produced by casting concrete into molds made from actual tree sections. Each stone has all the details of a real tree—bark, age rings, and cracks; the coloring is very woodlike, too. The pieces come in three sizes and can be used as a walk or for a complete patio. In fact, there are many ways to use these unique pieces from Coronado Products.

Prevent Weeds From Growing Between The Bricks

Plastic sheets placed under the mortarless patio can prevent weeds from growing up through the cracks. Warp's Carry-Home Coverall six-mil black (or clear) polyethylene makes a good weed shield. It comes in convenient packages of 20x25-foot sheets, although the same material is also available in 20x50-foot sheets of four-mil thickness. This sheeting also serves well as a covering over new concrete to prevent drying during the curing period, as a protective tarp, and as a moisture barrier. Coverall is a product of Warp Brothers, makers of many plastic household goods.

Building a Mortarless Patio

PLENTY OF PEOPLE would like to have a brick patio, but they shy away from building one due to the challenge of mortaring the bricks together. What would you say if someone told you that you could build a patio without any mortar? The following procedure will produce a long-lasting patio that has proven itself for many homeowners, and the ease with which you can make it will boggle your mind.

Regarding the bricks to use, the only thing of which you must make certain is that the bricks are SW (severe weathering) grade. Beyond the grade, only your personal taste and the availability of bricks in your area will dictate what you get. Since the bricks will be walked on, you should consider a darker shade that will show less dirt. Used brick is fine if you can locate what you want at a wrecking yard.

Pick out the spot where you want the patio to go, and make a rough layout with boards to see if the shape looks about right. You can estimate how many bricks you need just by determining the square footage. Since there are no mortar joints in this patio all you have to do is measure the brick and see how many it will take to equal the square footage you measured. Now you can build your new patio.

1. The first step is always the hardest. In this case, it is time to do the excavation. You need to dig down far enough to accommodate the thickness of the brick, plus a two-inch bed of sand. At the same time, you must keep water run-off in mind. Therefore, slope the area you are digging. The slope should be about a quarter inch per foot.
2. You should have a border around the perimeter of the patio to prevent bricks along the edge from sloughing off. You can elect either to stand the bricks on edge or to construct a redwood border. Whichever one you choose, dig a trench around the perimeter to accommodate the border plus a two-inch bed of sand.
3. Pour in the sand and tamp it down completely. When you get through, the compacted layer should be two inches thick. Dampen the sand as you tamp, but use only the fine spray adjustment on the garden hose nozzle.
4. At this stage, many people like to put down vapor barrier plastic sheets to prevent weeds from growing through their patios.
5. Put down your border for two sides of the patio only. If you are using bricks for your

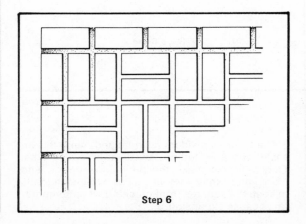

Step 6

Here Is What You Will Need

Materials

- SW grade bricks
- Wooden boards
- Redwood
- Sand
- Plastic sheet
- Nails
- Stakes
- Dry cement
- Measuring tape

Tools

- Shovel
- Garden hose
- Hammer
- Broom

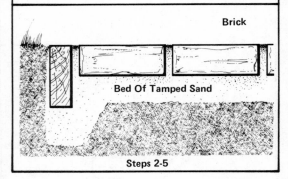

Steps 2-5

border, merely butt them end to end as you lay them on edge. Some people mortar the border, but you do not have to do so. If you are using redwood or another rot resistant wood for your border, just make a 2x4 frame by nailing the corners together in a butt joint. If stakes are necessary, put them on the outside and below the surface so that you can cover them.

6. Start laying the bricks from the corner, and work outward to cover the entire area. Use any pattern that you like, butting the bricks against the border and against each other as you go. If you notice any uneven places, take up the brick and either tamp in more sand or take some away to level the area.
7. After you lay all the bricks, you can install the other borders. By waiting until then, you make certain that the border will be as close as possible to the patio itself.
8. Now take handfuls of dry sand, scatter them over the patio, and sweep back and forth. The sand will go into and fill the cracks between the bricks.
9. Adjust your garden hose nozzle to its fine mist setting and spray the entire patio. The water will cause the sand to wash on down into the crack and out of sight.
10. When the surface is dry, repeat the sand treatment, sweeping and then spraying.
11. Next, mix dry cement to three parts sand. Sweep the mixture into the cracks and spray mist it down as you did the sand.

That is all there is to it. You now have yourself a patio that will last for many, many years. If you ever notice any areas that start to sink or if you spot a damaged brick, you can replace or repair such areas (even an individual brick) easily. Just take up the low or damaged bricks, add and tamp the sand underneath, and put the old bricks or their replacements back in the patio. Then, all that remains is to follow steps 8 through 11—but just for that area. Incidentally, you can use the same technique to render a quick but beautiful brick walkway.

Have A Pow-Wow On Your Patio

A somewhat different portable grill called the Pow-Wow, consists of a circular fire bowl with a barbecue grate, safety screen enclosure, and top-mount spark screen. Its shape makes the Pow-Wow a focal point on the patio. Big enough to be an impressive piece of yard furniture, the Pow-Wow—a unique idea from Hearth Craft—is small enough for easy moving and storage.

Outdoor Cookers Need Special Paint

To withstand the heat from your charcoal or gas fire, your outdoor cooker must be painted with a special formula like Zynolyte 1000F Hi-Temp. It's a self-priming spray paint that forms a flame-proof coating able to withstand temperatures over 1000 degrees F. It comes in six colors and can be used in many high heat situations. Of course, Zynolyte 1000F Hi-Temp is highly flammable before it dries.

Cook Outdoors Over Newspapers

You may not believe this, but you can cook a steak in six to eight minutes over four or five sheets of yesterday's newspaper crumpled into balls about the size of grapefruits. All you need is a Swaniebraai Newspaper Grill. Actually, the newspaper is the wick while the fat from the meat is the fuel. Although it seems mysterious, it works. Safe and cool and easy to light, no need for lighter fuel or briquets, the Swaniebraai Newspaper Grill cools in minutes. A most unusual device, it is made by Princess Winona Products, Inc.

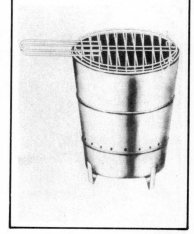

Building an Outdoor Cooker

THERE ARE SO many possibilities in design and types of barbeque grills that we would be hard pressed to come up with one that would be just what you wanted. What follows are some general guidelines to help you create a grill best suited for your needs.

If you decide to build a permanent barbeque grill, you can use stone, brick, or concrete block as the medium. If you already have a patio, you may wish to build on the edge of the patio surface. This precludes having to make a foundation or base for the grill. However, if it will take away too much from the space on the patio, extend it beyond the patio by providing a reinforced slab as a base. Put a bed of sand and/or gravel under the slab. Here are some things to consider when building a permanent outdoor cooker.

1. Be sure you check your local building codes before you build your barbeque grill.
2. Block out the cooker using bricks to outline its actual shape to be sure it does not stick out too far on to the patio. If it takes up too much of the patio, now is the time to move it, not after it is built.
3. Position the grill so that it will not be a smoke maker for the people on the patio.
4. If you do not want it to be adjacent to a patio, extend your slab out far enough in front of the grill to provide sufficient standing room.
5. When building the grill, you may want to think about adding a countertop for food preparation, a sink, and cabinet space for charcoal, starter, and cooking utensils. Now would also be the time to add underground wiring if you want electricity in the grill area.
6. If you are going to use the unit to gain privacy, put in a chimney. Most grills are more pleasant with a chimney anyway. Be sure the chimney top does not interfere with the house or trees.
7. Plan out the grill so that it is at a comfortable working level. The rule of thumb is around 32 to 34 inches, but you can make it higher or lower to meet your needs. The space under the firebox can be used as storage space with or without cabinet doors.
8. The firebox should be lined with firebrick. This is true whether you build your unit of brick, stone, or block. In working with firebrick, you do not soak them as you do other bricks. Try to use as small a mortar joint as you can. Use firebrick for the sides as well as for the bed.

9. Make the cooking area and firebox as large as you think you will ever need. For small meals, you can build your fire to one side. If you buy a metal grill, the size must conform to your specifications.
10. Reinforce the firebox underneath with steel rods that span the width with 3 to 4 inches to spare on each side. Space these about every 4 inches.
11. Provide for a cleanout door at the back, if possible. You can buy metal cleanout door units that can be set in place.
12. From a cleaning standpoint, it is best to have a grate that is removable, although some people set rods in mortar for this purpose.
13. Do not paint grills or grates that come in contact with food. Other metal parts, however, can be painted with high heat paint.

After the cooker is finished, keep it clean and watch for any cracks in the masonry. These should be repaired as soon as possible so they do not get bigger. Treat stains on this as you would on other brick, stone, or block structures.

Here Is What You Will Need

Materials

- Stone, brick, or concrete block
- Sand and/or gravel
- Cement slab
- Firebrick
- Mortar
- Metal grill
- Steel rods

Tools

- Tape measure
- Trowel

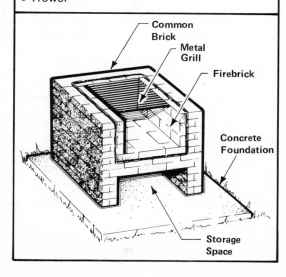

Common Brick — Metal Grill — Firebrick — Concrete Foundation — Storage Space

This Grill Is A Real Gas

Gas cooking has now moved outside, providing a much cleaner and easier way to have a cookout than grilling over charcoal. The Temco Regency Twin gas grill features a dual "X" burner with two infinite range heat controls, permitting you to cook two different dishes that require different heats. Or, you can warm on one side and cook on the other. Since the handle is on the side, you can avoid burning your fingers if there's a flare-up when you open the lid. The die-cast aluminum housing is rust-free and durable, as are the stainless steel burners and grids. You can get other Temco gas grills with a permanent mount post, on a patio stand, or on a portable cart.

Outdoors

Beautify Your Pool's Coping

The snap-on coping system called Nerak from GFA Products is made of Tenite Polyethylene from the Eastman Chemical Products Division of Eastman Kodak. It is resistant to weathering, chemicals, or freezing and is easily cleaned with regular household cleaners. After you fasten the mounting plates to the pool edge (simple hand tools are all you need) you can then snap the coping securely in place. Nerak coping sections come in various widths in straight, curved, and corner sections. Not only a beautifier, Nerak coping is also valuable as a safety measure in preventing poolside slips.

Pool Paint Must Be Special

With the constant exposure to water and chemicals, any paint used for the inside of a swimming pool must be quite special. There are several pool paints on the market. Pratt & Lambert's Pool Shield is a synthetic rubber based, alkali-resistant flat pool paint. As with any paint project, painting a pool demands that you follow directions. Remember that once you refill a pool, there's no opportunity for touch-ups. Wait at least 24 hours between painting and refilling for the paint to set up fully. Pool Shield comes in White, Swimming Pool Blue, and Swimming Pool Green; it is generally stocked by Pratt & Lambert paint dealers.

Baking Soda Belongs In Your Pool

Maintaining the proper pH level is very important in pool care. You may not believe it, but regular household baking soda will raise the pH if it's too low, and lower it if it's too high. Once you get the right pH, put in a pound of baking soda for each 10,000 gallons of water every week and you'll never have a pH problem again. Baking soda also helps clarify the water. It allows minute particles that are not trapped by your filter to attach themselves to larger particles. Soon your pool water will be sparklingly clean. If you'd like a folder on what baking soda can do for your pool, send a self-addressed stamped envelope to "The Baking Soda Common Sense Guide To Swimming Pool Care," Church & Dwight Company, Inc. (makers of Arm and Hammer Baking Soda), 2 Pennsylvania Plaza, New York, NY, 10001.

Swimming Pool Care

WITHOUT TRYING to make you a chemist, we will try to tell you what you can do to your swimming pool to keep it pretty and free from algae and bacteria. Without proper care, water in the pool can create a health hazard, become cloudy, turn green, smell bad, stain the pool, and ruin equipment. Keeping the pool water in good condition is easy, but requires almost daily effort.

The effort is not all that great, but unless you make it a regular habit, you will have problems. The keys to sparkling blue water are (1) filtration, (2) testing, (3) treating, and (4) cleaning. Here is what they mean:

1. Filtration. A clean, properly working filter is a must. The pump motor is the heart of the filter. It can run 24 hours a day for months on end and not wear out for years. It requires only a small amount of maintenance. Most are sealed and require no oiling. They do have to be kept free of leaves, weeds, and vines. Anything that covers the grids can cause overheating which can cause burned

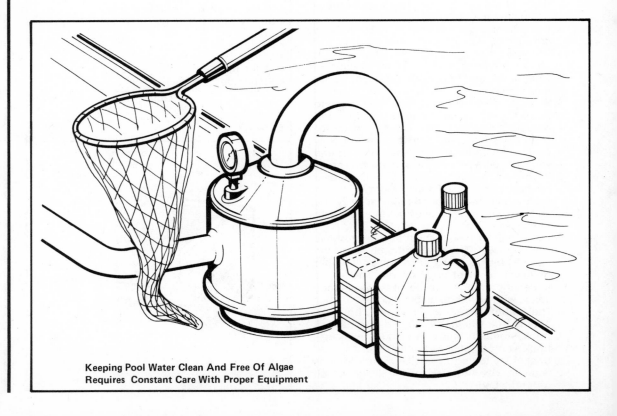

Keeping Pool Water Clean And Free Of Algae Requires Constant Care With Proper Equipment

Carpet Your Cracked Deck From A Can

If your pool deck is cracked, you should know about the spread-on material that can cover and fill those cracks. En-DUR-LON, a rubber-based material which winds up looking like a carpet, can be troweled on or applied with a roller. It requires no elaborate preparation. Just remove all dirt, grease, and oil. It usually requires two coats. In addition to covering concrete decks, En-DUR-LON can be applied to such surfaces as wood, metal, resilient flooring, and even ceramic tile. It produces a surface that will not rot or mildew, is easy to clean, and is slip-resistant for greater safety around the pool. A product of the W.J. Ruscoe Company and generally found at floor covering outlets. En-DUR-LON comes in green, gray, black, blue, and tile red.

Clean Out Leaves The Easy Way

If you have trees around your pool, then you know what a chore it is to get the leaves out. Fight the battle with a Jandy Leaf-Master. The Leaf-Master hooks to your garden hose, and when you turn the water on, it picks up leaves from the bottom of the pool and deposits them in the mesh bag. Not like the pool-cleaning vacuum that gets clogged with leaves easily, the Leaf-Master can be inverted to act as a quick surface skimmer for floating leaves. Your pool supply dealer most likely handles the Jandy Leaf-Master.

Deck Coping Seam Must Be Filled

Cracks that develop between the coping and the deck must be filled or else additional problems will plague your swimming pool. Dry Mix Concrete Company puts out a product called Krac-Kalk that is quite effective because it expands and contracts in response to temperature changes. Available in a cartridge for use with a caulking gun, Krac-Kalk demands little in terms of preparation; just clean the seam to be filled and be sure the surfaces are dry. For swim-

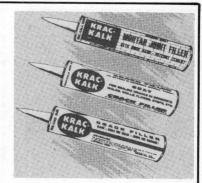

ming pool work, the gray-colored Krac-Kalk looks best.

out bearings. A pump motor will last longer if it has a cover over it. The cover should not be one that would restrict the flow of air, but one that would keep rain out, and more important keep hot summer sun from heating the housing to excess temperatures. Frozen bearings can be replaced, but unfortunately not by the homeowner, in most cases. Removal requires a bearing puller. Often it is better to buy a new motor if the old one is too old, because new bearings may not carry a warranty. A new motor will probably be guaranteed for a year. If you can take the motor in for repairs, it will cost much less than if you have someone come out to get it. Back to filtration. During the swimming season, check daily to see if you need to backwash. It is better to over filter than to not filter enough. Running the motor 24 hours a day is recommended by many experts.

2. Testing. Test every day during the season. You must get a test kit that will give you measurements of pH and chlorine. It is better if you can also test alkalinity. The term pH is the measure of acidity vs alkalinity. A high reading is too much alkaline, and low is too much acid. Over 7.8 is high and causes chlorine to lose effectiveness. Under 7.2 is low and causes irritation to the eyes, and may result in corrosion and filter deterioration. With a reading between 7.2 and 7.8 and regular maintenance, you can avoid pool problems.

3. Treating. To raise pH, you add soda ash as prescribed to bring it back to 7.2. Oddly enough, plain old baking soda will raise or lower the pH. It raises it fairly fast, but lowers it very slowly. However, once you get the pH set right, a pound for each 10,000 gallons per week will usually keep it within the desired range. Additionally, baking soda improves clarity. The next test is for chlorine. If the tester says to add chlorine, always add it. If the pH is right, the chlorine will immediately go to work to kill bacteria. Keep in mind that chlorine is used up faster with hot sunshine, with algae and bacteria in the

Here Is What You Will Need

Materials
- Soda ash
- Baking soda
- Chlorine
- ph test kit
- Laundry bluing

Tools
- Vacuum cleaner
- Pole brush
- Hone or whetstone

pool, and with foreign substances in the water. Also, during the swimming season, it is good to use super chlorinate. This is the addition of three to four times the normal amount of chlorine. You should do this during heat waves, heavy swimmer loads, when you see algae, and after heavy rains and dust storms.

4. Cleaning. With the pump doing its job of filtering the water, much of your cleaning is being taken care of. However, you must check the skimmers regularly. If you do not have an automatic cleaner, you should vacuum regularly. If all you have is fine dust on the bottom of the pool, you can brush the bottom while the skimmers are closed, and much of the dust will be pulled through the bottom drain. When leaves or trash get into the pool, get them out as soon as possible to avoid stains.

These are the things that keep the water blue, clean, and safe. If you want even bluer water, add a bottle of bluing from the laundry. It does nothing to clean the water, but does give it a deeper blue color.

Rust stains on the bottom of the pool can often be eliminated with a hone or whetstone. Tie the stone to the end of the pole brush and abrade away at the stain.

Seal Pool Cracks Under Water

It's nice to know that you need not drain your pool every time a crack develops. Just apply Ruscoe's Permanent-Sealer by squeezing it directly into the crack and forcing it in as far as possible. It dries under water in about 30 minutes. Permanent-Sealer has a nitrile rubber base and will not affect swimmers. In addition to the white Permanent-Sealer in a tube, Ruscoe also makes the compound in an aluminum color. Both colors come in tubes as well as cartridges for use with a caulking gun. It is made by W. J. Ruscoe Company.

Cut Pool-Heating Costs

Pour a liquid called Heet in your pool and you automatically form an invisible thermal film blanket that helps retain pool heat and thereby saves some of the energy required to run your pool's heater. Tasteless, odorless, and harmless to both you and your pool, Heet also reduces evaporation of pool water. An ounce of Heet covers about 75 square feet of surface water area. A product of Poolmaster, Inc. (a Division of American Sanitary), Heet can be found at most pool supply outlets.

Special Tool Removes Nails From Shingles

An ingenious tool from the Brookstone Company, allows a roofer to reach in under a shingle and remove nails without tearing up the shingle. Just hook the blade on the nail and then, yank the handle sharply; the tool lops off the nail head. A one-piece,

hand-forged, high-carbon, Sheffield steel tool that will last a lifetime, it is also a great tool for clapboard repairs and any other spot where nail heads are hidden. It can reach in as far as 19 inches.

Brush On Roof Patching Compound To Stop Leaks

Instant Patch, made by the Tremco Manufacturing Company, is an asphalt asbestos roof patching compound that can be applied with a brush. An easy way to patch when you know just about where the problem is but cannot track down the hole, Instant Patch also does a fine job around flashing materials and in some gutter repairs. Many roof repairs demand the thicker type cements, but anytime that the thinner brush-on type is adequate, use Tremco's Instant Patch. You should be able to find it in hardware and paint stores. They also market Instant Patch in a cartridge.

Leaks and Repairs

ROOF LEAKS can do all sorts of damage inside your home. Fixing the leak is often an easy task, but—since leaks are very elusive—locating the leak can take forever. Water can enter at one point in your roof and follow a rafter for many feet before it drips down onto the ceiling. Sometimes a leak occurs only when the wind is blowing from one direction and with enough force to blow rain in under a broken shingle or through some crack. You frequently have to be in the attic when it is raining in order to track down the spot, but the leak may even be in a place where you cannot spot it from inside the attic, then you have to look outside—but not while the roof is wet. Look for such things as missing shingles, split shingles, loose nails, or bad flashing. Once you find the leak, mark it well so that you can know where to go to work when the roof is dry.

Assuming that you have located the leak, you are ready to make some actual repairs. The following instructions are for a wood shingle roof.

1. You can either replace a split shingle or stop the leak in the old one. If you decide not to replace the shingle, try slipping a piece of flashing under the split or inserting some asphalt roofing paper under it. First, pry up the overlapping shingle with a flat garden spade, using your foot on the handle to apply pressure. If you cannot get the patch as far back under the shingle as you think it should go, use a hacksaw blade to cut away

Here Is What You Will Need
Materials
- Flashing or asphalt roofing paper
- Asphalt roofing cement
- Shingles
Tools
- Garden spade
- Hacksaw blade
- Propane torch

any nails that are in the way. Then apply asphalt roofing cement to anchor the patch. If you need to drive new nails that leave exposed heads, put a dab of the cement over each head.

2. Replace any missing shingles as soon as you notice their absence. Pry up the overlapping shingles, saw away any nails that prevent your getting the new shingle in far enough, and use a combination of cement and nails to anchor the new shingle.

3. If the problem involves the ridge shingles, your best bet is to go to a lumberyard and buy a bundle of ridges rather than try to piece them together.

For repairs on composition roof shingles, follow these instructions.

△ 1. Asphalt shingles with curled corners can be tamed easily by putting a dab of asphalt roofing cement about the size of a quarter under each and pressing the corner down.

△ 2. You can patch many holes or rips with roofing cement. Just lift up the shingle, dab the

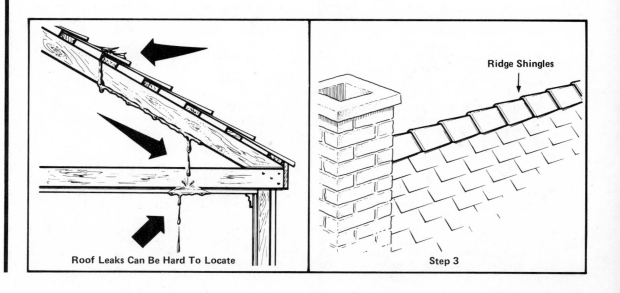

Roof Leaks Can Be Hard To Locate

Ridge Shingles

Step 3

Shingler's Hatchet Trims Wood Shingles Fast

Although it looks much like a Boy Scout hatchet, the Estwing 20-ounce shingling hatchet is designed for a specific purpose. Its thin blade is sharpened both along the regular blade edge and on the inside edge or heel. This is for trimming wooden shingles fast. The one-piece, solid steel nailing head is corrugated, and the nylon handle is cushion gripped; both are designed to hold up through many years of hard use. Anyone who plans to work with wooden shingles should have an Estwing shingling hatchet.

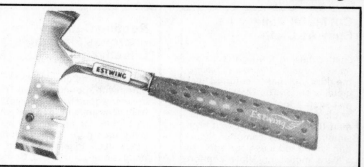

Chalk Line Keeps Shingles Straight

The chalk line is an invaluable tool for lining up rows of shingles. The reel-type chalk line, made by Evans-Aristocrat Industries, coats itself with chalk each time it is pulled out of its case. The reel is refillable with your choice of several chalk colors; blue is the most popular.

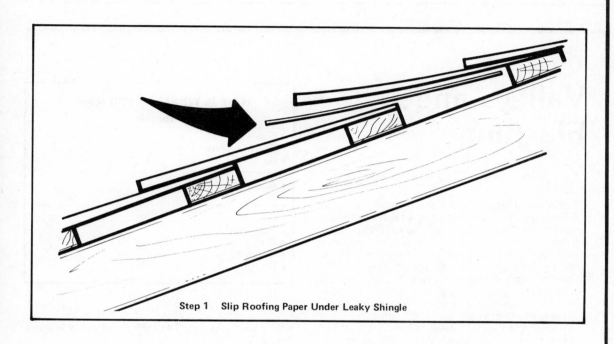

Step 1   Slip Roofing Paper Under Leaky Shingle

cement under the hole, and press the shingle back down.

△ 3. If you must replace a shingle, you can usually get to the nails holding the faulty shingle by raising the overlapping shingle. Raise it gently so as not to crack the shingle. Then loosen and remove the nails, and slip the bad section out. Put the new one in its place and renail using only two nails. Dab cement on the nail heads and on the overlapping shingle to anchor it down. You will find that warm composition shingles are much more pliable and, therefore, easier to work with. If

you cannot do your roof repair on a hot day, try running the flame from a propane torch across your shingles if they seem too brittle.

You can patch most flashing problems with asphalt roofing cement. The problem here is in locating the trouble. A gap in a flashing joint is easy to spot and easy to patch, but detecting a nearly invisible pinhole is something else again. When you see any spots that might possibly be such pinholes, cover them with cement. In addition, dab a little cement on any exposed nails in the flashing.

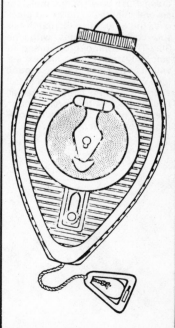

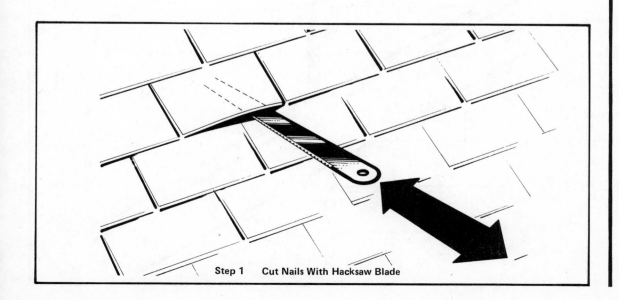

Step 1   Cut Nails With Hacksaw Blade

Roofs

Cut Metal Valleys As Easy As Cloth

Just as having the right scissors makes cutting cloth easy, having the right tool makes cutting sheet metal a snap. The Metal Wizz is just such a tool, and—best of all—it is priced for the home craftsman. Its serrated jaws keep it from slipping, and its compound cutting action reduces your effort to a bare minimum. Vinyl comfort grips make the Metal Wizz easy on your hands, and its effective safety latch is quite convenient. The Metal Wizz is made by J. Wiss & Sons, highly regarded manufacturers of all sorts of cutting tools.

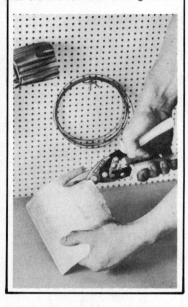

Patch Valleys With Roof Cement

If a hole develops in a valley, you can probably mend it with an asphalt roofing cement like Stay-Tite. To take care of a small hole, just squirt out the Stay-Tite and then use a putty knife or other flat tool to spread it over the hole. To patch a larger hole, cut a piece of metal to fit over the hole and then use the cement to glue the patch down. Push down on the metal for several minutes to hold it in place over the hole. After the patch has set, cover the edges with the Stay-Tite compound; spread it smoothly and remove any excess with a putty knife. It's also a good idea when installing valleys to put a dot of roofing cement over all nail heads; do this even though the nails will be covered with roofing material later on.

Roofing Cement Improves Flashing's Effectiveness

Most flashing problems can be cured with roofing cement. There are many good brands available in both cans and in the easier-to-use cartridges for application with a caulking gun. Gibson-Homans Black Jack Plastic Roofing Cement is one good brand. Cohesive as well as adhesive, it dries slowly and stays pliable so that it expands and contracts with temperature changes. In addition to sealing flashings, Black Jack Plastic Roofing Cement can be used as a general roofing patch to cover holes and hold down shingle edges. Gibson-Homans makes a variety of sealants, caulkings, and protective coatings.

Roofing Felt Underlays Valleys

Before installing metal valleys, be sure to put down roofing felt. A building paper of a strong tough base saturated with asphalt, roofing felt comes in rolls. Masonite Corporation's Roofing Division markets rolls of roofing felt 36 inches wide containing 216 square feet per roll. For valley underlayment, 30-pound felt is generally recommended.

Valleys and Flashing

Here Is What You Will Need

Materials

- Flashing
- Roofing cement
- Nails
- Mortar
- Roofing patch

Tools

- Putty knife
- Chisel
- Caulking gun
- Hammer

NO MATTER how good the shingles (or other material) and no matter how perfectly the job is done, it is impossible to get the roofing material so tightly against certain surfaces that no leaks will occur. These surfaces are where the roof line meets something like a wall or a chimney. Valleys in the roof can also lead to leaks. Therefore, these areas must be given special leak-prevention treatment and if a leak does occur, these would be the first areas to check.

To treat the problem areas where the roof line meets a wall or chimney, you apply galvanized metal, lead, copper, aluminum, or plastic flashing and then seal all joints with roofing cement or a similar compound. Roofing cement comes in ready-to-use bulk form or in cartridges for use with a caulking gun. The bulk is generally applied with a putty knife.

The following step-by-step instructions concern the replacement of flashing around a chimney, but the same general steps apply to other flashings.

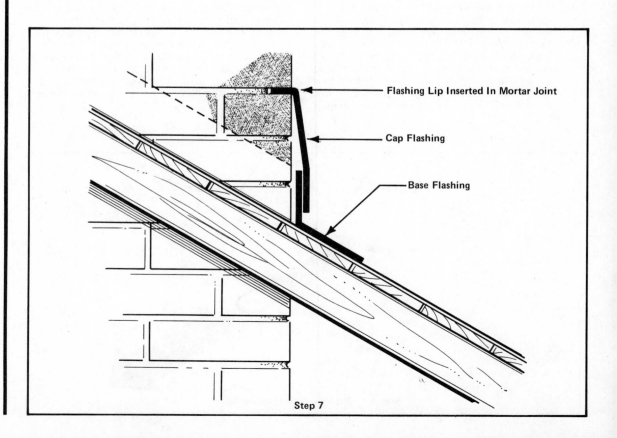

Flashing Lip Inserted In Mortar Joint

Cap Flashing

Base Flashing

Step 7

Roofs

Get Good Snips To Tailor Metal Flashing

Ridgid Metal Cutting Snips are perfect for cutting lightweight sheet metal of the type used for flashing. They operate just like a pair of scissors, with handles that can be used by right-handed or left-handed people. They also do a fine job of cutting composition roofing material, screening, wire, and flooring material. For heavier cutting, Ridgid's Aviation Snips offer compound action, a latch, and a comfortable vinyl handle.

Installing Vent Flashing Can Be A Snap

With Genova's Snap-Fit Roof Flashings, you can install flashing around vent stacks very easily. Just install the galvanized metal base (one size fits all), and then snap the neoprene collar into place. The collars—which come in three sizes to fit most roof pipe projections—create a watertight seal around the pipe, but be sure to apply asphalt roofing cement under the base to eliminate the possibility of leaks. Genova Snap-Fit Roof Flashings, available at lumberyards and plumbing supply houses, are made by Genova Products Company.

You Can Buy Aluminum Valleys In Rolls

Howmet Aluminum Corporation markets valley material in 10-foot long rolls. The material is .016 of an inch thick and comes in 14- and 20-inch widths. Since they will not rust or discolor, aluminum valleys can be left unpainted to weather to a soft gray. If your aluminum valleys come in contact with masonry or with a dissimilar metal, however, you should coat them with a bituminous paint to avoid electrolytic action between the surfaces. Moreover, you should only use aluminum nails. Attractive 5x7-inch aluminum flashing shingles as well as many other aluminum products are all available from the Building Products Division of Howmet Aluminum Corporation.

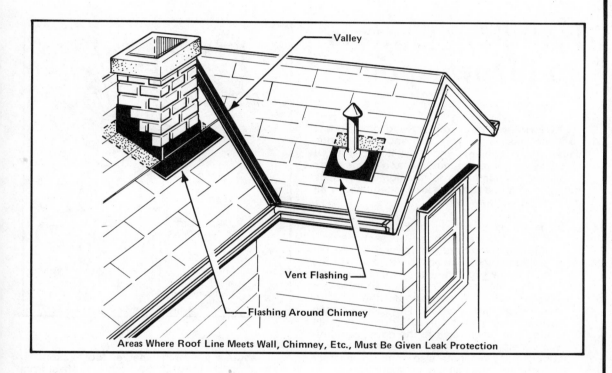

Areas Where Roof Line Meets Wall, Chimney, Etc., Must Be Given Leak Protection

1. Remove the old cap flashing (cap flashing is the outer or covering layer) that has come loose.
2. If necessary, remove the shingles around the flashing. Take care particularly with composition shingles because replacements may not be easy to find. Cautious prying can usually save shingles.
3. Remove the flashing and save it for use as a pattern.
4. Examine the base flashing to see if it needs to be replaced. If there is any doubt, replace it too, but be careful in removing it so as not to damage the roofing paper beneath it.
5. Chisel away all the old compound that held the flashing in place between the bricks.
6. Apply the front base flashing first, using liberal amounts of roofing cement to hold it in place. When nails must be used, be sure to cover nail heads with the cement. Bulk roofing cement, applied with a putty knife, is usually best for covering nails.
7. When all the base flashing is in place, replace the cap flashing, using as much of a lip going into the mortar joints as possible. This lip should be at least 1½ inches.
8. Set the cap flashing in place with either roofing cement or mortar, both of which are available in cartridges for use with a caulking gun.
9. Replace the shingles and cover all exposed

nail heads and all edges with roof cement.

Treat all vertical surfaces in this way, unless there is siding on the vertical surface. In such instances, bring the flashing up under the siding.

Pipes that stick out through the roof—such as vent pipes—must also be flashed. If the flashing around the pipes has gone bad, you can generally buy a complete flashing unit that slips over the pipe. Remove enough shingles above the vent to expose all of the old flashing, and then remove the old flashing. Slip the new unit in place and nail it down, covering all the edges and nail heads with cement. Then replace the shingles. Avoid exposed nail heads, but if they are necessary, cover them with the roofing cement.

Valleys are a different matter. Fortunately, most valley problems result from holes, and every effort should be made to patch rather than replace sections of roofing. When you locate a hole, cut a patch to fit over it and use roofing cement to hold it in place. After the patch and cement are in place, press down firmly so that there will be as little of the patch sticking up as possible. If the hole is under the shingles, pry up the shingles carefully and patch. Apply a dab of cement over all the nail heads in the valley flashing and over any exposed nails that you must drive into the shingles. Avoid exposed nail heads whenever possible.

Seal Flashing With Aluminum Tape

Flashband, a peel-and-stick self-adhesive aluminum flashing that comes in rolls, has a strong asphalt adhesive that will stick to almost any clean, dry surface of virtually all conventional building materials. Developed for professional roofers, Flashband is now available to the homeowner in rolls of two, three, six, and nine inches wide by 20 feet long. Water and air tight, it can be used to create a permanent seal around flues, chimneys, and skylights, but it also comes in a Patch Pak for smaller spot jobs. Flashband is made in England, but it is widely distributed in hardware stores and home centers in the United States by Evode Inc.

Roofs

Tape Holds Downspout Sections Together

Need a strong, smooth, self-adhesive foil tape that can hold downspout sections together and stop leaks? Arno's Aluminum Adhesive Tape will stick to almost any clean surface and is exceptional in its durability. Arno also makes a waterproof plastic-coated cloth adhesive, Ductape, that can hold sections of downspout together. It's primary use, however, is in sealing joints in heating and air conditioning ducts.

Hacksaw Cuts Guttering To Size

Although you shouldn't have to do much cutting when installing gutters and downspouts, be sure to use a good hacksaw equipped with a fine-toothed blade for whatever cutting must be done. The Millers Falls Hacksaw not only does a good job but is a pleasure to use besides. Able to handle both 10- and 12-inch blades, it has a lever tensioning device that makes blade changing quick and easy. The unbreakable tenite handle is quite comfortable, a fea-

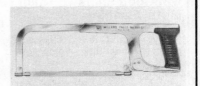

ture that is especially welcome on tougher jobs than sawing through lightweight guttering. Millers Falls is noted as a maker of quality tools, and this well-balanced hacksaw can only reinforce the company's enviable reputation.

Here's How To Win The Run-Off

A special drainage system consisting of corrugated plastic tubing and fittings is designed to carry the run-off from your downspouts away from your house to prevent seepage and consequent damage to your basement and foundation. Made by Advanced Drainage Systems, the corrugated tubing can be installed underground for appearance's sake, and there is also non-perforated tubing if you wish to carry the run-off into a dry well or out to the street. Be sure that such an installation complies with local building codes before you start digging.

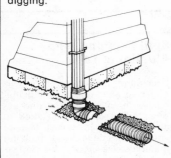

Consider The Advantages Of Aluminum Gutters And Downspouts

Lightweight aluminum gutters are very durable, and since they do not rust, they are more maintenance-free than conventional galvanized units. The do-it-yourselfer should appreciate the fact that, because aluminum guttering comes in longer sections, fewer joints are involved. In addition, it's so lightweight that much of the work can be done on the ground, after which the assembled system can be raised easily into position. Reynolds Colorweld Aluminum Gutters and Downspouts come in six bake-bonded colors to harmonize with every exterior color scheme. The finish is so durable that it almost never needs repainting. Reynolds gutters and downspouts are sold through lumberyards and building supply houses.

Installing Gutters and Downspouts

NOT HAVING good gutters and downspouts can wash away your soil and your plants, cause water problems under the house, rot out parts of your home's foundation, and create other problems too numerous to mention. If you lack gutters or if those you have are inadequate, by all means put on new ones.

1. Make a sketch of the roof. From this, you can determine the number of sections you will need. Standard gutter sections are ten feet long, and each section is joined to the next with a slip connector. Where the gutter turns, there must be either an outside or inside corner. A downspout should be installed at least every 35 feet, and for each downspout you will need a drop outlet, an elbow to reach back to the house, and another elbow to carry the water away from the house. Downspouts also come in ten foot sections, and each downspout should be secured by at least two straps. A strainer should go in each downspout, and end caps go over each end of each run of guttering; end caps are made for use on right and left ends. Supports should be placed about every 36 inches. By careful planning you can avoid delays, save trips to the supplier, and cut waste to a minimum.
2. After you have purchased the materials, lay them out on the ground around the house to be sure you have everything you need.
3. Establish a chalk line so that the gutters will slant toward all downspouts at a slope of

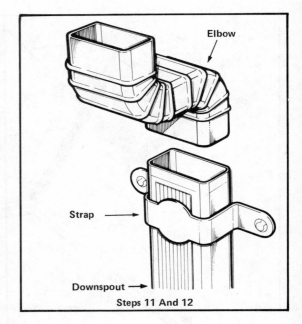

Steps 11 And 12

about a quarter inch per ten foot section.
4. Start with the end of the gutter farthest from the downspout.
5. Apply caulking to the end cap, and slip it in place.
6. Drill the holes for supports if necessary before raising the section.
7. Attach the section by installing supports every three feet; make sure that the gutter follows the chalk line.
8. Connect each section or different component with a slip connector that you have caulked along its edges.
9. If any cutting needs to be done, use a fine-toothed hacksaw and support the gutter from inside with a block of wood. File off any burrs to make installation easier.
10. Use a support on each side of a corner section.
11. When all of the guttering is up, slip elbows in place over the drop outlet.
12. Slip the downspout section in place, and install the straps near the top and bottom of the section to hold it flat against the wall. Use masonry nails if the wall is brick or concrete.
13. Attach elbows to the bottom of the downspout to lead water away from the house. Use as many extensions as are required, and pour concrete splash blocks if necessary.

If you buy prefinished guttering, then your work is done. If it is not painted, however, you must paint it yourself—that is, unless you installed gal-

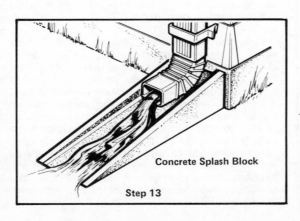

Concrete Splash Block

Step 13

Connect Downspout With Blind Rivets

Most downspout sections are first crimped and then forced together, but they are not actually fastened. As a result, they sometimes fail to hold together. You can connect them permanently, however, with the Star Blind Rivet Tool. The basic tool comes in kit form with changeable nose pieces to accommodate the four most popular rivet diameters, a generous variety of blind rivets, and a lightweight case in which to store the tool. Since it is a quick and easy way to fasten metal pieces—all work is

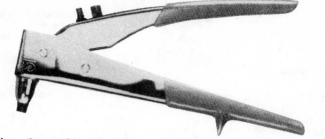

done from the outside—blind riveting has many home applications. You just drill a hole in the two sheets of metal, insert the correct size rivet in the tool, put

the other end of the rivet into the hole, and squeeze the tool's handles. The Star Blind Rivet Tool is a product of the Star Expansion Company.

Get The Right Angle From A Pro

The angle of guttering is crucial; you must make sure that it slopes enough to drain. The Pro Inclinometer and Level can handle this assignment and many more since it also acts as a square and plumb. The big four-inch dial renders fast and accurate readings. Sensitive to one half of one degree, the Pro Inclinometer and Level is housed in tough impact-resistant plastic that is not affected by heat or cold. It even has a grooved magnetized base for reading the angles of pipes or other round surfaces. It's made by the Pro Products Company, Inc.

Here Is What You Will Need
Materials
- Gutter sections
- Slip connectors
- Outside or inside corners
- Downspouts
- Drop outlets
- Elbows
- Downspout straps
- Strainers
- End caps
- Supports
- Caulking
- Chalk
- Wood block
- Masonry nails
- Concrete mix
- Zinc chromate primer
- Exterior house paint
- Asphalt roofing paint

Tools
- Hammer
- Drill
- Fine-toothed hacksaw
- File
- Paintbrushes

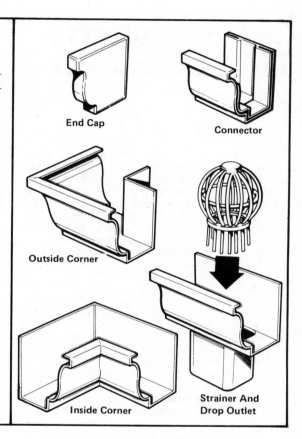

End Cap

Connector

Outside Corner

Inside Corner

Strainer And Drop Outlet

Hinged Downspout Moves Out Of Mower's Path

A clever device called Up The Downspout offers one big advantage over typical downspout extensions. It's hinged so that it can be lifted up and out of the way easily when you're mowing or edging. Long enough to carry water very far away from the house, Up The Downspout attaches to your old downspout extension or to any standard rain pipe. Made of high-impact polypropylene for durability, it is marketed by AAA Products Corporation.

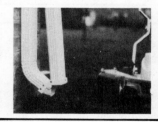

vanized metal sections. Galvanized metal does not accept paint until it has weathered for several months, and you should ask your dealer how long galvanized guttering should weather in your area

before painting. Use a zinc chromate primer to prepare gutters for painting, and then apply regular exterior house paint. Paint the insides of gutters with asphalt roofing paint.

Prepainted Guttering Saves Time And Trouble

Since galvanized metal is not the easiest material to paint, perhaps you should look into prepainted gutters. Reeves Style K Prepaint is available in all the different kinds of fittings and parts as well as in gutter and downspout sections. The Reeves five-step painting process leaves a very durable finish, but if you should happen to scratch the surface during installation, a matching white touch-up spray is available. Reeves products are from the Empire-Detroit Steel Division of the Cyclops Corporation.

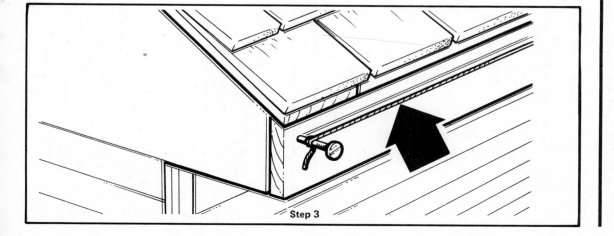

Step 3

Spray On Instant Galvanizing From A Can

If parts of your gutter and downspout system are not galvanized or have lost their galvanization to rust or corrosion, spray on LPS Instant Cold Galvanize. Not a paint, LPS Instant Cold Galvanize is 95 percent pure zinc; when applied, it generates a positive electric current that flows to the base metal. This electrochemical action fuses the zinc compound to the metal, resulting in a galvanization that equals the hot-dip process and can be relied upon for three or more years of protection. A product of LPS Research Laboratories, Inc., LPS Instant Cold Galvanize acts as a primer, should you wish to paint over it.

The Secret To Painting Inside The Downspouts

The rust that attacks downspouts often attacks from the inside. It would be great to protect the insides of downspouts with a coat of paint, but how do you get the paintbrush inside? Here's the trick that will do the job. First, you drop a string with a weight on it down through the downspout. Next, you tie a sponge to the bottom end of the string; use a sponge that must be compressed to fit inside the downspout. With the sponge in place inside the downspout, pour a quantity of paint into the downspout. Now, pull the string from the top to bring the sponge up through the downspout, spreading the paint as it moves upward. To be sure that you give the insides of your downspouts a good coating, repeat the trick after the first coat is dry.

End Leaks In Gutter Joints

You can seal end caps and joints against leaks with Stay-Tite Gutter Seal, a caulking made especially for this purpose. Available in a cartridge for use with a caulking gun, Stay-Tite Gutter Seal can be used on both galvanized steel and aluminum gutters of either the painted or unpainted variety. It can also be used for patching holes. Even though the connectors in your gutter system may seem to be watertight, take the time to caulk every joint; that way, you should never experience gutter leak problems. Stay-Tite Products Company, Inc., makes a complete line of home products, including an aerosol called Gutter Mender that can patch small holes in gutters by itself and larger holes when used in conjunction with a piece of metal window screen over the opening.

Care of Gutters and Downspouts

GUTTERS AND DOWNSPOUTS do require a little attention. Most importantly, they need to be kept clean. If the water cannot run along the gutters and pass through the downspouts, it will go over the sides and onto the ground. Gutters should always be cleaned after all the leaves have fallen in the autumn, and they may need to be checked at other times as well—depending on the type of trees you have around. For example, a mimosa tree drops blooms at one time, seed pods at another, and leaves at yet another.

1. Use a ladder that is tall enough to reach the gutters, and be sure to play it safe; move the ladder often so that you never have to reach far to either side.
2. Remove all the debris from the gutter. Use a discarded plastic plate scraper or a whisk broom to rake the leaves out of the gutter. If you clean the gutters with your hands, be sure to wear gloves.
3. Flush out the gutters with the garden hose.
4. Flush out the downspouts with the hose. If you discover that they are stopped up, use a plumber's snake to break through the clog. Then flush with the hose.

Here Is What You Will Need

Materials

- Paint thinner
- Window screen material
- Asphalt roofing cement
- Galvanized roofing nails
- Rivets or waterproof duct tape
- Work gloves

Tools

- Ladder
- Plastic plate, scraper, or whisk broom
- Garden hose
- Plumber's snake
- Wire brush
- Hammer
- Pop rivet tool
- Drill

Brush Out Debris
Step 2

Step 3

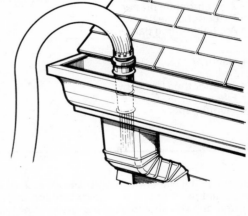

Holes In Both Sections

Pop Rivet

Pop Rivet Tool

Reattach Sections With Pop Rivets
Steps ○1 - ○4

A Safe Ladder Means A Safe Climb

When you climb a ladder, you want to be sure you're on a safe one. The Saf-T-Master ladder, part of the R.D. Werner ladder line, is an aluminum ladder of patented Alflo construction. It has 1¼-inch, round rungs in a modified I-beam frame, and the extension features a fixed aluminum locking mechanism for added safety. The top has a thermoplastic end cap, and the bottom has free-swinging safety shoes.

Seal Gutter Leaks With Tape

All you need is a pair of scissors to seal leaks in gutters, if you have Handi-Patch tape from the Gibson-Homans Company. Just cut off a piece and press it in place over the leak. Handi-Patch stays in place for years and adapts to any weather conditions. Due to its exceptional resilience and elongation characteristics, it will expand and contract in a temperature range of -65 to +180 degrees. Handi-Patch comes in rolls 2½ inches wide by 30 feet long.

Guard Your Gutters

If an ounce of prevention is worth a pound of cure, then the Conwed Gutter Guard is worth its weight in gold. By keeping leaves and debris out of your gutters, the Conwed Gutter Guard saves you from spring and fall gutter cleaning—a dangerous and distasteful job. More importantly, by keeping gutters free flowing, it prevents the kind of water buildup that causes roof damage. The tough polypropylene net won't rust, rot, or corrode, and it requires no special installation tools or skills. On roofs covered with flexible asphalt shingles, slip the Gutter Guard's back edge under the first row of shingles and the front edge under the gutter lip. Use ordinary scissors to cut Gutter Guard to fit around the hangers holding the gutter. Ends should overlap an inch or more. Made by the Conwed Corporation, Gutter Guard is marketed in 25-foot packages.

While you are cleaning, look for rust spots, holes, loose supports, and sags in the gutters and downspouts. Check the runoff to be sure the gutters are still pitched properly, and be sure the strainers are in place and unclogged.

Gutters with holes can be patched. For an easy way to patch them, follow these step-by-step instructions.

△ 1. Remove all rust and any other loose metal by cleaning the area with a wire brush. Cover the bad spot with paint thinner.
△ 2. Cut a patch from wire window screen material. The patch must cover the hole and extend about a half inch beyond it.
△ 3. Coat the area around the hole with asphalt roofing cement.
△ 4. Put the patch down over the cement and press it in place.
△ 5. Brush the cement over the screen.
△ 6. When the first coat sets up, cover it again with cement. You can patch tiny holes without using the screen; the cement will fill in by itself. You may have to apply several coats, however.

A gutter that sags usually has a loose hanger. There are three types of gutter hangers in use today. One type employs a gutter spike driven through a sleeve and into the roof board. If the spike comes loose, you can drive it back in with a hammer. Another type features a strap that is nailed to the roof under a shingle. Be sure to use galvanized roofing nails to resecure a loose strap,

then put a dab of roofing cement over the heads and old nail holes. The third type of gutter hanger is a bracket nailed to the fascia under the gutter. Since you may not be able to get to the loose nails with this type of gutter hanger, add an auxiliary support of another type to eliminate the sag. Sometimes a gutter sags because it lacks sufficient support points. There should be support points about every 36 inches along the run of gutter.

If an elbow or a section of downspout keeps coming off, the easiest way to attach it permanently is with a pop rivet tool. This is an inexpensive tool that installs rivets from the outside without your having to reach the inside surface. To install pop rivets, follow these steps.

○ 1. Place the two sections together.
○ 2. Using a drill bit of the size specified to accommodate the size rivet you have, drill through both pieces. Make two such holes, one on either side or one at the front and one at the back of the downspout.
○ 3. Insert the rivet into the hole in the tool, and then place the tip into the holes you drilled.
○ 4. Squeeze the handles of the tool together until the rivet shaft pops off. The rivet will then be permanently in place.

If you do not have a pop rivet tool and do not wish to buy one, you can use waterproof duct tape to hold the sections together. Although the tape holds well, taped sections look far less neat and attractive than riveted sections.

U-Can Patch Gutter Seams And Plug Holes

Hercules Chemical Company's U-can line of products for the do-it-yourselfer includes a good roof patching compound. U-can Make Roof Repairs features complete instructions on how best to use the product right on the distinctive yellow and black label. The U-can line also includes several top-quality products for making plumbing repairs.

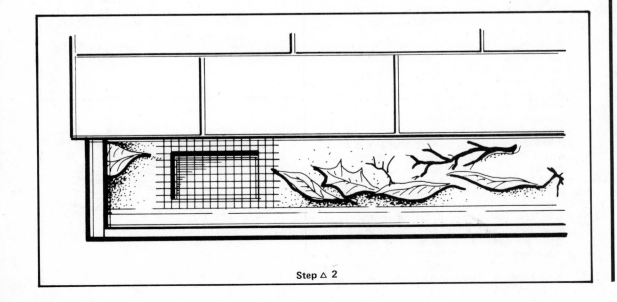

Step △ 2

Roofs

Snow Rake Helps Fight Winter Roof Problems

The Roof Snow Rake from Garelick Manufacturing Company is a handy tool for removing snow from roofs. If you leave the snow on the roof, you risk a moisture problem when the snow thaws and water backs up under the shingles. Such moisture can damage ceilings, walls, and furnishings, as well as the roof. The Garelick Roof Snow Rake features an angled pole and a big blade—24 inches wide and seven inches high—which enable you to get rid of the snow much more easily. It's even effective on low pitch roofs, two story homes, and other hard to reach areas. The handles come in 16- and 21-foot versions; extra five-foot handle extensions are available from the Housewares Division of Garelick Manufacturing Company.

Stop Ice And Snow Dams Along Roof Edges

By installing heat cables on a roof, you can eliminate frozen roof edges and thus prevent the build-up of dams that trap ice and snow; these ice and snow dams can cause roofs and gutters to develop leaks. Ready Heat Roof Cable Kits make it easy to prevent ice and snow dams. The kits contain varying lengths of heat cable, ranging from 20 feet up to 140 feet. Each kit contains the proper number of installation clips to secure the cable in place, as well as helpful instructions. Ready Heat Roof Cable Kits are products of Cox & Company, 215 Park Avenue, S., New York, NY, 10003.

Wrap-On Makes Roof Heater Tape

Wrap-On Company now makes a roof and gutter heat cable called Ice-Guard. Not only does Ice-Guard rid roofs of ice and snow, but it also provides an escape channel for all that it melts. Best of all, operation of Ice-Guard is economical, drawing only eight watts of power per foot of cable.

Use Only Outdoor Extension Cords Outside

Only heavy-duty extension cords specifically designated for outdoor operation should be used outside. A good example is Electricord's Heavy Duty Outdoor All Weather Extension Cord. It maintains its pliability in extreme cold where ordinary cords snap, crackle, and pop. The Pacific Electricord Company makes cords for both indoor and outdoor use.

De-icing

ICE AND SNOW on the roof may look pretty on greeting cards, but from the homeowner's standpoint, it is not all that great. Ice dams that form along the roof edges and in gutters can cause melting snow and ice to back up. This back up can get under the shingles, and if it works its way far enough under the shingles, you could develop a leak.

The weight of ice and snow can cause damage by itself. It is often heavy enough to loosen gutters and sometimes can even be too heavy for a roof or portion thereof to hold it. Snow and ice can cover roof vents for the plumbing system which results in slow running drains.

There are three basic methods of fighting this problem: (1) manually removing the ice and snow; (2) using roof snow guards; and (3) installing heat tapes. Here are the advantages and disadvantages of each.

1. If you could use a long handled roof type snow shovel or any other tool that would rake away the snow for several feet back along the roof edge, much of the problem would be solved. If snow and ice do not build up here, you will not have ice dams when it starts to melt on the roof. Not having snow along the edge also does away with snow falling on people underneath. However, it is not always possible to get out and do the work when it needs to be done. Once the snow starts to turn into hard ice underneath, there is not much you can do with a broom or shovel.
2. Snow guards attach to the roof and prevent avalanches. However, they can actually do more damage than good because they sometimes cause ice dams to form under the pile of snow that they have stopped from sliding down on you.
3. The best control for winter roof problems is with heat tapes. These are electrical tapes that are installed in gutters and along roof edges. They can be turned on or plugged in during the snow and ice season and will keep the snow and ice from forming along this strip. This positively prevents ice dams. It also stops avalanches to a large degree. The tape keeps the gutter open to carry away the melted snow and ice. These heat tapes are easily installed and can be left in place year round. Different brands are installed in different ways. Each maker of such tapes includes instructions and sug-

gestions for installation. The time to install these is not during a snow storm; they should be put in long before winter arrives. Be sure to use outdoor extension cords of the proper size.

While there is a covering of snow on the roof, use this as an opportunity to check for heat loss. Before you turn on your heat tapes and before the snow builds up very high, walk out far enough away from the house to be able to see the roof. See if there are any areas where the snow has melted. Around a chimney in use, is expected. If there are patches in the middle of a roof area for no apparent reason, find out how your home is losing heat.

Here Is What You Will Need

Materials

- Heat tapes
- Outdoor extension cord

Tools

- Ladder
- Snow shovel or broom

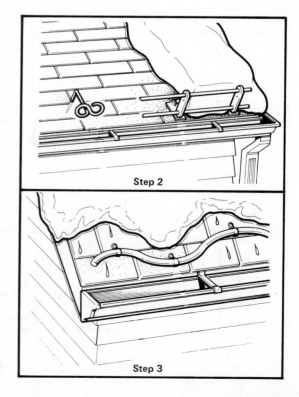

Step 2

Step 3

Hook Your Ladder On The Roof

When working on a steeply pitched roof, you must anchor your ladder securely. A gadget called the Saf-T-Arm attaches to any type of straight ladder and makes using the ladder on the roof much safer. With an arm span of 48 inches, the Saf-T-Arm has a definite stabilizing effect, and its no-mar tips also prevent slipping. Saf-T-Arm can be ordered from Gregory Rennie, 165 Newbury Street, Boston, Massachusetts 02116.

Hip Roofers Wear A Hip Pad

A hip pad is not only an article of roof safety but also a clothing protector. The cushioned pad makes your work much more comfortable, too. You may encounter some difficulty in locating a hip pad, but you can always order one by mail from McGuire-Nicholas, 6223 Santa Monica Boulevard, Los Angeles, California 90038.

Roof Safety

ROOFTOP WORK should always be considered dangerous. When you become blasé about walking on a sloped surface high above the ground, you start getting careless and that's when mistakes occur. On the other hand, there's no reason to be terrified of being on the roof. Just always be aware of the danger and exercise caution, while at the same time maintain your confidence that you've taken all precautions and are, therefore, safe.

Here are some confidence-building safety rules to follow any time you venture out on your roof.

1. Never go out on a roof that is damp. And remember that rain isn't the only source of moisture; morning dew can also cause a damp roof.
2. If you have vision problems or inner ear problems, never venture out on the roof.
3. Don't start a roof repair job when you're tired.
4. Inspect the roof from inside before going out. Try to locate the problem beforehand, thereby spending less time on the roof. Try also to spot damaged places or rotted wood that might give way under your weight. Probe suspect wood with an ice pick, and repair from within wherever possible.
5. Always wear sneakers or crepe-soled shoes, and test your shoes' traction carefully before you start your work. Make sure the laces are tied securely.
6. Avoid bulky or tight clothes that restrict your agility.
7. Tie a rope to a chimney or to a hook over the ridge so you'll have something to hold onto. Ladders can be rigged with ridge hooks or with one of the several safety devices you can buy that anchor them to the ridge. Once anchored, the ladder gives you very sure footing.
8. Check out the possibility of wearing a harness around your chest that you can anchor either to the chimney or to something on the ground on the other side of the ridge.
9. Watch out for overhead power lines and power lines entering your house.
10. Make sure your TV antenna is grounded.
11. Pick calm days for your ascent; even a slight wind can be dangerous.
12. Never work on a roof when an electrical storm is expected.
13. Work low to the surface; stay in a crouch or even a crawl whenever possible.

Here Is What You Will Need

Materials
- Sneakers or crepe-soled shoes
- Rope
- Chest harness

Tools
- Ice pick
- Ladder
- Ridge hook

14. If you begin to feel overly nervous, sit down and scoot back to safety.

Working on your roof for the first time will naturally be a little scary, but if you take the necessary precautions, you'll quickly gain confidence. Just remember to take it slow and play it safe.

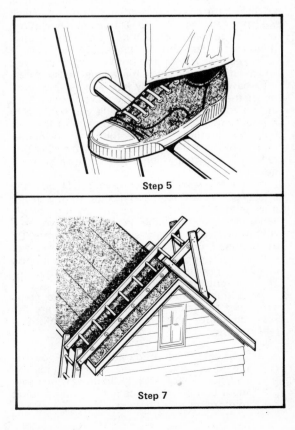

Step 5

Step 7

Rope Aids In Roof Safety

A sturdy rope is one vital ingredient in roof safety. Most lumberyards and some hardware stores carry rolls of rope, although some have packaged rope. The Jackson Rope Corporation markets several different types of rope. For the roof work, buy a strong nylon, polypropylene, or manila rope. Jackson offers all these as does The Cordage Group.

Stripper Beats Your Mouth For Holding Nails

Many roofers store nails in their mouths to have a supply ready when needed, but a nail stripper accomplishes the same objective in a much safer way. Wear the nail stripper on an angle, and the nails will line up and come out point down. All you do is roll the nail out the end of the stripper with your thumb, and you're ready to go. Lumberyards catering to the building trades may stock nail strippers, but if you can't locate one, drop a note to Roofmaster Products Company, P.O. Box 63167, Los Angeles, California 90063 and ask about prices. When ordering, be sure to specify whether you want one made for right-handed or left-handed use.

Brick and Masonry

For Small Jobs, Buy Premix In Sacks

For the homeowner who does only occasional small concrete jobs, premixes are the answer. In one bag you get all the ingredients, properly proportioned and mixed. All you add is water and work. Sakrete is probably the best-known brand in premixed concrete. Sakrete cement mixes come in three forms: concrete mix, sand mix and mortar mix. The regular concrete mix contains rocks and is formulated for such tasks as setting posts, pouring curbs, etc. The sand mix is the same except that it has no gravel and is intended for patching, topping, and other thin concrete projects. The mortar mix is specially formulated for brick laying and filling loose mortar joints. Be sure to follow the mixing directions on the bag, taking special care not to add more than the prescribed amount of water. If you plan to use only part of the bag, mix up all the dry ingredients before pouring any from the bag; they tend to settle and separate. You can find Sakrete in hardware stores, lumberyards, and home centers.

You Can't Complete The Job Without Finishing Tools

You'll need several finishing tools in the course of completing an average concrete job. The Marshalltown Trowel Company makes every concrete tool you might require. The magnesium bull float can be fitted with either a magnesium or fiberglass handle. Marshalltown also makes a wooden float. The Marshalltown metal finishing trowel, in the company's Xtralite line, has a spring steel blade and aluminum mounting. Marshalltown also makes a long-handled metal trowel, a groover for creating joints between slabs, and an edger for rounding off the edges of a slab.

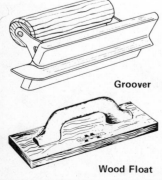

Groover

Wood Float

Stroll Your Own

Roll-A-Mix Company markets an ingenious concrete mixer called Stroll-A-Mix. You just add the ingredients and push the unit around for two to three minutes; as you stroll, the concrete gets mixed. Pouring is easy, and the mixer can handle up to 100 pounds of concrete. Since the mixer vat is made of polyethylene, the Stroll-A-Mix is as light as you can expect a concrete mixer to be. For more information about this creation, contact Roll-A-Mix, 1083 Bloomfield Avenue, West Caldwell, New Jersey 07006.

You'll Need A Hoe For Hand Mixing

Many people use a mortar mixer hoe for mixing concrete. The Atlas hoe is a heavy-duty tool, featuring a big 10x6-inch blade which helps the mixing go faster. The 66-inch handle fits into an eight-inch Tapertite ferrule. Atlas makes a full line of industrial quality shovels, scoops, wheelbarrows, and rakes, all designed for rugged use and long life. Atlas Tools are made by the Union Fork & Hoe Company.

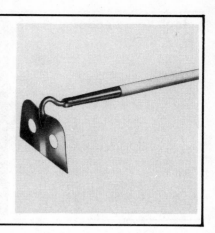

Primer on Concrete Mixing and Finishing

THERE ARE three basic ways to obtain concrete mix when it becomes necessary for a project. You can buy pre-mixed concrete by the bag. It contains all the ingredients, except water, and includes cement, sand, and aggregate or gravel. Or, you can buy these ingredients separately and mix them yourself. The third way, when you have a really big job, is to order the number of cubic yards you will need from a company that can send a truck and pour ready mixed concrete into your forms.

The key to what method you use is the size of the job. Smaller jobs are usually done best with the pre-mix. These would include setting a post, pouring a few stepping stones, and other small jobs. Mix-it-yourself jobs would be those where a few cubic feet of concrete mix are needed such as setting all the posts for a fence or pouring a small walk or even a small patio. The ready-mix method would be for big jobs such as a driveway, a foundation for an addition, or a large patio.

The easiest way to find out how much mix you will need is to get a chart. Places that sell concrete may have one. The ready-mix people may drop one in the mail to you. However, if you do not have access to one, there is a formula you can use to figure it out. Take the square footage of the surface, and multiply it by the thickness in inches, then take the answer and divide it by 324. This tells you how many cubic yards of mix you will need.

With a pre-mix, all you need do is add the proper amount of water and mix thoroughly. If you only need part of the bag, mix the dry ingredients while they are still in the bag. If they have been sitting for a long time, they tend to separate. Be sure to use no more than the required amount of water. Many people make the mistake of using too much water to get the mixture made more quickly. This weakens the mix however.

For a mix-it-yourself job, here are the steps from start to finish. The finishing steps are the same no matter which method you use to obtain the concrete.

1. Take care of all preparation before you begin the mixing process. This includes excavation if necessary, building of forms, laying a bed of sand if called for, and putting reinforcing steel in place.

Here Is What You Will Need

Materials

- Cement
- Sand
- Gravel
- 1x12 boards
- Nails
- Air entraining agent
- Long 2x4
- Plastic sheet, canvas tarp, or burlap

Tools

- Tape measure
- Saw
- Hammer
- Shovel
- Hoe
- Wheelbarrow
- Bull float
- Edgers
- Jointers
- Steel finishing trowel
- Garden hose

2. Figure out how much concrete you will need, then determine how much sand and gravel you will need.

3. Carefully measure in the ingredients. For this, it is good to know that a standard sack of cement is one cubic foot. Make a bottomless box one foot deep and one foot square, without a top or bottom. This will help you get the right proportion of the other dry ingredients. If the mix called for is a 1:2:3 (1 part cement, 2 parts sand, and 3 parts aggregate), you need only shovel the sand into the box, and when full, lift it up, move it over and fill it again. Do the same with the gravel, and you will get exact measures very quickly.

4. Mix the dry ingredients first unless you are using a cement mixing machine.

5. Measure out the amount of water you will need. If you have used wet sand, use less water. Never use more than 6 gallons of water per sack of cement in the mix. Wet sand could cut it down to 4½ gallons.

6. Start with only part of the water, and mix back and forth, gradually adding more water. The idea is to mix until every grain of sand is covered with the gray paste-like cement. Often after you have poured all the water in, it will appear that you will never attain the proper mix. Just hang in there, though, and keep mixing. It will blend. The

Have Big Jobs Mixed

For really big concrete jobs like pouring a driveway, you may do well to have someone else do the mixing. Try to find a company with trucks that carry all the ingredients but which do not actually mix the concrete until they arrive at the work site. You will get fresher concrete from such a truck, and fresher concrete means a longer time for you to smooth and finish. Many of these trucks are equipped with meters to measure out how much concrete they pour. That means you only pay for the amount you use.

Coat Your Concrete With A Weatherproof Sealer

A do-it-yourself crystal clear coating for sealing concrete and stone surfaces is now being manufactured and marketed nationally by Resin Systems, Inc. Called Congard, the all-year, all-weather coating can be applied easily with a standard roller, brush, or mop. It dries in an hour, seals the surface so that it is impervious to most common corrosive chemicals including rock salt, and prevents the concrete from staining, cracking, spalling, or powdering. Congard is ideal protection for porches, patios, steps, walkways, basements, garages, and driveways—wherever wear, water, or weather conditions tend to damage the surface. It answers the need for weatherproof protection against the freeze-thaw-crack-chip cycle which ruins concrete. It is available in one-gallon cans (one gallon covers approximately 400 square feet) at paint, hardware, and garden supply stores.

mixing can be done with a hoe in a wheelbarrow, or it can be done in a mixing box or on a flat concrete surface. If using a mixer, let it run for one to three minutes.

7. If your concrete will be subjected to freezing, use an additive called an air entraining agent such as Darex. Follow the directions closely. This adds microscopic bubbles to the mix, and when it sets up, these cavities help compensate for the expansion and contraction from freezing and thawing.
8. Pour the mix into the forms. Pour it as near as possible to where it should go. Do not pour piles and then move them together.
9. Spread the mix with a flat shovel or a hoe. Never use a rake as it tends to separate the aggregate from the rest of the mix.
10. Once spread, strike off the top with a 2x4 or some other type of flat board. This is usually best done by starting at one end of the project, and using a striker that will span from one form to the other, pull the striker across the surface with a back and forth sawing motion to remove the excess.
11. Next, use a bull float to fill in any voids and to push larger aggregate down below the surface. Do as little work on the surface as possible.
12. Run edgers and jointers where these tools are needed.
13. The floating will cause the surface to have a sheen from the water. When this disappears, you are ready for hand floating. The float is moved in an arc-like motion across the surface. This is done with either a wooden or metal float. It levels and pushes down any rock that is at the surface. For many projects, this rough finish is fine.
14. If a smoother finish is desired, wait until the sheen from the hand floating has disappeared. Then use a steel finishing trowel. Hold this tool at an angle so the edge toward the movement is tilted up. Otherwise it will dig into the surface. Rejoint and edge.
15. Once the desired finish is attained, allow a full week for curing. During this time, the concrete should not be allowed to dry out. It is best to cover the concrete to help hold in the moisture. Check the concrete each day, and using the hose set to a fine mist, add moisture if necessary. The concrete can be covered with a plastic sheet, canvas tarp, or burlap. Be sure the spray is a fine mist as big drops of water may pit the surface.

Step 6

Step 10

Wood Float

Tamp Down Earth And Sand To Improve Concrete Work

An inexpensive tamper like the one from Marion Tool Corporation can be a great help in achieving a solid base for your concrete work. It measures 8x10 inches, a good size for a hand tamper. Wooden-handled tampers like this one should occasionally be treated with a coat of boiled linseed oil. The linseed oil preserves both the handle and your hands. Marion Tool Corporation specializes in popularly priced tools.

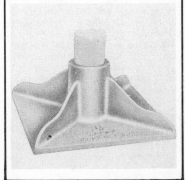

That is the basic procedure for concrete mixing and finishing. If you have ready-mix delivered, be sure to have all your preparation done before the truck arrives, and have plenty of help to get the

concrete mix spread and finished before it sets up.

Start off with a small concrete project to get the feel of finishing, and then work up to a larger job. It is hard work, but it can save lots of money since labor is a big factor in concrete work.

Brick and Masonry

Bonding Liquid Works Like A Glue For Concrete

Franklin Concrete Adhesive is like a glue that makes new concrete stick to the old. It creates a permanent bond, and without it your patching efforts may not last long. This liquid bonder, which comes ready to use, can be used on almost any surface. Available in pints, quarts, and gallons, Franklin Concrete Adhesive is a product of the Chemical Industries Division of the Franklin Glue Company.

Concrete Chipping Requires Hefty Hammer

You should use a rugged and hefty hand-drilling hammer for concrete chipping. The one from the Great Neck Saw Manufacturers, Inc., features polished faces on a blue-painted head. It has a comfort grip hickory handle that is 10 inches long, and you can take your choice of 32-, 48-, and 64-ounce head weights. Always be sure to wear safety goggles when you chip concrete with a hand-drilling hammer.

Some Tips For Storing Leftover Dry Cement

Almost always, when you complete a concrete repair project you find yourself with some unused, unmixed dry cement leftover. If you leave the cement in the bag and store the bag improperly, you'll come back to find a big blob of hardened concrete the next time you need it. To prevent losing leftover dry cement, transfer it from the bag into two-pound coffee cans with plastic lids. The cans will keep your powder dry, and the concrete will be ready the next time you need it.

Wheelbarrow Is Good For Mixing And Hauling

A good example of what a sturdy wheelbarrow should be is Big Red, Kelley's KC-5 heavy-duty home and farm wheelbarrow. It has great balance even with a full load of five cubic feet of wet concrete—about 411 pounds. The legs, braces, and nose piece are chaneled heavy-duty steel, and it is available with either wood or tubular handles. The one-piece drawn tray with rolled edges is made of 16-gauge metal. The Kelley Manufacturing Company makes larger and smaller wheelbarrows as well as a line of galvanized garbage cans and buckets.

Patching Holes in a Concrete Slab

QUITE FREQUENTLY, the surface of a concrete drive, walk, or patio gets crumbly, and before long you notice some big holes. Such holes can cause sprained ankles, and when they occur in your driveway they are rough on tires. You would be wise, therefore, to patch small holes before they become big problems. Most patches, though, come out after a while, and then you are right back where you started. Do it right with the following method, however, and your patch will stay put.

Here Is What You Will Need

Materials
- Ready (sand) concrete mix
- Concrete bonding agent
- Tarp or plastic sheet

Tools

● Hammer	● Trowel
● Chisel	● 2x4
● Garden hose	● Wooden float
● Paintbrush	● Metal float
● Metal wheelbarrow	● Push broom

1. Remove every last bit of the loose concrete, and then hose out the cavity until it is perfectly clean.
2. Get a sack of ready mix (called a sand mix) and a small can of a bonding agent. The bonding agent is the key to creating a patch that is bonded permanently to the old concrete. You can buy patching mix that includes a bonding agent, but if you are patching many holes, the cost of the mix might be prohibitive.
3. Remove any standing water in the hole.
4. Brush on the bonding agent, following the manufacturer's directions.

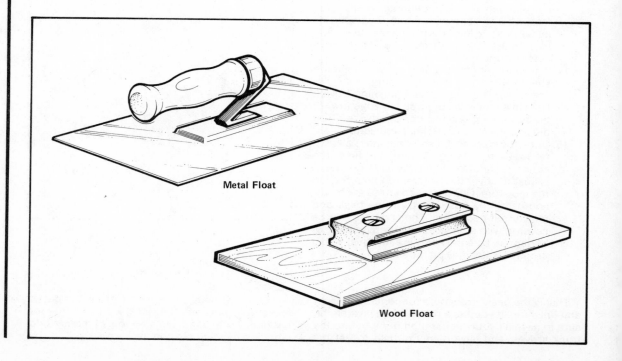

Metal Float

Wood Float

Pre-Mixed Dry Concrete Just Needs Water And Work

Quikrete is another brand of pre-mixed dry concrete that you can find almost everywhere. It's all ready to go; all you add is water and work. When you buy a bag and use just part of it on a small patching job, be sure to take care of the leftovers. If you store the bag where moisture can get to it, you'll probably find a giant lump of concrete when you need it the next time. Never store bagged cement on a bare concrete floor—at least put a wooden base under the sack—and if possible transfer the leftover cement to a waterproof container.

Epoxy-Vinyl Concrete Repair Mix Fills Holes For Keeps

Poxymix Concrete Repair Mix comes in dry form and is prepared by mixing with water. Ideal for fixing step edges or other small repair chores, it can also be used for patching holes in drives or walks, resurfacing, or tuckpointing. It bonds securely to the old surface, but the old surface must be dry for best results. An epoxy and vinyl compound, it dries to a light gray and can be feathered smooth; if used for resurfacing, Poxymix can be used in a layer as thin as $\frac{1}{16}$ of an inch. Available in small three-pound cans as well as in larger quantities, Poxymix is marketed by the Manhattan Brush Company.

5. Prepare the sand mix according to directions. Make sure that each grain of sand is coated with the gray mix, and make sure to use only the prescribed amount of water. A watery mix may be easier to work with, but it loses much of its strength. A metal wheelbarrow makes an ideal container for mixing.
6. Pour the mix into the hole, and then use a trowel to poke it in place completely.
7. Rake a 2x4 across the top to level the patch.
8. When the water sheen disappears, start to smooth the patch with a wooden float. You will soon see some water back on the surface, and when you do notice a sheen again stop the smoothing process.
9. If additional smoothing is necessary, wait until the surface sheen goes away again, and then smooth with a metal float. Remember, though, that most outdoor concrete projects should have a fairly rough finish for better traction. Pulling a push broom across the surface gives you the kind of finish you generally need.
10. When the water disappears again, cover the patch with a tarp or a sheet of plastic.
11. Remove the tarp or plastic sheet every day,

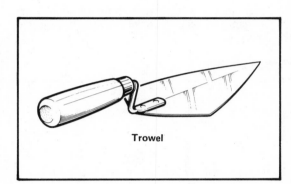

Trowel

adjust the nozzle on a garden hose to fine mist, and spray the concrete lightly. If possible, repeat this process for six days, recovering the patch after each spraying. What you are doing is letting the concrete cure. Curing is very important, since those who fail to do it—permitting the new concrete to dry out too fast—end up with a new crop of holes to patch in very short order.

Carbide Cuts Concrete

The New England Carbide Tool Company, Inc., makes several tools for cutting, drilling, and abrading concrete. A quick way to undercut concrete for patching would be to use a New England Masonry Cutting Blade in your circular saw. Sized to fit most home saws, these blades feature a unique adapter that allows them to go on all shaft sizes. Each blade comes with the adapter. New England Carbide also puts out a line of carbide-tipped drill bits.

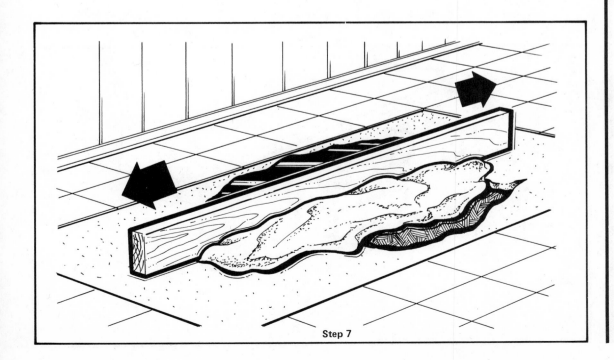

Step 7

Brick and Masonry

Cold Chisel Is A Hot Tool For Undercutting

Cold chisels, made in one piece of a good grade tool steel, are used for chipping concrete and for cutting metal. Great Neck Saw Manufacturers, Inc., makes a fine cold chisel as part of a wide line of hand tools. Classified according to the shape of their points, chisels commonly available include the flat, cape, diamond point, and round nose. Be sure to match the size of the hammer you use with the chisel and the work. A lightweight hammer would produce little effect on a large chisel because the chisel itself would absorb all of the force of the blow.

Special Tools Give Edge To Concrete Steps

If you've ever wondered just how the pros get a nice rounded edge on concrete steps, the answer is that they use special step edger tools. Easco makes economically priced yet well-made step-edger tools out of durable cast iron. Two are curved step edgers; another is a tool for working square edges as well as for use on outside corners; and still another is for forming inside corners or for use on the bottom of the step where the next step begins.

Safety Goggles Are A Must When Chipping Concrete

Any time you strike a cold chisel or use any tool for chipping concrete or masonry, be sure to wear safety goggles. Don't risk an eye injury. Xtralite Softies from Shoplyne have a flexible frame that conforms to your facial contours for a fair degree of comfort. Shoplyne makes other safety equipment for the home handyman, including ear plugs, dust masks, face shields, hard hats, and welders' protective equipment. Shoplyne Safety Products are made by the Fibre-Metal Products Company.

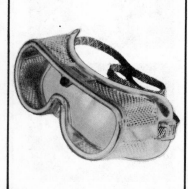

Patching Concrete Steps

THE EDGES OF concrete steps receive a great deal of wear and rough treatment, and in most cases, they can take it. Once edges start to fall apart, however, they keep on until after a while there is not much left. Not only do crumbled steps look bad, but they also pose a real safety hazard. Since patching damaged concrete steps is a fairly easy repair, why not fix them up now? Here is all you do.

1. Undercut the crumbling edge with a hammer and cold chisel. Undercutting is the process of cutting a "V" back into the solid concrete so that the patch will have a better chance of locking in place.
2. Remove all loose concrete, and clean the area thoroughly with the strong spray of the garden hose.
3. Build a form by placing a board against the riser and securing it with several bricks; that should hold the board firmly in place. Select two planks that are wide enough and tall enough and place them against the sides. Then angle a 2x4 as a brace, and nail it in place. Make sure that the top of your form is level with the step.
4. Paint the area to be covered with a concrete bonding agent, following the directions on the can. You can find concrete bonding

Here Is What You Will Need

Materials

- Wood planks
- Bricks
- 2x4
- Nails
- Concrete bonding agent
- Ready-mixed concrete
- Tarp or plastic sheet

Tools

● Hammer	● Paintbrush
● Cold chisel	● Trowel
● Garden hose	● Wooden float

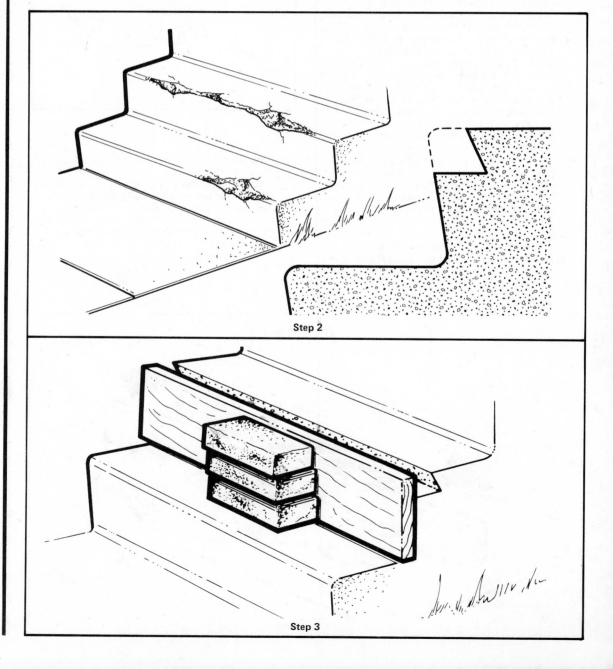

Step 2

Step 3

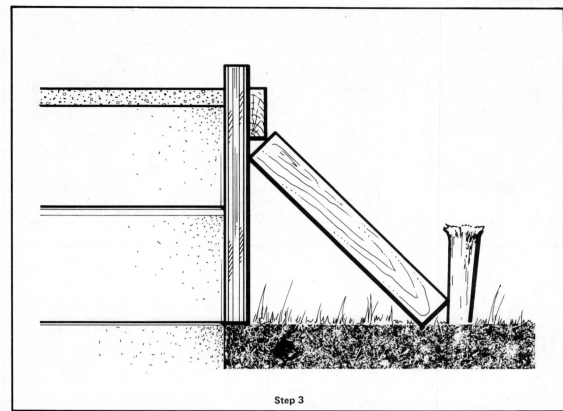

Step 3

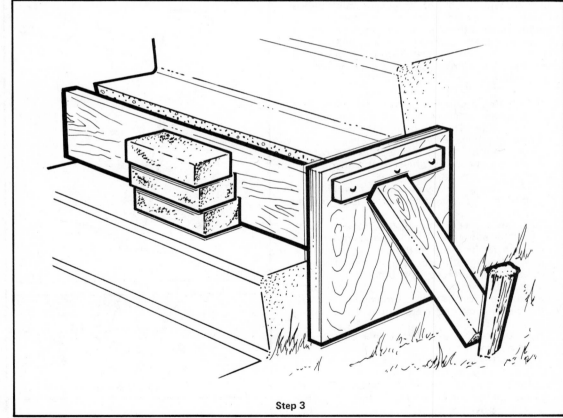

Step 3

agents at any hardware store.

5. Use ready-mixed concrete of the sand mix formula. Add no more water than the directions specify, and mix completely until every grain of sand is coated with the cement.
6. Use a trowel to poke the concrete mix in place, and check to be sure that you leave no air spaces back in the "V."
7. Finish off the concrete patch so that it is level with the rest of the step. You can use your trowel or a wooden float to get the patch level.
8. Make the patch match the texture of the rest of the step, and then cover it with a tarp or a plastic sheet.
9. The next day, and each succeeding day for five days, lift the cover and spray the new concrete with water. Adjust the hose nozzle to its fine mist setting.

You can remove the forms as soon as the concrete patch sets up, but by leaving them in place during the curing process, you reduce the likelihood of someone accidentally stepping on the patch before it is fully cured.

Brick and Masonry

Try To Crack This Hose

The quality of a garden hose has little effect on its ability to clean away concrete chips or mortar dust unless it cracks and the water never makes it to the nozzle. Cracking simply cannot happen with a Colorite Garden Hose. So flexible that you can kink it, twist it, crimp it, and run over it with your car without damage, it never gets stiff or brittle. The Colorite Garden Hose is a product of Colorite Plastic Company, makers of a wide range of plastic hoses.

Concrete Patch Comes In A Can

Coughlan Permanent Concrete Patch is made with vinyl acrylic resins, and all you need to do is add water and apply. Once it fills the cracks in concrete or cinder block, it bonds to the old surface with incredible strength. It can be applied in a very thin layer (down to $\frac{1}{16}$ of an inch), is easy to smooth and finish, and it dries to a gray concrete color—about as close as you can get with any type patching material. Coughlan Permanent Concrete Patch, from the

Coughlan Products Company, comes in 3¾-pound cans.

Sta-Patch Eliminates Need For Surface Preparation

Sta-Patch is a vinyl adhesive patcher for concrete and stucco that requires no surface preparation such as undercutting, etching, or priming. Just mix it with water according to the instructions until it reaches a putty consistency, put it in place, and smooth or roughen to match the rest of the surface. It sets in an hour and hardens in a day

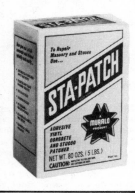

Concrete Bonding Agent Sticks New To Old

Just brush, roll, or spray Elmer's Concrete Bonder over old concrete, and you create a tacky surface for the application of new concrete. It requires no etching of the old surface—just clean and flush, and then apply Elmer's Concrete Bonder to the damp surface. You can also add the bonder to the concrete mix for greater strength, resiliency, and minimum cracking; the bonder acts as a fortifier. Elmer's Concrete Bonder cleans up with water and works equally well for plaster, stucco, or masonry. All Elmer's products are made by Borden.

Cracks in Concrete

CONCRETE CRACKS just grow and grow. The small crack running across the patio today will become a chasm between two smaller patios in very short order. Moisture and temperature changes push at the sides of the crack as more of the surface inside comes loose, and before long you have your own Royal Gorge. Patching can stop the crack's progress. So get cracking and start patching.

1. Use a cold chisel to convert the crack to a groove which is at least an inch deep and ½ inch wide. When chipping concrete, always wear goggles to protect your eyes. In addition, cut an "X" in a plastic coffee can lid and slip it over the chisel to shield you from flying fragments.
2. Undercut the groove to make it wider at the bottom; undercutting helps lock in the patch.
3. Brush and wash out all the loose concrete with a stiff broom and strong spray from your garden hose. If the crack goes all the way through the slab, tamp in a sand base.
4. Leave all surfaces wet, but get rid of any standing water.
5. Coat all surfaces with a creamy mix of Portland cement and water, or use a bonding agent.
6. Prepare either a stiff sand mix or one with small gravel.
7. Tamp the mix into the crack with a small trowel or putty knife.
8. When the new concrete begins to stiffen (usually about 45 minutes later), smooth it with a trowel or a 2x4.
9. Let the patch cure six days.

Here Is What You Will Need

Materials
- Portland cement or concrete bonding agent
- Plastic coffee can lid
- Sand or gravel mix
- 2x4

Tools
• Cold chisel	• Stiff broom
• Hammer	• Garden hose
• Goggles	• Small trowel or putty knife

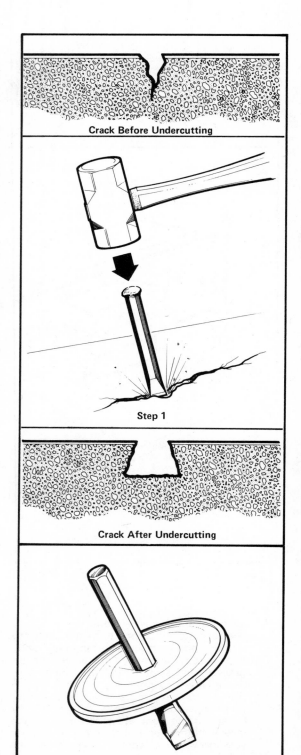

Crack Before Undercutting

Step 1

Crack After Undercutting

Step 1

Driveway Coater Combines Squeegee And Spreader

The Ardmore Double Blade Driveway Coater has a serrated hard rubber blade on one side for spreading blacktop material quickly and easily and a squeegee on the other side for smoothing, removing excess, and for applying sealer. The blade is 12 inches wide and the lightweight aluminum handle is a full 48 inches long. If you have any blacktop surfaces around your home, you'll be applying sealer often enough to warrant buying this handy tool. Actually, it's inexpensive enough that you need not use it more than once to make it a good investment. The Ardmore Manufacturing Company Inc., makes many other squeegee products.

Sakrete Makes Black Top Patch And Sealer

Sakrete's Black Top Patch comes ready to use right from the sack and requires absolutely no mixing. Just pour it into the clean chuck hole or cavity and tamp it down firmly. You can drive over the patch immediately. Sakrete Black Top Sealer is also ready to use applied from the bucket with a squeegee or broom. It seals the surface to prevent moisture from going down into the blacktop to cause cracks and holes and it prolongs the life and improves the appearance of your driveway. To patch wide cracks, mix Sakrete Black Top Sealer with sand to create a slurry, then force this slurry into the crack and smooth. After the patch has cured, coat the entire blacktop surface with Black Top Sealer for a uniform appearance.

Repairing Blacktop Surfaces

THE SAME PROBLEMS—ruined tires and sprained limbs—that accompany holes in concrete also present themselves with holes in an asphalt driveway. In a sense, however, the asphalt problems are worse. Once asphalt starts to slough away, the hole spreads, and before long you have a major resurfacing project on your hands. Fortunately, you can buy blacktop cold patch in a bag that requires no mixing. You just pour it from the sack to stop the spread of holes in blacktop.

1. Chip away at the loose asphalt material until you reach a solid surface.
2. Brush out all of the loose material.
3. Pour in the blacktop patch from the sack, adding enough to make the patch about a half inch higher than the surrounding area.
4. Use the back of your shovel or rake to pack the patch down thoroughly. If you can pack the patch material below the surrounding surface, pour in more and tamp it down. Just make sure that the patched area is level with the rest of the driveway. You can drive your car over the new patch immediately.

There are blacktop sealers on the market that will prolong the life of your driveway. They come ready to use and require no heating (as did the old-fashioned asphalt toppings). Nonetheless, you will get a better seal if you apply the material during a summer heat wave. Most blacktop surfaces should be sealed about every two years. The sealer can also be used for filling wide cracks. You just mix the sealer with sand to form a slurry mix, and then force the mix into the crack.

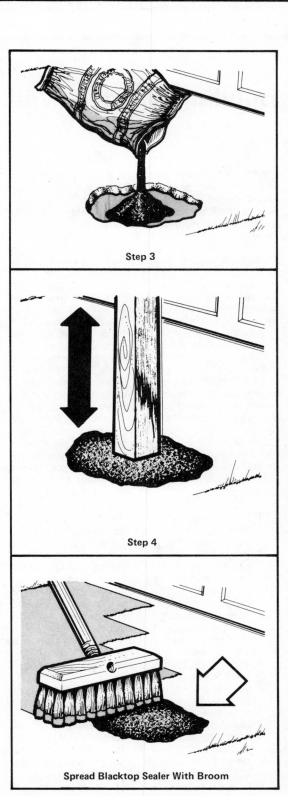

Step 3

Step 4

Spread Blacktop Sealer With Broom

Here Is What You Will Need

Materials

- Blacktop patch
- Blacktop sealer
- Sand

Tools

- Chisel
- Brush
- Shovel or rake
- Trowel
- Broom

Crack Sealer Dries Tough

A blacktop crack sealer that withstands harsh weather, dries quickly, and cleans up easily has been developed by Borden Chemical's Consumer Products Division. Formulated for driveways and a host of other asphalt jobs outside the house, Elmer's Acrylic Latex Blacktop Crack Sealer may be walked on after one hour and cures tough overnight. It is also recommended as a sealer for gutters, chimney flashing, roof leaks, and above-ground foundations. Elmer's Acrylic Latex Blacktop Crack Sealer comes in an 11-ounce cartridge and can be used with any conventional caulking gun.

Tamp Down Blacktop Patch

You can tamp down Handi-Gard Driveway Patching Compound with a scrap of 2x4 and a small sledge hammer. Handi-Gard comes ready to use; merely pour enough in the hole to stick up about a half inch above the rest of the surface, and then tamp it down. After tamping, add more compound and continue tamping until the surface of the patch is even with its surroundings. Handi-Gard Driveway Patching Compound is a product of the Gibson-Homans Company.

Brick and Masonry

Your Level Should Be Exact

Keeping your work plumb and level is no problem with an exacting instrument from the Exact Level & Tool Manufacturing Company, Inc. Exact modestly tabs their levels "the Best in the World," and supports the boast with easy-to-read vials—accurate within .010 inch in both level and plumb—and warp-proof, scratch-proof, and abrasion-resistant frames. Exact also makes metal rules, squares, floats, plumb bobs, aluminum C-clamps, and other fine tools.

Keep Your Line Taut

You must maintain a taut line in brickwork or else the bricks in the center of the course will dip. The special tools to help achieve the tightest line possible are called line blocks or corner ties. You attach the plastic line blocks to each corner before laying a course of bricks. Since you do the corners first, the line block enables you to keep the in-between bricks straight. The UB Tool Company makes line blocks and markets them through building supply houses that carry other concrete and masonry tools. Be sure to use a strong line, like one bearing the Eagle brand from the Samson Cordage Works.

A Bricklaying Kit For The Serious Amateur

The people at Weekender Products have put together a complete bricklaying kit that contains every tool and accessory needed for professional quality concrete work. The kit includes a forged steel pointing trowel, a brick trowel with a 10-inch blade, a forged steel bricklayer's hammer, two double-blade caulking trowels, a pair of bricklayer's corner blocks, a 48-inch aluminum frame level, a spring joint extension rule, and a copy of the Easi-Bild book *Bricklaying Simplified*. It comes with a heavy-duty 20x6x13-inch canvas bag to carry all the gear except

the level. Write to Weekender Products, 511 Osage, Kansas City, Kansas 66110 for more information about item No. 80-114 in the Weekender Catalog.

Build A Concrete Block Wall Without Mortar

Normally, you lay concrete blocks as you would bricks, but with Surewall Surface Bonding Cement you can join the blocks without mortar joints. All you need do is stack the blocks and trowel on Surewall. The compound is a mixture of white cement and fibers, and when applied properly, it creates a wall that is as strong or stronger than a wall with mortar joints. Surewall also decorates the wall and protects it from water penetration. A great way to make outbuildings, enclose a carport, build a barbeque grill—as well as construct concrete block walls—Surewall Surface Bonding Cement is made by W.R. Bonsal Company.

Building a Brick Wall

WITH PATIENCE and a little know-how you can do a fairly good job of bricklaying. You may not be anywhere near as fast as a pro, but you can end up with the same results. It is best to start with a small job and gradually work up to bigger jobs. Here are some very basic steps in bricklaying.

The first step is planning. Try to lay out your job so that it will come out to either an exact number of bricks in length or the number plus an exact half of a brick. This can be done by figuring the length of each brick as 8½ inches. The bricks actually measure eight inches with an extra half inch for the mortar joints. This half inch joint is suggested for the new bricklayer. Figure the half brick as 4¼ inches which includes the joints. The nominal height, also including the joints, is 2¾ inches.

To estimate how many bricks you will need, determine the square footage and figure 6.8 bricks per square foot with these half inch joints. If you drop the joints in size down to ¼ inch, you will use almost an entire brick more per square foot. For your first job, use a pre-mix of the mortar mix variety. All you need to do is add water. Later on you can mix cement, lime, and sand yourself to make a mortar mix. Here is how the bricklaying goes.

1. Be sure to have a solid footing for the bricks, poured concrete is best. It should extend down below the frost line and up above the grade if possible.
2. Lay out the walls with stakes and lines. Use them to establish corners and carefully mark each one. Lay down a thin bed of mortar on which to make the lines for the corner. Extend these lines for several feet in both directions from each corner. Use a straight board and mark in the wet bed with your trowel.
3. Wet down the brick pile with the hose and keep the bricks damp.
4. Start in one corner and lay a half inch bed of mortar long enough for about six bricks. Do not cover up your lines.
5. Lay the corner brick and carefully line it up with both lines in that corner. Check it with the level to be sure it is level. Bring your line down to be sure the brick is aimed directly at the corner at the other end of the wall.
6. Spread a generous amount of mortar on

Here Is What You Will Need

Materials

- Pre-mixed mortar
- String or twine
- Wooden stakes
- Bricks
- Nails
- Muriatic acid

Tools

- Tape measure
- Mortarboard
- Trowel
- Level
- Hammer
- Garden hose
- Brush
- Jointer

each end of another brick. This step is called "buttering". Place this brick in the mortar bed and slide it against the first brick. Use the handle of the trowel to push the brick down to the proper level.

7. Repeat this until you have six bricks lined up.
8. Now go back to the corner and work along the line going in the other direction in the same manner as the first six bricks were layed.
9. Put another bed of mortar on top of this first course of bricks and lay about five bricks out in each direction following the same buttering and leveling procedure. Check after each course to be sure the bricks are lined up in every way and that the course is level.
10. Continue until you have built a sort of pyramid in the corner that is about four courses high.
11. Now, build the same sort of pyramid in the other corners.
12. Next, start to lay the bricks in between the corners on the first course. Work from both ends toward the center, laying down a full bed joint. (If the footing was not level, use the mortar joint to compensate. The bricks in the first course should be level.)
13. The last brick in the center is the closure brick. Vary the size of the joints here to compensate, if necessary.

Brick and Masonry

You Need A Brick Hammer For Brick Work

Although it is possible to cut bricks with a regular hammer, you'd be wise to invest in a brick hammer if you plan to do much work with bricks. The Rocket brand brick hammer from the True Temper Company has a forged steel head that weighs 24 ounces and is permanently anchored to the handle so that it cannot loosen or fly off. The handle is an oval-shaped, chrome-plated tubular, heat-treated shaft with a grip especially made to absorb shock. True Temper also makes a wooden-handled brick hammer that comes with or without the cushioned grip.

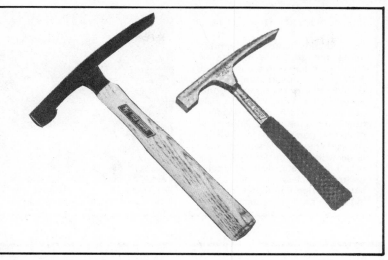

Wide Chisel Is Made Especially For Brick Work

The wide, flat chisel called a bricklayer's chisel usually has a 3½- or 4-inch blade. The Target Head Brick Chisel from the Damascus Steel Products Company features a beveled striking face to minimize mushrooming and one-piece drop-forged steel construction. A heavy-duty tool, this chisel can cut bricks, and it is quite handy for removing damaged bricks that must be replaced. To get the best from such a chisel, be sure to use a hammer that is heavy enough to do the job. Naturally, you should always wear safety goggles when using a bricklayer's chisel.

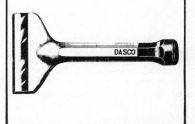

14. Collect the oozing mortar that is squeezed out as you go. Put back on your mortarboard or hawk for reuse.
15. Before the mortar sets up, the joints must be worked. Know ahead of time which of the various joints you will use and have the proper tool to make them. Do this work before the mortar gets hard. On hot days, this can become a critical step that has to be done fairly quickly. Do the verticals first and then the horizontals.

These are the basic steps, but there are some other things that will be helpful to know about. First of all, make yourself a brick rule or story pole. This is a board cut to the height of the brick work. It is then marked off with lines to indicate each course of bricks including the mortar joints. The lines should indicate where the top of each brick would be. With this, you can be sure that each course is at the right height.

You will also wish to constantly use your level to check both the plumb of the wall as well as the level.

There are masonry lines that attach to the corners, or you may attach the line to nails that are poked into the wet mortar to let you use a line as a guide for every course. Be sure to move it up each time, and you will end up with a straighter wall.

After you are through with the bricklaying, use a brush to remove any burrs or leftover mortar. In a situation of fast drying, do this as you make the joints. Do not use a brush stiff enough to leave its mark in the mortar joints. If any of this got away from you and hardened, remove it later with a wire brush.

If there is a gray cast to the bricks, it is from masonry you got on the bricks. It can be cleaned away with a very diluted solution of muriatic acid. Use about one part acid to 10 parts water. Observe all the caution notices on the acid container. Use a stiff scrub brush and start at the top and work down. After the acid stops its action, flush it away completely.

After you have tackled a simple project, you may wish to get involved in something more complicated. The procedure will be about the same, but there can be any of several different bonds (patterns). There are also different types of bricks that measure different from those mentioned here. The same principles are used in stone work as well as in using concrete blocks. There are some differences, so before you move on to bigger and better projects, do some additional reading on advanced brick work. Check your library for such books.

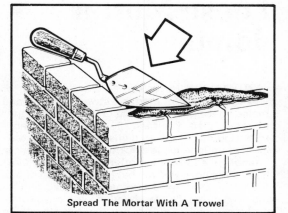
Spread The Mortar With A Trowel

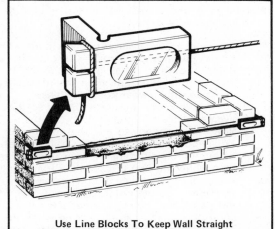
Use Line Blocks To Keep Wall Straight

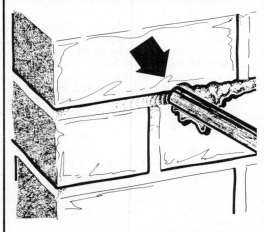
Remove Excess Mortar With A Jointer

Versatile Brick Trowel Is A Must

The brick trowel is the tool to use to lay mortar beds, butter bricks, mark and scribe in wet mortar, and to do some tuckpointing. You can tap bricks in place in the mortar bed with the trowel's handle, and, after some practice, you can even use a trowel to break bricks. Trowels come in a wide variety of sizes and shapes. Easco Tools, Inc., manufactures a quality line of trowels, as well as hammers, hatchets, and tools for masonry and plastering.

Line Level Works Well On Long Brick Walls

The line level hooks onto a cord stretched across the entire length of a wall, and is usually left in place while a course of bricks is being laid; then it is moved on up. The Ridgid line level is made of lightweight high-strength aluminum. It locks on and unlocks from the cord quite easily, and since it measures only three inches long, it can be carried in a pocket without difficulty. An accurate tool, it has a flat base for surface leveling. Ridgid Tools are made by the Ridge Tool Company.

253

Brick and Masonry

Gun Down Loose Mortar Joints

Weldwood packages Concrete Patch in cartridges for use with a caulking gun. A quality product that is easy to use, Weldwood Concrete Patch is available at many hardware and paint stores. Weldwood also markets caulks, wood preservatives, as well as an adhesive for almost every conceivable home repair. Weldwood Products is part of Roberts Consolidated Industries, a subsidiary of Champion International.

Buy Concrete In A Tube

For patching cracks in mortar joints and concrete, nothing is easier than applying a compound with your caulking gun. Macco Liquid Patch is one of many good brands on the market. You can control the width of the bead by how you cut the spout. After gunning the compound into place, you can smooth or shape the material with a putty knife or joint tool. Liquid Patch will fill cracks up to one inch wide in one application. It dries a light gray, matching the color of concrete as close-

ly as any patching product can. Liquid Patch is made by the Mac-

co Adhesives Division of Glidden Coatings and Resins.

Jointer Puts Finishing Touches On Mortar Joints

There are a number of tools you can use to rake mortar joints, but nothing quite does the job of the jointer. Different jointers are designed to create differently shaped mortar joints. C.S. Osborne & Company makes jointers as well as tools for electricians, carpenters, plumbers, and the home handyperson.

Hawk Is A Handy Mortar Holder

The hawk is a tool designed to hold a supply of mortar or plaster so you need not go back to the main supply as often. It's particularly handy when repointing joints between bricks. In addition to the hawk, the Harrington Tool Company offers hundreds of tools for brick, plaster, and concrete work. If you don't wish to invest in a hawk, you can make your own out of a square of hardboard or marine plywood and a piece of an old broom handle. Fasten the handle to the board with a wood screw.

Tuckpointing In A Tube Fills Brick Joints Fast

Mr. Thinzit Concrete Crack Fix can be gunned into the cleaned crack between bricks and then easily tooled to match the other joints. Whatever tool you use, you'll reduce the likelihood of it sticking and pulling the compound away if you dip the tool into paint thinner or a soap solution. Mr. Thinzit Concrete Crack Fix, from the Michlin Chemical Corporation, dries fast to a gray mortar-like color.

Tuckpointing Loose Mortar Joints

TUCKPOINTING is sort of a weird name for removing old mortar between bricks and replacing it with new. Loose or crumbling mortar must be replaced or it will allow moisture to penetrate, and moisture can damage the interior wall. In addition, one loose brick tends to cause more crumbling and loose mortar outside. The next thing you know, you will have a whole wall of bad mortar joints to fix. Therefore, go ahead and fix them now, before the situation gets any worse. Just buy a sack of mortar mix that has everything already in it except the water, and your tuckpointing should be a snap.

1. Clean out the loose or crumbling joints with a cold chisel and hammer. Cut down to a depth of at least a half inch, attacking the vertical joints first and then the horizontal ones. Be sure to wear safety goggles.
2. Turn the hose on the cleared joint to flush away all loose mortar and dust.
3. Now you are ready to mix the new mortar. You should know that the mix will probably be an entirely different shade when it dries than when you first mix it. Mix a trial batch and apply it to a piece of corrugated board. The porous cardboard will suck out most of the water, and the mortar that is left will be about the same shade it will be when dry. The next step is to add some color (available at hardware stores) to the mortar so that it will match the rest of the walls. When you arrive at a match on the cardboard, you will have a good idea of what the wet mix should look like to achieve the desired results.
4. Dampen the joints to be tuckpointed.
5. Force mortar into the joints with a trowel, filling the vertical joints first and then the horizontals. Press the mortar into the new joints firmly to make certain that you leave no cavities.
6. Now—before the mortar sets up—you must make the new joints look the same as the old. On a hot or warm and windy day, the mortar will dry out quickly, so you must work fast. Scrape off the excess mortar before you start pointing, and then use a jointer tool or a trowel to achieve the desired effect.
7. After the mortar sets up, take a stiff brush and clean the face of the bricks.

Here Is What You Will Need

Materials
- Mortar mix
- Corrugated cardboard
- Mortar coloring

Tools
- Cold chisel
- Hammer
- Safety goggles
- Garden hose
- Trowel
- Jointer tool or short piece of pipe
- Stiff brush

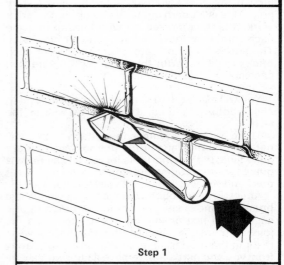

Step 1

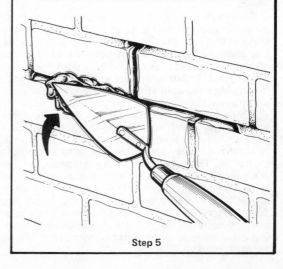

Step 5

Pointing Trowel Is Small And Handy

There is a small trowel that looks just like a bricklayer's trowel except for its size; it's called a pointing trowel. While too small for buttering bricks as effectively as its larger brother, the pointing trowel is much easier to handle for any kind of pointing purpose. Murray-Black makes a fine point-

ing trowel. When you're done with the job, clean the trowel thoroughly. Mortar left on a trowel becomes very difficult to remove

once it sets. If the surface of the blade doesn't feel slick after cleaning, use fine steel wool for smoothing.

Get A Good Bucket For Brick Work

A bucket of water comes in handy for brick and masonry work. You'll use it for keeping your tools clean as well as for soaking the bricks. If you need to buy one, consider a Fortex Rubber Bucket. Made of heavy-duty reinforced molded rubber, the Fortex Rubber Bucket comes in all sizes, many with graduated markings for measuring. Fortex Rubber Buckets won't rust or dent, and they resist the effects of plaster, acids, grease, detergents, and paints; hardened concrete will not stick to the bucket's surface. Fortex Rubber Buckets are products of Texamar Enterprises, Inc.

Replacing a Brick

A LOOSE BRICK should be reattached and a damaged brick should be replaced. Just buy a sack of mortar mix and you are ready to go to work. After you mix up a batch of the mortar, you should be able to get the loose brick back in place before it falls out and creates an even bigger headache.

1. Remove the mortar around the loose or damaged brick with a hammer and chisel. If the brick is already damaged, you can use a chisel to break it up too. If the brick is just loose, though, be careful not to break it as you chip the mortar to get it out. You will want to use the brick again in a few minutes.
2. After the brick comes out, chip away all the mortar that is still clinging to it.
3. Place the brick into a bucket of water.
4. Go back to the hole and chip away all remaining mortar. You may have to use a wire brush to get the hole really clean. When you get all the mortar out, hose down the cavity.
5. Mix the mortar, adding coloring to shade the mixture so that it matches the rest of the wall.
6. Lay a bed of mortar down on the damp floor of the hole where the brick will go.
7. Take the brick out of the bucket of water, but do not dry it; just shake off any surface water. Butter the two ends and the top of the brick with mortar.

Here Is What You Will Need
Materials
- Mortar mix
- Mortar coloring
- Replacement brick
- Bucket

Tools
- Hammer
- Cold chisel
- Wire brush
- Garden hose
- Trowel

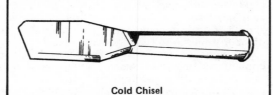

Cold Chisel

8. Insert the brick in the hole and press it in place, lining it up with the other bricks.
9. Use your trowel to force back into the cavity all the mortar that was pushed out when you inserted the brick.
10. Clean away any excess mortar.
11. Now—before the mortar sets up—make the new joints match the old ones. Remember that mortar dries faster on a hot or windy day.

Brick Handling Can Be Hard On The Hands

One accessory every brick handler needs is a pair of heavy work gloves. Heavy-duty gloves, like those bearing the White Mule Brand from the Wells Lamont Corporation, will protect you from hurting your hands while handling bricks. White Mule work gloves feature leather in all areas subject to harsh wear; the remainder is made of heavy cotton. The gloves have elastic straps at the wrist, rubberized cuffs, and leather knuckle straps. Wells Lamont makes every conceivable type of work glove, and all are of excellent quality.

Rake Your Joints With A Roller Skate

Nicknamed the "roller skate," the joint raker from Red Devil Inc., can be adjusted for depth by a mechanism that holds the nail at the precise depth required. The nail is front mounted to prevent any clogging as the tool zips through its work. Red Devil's joint raker features a lightweight aluminum handle and smooth rolling wheels. Red Devil markets dry concrete patching compound and a fast-setting anchoring cement as part of their masonry line, which includes trowels, floats, groovers, and edgers.

Step 8

Heating and Cooling

Pre-Kool Saves Energy, Lowers A/C Expense

The MasterWorks Pre-Kool unit is a new creation that can be a real energy saver for central air conditioning units. A separate unit that you set up next to the outside compressor/condenser so that it is adjacent to the condenser coil, Pre-Kool pumps water through a special media where it evaporates and draws heat off of the air conditioning condenser coils. This heat removal process enhances

the efficiency of the air conditioner and thereby reduces the amount of energy expended in keeping your home cool. Write to MasterWorks, Inc., 4606 College Park Drive, Dallas, TX 75229.

Electrostatic Air Cleaners Fit Central Units

Although your central heating/air conditioning unit filters the air, plenty of contaminants flow through even the cleanest of homes. Soot, smoke, cooking grease, and bacteria lurk in the air you breathe. An electrostatic air cleaner, like the one from General Electric, catches and holds most of the contaminating substances that would otherwise be blown

back through your home. Not an inexpensive addition, the GE Electrostatic Air Cleaner fits right into most central heating and air conditioning units.

Troubleshooter's Guide To Central Air Conditioning

There is a little booklet that despite its few pages explains just about everything that can go wrong with your central air conditioning and provides the remedy for every problem. Some repairs can be handled by the average homeowner, while others require the skill, knowledge, and equipment of professional air conditioning repairmen. Titled *$35.00 An Ounce or Air Conditioning Service Made Easy* by Joy A. Stoker, it's available by mail-order only from Air Conditioning Training, Rt. 13, Box 247, Ft. Worth, Texas 76119. It is an expensive little booklet, but if it saves you the cost of a single service call, you'll be money ahead.

Capture Waste Heat That Goes Out The Vent Pipe

The vent pipe or flue that carries away unwanted products of combustion also carries away a great deal of heat. Some of that heat can be captured with a Recyclo-Heater, a device that fits around the flue near the furnace. The unit absorbs heat through a metallic conductive media and then blows out clean heated air. Installation is a snap because the unit wraps around the flue pipe and snaps in place. The fan motor plugs into a regular wall socket, and a thermostat turns the fan off when the pipe cools. You can even attach flexible ducting to carry heat from this new source to where your house needs it most. Recyclo-Heaters are made by General Products Corporation.

Central Heating and Air Conditioning

THERE ARE SOME problems in a central heat and air conditioning unit that should not be tackled by the novice do-it-yourselfer. On the other hand, there are a number of things that you should do and which you can do with a minimum of tools, training, and experience.

The biggest enemy of your central heating and cooling system is dirt. Many homeowners know that there is a filter in the unit that needs to be cleaned or changed periodically, but most rely on the preseason inspection by a serviceman for filter maintenance. Once or twice a year, though, is not enough. In fact, many units need a filter change once a month. If your heating/cooling unit has a permanent type filter, clean it according to the instructions on the unit itself. Many models must be sprayed after you clean them with a filter coating chemical available at hardware stores. Fortunately, most units have disposable filters that are very inexpensive and easy to change.

Here Is What You Will Need

Materials

- New filters
- Filter coating chemical
- Household bleach
- Duct tape
- Lightweight oil
- Belt dressing

Tools

- Screwdriver
- Toothbrush
- Brush
- Canister vacuum cleaner
- Suede brush
- Hand mirror

1. The filter is usually located in the furnace unit between the blower and the return air vent. Look right next to the blower, and when you find it, remove the filter access panel on the front of the unit.
2. Remove the old filter. It is either held in

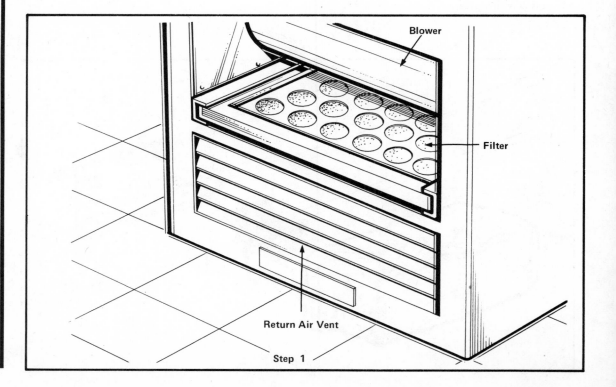

Blower

Filter

Return Air Vent

Step 1

Air Flow Is Important

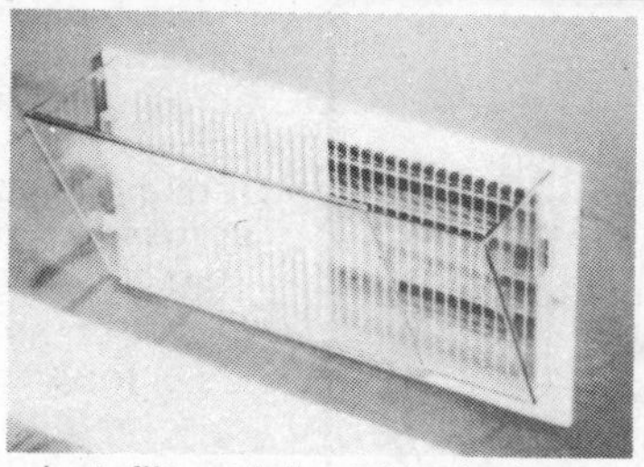

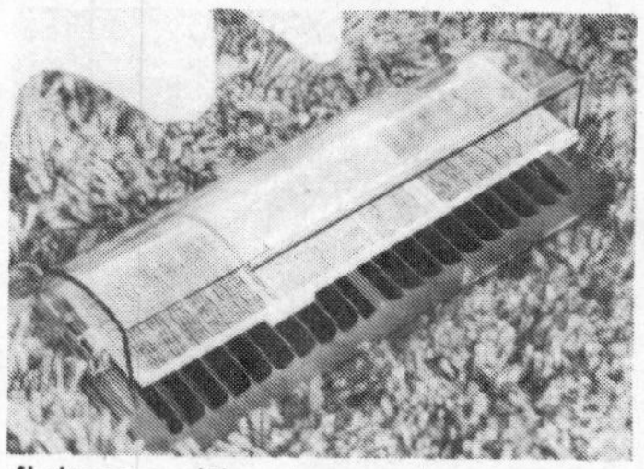

Because heat rises, the direction of air flow in a heating and cooling system is quite important. In the winter, you need to direct the warm air toward the floor, while in the summer, you should try to aim it upward. You can accomplish this feat with inexpensive clear plastic deflectors that are held in place on the vent registers by small magnets or by Velcro. Deflect-O deflectors come in several styles for different types of registers. There is even a model with a dust filter. Adjustable in length and reversible for changes in the seasons, these Deflect-O units provide an excellent way of controlling air flow and increasing efficiency without spending a great deal of money. A comparable brand of deflectors in wide distribution is Deflex from Aristo-Mat.

place by some sort of device that you can see, or it is in a slot. The size of the filter should be printed on its sides or ends. If you have a poor memory, write the size on a piece of tape and attach it to the filter access panel.

3. Install the new filter. Make sure that the arrow on the filter is aimed in the same direction that the air flows.
4. Be sure to replace the access panel.

What most homeowners fail to realize is that there are other places besides the filter where dirt can disrupt your heating/cooling unit. The blower or fan that moves air from the unit out through the ducts can get dirty, too. This is particularly true with a squirrel-cage type fan. When the openings get clogged, the fan cannot move enough air, and the system runs inefficiently. Here are some blower cleaning instructions.

△ 1. Turn off all electric power to the unit by tripping the circuit breaker switch. Make sure the current is off before you start working on the blower.
△ 2. Remove the filter access panel. The fan is usually held in a track by sheet metal screws. Remove the screws.
△ 3. The fan unit will slide out.
△ 4. If the electric cord to the fan unit is not long enough for you to slide the unit all the way out, disconnect the wires after noting exactly how they are hooked up.
△ 5. To clean the blower, you must brush off each fan blade. An old toothbrush may be the biggest brush you can get into the spaces between blades.
△ 6. Also brush the entire area around the blower; here you can use a larger brush.
△ 7. Go over the fan unit with a hose type vacuum cleaner to remove all the dirt you loosened.
△ 8. Replace the fan assembly; make sure that you secure it with the screws or bolts you removed earlier.

With an air conditioning unit, you have additional cleanup chores outside as well as those inside. The inside cleanup concerns the evaporator, which is rather difficult to reach. The evaporator is located just forward of the furnace in a small metal box called a plenum. The blower sends air through the furnace and then through the evaporator just before the air goes into the duct system. If you change filters monthly, the evaporator should never get very dirty, but you should clean it every year in any case. Here is how to reach and then clean the evaporator.

(Continued on following page)

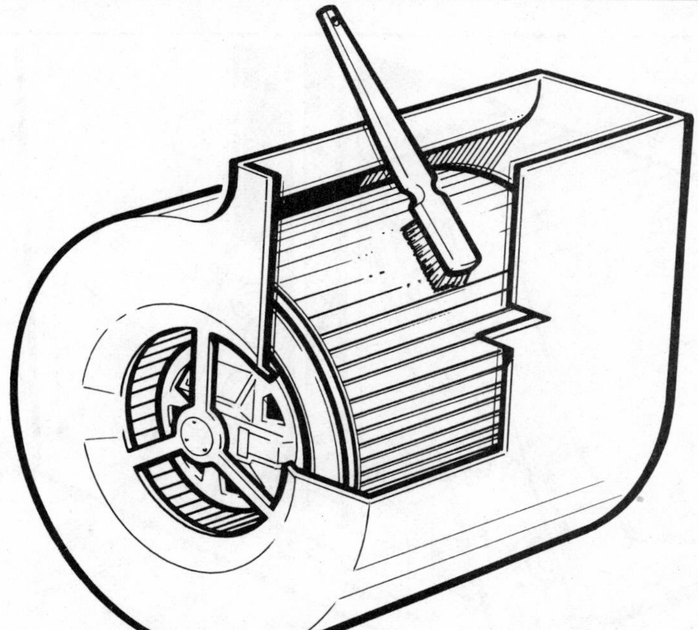

Step △ 5

Heat Pump Can Answer Heating/Cooling Needs

In many parts of the country, a new comfort conditioner is taking the place of central heating and air conditioning units. Called the Heat Pump, it pumps heat out of the house in summer and brings heat from the outside air inside during winter. Yes, even cold air has some heat, and the heat pump finds it; but in very cold weather, a heater assists the pump. Actually, it is only practical in climates where you need both heating and cooling. Since it is totally electric, the heat pump will be unaffected by the possible future of natural gas or fuel oil; but if the cost of electricity keeps going up, its attractiveness may be diminished somewhat. General Electric, Westinghouse and Chrysler Airtemp are all in the heat pump race.

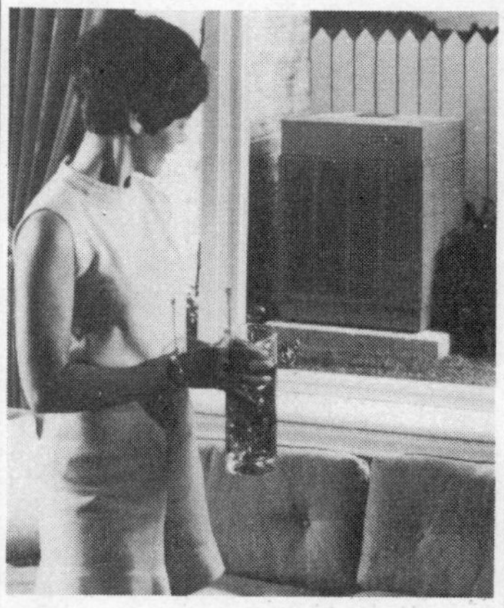

Thermostat Registers Control Individual Rooms

Does your central heating system make you swelter in one room while you freeze in another? You might be able to correct this situation with Trol-A-Temp registers or dampers. These motorized devices are controlled by separate thermostats that automatically send heated or cooled air where you need it and when you need it. The thermostat in any room automatically opens the corresponding register or damper and automatically turns on the system. Likewise, the thermostat can shut off the register or damper, and—providing all of the other thermostats are not in need of heating or cooling—turn the system off. Trol-A-Temp registers and dampers come in a number of different styles to fit into just about any type of central heating/cooling system.

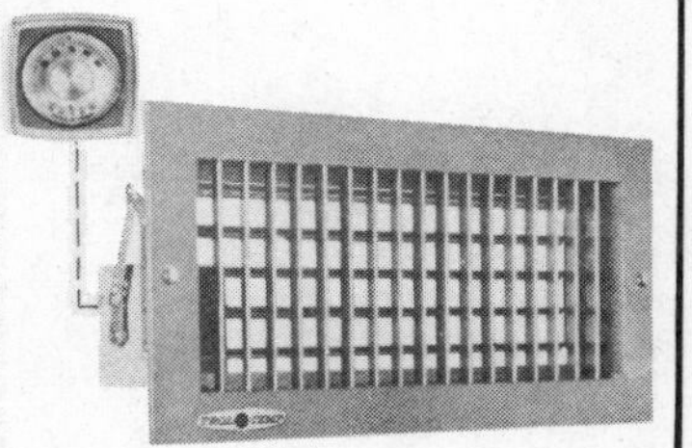

Heating and Cooling

Air Filters Are Key To Efficiency

Clean air filters in your heating and cooling systems are the key to efficiency. Inexpensive and easy to replace, most air filters are merely thrown away when they get dirty. You might, however, wish to look into permanent filters that you can clean and reuse. The all-aluminum Phifer Air-Weave filters can be cut to fit your heating/cooling system with tin snips or even kitchen scissors. They should be cleaned about every month. Vacuum them first, and then wash them with soap and water. After they are clean and dry, spray them with a dust attracting filter coater like Alfcoater. There are also fiber-type permanent filters, but the aluminum ones are easier to clean and last much longer.

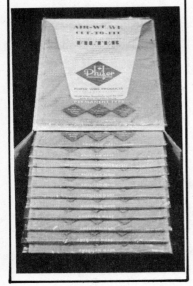

Unwrapped Ducts Cost You Money

Any ducts that are not properly insulated cost you money during both the heating and the cooling seasons. Certain-teed's Standard Duct Wrap Insulation offers permanent, fire-safe insulation performance, and the factory-applied vapor barrier stops ducts from sweating—a cause of many a ruined ceiling. Available in 1½- and two-inch thicknesses, Certain-teed's Standard Duct Wrap Insulation comes in rolls of 75 feet for the two-inch type or 100 feet for the thinner wrap. Both rolls are four feet wide. Certain-teed also makes duct liner material for ducts that must be fabricated, as well as a complete line of ducts in all sizes and shapes.

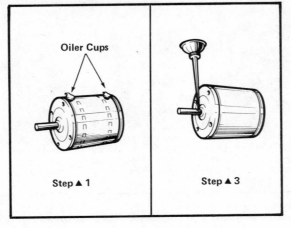

Oiler Cups

Step ▲ 1   Step ▲ 3

(Continued from previous page)

o   1. Cut the electric power to the unit by tripping the circuit breaker switch. Make sure that the current is off before you start working.
o   2. Remove the foil wrapped insulation at the front of the plenum. It is probably taped in place. Remove it carefully because you will have to replace it later.
o   3. Once the insulation is off, you will see the access plate which is held on by several screws. Remove the screws and the plate will come off.
o   4. In some cases, you will now be able to reach all the way back to clean the entire area. If not, slide the evaporator out a little. You can slide it even though the evaporator has rigid pipes connected to it, but be sure not to bend the pipes.
o   5. Use a suede brush to clean the entire underside of the evaporator unit. A large hand mirror can be very helpful in letting you see what you are doing.
o   6. Clean the tray located below the evaporator unit. This tray carries away condensation from the evaporator, and if it gets dirty it can clog up. Next, pour some household bleach into the hole in the tray to get rid of any fungus that may be forming.
o   7. Put the evaporator unit back in place, reinstall the plate, and tape the insulation back over it. Check for any air leaks and cover with duct tape.

The outside cleaning must be done at the condensing unit. The unit has a fan that moves air across the condenser coils. You must clean the coils on the intake side. Check while the unit is running to ascertain which direction the air moves across the coils. After you know this, then you can start cleaning.

□   1. Cut all the electric power to the unit by tripping the circuit breaker switch. Make sure that the current is off before you start working.
□   2. Cut down any grass, weeds, or vines that have grown up around the condensing unit. They could be obstructing the flow of air.
□   3. Use a brush to clean away all the dirt that has collected on the fins. Brushing works better than spraying with a garden hose because water can turn part of the dirt into mud and compact it between the fins.

In addition to cleaning, you should be sure to lubricate parts of your heating/cooling unit. Cut off the power if you have to reach inside to oil. Here are the spots to lubricate.

▲   1. The blower motor has oiler cups. Lift the cups and squirt in from five to ten drops of lightweight oil at the beginning of each season.
▲   2. If the blower motor is belt driven, spray belt dressing on the belt once a year and any time you hear the belt squealing.
▲   3. Apply lightweight oil to the fan motor in the condensing unit at the start of each season. If the fan blade is aimed upward, look for a rubber or plastic cover over the oiler cup. Lift the cover to oil, and put in no more than five to ten drops. If the fan faces out, look for oiler cups on the motor housing. To reach them, you must remove the access plate. If there are no oiler cups, you may have a sealed unit. Sealed units do not need oiling, but it is a good idea after about four years to squirt oil around the spot where the shaft enters the motor. A felt pad there tends to dry out.

These simple care and maintenance steps will make your unit work more efficiently and thus reduce your utility bills. They should also cut down on those very expensive repair bills you were paying every year.

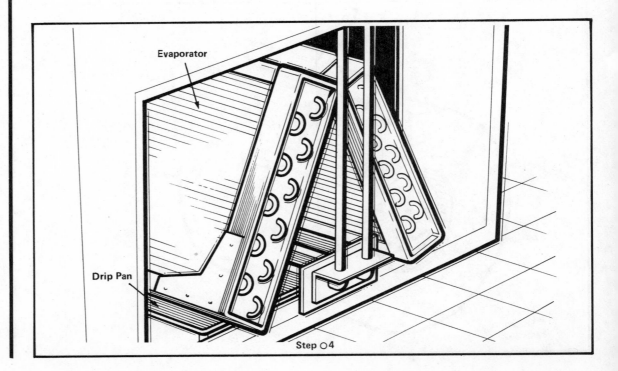

Evaporator

Drip Pan

Step O 4

Forced Air Heaters Need Filters

A dirty filter on a forced air system can seriously retard the system's efficiency. Many homeowners prefer the inexpensive disposable filters, but such filters should be changed often. Amer-Glas filters, made by the American Air Filter Corp., come in all forms: hammock type, filter media rolls that can be cut to fit, and the individual filters in the Amer-Glas II line. The Amer-Glas II filters contain a media that shows dirt faster.

Adjustment Ratchet Wrench Makes Furnace Work Fast

If you'd like a new wrench that works twice as fast as an ordinary wrench on pipes, nuts, or bolts, buy yourself a Weil Adjustamatic Ratchet Wrench. It does the work of an adjustable, open-end, box, or pipe wrench and does the work better and faster due to its ratchet feature. It can be used with one hand and is self adjusting to a sure, three-point grip. Precision engineered, made of drop-forged

steel, fully ground and polished with a chrome finish, the Weil Adjustamatic Ratchet Wrench comes in four sizes; you may want all four after you try one.

Gas Lines Take Gas Fittings

While some plumbing fittings can be used on gas lines, in many instances it is best to use fittings specifically designed for gas lines. For example, the Rockwell Gas Stop from Rockwell International is made of brass and is equipped with a solid lever handle with an integral check. Rockford-Eclipse Division of Eclipse Fuel Engineering Company also makes gas cocks and valves, and Rockford's Gas Stop Lubricants should be used in all gas valves. There are different formulations for different types of gas and different situations.

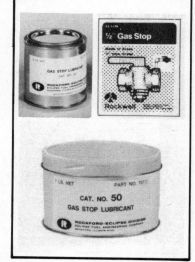

Gas Burners

ALTHOUGH MORE expensive than fuel oil in many parts of the country, natural gas is generally the more popular and preferred source for heat. Natural gas burns cleaner than fuel oil, and most natural gas furnaces present far fewer operational difficulties. In fact, the problems that do afflict natural gas furnaces usually have little to do with the fuel source itself; instead, they typically involve the thermocouple, the pilot, or some aspect of the electrical hookup. And despite the fact that natural gas costs more (and its price is rising steadily), the natural gas furnace is less costly both to buy and to install than its fuel oil counterpart.

The basic bit of maintenance that you can perform on your gas burner is to change or clean filters at the prescribed periods. If some serious difficulty afflicts your furnace, by all means call in a professional repairman. There are, nonetheless, some simple repairs which you can perform yourself and save the cost of an unnecessary service call.

1. If the pilot goes out, check the orifice to see

Here Is What You Will Need

Materials

- Replacement filters
- Replacement thermocouple
- Replacement thermostat
- Replacement fuse

Tools

- Needle

Burner
Thermocouple Tube
Bracket
Bracket Nut

whether it is clogged; if it is, clean it out with the point of a needle. A faulty pilot may well signal a problem with the thermocouple, however. Replace the thermocouple if it is no longer functioning properly, but before you replace it, check to make sure that the pilot flame is bathing it satisfactorily. You can adjust the pilot flame to bathe the tip of the thermocouple by following the instructions in the furnace owner's manual.

2. If the burner itself fails to light, the first thing to check, of course, is the pilot. If the problem isn't the pilot, it may be a faulty gas valve that is sticking when it shouldn't. Tap the gas valve sharply with your knuckles. Another possible cause is a faulty thermostat. Turn the thermostat to a higher setting; if the gas burner goes on only when the thermostat is set much higher than it should be, replace the thermostat. The only other possible cause that you should investigate for the burner not functioning is that no electrical current is reaching the furnace. Check for a blown fuse or tripped circuit breaker switch and replace or reset as necessary.

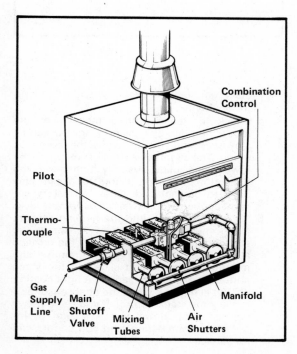

Combination Control

Pilot
Thermocouple
Gas Supply Line
Main Shutoff Valve
Mixing Tubes
Air Shutters
Manifold

A Gas Furnace From GE

Despite the corporate name, General Electric makes fine gas furnaces. GE Executive furnaces—available in heating capacities of 100,000, 130,000, and 165,000 BTUH—offer modulation control. Through three different flame levels and three different fan speeds, Executive furnaces automatically provide closely controlled temperatures. Heat flow changes from the high level on frigid below-zero winter days to the medium level on most winter days to the quiet low level on brisk spring and fall mornings. GE's sensitive solid-state thermostat helps maintain close temperature control. Executive furnaces can be fitted with a top-of-the-line air conditioner, electronic air cleaner, and/or a power humidifier to equip your home for total year-round comfort control.

Heating and Cooling

Williamson Five-In-One Provides Year-Round Comfort

One oil-fired unit that does nearly everything you could expect from a heating/cooling system is the Williamson Five-In-One. In addition to being a furnace and air conditioner, it serves as an electronic air cleaner, a humidifier, and a dehumidifier. Designed to provide total year-round comfort, the Williamson Five-In-One heats, cools, purifies the air electronically, and humidifies or dehumidifies as needed. If you need a new oil heater, call your local Williamson dealer for more information about the Five-In-One.

Auxiliary Heater Burns Kerosene

Although it may sound like a throwback to the 19th century, the kerosene-burning auxiliary heater—thanks to modern engineering—can be a safe, clean-burning, odorless, and very effective small space heater. Ideal for supplying heat to a room that is always too cool because the main heater's circulation fails to warm it sufficiently, the kerosene heater is also made for people who live in moderate climates where central heating would be impractical for handling the few cool days each year. One good kerosene burner is the Happy II Radiant Heater made by Greenford Products, Inc. Its cost of operation totals about 1½¢ per hour.

BernzOmatic Kit Burns Mapp Gas

BernzOmatic markets a special torch for use with Mapp gas. Called the Super Torch with Cyclone Jet Burner, this new type torch delivers a rotary action flame that heats faster and burns hotter. While it is a brazing tool, it joins most metals as completely as if they were welded. The BernzOmatic kit, which costs little more than a propane torch kit, includes two torches—one for fine flame and one for a heavy flame; two each of three different brazing rods; a spark lighter; a pair of protective glasses; a complete guide to using the Super Torch; a handy cylinder stand; and a cylinder of Mapp gas. These components are available separately if you don't need the entire kit. The Super Torch can sweat solder any heating and cooling installation.

Oil Burners

OIL-FIRED BURNERS are used in many sections of the country as the basic heat source for a warm air heating system, a hot water heating system, or a steam heating system. Most of the home oil systems in use today are called pressure burners. A high-pressure spray combines with a blower to send a fine mist of oil into the combustion chamber, where the oil is ignited by an electric spark. The oil continues to burn, of course, as the mist continues to be sprayed.

Although oil burners are generally reliable, hard-working systems that provide years of trouble-free service, you must know how to maintain them properly. Here are the steps in maintaining an oil burner:

1. Keep the fan motor lubricated according to the instructions in your owner's manual. Most motors require the application of an electric motor oil.
2. Keep the blower clean. Again, follow what the manual says, but be sure to shut off the current. A small skinny brush usually works best.
3. Keep the stacks free of soot deposits by dismantling the stacks and bringing each section down sharply against the newspaper-covered floor. Be sure to seal the

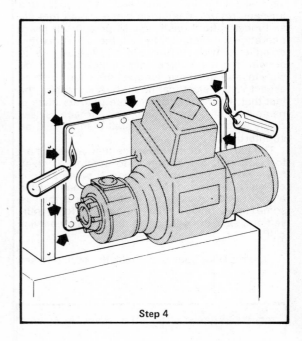

Step 4

stack connections properly when rejoining the sections.

4. Check for leaks around the rim of the mounting plate by passing a lighted candle slowly around the rim while the burner is going. The slightest leak will suck the flame toward the plate. Usually tightening the bolts stops the leak; if not, the gasket may need to be replaced. Often refractory cement applied around the rim, stops any leak.
5. About two months into the heating season, clean and inspect the heat sensor in the stack control. Cut off current to the furnace at the electrical entry box, remove the mounting screws, and slide out the stack control to expose the sensor. A light coating of soot is normal; clean the heat sensor and replace the stack control. If you see a heavy coat of soot, however, it's a sign of incomplete combustion, and you should call for service.

Here Is What You Will Need
Materials
- Electric motor oil
- Replacement fuses
- Kerosene
- Candle
- Refractory cement
Tools
- Small brush

Handy Level Fits In Your Pocket

The pocket level from Mayes Brothers Tool Manufacturing Company is as accurate as any level around. It features a protected bubble vial, a sturdy pocket clip, and a hang-up hole for pegboard storage. Naturally, this mini level can be used on all flat surfaces, but it also has a V-grooved bottom so that it sits on pipe or conduit. Its lightweight aluminum construction means that you hardly know you're carrying it until you need it. All furnaces work best when they are level.

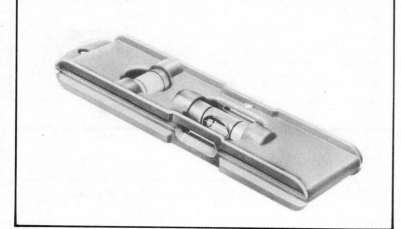

Plumbing Tools Can Handle Furnace Work

Many of the tools designed for solving plumbing problems come in handy when working on furnaces and heating systems. For example, the 10-inch adjustable plumber's pliers made by Kirkhill, Inc., are great for furnace work and a host of other household tasks in addition to plumbing chores. Made of forged steel, the pliers are equipped with comfortable grips. Kirkhill markets a full line of plumbing parts as well as other plumbing tools.

If The Fuel Crisis Really Gets Bad . . .

The fuel shortage has made some people seek alternative heating methods to oil-burning furnaces. If wood is plentiful, try the J-E Wood Circulator Home Heater. Called Hearth-Flo, it features an inner unit constructed of heavy-gauge steel and a firebox lined with firebrick that won't expand or burn out. The outer cabinet is finished in two-tone (brown and beige) high-temperature baked-on enamel. The louvered top guides the heat in all directions, while a non-electric thermostat controls the air intake, sending fresh air to the fire—and thus more heat into the room—when needed. An optional thermostatically-controlled blower pulls heat from the ceiling forcing it over the inner unit and then out over the floor. Hearth-Flo is made by the Jackes-Evans Manufacturing Company and is available where other heating systems are sold.

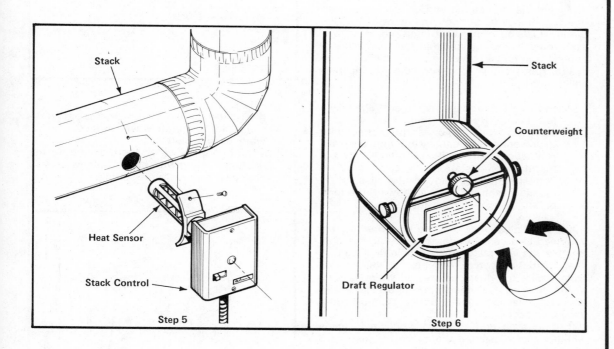

Step 5

Step 6

6. Inspect the air draft regulator. It should close when the unit goes off and be slightly open when the burner is on. You can adjust the air draft regulator easily by turning the counterweight.
7. Consult the manual regarding the proper adjustment of the spark gap, the air tube shutter, and all other components requiring adjustment.
8. Call in a pro to clean, adjust, and inspect the unit prior to the onset of winter.

If the unit fails to run, here are some of the steps you can take to get it going again.

△ 1. Check to be sure the switch is on; if it is, push the reset button if the unit has one.
△ 2. If nothing happens, check the fuse or circuit breaker switch to see whether the power is still on. If you find that the fuse or circuit breaker is the problem and after you put in a new fuse or reset the switch it goes out again, you know that your system has a short. Repair it or have it repaired immediately.
△ 3. If the burner works spasmodically or sputters before going out completely, you probably have a dirty oil filter. Check your owner's manual for instructions on getting to the filter and on bathing the filter in kerosene. Use caution as kerosene is flammable.
△ 4. Make sure you have enough fuel oil.
△ 5. Move the thermostat up to a higher than normal setting. Check the accuracy of the thermostat.
△ 6. If you have a steam system, be sure the water level in the boiler is adequate.
△ 7. If you have a hot water system, check the recirculating pump to make certain that it is moving the water around as it should. If the water does not circulate, the burner system does not operate.

You Can Get Replacement Parts For Your Oil System

In areas where oil heating is popular, hardware stores and plumbing suppliers generally stock a variety of replacement parts for oil-burning furnaces. Many of these parts are manufactured by Hancock-Gross. Since these parts are generally sold from bins and do not come with instructions, however, you'll certainly need the owner's manual or professional help before tackling any repairs. Remember that one cardinal rule of working with a heating system is that you don't mess with it unless you know precisely what you're doing.

Heating and Cooling

Honeywell Controls All Temperatures

The Honeywell name has long been considered a leader in the thermostat field, making controls for all sorts of heating and cooling systems. The familiar round Honeywell thermostat can be found in homes all across the country. An accurate thermostat for heating and cooling, it has an outstanding track record for longevity, though it is easily and inexpensively replaceable. Honeywell also makes a Chronotherm unit that provides automatic temperature control;

the device can be set to switch the temperature setting up and down every night. This energy saver replaces any 24-volt two-wire thermostat; a separate transformer is provided for the clock.

Cordless Thermostat Control Cuts Fuel Bills

A cordless automatic thermostat control called Thermotimer from the Thermotrol Corporation turns your thermostat down at night and back up again the following morning. Powered by a "C" battery, Thermotimer cuts heating costs and saves valuable energy. You merely set the control for the low and high temperatures you want and for the time you want the changes from one to the other to go into operation. The Thermo-

timer device fits over most conventional round thermostats.

Make Your Automatic Control Even More Automatic

The thermostat is in itself a device that automatically maintains the temperature inside your home. But by adding a Fuel Sentry unit, you can make your thermostat even more automatic. Fuel Sentry turns the heat down at night and then back up before you get up in the morning. Similarly, it can be set to turn on the air conditioning an hour or so before you get home in the afternoon or evening. No more getting up to a cold house in the winter; no more coming home to a hot box in the summer. Most importantly, Fuel Sentry provides an excellent way to save energy and not lose your temper in the process. Easy to install.

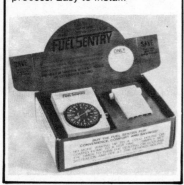

Replace A Worn-Out, Inaccurate Thermostat

There are replacement thermostats available for just about any heating/cooling or just heating system. Jade offers three different models, vertical and horizontal units and an adapter with cover plate to replace round units. A Jade thermostat is available for every type of energy system—natural gas, electric, propane gas, or oil. The decorative as well as accurate units all have easy-to-read numbers and positive "off" settings.

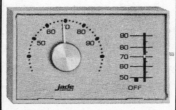

Checking and Changing a Thermostat

IF YOU HAVE a thermostat in your home that controls the heating and/or cooling of your house, you may be perfectly happy with it. If the thermostat is no longer calibrated properly, however, you can never be sure that you are heating or cooling your house to the temperature setting you desire. Here is how to check your thermostat's calibration.

1. Tape a glass tube thermometer to the wall a few inches from the thermostat. Place a small tab of padding under the thermometer to prevent it from actually touching the wall.
2. Wait about ten to fifteen minutes for the thermometer to stabilize.
3. Compare the reading on the glass thermometer with the needle showing the temperature on the thermostat.

If there is a variance of more than one degree, you need to do something about the thermostat. Remove the face plate—usually held in place by a snap-in friction catch—and inspect the mechanism inside for dust particles. If there is dust inside, blow it away either with your breath or with an empty plastic squeeze bottle. Do not use a vacuum cleaner.

If there is no dust problem, you must decide whether to replace the thermostat or just learn what each setting means in terms of real temperature. If you wish to put in a new unit, here are the basic steps.

△ 1. With the face plate off of the old unit, look for the mounting screws. Remove the screws to release the unit from the wall.
△ 2. Remove the wires coming from the wall by turning the screws on the back of the thermostat unit counterclockwise. Take care not to let the loose wires fall down between the walls.
△ 3. Clean the exposed wires by scraping them with a knife until the wire ends shine.
△ 4. Attach the wires to the new thermostat. Be sure that the new unit operates on the same voltage.
△ 5. Push the excess wire back into the wall.
△ 6. Tape up the opening to prevent cold air inside the walls from affecting the thermostat.
△ 7. Install the mounting screws to secure the new unit to the wall. If the thermostat has a mercury tube, set the unit against a level

Here Is What You Will Need
Materials
- Tape
- Tube-type thermometer
- Padding
- Replacement thermostat
Tools
- Plastic squeeze bottle
- Screwdriver
- Knife
- Level
- Razor blade

during installation. A mercury tube thermostat is more accurate when it is level.
△ 8. Snap the face plate in place.
△ 9. Make sure that the new thermostat turns the heating/cooling unit on and off when you change the temperature setting.

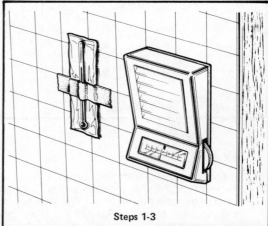

Steps 1-3

Step △1

Have Baseboard Heat Without Plumbing Connections

You can install permanent hot water baseboard heating without having to make any plumbing connections whatsoever. Intertherm units are completely self contained (except for the connection to electric current), use no blowers or motors, and are completely silent. They create heat by running water in hermetically-sealed copper tubing through a long finned area that heats the water. The water, in turn, heats the air around it, and the heated air rises out of the unit, drawing in cold air from the bottom to start circulation. Since Intertherm units heat the water only to the temperature needed to warm the air, they are exceptionally safe and economical baseboard heaters.

Heater Receptacle Makes Sense

One very practical add-on for an electric baseboard system is a duplex receptacle. If you need another wall outlet it makes good sense to tie in to the heater wiring rather than cut into the wall. Nelco makes a duplex receptacle that attaches easily to the Nelco baseboard heating system, which is known for its quiet, safe, and efficient operation. In its durable baked epoxy coating as well as its style, the Nelco duplex receptacle matches the Nelco baseboard heating system.

Electric Baseboard Units

ANY HEATING system that involves electricity is going to be costly, but the electric baseboard system has some advantages that may make its extra operational expense worthwhile. Baseboard units constitute the nearly ideal accessory system to augment an inadequate central heating system. They are great for handling the heating requirements of a new room because they can be installed so easily; they require no plumbing or ducting, and many just plug into a wall outlet. And since they hug the wall, they don't take up much floor space.

Electric baseboard heating is clean and quiet. Heat is sent into the room by convection, so there is no noise from a fan. Each room can be individually heated and controlled by its own thermostat, usually built into the baseboard unit.

There are no routine maintenance tasks, and nearly all problems are electrical. Here are the basic remedial steps to take if you discover that no heat is coming out of your electric baseboard heater.

1. Check for a blown fuse or tripped circuit breaker switch. Replace the fuse or reset the circuit breaker switch.
2. Shut off the current and then carefully inspect the unit's wiring; check both by looking at the wiring and by testing it with a continuity tester.

Here Is What You Will Need

Materials
- Replacement fuse
- Electrical wire
- Replacement heating element
- Replacement thermal cut-off safety device
- Replacement thermostat

Tools
- Continuity tester

3. Remove any obstruction that could be impeding the air flow. Something may have fallen into the unit, or the drapes or a piece of furniture may be blocking the air flow. Once you remove the obstructions, push the reset button.
4. Check the heating element with a continuity tester. If it is defective, replace it according to the instructions in your owner's manual, or have a professional repairman replace it for you.
5. Check the thermal cut-off safety device with the continuity tester. This device shuts the unit off when a problem exists. If it is faulty, however, it will prevent the unit from running. Replace the cut-off device if it proves defective.
6. Check the thermostat and replace if it is defective.

Portable Baseboard Heaters Travel To Trouble Spots

With a portable baseboard heater like Emerson's PBH model, you correct any heating trouble spot in your home. Less than four inches deep, it can fit snugly against the wall; yet its 49 inch length spreads heat over a wide area. The built-in adjustable thermostat allows you to set the heat level you desire, and since there is no fan or motor, the Emerson Portable Baseboard Heater is whisper quiet. A safe unit (UL Listed) with grounded plug and thermal protectors, its heating elements float in nylon bushings to handle contraction and expansion. The sandalwood baked enamel finish is attractive but unobtrusive, while the carrying handle and feet are quite functional in moving and setting up the unit in different locations.

Duct System Doubles As Baseboard Heater

Thermo-Base is a system that converts standard ducts for the central heating into baseboard units. By changing velocity pressure into static pressure, Thermo-Base produces full end-to-end heat distribution delivered at low velocity with no blasts of air. You can get Thermo-Base — a creation of Leigh Products, Inc. — in three-, five-, and eight-foot lengths in your choice of beige or English\Walnut finishes.

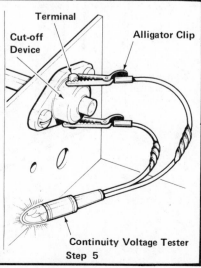

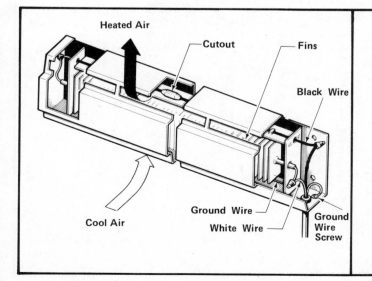

Heated Air — Cutout — Fins — Black Wire — Ground Wire — White Wire — Ground Wire Screw — Cool Air

Terminal — Cut-off Device — Alligator Clip — Continuity Voltage Tester Step 5

Heating and Cooling

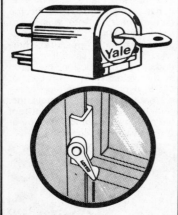
Window Air Conditioning Units

ALTHOUGH COMMONLY called a window air conditioner, a room air conditioner can be installed in a wall as well. No matter where it is mounted, however, it functions by venting hot air from both the fan motor and the condenser to the outside. One of the more powerful units can generally handle the cooling requirements of more than the room in which it is installed; in fact, if the paths of air circulation permit, one (or possibly two) room air conditioners of substantial capacity can cool an entire apartment.

Although repairing a room air conditioner can get complicated, routine maintenance is quite simple. Just follow these steps.

1. Lubricate the fan motor according to the instructions in your owner's manual.
2. Clean or replace the air filter at the beginning of each summer season.
3. Clean and inspect the coil fins. If you discover that the fins are crimped or bent, straighten them with a fin comb.
4. Vacuum the condenser coils and evaporator coils to rid them of dust and dirt.
5. Clean the drain tube that carries off condensate.

When preventive maintenance fails and the room air conditioner either fails to function at all or functions unsatisfactorily, the following procedures should get it going again.

△ 1. If nothing happens when you turn the unit on, check the fuse or circuit breaker and replace or reset as necessary. It is possible, of course, that no current is reaching the unit due to a faulty plug and/or cord. Check

and replace any defective electrical parts.

△ 2. When the air conditioner blows warm air, either the temperature control knob (which is actually a thermostat) is faulty or the compressor has gone bad. Check the knob with a continuity tester and replace it if faulty. If the knob is still working, call in a profes-

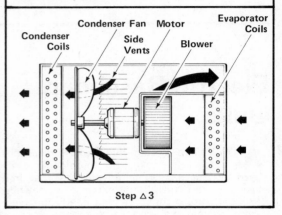

Step △3

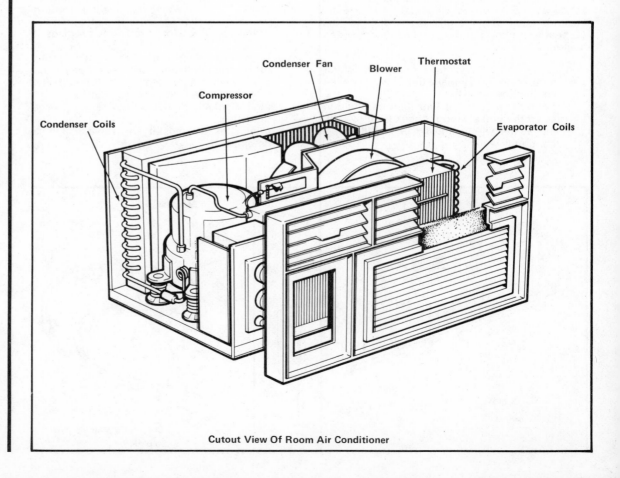

Cutout View Of Room Air Conditioner

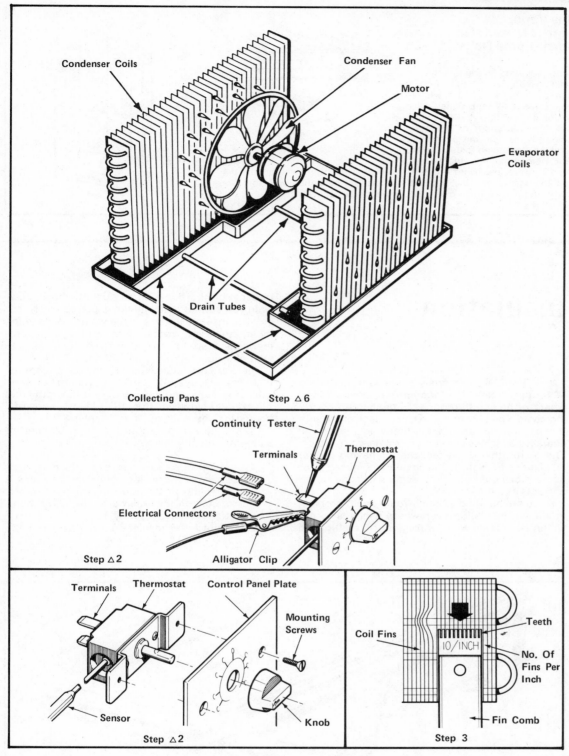

Condenser Coils

Condenser Fan

Motor

Evaporator Coils

Drain Tubes

Collecting Pans

Step △ 6

Continuity Tester

Terminals

Thermostat

Electrical Connectors

Alligator Clip

Step △ 2

Terminals

Thermostat

Control Panel Plate

Mounting Screws

Coil Fins

10/INCH

Teeth

No. Of Fins Per Inch

Sensor

Knob

Fin Comb

Step △ 2

Step 3

sional repairman to install a new compressor.

△ 3. When the air conditioner blows cool air but not enough of it, check the fan first. You may well find that the bearings are in need of lubrication or that the fan motor requires replacing. Insufficient air flow is also a common result of a lack of routine maintenance; clean or replace the filter, straighten and clean bent fins, and vacuum the condenser and evaporator coils. The flow of air might be hampered, however, by the evaporator icing over; check the blower and make sure that the set screw is tight on the shaft.

△ 4. A compressor that cuts in and out spasmodically may indicate merely that the condenser coils need vacuuming or that some obstruction (like drapes or furniture) must be moved out of the way. It may also indicate that the sensor bulb is out of position; the bulb should be in the return air flow but not touching any of the coils.

△ 5. If your air conditioner seems exceptionally noisy, check the fan blades and the motor bearings. The blades may require straightening and/or cleaning, and the motor bearings may require lubrication. The noise may also be due to the air conditioner being loose in its mountings; tighten it down or install additional supports as required. Also make sure that the set screw holding the blower to the shaft is tight.

△ 6. Water dripping inside your house from the air conditioner can usually be corrected by repositioning the unit so that it tilts toward the outside or by cleaning the drain tube. If the excess moisture is caused by condensation (a common problem in humid areas), install a drain pan made especially for this purpose.

Heating and Cooling

Styrofoam Enters The Home Insulation Field

Styrofoam is becoming a factor in the insulation field. In any remodeling project you'll find sheets of Styrofoam TG in a form to go under new shingles, under new siding, over concrete slab floors, under existing ceilings, and in crawl spaces. Styrofoam TG has been used for years as an insulation in refrigeration and is now coming into its own for use in homes. Dow Chemical produces Styrofoam TG and markets Styrofoam TG insulation materials, but several other companies—including Amspec, Inc.—use it in their insulating products as well.

Loose Fill Is The Least Costly Insulation

Usually, the least expensive insulation you can add to your attic is loose fill. Available by the bag and poured in place and then raked level, loose fill can also be blown into place, but that requires professional equipment. Owens-Corning Fiberglas Corporation makes Fiberglas Blowing Wool for this purpose, as well as Fiberglas insulation in many other forms.

Buy Vapor Barrier Material In Carry-Home Rolls

Warp Brothers markets rolls of plastic material in thicknesses from two to six mils and in widths from three to 20 feet. Called Carry-Home Coverall, the material makes a fine vapor or moisture barrier in the four-mil or thicker versions. If you plan to use it in an attic, remember that the barrier goes between the living quarters and the insulation. Just lay the Carry-Home Coverall over the joists, and the weight of the loose-fill insulation will hold the vapor barrier in place.

Insulation

AS THE ENERGY crisis brings with it soaring utility rates, the homeowner needs to do whatever he can to reduce his heating and cooling costs. The best thing he can do is to make sure that his home is insulated properly; insulation will actually pay for itself in long-term energy savings. There are other good reasons for having proper insulation, though. Good insulation makes your home more comfortable, deadens outside noise, and acts as a fire retardant.

If you are building a home, you face no problem in placing insulation everywhere it needs to go: within all outside walls, throughout the attic, and under your new floors. In an existing house, however, you cannot reach all those places easily, but you can insulate the one place where you lose the most efficiency during both winter and summer—the attic. In most cases, you can insulate your attic yourself with little difficulty.

There are two basic types of insulating material, blanket and loose-fill. Blanket insulation comes in rolls or in batts, and you can buy it in widths that fit exactly between the attic joists. Loose-fill comes in bags, and you pour it in place.

Here is how to go about installing blanket insulation in an unfinished attic.

1. Lay wide boards across the joists to serve as walkways. The surface between the joists is the ceiling of the room below, and unless you stay on the walkways, you could damage that ceiling severely.
2. If there is no insulation whatsoever in the

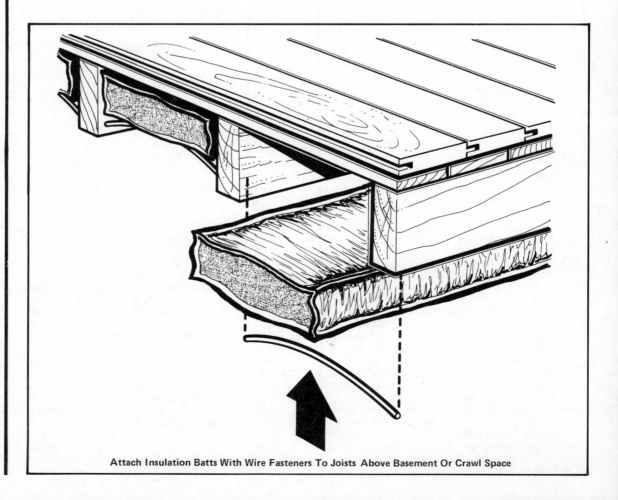

Attach Insulation Batts With Wire Fasteners To Joists Above Basement Or Crawl Space

Stapling Hammer Quickens Insulation Installation

When installing batts or rolls of insulation that must be stapled in place against studs or joists, you'll find that a stapling hammer will do an even faster job than the regular staple gun. The Bostitch Model H2B is a lightweight tool that is well balanced and easy to use. Bostitch makes several other stapling hammers as well as many types of regular staplers.

Unfaced Batts Tops For Supplementing Attic Insulation

If your existing attic insulation is not adequate, consider adding insulation batts or blankets that lack any vapor barrier. An example of this type of insulation is Reinsul made by Johns-Manville. An unfaced fiberglass insulation specially made for upgrading attic insulation, Reinsul does not need to be fastened to the joists in the attic floor; it just rests on top of the old insulation. Johns-Manville makes many other insulating products.

Don't Get Ripped Off On Pumped-In Insulation

The newest type of home insulation is the foam that is pumped into the cavities of your walls. Once inside, the foam expands and sets up, forming good insulation for interior rooms. Some companies which handle these applications are better than others; check carefully by talking to previous customers before agreeing to have the work done by any insulation firm.

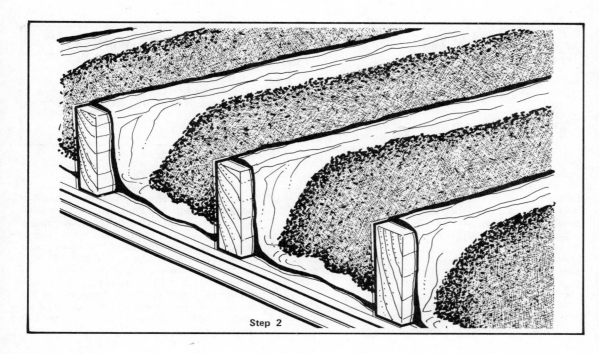

Step 2

Foil-Faced Insulation Adds Reflective Thermal Value Plus Vapor Barrier

Aluminum foil on the face of insulation batts or rolls enhances the effectiveness of the insulation, the reflective thermal value being in addition to the R-value given the insulation. Certain-teed foil-faced fiberglass insulation comes in rolls or in batts. The six-inch batts would be used in an attic, while the 3½-inch would be excellent for use in walls. This type of insulation is not to be used as an addition to insulation already in the attic, however, because the foil acts as a vapor barrier and the vapor barrier should always be directly against the attic floor. It makes excellent new insulation, though. Certain-teed markets other types of insulation as well as a variety of products for the home.

attic at present, you should install a vapor barrier. You can buy blanket insulation that has a vapor barrier on it, or you can put down a two mil polyethylene sheeting. Place the vapor barrier right next to the ceiling with the insulation on top. If you are merely adding to the thickness of the existing insulation, you can install blankets that do not have a vapor barrier.

3. Blankets need not be attached. Just lay them between the joists. If the blanket insulation comes in rolls, cut what you need to fit a specific length. Be sure not to cover the eave vents.
4. Fill odd spaces that will not accommodate a complete blanket either by cutting a section of blanket to fit or by stuffing scraps into the opening.
5. Work around obstructions like ducts, wiring, or pipes. If you cannot work the blankets around a particular obstruction, try placing a single bag of loose-fill insulation in the problem area.
6. Be careful not to let the material fall through or cover the eave vents.

If the attic floor is finished or if you plan to finish it later, use blanket insulation and staple it between the rafters. Once again, keep the vapor barrier toward the inside of the house.

To insulate under the floors of an existing home, go down to your basement or crawl space

and staple batts of insulation to the joists. Instead of stapling, though, you can use the special wires made for this purpose. The wires have points to go into wood, and they are bowed in order to hold the insulation between the joists.

Putting insulation between the walls of an existing home is not a do-it-yourself job for the average homeowner. The insulation should be blown in. Firms that do this sort of work make openings in the walls between each pair of studs and then blow the material in. If you are building an addition onto the house or finishing a garage or basement, however, you can install wall insulation by stapling the blanket type in place when only the framing is up. Be sure to save all the scraps for use around windows, doors, and electrical outlets and switches.

Here Is What You Will Need
Materials
- Blanket and/or loose-fill insulating material
- Wide boards
- Polyethylene sheeting
- Staples
- Insulation support wires

Tools
- Staple gun
- Knife or scissors

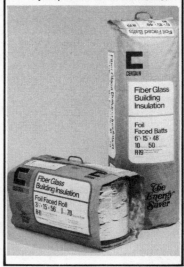

Heating and Cooling

Midget Louvers Solve Giant Problem

An easy way to ventilate your home is with Midget Louvers. Small vents that can be added to walls, overhangs, gable ends, and other places, Midget Louvers are easily installed. Just drill the proper size holes, and then push the Midget Louvers in place; they hold themselves in place with special fasteners. The Midget Louver Company manufactures these vents in a number of styles and sizes.

Gable-Mount Electric Vents

Some roofs simply do not lend themselves to the addition of a vent fan. In such cases, the Kool-O-Matic gable electric ventilator comes in handy. Furnished completely assembled—including a pre-wired, adjustable thermostat and an automatic wall shutter—this wall-mounted attic space ventilator features an all-aluminum enclosed venturi housing for maximum efficiency and a permanently lubricated motor.

Ventilators For Brick Walls

If you plan to put a vent into a brick or cinder block wall or even in a foundation wall, you'll be happy to know that there are special vents made for all these places. The brick ventilator from Leigh Products is exactly the size of a brick, and comes with a front flange to space the mortar joint. Since the flange channels out water and the galvanized steel louvers (backed by screens to keep bugs out) deflect rain and snow, the Leigh brick ventilator is self-draining. Leigh also makes ventilators to fit in block walls and others that can be set in foundation walls. Some of the latter have dampers that can be closed from the outside.

Ventilator Also Removes Attic Humidity

Kool-O-Matic offers an attic ventilator equipped with both a thermostat and a humidistat. It turns on when the temperature in the attic reaches 100 degrees and shuts off when the temperature drops to 85 degrees. As a result, this unit helps keep your home cooler during summer and saves on air conditioning costs. The humidistat turns the unit on when the humidity reaches 90 percent, and the Kool-O-Matic removes moisture-laden air that could damage the attic. Available in a number of different models, the Kool-O-Matic Ventilator can be installed on a sloping roof, on a flat one, or even vertically on gable ends.

Ventilation

TOO MANY people think that vents in your home just serve to make the house cooler during the summer. But cooling is only one aspect of ventilation. Vents are also there to let moisture out, during both summer and winter. Homeowners who close off all the vents in the winter frequently find that they have problems with trapped moisture. Proper use of exhaust fans and other methods of ventilation is, therefore, crucial to keeping your home cool in the summer and dry all year round.

Here are the places within the home where exhaust fans or other ventilation devices should be considered:

1. Attic ventilation is of prime importance. Since heat rises, intense heat can collect in the attic during the summer if proper ventilation is lacking. The rising air can also carry moisture which must be removed as well. Soffit vents coupled with adequate gable louvers provide a natural way for the attic to be ventilated. An attic fan is an even better solution to this ventilation problem. The attic fan draws outside air through open windows to replace the hot air that rises from the house. A roof ventilator fan achieves the same objective, but it does so by drawing air up through the soffit vents to replace the hot air it dispels.

Here Is What You Will Need
Materials
- Attic fan
- Roof ventilator fan
- Window exhaust fan
- Range vent
- Wall vents

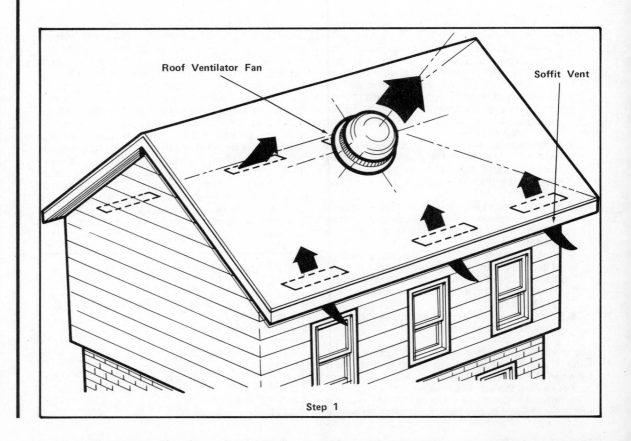

Roof Ventilator Fan

Soffit Vent

Step 1

Vent System Covers Roof Ridge

What could be simpler than a system that takes advantage of the fact that warm air rises by providing an escape outlet for hot air all along the roof ridge? The aluminum alloy Vent-A-Ridge unit maintains a low profile and blends right into the roof line. Since the unit uses no fan, it requires no energy, and it blocks out rain and snow because all openings are on the underside of a horizontal surface. Replacement air comes in through soffit vents, and the man-

ufacturer—HC Products Company —recommends that all other attic vents be closed, leaving only the Vent-A-Ridge and the soffit vents

to do the job. The competent do-it-yourselfer can install the Vent-A-Ridge System in a day's time.

Exhaust Fan Also Lights The Way

The combination ceiling light/exhaust fan from the Ritenhouse Division of Emerson-Chromalox may be just what you need in your bathroom ceiling. It features a very quiet exhaust fan and improved lighting through the use of a prismatic dropped bowl polycarbonate diffuser. The unit installs between standard ceiling joists.

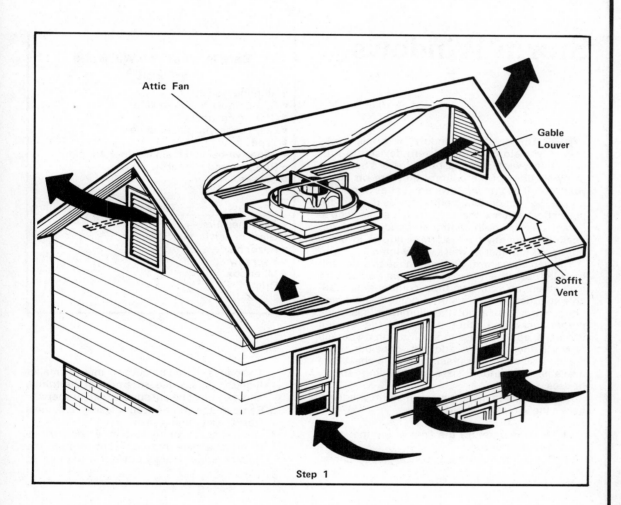

Attic Fan
Gable Louver
Soffit Vent

Step 1

Turbine Vents Cool Attic With Wind Power

Turbine coolers are more than 100 years old, but not until recently have they become popular for home use. The Wisper Cool turbine vent is turned by the breeze, and as it turns, it removes hot air from the attic below. Wisper Cool features a noiseless jewel-type ball bearing with permanent lubrication. The key to satisfactory operation is adequate louver area to allow outside air to come in and flow through the attic. Although it does require a little nerve to cut a hole in your roof, installation by the homeowner is easy and requires no special tools. A 12-inch Wisper Cool can handle about 600 square feet of attic floor space. A 14-inch model is also available.

AN ENERGY SAVING Product

2. Bathrooms that suffer from excess moisture during baths or showers can often be cured by just opening a window. If the open window is not enough, however, consider installing an exhaust fan or perhaps even a skylight that can be opened to let nature carry away moist air.
3. Excessive moisture in the kitchen can be diminished with the help of a range vent. A clean filter in the vent is quite important, and since much of the moisture removed from the kitchen is grease laden, the vent filter must be checked frequently to avoid clogs. If the range vent by itself cannot handle all the moisture created by cooking and washing dishes, consider installing a vent fan.
4. Laundry rooms should have a ventilation system. Dryers generally are vented to the outside, but dryers are not the only moisture

makers in your laundry room.
5. Basements often suffer from moisture problems from the condensation caused by cold and warm air meeting. An exhaust fan is usually the best solution.
6. Crawl spaces under the house need cross ventilation to prevent the build-up of moisture. Usually, the local building code specifies a certain amount of vent space per square foot, but you can add vents if your present situation is too wet.

Often, moisture in the home has no way of escaping and pushes its way out right through the walls. It may pass through wood and other materials without bothering them, but when excessive moisture reaches the paint job, it bubbles and cracks the paint causing peeling. This problem can often be eliminated by installing small vents in the wall.

Heating and Cooling

Make Do-It-Yourself Storm Windows From Kits

You can create a rather neat looking storm window from a kit marketed by Plaskolite, Inc. The In-Sider Storm Window System involves sheets of clear rigid plastic and softer trim material that fits around the edges of the sheet. When cut to window size (the sheets come in different sizes to fit many standard windows), the trim fits around the sheet to hold it in place and at the same time make the installation airtight. Installed from inside the house—the storm window goes inside the regular window—In-Sider windows eliminate the difficulties and dangers of an outside climb. They stay securely in place, but can be removed for cleaning or when you want fresh air. Look for the In-Sider display at hardware stores and home centers.

Reynolds Components Create Do-It-Yourself Storm Window Frames

With aluminum storm sash sections and aluminum corner locks from Reynolds Aluminum—plus the glass or acrylic of your choice—you can put together your own storm windows. Just measure the storm sash sections and then saw them with a fine-toothed hacksaw or even a coping saw. Plastic glazing chan-

nels fit around the pane to hold it in place in the aluminum frame and render an airtight seal. You can also make your own window screens with Reynolds aluminum frame components.

Storm Windows

THE TERM "storm window" is a misnomer. Maybe storm windows were devised to protect against winter storms, but in today's homes in many sections of the country they are on guard year round. Storm windows are just as important for peak air conditioning efficiency as they are for protection against the cold, and people whose homes possess both central air conditioning and heating frequently have storm windows in place during the summer as well as the winter.

You can have storm windows made to order and installed, buy them and install them yourself, or make them on your own from components available at larger hardware stores, home centers, and lumberyards. Price out the aluminum sash, the corner locks and other hardware, the glazing channels, and the glass to see if doing it yourself is worth the effort. In addition, consider using plastic instead of glass; acrylic plastic sheets are available in various sizes at building supply houses.

If you decide to make your own storm windows, here's the way to go about it.

1. Measure carefully the area where the storm windows will go.
2. Cut or have cut the glass or plastic panes.

Here Is What You Will Need
Materials
- Aluminum sash
- Corner locks and hardware
- Glazing channels
- Glass or acrylic plastic sheets
- Tape
- Adhesive-backed foam weatherstripping
- Brackets and hangers
- Screws

Tools
- Tape measure
- Glass or acrylic plastic cutter
- Razor blade
- Hacksaw
- Miter box
- Drill

The panes should be cut 1⅛ inches smaller than the outside measurement of the frame, and they must be cut square to fit properly.

3. Remove the rubberized glazing channels from the aluminum sash.
4. Use a sharp razor blade to miter the corners of the channels, but don't cut through the outside edge. Merely cut out a triangle so

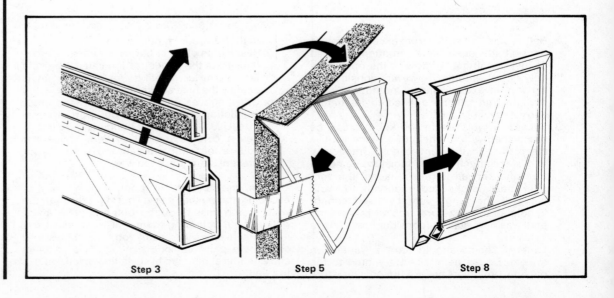

Step 3   Step 5   Step 8

Put A Sturdy Latch On Your Storm Door

If your storm door latch fails for any reason, you can install a quality replacement with a minimum of difficulty. The Storm King push button replacement latch generally requires no installation redrilling. It features a modernistic design and is made of sturdy die-cast construction with an aluminum finish. A push button opens the latch from the outside, while a lever handle operates the handle

from the inside; a key-lock version is also available. The Storm King replacement latch is made by the

S-B Manufacturing Company and is available at hardware stores and home centers.

Convert Your Screens To Storm Windows

While they can never be as good as actual storm windows, window screens and screen doors can be converted to weather protectors by attaching plastic film to them. Arvey Corp., markets a kit called Easy Does It that includes R-V Lite plastic film plus fiber strips and enough nails to make the conversion. The kits vary in size to take care of one, two, or four windows, and there are even kits to convert a screen door into a storm door. The clear plastic film, which lets light in and allows you to see out, forms a barrier between the cold air outside and the window pane. Although the converted screens cannot do the work of storm windows, they do a good job of eliminating drafts and are surely preferable to direct contact with Jack Frost.

the miter can be made where the channel edges will be whole except where the two ends meet.

5. Slip the channels around the edges of the pane, using tape to hold them in place if necessary.

6. Use a hacksaw and miter box to miter the aluminum sash pieces.

7. Install the corner lock hardware in the two side pieces.

8. Fit the top and bottom sash pieces over the glass and glazing channel. Then install the side pieces.

9. Attach adhesive-backed foam weatherstripping all the way around the inside edge of the frame to seal out air leaks.

10. Mount the storm window with brackets and hangers made for mounting purposes, or

—if you intend to leave the storm windows up year-round—drill through the frames and mount them with screws.

One of the benefits of storm windows other than their fuel saving advantages is the fact that they help to curb window sweating. If you do see sweating on your storm windows, however, you would be wise to check the seal. If the sweating is on the inside window, it indicates that your storm window is not adequately sealed and is allowing cold air to seep in. If the sweating is on the inside of the storm window, it indicates that the interior window is leaking warm air into the space between the two windows.

Insofar as regular maintenance is concerned, you need only keep the panes clean and be on the lookout for pitting or oxidation of the aluminum.

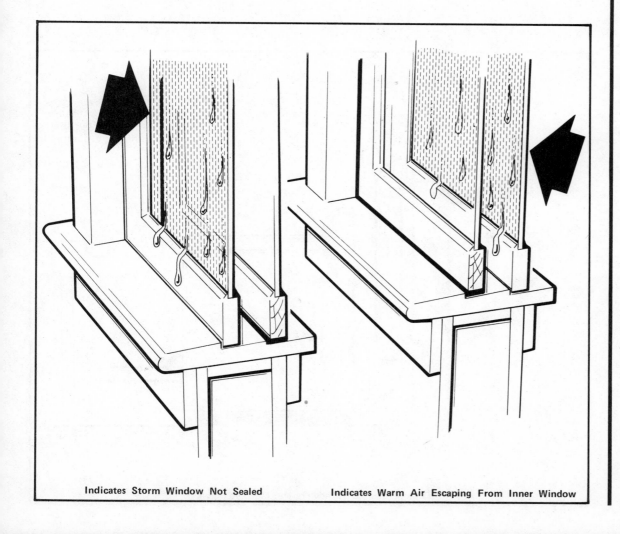

Indicates Storm Window Not Sealed   **Indicates Warm Air Escaping From Inner Window**

Storm Windows Are Over-The-Counter Commodities

If you have standard sized windows, you probably can purchase storm windows at your local lumber or hardware dealer. While the retailer may not have what you need in stock, he can show you samples of what is available and then order whatever you want. If he carries the line from Croft Metals, Inc., he can order Croft Combination Storm and Insulator windows in all the standard sizes. Croft also makes storm window/screen units that can be raised and lowered.

Heating and Cooling

Humidity Control

THE AMOUNT OF moisture in the air within your home not only has an enormous effect on your comfort, but can also cause great damage to your house and its furnishings. Occasional abnormal humidity conditions may not require any corrective action, but prolonged periods of excessive or insufficient humidity should not be ignored.

Your home can become too dry during the winter as moisture-deficient heated air circulates through every room. The lack of moisture in the air can make you feel cold, despite the fact that the thermostat registers a comfortable temperature. Conversely, having adequate humidity allows you to be comfortable with temperatures several degrees lower, thus allowing you to save on your heating bill. Low humidity also causes discomfort in other ways: cracked lips, dried skin, and chapped hands; some people even develop ticklish throats and stuffy noses in a dry home. Furniture dries out too; loose joints and squeaks signal further—possibly permanent—damage to come. Lack of humidity also creates that annoying side effect—static electricity.

There are a number of steps you can take to add moisture to your home during winter.

1. Place containers of water near your home's heating source. The water will evaporate and moisten the dry air that circulates throughout your house. This can help, but generally cannot cure a low-humidity problem.
2. Install a humidifier unit as part of your central heating system. Which type you add depends upon the type of heating in your home.
3. Purchase one or more free-standing humidifiers if your central heating system cannot readily accommodate a built-in humidifier unit.

About all there is to maintaining a humidifier is to keep it clean and maintain the fan motor as you would any other. The owner's manual is the best guide for maintenance, but the most common problems stem from the fact that water leaves minerals behind after it evaporates. These mineral deposits form scales which can hamper the operation of the unit. With some units, a fungus forms and an odor develops.

The opposite problem, too much moisture in the air, can make you feel uncomfortably hot in the summertime. Most humidity excesses are caused by cooking, doing laundry, running a dryer, taking showers, and washing floors. High humidity levels resulting from such typical activi-

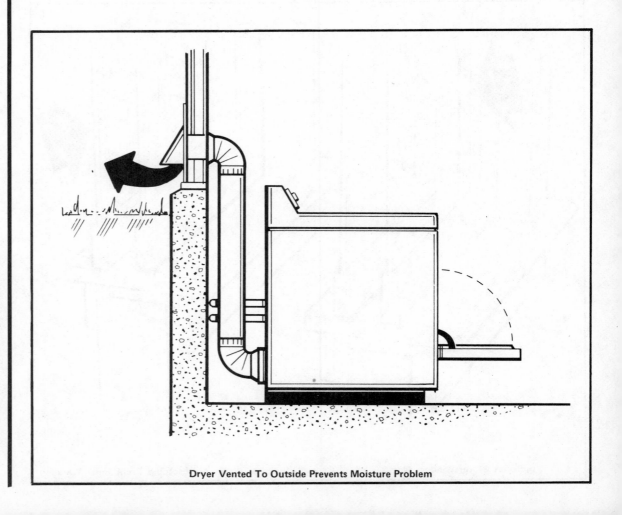

Dryer Vented To Outside Prevents Moisture Problem

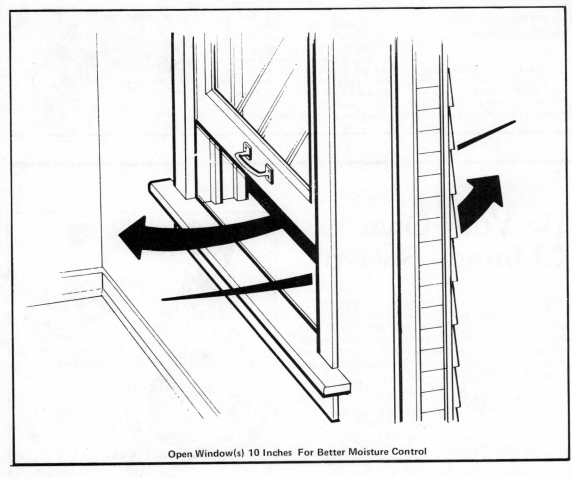

Open Window(s) 10 Inches For Better Moisture Control

The humidifier or dehumidifier you own may or may not have adequate controls to test the humidity in the room. If not, consider installing the handsome Honeywell Humidity Controller. Designed for wall mounting at the most advantageous location in the living area of your home, it can also be mounted on the return air duct to measure the humidity level of air coming from the living areas. Several models are available for either humidification or dehumidification control. All are easy to install and feature fingertip adjustment controls.

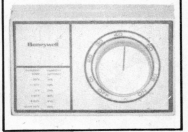

A Chemical Dehumidifier Can Help

If you have a small area with a humidity problem, see what Hum-i-dri—an easy-to-use chemical dehumidifier—can do. It comes in a 12-ounce plastic container, and all you have to do is remove the lid and put it in the room. Hum-i-dri is made by Malco Products, Inc.

Fight Humidifier Scale And Odors

Water poured into a humidifier contains all sorts of chemicals, and after the water has been sent into the air, the chemicals are left behind to form scale and deposits that can clog the humidifier, create odors, and even cause breakdowns. Cosco Chemicals Inc., markets two products for humidifier units; it dissolves the minerals that have formed. The other product, Solution 24 is for use with manually filled units; it prevents the build-up of scale and controls odors. These products will help to keep your humidifier working better longer.

ties can generally be corrected by a dehumidifier.

A dehumidifier consists of a fan that draws air into the unit and passes it over refrigerated coils, causing the air to condense on the coils. It then drips off into a collection tray and is carried off through a hose to a drain. Sometimes the unit cannot be hooked up conveniently to a drain, and in such cases it must be hand emptied. If that is your situation, be sure to get a unit that offers easy access to the drain container.

Like the humidifier, the dehumidifier requires little maintenance by the homeowner other than cleaning. It is most important that you keep the coils clean. Use a canister vacuum cleaner with a brush attachment, or if this type vacuum is not available, just brush the coils clean.

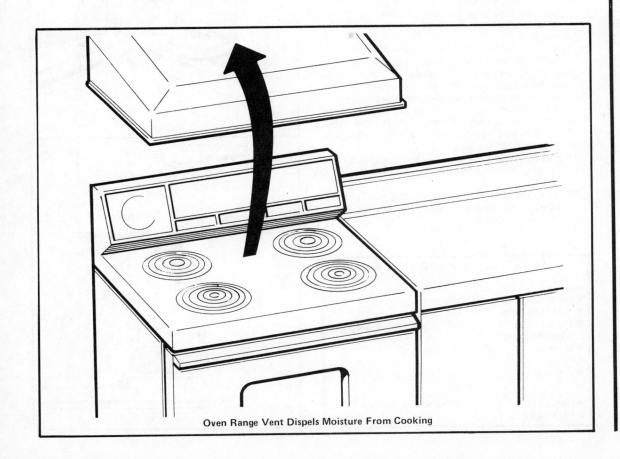

Oven Range Vent Dispels Moisture From Cooking

Heating and Cooling

Hearth Accessories Are More Than Ornaments

Cleaning out the residue after the chimney sweeping is done is the finishing touch. The shovel from the fire set made by Hart Fireplace Furnishings can handle such an assignment. But what do you use to carry out this residue? The ornamental fireside bucket that matches the fire set makes a nice decorative touch, but you should really have a larger metal pail around for chimney sweeping purposes.

The Kelley pail is made of heavy-duty pre-galvanized sheetware and can withstand a great deal of abuse.

Remove Smoke Stains From Brick

Imagine those smoke-stained fireplace bricks looking clean again! Sure Klean Fireplace Cleaner, a yellow liquid blend of chemicals and wetting agent formulated especially to clean brick and stone, is a real smoke eater. Just spray it on, let it stand two or three minutes, and then wipe with a damp rag or sponge. Heavy stains may require additional treatment, but you are sure to see marked improvement as Sure Klean Fireplace Cleaner cleans away smoke, carbon film, and dirt. A formulation of the Process Solvent Company, Sure Klean is a powerful chemical solution, and you must handle it carefully.

Arm Chair Chimney Sweeping

While you're sitting comfortably enjoying the fire, you can also be cleaning the chimney. Just sprinkle Chimney Sweep Fireplace Powder on the burning logs. As the powder burns it destroys soot up in the chimney, creates a better draft and therefore a better fire, and even makes the flames sparkle in a brilliant rainbow of colors. Chimney Sweep Fireplace Powder is made by Coughlan Products, Inc.

Ash Pit Keeps Fireplace Clean

If you are building a fireplace or having one built, be sure to install an ash pit. The ash pit consists of two items—an ash dump unit and a cleanout door—that you can obtain from the Heatilator Fireplace Division of Vega Industries. The ash dump, installed in the hearth, allows ash disposal into the cleanout pit. The cleanout door provides either exterior or basement access to the ash pit. Both Heatilator products make cleaning your fireplace much less messy.

Be Your Own Chimney Sweep

THE HOME fireplace chimney usually requires little in the way of repairs, but you should clean it every so often. Although not one of your more pleasant jobs, cleaning the chimney will make your fireplace operate more efficiently next winter. Here is how to make cleaning the chimney a do-it-yourself project.

1. Open the damper.
2. Seal off the fireplace opening from the room by attaching a heavy plastic sheet or a scrap piece of plywood with masking tape. Make sure that there are no cracks or leaks.
3. Fill a burlap bag with straw, excelsior, or wadded paper, and then put in a brick or two for added weight.
4. Fasten the bag securely to a rope.
5. Climb up on the roof on a day you are certain that the roof is completely dry. Be sure to wear sneakers for good traction; some people even tie a rope around themselves and the chimney.
6. Lower the bag down one corner of the chimney until it hits bottom.
7. Raise the bag up and down several times.
8. Now move the bag around the perimeter of the opening (move it about a foot each time) and repeat step 7. Then get down off the roof.
9. If your fireplace has an outside door, open it and remove the soot that you loosened.
10. Wait for an hour or so while the dust settles before removing the plastic sheet or plywood covering from the fireplace opening.
11. With the opening uncovered, take a large hand mirror and a flashlight and hold them so that you can inspect the chimney. Look for any obstructions.
12. Put on gloves, reach over the damper to the smoke shelf, and gently clean away the debris.
13. Vacuum out the fireplace, and if you have an attachment that will reach the smoke shelf, vacuum it as well.

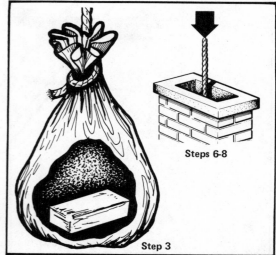

Steps 6-8

Step 3

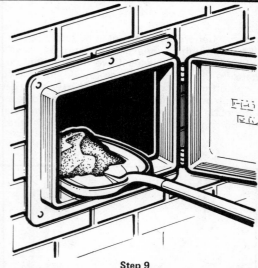

Step 9

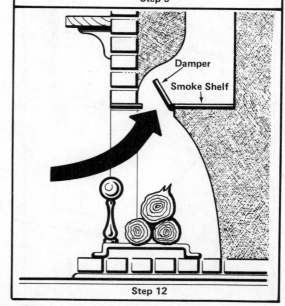

Damper

Smoke Shelf

Step 12

Here Is What You Will Need

Materials

- Plastic sheet or plywood scrap
- Masking tape
- Burlap bag filled with straw, excelsior, or wadded paper
- Bricks
- Rope
- Gloves

Tools

- Hand mirror
- Flashlight
- Vacuum cleaner

Pilot Lights

MOST APPLIANCES heated by natural gas have pilot lights to provide instant heat when you need it. No matter whether the pilot is on a hot water heater, a furnace, a range, or a clothes dryer, they are all quite similar. While the best guide for any appliance is the owner's manual, here are some general tips for lighting and maintaining pilot lights.

1. If the pilot is out, check to be sure that the gas cutoff valve and the gas cock (the "on-off" knob at the gas valve) are both at the full "on" position.
2. Unless otherwise specified, turn the gas cock to its "off" position and wait five minutes.
3. Turn the gas cock to the "pilot" position.
4. Hold a lighted match to the pilot and push the reset button down. Keep the button depressed for 30 seconds, and make sure that the pilot stays lighted during the entire interval.
5. Release the reset button; the pilot should keep burning.

If you cannot get the pilot lighted, there is probably something obstructing the flow of gas. Check the tiny orifice for clogging, and clean it if necessary.

If the pilot catches but goes off when you release the reset button, try holding the button down again for an additional 10 to 15 seconds. If it still fails to stay on, you either have a thermocouple that is defective or one that is not positioned properly in the flame of the pilot. The flame from the pilot should bathe the top half inch of the thermocouple rod (the sensor tube). If it does not, loosen the bracket nuts and reposition the rod. In case you are wondering what the thermocouple does, it acts as a safety cutoff for the gas valve. When the pilot is lighted, the heat generates a slight electric current in the thermocouple which then allows gas to come from the gas valve. When the pilot goes out, the thermocouple stops sending the current, and the gas supply stops. If the thermocouple is faulty, replace it.

△ 1. Purchase a new thermocouple of the same type, making sure that the lead-in tube is the

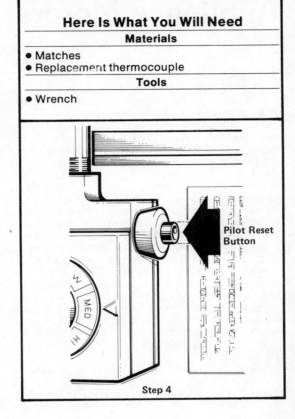

Here Is What You Will Need

Materials
- Matches
- Replacement thermocouple

Tools
- Wrench

Pilot Reset Button

Step 4

same length as the old one.
△ 2. Remove the bracket nut (or nuts) that hold the thermocouple unit next to the pilot.
△ 3. Unscrew the connection nut that holds the other end of the thermocouple to the gas valve.
△ 4. Position the tip of the new unit so that about its top half inch will be bathed by the pilot flame. Secure it with the bracket nut or nuts.
△ 5. Be careful not to kink the thermocouple's lead-in tube when maneuvering the other end into position at the gas valve.
△ 6. Turn the connection nut finger tight, and then just a quarter turn more with a wrench.
△ 7. Relight the pilot.

The pilot flame should be steady, blue in color, and strong enough to reach out beyond the tip of the thermocouple.

Thermocouple Makes Pilot Operation Safe

Replacement thermocouple units, like the one from Jade Controls, come with complete installation instructions. Most home pilot lights take one of the standard thermocouple models, but you may have to order an unusual size. There are also thermocouples for use when the limit switch is wired in series circuit with the thermocouple. If this is the case in your situation, be sure to get a junction block replacement thermocouple.

Here's A Pilot Lighting Trick

Rather than burn your fingers with a short match while trying to ignite a recessed pilot light, why not rig up a gadget that gives you the extra reach you need? Secure a small alligator clip to the end of a 12-inch piece of coat hanger wire. The clips with round openings are the easiest to connect. Then put a match in the teeth of the clip, light the match, and then ignite the pilot. Your hand will be a foot away when the pilot catches.

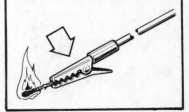

Parts Centers Can Help

Many large appliance companies operate well-stocked parts centers in various locations across the country. Your appliance owner's manual may contain a list of these locations, but if not, check the Yellow Pages to find the nearest parts center for your particular appliance brand. By writing or calling the center with the appropriate part number, part description, and appliance model number, you should be able to obtain the exact replacement or a compatible substitute for the worn or damaged component.

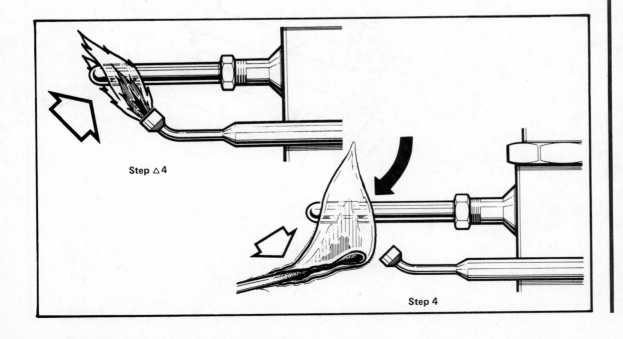

Step △ 4

Step 4

Mechanical Monsters

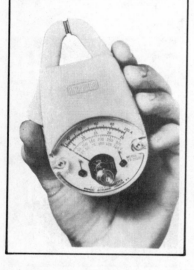
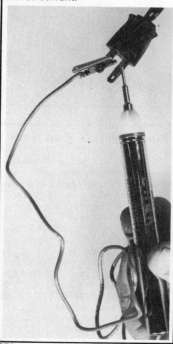
Appliance Motors

SINCE MOST electrical appliances have motors, let us discuss the various types that are used in today's modern appliances.

The universal motor, easily recognized by the brushes that conduct current from the field to the rotor, is the only motor that you are likely to find in an appliance that has coils of wire wound in the rotor as well as in the stator. It is called a universal motor because it operates on either alternating current (AC) like that found in a home, or direct current (DC) like that which comes from a battery.

The universal motor is powerful at low speeds, and it is capable of reaching very high speeds. In most appliances in which universal motors are used, some sort of speed control is necessary.

Many small appliances—fans, can openers, and others where low turning force or torque is required—use shaded-pole motors. You will recognize shaded-pole motors by the heavy shading coil (a heavy conductor) which cuts across the stator laminations (the many pieces of metal that are bonded together and around which the field coils are wound).

Many battery-operated appliances, such as electric knives, utilize miniature DC motors. Though small in size, these motors provide sufficient power to do the job for which they are designed.

Clock motors or synchronous motors are found in many appliances, from the smallest to the largest. In the small alarm clock, the motor turns the hands; on the largest refrigerator, the motor initiates the defrost cycle. Although synchronous motors lack power, they can be connected to a team of drive gears to turn such fairly heavy mechanisms as washer timers or defrost timers on refrigerators—or other primary mechanisms that are intended to turn very slowly.

Split-phase motors are used on some larger appliances, even though their starting torque or turning force is limited. They are often found on washing machines, dryers, and dishwashers. Capacitor motors, similar to split-phase motors, provide higher starting torque for heavy-duty applications.

Care for small appliance motors is simple and results in longer life. Motors of all types have the same basic needs—they must run cool, which means that air must circulate around and through them. The owner's manual that came with the appliance will be your best guide for maintaining your appliance motor. In its absence, however, follow these few maintenance tips.

1. Keep all motors dusted and free of lint or dirt. Dirt and grime should not be allowed to build up—an occasional cleaning is a good practice. If the dirt cannot be wiped away easily, use a vacuum cleaner.
2. If the motors have oil caps on the end bells where the rotor shaft comes out of the motor housing, lubricate them sparingly with a light machine oil at least once a year.
3. Make sure that the belts attached to the motors are never too tight. Generally, a belt attached to a motor should be adjusted to have about ¼-inch of play between the motor and the nearest pulley.
4. Always use the appliance only for the uses it was intended for. Do not force it to do things beyond its strength or capabilities.

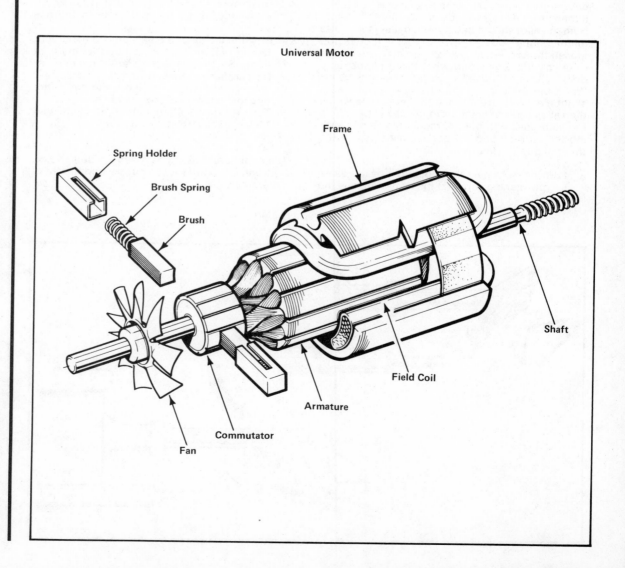

Universal Motor

Spring Holder
Brush Spring
Brush
Frame
Shaft
Field Coil
Armature
Commutator
Fan

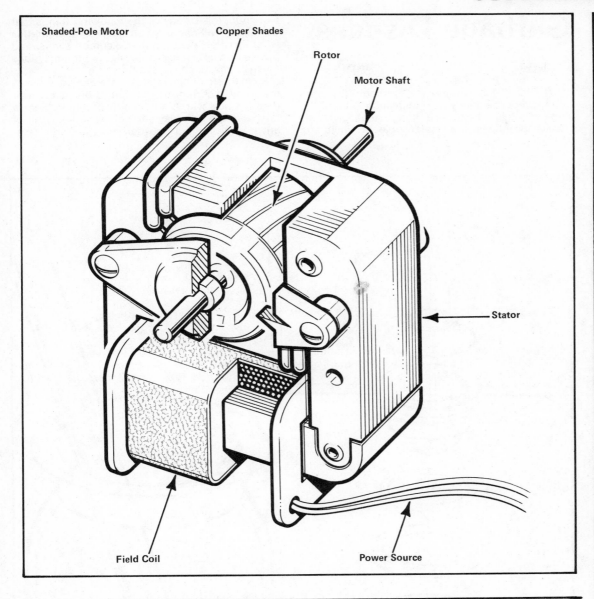

Shaded-Pole Motor   Copper Shades

Rotor

Motor Shaft

Stator

Field Coil

Power Source

Small Appliance Motors Troubleshooting Chart

Caution: Unplug appliance before inspecting or repairing. Do not reconnect power until job is completed or while any wiring connections are exposed.

PROBLEMS	CAUSES	REPAIRS
Motor will not run or runs off and on	1. No power.	1. Check cord, plug, wall outlet, fuse or circuit breaker, or for loose wire inside.
	2. Faulty brushes or brush springs.	2. Replace brushes or brush springs as necessary.
	3. Faulty switch.	3. Replace switch.
Motor will not shut off	1. Short in switch.	1. Replace switch.
Motor overheats	1. Needs lubrication.	1. Lubricate bearings according to owner's manual. (If specified lubricant is not known, use 20 weight non-detergent motor oil.)
	2. Motor dirty or air intake clogged.	2. Clean with vacuum cleaner.
Noisy motor	1. Bearing loose, worn or dry.	1. Tighten, replace or lube.
	2. Blades of fan hitting.	2. Straighten.
Fuses blow or circuit breaker switch trips	1. Short.	1. Check cord for loose connection inside.
	2. Frozen bearings.	2. Lubricate.
Sparking	1. Brushes or brush springs faulty.	1. Replace. (New brushes spark until worn to conform.)

V.O.M. Is Only For Experienced Appliance Repairers

The letters "V.O.M." stand for Volt-Ohm-Milliammeter, an appliance testing device that is beyond the scope of the average homeowner, but a tool that every advanced appliance repairer should own. The Triplett Model 310 is a very compact and rugged unit, and it is self shielded for use in strong magnetic fields. Most of the good V.O.M. testers currently on the market come with instruction manuals.

Pennz-Guard Spray Lube Dries Electric Motors

The Pennzoil Company's Gumout Division markets a spray lube called Pennz-Guard. It, like many of the other spray lubes, is excellent for drying out electric motors, making them operable almost immediately. Because Pennzoil is best known for its automotive products, you probably stand a better chance of finding Pennz-Guard in an auto supply outlet than in a hardware store.

Build Your Own V.O.M.

If you really get into appliance repairs, you may just want to build your own V.O.M. meter. The Heathkit general purpose V.O.M. unit comes in kit form, and like all top quality Heathkits, it comes with such detailed and easy-to-understand instructions that success is nearly assured. Heathkit also markets kits for several other types of testers and meters. Check with your local Heathkit store or write to the Heath Company, Benton Harbor, MI 49022 for a catalog.

Replace Ancient Disposer Stopper To Keep Your Sink Looking Good

An aged disposer stopper can become an eye-sore in your sink, but finding a new one is easy. Kirkhill offers a replacement stopper that fits all standard home garbage disposers. If the stopper you have is just dirty or coated with a fungus underneath, you may be able to restore it. Just soak it in regular laundry bleach to clean the rubber and remove the fungus.

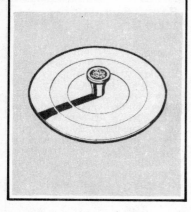

Splash Guard Saves Splatters

One of the least expensive items that wears out on a kitchen disposer is the rubber splash guard that fits in the opening. The splash guard allows you to push garbage through as the several slits radiating from the center hole bend downward, but when garbage is in the disposer, these flanges snap back up to prevent splashing; water, of course, can still go into the disposer. Hancock-Gross's replacement splash guard snaps in the sink drain with a reinforced snap ring to hold it in place. It fits all standard home garbage disposers.

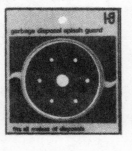

Garbage Disposer

IT IS LITTLE wonder why garbage disposers will occasionally get indigestion with all the junk we feed them. The things that generally cause problems are metal objects, including aluminum foil, or any of the following things that we think it will chew up: strings, cloth, cigarettes with filter tips, paper, bones, seafood shells, and pieces of glass. Once in awhile the unit may take these things, but not very often.

Such foreign objects must be removed. Be sure the electric current to the unit is off before you reach in, however. After the bulk of the problem is removed, the unit may still not work; a tiny bit of grit may be lodged between moving parts. Usu-

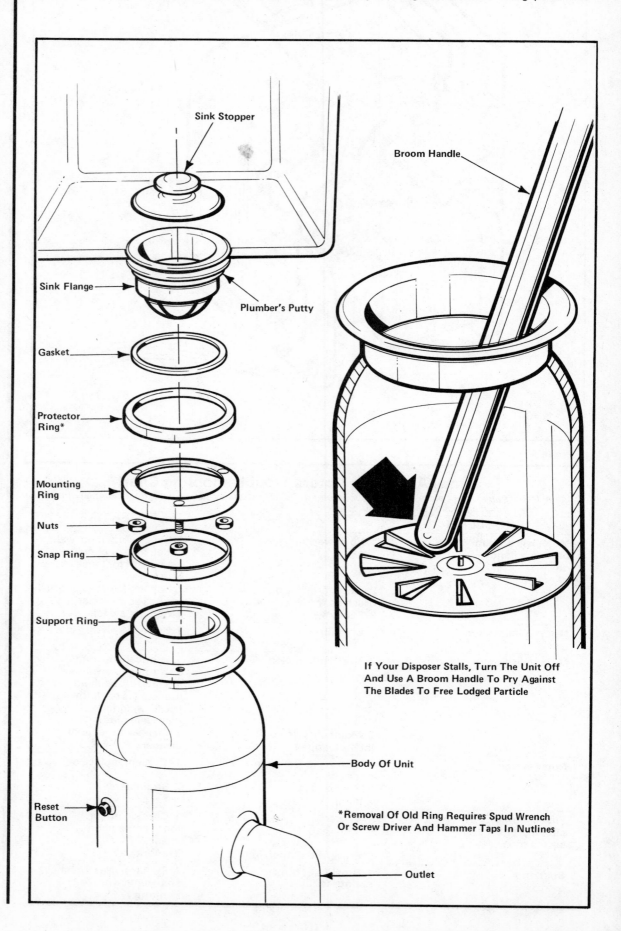

If Your Disposer Stalls, Turn The Unit Off And Use A Broom Handle To Pry Against The Blades To Free Lodged Particle

*Removal Of Old Ring Requires Spud Wrench Or Screw Driver And Hammer Taps In Nutlines

Labels in diagram: Sink Stopper, Broom Handle, Sink Flange, Plumber's Putty, Gasket, Protector Ring*, Mounting Ring, Nuts, Snap Ring, Support Ring, Body Of Unit, Reset Button, Outlet

ally, moving the parts just the least bit will dislodge the particle. Some units have a crank that fits underneath which you turn to dislodge an object. If yours is not outfitted with this feature, insert the end of a broom handle into the drain, angled so it can push against the impeller blades. Push at several points. Then remove the handle and switch the unit on. This will usually do the job.

Some disposers have a reset button on the bottom of the unit. This will trip when the disposer bites into something it should not. It must be pushed after the blockage is cleared.

Odors can often be removed by packing the disposer with ice cubes. This is noisy, but effective. Follow this by feeding in a half of a lemon. There are products specified for use in disposers to clean and deodorize. Drano markets one (not regular Drano liquid). Be sure not to use regular drain cleaners.

If it ever becomes necessary to replace a disposer, here are the basic installation steps. The procedure may vary with different brands, but this will give you the general idea of what you will be getting into.

1. Remove the drain pipe under the sink.
2. Remove the old sink flange, as well as the sealing material and any gaskets from the sink.
3. Place a bed of plumber's putty around the opening and around the underside of the sink flange unit.
4. Insert the flange into the opening and press it down into place. Once it is in place, do not rotate the flange; you could break the seal.
5. Remove the excess putty from around the flange.
6. Now you are ready to go below the sink. Slip

the gasket over the underside of the sink flange, followed by the protector ring with the flat side up. The mounting ring—which has three threaded pins inserted in it—follows the protector ring.

7. While holding these parts in place above the groove on the flange, push the snap ring up along the flange until it snaps into the groove. One word of caution about the snap ring: if you spread it, it can become too loose to hold in place around the groove. You may find it slow to push the snap ring in place, but it will go. Make sure it fits firmly in the groove.
8. The threaded pins have screw slots which must be uniformly tightened against the protector ring to hold it and the gasket snugly against the bottom of the flange.
9. Now, lift the disposer unit and put it in place. Match the holes in the disposer with the threaded pins, but before tightening the nuts that hold the unit in place, rotate the disposer so that the outlet pipe lines up with the drain pipe. Tighten the nuts.
10. Now you are ready to hook up the drain. Use slip nuts and remember that the parts of the trap can be maneuvered around so that they will fit together. If this is a replacement unit, you will have no problem. If it is a new installation, you may have to buy and install some extra pipe sections. A common trap for both the disposer and the other side of the sink is acceptable.
11. Test the installation and the unit for leaks.
12. Before you plug in the unit, reach inside to see whether you dropped any tools in there. Now you can start throwing the garbage down the sink.

Garbage Disposers Troubleshooting Chart

Caution: Disconnect unit before inspecting or repairing. Do not reconnect power until job is completed or while any wiring connections are exposed.

PROBLEMS	CAUSES	REPAIRS
Disposer fails to operate	1. No voltage to receptacle or blown fuse on line.	1. Test the receptacle with a table lamp. If the disposer is wired directly, replace the blown circuit fuse.
	2. Overload protector kicked out.	2. Depress the reset button, which is usually located on the bottom of the disposer.
	3. Foreign object jamming the impeller	3. Free the foreign object by inserting a wooden stick (broom handle) and prying against the jammed impeller.
	4. Defective relay switch, capacitor, or motor.	4. Call in a service technician.
Disposer leaks	1. Loose sink flange connections.	1. Check the connections and tighten.
	2. Impeller or seals leaking.	2. Call in a service technician.
Disposer makes excessive noise	1. Foreign object in disposer.	1. Remove the foreign object.
Disposer emits a foul odor	1. Insufficient flushing of food particles.	1. Grind up a hopper full of ice, followed by lemon. Flush, using plenty of cold water.
Water fails to flow out	1. Clogged drain line.	1. Clean the drain line, but do not use a chemical cleaner. Use only a special cleaner made for garbage disposer purposes.
	2. Worn shredder.	2. Call in a service technician.

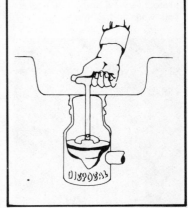

Mechanical Monsters

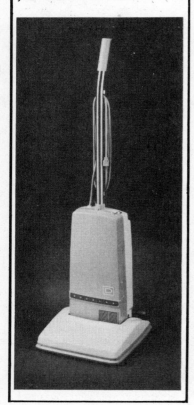
Vacuum Cleaners

VACUUM CLEANERS exist in two distinct forms. In the canister vacuum, a universal motor powers a large fan (or impeller) which pushes air out of the vacuum. Often, several impellers are stacked to create better efficiency. As air goes out, other air is drawn in to replace that which has been evacuated. The canister is designed in such a way that the new air comes from the inlet into which you plug the vacuum hose.

You attach the special cleaning tools at the opposite end of the hose. These tools include brushes or wands which help to dislodge dust and lint from floors, walls, crevices, etc. The dust and lint then pass through the wand (the stiff metal or plastic tube attached to the end of the hose), through the flexible hose, and into the vacuum canister itself. Here, a special bag acts as a filter. The bag is designed so that air can pass through, but not even the tiniest particles of lint, dust, and dirt can escape—these particles are, instead, trapped and held within the bag.

Since the air must also pass across the impellers and across the motor windings—cooling them as it leaves the vacuum—another protective filter is provided at the motor. If this filter becomes clogged, dust and dirt can damage the motor assembly (particularly the bearings).

In the upright vacuum, the motor is designed to drive a revolving brush in addition to the air flow mechanism. The upright is superior to the canister for carpet cleaning because its revolving brush can dislodge deep dirt near the base of the nap. The machine's suction then carries the soil-laden air into a porous bag which is usually suspended from the handle on most upright models.

Several of the newer and more expensive canisters also have an accessory attachment to give them the versatility of the upright vacuum. They come with a motorized revolving brush (the motor is self-contained within the accessory itself) which you can put on the canister much as you would any ordinary carpet attachment. The accessory device combines the strong suction from the canister with the attachment's revolving brush action to provide excellent cleaning of deep-down carpet fibers. Since the suction is independent of the attachment, the only maintenance problems that the revolving brush accessory could offer would involve bearing, motor, and belt replacements within the unit itself.

One of the most common problems to strike any vacuum cleaner is a lack of suction. If you notice such a problem, here is what you should do.

1. Turn off the vacuum and remove the hose.

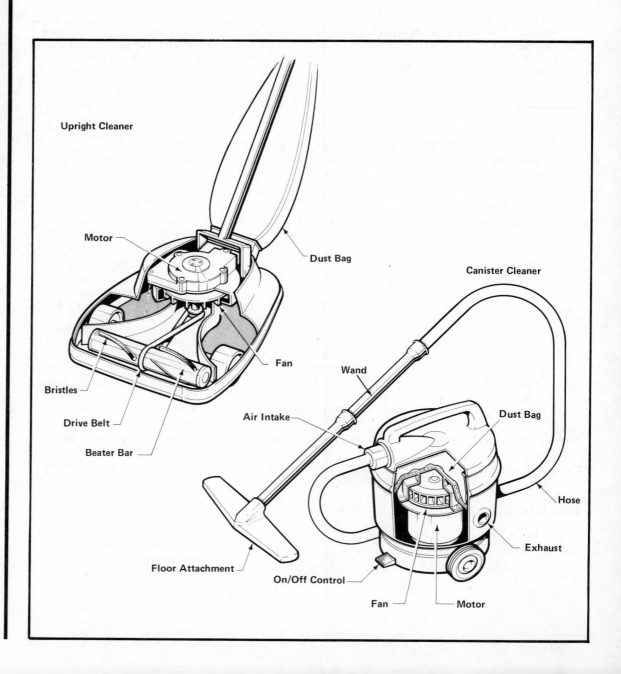

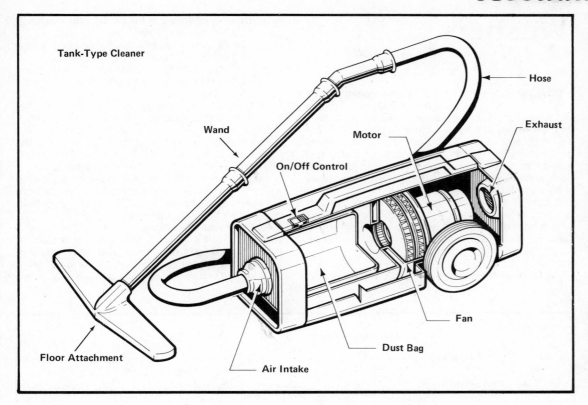

Tank-Type Cleaner

Hose

Wand

Motor

Exhaust

On/Off Control

Fan

Floor Attachment

Dust Bag

Air Intake

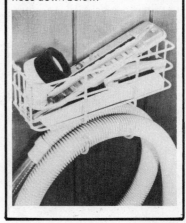

2. Turn the vacuum back on and place your hand across the air inlet to see whether suction exists there. If it does, then the blockage problem is in the hose. Nails, toothpicks, etc., can become wedged diagonally in the hose and prevent your vacuum cleaner from operating as it should. Most hose blockage problems are easy to remedy.
3. Remove the hose from the vacuum and take it outside.
4. Push an ordinary garden hose (one that is of a smaller diameter, of course) through the vacuum hose. The garden hose should dislodge any foreign objects within the vacuum hose.
5. If there is no suction at the inlet, then the problem is within the vacuum itself.
6. Check to be sure that the bag is empty. A full bag prevents air from passing, with the result, of course, that no suction can be produced. Empty (or change) the bag regularly.
7. Check the protective motor filter whenever you empty the bag. Since many of these filters are washable, you should have no difficulty in keeping it clean. A filter that becomes severely blocked can cause a reduction in suction and can even produce motor damage. If the filter begins to tear, however, replace it; some manufacturers even recommend that you replace the filter annually whether it is torn or not. Never operate a vacuum cleaner that does not have its protective motor filter in place.

Vacuum Cleaners Troubleshooting Chart

Caution: Unplug appliance before inspecting or repairing. Do not reconnect power until job is completed or while any wiring connections are exposed.

PROBLEMS	CAUSES	REPAIRS
Motor will not run	1. No voltage reaching vacuum. 2. Damaged power cord. 3. Worn motor brushes. 4. Bad on-off switch. 5. Damaged motor.	1. Check the condition of the receptacle with a table lamp. 2. Replace the cord. 3. Replace the brushes. 4. Replace the switch. 5. Repair if possible; replace if necessary.
Vacuum cleaner emits shock when motor is started	1. Wire has come loose and is grounded against unit's case or the motor windings are grounded.	1. Take the vacuum cleaner to a professional service technician; do not use the appliance again until the fault ground is found and repaired.
Upright vac is hard to push	1. Carpet height adjustment set too low (too close to floor). 2. Worn-out brushes. 3. Brush spindles need lubrication.	1. Raise the carpet height adjustment. 2. Replace the brushes. 3. Follow the diagram in your owner's manual for proper lubrication.
Lack of suction	1. Foreign object in the base or attachments. 2. The bag or protective filter is full.	1. Check the hose and clear any blockage. 2. Replace or empty the bag; replace the filter.

Screens Extend Washer Life

Screens on the faucets from which water enters the washer are a must to keep sediment from entering the lines. If the screens on your washer faucets are either non-existent or non-effective, put in good ones right away. Montgomery Ward sells the screens you need plus the high-pressure hose that conveys the water from the faucets to the washing machine.

Replacing A Washer Pump Is A Do-It-Yourself Project

There is also a pump made especially for your brand of washer. Once you get the right pump, replacement normally involves only a few simple steps. Drain the unit, and disconnect it from the plumbing and electrical systems. If you decide to work with the washer face down, be sure to pad the floor before tilting it over. Then loosen the motor mounting bolt and move the motor to slacken the belt. Remove all hoses from the pump, and then take out the pump's mounting bolts which hold it in place. Once you get the old pump out, just reverse the procedure to install the new one.

Save Installation Sheets

Whenever you have any new appliance installed, save the instruction sheets, which the installer usually leaves behind.

Washers

FROM POUNDING clothes clean on rocks by the river to the modern clothes washer is a big jump, and the complexity of the equipment is proportionally an even bigger jump. There are many complicated systems within the unit. Many of these parts require special equipment to test and to track down problems. However, there are several common problems that the average homeowner can handle by himself.

A slow filling washer can be the result of clogging in the tiny screens that are in place in the line where both hot and cold water enter the machine. Caution: Never work inside the unit without shutting off current to the unit.

1. Turn off the faucets and unscrew the hoses that are attached to the back of the washer.
2. The screens may have to be pried out.
3. The domed strainers can be cleaned with a stiff brush.
4. In reattaching the hoses, put them on hand tight, and then add a quarter turn more with pliers.
5. Check to be sure there are no leaks after replacing the hoses.

The hoses mentioned above, as well as the hoses within the actual unit, can develop leaks. They are easy to replace. They are held in place by spring-type hose clamps that must be squeezed with pliers to loosen. Be ready to catch water from the hoses with a towel. In addition, belts may wear or break and need to be replaced.

Anytime you work on a washer, make sure to check the unit with your level when it is back in place. An unlevel unit has to labor much harder, will wear out sooner, will not be as quiet as it should, and will not do as good a job.

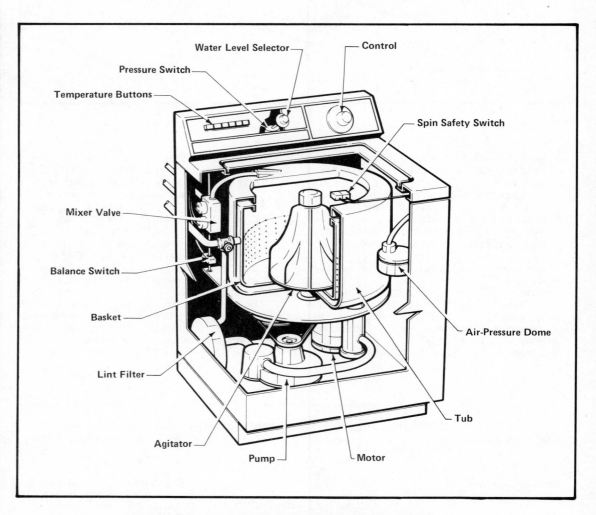

Clothes Washers Troubleshooting Chart

Caution: Unplug appliance before inspecting or repairing. Do not reconnect power until job is completed or while any wiring connections are exposed.

PROBLEMS	CAUSES	REPAIRS
Washer does not fill with water	1. Water shut-off valves on supply pipes closed.	1. Open the valves.
	2. Water-inlet hoses kinked or knotted.	2. Straighten out the hoses.
	3. Clogged water-intake screens.	3. Remove the screens and clean out the sediment.
	4. Defective water-valve solenoid.	4. Remove the leads from the valve, and test them with a continuity tester. If the solenoid coil is open, replace it.
	5. Defective water valve.	5. Disassemble the water valve and inspect all parts for damage. Replace a bad part with a new one, if possible. If not, replace the entire valve.

PROBLEMS	CAUSES	REPAIRS
	6. Defective timer.	6. Test the timer with a continuity tester, and replace the timer if it is faulty.
	7. Defective water temperature switch or water level pressure switch.	7. Test the switches with a continuity tester and replace if faulty.
	8. Open circuit in timer, in water solenoid valve coil, or in connecting wires.	8. Once you are sure that the machine is unplugged, use a continuity tester to check for a complete circuit from the line cord plug prong to the solenoid; also make a continuity check between the two solenoid terminals. There should be continuity from "source to load" — from the line cord plug to the motor lead wire — when the timer is set to wash. Be sure that washer is unplugged.
Agitator does not work	1. Broken drive belt.	1. Replace with a new belt.
	2. Drive belt is too loose and slipping.	2. Tighten the belt until the belt tension is such that the belt can be deflected no more than ½ of an inch.
	3. Defective transmission.	3. Place the control knob timer in its "Wash" position. Remove the drive belt, and turn the transmission pulley by hand in the direction of agitation, which is generally clockwise. If the agitator is not driven by this action, the transmission is probably bad and should be overhauled or replaced.
	4. Defective timer or water level pressure switch.	4. Test the timer and switch with a continuity tester while tub is full of water. Replace faulty parts.
Water drains from machine during wash and rinse cycles instead of at the end of the cycle	1. Drain hose may be positioned lower than the water level in basket. This creates a vacuum and water siphons out.	1. Reposition the drain hose so that is higher than the highest water level in the basket.
Machine does not spin at all or does not spin at correct speed	1. Broken drive belt.	1. Replace with a new belt.
	2. Slipping drive belt.	2. Tighten the belt.
	3. Loose motor drive pulley.	3. Tighten the pulley set screw.
	4. Defective drive clutch.	4. With washer unplugged, dial the control knob (timer) to its "Spin" position. Remove the drive belt and turn the clutch by hand. If there is a strong resistance, the clutch is bad and should be replaced.
	5. Spin brake does not release or transmission is frozen.	5. The spin brake and transmission are attached. Place the control knob (timer) in its "Spin" position. Remove the drive belt, and turn the brake stator. It should move freely. If the brake stator binds, the brake assembly or transmission is defective. Have one or both repaired.
	6. Defective timer.	6. Test according to manufacturer's recommended procedure and replace if faulty.
	7. Open circuit.	7. Use a continuity tester to check for complete circuit from line cord to solenoid terminals.
	8. Too much detergent.	8. Reduce the amount of detergent you use.
	9. Clutch needs adjusting (disc type).	9. Adjust the nut or the clutch actuating shaft.

Dual-Action Agitator Rolls Over Clothes

Many Sears Kenmore washers feature a special agitator that causes greater rollover of the wash load and thus produces cleaner clothes. The bottom plate paddles back and forth while the center post rotates and augers the laundry downward. This dual-action agitation results in the load being rolled over about seven times per cycle. Standard equipment on several new Sears Kenmore washers, the dual-action agitator is also available as a replacement for many older Sears Kenmore models.

Take The Pressure Off Washer Hoses

The Dual-Protector Valve from Chatham Brass Company, Inc., is a valuable accessory for your automatic washing machine. It has a lever that allows you, with just a flick of the finger, to cut off both the hot and cold water. An easy item to install, the Dual-Protector Valve relieves the pressure on the hoses, gives them longer life, and eliminates the danger of a flood should a hose rupture. It is available in either a chrome or brass finish.

Maytag Washers Save Energy

Maytag has introduced new energy-saving features on automatic clothes washers. For example, all the new automatics provide wash water temperatures from hot to cold, and all provide for a cold-water rinse with any wash temperature selected. Maytag Model A608 offers these features plus a bleach dispenser.

Save Energy Without Sacrificing Performance

By using cold-water rinses for every wash load, you can save a good deal of energy without reducing the quality of the washing process. Since rinsing is a dilution process, a cold rinse is just as effective as a warm one. You can also save energy by setting the water-level control (most newer machines have one) to correspond to the size of your load. These simple suggestions can add up to many dollars saved over the course of a year.

Mechanical Monsters

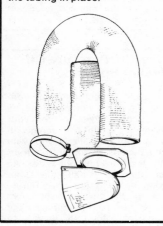

Dryers

THE CLOTHES DRYER consists of a cabinet surrounding a motor-driven drum. Clothing placed inside the drum tumbles through air which has been warmed by a heater and pulled into and through the drum by an exhaust fan. These three basic components—heat, air flow, and tumbling action—must be present for a clothes dryer to operate properly. Actually, the clothes dryer is a very simple appliance. When it is operating properly, it can dry your clothing quickly and safely, but the appliance must be kept in proper operating condition and it must be used correctly.

The motor that drives the drum is usually located at the base of the dryer. You can get at it by removing either the front panel or the rear service panel, but be sure to unplug the dryer before attempting any motor service or repairs. In the case of a gas dryer, be sure that the gas line is turned off before you open up the appliance or pull it away from the wall.

The motor drives a belt, which in most newer dryers completely surrounds the outside of the drum. Many of these belts have an odd appearance—almost flat like a rubber band. If you look at the belt closely, however, you can see that it has a number of grooves on one side to give the belt greater gripping power. Near the point where the belt is attached to the small motor pulley, a spring-loaded wheel (called an idler) maintains tension on the belt as the drum turns. Since the drum itself acts as a very large pulley and the motor has a very small one, tremendous speed reduction is obtained. Most drums rotate at around 50 rpm. Any faster and centrifugal force would tend to hold the clothing against the side of the drum rather than allowing it to tumble.

The dryer's heat source can be either an electric heating element or a gas burner. In either case, the heat source is usually located within a box that has both an inlet and an outlet. Air flows in through the box where it is heated, and then it is blown into the drum by a fan. Since the drum is a sealed container when the dryer door is closed, the exhaust fan must pull air through the opening and into the heater box to replace that expelled by the fan. The heated air flows into the drum, where it absorbs moisture from the clothing, and it is then exhausted to the outside of your home through the vent.

The heat level is quite important. Heat must be controlled at the proper temperature for the type of clothing that is in the dryer. Most dryers have one thermostatic control set to operate around 145 degrees F., but some dryers offer an adjustable thermostat which you can set according to the nature of the load you are drying. The adjustable thermostat can range from 120 degrees for delicate clothing to 155 degrees for heavy cottons and linens. You can check your dryer's temperature by inserting a candy or meat thermometer in the exhaust vent at the point where the vent is attached to the dryer. The machine's temperature sensors are usually located within the exhaust duct, just inside the dryer.

There is another thermostat in your dryer, but it is there for safety purposes only. The safety thermostat shuts off the heating element or burner when the temperature in the dryer exceeds 200 degrees. Normally, your dryer will never even approach 200 degrees; it gets that hot only in cases where the thermostat sticks, the heating element becomes grounded, or the air flow through the dryer is blocked. The following paragraphs list some of the things you should and should not do to your clothes dryer.

1. Most dryers that were built within the past few years have sealed-for-life lubrication. If you ever disassemble the dryer for any reason, however, you must be sure that all bearing surfaces are lubricated; use the manufacturer's recommended lubricant. One important spot to check is around the

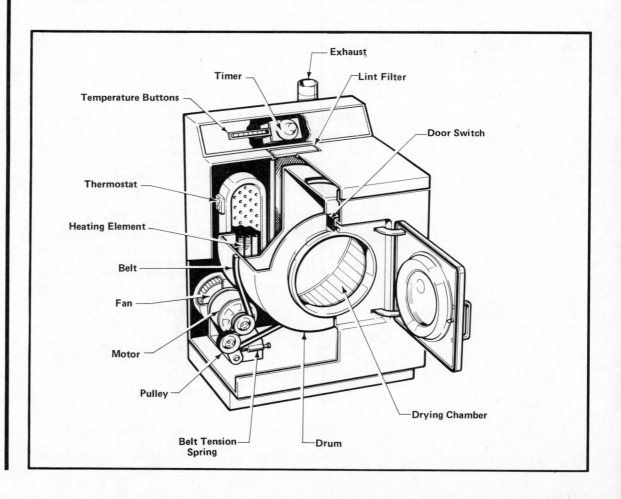

front edge. The drum of many modern dryers is supported on rollers at the rear, while in front the flange of the door opening serves as a bearing surface. If the surface appears to be dry, lubricate it according to the manufacturer's instructions.

2. One of the most important preventative maintenance tasks you can do for your dryer is to clean the lint filter prior to drying every load. If the filter becomes completely clogged, some lint can escape and create jamming problems elsewhere in the dryer. Even a partial blockage reduces the dryer's efficiency and limits its capabilities. Most importantly, though, a clogged dryer can be a fire hazard. Lint from many fabrics—particularly synthetics—is highly combustible.

3. The vent is designed to carry heat and moisture away from the dryer to the outside of the house. While the vent may seem to waste a great deal of heat which could be put to use, remember that the warm air is heavy with moisture after it passes through the dryer. Were this air to be recirculated through the dryer, the appliance's efficiency would suffer greatly, since the air simply could not hold much additional moisture. Moreover, the same air is circulated through the dryer motor to help cool it. The hotter the air is, the hotter the motor will run.

4. Although it is very tempting to place large quantities of clothing in the big drum, remember that the clothing needs a great deal of space for tumbling. Never dry more than a single washer load in a single dryer load, and never try to bake your clothes completely dry. Most clothes should be allowed to retain a slight amount of moisture.

5. Once a year unplug the dryer or turn off the gas supply, remove the service panel, and vacuum away any lint or dust in the vicinity of the motor. Regular cleaning keeps lint away from the bearings, and it helps maintain clean air passageways. It also reduces the possibility of a fire.

Clothes Dryer Troubleshooting Chart

Caution: Unplug appliance before inspecting and repairing. Do not reconnect power until job is completed or while any wiring connections are exposed. If you suspect a leak in a gas appliance, turn off the gas supply, extinguish all open flames, open windows or doors, and leave the area. Never search for a leak with a match or any other sort of open flame. Call an authorized technician or your utility company for a complete check before operating the appliance.

PROBLEMS	CAUSES	REPAIRS
Dryer fails to run	1. Blown fuse.	1. Replace fuses in the dryer circuit.
	2. Broken belt.	2. Unplug the dryer, remove the service panel, and replace the broken belt with the manufacturer's specified part. Be sure to apply proper tension to the new belt.
	3. Defective door safety switch.	3. Check the switch with a continuity tester. Replace the switch or adjust the linkage.
	4. Defective timer.	4. Check the contacts to the heating element, and replace the timer if the contacts are open when they should be closed.
Dryer runs, but there is no heat	1. Insufficient voltage reaching appliance.	1. Replace both fuses to the appliance.
	2. Thermostat(s) open.	2. Test with a continuity tester when the machine is cool and replace any defective thermostat.
	3. Thermostat or timer turned to air position.	3. Set the thermostat or timer to the correct position.
Clothes not drying sufficiently	1. Lint filter clogged.	1. Remove and clean the lint filter.
	2. Dryer is overloaded with clothing.	2. Dry only one washer load at each dryer cycle.
	3. Timer set incorrectly.	3. Set timer for longer drying time.
	4. Clothing too wet when placed in dryer from washer.	4. Check the washer's operation.
	5. Circuitry to heating element open.	5. Test the circuitry with a continuity tester, and replace any defective component.
Dryer runs noisily	1. Lint buildup behind drum.	1. Unplug the dryer and remove the lint buildup. This can sometimes be accomplished by pressing a stiff brush through the perforations in the drum.
	2. Bearings either worn or in need of lubrication.	2. Check bearings; clean and lubricate them if necessary.
	3. Slipping belts.	3. Check belt tension and adjust it properly. Wraparound belts must be properly tensioned by the idler.
	4. Lint in blower fan.	4. Remove the fan and clean the lint from it.

Exhaust Kits Make Venting Easy

If you are a homeowner planning to install your own dryer, your best bet is to buy a kit that comes complete with everything you need to pipe the moist exhaust air outside. The Montgomery Ward exhaust kit contains the vent hood, wall unit, adjustable elbows, and the sections of pipe. The shorter and straighter the exhaust pipe, the better. Twenty-two feet is the maximum (some dryers with inferior exhaust systems cannot make it that far), and you should deduct three feet for every right angle bend.

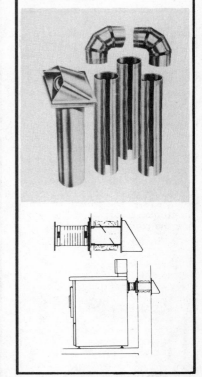

Mother Nature Can Dry Clothes Too

Not everyone wants or has room for an automatic clothes dryer. Such people hang their clothes on lines either indoors or out. If you count yourself in the latter group, you should know about a gadget that mounts on any flat surface and lets you reel out clothesline when you need it. The Cordomatic Clothesline contains 20 feet of white plastic line that is housed in the wall-mounted casing. The line reels out easily, and the ring on its end allows you to attach the line to a hook on a tree, a post, or a wall. Ideal for the apartment dweller who needs an indoor clothesline, the Cordomatic is sold in retail stores and by mail from Almatex International, 3569B Bristol Pike, Cornwell Heights, Pennsylvania 19020.

Dishwashers

Dishwasher Tailpiece Is A Drain

Since the dishwasher has a pump to remove waste water, there is no need to have a drain directly beneath the unit. If you have a disposer in a nearby sink, for example, the dishwasher waste water can be pumped through it. You can also direct the dishwasher waste water directly into the sink drain by replacing a section of the drain pipe with the Hancock-Gross Y-tailpiece connector. Both the disposer and sink drain connections apply only to under-the-counter dishwashers.

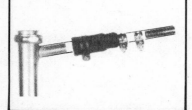

Dishwasher Hook-Up Kit Can Save You Money

Several companies market kits enabling the do-it-yourselfer to hook up a replacement dishwasher with a minimum of trouble and a maximum amount of money saved. GE's kit not only works for GE dishwashers; it allows you to install just about any other type with a minimum of difficulty. The kit comes with very complete instructions and probably every part you will need, though in some cases you may have to buy a few additional components.

NOT ONLY DOES the automatic dishwasher solve the age old problem of, "Who will do the dishes?", but it also gets the dishes a lot cleaner than even the best hand washing job. And, in most cases, it does a good job of killing bacteria. It does all this while using a lot less water than the old way and without a great amount of electricity being consumed.

Although the dishwasher is a complicated machine, there are several things that the homeowner can solve by using the troubleshooter's guide. One very complicated unit is the timer. You do not have to know how this gadget works to ascertain that it needs to be replaced. Here are the steps in replacing a timer.

1. Turn off the electric power to the unit and do not disconnect any of the wires until you are ready to put in the new unit.
2. Remove the panel from the dishwasher so the timer will be exposed. Most knobs pull straight off.
3. Hold the new timer next to the old one, and change the wires one at a time from the old to the new. That way, you will not get them crossed up.
4. To disengage the wires, pull them straight off, and then slide them on the new terminals.
5. Now remove the screws holding the old timer and replace it with the new one.

The spray arm or arms and the screen below can get clogged with particles and can be removed easily for cleaning with a brush in the sink. A knurled nut above the arms can be unscrewed for removal.

The pump can also become clogged. Consult your owner's manual for the removal sequence of parts for replacing impellers, and follow this same procedure to get to and clean the pump. It is best to replace any O rings you remove with new ones even though the old ones may look all right. If you do not have the manual, be sure to keep track of where everything goes with a rough sketch as you remove parts so they can go back in the right place.

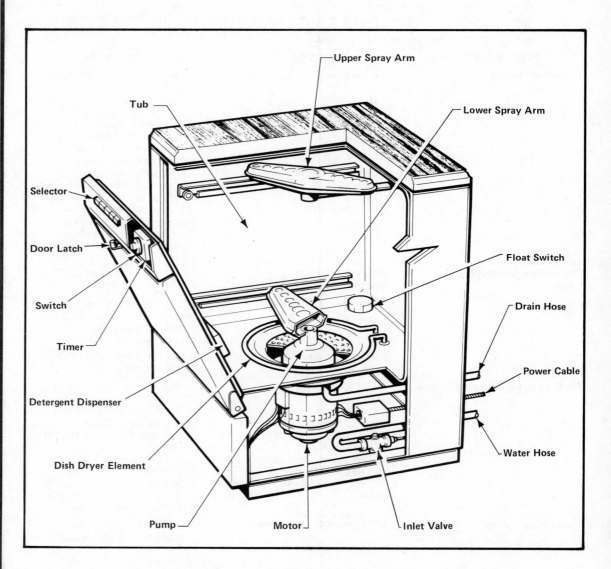

Dishwashers Troubleshooting Chart

Caution: Unplug appliance before inspecting or repairing. Do not reconnect power until job is completed or while any wiring connections are exposed.

PROBLEMS	CAUSES	REPAIRS
Dishwasher leaks	1. Loose or worn door gasket.	1. A torn, flattened, or hardened gasket should be replaced. Position the gasket tightly around the door.
	2. Broken door hinge.	2. Replace the hinge.

PROBLEMS	CAUSES	REPAIRS
	3. Fitting on the water-inlet line leaks or the line is ruptured.	3. Tighten the compression nut to stop the fitting from leaking. If the line is damaged, replace it.
	4. Defective motor seal.	4. If water leaks from around the motor shaft, replace the seal.
	5. Loose hose clamp.	5. Check and tighten all hose clamps.
Dishwasher does not operate	1. Door is not closed and latched.	1. Door must be closed and latch locked.
	2. Cycle selection button is not fully engaged.	2. Depress the cycle button all the way.
	3. Blown fuse or tripped circuit breaker.	3. Replace the bad fuse or reset the circuit breaker. If the fuse blows or the circuit breaker trips again, there is an electrical defect. Call a serviceman immediately. Do not operate the appliance.
	4. Defective door switch.	4. Test the switch with a continuity tester while depressing the switch button. Replace the switch if it is open.
	5. Defective timer.	5. Turn the timer dial by hand very slowly with the door latched and the wash cycle button engaged. If the timer fails to turn the dishwasher on, it is probably defective and must be replaced.
	6. Defective motor.	6. Call in a service technician.
Dishwasher fails to fill	1. Shut-off water valve partially or fully closed.	1. Check the shut-off valve on the line leading to the dishwasher; open it fully.
	2. Water pressure is too low.	2. Water pressure must be at least 15 pounds per square inch; call your local water company.
	3. Clogged water-inlet screen or damaged water valve.	3. Most water valves are equipped with screens to trap deposits. Disassemble and clean the screen. If the parts are heavily calcified, replace the entire water-inlet valve assembly.
	4. Defective water-valve solenoid.	4. Check the solenoid with a continuity tester. Replace the solenoid if it is open.
	5. Faulty float switch.	5. Some dishwashers are equipped with a float switch in the tub that controls the water valve. Test the float by picking up the float with your finger and letting it drop. You should hear a "click," and the float arm should fall squarely on the float switch. If it does not, replace the float assembly.
Dishwasher fails to drain	1. The drain hose is kinked or clogged.	1. Remove the drain hose and straighten it; make sure that the hose is not clogged and reinstall it.
	2. Damaged or defective pump.	2. Remove and disassemble the pump. Clean away any clogged material. Be sure that all particles are removed; otherwise, the pump can be damaged.
	3. Stuck timer.	3. If the timer does not advance by itself, it is probably defective. Replace it.
	4. Defective pump motor.	4. Advance the timer to its drain phase. If the motor hums, look for impeller obstructions. If the impeller is free, the pump motor wiring is probably defective. Replace the pump motor.

Here's An Energy Saver On Wheels

You can roll out Frigidaire's Electri-Saver portable dishwasher and save energy in the process. The unit's pushbutton option of "no heated dry" cuts energy use on a normal soil cycle up to 30 percent. The Electri-Saver also has a quick-wash cycle and a triple-wash pots and pans cycle. The control panel, redesigned for better visibility, is larger than on previous Frigidaire models.

It's No Sweat With Paste Solder

Installing or repairing a dishwasher often requires sweat soldering copper fittings (as do other plumbing chores which involve copper tubing). One product that makes the job easier is brushable SWIF solder paste from Hercules. SWIF is available at hardware stores and comes with complete instructions.

Dishes Get Washed Behind Glass

Whirlpool's SDU9000 built-in dishwasher is available with an optional kit with which you can give the unit the popular black-glass look. New design features include high-sided racks for better china and glassware protection and an upper rack that is adjustable in height and tilt. Three pushbuttons provide a full range of energy options. With these settings, you can add heat to the washing cycle, heat to the drying cycle, or no heat to either washing or drying. A concealed door latch is located behind the console.

Mechanical Monsters

Refrigerators

WHILE THE REFRIGERATOR is a sturdy appliance and gives years of almost trouble-free service, there are still things that you, the homeowner, can do to make sure it stays trouble-free.

1. Cleaning the condenser coils about four times a year is an absolute must. A build-up of dust cuts down on the efficiency. A tank type vacuum cleaner with a brush attachment works well. While you are at it, clean dust off everything else.
2. Many refrigerators will have a pan underneath to catch condensate water. Check this each time you vacuum. If it is not regularly cleaned, it will collect particles of food that will cause odors.
3. If your unit is not self defrosting, you should watch the frost build-up, and when it approaches ¼ of an inch, defrost it. Otherwise, the layer of frost will act as an insulator and cut down on the efficiency.

There are also some controls that you should check on, and if they are faulty, they should be replaced. Often, the trouble is in the setting control. You should check the temperature in both the refrigerator and the freezer to be sure that the controls are set at the most economical setting. The temperature in the freezer should be between zero and five degrees. Here is how to test it.

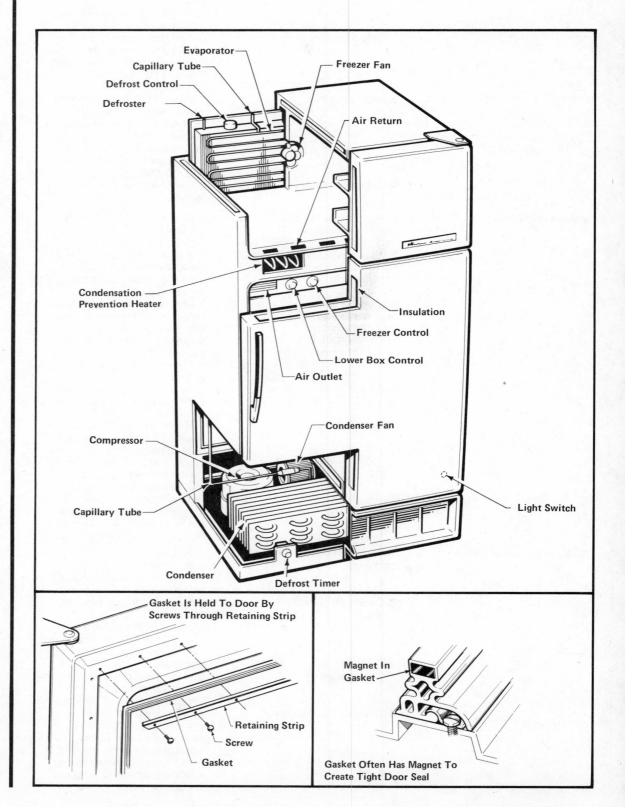

△ 1. Place the thermometer between packages that have been in the freezer for at least twenty-four hours. If the reading is below zero or above five degrees, reset the freezer thermostat up or down accordingly.

△ 2. The temperature in the refrigerator part should be between 34 and 37 degrees. Put the thermometer in the refrigerator long enough to get an accurate reading. The refrigerator temperature control should be set up or down to bring it within range.

△ 3. Check for a faulty door gasket by closing the door on a dollar bill.

△ 4. With the door closed, tug at the dollar. If it comes out without much resistance, the seal is not right.

△ 5. Make this dollar test at several other places around the doors.

Dirt on the gasket and loose hinges can also prevent a tight seal. However, if it is determined that a new gasket is in order, get the new one before you take off the old. Normally, the gasket will be of the type that has magnets inside to hold the door closed. It will be held to the door by screws through a metal retainer strip, an inner door facing, and then into the door.

○ 1. To get at the screws, usually the old gasket will have to be peeled back.

○ 2. Remove the screws in the top half and install the new gasket across the top. This prevents the entire inner door facing and shelves from coming off, which would happen if all the screws were removed at once.

○ 3. With the new gasket in place, make sure that it makes contact all the way around. Smooth and even it out with your hands. If there are big kinks, rub it with hot towels.

Ice maker problems occur when the strainer in the water line entry gets clogged. It can be reached usually by cutting the water supply off and unscrewing the hose type connector on the back of the box. Clean the strainer with an old toothbrush.

Put Your Refrigerator on Wheels

You generally do not move large appliances around much, and yet they should be moved periodically so that you can clean the area around and beneath them. Hemco appliance rollers makes moving these monsters easy. Best used for refrigerators and freezers, the Hemco Model SAR-12 is a heavy-duty steerable roller set. The steering lever lets you move the appliance anywhere, although Hemco also makes nonsteerable models if you merely want to move the appliance out for cleaning. Model SAR-12 is strength tested for 3000 pounds, and it is guaranteed for the life of the appliance. Once in place under the appliance, the rollers stay securely without your having to attach them. Hemco stands for the Home Equipment Manufacturing Company.

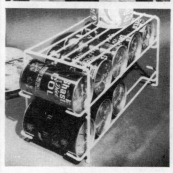

Refrigerators Troubleshooting Chart

Caution: Unplug appliance before inspecting or repairing. Do not reconnect power until job is completed or while any wiring connections are exposed.

PROBLEMS	CAUSES	REPAIRS
Food storage compartment is too warm	1. Door is opened too often.	1. Open the door only when absolutely necessary.
	2. Thermostat is set at too high a temperature.	2. Readjust thermostat to a lower temperature setting.
	3. Door does not seal tightly.	3. Test the seal by closing the door on a dollar bill. If there is no resistance when you pull on the bill, the door needs adjusting.
	4. Light bulb stays on after door is closed.	4. Test by depressing light bulb button near door. If bulb does not go out, replace defective switch.
	5. Defective defrost system on a frostless refrigerator.	5. Test the defrosting components and replace them if they are faulty
Compressor runs excessively or never stops running	1. Thermostat is set at too high a temperature.	1. Readjust thermostat to a lower temperature.
	2. Door does not seal tightly.	2. Test the seal by closing the door on a dollar bill. If there is no resistance when you pull on the bill, the door needs adjusting.
	3. Condenser is coated with dust or dirt, preventing refrigerant from liquifying.	3. Remove dust or dirt from condenser coil with a vacuum cleaner to allow air to circulate and cool vaporized refrigerant.
Compressor does not function	1. Fuse is blown or circuit breaker is tripped.	1. Replace fuse or reset circuit breaker.
	2. Thermostat is defective.	2. Test thermostat for continuity and replace if faulty.
	3. Timer is defective.	3. Test timer and replace if faulty.
	4. Relay is defective.	4. Test relay and replace if faulty.
	5. Compressor is broken.	5. Install new compressor or have old one fixed.
Refrigerator is excessively noisy	1. Unit is not level.	1. Check the refrigerator's position with a carpenter's level, and reposition the unit if required.
	2. Compressor is loose in its mountings.	2. Tighten compressor mountings.
	3. Tubing hits against cabinet.	3. Reposition tubing so that it cannot strike the cabinet.
	4. Clogged condenser.	4. Vacuum away lint and dust.
	5. Condenser fan inoperative.	5. Oil fan, or replace it if necessary.

Ice Tray Rack Ends Freezer Storage Woes

If you lack storage space in the freezer compartment above your refrigerator, the freezer rack from Grayline Housewares may solve the problem. Only three inches high so that a pair of ice trays easily slide underneath, the Grayline rack can accommodate a good supply of frozen foods. Like most of Grayline's storage helpers, the freezer rack is made of rigid steel wire frames covered with cushion-coated vinyl. Grayline also comes to the rescue of the crowded refrigerator with its beverage can dispenser. It holds 10 beer or soft drink cans, and as a can is removed, another rolls forward for easy access. The top shelf of the can dispenser serves as yet another storage area.

Mechanical Monsters

Ranges (Gas)

IN A GAS RANGE, the heat for both the surface burners and the oven emanates from an open flame. The fuel may be either natural gas or one of several types of bottled gas, but the operation in either case is the same. The gas burner operates by combining the fuel from the supply line with the correct proportion of air for burning that is thorough and clean. The fuel enters the burner assembly through an orifice, which is simply an opening sized to provide the proper amount of gas flow. The gas stream pulls air in through an open shutter behind the orifice, and as the mixture flows on through the burner tube to the burner itself, the air and gas mix thoroughly. By the time it reaches the burner, the air/gas mixture is ready to meet the pilot or the burner flame. Burning then occurs with an odorless and soot-free flame.

Air must be mixed with the fuel supply in the proper proportion to provide a clean-burning and efficient flame. You can judge the quality of the air/fuel mixture by observing the flame. If the flame is yellow, you know that there is insufficient air; if the flame tends to pull away from the burner,

you know that there is too much air. You can regulate the quantity of air by adjusting the shutter, which is located at the point where the burner meets a pipe near the front of the range.

1. Loosen the screw and adjust the shutter to render the correct flame.
2. Close the shutter until the flame turns yellow.
3. Open the shutter slowly until the yellow tips of the flame just disappear. You should see a distinct cone-shaped flame with soft blue tips. The flame is hottest at the points of the tips, and coolest at their base.
4. Retighten the screw.

The heat output from each surface-unit burner is usually regulated by a separate control valve. This valve opens and closes an internal passageway, allowing more or less gas to flow through the orifice. The amount of gas that flows through the orifice automatically adjusts the air mixture; a smaller amount of gas flow allows a smaller quantity of air to enter the air shutter.

The oven thermostat on many gas ranges operates exactly like the thermostat on most electric ranges. A sensing tube runs from the thermostat into the oven chamber. Inside the tube, a liquid responds to heat changes by expanding or contracting, which in turn opens or closes a switch

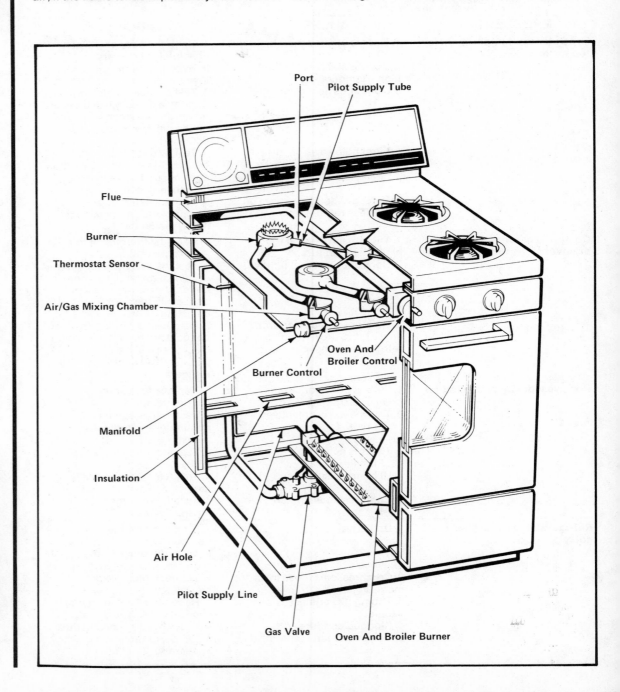

within the body of the thermostat. The switch controls an electrical coil, called a solenoid, located on the gas line. The solenoid, consisting of coils or wire that are wound around a central armature or plunger, concentrates the magnetic force generated by the electricity flowing through the wires. When the coil is energized, the plunger moves, opening or closing the gas line to the oven burner as required to maintain a specific temperature setting.

Some oven thermostats operate directly on the gas line, moving a bellows arrangement to open or close a disk which, in turn, permits or blocks the flow of gas through the line. Some of these valves modulate—that is, they open or close the gas line gradually rather than instantaneously. A modulating valve reduces any temperature overshooting, and it helps maintain a more constant temperature level.

You can adjust the thermostat of a gas range if the temperature within the oven varies by more than 25 degrees from the setting on the knob.

1. Check the oven temperature by placing an accurate thermometer in the center of the oven cavity.
2. Allow the oven burner to stabilize for 30 minutes.
3. If you find a great disparity between the thermometer reading and the knob setting, remove the thermostat knob and look for an adjusting screw. You may find the screw within a hollow thermostat shaft, or you may find it on a movable scale at the rear of the knob skirt.
4. Move the screw or scale until the setting on the knob corresponds with the actual oven temperature.

Gas ranges require little in the way of service. Their electrical components—timer, thermostat, and valve—are subject to failure, but they rarely do fail. Just make sure that the timer is set to a manual or to an operating position when you want to use the oven. Here are some helpful maintenance tips.

1. Gas burners require cleaning from time to time. Before you perform any sort of service procedure, however, be sure that you shut off the gas supply and unplug the range.
2. You can disassemble many burners, soak them in hot soapy water, and then brush them with an old toothbrush to remove food particles.
3. If you notice that a burner is starting to clog, you can prevent the clog from worsening by cleaning the blocked orifice with a wooden toothpick.
4. If you see that the heat output from a particular burner is reduced below its normal level, use only a soft object (like a toothpick) for cleaning. Since metallic objects can enlarge the orifice openings, they should not be used for cleaning.
5. Should a pilot light become clogged, it might be necessary to unscrew the orifice tip itself and clean the orifice from the inside. The opening in the orifice is generally too small to be cleaned from the outside.
6. If a burner is hesitant when you turn on the gas supply, check to be sure that the pilot flame is adjusted correctly and that the connecting tubes from the pilot to burner are in place.

Turn off the gas supply and pull the plug before you attempt any gas range repair. If you smell a gas leak, be sure to call a technician immediately to inspect the range, and do not use the range until it has been examined thoroughly. Open the windows to provide plenty of ventilation, and extinguish any open flames. Natural gas itself has no odor, but the gas company adds an artificial odor to help you detect leaks in gas lines. A leak indicates a situation that is potentially very hazardous. Should you ever smell raw gas in your home, call professional service personnel immediately.

Shield Your Stove As You Clean It

Some cleaners are hard on appliance finishes, but Appliance Magic from Magic American Chemical Company cleans without scratching or streaking and leaves a fine film of silicone to form a tough shield on the surface. The largest-selling cleaner-polish for ranges, refrigerators, stainless steel, copper, and chrome, Appliance Magic removes all the dirt, film, and soil that any kitchen produces: food stains, cooking grease, etc. You can use Appliance Magic on appliances of any color.

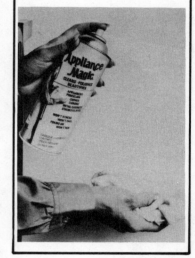

Convection Cooking Is Quick

Tappan has brought the speed of convection cooking to the home gas range. Convection cooking, in which a stream of hot air is directed at the food, has been used extensively in restaurants because it means faster cooking and no pre-heating. Due to its automatic oven ignition system and cooking speed, the Tappan Convectionaire (available with a self-cleaning oven) can save as much as 37 percent of the energy consumed by a conventional gas oven.

Gas Ranges Troubleshooting Chart

Caution: Unplug the range, turn off the gas supply, and use care in handling when servicing, inspecting, or adjusting the range. Replacement parts should only be done by a technician. If you suspect a leak in a gas appliance, turn off gas supply, extinguish all open flames, open windows or doors, and leave the area. Never search for a leak with a match or other open flame. Call an authorized technician or your utility company for a complete inspection before operating the appliance.

PROBLEMS	CAUSES	REPAIRS
Range fails to operate	1. Gas supply shut off.	1. Make sure that the gas is open.
	2. Defective regulator on supply line.	2. Call in an authorized gas technician.
	3. No power to range.	3. Check the electrical receptacle with a table lamp; repair the receptacle if required.
	4. Fuse or circuit breaker in range is open.	4. Check the fuse and replace it if it is open. Reset the circuit breaker.
	5. Pilot flame extinguished.	5. Relight the pilot.
	6. Thermostat defective.	6. Have an authorized technician replace the thermostat.
	7. Timer switch open.	7. Set the timer switch to manual or normal position.
Dirty (sooty) flame	1. Clogged air shutter opening.	1. Check and clean opening.
	2. Air shutter not adjusted properly.	2. Adjust the air shutter to render a good flame.
Surface burners "pop" when turned on	1. Conduction tubes from burner to pilot burner are out of place.	1. Check and place tubes in proper position.
	2. Pilot set too low.	2. Adjust the pilot to proper height (usually about ¼ of an inch).

Mechanical Monsters

Ranges (Electric)

MOST ELECTRIC ranges employ a sheath-type enclosed nichrome heating element to provide a controlled amount of heat to the cooking surface and to the oven cavity. The heating elements on the top of the range are shaped to make the maximum amount of contact with the bottom of your pots and pans. It is quite important that your cooking utensils be flat and in good condition, however. Otherwise, the pan can produce "hot spots" in the element, and hot spots reduce the life of the element as well as yield poor cooking results.

The cook-top elements—or surface units as they are called—can usually be removed easily. On many newer ranges, in fact, the surface units simply plug into a special receptacle at the rear, while on some other ranges, the units are hinged to make their wiring accessible.

Some electric ranges include a thermostat control on one of the surface units. Usually a solid state type of resistor, this thermostat changes resistance according to the amount of heat you set on the control. The thermostat control has a heat sensor that rests lightly against the pan bottom, and the control adjusts the element to maintain an exact temperature level at the bottom of the pan. It is absolutely essential, however, that your pan have a flat surface that meets the sensor squarely.

Some new ranges have flat ceramic tops over the elements; heat is transferred from the element through the ceramic material to your pots and pans. Sometimes, separate thermostatically-controlled switches are used to provide controlled heat to each section of the flat-top range. Be sure to follow the manufacturer's recommendations for cleaning these ranges, and always treat the ceramic surfaces with great care.

Many surface-element problems are related to a burned-out element or to a poor wiring connection either at the element receptacle or where the wire is attached to the element. You can repair any of these connections easily, but be sure to turn off the power supply and unplug the range before attempting to fix any part of your range.

It is possible for an element's inner coil to be grounded to its sheathing. If this happens, the coil can actually burn a hole through the outer surface of the element. Sometimes the hole is visible, but if it is not, test the element.

1. Use a continuity tester, and if you discover a fault, obtain a replacement element from an appliance parts distributor.
2. Record the color of each wire and the terminal to which it is connected before you disassemble the faulty element. Rewiring the replacement element should not offer any problems.
3. If a wire should break or burn away from the element or receptacle, install a special high-temperature terminal.
4. Be sure that all the wiring connections are tight, and if any connections appear to be corroded, polish them with a file or sandpaper until they are bright and shiny.

Heat from a poor connection is usually the cause of such corrosion, and if you fail to clean it, the connection is sure to malfunction again.

The oven has a capillary-tube thermostat to detect and maintain the proper temperature levels. The thermostat is usually not serviceable; if part of the thermostat fails, the entire control must be replaced. If the thermostat is out of calibration by more than 25 degrees, however, you usually can adjust it.

1. Place a good thermometer as near to the center of the oven as possible, and set the thermostat to a temperature in the medium range.
2. Allow the oven to stabilize for approximately 30 minutes before taking a reading.
3. If there is a great disparity between the thermometer reading and the thermostat setting, remove the thermostat knob and look for a calibration screw; you may find the screw within a hollow shaft or on the front of the control.
4. Turn the screw to correct the thermostat setting.
5. In other electric ranges, the skirt on the back of the thermostat knob is adjustable. Loosen the screw and adjust the position of the skirt to get the thermostat knob indicator to the correct temperature.
6. If the thermostat moves out of calibration

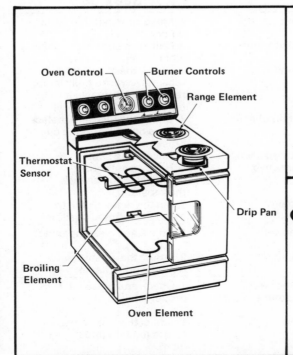

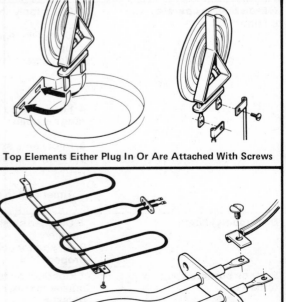

Top Elements Either Plug In Or Are Attached With Screws

Loosen Mounting Screws To Remove Oven Element

again install a new thermostat.

If a heating element in an oven fails to operate, and you have verified with the continuity tester or by visual inspection that it is defective, remove it from the oven by loosening the mounting screws at the rear of the oven. When you pull the defective element forward, enough connecting wiring should come with it to allow you to remove the wire from the old element and to attach it to the new element. Naturally, the power must be turned off before you attempt such a repair. In addition, make sure that the wiring connections are bright and shiny before you install the new element.

Many ranges have a timer connected to the oven circuit to turn the oven on and off at preset intervals. Although a convenience feature, the timer, ironically, is frequently the cause of people thinking that their ranges are defective. The timer controls can keep the oven from operating if they are inadvertently moved out of position. Therefore, if your oven fails to function, make certain that the timer is in the manual or normal position. It is easy to move the timer controls out of position accidentally when you clean the range.

The outlet and light are usually connected to the 110-volt circuit independent of the other range circuits. Generally, a separate fuse (located beneath the elements) or a circuit breaker (on the control panel) protects the outlet and light circuit. If the outlet or light ever fails to operate, check the condition of the fuse or the position of the circuit breaker.

If the entire range fails to operate—or if it operates only at a low temperature—chances are that one or both of the main fuses in your home's electrical circuit to the range have blown. If they are cartridge-type fuses, you must check them with a continuity tester or replace them with new ones. If the range circuit is protected by a circuit breaker, simply reset it to restore the range's power supply. Of course, you should try to determine why the fuse blew or the circuit breaker tripped.

Electric Ranges Troubleshooting Chart

Caution: Unplug appliance before inspecting or repairing. Do not reconnect power until job is completed or while any wiring connections are exposed.

PROBLEMS	CAUSES	REPAIRS
Oven light fails to operate	1. 15-amp fuse blown. 2. Inoperative switch.	1. Replace the fuse. 2. Check for continuity at the switch terminals. If there is no continuity, replace the switch.
Convenience outlet inoperative	1. 15-amp fuse blown. 2. Clock-timer switch. 3. Defective clock-timer switch.	1. Replace the fuse. 2. Set the clock for automatic operation. 3. Check the switch for continuity. If it lacks continuity, replace the clock-timer or the switch (if available).
Single surface element inoperative	1. Burned-out element. 2. Defective terminal block. 3. Loose wires. 4. Defective infinite switch.	1. Check the element for continuity; if it is open, replace it. 2. Replace the terminal block. 3. Clean the terminals and connect the wires. 4. Replace the switch.
Surface element overheats	1. Defective infinite switch.	1. Replace the switch.
Oven will not operate manually	1. Timer not set for manual operation.	1. Set the timer for manual operation.
Self-cleaning oven door will not open	1. Self-cleaning switch is not turned off. 2. Main circuit breaker tripped or fuse blown. 3. Door latch motor defective. 4. One or more of the following switches is defective: motor limit switch, door switch, self-cleaning switch, oven thermostat. 5. Broken or loose wires or terminals. 6. Cooling period following self-cleaning is not completed.	1. If you cannot turn the switch off, it is defective; replace it. 2. Reset the circuit breaker or replace the fuse. 3. Check the continuity of the motor and replace it if the motor lacks continuity. 4. Check the continuity of the switches, and replace any of them that are defective. 5. Check for broken or loose wires and repair any that you find. 6. Wait until lock light goes out.
Oven overheats	1. Defective thermostat. 2. Relay sticking. 3. Defective or miswired limit switch on a self-cleaning oven. 4. Thermostat bulb not installed properly in oven.	1. Adjust or replace the thermostat. 2. Replace the relay. 3. Replace the switch or correct the wiring. 4. Install the thermostat bulb correctly.

Mechanical Monsters

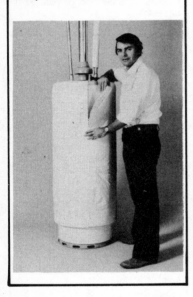

Hot Water Heater Maintenance

POSSIBLY THE sturdiest appliance you will ever own is your hot water heater. Most new units carry a guarantee on all parts, with an even longer guarantee (often up to 10 years) on the tank. Whether you have a gas, electric, or oil-heated unit, usually the only maintenance you need to do is drain periodically to prevent sediment from building up in the tank. In many areas you may need to drain monthly, depending on the hardness of the water and on the type of chemicals added. Here is how to drain your hot water heater.

1. Make sure that the drain valve turns easily. If it does not, it may have frozen from not being used for a long period of time. If it is frozen, attach a garden hose to the faucet so that when you do get the drain valve open and then cannot close it readily, you will be able to direct the water either into a drain or outside the house.
2. Perform this maintenance step early in the morning before anyone has used the hot water to insure that the sediment has settled to the bottom of the tank.
3. Open the drain valve and let a few pints of water flow into a bucket or small container.
4. Keep draining until the water runs clear. When it does run clear, your draining chore is done.

Once you do this task several months in a row, you will know how often it needs to be done. Sometimes, twice a year is all the draining required. By keeping the sediment out, you will have a more efficient and less noisy hot water system, and you will prevent future problems from developing in the tank and in the hot water pipes.

For a more efficient and longer lasting hot water heater, keep the heat control at a moderate setting. The temperature control knob on most heaters has "warm," "normal," and "hot" settings. The "normal" setting, usually about 140 degrees, is about all the heat you need. If you set the water heater control too high, it can create steam and cause knocking noises in the pipes.

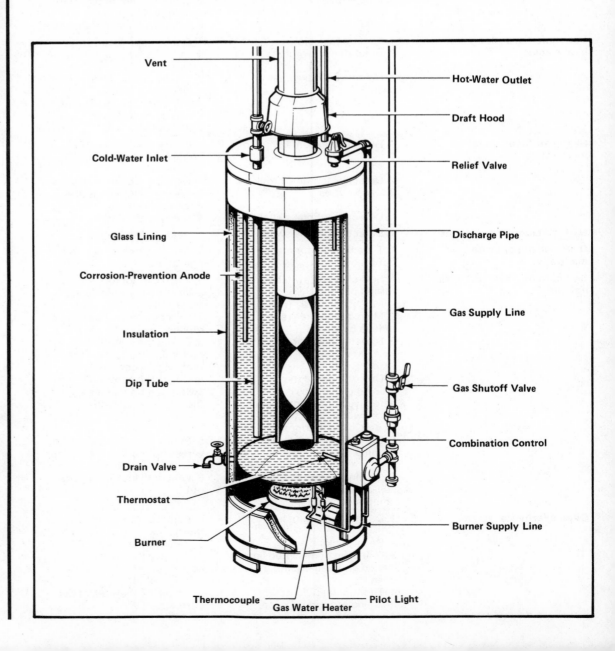

Vent · Hot-Water Outlet · Draft Hood · Cold-Water Inlet · Relief Valve · Glass Lining · Discharge Pipe · Corrosion-Prevention Anode · Gas Supply Line · Insulation · Dip Tube · Gas Shutoff Valve · Combination Control · Drain Valve · Thermostat · Burner Supply Line · Burner · Thermocouple · Gas Water Heater · Pilot Light

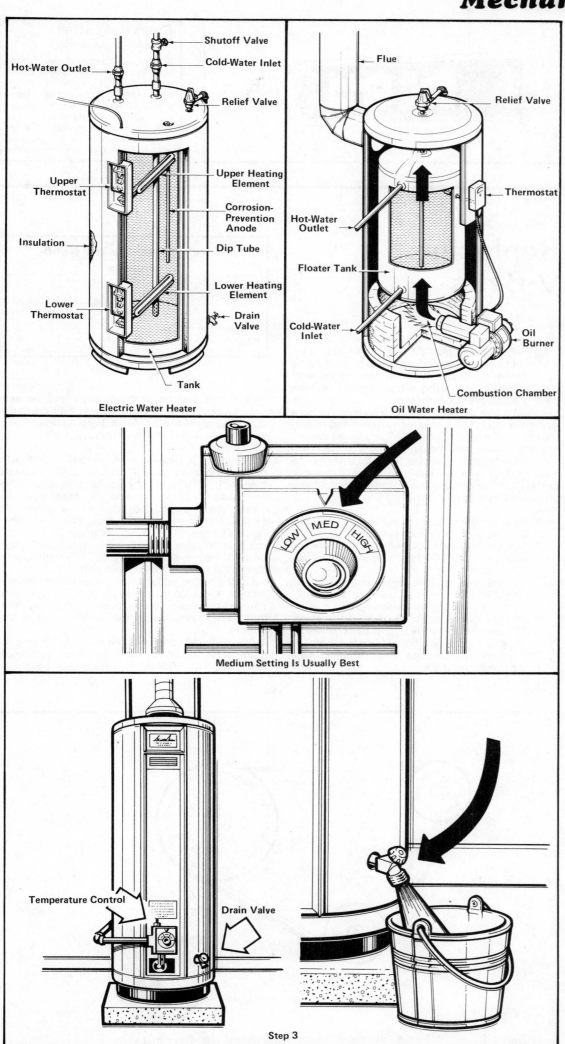

Electric Water Heater

- Hot-Water Outlet
- Shutoff Valve
- Cold-Water Inlet
- Relief Valve
- Upper Thermostat
- Upper Heating Element
- Corrosion-Prevention Anode
- Insulation
- Dip Tube
- Lower Thermostat
- Lower Heating Element
- Drain Valve
- Tank

Oil Water Heater

- Flue
- Relief Valve
- Thermostat
- Hot-Water Outlet
- Floater Tank
- Cold-Water Inlet
- Oil Burner
- Combustion Chamber

Medium Setting Is Usually Best

LOW MED HIGH

Step 3

- Temperature Control
- Drain Valve

Hot Water Dispenser Is Ready When You Are

A second cup of instant coffee is only an instant away with In-Sink-Erator's Steaming H_2O Tap. It is an at-the-sink hot water dispenser that provides 190-degree water for making instant coffee, tea, hot cereal, soups, and other fast foods. It can be installed by a handy do-it-yourselfer.

Small Water Heater Performs Mightily

A compact electronic water heater from Chronomite Labs provides continuous and instantaneous hot water at 98 percent efficiency. The unit, installed at the point of hot water use, only functions upon demand for hot water. While it can be used to serve hot water needs in the home (by putting one at each tap where hot water is needed), it is designed primarily for use in mobile homes, recreational vehicles, vacation homes, and boats.

Hook Up Your Water Heater Yourself

If you plan to replace your water heater, you'll be happy to know that you can buy flexible copper water heater connectors. EZ Plumb makes such connectors in various lengths from 12 to 24 inches. They eliminate sweat soldering, threading, require no special tools, and can be bent up to 180 degrees. These connectors are also great if you need to replace a broken connector pipe on your existing heater.

Mechanical Monsters

Replacing V-Belts

SEVERAL APPLIANCES and numerous other mechanical monsters use belts to drive some or all of the moving parts. When you go through the frustration of having a belt break and then having to change it, you may wonder why they even use a belt for this purpose. However, using a belt drive results in a simpler system, thus reducing the cost in manufacturing. The simpler system actually means less possibility of a breakdown later on. The belt has give, and thus takes the stress off of less flexible and more expensive parts. The following service tips should help if you encounter a problem.

1. To get at the belt, you may have to remove a back panel, front panel, or top.
2. To work on a belt, you may have to turn the appliance over. Always disconnect the power to the unit.
3. A loose belt is probably one that is just stretched. Depending upon the appliance, tightening is done by loosening and moving another part in order to take up the slack. The part to be moved may be a pulley, a wheel, a tension spring, or even the motor. If you cannot figure out what to do, consult the owner's manual.

Here Is What You Will Need

Materials
- Belt dressing
- Replacement belt

Tools
- Steel tape measure
- Level

4. A belt that occasionally slips and squeals can be corrected by applying belt dressing. This gives the belt extra gripping power, and also prevents the belt from cracking.

Replacing a broken or worn belt starts with getting the right size. If you have the owner's manual, it will give you the size and number of the belt needed. If not, the width is determined by measuring across the outside surface of the belt. That is the easy part, and most people do that right. The length, however, is measured around the outside edge of the pulleys—not down in the groove. Use a steel tape rule, if possible, and follow the path of the belt from end to end.

For the actual replacement, refer to the owner's manual if it is available. If not, look for movable parts as discussed above on belt tightening. You may have to remove parts in order to get at the pulleys.

After it is properly in place and tensioned correctly, apply a belt dressing. When the appliance is ready to go, check to be sure it is level again.

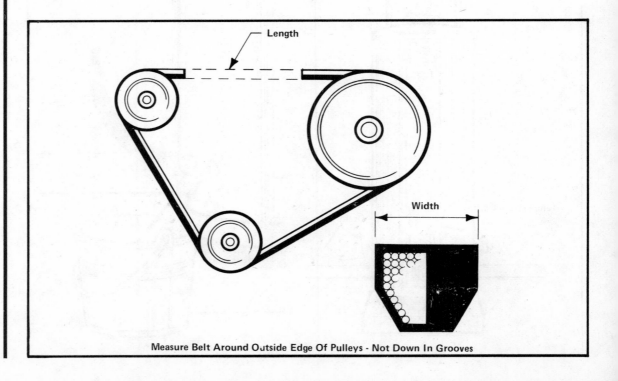

Measure Belt Around Outside Edge Of Pulleys - Not Down In Grooves

Sewing Machines

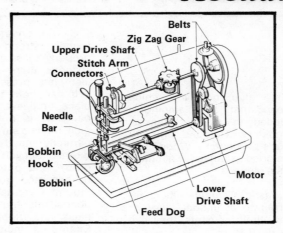

IT IS ALWAYS amazing that a woman who shys away from the simplest fix-it task will know exactly what to do when her sewing machine goes on the fritz. If you are not among that number, examine the troubleshooter's guide the next time there is a problem, and you will probably find out what to do.

Since it is electric, many things have to be right for the current to reach the machine: the outlet has to be live, the cord and plug have to be functioning, and the switch has to be working. Also, most machines need to be oiled about every three sewing hours. Your owner's manual is your best guide to be sure you have not missed any of the oiling points. Take care not to over oil, and use a good machine oil. Belts can become loose or break and may need replacing. An incorrect needle can cause the machine to malfunction as can a needle that is loose or one that is bent.

For a long, trouble-free life, give your machine periodic cleaning at regular intervals. Also, do not ask your machine to do more than it is capable of. Some machines are built to sew through canvas tents, but many are not. The extra strain can be injurious.

Sewing Machine Troubleshooting Chart

PROBLEMS	CAUSES	REPAIRS
Machine will not run	1. No power.	1. Check cord, plug, outlet and fuses or circuit breaker. Then check on-off switch.
Motor runs but machine will not	1. Needs oil.	1. Lube (This should not happen all of a sudden. You should first notice the machine getting noisy).
	2. Controls set wrong.	2. Check setting.
	3. Belt slips or is broken.	3. Examine belt and also make sure set screws on pulleys are not loose.
	4. Thread jamming bobbin.	4. Remove excess thread.
Will not stitch	1. Needle bent, loose, or in wrong.	1. Check and correct.
	2. Wrong needle.	2. Replace.
	3. Threaded wrong.	3. Rethread.
	4. Bobbin empty.	4. Rewind.
	5. Bobbin in wrong.	5. Remove and reinstall.
	6. Thread too heavy for needle.	6. Use heavier needle or lighter thread.
Needle breaks	1. Wrong needle or bent needle.	1. Replace.
	2. Needle in wrong.	2. Reinstall.
	3. Needle plate loose or foot loose.	3. Tighten.
	4. Wrong needle plate or wrong foot for stitch.	4. Change to proper plate or foot.
	5. Bobbin in wrong.	5. Remove and reinstall.
Machine is noisy	1. Dirty or needs oil.	1. Clean and oil.
Labors slowly	1. Dirty or needs oil.	1. Clean and oil.
	2. Controls set wrong.	2. Check to see if bobbin winder is engaged.
Thread breaks-Needle	1. Threaded wrong.	1. Rethread.
	2. Tension too great.	2. Reset.
	3. Wrong, bent or damaged needle.	3. Replace.
	4. Needle in wrong.	4. Reinstall.
	5. Faulty thread.	5. Use better quality thread.
Thread breaks-Bobbin	1. Damaged bobbin or case.	1. Replace.
	2. Bobbin wound too tight.	2. Rewind.
	3. Knots or snarls in thread.	3. Rewind.
	4. Case in wrong.	4. Reinstall.
	5. Faulty thread.	5. Use better quality thread.

This Household Oil Is A Household Word

Probably the best-known name in machine oil is 3-In-1. Used wherever there is a call for lightweight lubricating oil, 3-In-1 is generally found in close proximity to the home sewing machine. It is a product of Boyle-Midway, Inc.

Teflon Moves Into The Sewing Room

Pentapco, Inc., has introduced sewing machine needles that are Teflon-F coated. Teflon-F coated needles reduce friction because they enter the material more easily, and this reduced friction means less wear and tear on the machine. The needles themselves stay sharper longer, and, of course, they never rust.

Tiny Tool Tip

If your sewing machine did not come with an accessory tool kit, you'll probably need to go out and buy a very small screwdriver. If your hardware store doesn't carry ones that are small enough, your local optical merchant probably does. Many opticians sell tiny screwdrivers for tightening screws on eyeglasses, but you will find one handy for a host of delicate jobs, including sewing machine repairs.

A Sophisticated Machine Makes Sewing Simple

Singer's Athena 2000 exemplifies how solid-state electronics can simplify a complicated product. The most advanced machine in the world, it represents the biggest technical change in sewing since Singer electrified machines in 1884. With the touch of a button, it can deliver 24 different stitches without cam changing or dialing.

Adhesives

IF YOU FAIL to use the right adhesive in the proper manner, you'll end up with a poor joining job every time. The key to finding the right glue for the materials to be joined lies in reading the label on the adhesive. Generally speaking, the manufacturer will tell you what materials the glue is formulated to hold. If the label doesn't mention your particular material, look further and you'll probably find exactly what you need. There is an adhesive for almost every combination of materials you might consider joining. Large hardware and paint stores stock a wide variety of adhesives, but sometimes you must go to a specialty supplier to find adhesives for unusual plastics or for specialized marine adhesives.

Here's some information on the adhesives which do-it-yourselfers use most frequently.

White Glue (PVA-Polyvinyl Acetate). A ready-to-use glue that is among the most popular types sold, PVA glue is water soluble, so it must be used only for interior applications. Excellent for general wood gluing, it dries clear. The best-known brand is Elmer's Glue-All, but there are plenty of other good ones available, including USG's Durabond, Weldwood's Home Safe White Glue, and Franklin Glue Company's Evertite. Most manufacturers package white glue in a squeeze bottle, making it as easy to use as any adhesive could be.

Aliphatic Resin Glues. Ready-to-use and possessing many of the same qualities as white glue, aliphatic resin glue is beige in color, but dries clear. Though considered more moisture resistant than white glue, it is not waterproof. It is stronger and tackier than

white glue, however, which means that less clamping is needed in many instances. Franklin's Titebond and Elmer's Carpenter's Wood Glue are good examples of aliphatic resin glues.

Plastic Cement. Often referred to as model glues or household cements, they can be used to glue glass, wood, and plastic. Duro Cement, Elmer's Clear Household Cement, and Scotch Super-Strength are among the more popular plastic cements. Many have now been rendered "non-sniffable," and if you have children, you'd do well to stick with those. Follow directions for curing time, temperature and clamping.

Rubber-Based Adhesive. Rubber-based adhesives are waterproof and are capable of gluing practically anything — metal to metal, glass to metal, cloth to cloth, wood to concrete, etc. Such brands as Black Magic, Gripit, and ScotchGrip are well-known rubber-based adhesives.

Latex-Based Adhesive. Often used in carpet applications, latex-based adhesives form a tough but flexible bond that can withstand washing. These quick-drying adhesives include the various indoor/outdoor carpet cements, Sears Stitchless Mender, and many others.

Mastic Adhesive. Usually available in cartridges for use with a caulking gun, the mastic adhesives are formulated for holding ceiling tiles, wall paneling, and floor tiling.

Silicone Sealant. Silicone sealants are particularly useful in filling gaps around tubs and sinks. GE and Dow both market popular silicone sealants.

Cyanoacrylate Glue. Extremely strong when used properly, these glues set up in seconds; there is no need for clamping pressure because you can hold the pieces in place until set. Since cyanoacrylate is not a gap-filler glue, the two surfaces must be perfectly mated. All manufacturers direct you to use "just a drop," and poor results can be expected from using too much. Cyanoacrylate glue bonds metal to metal, glass to glass, and rubber to rubber. Examples include Eastman 910, Super Glue-3, and Crazy Glue.

Resorcinol Glue. A two-part wood glue—the components being a powder and a liquid—resorcinol glue is great for outdoor use as it is completely waterproof and very strong. Elmer's Waterproof and any number of other glues that have "Resorcinol" in their name are included in this category.

Contact Cements. These cements are used for bonding plastic laminates to counter tops, as well as several other materials to wood. Once the two surfaces touch, that's it. The bond is instantaneous, and there can be no adjusting to make things fit. You get no second chance. By slipping sheets of wax paper or wrapping paper between the two surfaces, though, you can align the materials before contact is made. You will see a few trade names like Pliobond, but most of the major glue makers simply label their products "Contact Cement."

Epoxy Glue. Another two-part adhesive, consisting of a resin and a hardener which you generally mix in equal amounts, epoxies can be used for almost every glue job, but they are still too expensive for use on large jobs where less-expensive adhesives will do. Completely waterproof, epoxy glues come either clear or opaque. Formulas vary widely and, therefore following the specific instructions for the brand you purchase is a must. Most epoxies require long curing periods, some up to 48 hours, but there are quick-setting types like Duro E-Pox-E 5 that sets in only five minutes. There are many brands, but almost all include the word "Epoxy" in the name.

Once you find the right adhesive, the next thing to do is read the directions. The manufacturer has spent time and money to describe how to use the product best. If the direc-

tions say to leave the pieces clamped together for 24 hours, don't think you can cheat just because the joint is dry to the touch. If the temperature tolerances specify use between 65 and 80 degrees, don't try to glue materials in your garage on a cold day.

The next key to good gluing rests in proper clamping pressure. Clamping, in most cases, must be uniform across the entire joint and done so that enough pressure is exerted to squeeze out excess glue but not so great as to force it all out. There are many different types of clamps, sometimes you have to improvise your own pressure-exerting devices. A good example would be where you are gluing a wide flat piece in place, and all you need is extra weight to push downward. Here you might employ books, bricks, or a container of water. Another example would be where there is a long glue line involved. You will find that nailing blocks can take the place of a multitude of clamps. After you wait the proper set-up time, you merely pry the blocks out.

BONDS IN 4 TO 6 MINUTES

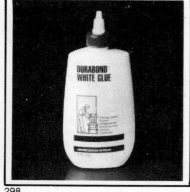

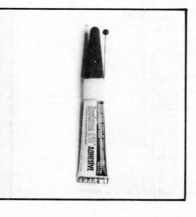

Abrasive Chart

CHOOSING THE proper abrasive for a particular job usually means the difference between mediocre results and a truly professional appearance. Most home handymen still refer to various grades of "sandpaper," but the proper term for these sanding sheets is "coated abrasives." There are four primary factors to be considered when selecting any coated abrasive: (1) the abrasive mineral, the type of rough material; (2) the grade, the coarseness or fineness of the mineral; (3) the backing, paper or cloth; and (4) the coating, the nature and extent of the mineral on the surface.

Paper backing for coated abrasives comes in four weights: "A," "C," "D," and "E." "A" (also referred to as "Finishing") is the lightest weight for the lightest sanding work. "C" and "D" (also called "Cabinet") are for heavier work, while "E" is for the toughest jobs.

The coating can either be "Open-Coated" or "Closed-Coated." "Open-Coated" means that the grains are spaced so as only to cover a portion of the surface; an open-coated abrasive is best used on gummy or soft woods, soft metals, or on painted surfaces. "Closed-Coated" means that the abrasive covers the entire area. Naturally, closed-coated abrasives provide maximum cutting, but they also clog faster; a closed-coated abrasive is best used on hard woods and on hard metals.

There are three popular ways to grade coated abrasives. The "Simplified Markings" (fine, very fine, etc.) provide a general description of the grade. "Grit" actually refers to the number of mineral grains which, when set end to end, equal one inch. The commonly used "O" symbols are more or less arbitrary. The coarsest grading under this system is 4½, and the finest is 10/0 (or 0000000000).

Although the coated varieties definitely include the most popular forms of abrasives, there are other types of finishing abrasives that you should know about. The best known of these other types are pumice, rottenstone, rouge, and steel wool. Pumice is a volcanic abrasive powder used for fine finishing; it is generally lubricated with water or oil and runs from 0000 to 0 in coarseness. Rottenstone is a fine powder, finer even than pumice, that is used to render a high sheen. Rouge is an abrasive powder used primarily in the polishing of metal. Steel wool comes in a wide selection of coarsenesses, and you should be careful to apply the correct grade of steel wool to the work you have at hand.

Most Widely Used Coated Abrasives

Abrasive	Backing	Grades (readily available)	Broad Uses
Flint	Paper (A, C, & D weights)	Extra coarse through extra fine	Small hand sanding, wood-removing, paint. Clogs fast but very cheap. Great for gummy surfaces that would clog any paper used.
Garnet	Paper (A, C, & D weights)	Very coarse through very fine	Hand shaping and sanding of wood. Also for cork and composition board. Cuts better and lasts longer than flint.
Aluminum Oxide	Paper (A, C, & D weights)	Very coarse through very fine	Hand or power sanding or shaping of wood. Also for metals, paint smoothing, or end-grain sanding.
	Cloth	Very coarse through fine	Mostly used for belt sanders.
Silicon Carbide	Waterproof paper (A weight)	Very coarse through super fine	To smooth coats on wood, metal, etc. For sanding floors, glass, or plastics. Used wet with water or oil.
Emery	Cloth	Very coarse through fine	General light metal polishing. Removing rust and corrosion from metal. Can be used wet or dry.
Crocus	Cloth	Very fine only	Super high-gloss finishing for metals.

Comparative Grades And Uses

Grit	"O" Symbols	Simplified Markings	Uses
600 500	None None	Super fine	High satinized finishes— wet sanding.
400 360 320	10/0 None 9/0	Extra fine	High finish on lacquer, varnish or shellac top-coats—wet sanding.
280 240 220	8/0 7/0 6/0	Very fine	Finishing undercoats or top paint coats—leaves no sanding marks—dry sanding.
180 150	00000 0000	Fine	Final sanding of bare wood—smoothing a previously painted surface.
120 100 80	000 00 0	Medium	General wood sanding— plaster smoothing— preliminary smoothing of previously painted surface.
60 50 40	½ 1 1½	Coarse	Rough sanding of wood— paint removal.
36 30	2 2½	Very coarse	Rust removal on rough finished metal.

Steel Wool Grades And Uses

Grade	Uses
0000— super fine	Primarily used by the home handyman in rubbing-down after the final lacquering, shellacking, or varnishing.
000— extra fine	Removes paint spots from woods— cleans polished metals such as stainless steel or chrome.
00— fine	When used with linseed oil will satinize or dull a high-luster finish on wood.
0— medium fine	OK for use in brass finishing— removes stains from kitchen and bathroom tiles and from better cookware.
1— medium	Removes rust from cast iron—cleans heavier cookware—cleans glazed tiles— removes shoe and furniture marks from wood floors.
2— medium coarse	Removes scratches from brass—removes paint from ceramic tiles—used to rub-down floors between coats of finish.
3— coarse	OK for use in removing paint spots on linoleum—removes paint from furniture before refinishing.

Plywood Grading

KNOWING EVERYTHING you can about plywood can save you money as well as mean the difference between a successful project and one that fails. For example, there's no reason for you to buy an expensive piece of plywood that's perfect on both sides if only one side will ever be seen. Similarly, there's no sense in paying for ⅝ of an inch thickness when ¼ inch plywood is really all you need. Plywood also comes with different glues, different veneers, and different degrees of finish. By knowing about all these characteristics you may be able to save quite a bit of money, and you certainly will improve your chances of getting the right material for the work you have in mind.

Plywood is, in several respects, better than lumber for particular projects. It's strong, lightweight, and rigid. Its high impact resistance means that plywood does not split, chip, crack all the way through, or crumble; the cross-laminated construction restricts expansion and contraction within the individual plies. Moreover, you never get "green" wood with plywood. Easy to work from cutting to fastening to finishing, plywood is available at many large home centers and hardware stores as well as at lumberyards.

When you buy a sheet of plywood, you know exactly what size you're getting. A 4x8-foot sheet of ¾-inch plywood measures exactly four feet by eight feet and is ¾ of an inch thick. This contrasts with the distinction between nominal and actual measurements that affects other types of lumber.

When you buy plywood, look for a back-stamp or edge-marking bearing the initials APA or DFPA. APA stands for American Plywood Association, while DFPA is the Douglas Fir Plywood Association. These two organizations represent most of the plywood manufacturers and they inspect and test to insure that plywood quality is high and that grading is accurate. Their stamp is your assurance that what you see is what you get.

Plywood is broadly categorized into two types: Exterior and Interior. Exterior plywood is made with nothing but waterproof glue, and you should always select Exterior for any exposed application. Interior, made with highly resistant glues, can actually withstand quite a bit of moisture. There is Interior plywood made with IMG (intermediate glue), which is resistant to bacteria, mold, and moisture, but no Interior plywood is made for use outside. The reason is that in most cases the inner plies of Interior plywood are made of lower grade woods.

The most critical plywood grading category for most home projects is the appearance grade of the panel faces. Check the chart "Plywood Grading For Panel Faces" before you buy any plywood.

Standard plywood can be made from more than 70 different woods, and the chart "Classification Of Species" organizes these woods into five groups on the basis of stiffness and strength. The lower the group number, the greater the stiffness and strength.

The "Plywood Grades" charts indicate the various uses for each grade. The first letter indicates the face grade, while the second indicates the back grade.

Now you know enough to buy the right plywood!

Plywood Grades For Interior Uses

Grade (Interior)	Face	Back	Inner Plies	Uses
A-A	A	A	D	Cabinet doors, built-ins, furniture where both sides show.
A-B	A	B	D	Alternate for A-A. Face is finish grade, back is solid and smooth.
A-D	A	D	D	Finish grade face for paneling, built-ins, backing.
B-D	B	D	D	Utility grade. One paintable side. For backing, cabinet sides, etc.
C-D	C	D	D	Sheathing and structural uses such as temporary enclosures, subfloor. Unsanded.
Under-layment	C-Plugged	D	C and D	For underlayment or combination sub-floor-underlayment under tile, carpeting.

Plywood Grades For Exterior Uses

Grade (Exterior)	Face	Back	Inner Plies	Uses
A-A	A	A	C	Outdoors, where appearance of both sides is important.
A-B	A	B	C	Alternate for A-A, where appearance of one side is less important. Face is finish grade.
A-C	A	C	C	Soffits, fences, base for coatings.
B-C	B	C	C	For utility uses such as farm buildings, some kinds of fences, base for coatings.
C-C (Plugged)	C-Plugged	C	C	Excellent base for tile and linoleum, backing for wall coverings, high-performance coatings.
C-C	C	C	C	Unsanded, for backing and rough construction exposed to weather.

Plywood Grading For Panel Faces

Symbol	Description
N	The best! "N" stands for "natural finish." No flaws or defects.
A	Often usable when "N" is not available. Smooth and paintable, "A" can be used for many furniture applications
B	Solid surface veneer in which tight knots and circular plugs may appear.
C	To be used only where it will not be seen. "C" grade plywood can have 1- to 1½-inch knotholes, providing the total knothole area falls within a certain limit. It also has limited splits.
C PLGD.	An improved "C," "C-Plugged" has smaller splits and its knotholes are limited to ¼x½ inches, but it is also to be used only where it will not be seen.
D	Strictly for out-of-sight purposes. "D" plywood has knots and knotholes up to 2½ inches and can even have larger ones within a specified ratio.

Classification Of Species

Group 1	Group 2		Group 3	Group 4	Group 5
Apitong, (a), (b)	Cedar, Port Orford	Maple, Black	Alder, Red	Aspen	Basswood
Beech,	Cypress	Mengkulang (a)	Birch, Paper	Bigtooth	Fir, Balsam
American	Douglas Fir 2 (c)	Meranti, Red (a), (b)	Cedar, Alaska	Quaking	Poplar, Balsam
Birch	Fir	Mersawa (a)	Fir, Subalpine	Cativo	
Sweet	California Red	Pine	Hemlock, Eastern	Cedar	
Yellow	Grand	Pond	Maple, Bigleaf	Incense	
Douglas Fir 1 (c)	Noble	Red	Pine	Western Red	
Kapur	Pacific Silver	Virginia	Jack	Cottonwood	
Keruing (a), (b)	White	Western White	Lodgepole	Eastern	
Larch, Western	Hemlock, Western	Spruce	Ponderosa	Black (Western	
Maple, Sugar	Lauan	Red	Spruce	Poplar)	
Pine	Almon	Sitka	Redwood	Pine	
Caribbean	Bagtikan	Sweetgum	Spruce	Eastern White	
Ocote	Mayapis	Tamarack	Black	Sugar	
Pine, Southern	Red Lauan	Yellow Poplar	Engelmann		
Loblolly	Tangile		White		
Longleaf	White Lauan				
Shortleaf					

(a) Each of these names represents a trade group of woods consisting of a number of closely related species.

(b) Species from the genus Dipterocarpus are marketed collectively, Apitong if originating in the Philippines; Keruing if originating in Malaysia or Indonesia.

(c) Douglas fir grown in the states of Washington, Oregon, California, Idaho, Montana, Wyoming, and the Canadian Provinces of Alberta and British Columbia shall be classed as Douglas fir No. 1. Douglas fir grown in the states of Nevada, Utah, Colorado, Arizona and New Mexico shall be classed as Douglas fir No. 2.

(d) Red Meranti shall be limited to species having a specific gravity of 0.41 or more based on green volume and oven dry weight.

Woods

SINCE WOOD IS such important material throughout the whole house, you should know all you can about it. If you want to get truly in-depth information about any particular specie, ask your lumber dealer for the address of the association of producers marketing that specie. For most do-it-yourselfers, though, a good grounding in the basics of wood and lumber should be sufficient.

Woods are separated into two classifications—hardwoods and softwoods. This distinction does not refer to the actual hardness or softness of the wood itself; some so-called softwoods, in fact, are harder than some hardwoods. The term is botanical. In simple terms, hardwoods come from deciduous or broad-leaf trees, while softwoods come from coniferous or needle-bearing trees. The "Wood Species Table" describes some of the more popular species and covers their most widely accepted uses.

One of the most confusing things about buying lumber concerns the way it is measured. You ask for a 2x4, but the lumber you get is neither two inches thick nor four inches wide. Actually, the wood once did measure two inches by four inches (the nominal size), but after it was processed and dried, the two inches shrunk to 1½ and the four inches came down to 3½.

"Board Feet" is how lumberyards determine the quantity of lumber for pricing. A board foot is a linear foot-long board that is an inch thick and a foot wide. Linear measurements, unlike the nominal figures, reflect the actual amount of lumber you get. If you order a board eight feet long, that's exactly what you receive and are billed for. The width and length are figured according to nominal size, however, which you don't get. Most home centers (and lumberyards catering to the do-it-yourself trade) price lumber by the linear foot, making it easier for most people to calculate what they need to buy. Molding, trim, dowels and poles are also sold by linear measure.

Lumber grading is confusing because there are differences between the grades of hardwood and softwood. The "Hardwood Grades" and "Softwood Grades" charts should give you a good idea of how the grading systems work. If you have any doubts about what you need or what you're getting, describe your project to the lumber dealer and ask for his advice.

Hardwood Grades

First Grade	91⅔ percent of the total surface (both sides) is clear of defects.
Second Grade	83⅓ percent of the total surface (both sides) is clear of defects.
F.A.S. (Firsts And Seconds)	The above two grades are usually sold in combination.
Select	One side must be at least second grade, and the other must be #1 Common.
#1 Common	66⅔ percent of the total surface is clear of defects.
#2 Common	50 percent of the total surface is clear of defects.

Softwood Grades

(The grades are the same, but standards vary with different species. The standards below are for white pine.)

B & Better Select (#1 and #2 clear) Supreme	Contains only minute blemishes.
C Select (Choice)	May have small sound knots or torn grain.
D Select (Quality)	Larger imperfections, but still sound.
#1 Common	Contains sound, tight knots and very few blemishes.
#2 Common	Flaws are more pronounced, but knots are still sound and tight.
#3 Common	Contains loose knots, as well as more pronounced flaws.
#4 Common	Bigger, looser knots, and even knotholes.
#5 Common	All that's required is that the board holds together.

Wood Species Table

Species	Uses	Freedom From Shrinkage & Swelling	Freedom From Warping	Hardness	Workability	Bending Strength	Filler Needed	Requires Stain
Ash	Tool handles, furniture, oars, baseball bats.	Medium	Medium	Medium to high	Hard	High	Heavy	Yes or no
Basswood	Furniture parts, woodenware. (Can be disguised as other woods.)	Low	Medium	Low	Easy	Low	None	Always
Beech	Furniture flooring, woodenware.	Low	Low	High	Hard	High	Thin	Yes or no
Birch	Furniture, cabinet work, millwork, dowels (Can be made to look like cherry.)	Low	Medium	High	Hard	High	Thin	Yes or no
Cherry	Furniture, caskets.	Medium	High	Medium to high	Hard	High	Thin	Never
Chestnut	Furniture, frames (often stained to look like walnut or oak).	Medium	High	Medium	Medium	Low	Heavy	Yes or no
Elm	Veneers, furniture.	Low	Medium to low	High	Hard	Medium	Heavy	Yes or no
Gumwood	Furniture (often stained to look like mahogany), veneers.	Low	Low	Medium	Medium	Medium	Thin	Always
Mahogany	Furniture, veneers.	High	High	High	Medium to easy	High	Medium	Never
Maple	Flooring, woodenware, furniture.	Low	Medium	High	Hard	Medium to high	Thin	Never
Oak	Furniture, floors, store fixtures.	Low	Medium	High	Hard	High	Heavy	Yes or no
Pine	Furniture (often unfinished).	Medium to high	High	Low	Easy	Low	None	Always
Poplar	Furniture (simulates other woods with staining).	Medium	Medium	Low	Easy	Medium	None	Always
Walnut	Gunstocks, paneling, fine furniture.	Medium to high	High	High	Medium	High	Medium	Never

Screw Chart

PROBABLY THE BEST all-round fastener for do-it-yourselfers is the screw. Nails go through wood easier, but screws have the ability to pull two pieces of wood together and create a tighter joint. Naturally, the threads of a screw hold tighter than the plain shank of a nail.

Wood screws are sized according to length and diameter. Lengths are expressed in inches and fractions of inches, while diameters are expressed in gauge numbers. The length is the amount of the screw that actually goes into the material; a round-head screw or any other kind in which the head sticks up above the surface is measured from where the bottom of the head touches the wood. A countersunk screw is measured from the top of its head since the entire screwhead included—penetrates the material. The gauge of a screw

is measured at the widest part of its body.

In choosing screws for a wood project, you should select ones that are long enough to bite firmly into the second piece of wood without coming all the way through it. The selection of the gauge depends on the strength needed in the joint. The bigger the gauge, the stronger the joint.

The two basic types of screws are the slotted (or regular) head and the Phillips head. The slotted-head screw has a single notch across the head, while the Phillips-head screw has a sort of cross. You must use only a slotted screwdriver for driving and removing slotted screws, and only a Phillips screwdriver on Phillips-head screws. The wrong tool can ruin the screw, making it impossible to remove.

When selecting the type of screwhead you want to use, you must take into consideration whether the screws will be seen or not. Some screwheads are much more decorative than others. Also consider whether the head will be exposed to moisture or not.

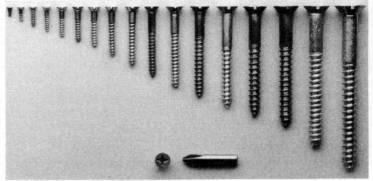

(Photo Courtesy: S.D. Warren Company)

Screws are made in several different metals and finishes, and each type is made for specific purposes.

Pilot holes are very important when you are driving screws. Not only does a pilot hole make insertion of the screw easier, but it also governs the screw's holding power. Basically, the pilot hole must be almost as deep as the length of the screw and slightly smaller than the screw's diameter. Often, you can just guess at these measurements and produce a good pilot hole, but there is a better way. Use the screw

chart below to determine what you need for the correct hole.

If the screw is not threaded all the way up, you must make a special hole for the unthreaded portion—called the shank—in addition to the pilot hole, which is for the threaded portion. Moreover, the type of drill bit you use makes a difference because bits carry different designations. On top of all this, the pilot hole for a screw going into a softwood is different than the one for a screw going into a hardwood. Therefore, study the chart carefully when you need to drill pilot holes.

Gauge Number	Decimal Diameter	Fractional Diameter	Shank Hole Twist Bit	Shank Hole Drill Gauge	PILOT HOLE HARDWOOD Twist Bit s	HARDWOOD Twist Bit p	HARDWOOD Drill Gauge s	HARDWOOD Drill Gauge p	SOFTWOOD Twist Bit s	SOFTWOOD Twist Bit p	SOFTWOOD Drill Gauge s	SOFTWOOD Drill Gauge p	Auger Bit Number	Threads Per Inch	Lengths Usually Available
0	.060	1/16-	1/16	52	1/32	—	70	—	1/64	—	75	—	—	32	1/4-inch
1	.073	5/64-	5/64	47	1/32	—	66	—	1/32	—	71	—	—	28	1/4-inch
2	.086	5/64+	3/32	42	3/64	1/32	56	70	1/32	1/64	65	75	3	26	1/4 to 1/2-inch
3	.099	3/32+	7/64	37	1/16	1/32	54	66	3/64	1/32	58	71	4	24	1/4 to 5/8-inch
4	.112	7/64+	7/64	32	1/16	3/64	52	56	3/64	1/32	55	65	4	22	3/8 to 3/4-inch
5	.125	1/8-	1/8	30	5/64	1/16	49	54	1/16	3/64	53	58	4	20	3/8 to 3/4-inch
6	.138	9/64-	9/64	27	5/64	1/16	47	52	1/16	3/64	52	55	5	18	3/8 to 1-1/2-inch
7	.151	5/32-	5/32	22	3/32	5/64	44	49	1/16	3/64	51	53	5	16	3/8 to 1-1/2-inch
8	.164	5/32+	11/64	18	3/32	5/64	40	47	5/64	1/16	48	52	6	15	1/2 to 2-inch
9	.177	11/64+	3/16	14	7/64	3/32	37	44	5/64	1/16	45	51	6	14	5/8 to 2-1/4-inch
10	.190	3/16+	3/16	10	7/64	3/32	33	40	3/32	5/64	43	48	6	13	5/8 to 2-1/4-inch
11	.203	13/64-	13/64	4	1/8	7/64	31	37	3/32	5/64	40	45	7	12	3/4 to 2-1/4-inch
12	.216	7/32-	7/32	2	1/8	7/64	30	33	7/64	3/32	38	43	7	11	7/8 to 2-1/2-inch
14	.242	15/64+	1/4	D	9/64	1/8	25	31	7/64	3/32	32	40	8	10	1 to 2-3/4-inch
16	.268	17/64+	17/64	I	5/32	1/8	18	30	9/64	7/64	29	38	9	9	1-1/4 to 3-inch
18	.294	19/64-	19/64	N	3/16	9/64	13	25	9/64	7/64	26	32	10	8	1-1/2 to 4-inch
20	.320	21/64-	21/64	P	13/64	5/32	4	18	11/64	9/64	19	29	11	8	1-3/4 to 4-inch
24	.372	3/8	3/8	V	7/32	3/16	1	13	3/16	9/64	15	26	12	7	3-1/2 to 4-inch

s = slotted head   **p = Phillips head**

Think Metric

THE METRIC SYSTEM will, without a doubt, become the standard system of measurement in the United States in the years to come. How long it will take before Americans use the metric system as easily as they use such designations as inches, feet, yards, ounces, pounds, quarts, gallons, and Fahrenheit temperature gradations no one can predict accurately. But no one can deny that within the relatively near future we will be hearing more and more about centimeters, meters, kilometers, grams, kilograms, milliliters, liters, and Celsius (centigrade) temperature gradations.

The meter is the basic unit for measuring length in the metric system. A little longer (39.37 inches) than a yard, the meter can be divided into 100 centimeters and 1000 millimeters. A kilometer measures 1000 meters long, which equals approximately one half mile.

The term "mass" is more commonly used in the metric system for what we normally call "weight," although for most purposes "weight" is an acceptable metric term. The kilogram is the basic unit for measuring mass in the metric system. The equivalent of slightly more than two pounds, the kilogram is just about what one liter of water weighs. One thousand kilograms equal a metric ton, while—in the opposite direction—1/1000 of a kilogram equals one gram.

In measuring volume via the metric system, the basic unit is the liter. A liter is slightly larger than one quart. Thus, there are slightly fewer than four liters in the gallon. The common division of the liter is into thousandths, called milliliters.

The degree, of course, is the standard unit of measurement in both the Fahrenheit and Celsius temperature scales. Gabriel Fahrenheit, a German physicist who developed the thermometer bearing his name in 1714, based his temperature measuring system on 180 equal units between the freezing and the boiling points of water. But since he used the coldest temperature to which he could reduce mercury as his zero point, there is a difference of 32 degrees between zero and the degree measurement at which water freezes according to the Fahrenheit thermometer.

A Swedish astronomer, Anders Celsius, developed a different temperature-measuring system in 1742. Setting the freezing point of water at zero degrees and the boiling point of water at 100 degrees, Celsius then was able to mark off degrees as 1/100 of the distance between water's freezing and boiling points. Thus, zero degrees Celsius (also called centigrade) equals 32 degrees Fahrenheit, and 100 degrees Celsius equals 212 degrees Fahrenheit. To convert from Fahrenheit measurements to Celsius measurements, you must first subtract 32 and then multiply the resulting Fahrenheit figure by 5/9. For example, if the outside temperature measures a pleasant 77 degrees Fahrenheit, the corresponding Celsius figure would be 25.

To Convert To Metric			To Convert From Metric		
To Convert From	To	Multiply By	To Convert From	To	Multiply By
Length			**Length**		
inches	centimeters	2.54	millimeters	inches	0.03937
inches	meters	0.0254	centimeters	inches	0.3937
feet	centimeters	30.48	meters	feet	3.2808
yards	meters	0.9144	meters	yards	1.094
miles	kilometers	1.609	kilometers	miles	0.62137
Area			**Area**		
square inches	square centimeters	6.452	square centimeters	square inches	0.155
square feet	square meters	0.0929	square meters	square feet	10.765
square yards	square meters	0.836	square meters	square yards	1.196
square miles	square kilometers	2.589998	square kilometers	square miles	0.3861
acres	hectares	0.40468	hectares	acres	2.471
Mass			**Mass**		
ounces	grams	28.34952	grams	ounces	0.03527
pounds	kilograms	0.453592	kilograms	pounds	2.20462
tons (short) (2000 lbs.)	metric ton (tonnes)	0.907185	metric tons (tonnes) (1000 kg.)	tons (short)	1.10231
Volume			**Volume**		
fluid ounces	milliliters	29.57353	milliliters	fluid ounces	0.0338
pints	liters	0.47318	liters	pints	2.11338
quarts	liters	0.946333	liters	quarts	1.05669
gallons	liters	3.7853	liters	gallons	0.2642
cubic feet	cubic meters	0.028317	cubic meters	cubic feet	35.3145
cubic yards	cubic meters	0.76456	cubic meters	cubic yards	1.30795
Additional approximate measures: a teaspoon is about 5 milliliters a tablespoon is about 15 milliliters a cup is about 0.24 liters					
Temperature			**Temperature**		
Fahrenheit	Celsius (centigrade)	5/9 after subtracting 32	Celsius (centigrade)	Fahrenheit	9/5 and then add 32

Our Catalog of Catalogs

Barap Woodworkers & Hobbyists Catalog. The Barap Catalog contains hundreds of hard-to-find supplies and tools for the home craftsman. Write to Barap Specialties, 835 Bellows, Frankfort, Michigan 49635. Nominal charge for catalog.

Brookstone Hard-To-Find Tools. Frustrated at not finding specialized tools at the hardware store? Send for the Brookstone Catalog. If somebody makes the tool you need, chances are that Brookstone stocks it. Everything in the Brookstone Catalog is quality merchandise, and all orders are filled and shipped as soon as they are received. Write to the Brookstone Company, Peterborough, New Hampshire 03458.

Burpee Seed Catalog. You can buy more than 1400 vegetables, flowers, shrubs, trees, and garden aids through the mail from this 100-year-old company. Write to W. Atlee Burpee Company in Warminster, Pennsylvania 18974 or Clinton, Iowa 52732 or Riverside, California 92502, depending upon which location is nearest your home.

Constantine Woodworkers Catalog. Constantine carries everything for the woodworker, from tools to veneers. All are quality products. Write to Constantine, 2059 Eastchester Road, Bronx, New York 10461. Nominal charge for catalog.

Craftsman Wood And Woodshop Supply Catalog. You can order fine domestic and imported hardwoods plus everything for your shop—hand and power tools and much more—from Craftsman Wood Service, 2729 South Mary Street, Chicago, Illinois 60608. Nominal charge for catalog.

Edmund Scientific Catalog. The Edmund Scientific Catalog consists of 172 pages filled with more than 4500 unusual items for hobbyists, schools,

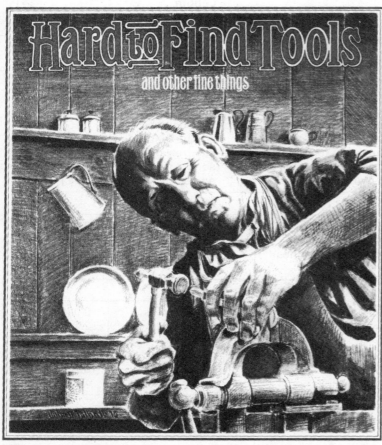

Brookstone Company
Peterborough, New Hampshire

Automotive Accessories, page 10 • Gourmet Kitchen, page 20 • Distinctive Necessities, page 22 • Garden Tools, page 58

and industry. Write to Edmund Scientific Company, 300 Edscorp Building, Barrington, New Jersey 08007.

Emperor Clock Catalog. Case kits, movements, dials, and finished clocks are all available through the mail from the Emperor Clock Company, Fairhope, Alabama 36532.

Harris Seed Catalog. Not only does the Harris Catalog present just about every seed variety for the home gardener, but it also supplies valuable instructional material. Write to the Joseph Harris Company, Inc., 48 Moreton Farm, Rochester, New York 14624.

Heathkit Electronic Kit Catalog. Heath manufactures do-it-yourself kits for everything from door chimes to color TV. The kits are complete, and the instructions are easy to follow. You'll be amazed at what you can do. Write to the Heath Company, Benton Harbor, Michigan 49022.

Jensen Catalog. Each issue of the Jensen Catalog contains tool tips, technical data, and other useful information as well as more than 2800 top-quality, hard-to-find tools for electronic assembly and precision mechanics. Write to

Jensen Tools and Alloys, 4117 North 44th Street, Phoenix, Arizona 85018.

Lamb Nursery Catalog. You can order hardy plants—including perennials, rock plants, flowering shrubs, and many others—through the mail from Lamb Nurseries. The Lamb Catalog not only tells you what is available, but even teaches you how to pronounce all the names. Write to Lamb Nurseries, 101 E. Sharp, Spokane, Washington, 99202.

Maximum Security Catalog. You'll find a host of alarms, locks, safes, and other security items in the Maximum Security Catalog. Write to Maximum Security Center, Inc., 241 South Elmwood Avenue, Buffalo, New York 14201. Nominal charge for catalog.

Minnesota Woodworkers Supply Company Catalog. Everything for the woodworker from veneers and moldings to sophisticated tools, can be found in the Minnesota Woodworkers Supply Company Catalog. All products are of good quality, and order fulfillment is prompt. Write to Minnesota Woodworkers Supply Company, Industrial Boulevard, Rogers, Minnesota 55374.

Whole House Knowledge Miscellany

mountain west
alarm supply co.

Morgan Veneer Catalog. Choose from 90 varieties of veneers and inlays at reasonable prices. The Morgan Veneer Catalog also offers some valuable instructional material. Write to Morgan Veneers, 915 E. Kentucky Street, Louisville, Kentucky 40204.

Mountain West Alarm Catalog. Mountain West handles everything for home, business, and personal security—including many items which you probably cannot find locally. Write to the Mountain West Alarm Supply Company, 4215 N. 16th Street, Phoenix, Arizona 85016.

The NC Flasher. Although it is the catalog of National Camera, NC Flasher covers much more than photographic gear. In addition to all sorts of electronic gadgets, the catalog contains tools for specialized hobbies and crafts as well as for the home. Write to National Camera, 2000 West Union Avenue, Englewood, Colorado 80110.

Rain by Mail. You can order lawn sprinkler and drip systems by mail via a catalog that lists all the components, plus design guides and instructions. Write to Rain by Mail, 1781 Andrews Street, Tustin, California 92680. Nominal charge for catalog.

Silvo Tool Catalog. In its 168 pages, the Silvo Tool Company presents thousands of brand-name tools. For a copy of the catalog, write to the Silvo Hardware Company, 107 Walnut Street, Philadelphia, Pennsylvania 19106. Nominal charge for catalog.

Stark Brothers Nursery Catalog. Choose from more than 350 varieties of plants, ranging from trees to vegetables. The map in the catalog helps you make sure that what you order will grow well in your area. Write to Stark Brothers Nurseries and Orchards Company, Box A 16976, Louisiana, Missouri 63353.

U.S. General Tool And Hardware Catalog. Want to buy nationally known brands of tools and shop materials at bargain prices? U.S. General is the outfit to contact. Write to the U.S. General Supply Corporation, 100 General Place, Jericho, New York 11753. The nominal charge for the catalog can be credited to your first order.

Weekender Products Catalog. This is a delightful catalog that's fun to read. The variety of quality tools and products is enormous, and you'll find some handy hints along the way. Write to Weekender Products, P.O. Box 2301, Kansas City, Kansas 66110.

Whittemore Stained Glass Catalog. Kits, tools, books, supplies, and ideas for the stained glass hobbyist can be found in abundance in the Whittemore Stained Glass Catalog. Write to Whittemore, Box A 2065, Hanover, Massachusetts 02339. Nominal charge for catalog.

Woodcraft Tool Catalog. You can find more than 1000 hard-to-find woodworker tools in the Woodcraft Tool Catalog. Write to Woodcraft, 313 Montvale Avenue, Woburn, Massachusetts 01801. Nominal charge for catalog.

The Yankee Wood Craftsman Catalog. The quality-conscious woodworker will find that The Yankee Wood Craftsman Catalog is a dream come true. It is filled with all the tools and supplies a person needs to create beautiful things from wood. All products are carefully selected, for there is nothing on these pages that is not of exceptional quality. Write to the Garrett Wade Company Inc., 302 Fifth Avenue, New York, New York 10001.

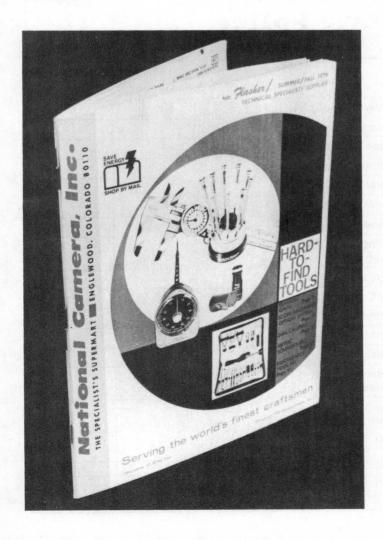

The Yankee Wood Craftsman
Garrett Wade
Company Inc.

Whole House Phone Directory

Jot down phone numbers for people you may need to contact in the course of running your home.

Emergency:

Police Dept. _____ Fire Dept. _____

Doctors' Offices Ambulance _____

Dr. _____ Hospital _____

Dr. _____ Sheriff's Dept. _____

Dr. _____ State Police _____

Others:

	Name Of Firm	Number	Ask For
Air Conditioning Repair			
Appliance Repair			
Attorney			
Better Business Bureau			
Builder			
Building Supply			
Burglar Alarm Service			
Cabinet Maker			
Carpenter			
Carpet Cleaner			
Electrical Supplies			
Electrician			
Floor Repair			
Foundation Work			
Furniture Repair			
Garden Shop			
Glazer			

	Name Of Firm	Number	Ask For
Hardware Store			
Home Center			
House Leveling			
Insurance Agent			
Iron Work			
Lending Agency			
Lumberyard			
Moving And Storage			
Patrol Service			
Pest Control			
Plumber			
Plumbing Supplies			
Roofer			
Swimming Pool Service			
Television Repairs			
Utility Companies Electric			
Gas			
Telephone			
Water			

Directory of Manufacturers

AAA Products Corp.
1122 W. Northbranch Dr.
Oak Creek, WI 53154

A B Chance Co.
210 N. Allen St.
Centralia, MO 65240

Abitibi Corp.
Building Products Div.
3250 W. Big Beaver Rd.
Troy, MI 48084

AC Horn Div.
Dewey & Almy Chemical Co.
62 Whittemore Ave.
Cambridge, MA 02134

Acme Mfg. Co.
7500 State
Philadelphia, PA 19136

Acorn Mfg. Co.
Box 31, School St.
Mansfield, MA 02048

Adams Products Co. Inc.
PO Box 986
Oxford, NC 27565

Adjustable Clamp Co.
433 N. Ashland Ave.
Chicago, IL 60622

Adjusta-Post Mfg. Co.
PO Box 71
Norton, OH 44203

Advanced Drainage Systems Inc.
3300 Riverside Dr.
Columbus, OH 43221

AG-Drip Sales, Inc.
3156 E. LaPalma Ave. Ste. J
Anaheim, CA 92806

Air Conditioning Training
Rt. 13 Box 247
Ft. Worth, TX 76119

Ajax Home & Van Equipment Co. Inc.
3325 Ferguson Rd.
Fort Wayne, IN 46809

Akro-Mils
1293 S. Main
Akron, OH 44309

Albion Engineering Co.
1572 Adams Ave.
Philadelphia, PA 19124

Allastics
Div. of Kusan Inc.
3206 Belmont Blvd.
Nashville, TN 37212

Allied Plastics Inc.
1663 Hargrove Ave.
Gastania, NC 28052

Allway Tools Inc.
1513 Olmstead Ave.
Bronx, NY 10462

Almatex International
3569 B Bristol Pike
Cornwell Heights, PA 19020

T. A. Altender & Sons
1217 Spring Garden
Philadelphia, PA 19123

American Air Filter Co. Inc.
Box 21127, Standiford Station
Louisville, KY 40221

American Art Clay Co. Inc.
4717 W. 16 St.
Indianapolis, IN 46222

American Fluorescent Corp.
238 N. Oakley Blvd.
Chicago, IL 60612

American Grease Stick Co.
PO Box 729
Muskegon, MI 49443

American Machine & Tool Co. Inc.
4th & Spring Sts.
Royersford, PA 19468

American Olean Tile
Div. National Gypsum Co.
1000 Cannon Ave.
Lansdale, PA 19446

American Optical Corp.
A O Safety Products
14 Mechanic
Southbridge, MA 01550

American Safety Razor Co.
Industrial Products Div.
100 Park Ave.
New York, NY 10017

American Standard Inc.
40 W. 40th St.
New York, NY 10018

American Steel Wool Mfg. Co. Inc.
42-24 Orchard
Long Island City, NY 11101

Amerock Corp.
4000 Auburn
Rockford, IL 61101

Amprobe Instrument
630 Merrick Rd.
Lynbrook, NY 11563

Anchor Continental Inc.
PO Box 5867
2000 S. Beltline Blvd.
Columbia, SC 29205

Anglo-American Distribution Ltd.
401 Kennedy Blvd.
Somerdale, NJ 08083

Arco Products Corp.
110 W. Sheffield Ave.
Englewood, NJ 07631

Ardmore Mfg. Co. Inc.
3945 N. Western Ave.
Chicago, IL 60618

Aristo-Mat Inc.
1718 E. 75th
Chicago, IL 60649

Arkansas Abrasives Inc.
PO Box 1298
Hot Springs, AR 71901

Arlyn Industries Ltd.
White Rock
British Columbia, Canada

Armco Steel Corp.
703 Curtis
Middletown, OH 45042

Armstrong Cork Co.
Liberty St.
Lancaster, PA 17604

Armstrong Paint Co.
1330 S. Kilbourn Ave.
Chicago, IL 60623

Arno Adhesive Tapes Inc.
Sub. Scholl Mfg. Co.
PO Box 301
Michigan City, IN 46360

Arnold Industries Inc.
PO Box 2790
3011 Council St.
Toledo, OH 43606

Arrow Fastener Co. Inc.
271 Mayhill
Saddle Brook, NJ 07662

Artcraft Industries
Div. Enamel Products &
Plating Co.
3500 Walnut St.
McKeesport, PA 15132

Arvey Corp.
3500 N. Kimball Ave.
Chicago, IL 60618

Auth Electronic Co.
Div. Sta-Rite Industries Inc.
505 Acorn
Deer Park, NY 11729

Aven
Div. of Firth Brown Tools Ltd.
Sheffield, England

Azrock Floor Products
PO Box 531
San Antonio, TX 78292

Barclay Industries Inc.
65 Industrial Rd.
Lodi, NJ 07644

Bauer Corp.
1505 E. Bowman
Wooster, OH 44691

H. Behlen & Brothers Inc.
PO Box 698
Amsterdam, NY 12010

Behr Process Corp.
1603 W. Alton St.
Santa Ana, CA 92702

Belden Corp.
2000 S. Batavia Ave.
Geneva, IL 60134

Belwith International Ltd.
PO Box 1057
7600 Industry Ave.
Pico Rivera, CA 90660

Bendix Mouldings Inc.
Sub. Lightron Corp.
235 Pegasus Ave.
Northvale, NJ 07647

BernzOmatic Corp.
740 Driving Park
Rochester, NY 14613

Bestop Mfg. Co.
PO Box 318
Boulder, CO 80302

Bethlehem Steel Corp.
Bethlehem, PA 18016

Bissell Inc.
2345 Walker Rd. NW
Grand Rapids, MI 49504

Black & Decker Mfg. Co.
E. Joppa Rd.
Towson, MD 21204

Boltmaster Corp.
119 Bond
Elk Grove Village, IL 60007

Bon Ami Co.
Faultless Starch
1025 W. 8th St.
Kansas City, MO 64101

Bond Chemical Products Co.
2103 W. Fulton
Chicago, IL 60612

Bondex International Inc.
Box 88
Brunswick, OH 44212

W.R. Bonsal Co.
PO Box 38
Lilesville, NC 28091

Borden Chemical
Div. Borden Inc.
1500 Touhy Ave.
Elk Grove Village, IL 60007

Boss Mfg Co.
221 W. First St.
Kewanee, IL 61443

Bostitch
Div. Textron Inc.
Briggs Dr.
East Greenwich, RI 02818

Bowers Mfg. Co. Inc.
PO Box 638
Chester, PA 19016

Bowmar Instrument Corp.
8000 Bluffton Rd.
Ft. Wayne, IN 46809

Boyle-Midway
685 Third Ave.
New York, NY 10017

Bradley Corp.
PO Box 348
Menomonee Falls, WI 53051

Brainerd Mfg. Co.
115 N. Washington St.
East Rochester, NY 14445

Braun Mfg. Co. Inc.
1657 N. Kostner Ave.
Chicago, IL 60639

Bric-Mold Corp.
70 Jerusalem Ave.
Hicksville, NY 11801

Brink & Cotton Mfg. Co.
67 Poland St.
Bridgeport, CT 06605

Brock Co.
1042 Olive Hill Ln.
Napa, CA 94558

Brookstone Co.
123 Vose Farm Rd.
Peterborough, NH 03458

Buck Knives Inc.
PO Box 1267
1717 N. Magnolia
El Cajon, CA 92022

Buckner Industries Inc.
PO Box 2322
Fresno, CA 93708

Burgess Vibrocrafters Inc.
Grayslake, IL 60030

Bussman Mfg.
University at Jefferson
St. Louis, MO 63107

Samuel Cabot Inc.
1 Union
Boston, MA 02108

Caldwell Mfg. Co.
Box 444
Rochester, NY 14602

Cal-Tuf Glass Corp.
1100 S. Meridian Ave.
Alhambra, CA 91803

Campbell Chain
3990 E. Market St.
York, PA 17402

HD Campbell Co.
Campbell Bldg.
Rochelle, IL 61068

Cane & Basket Supply Co.
1283 Cochran Ave.
Los Angeles, CA 90019

H O Canfield Co. of Virginia Inc.
Sub. The Pantasote Co.
Park II, PO Box 1800
Greenwich, CT 06830

Carborundum Co.
PO Box 337
Niagara Falls, NY 14302

Carpet Products Co.
River Rd.
Central Square, NY 13036

Casaplanta
16129 Cohasset St.
Van Nuys, CA 91406

Celotex Corp.
PO Box 22602
Tampa, FL 33622

Century Drill & Tool Co.
322 S. Green St.
Chicago, IL 60607

Cerro Corp.
39 S. LaSalle St.
Chicago, IL 60606

Certain-teed Products Corp.
750 E. Swedesford Rd.
Valley Forge, PA 19482

Chair-Loc Co.
PO Box 45
Lakehurst, NJ 08733

Channellock Inc.
1306 S. Main
Meadville, PA 16335

Charles Paint Research Inc.
2401 E. 85th St.
Kansas City, MO 64132

Chason Industries
Div. Waxman Industries
24455 Aurora Rd.
Bedford Heights, OH 44146

Chatham Brass Co. Inc.
1500 W. Blancke St.
Linden, NJ 07036

Chemik Labs, Inc.
PO Box 24884
Dallas, TX 75224

Chempar Chemical Co. Inc.
260 Madison Ave.
New York, NY 10016

Chempro Corp.
5400 Memorial Dr., Ste. 414
Houston, TX 77007

Chicago Specialty Mfg. Co.
7500 Linder Ave.
Skokie, IL 60076

Chronomite Laboratories
21011 S. Figueroa
St. Carson, CA 90745

Chrysler Airtemp
1600 Webster
Dayton, OH 45404

Church & Dwight Co. Inc.
2 Pennsylvania Plaza
New York, NY 10001

Ciba-Geigy Chemical Corp.
Agricultural Div.
PO Box 11422
Greensboro, NC 27409

Clauss Cutlery Co.
223 N. Prospect
Fremont, OH 43420

Cling-Surface Co.
1048 Niagara
Buffalo, NY 14213

Clopay (Overhead Door Div.)
Clopay Square
Cincinnati, OH 45214

Clorox Co.
7901 Oakport
Oakland, CA 94621

Closet Maid Corp.
PO Box 304
720 SW 17th St.
Ocala, FL 32670

Cluster Shed Inc.
Hartland, VT 05048

Coastal Chemical
190 Jony Drive
Carlstadt, NJ 07072

Colorite Plastics Co.
101 Railroad Ave.
Ridgefield, NJ 07657

Commodore Vanity Co.
7735 Kester Ave.
Van Nuys, CA 91405

Congoleum Industries Inc.
195 Belgrove Dr.
Kearny, NJ 07032

Conolite
Div. Woodall Industries Inc.
425 Maple Ave.
Carpentersville, IL 60110

Continental Marketing
11272 Kelly
Los Alamitos, CA 90720

Conwed Corp.
332 Minnesota St.
St. Paul, MN 55101

Cook Paint & Varnish Co.
PO Box 389
Kansas City, MO 64141

Cooper Group
PO Box 728
Apex, NC 27502

Cordage Group
Div. Columbian Rope Co.
309 Genesee St.
Auburn, NY 13021

Cordomatic
1724 W. Indiana Ave.
Philadelphia, PA 19132

Corning
Div. Corning Glass Works
Corning, NY 14830

Cosco Chemicals Inc.
25 Beachway Dr.
Indianapolis, IN 46224

Coughlan Products Inc.
29 Spring
West Orange, NJ 07052

Cox & Co.
215 Park Ave. S.
New York, NY 10003

CPM Corp.
Arlington, NJ 07032

Craftsman Wood Service Co.
2727 S. Mary St.
Chicago, IL 60608

Craftwood Corp.
PO Box 62
Oconomowoc, WI 53066

Creative Tools Inc.
309 County St.
Bennington, VT 05201

Cresline Plastic Pipe Co. Inc.
955 Diamond Ave.
Evansville, IN 47717

Crost Metal
3951 Thomas St.
McComb, MI 39648

Croton Craft
2 Memory Lane
Croton-On-Hudson, NY 10520

Crown Chemicals
4995 N. Main
Rockford, IL 61101

Cyclone Seeder Co. Inc.
PO Box 68
Urbana, IN 46990

Dacor Inc.
65 Armory
Worcester, MA 01601

Dalton Mfg. Co.
130 S. Bemiston
Clayton, MO 63105

Damascus Steel Products Corp.
2215 Kishwaukee St.
Rockford, IL 61101

DAP Inc.
PO Box 277
5300 Huberville Ave.
Dayton, OH 45401

Darworth Inc.
PO Box K
Avon, CT 06001

Daubert Chemical Co.
Consumer Products Div.
1200 Jorie Blvd.
Oakbrook, IL 60521

Dayton Electric Mfg. Co.
5959 W. Howard St.
Chicago, IL 60648

d-CON Co. Inc.
90 Park Ave.
New York, NY 10016

Decocraft Inc.
208 Russel Pl.
Hackensack, NJ 07601

Decro-Wall Corp.
375 Executive Blvd.
Elmsford, NY 10523

Deflect-O Corp.
PO Box 50057
7035 E. 86th St.
Indianapolis, IN 46250

Deft Inc.
17451 Von Karman Ave.
Irvine, CA 92714

Del Mar Woven Wood Co.
390 Central Ave.
Bohemia LI, NY 11716

deMert & Dougherty Inc.
333 Skokie Blvd. Ste. 101
Northbrook, IL 60062

Devoe Paint Div.
Celanese Coatings
1 Riverfront Plaza
Louisville, KY 40202

Disston, Inc.
601 Grant St.
Pittsburgh, PA 15219

Dog Dor Co.
Box 662
Reseda, CA 91335

Door Products
PO Box 584
Bensenville, IL 60106

Double J. Systems, Inc.
1305 S. Strong Ave.
Copiague, NY 11726

Douglas Div.
Scott & Fetzer Co.
141 Railroad St.
Bronson, MI 49028

Dow Chemical Co.
Midland, MI 48640

Dow Corning
Consumer Products Div.
Midland, MI 48640

Dowling Miner Magnetics Corp.
124 Paul Dr.
San Rafael, CA 94903

Drackett Co.
5020 Spring Grove Ave.
Cincinnati, OH 45232

Dremel Mfg.
Div. Emerson Electric Co.
PO Box 518
Racine, WI 53401

Dresser Industries
Tool Group Marketing Div.
3201 N. Wolf Rd.
Franklin Park, IL 60131

Drip-EZE
Controlled Water Emission
Systems
585 Vernon Way
El Cajon, CA 92020

Dry Mix Concrete Co.
Sakrete & Far-Go Products
10352 Franklin Ave.
Franklin Park, IL 60131

Duo-Fast Fastener Corp.
3702 River Rd.
Franklin Park, IL 60131

E. I. du Pont de Nemours & Co.
Consumer Products Div.
1007 Market St.
Wilmington, DE 19898

Donald Durham Co.
PO Box 804
78 Jefferson
Des Moines, IA 50304

Duro Art Supply Co.
1832 Juneway Ter.
Chicago, IL 60626

Eagle Mfg.
45 Court Square
Long Island City, NY 11101

Easco Tools Inc.
3 Turnpike Rd.
Windsor Locks, CT 06096

Eastman Kodak Co.
343 State
Rochester, NY 14650

Easy Heat/Wirekraft
Div. W. R. Grace
31977 U.S. 20 E.
New Carlisle, IN 46552

Elco Industries Inc.
1111 Samuelson Rd.
Rockford, IL 61101

Eller Mfg. Co. Inc.
733-735 Livonia Ave.
Brooklyn, NY 11207

Elmer
Borden Chemical
180 E. Broad St.
Columbus, OH 43215

Emco Specialties Inc.
PO Box 853
2121 E. Walnut
Des Moines, IA 50317

Emerson Electric Co.
8100 W. Florissant Ave.
St. Louis, MO 63136

Empire-Detroit Steel Div.
Cyclops Corp.
137 Iron Ave.
Dover, OH 44622

Enderes Tool Co. Inc.
PO Box 691
Albert Lea, MN 56007

ENM Co.
5350 Northwest Hwy.
Chicago, IL 60630

ESB Inc.
Atlas Minerals & Chemicals
Div.
Merztown, PA 19539

Esmay Products, Inc.
Box 547
Bristol, IN 46507

Estwing Mfg. Co. Inc.
2647 Eighth St.
Rockford, IL 61101

Evans-Aristocrat Industries
768 Frelinghuysen Ave.
Newark, NJ 07114

Evans Rule Co.
768 Frelinghuysen Ave.
Newark, NJ 07114

Evode Inc.
401 Kennedy Blvd.
Somerdale, NJ 08083

Exact Level & Tool Mfg. Co. Inc.
100 W. Main St.
High Bridge, NJ 08829

Excell Chemical Products Co.
Philadelphia, PA 19127

Exelon
1712 F Newport Circle
Santa Ana, CA 92705

E-Z Paintr Corp.
4051 S. Iowa Ave.
Milwaukee, WI 53207

E Z Plumb
Div. United States Brass Corp.
PO Box 37
Plano, TX 75074

Farberware
Div. LCA Corp.
1500 Bassett Ave.
Bronx, NY 10461

William Farwell
Rutland, VT 05701

Fedders Corp.
Edison, NJ 08817

Federal Housewares Co.
3600 W. Pratt
Chicago, IL 60645

Ferum Co. Inc.
815 E. 136th St.
Bronx, NY 10454

Fibre-Metal Products Co.
Box 248
Concordville, PA 19331

Flecto Co. Inc.
1000 45th
Oakland, CA 94607

Fletcher-Terry Co.
Spring Lane
Farmington, CT 06032

Flintkote Co.
Flooring Div.
480 Central Ave.
E. Rutherford, NJ 07073

Flood Co.
Hudson, OH 44236

Fluidmaster Inc.
1800 Via Burton
Anaheim, CA 92805

Focal Point, Inc.
3760 Lower Rosewell Rd.
Marietta, GA 30060

Formby Refinishing Products Inc.
PO Box 788
Olive Branch, MS 38654

Fort Steuben Metal Products Co.
PO Box 268
Weirton, WV 26062

Franklin Glue Co.
2020 Bruck St.
Columbus, OH 43207

Frantz Mfg. Co.
Sterling, IL 61081

Freedman Artcraft Engineering Corp.
PO Box 228
Charlevoix, MI 49720

Frigidaire
Div. General Motors Corp.
300 Taylor
Dayton, OH 45401

Fuel Sentry Corp.
79 Putnam St.
Mount Vernon, NY 10550

H. B. Fuller Co.
2400 Kasota Ave.
St. Paul, MN 55108

Fuller Tool Co. Inc.
152-35 10 Ave.
Whitestone, NY 11357

Fulton Corp.
PO Box 109
Fulton, IL 61252

GAF Corp.
Building Products Group
140 W. 51st St.
New York, NY 10020

Galaxy Chemical Co. Inc.
1620 S. Canal St.
Chicago, IL 60616

Garco Mfg. Co.
2219 W. Grand Ave.
Chicago, IL 60612

Garelick Mfg. Co.
644 2nd St.
St. Paul Park, MN 55071

Garrett Wade Co. Inc.
302 Fifth Ave.
New York, NY 10001

Gates Rubber Co.
999 S. Broadway
Denver, CO 80222

Georgia-Pacific Corp.
900 SW Fifth Ave.
Portland, OR 97204

General Bathroom Products Corp.
2201 Touhy Ave.
Elk Grove Village, IL 60007

General Electric Co.
1285 Boston Ave.
Bridgeport, CT 06602

General Finishes
1580 S. 81st St.
Milwaukee, WI 53214

General Hardware Mfg. Co. Inc.
80 White St.
New York, NY 10013

General Products Corp.
150 Ardade St.
West Haven, CT 06516

General Wire Spring Co.
1101 Thompson Ave.
McKees, PA 15136

Genova Inc.
300 Rising
Davison, MI 48423

Gerber Wrought Iron Products Co.
Gerber Industries Inc.
1510 Fairview Ave.
St. Louis, MO 63132

Louis M. Gerson Co.
15 Sproat
Middleboro, MA 02346

Gibson Good Tools Inc.
75 Pearl
Sidney, NY 13838

Gibson-Homans Co.
2366 Woodhill Rd.
Cleveland, OH 44106

Gilbert & Bennett Mfg. Co.
Georgetown, CT 06829

Giles & Kendall Inc.
PO Box 188
Huntsville, AL 35804

Gill Mechanical Co.
PO Box 5529
Eugene, OR 97405

Gilmour Mfg. Co.
Div. R. M. Smith Inc.
PO Box 486
Somerset, PA 15501

Glidden Coatings & Resins Co.
Glidden-Durkee Div.
900 Union Commerce Bldg.
Cleveland, OH 44115

Globe Products Corp.
2000 E. Federal
Baltimore, MD 21213

Goldblatt Tool Co.
511 Osage
Kansas City, KS 66110

Gold Bond Building Products
325 Delaware Ave.
Buffalo, NY 14202

Golden Star Polish Mfg. Co. Inc.
400 E. 10th Ave.
North Kansas City, MO 64116

Gold Seal Co.
210 N. 4th St.
Bismarck, ND 58501

Goodyear Tire & Rubber Co.
1114 Market
Akron, OH 44316

Greenford Products Inc.
64 Old Orchard
Skokie, IL 60076

GQF Mfg. Co.
Box 8152
Savannah, GA 31402

Granberg Industries Inc.
200T Garrard Blvd.
Richmond, CA 94804

Cliff Granberry Corp.
PO Box 9505
Dallas, TX 75214

Grayline Housewares Inc.
1616 Berkley St.
Elgin, IL 60120

Great Neck Saw Manufacturers Inc.
165 E. 2nd St.
Mineola LI, NY 11501

Greenview Mfg. Co.
2557 N. Greenview Ave.
Chicago, IL 60614

Gries Reproducer Co.
129 Beechwood Ave.
New Rochelle, NY 10801

Earl Grissmer Co. Inc.
712 E. 64th St.
Indianapolis, IN 46220

Guardian Service Security Systems
12637 Beatrice St.
Los Angeles, CA 90066

Gulf Oil Co.-U.S.
PO Box 1403
Houston, TX 77001

Gumout Div.
Pennzoil Co.
2686 Lisbon Rd.
Cleveland, OH 44104

GX International Inc.
Sub. Bridgeport Chemical Corp.
2610 NE 5th Ave.
Pompano Beach, FL 33064

Hager Hinge Co.
139 Victor St.
St. Louis, MO 63104

Hancock-Gross
401 N. 21st St.
Philadelphia, PA 19130

H & G Industries
6 Main St.
Belleville, NJ 07109

Russell Harrington Cutlery Inc.
44 River
Southbridge, MA 01550

Harrington Tools, Inc.
4316 Alger St.
Los Angeles, CA 90039

Hart Fireplace Furnishings
Box 9
New Albany, IN 47150

Hartline Products Co. Inc.
2186 Noble Rd.
Cleveland, OH 44112

HC Products
PO Box 68
Princeville, IL 61559

Heath Co.
Benton Harbor, MI 49022

Heatilator Fireplace
PO Box 409
Mt. Pleasant, IA 52641

Helistrand Inc.
707 E. Yanonali
Santa Barbara, CA 93103

Hemco Home Equipment Mfg. Co.
14481 Olive St.
Westminster, CA 92683

Henkel Inc.
480 Alfred Ave.
Teaneck, NJ 07666

Hercules Chemical Co. Inc.
U-Can Div.
84 Fifth Ave.
New York, NY 10011

Hide-A-Pipe Co.
510 South Ave. W.
Westfield, NJ 07090

Hillwood Mfg. Co.
21700 St. Clair Ave.
Cleveland, OH 44117

Homelite Div. Textron
PO Box 7047
14401 Carowinds Blvd.
Charlotte, NC 27217

Honeywell Inc.
Honeywell Plaza
Minneapolis, MN 55408

Hopkins Agricultural Chemical Co.
Madison, WI 53701

Howard Hardware Products Inc.
PO Box 589
38 Davey
Bloomfield, NJ 07003

Howard Mfg. Co.
67th Ave. N.
Kent, WA 98031

Howmet Aluminum Corp.
Building Products Div.
6235 W. 73rd
Bedford Park, IL 60501

Huron Products Co.
555 Moore Ave.
Bellevue, OH 44811

Hyde Tools Mfg. Co.
Southbridge, MA 01550

Illinois Bronze Powder & Paint Co.
300 E. Main St.
Lake Zurich, IL 60047

Imperial Screen Co.
5336 W. 145th St.
Lawndale, CA 90260

Independent Nail Inc.
106 Hale
Bridgewater, MA 02324

Indestro Mfg. Co.
2649-59 N. Kildare Ave.
Chicago, IL 60639

Industrial Petrolic Corp.
1525 Bassett Ave.
Bronx, NY 10461

Innovative Audio Systems
Wheeling, IL 60090

In-Sink-Erator
Div. Emerson Electric Co.
4700 21st St.
Racine, WI 53406

International Paper Co.
Long-Bell Div.
PO Box 579
Longview, WA 98632

International Steel Wool Corp.
PO Box 936
1805 Commerce Rd.
Springfield, OH 45501

Ironworks Hill
Box 191
Brookfield, CT 06804

Irwin Auger Bit Co.
92 Grant Ave.
Wilmington, OH 45177

Jackes-Evans Mfg. Co.
4427 Geraldine Ave.
St. Louis, MO 63115

Jack-Post Corp.
PO Box 252
Galen, MI 49113

Jack The Stripper
1373 Freeport Dr.
Mississauga, Ontario, Canada

Jade Controls
PO Box 271
Montclair, CA 91763

Jandy
27 Larkspur
San Rafael, CA 94901

Jefferson Screw Corp.
691 Broadway
New York, NY 10012

Jenn-Air
3035 Shadeland
Indianapolis, IN 46226

Jer Mfg. Inc.
280 River
Coopersville, MI 49404

Jiffy Inc.
3100 Admiral Wilson Blvd.
Pennsauken, NJ 08109

Johns-Manville Corp.
Greenwood Plaza
Denver, CO 80217

C J Johnson Co.
Bradford, PA 16701

Johnson Wax
S C Johnson & Son
1525 Howe St.
Racine, WI 53403

Johnson Products Co. Inc.
2072 N. Commerce St.
Milwaukee, WI 53212

Jordan Industries Inc.
3030 NW 75th St.
Miami, FL 33147

Judsen Rubber Works Inc.
4107 W. Kinzie St.
Chicago, IL 60624

Kagil Corp.
14 Golf Rose Shopping Ctr.
Hoffman Estates, IL 60172

E A Karay Co. Inc.
10 Columbus Circle
New York, NY 10019

Kedman Co.
Box 25667
Salt Lake City, UT 84125

F D Kees Mfg. Co.
700 Park Ave.
Beatrice, NE 68310

Kelley Mfg. Co.
PO Box 1317
4800 Clinton Dr.
Houston, TX 77001

Kentile Floors Inc.
58 Second Ave.
Brooklyn, NY 11215

Kindergard Corp.
3357 Halifax St.
Dallas, TX 75247

King Cotton Cordage Co.
Div. John H. Graham Co. Inc.
617 Oradell Ave.
Oradell, NJ 07649

Kirkhill Inc.
12021 Woodruff Ave.
Downey, CA 90241

Kirsch Co.
309 Prospect
Sturgis, MI 49091

Klise Mfg. Co.
601 Maryland Ave. NE
Grand Rapids, MI 49505

Knape & Vogt Mfg. Co.
2700 Oak Industrial Dr. NE
Grand Rapids, MI 49505

Koehring Atomaster Div.
PO Box 719
Bowling Green, KY 42101

Kool-O-Matic Corp.
1831 Terminal Rd.
Niles, MI 49120

Koppers Co. Inc.
Pittsburgh, PA 15219

Kwikset Sales & Service Co.
Sub. Emhart Corp.
516 E. Santa Ana
Anaheim, CA 92803

Lafayette
Timing Controls & Clocks
52 Bypass
Lafayette, IN 47902

Lake Chemical Co.
250 N. Washtenaw Ave.
Chicago, IL 60612

Landers Import-Export Co. Inc.
PO Box 736
East Hampton, NY 11937

L & L Mfg. Inc.
14056 Vale Court
Eden Prairie, MN 55343

Lawrence Brothers
Sterling, IL 61081

Lebanon Chemical Corp.
Greenview Lawn & Garden
Products Div.
PO Box 317
Lebanon, PA 17042

Lehigh Sales & Products Inc.
Allentown, PA 18105

Leigh Products Inc.
1870 Lee
Coopersville, MI 49404

Leviton Mfg. Co. Inc.
59-25 Little Neck Pkwy.
Little Neck, NY 11362

Little Giant Industries Inc.
138 W. 2260 S.
Salt Lake City, UT 84115

Litton Industries
360 N. Crescent Dr.
Beverly Hills, CA 90210

LOK-BOX, Inc.
RD No. 9
Boxwood Lane
York, PA 17402

Loxem Mfg. Corp.
1201 Exchange Dr.
Richardson, TX 75080

LPS Research Laboratories
2050 Cotner Ave.
Los Angeles, CA 90025

Lufkin-The Cooper Group
PO Box 728
Apex, NC 27502

Lustre Line Products
Richmond & Norris Sts.
Philadelphia, PA 19125

Macco Adhesives
30400 Lakeland Blvd.
Wickliffe, OH 44092

Macklanburg-Duncan Co.
PO Box 25188
Oklahoma City, OK 73125

Magic American Chemical Corp.
23700 Mercantile Ave.
Cleveland, OH 44122

Magic Chef
Cleveland, TN 37311

Magic Crystal
PO Box 75128
Los Angeles, CA 90075

Magnolia Products
701 Beach Blvd.
Pascagoula, MS 39567

Malco Products Inc.
Annandale, MN 55302

Manhattan Brush Co. Inc.
42 W. 18th St.
New York, NY 10011

Mantrose-Haeuser
Div. Millmaster Onyx Corp.
99 Park Ave.
New York, NY 10016

Marion Tool Corp.
PO Box 365
Marion, IN 46952

Marshall-McMurray Co.
1238 W. First St.
Los Angeles, CA 90026

Marshalltown Trowel Co.
Marshalltown, IA 50158

Martin Senour Co.
Div. Sherwin-Williams Co.
1370 Ontario Ave. NW
Cleveland, OH 44113

Marvel Industries Inc.
Dayton Walthers Div.
PO Box 8
Fayette, OH 43521

Masonite Corp.
29 N. Wacker Dr.
Chicago, IL 60606

MasterWorks Inc.
4608 College Park Dr.
Dallas, TX 75229

Mayes Brothers Tool Mfg. Co.
PO Box 1018
Johnson City, TN 37601

Mayhew Steel Products Inc.
Shelburne Falls, MA 01370

Maytag Co.
Newton, IA 50208

WH Maze Co.
100 Church
Peru, IL 61354

Mr. Chain
Div. M-R Products Inc.
1805 Larchwood
Troy, MI 48084

MTI Digital Instruments Div.
7051 Wilson Ave.
Chicago, IL 60656

McCloskey Varnish Co.
7600 State Rd.
Philadelphia, PA 19136

McGill Metal Products Co.
303 S. Morgan St.
Wheaton, IL 60187

Geo. W. McGuire Co. Inc.
150-31 12th Ave.
Whitestone, NY 11357

McGuire-Nicholas
6223 Santa Monica Blvd.
Los Angeles, CA 90038

Mechanical Plastics Corp.
151-5 W. Industry Court
Deer Park, NY 11729

Mercer Plastics Co. Inc.
1 Jabez St.
Newark, NJ 07105

Metal Industries
Box 1299
Ontario, CA 91762

Metalco Industries
Div. Metal Tile Corp.
258 Herricks Rd.
Mineola LI, NY 11501

Michlin Chemical Corp.
9045 Vincent
Detroit, MI 48211

Micro-Lambda
Winter Park, FL 32789

Midget Louver Co.
800 Main Ave.
Norwalk, CT 06852

Millers Falls Co.
57 Wells
Greenfield, MA 01301

Miller Studio Inc.
734 Fair Ave. NW
Philadelphia, OH 44663

**Minnesota Woodworker's
Supply Co.**
Industrial Blvd.
Rogers, MN 55374

Minwax Co. Inc.
72 Oak
Clifton, NJ 07014

Modern Industries Inc.
515 Olive Ave.
Vista, CA 92083

Modern Methods Inc.
PO Box 370
2208 W. 2nd St.
Owensboro, KY 42301

Montgomery Ward
618 W. Chicago Ave.
Chicago, IL 60607

Benjamin Moore & Co.
Chestnut Ridge Rd.
Montvale, NJ 07645

Moore Push Pin Co.
113-125 Berkley
Philadelphia, PA 19144

Mortell Co.
550 N. Hobbie Ave.
Kankakee, IL 60901

**Mountain West Alarm Supply
Co.**
4215 N. 16th St.
Phoenix, AZ 85016

M-P Corp.
6466 Chene St.
Detroit, MI 48211

Multi-Purpose Ladder Co. Inc.
4400 E. LaPalma Ave.
Anaheim, CA 92807

Muralo Co. Inc.
148 E. 5th St.
Bayonne, NJ 07002

Murray-Black Co.
552 W. State
Springfield, OH 45501

My-Ro Products Inc.
1736 N. Second St.
Milwaukee, WI 53212

NanKee Co. Inc.
Engineers Lane
Farmingdale, NY 11735

National Casein of California
3535 W. MacArthur Blvd.
Santa Ana, CA 92704

National Consumer
888 Toulon
Pacific Palisades, CA 90272

National Gypsum Co.
Gold Bond Bldg. Products Div.
325 Delaware Ave.
Buffalo, NY 14202

National Mfg. Co.
PO Box 577
Sterling, IL 61081

National Recessed Cabinets
3930 NW 25th St.
Miami, FL 33142

National Seat Mfg. Corp.
186-202 Spruce
Winchendon, MA 01475

National Solvent Corp.
955 W. Smith Rd.
Medina, OH 44256

James Neill (USA) Inc.
British Distribution Services
417 Woodmont Rd.
Milford, CT 06460

**Nelco Electric Heating & Air
Conditioning Div.**
Square D Co.
1601 Mercer Rd.
Lexington, KY 40505

New York Bronze Powder Co. Inc.
515 Dowd Ave.
Elizabeth, NJ 07201

New Delphos Mfg. Co.
102-125 S. Pierce
Delphos, OH 45833

Newell Window Products Co.
916 S. Arcade Ave.
Freeport, IL 61032

Newell Workshop
19 Blaine Ave.
Hinsdale, IL 60521

Nibco Inc.
500 Simpson Ave.
Elkhart, IN 46514

Nichols-Homeshield Inc.
1000 N. Harvester Rd.
West Chicago, IL 60185

Nicholson File Co.
Cooper Group
PO Box 728
Apex, NC 27502

Niemi Enterprises
21370 Applewood Dr.
California City, CA 93505

Normark Corp.
1710 E. 78th St.
Minneapolis, MN 55423

Norris Industries
Div. Weiser Co.
4100 Ardmore Ave.
South Gate, CA 90280

Northland Wood Products Co.
203 Northfield Rd.
Northfield, IL 60093

Norton Co.
1 New Bond
Worcester, MA 01606

Nu-Tone
Div. Scovill
Madison & Red Bank Rds.
Cincinnati, OH 45227

Oatey Co.
4700 W. 160th St.
Cleveland, OH 44135

O'Malley Valve Co.
4228 8th Ave. S.
St. Petersburg, FL 33711

Omega Precision Hand Tool Co.
18-39 128th St.
College Point, NY 11356

Onan Corp.
1400 73rd Ave. NE
Minneapolis, MN 55432

C. S. Osborne & Co.
125 Jersey St.
Harrison, NJ 07029

Overhead Door Corp.
6250 LBJ Freeway
Dallas, TX 75240

Owens-Corning Fiberglas Corp.
PO Box 901
Toledo, OH 43601

Pacific Electricord Co.
PO Box 10
747 W. Redondo Beach Blvd.
Gardena, CA 90247

Padco Inc.
2220 Elm St. SE
Minneapolis, MN 55414

Paint Master Industries Inc.
45 W. 17th St.
New York, NY 10011

Panef Mfg. Co.
5700 W. Douglas Ave.
Milwaukee, WI 53218

Park Mfg. Co.
Div. Triangle Corp.
Grant Park, IL 60940

Parker Mfg. Co.
PO Box 644
Worcester, MA 01613

Parker Metal Corp.
85 Prescott
Worcester, MA 01605

Pendleton Studios
2708 Boll St.
Dallas, TX 75204

J C Penney
1301 Ave. of the Americas
New York, NY 10019

Permatex Co. Inc.
PO Box 1350
West Palm Beach, FL 33402

Petersen Mfg. Co. Inc.
PO Box 337
De Witt, NE 68341

Phifer Wire Products Inc.
PO Box 1700
Tuscaloosa, AL 35401

Philstone Nail Corp.
57 Pine
Canton, MA 02021

Pierce & Stevens Chemical Corp.
PO Box 1092
Buffalo, NY 14240

Pioneer Rubber Co.
408 Tiffin Rd.
Willard, OH 44890

Plaskolite Inc.
PO Box 1497
Columbus, OH 43216

Plasti-Kote Co.
1000 Lake Rd.
Medina, OH 44256

Arthur I. Platt Co.
24 Coolidge Ct.
Fairfield, CT 06430

Plumb Craft Mfg.
24455 Aurora Rd.
Bedford Heights, OH 44146

Plumb Tools
Ames Div. Mc Donough Co.
PO Box 1774
Parkersburg, WV 26101

Poolmaster Inc.
PO Box 2288
160 Jefferson Dr.
Menlo Park, CA 94025

Post Hold Inc.
1440 Willow St.
Chicago, IL 60622

Pour-Ezee
Weil Tool Co. Inc.
192 Vincent Ave.
Lynbrook, NY 11563

Power Products Div.
DESA Industries
25000 S. Western Ave.
Park Forest, IL 60466

PPG Industries
One Gateway Center
Pittsburgh, PA 15222

Pratt & Lambert Inc.
PO Box 22
Buffalo, NY 14240

Precision Valve Corp.
700 Nepperhan Ave.
Yonkers, NY 10703

Prestolite Electrical
Div. Eltra Corp.
511 Hamilton
Toledo, OH 43694

Process Solvent Co.
Box 4437
Kansas City, KS 66104

Pro Products Co. Inc.
7440 Forest Hills Rd.
Rockford, IL 61111

Purcell Miller Co.
PO Box 245
New Lenox, IL 60451

Qest Products Corp.
PO Box 201
Elkhart, IN 46514

Quadmatic Industries Inc.
PO Box 337
Dorchester, WI 54425

Quaker City Mfg. Co.
701 Chester Pike
Sharon Hill, PA 19079

Quaker Industries Inc.
90 McMillen Rd.
Antioch, IL 60002

Quality Steel Products Inc.
1551 Central St.
Stroughton, MA 02072

Quickee Inc.
Bridge St. Ext.
Catasauqua, PA 18032

Quicker Sticker
204 W. 50th
Loveland, CO 80537

Quikrete Co.
733 E. Dublin-Granville Rd.
Columbus, OH 43229

Radiator Specialty Co.
PO Box 10628
Charlotte, NC 28201

Rain Bird National Sales Corp.
7045 N. Grand Ave.
Glendora, CA 91740

Rain Jet Corp.
301 S. Flower
Burbank, CA 91503

Rake-O-Matic
Box 907
Oswego, IL 60543

Rancher Fence Post Driver
Corsicana Grader & Machine Co.
Box 1699
Corsicana, TX 75110

RAP Products Inc.
PO Box 459
Bay City, MI 48706

Rathbone Chesterman Ltd.
Birmingham, England

Raylor Co.
Box 8366
Long Beach, CA 90808

Red Devil Inc.
2400 Vauxhall Rd.
Union, NJ 07083

Redwood Domes
PO Box 666
Aptos, CA 95003

Gregory Rennie
165 Newbury St.
Boston, MA 02116

Resins & Chemicals Co.
3926 Huston Ave.
Cincinnati, OH 45212

Resin Systems Inc.
25-29 50th St.
Woodside, NY 11377

Reynolds Metals Co.
6601 W. Broad St.
Richmond, VA 23261

Richards-Wilcox Mfg. Co.
310 Third St.
Aurora, IL 60507

Richdel Inc.
1235 W. Glenoaks Blvd.
Glendale, CA 91201

The Ridge Tool Co.
Sub. Emerson Electric Co.
400 Clark St.
Elyria, OH 44035

Ringer Corp.
6860 Flying Cloud Dr.
Eden Prairie, MN 55343

**Rittenhouse Operations
Chromalox Div.**
Emerson Electric Co.
Honeoye Falls, NY 14472

Rival Mfg. Co.
36th & Bennington
Kansas City, MO 64129

Rockford-Eclipse
Div. Eclipse Fuel Engineering Co.
1100 Buchanan
Rockford, IL 61101

Rockford Products Corp.
Packaged Products Div.
PO Box 6306
Rockford, IL 61110

Rockwell International
Power Tool Div. Consumer Products
Ste. 303, 3171 Directors Row
Memphis, TN 38131

Roe International Inc.
PO Box 471
217 River Ave.
Patchogue, NY 11772

Roll-A-Mix
1083 Bloomfield Ave.
W. Caldwell, NJ 07006

Ronson Corp.
1 Ronson Rd.
Woodbridge, NJ 07095

Roofmaster Products Co.
PO Box 63167
Los Angeles, CA 90063

Rosco Tools Inc.
PO Box 397
100 Landing Ave.
Smithtown, NY 11787

Rotocrop USA Inc.
58 Buttonwood St.
New Hope, PA 18938

Rubbermaid Inc.
1147 Akron Rd.
Wooster, OH 44691

David Rubin, Art Specialist & Restorer
42 Somerset St.
Springfield, MA 01108

Rudolph Industries
196 E. 25th St.
Holland, MI 49423

W J Ruscoe Co.
483 Kenmore Blvd.
Akron, OH 44301

Rust-Oleum Corp.
2301 Oakton
Evanston, IL 60204

Rutt Custom Kitchens, Inc.
Goodville, PA 17528

Sabre Saw Chain Inc.
PO Box 272
LaSalle Stations
Niagara Falls, NY 14304

Safe Hardware Corp.
Div. Emhart Corp.
225 Episcopal Rd.
Berlin, CT 06037

Sakrete Inc.
PO Box 17087
Cincinnati, OH 45217

Samson Cordage Works
99 High St.
Boston, MA 02110

Sandvik Steel Co.
Saws & Tools Div.
1702 Nevins Rd.
Fair Lawn, NJ 07410

Savogran
PO Box 130
Norwood, MA 02062

S-B Mfg. Co.
11320 Watertown Plank Rd.
Milwaukee, WI 53226

SBI Inc.
936 National Ave.
Addison, IL 60101

Scandecor Inc.
1105 Industrial Hwy.
Southampton, PA 18966

Schaul Mfg. Co.
796 E. 105th St.
Cleveland, OH 44108

H. J. Scheirich Co.
Box 21037
Louisville, KY 40221

Schlage Lock Co.
PO Box 3324
San Francisco, CA 94119

Schrade Cutlery Corp.
30 Canal
Ellenville, NY 12428

Schulte Corp.
11450 Grooms Rd.
Cincinnati, OH 45242

Scotch
Brand name of 3M Co.
3M Center
St. Paul, MN 55101

Scott's Liquid Gold Inc.
4880 Havana
Denver, CO 80239

O. M. Scott & Sons Co.
Marysville, OH 43040

Screen Patch Co.
1012 James Blvd.
Signal Mtn., TN 37377

Sears, Roebuck and Co.
Sears Tower
Chicago, IL 60684

Seymour of Sycamore Inc.
917 Crosby Ave.
Sycamore, IL 60178

Seymour Mfg. Co.
500 N. Broadway
Seymour, IN 47274

Sharon Bolt & Screw Co. Inc.
60 Pleasant St.
Ashland, MA 01721

Shelby Standard Inc.
PO Box 525
110 Broadway
Shelby, OH 44875

Shell Chemical Co.
2401 Crow Canyon Rd.
San Ramon, CA 94583

Shepherd Products US Inc.
203 Kerth
St. Joseph, MI 49085

William Shine Design Co. Inc.
31A E. Dale Dr.
Monroe, CT 06468

Shopmaster
6600 Washington Ave. S
Eden Prairie, MN 55343

Shopsmith, Inc.
320 N. Second St.
Tipp City, OH 45371

Shop-Vac Corp.
2323 Reach Rd.
Williamsport, PA 17701

Simer Pump Co.
5960 Main St. NE
Minneapolis, MN 55432

Simonds Cutting Tools
Wallace Murray Corp.
PO Box 500
Fitchburg, MA 01420

Simplex Security Systems Inc.
10 Front
Collinsville, CT 06022

Singer Co.
Industrial Sewing & Knitting
Div.
275 Centennial Ave.
Piscataway, NJ 08854

Skil Corp.
5033 Elston Ave.
Chicago, IL 60630

Skokie Saw & Tool Co.
2105 Production Dr.
Louisville, KY 40299

R & G Sloane Mfg. Co. Inc.
Sub. Susquehanna Corp.
7606 N. Clybourn Ave.
Sun Valley, CA 91352

SMC
Specialty Mfg. Co.
2356 University
St. Paul, MN 55114

Soss Mfg. Co.
PO Box 8200 Harper Sta.
Detroit, MI 48213

Spacemaster Home Products
Div. Garcy Corp.
2501 N. Elston Ave.
Chicago, IL 60647

Spartan
S. Parker Hardware Mfg. Corp.
27 Ludlow
New York, NY 10002

Spear & Jackson Inc.
4767 Clark Howell Hwy.
College Park, GA 30349

Specialty Mfg. Co.
2356 University Ave.
St. Paul, MN 55114

Spin-Thru
General Wire Spring Co.
PO Box 8558E
Pittsburgh, PA 15220

Standard Dry Wall Products
7800 NW 38th St.
Miami, FL 33166

Standard Tar Products Inc.
2456 W. Cornell St.
Milwaukee, WI 53209

Stanley Tools
Div. Stanley Works
New Bern, NC 28560

Star Bronze Co.
803 S. Mahoning
Alliance, OH 44601

Star Expansion Co.
Mountainville, NY 10953

Stauffer Chemical Co.
Plastics Div. - Decorative
Interior Products
Newburgh, NY 12550

Stay-Tite Products Co. Inc.
PO Box 9128
14701 Industrial Ave.
Cleveland, OH 44137

Steel City Corp.
190 N. Meridian Rd.
Youngstown, OH 44509

Sterling Clark Lurton Corp.
184 Commercial
Malden, MA 02148

312

Stove Hospital
Ron Anderson
715 Liberty St.
Dallas, TX 75204

Sunbeam Appliance Service Co.
5600 W. Roosevelt Rd.
Chicago, IL 60650

Sunnyside Products Inc.
5530 N. Wolcott Ave.
Chicago, IL 60640

Superior Fastener Corp.
9536 W. Foster Ave.
Chicago, IL 60656

Superior Graphite Co.
20 N. Wacker Dr.
Chicago, IL 60606

S/V Tool Co.
301 N. Main St.
Newton, KS 67114

Swedlow Inc.
7350 Empire Dr.
Florence, KY 41042

Swingline Inc.
32-00 Skillman Ave.
Long Island City, NY 11101

Switchpack Systems Inc.
Del Mar, CA 92014

Synkoloid Co.
PO Box 60937
Los Angeles, CA 90060

TACO
Trans-Atlantic Co.
440 Fairmount Ave.
Philadelphia, PA 19123

T & R Chemicals Inc.
PO Box 216
El Paso, TX 77941

Tappan Appliance Group
Tappan Park
Mansfield, OH 44901

Teco (Timber Engineering Co.)
5530 Wisconsin Ave.
Washington, DC 20015

Teledyne Mono-Thane
1460 Industrial Pkwy.
Akron, OH 44310

Tel Products, Inc.
7801 Bass Lake Rd.
Minneapolis, MN 55428

Texamar Enterprises, Inc.
310 Madison Ave.
New York, NY 10017

Thermal Metal Products Corp.
1300 E. North Ave.
Baltimore, MD 21213

Thermotrol Corp.
29400 Stephenson Hwy.
Madison Heights, MI 48071

Thermwell Products Co. Inc.
150 E. 7th St.
Paterson, NJ 07524

Thorsen Tool Co.
PO Box 20678
2527 Willowbrook Rd.
Dallas, TX 75220

3M Co.
3M Center
St. Paul, MN 55101

Torch Products Co.
654 Crofton SE
Grand Rapids, MI 49507

Toro Co.
8111 Lyndale Ave. S
Minneapolis, MN 55420

Tower Mfg. Corp.
Madison, IN 47250

Tremco
10701 Shaker Blvd.
Cleveland, OH 44104

Trewax Co.
PO Box A
5631 S. Mesmer
Culver City, CA 90230

Triplett
Corner of Harmon and Poplar
Sts.
Bluffton, OH 45817

Trojan
Div. Ritchie Industries Inc.
Conrad, IA 50621

Trol-A-Temp
Div. Trolex Corp.
725 Federal Ave.
Kenilworth, NJ 07033

Trophy Products
9712 Old Katy Rd.
Houston, TX 77055

True Temper Corp.
1623 Enclid Ave.
Cleveland, OH 44115

Tru-Test
Cotter & Co.
2740 Clybourn Ave.
Chicago, IL 60614

Tuff-Kote Co. Inc
210 Seminary Ave.
Woodstock, IL 60098

Turen Inc.
2 Cottage Ave.
Danvers, MA 01923

Turner Co.
821 Park
Sycamore, IL 60178

U-Fasten-It
3301 Colerain Ave.
Cincinnati, OH 45225

Underwriters Laboratory Inc.
Northbrook, IL 60062

Union Fork & Hoe Co.
500 Dublin Ave.
Columbus, OH 43216

United Gilsonite Laboratories
PO Box 70
Jefferson Ave.
Scranton, PA 18501

United Merchants Div.
1407 Broadway
New York, NY 10018

United States Borax & Chemical
Corp.
Los Angeles, CA 90010

United States Ceramic Tile Co.
1375 Raff Rd.
SW Canton, OH 44710

U.S. Expansion Bolt Co.
PO Box 1589
500 State
York, PA 17405

U.S. Floor Systems Inc.
Drawer 18424
Raleigh, NC 27609

United States Gypsum Co.
101 S. Wacker Dr.
Chicago, IL 60606

United States Purchasing
Exchange
5260 Vineland Ave.
North Hollywood, CA 91601

Universal Metal Products Co.
Div. Reflect-O-Lite Corp.
260 Matzinger Rd.
Toledo, OH 43612

U-Plumb-It
Future Pak
619 Redna Ter.
Cincinnati, OH 45215

Urethane Arts Inc.
Far Rockaway, NY 11691

USM Corp.
Consumer Products Div.
Muhlenberg Industrial Mall
4408 Pottsville Pike
Reading, PA 19605

USM Corp.
504 Mt. Laurel Ave.
Temple, PA 19560

Utica Tool Co. Inc.
Cameron Rd.
Orangeburg, SC 29115

Vaco Products Co.
510 N. Dearborn St.
Chicago, IL 60610

Val-A Co.
700-710 W. Root St.
Chicago, IL 60609

Vaughan & Bushnell Mfg. Co.
11414 Maple Ave.
Hebron, IL 60034

Lillian Vernon
510 S. Fulton Ave.
Mount Vernon, NY 10550

Vigilant Products Co. Inc.
27 Main St.
Ogdensburg, NJ 07439

Viking Sauna
909 Park Ave.
San Jose, CA 95126

Vise-Grip
Petersen Mfg. Co. Inc.
PO Box 337
De Witt NE, 68341

VSI Fasteners
3064 E. Maria
Compton, CA 90221

Wal-Rich Corp.
35-12 Skillman Ave.
Long Island City, NY 11101

Jim Walter Corp.
PO Box 22601
Tampa, FL 33622

Warner Mfg. Co.
13435 Industrial Park Blvd.
Minneapolis, MN 55441

Warp Brothers
4647 W. Augusta Blvd.
Chicago, IL 60651

The Warren Group
PO Box 68
Hiram, OH 44234

Watco-Dennis Corp.
1756 22nd St.
Santa Monica, CA 90404

Water Master Co.
13 S. 3rd Ave.
New Brunswick, NJ 08904

WD-40 Co.
1061 Cudahy Place
San Diego, CA 92110

Weekender Products
PO Box 2301
511 Osage
Kansas City, KA 66110

Weil Tool Co. Inc.
192 Vincent Ave.
Lynbrook, NY 11563

Wej-It
Sub. Allied Products Corp.
500 Alter St.
Broomfield, CO 80020

Weldwood Products
Dept. B
600 N. Baldwin Park Blvd.
City of Industry, CA 91790

Wellington Puritan Mills Inc.
Madison, GA 30650

Wells Lamont Corp.
6640 W. Touhy Ave.
Chicago, IL 60648

Wen Products Inc.
5810 Northwest Hwy.
Chicago, IL 60631

R.D. Werner Co. Inc.
Greenville, PA 16125

West Bend Co.
400 Washington St.
West Bend, WI 53095

Western Auto Supply Co.
2107 Grand Ave.
Kansas City, MO 64108

Western Wire Products Co.
1451 S. 18th St.
St. Louis, MO 63104

Westinghouse Electric Corp.
Industrial Equipment Div.
PO Box 300
Sykesville, MD 21784

Westvaco
Westvaco Bldg.
299 Park Ave.
New York, NY 10017

Whirlpool Corp.
Benton Harbor, MI 49022

J.C. Whitlam Mfg. Co.
Chemical Div.
PO Box 71
Wadsworth, OH 44281

Wickliffe Industries
PO Box 286
Wickliffe, OH 44092

Edwin L. Wiegand
Div. Emerson Electric Co.
7598 Thomas Blvd.
Pittsburgh, PA 15208

Williamhouse Regency Co.
Blisscraft of Hollywood
13007 W. Western Ave.
Gardena, CA 90249

Williamson Co.
3500 Madison Rd.
Cincinnati, OH 45209

Williams Products
1750 Maplelawn Blvd.
Troy, MI 48084

Willson Products Div.
ESB Inc.
PO Box 622
Reading, PA 19603

Wilmod Co. Inc.
200 W. 57th St.
New York, NY 10019

Wingaersheek Inc.
2 Dearborn Rd.
Peabody, MA 01960

Wire Products Co.
111 N. Douglas
Hortonville, WI 54944

Wisper Kool
Triangle Engineering Co.
PO Drawer 38271
Houston, TX 77088

J. Wiss & Sons Co.
400 W. Market St.
Newark, NJ 07107

Wood Davies & Co. Ltd.
184 Front St.
East Toronto, Ontario M5a 1E6

Woodhill Chemical Sales Corp.
PO Box 7183
18731 Cranwood Pkwy.
Cleveland, OH 44128

Woodstream Corp.
Lititz, PA 17543

Wooster Brush Co.
604 Madison Ave.
Wooster, OH 44691

H L Worden Co.
Granger, WA 98932

Wrap-On Co. Inc.
341 W. Superior
Chicago, IL 60610

Wright-Bernet Inc.
1524 Bender Ave.
Hamilton, OH 45011

Wrightway Mfg. Co.
371 E. 116th St.
Chicago, IL 60628

X-Po Instrument Co. Inc.
19D Gardner Rd.
Fairfield, NJ 07006

Yale
Eaton Corp. Lock & Hardware
Div.
PO Box 25288
Charlotte, NC 28212

York Industries Corp.
6 Hoffman Pl.
Hillside, NJ 07205

Z-Brick Co.
Div. VMC Corp.
2834 NW Market
Seattle, WA 98107

Zenith Metal Products Corp.
723 Secane Ave.
Primos, PA 19018

Zephyr Mfg. Co.
400-410 W. 2nd St.
Sedalia, MO 65301

William Zinsser & Co. Inc.
39 Belmont Dr.
Somerset, NJ 08873

Zynolyte Products Co.
15700 S. Avalon Blvd.
Compton, CA 90224

Index of Recommended Products

AAA Up the Downspout, 239
Accelerator Compost Bin, 220
Acme Ventrol Dryer Vent Kit, 284
ABRASIVES
 Arkansas Abrasives Indian Mountain Sharpening Stones, 210
 Carborundum Emery Cloth, 6; Sharpening Stones, 211
 Howard Hardware Sandpaper, 130
 Jack The Stripper, 135
 Norton Bear Sanders, 116
 Plasplugs Quiksand, 154
 Synkoloid Rottenstone, 137
 3M Press'N Sand Sanding Discs, 160; Resinite Sanding Discs, 45
Acorn Butterfly Hinges, 168
ACRYLIC SHEETING
 Swedlow Swedglaze Acrylic Sheeting, 86
Adams Big Job Paint Kit, 114
ADHESIVES
 Carpet Products Mr. Quick Adhesive, 50
 Chair-Loc, 125
 Craftsman Wood Service Plastic Resin Glue, 128
 Elmer's Carpenter's Wood Glue, 125; Cove Base Adhesive, 62; Heavy Grip Cement, 43; Latex Base Contact Cement, 157; Two-Part Waterproof Glue, 38; Waterproof Glue, 38; Wood Glue, 125
 Franklin Glue Evertite, 246
 Goodyear Plio-Nail Panel Adhesive, 63
 Henkel Wallpaper Pastes And Adhesives, 84
 Magic American Magic Liquid Stitch, 99
 Michlin Mister Thinzit Panel Adhesive, 82
 Murray-Black Paste-Bak, 73
 National Casein "DR" Powdered Resin Glue, 161
 US Ceramic Quick Set Adhesive, 51
 USG Exterior Carpet Adhesive, 228; Wal-Lite Ceiling Tile Adhesive, 78
 USM Bostik Spray Glue, 200
 Val-A Tehr-Greeze Fabric Cement, 59
Adjusta-Post Telescoping Supports, 34
Advanced Drainage System, 238
AIR CLEANERS
 GE Electrostatic Air Cleaner, 256
AIR CONDITIONER COVERS
 Allied Plastics Air Conditioner Covers, 264
Ajax Earth Mounts, 222
Akro-Mils Bench-Mate, 205; Drill-Mate, 206; Quik-Pik, 205; Saw-Mate/Sander-Mate, 206
ALARMS
 Guardian Service Pre-Entry Door Alarm, 148
 Kwikset Exterior Alarm Bell, 149
 Loxem Door Chain Alarm, 148
 J.C. Penney Gard-Site Security System, 149
 Sunbeam Stop Alarm, 145
Albion Caulking Gun, 53
Alcan Aluminum Patio Roof, 229
Alfcoater, 258
Allastics Cellwood Door Systems, 102
Allied Plastics Air Conditioner Covers, 264
Allway Master Saw, 170
T.A. Altender Straightedge, 88
Amer-Glas Heater Filters, 259
American Art Clay Rub 'N Buff Decorator Finish, 140
American Carpet Cutter Knife, 50
American Fluorescent Convert-A-Lite, 30
American Grease Stick Sil-Glyde, 85
American Olean Easy-Set Tile System, 51
American Optical Safeline Safety Hat, 201
American Steel Wool, 135
Amerock Tri-Roller Drawer Slide, 195
AMMETERS
 Amprobe Snap-On Ammeter, 276

Amprobe Snap-On Ammeter, 276
AMT Power Tools, 202
Anchor Continental Weatherstripping Tapes, 111
ANCHORS
 A.B. Chance Keep-Stakes Anchors, 192
 Jordan Jord-EZE Plastic Anchors, 74
 US Expansion Bolt Yellow Jacket Anchor, 98
 Wej-It Expansion Bolts, 228
ANTI-STATIC PRODUCTS
 End Stat, 48
 Merix Anti-Static, 48
 Stat-O-Cide, 48
 Vigilant Products D' Stat, 48
ANTIQUING
 American Art Clay Rub 'N Buff, 140
 Martin-Senour Antiquing Kit, 140
APPLIANCE CORDS
 Belden Appliance Cords, 32
 Eagle Cord Connectors, 32
 GE Appliance Cords, 32
APPLIANCE ROLLERS
 Hemco Model SAR-12 Roller Set, 289
APPLIQUES
 Bendix Mouldings Plant Ons, 141
 Con-Tact Tile Appliques, 52
Arco Dial-A-Dado Saw Washers, 154; Dowel Centers, 127; Wire End Brush, 116; 3-Way Plane, 109
Ardmore Double Blade Driveway Coater, 251
Aristo-Mat Deflex Deflectors, 257
Arkansas Abrasives Indian Mountain Sharpening Stones, 210
Arlyn Industries Cutter, 157
Arm and Hammer Baking Soda, 232
Armco Steel Sheffield A to Z Nails, 33, 54
Armstrong Cork Steel Channels, 79; Decorator Ceiling Tiles, 79; Gourmet Chandelier Tile, 79; "How To Install Do-It-Yourself Carpet," 46; Integrid Suspended Ceiling System, 81; Solarian Place 'N Press Tiles, 43
Armstrong Paint Du-Kwik Acrylic Latex Enamel, 193
Arno Aluminum Adhesive Tape, 238; Carpetak Tape, 47; Electrical Tape, 32
Arnold Mower Bags, 226; Mower Blade Sharpener, 216

Arrow T-50 Staple Gun, 78
Artcraft Awnings, 265
ARTIFICIAL BRICKS AND STONES
 Bric-Mold Brick Molds, 66
 Brock Brick 'N Wire, 67
 Dacor Miracle Bricks, 66; Stones, 67
 Masonite Roxite Brick Panels, 66
 Modern Methods Brickettes Mini-Panel, 67
 Z-Brick, 67
Arvey Easy Does It Kits, 271
Atomaster Reddy Heater, 203
AUGERS
 Chicago Specialty Drainmaster Power Drain Auger, 15
 Tuffy Drain Cleanout Auger, 15
 U-Plumb-It Flat Sewer Auger, 15
 Wrightway Tuffy Closet Auger, 18
Auth Electric Medicine Cabinet, 172
AWLS
 General Hardware Scratch Awls, 94
AWNINGS
 Artcraft Awnings, 265
Azrock Hampshire Brick Vinyl Tiles, 43
BAG HOLDERS
 Specialty Bag Butler, 219; Yard N' Garden Cart, 219
BAKING SODA
 Arm and Hammer Baking Soda, 232
Barclay Filigree Hardboard Panels, 163; World of Wood Beams, 82
Bartlett Two-Hand Pruner, 218
Bauer Aluminum Ladder, 33
BEAM SUPPORTS
 Adjusta-Post Telescoping Supports, 34
 Montgomery Ward Heavy Duty Jack Screw, 34
H. Behlen & Brother Shellac Sticks, 133
Behr Process Build 50 Finish, 141; Spray Stain and Sealer, 137
Belden Appliance Cords, 32
Belwith Accuride Drawer Slides, 130; Lock Plate, 144
BENCH GRINDERS
 Wen Bench Grinder, 211
Bendix Mouldings Wood Carvings, 141
Benjamin Moore Regal Latex Enamel, 113
BernzOmatic BernzCutter Cutting Tool, 156; 70-piece Tool Set,

313

202; Spark Plug Socket Set, 217; Super Torch, 260; Thermo Fogger, 188
Bestop Super-Horse Sawhorses, 204
Bethlehem Steel Scotch Nails, 176
BICYCLE STORAGE
Continental Bike Keeper, 196
Montgomery Ward's Bike Rack, 196
Sears Bike Storage Lift, 197
Spacemaster Bike Bin, 197
Bissell Century Carpet Sweeper, 48; Dry Carpet Cleaner, 48; Spin-foam Rug Shampooer, 48
Black & Decker Circular Saw, 55; De-Walt Deluxe Power Shop Saw, 202; Finishing Sander, 163; WorkMate, 205
BLACKTOP PATCH AND SEALER
Elmer's Acrylic Latex Blacktop Crack Sealer, 251
Gibson-Homans Handi-Gard Driveway Patching Compound, 251
Sakrete Black Top Patch, 251; Black Top Sealer, 251
BLACKTOP SPREADER
Ardmore Double Blade Driveway Coater, 251
BLIND RIVET TOOLS
Star Blind Rivet Tool, 239
Blisscraft Every Room Organizer Spice Rack, 164
Blue Lustre Carpet Shampoo, 48; Shampooer, 48
BOILER PLUGS
Hancock-Gross Boiler Repair Plugs, 9
Boltmaster Steel Shelving Parts, 152
Bon Ami Polishing Cleanser, 288
Bond Chemical Crystal Tack-Cloth, 136
Bondex Tile Grout, 51
W. R. Bonsal Surewall Surface Bonding Cement, 252
Boss Horsehide Work Gloves, 225
Bostitch H2B Stapling Hammer, 267
Bowers Replacement Faucet Handles, 12
Bowmar Digital Combination Entrance Control, 148; Trap Mat, 148
Boyle-Midway 3-in-1 Lubricating Oil, 297
BRACES
Hager Corner Braces, 41
BRACKETS
Dalton Hang-it-all Brackets, 221; Sawhorse Brackets, 205
Bradley Bradtrol Valve, 13
Brainerd Decorative Cabinet Hardware, 184
BRICK LAYING KITS
Weekender Products Bricklaying Kit, 252
Bric-Mold, 66
Brink & Cotton Clamp-It C-Clamp, 108; Edging Clamp, 151
Brock Brick 'N' Wire, 67
Brookstone Shingle Nail Remover, 234
Buck Knives, 41
BULL FLOATS
Marshalltown Bull Float, 244
Burgess Fluidic Sprinkler, 215; Shower Stick Sprinkler, 215
Bussman Fuse Pullers, 23; Fustat Type S Fuse, 23
CABINET HARDWARE
Brainerd Decorative Cabinet Hardware, 184
Hager Hinge Cabinet Hardware, 154
Kindergard Latches, 192
National Cup Pulls, 163
Safe Cabinet Hinges And Catches, 171
Stanley Classic Brassware, 181
CABINETS
Emco Modular Shelves And Cabinets, 166
Long-Bell Cabinet Components, 170

National Recessed Cabinets Handy-Can Cupboard, 168
Cabot Bleaching Oil, 223; Decking And Fence Stains, 223
Caldwell Sash Balance, 91
Cal-Tuf Glass Shelves, 167
Campbell Sash Chain, 90
CANE
Cane And Basket Supply Pre-Woven Cane, 142
Minnesota Woodworkers Paper-Cane, 142
Newell Caning Kit, 142
Cane And Basket Supply Pre-Woven Cane, 142
Canfield Copper Mate Paste Flux, 6; Quality Solder Roll, 6
Carborundum Emery Cloth, 6; Sharpening Stones, 211
CARPET JOINERS
Mercer Plastics Universal Joiner, 47
Carpet Products Mr. Quick Adhesive, 50
CARPET SHAMPOOS AND CLEANERS
Bissell Dry Carpet Cleaner, 48; Spin-foam Shampooer, 48
Blue Lustre Carpet Shampoo, 48; Shampooer, 48
Coastal Chemical Rid-Spot, 49
Dracket Renuzit, 49
US Floor Systems Steamex, 49
Zynolyte Rug-Mate, 49
CARPET STRETCHERS
C. S. Osborne Knee Kicker, 46
CARPET TACK STRIPS
Sears Tack Strips, 46
Casaplanta Casa Mini Greenhouse, 227
CASTERS
Chason Nail-On Swivel Glides, 129; Wheelees Casters, 129
Shepherd Saturn Casters, 129
CATCHES
Jiffy Hardware Friction Catch, 175; Spring And Roller Catch, 174
Safe Cabinet Hinges And Catches, 171
CAULKING AND CAULKING TOOLS
Albion Caulking Gun, 53
Darworth Polyseamseal Caulk, 100; Seamseal Rubber Caulk, 100
Dry Mix Concrete Krak-Kalk, 233
Dura Bond Tube Caulk, 101; Utility Caulk, 101
Elmer's Acrylic Latex Caulk, 101
GE Silicone Bathtub Caulk And Seal, 53
GX International Space Age Caulk, 190
Macco Adhesives Liquid Seal Tub & Tile Caulk, 53; Super Caulk, 100
Michlin Chemical Caulking Gun, 100
Mico Caulking Tools, 53
Murray-Black Plaster-Stik, 61
My-Ro Tub 'N Wall Seal-A-Crack, 53
Ruscoe Permanent Sealer, 233
Stay-Tite Gutter Seal, 240
USG Durabond Acrylic Caulk, 101; Butyl Caulk, 101; Tub Caulk, 53; Utility Caulk, 101
CEDAR PANELS
G & K Cedar Panels, 177
CEILING BEAMS
Barclay World of Wood Beams, 82
Emco Decorator Beams, 82
Williams Archcraft Ceiling Beams, 83
CEILING PANELS
Certain-teed Ceiling Panels, 80
Leigh Light Diffusing Panels, 80
USG Wal-lite Ceiling Panels, 80
CEILING TILE
Armstrong Decorator Ceiling Tiles, 79; Gourmet Chandelier Tile, 79; Integrid System, 81

Gold Bond Ceiling Tiles, 78
USG Wal-lite Ceiling Tile, 79
CEILING TILE SUPPORTS
Armstrong Cork Company Steel Channels, 79
Gold Bond Ceiling Grid Kit, 81; Clip Strip Ceiling Tile Channels, 78
CEMENT COLORS
Dewey & Almy Chemical Colorundum Dry-Shake Colors, 229
Dry Mix Concrete Far-Go Cement Colors, 229
Century Drill & Tool Drill Stop, 161
CERAMIC TILE
American Olean Easy Set Tile System, 51
Cerro Copper Cinch-Pipe, 7
Certain-teed Duct Wrap Insulation, 258; Ceiling Panels, 80; Fiberglass Insulation, 267
CHAINS
Campbell Sash Chain, 90
M-R Products Mr. Chain, 165
CHAIN SAWS, see SAWS, POWER
CHAIN SAW SUPPLIES
Nicholson Chain Saw File Guide, 224
Sabre Saw Chain, 225
Textron Safe-T-Tip, 224
Chair-Loc, 125
CHALK LINES
Evans-Aristocrat Chalk Line, 235; Chalk-Mor Plumb Bob And Chalk Line, 159
Irwin Strait-Line Chalk Line Reel, 59
A.B. Chance Keep-Stakes Anchors, 192
Channellock Aviation Snips, 80; Model 415 Pliers, 12
Charles Paint Deglosser, 116
Chason Nail-On Swivel Glides, 129; Wheelee Casters, 129
Chatham Brass Dual-Protector Valve, 283
Chemik Max-44 Mildew Remover, 185
Chempar RoZol Rat & Mouse Killer, 189
Chempro Jomax Mildew Remover, 185; Mil-X Mildew Remover, 185
Chicago Specialty Drainmaster Power Drain Auger, 15; Shur-Seal Pipe-Stik, 11; Toilet Seat Hinge, 19
CHISELS
Dasco Cold Chisel, 35; Concrete Point, 35; Target Head Brick Chisel, 253
Great Neck Saw Cold Chisel, 248
Mayhew Steel Ambertuf Butt Chisel, 109
Sandvik Fish And Hook Chisels, 175
Stanley Electrichisel, 126
Chromalox Adapt-O-Matic 293; Heating Elements, 293
Chronomite Labs Water Heater, 295
Chrysler Air-Temp Heat Pump, 257
Church Toilet Seat, 19
Ciba-Geigy Spectracide, 188
CLAMPS
Brink & Cotton Clamp-It, 108; Edging Clamp, 151
Exact C-Clamp, 181
Hargrave Mitre Frame Clamp, 76
Jorgensen Band Clamp, 126; Handscrew, 126; Pony Clamp, 126
Vise-Grip C-Clamp, 180
Clauss Rug Shears, 47
Clay Tenon Saw, 180
Cling-Surface TFE Dry Film Lubricant, 41
Clopay Overhead Door Cables And Pulleys, 106
Clorox Formula 409, 44; Liquid-Plumr, 15
Closet Maid Space Builder Units, 173
CLOTHESLINES
Cordomatic Clothesline, 285

Cluster Sheds, 227
Coastal Chemical Rid-Spot, 49
Colorite Garden Hose, 250
Columbian Long Jaw Hinged Vise, 7; Woodworker's Vise, 126
Commodore Vanities, 171
Como Plastics SF Bi-fold Door, 102
COMPOST SUPPLIES
Accelerator Compost Bin, 220
Ringer Compost Bin Kit, 220; Compost Maker Flakes And Tablets, 220; Killer Kane; 220
CONCRETE BONDERS
Elmer's Concrete Bonder, 250
Franklin Concrete Adhesive, 246
CONCRETE MIXES
W. R. Bonsal Surewall Surface Bonding Cement, 252
Quikrete Concrete Mix, 247
Sakrete Premixed Concrete, 244
CONCRETE MIXERS
Stroll-A-Mix Concrete Mixer, 244
CONCRETE PATCHES
Coughlan Permanent Concrete Patch, 250
Dry-Mix Concrete Krak-Kalk, 233
Hartline Products Rockite, 249
Macco Liquid Patch, 254
Manhattan Brush Poxymix Concrete Repair Mix, 247
Michlin Mr. Thinzit Cocrete Crack Fix, 254
Muralo Sta-Patch, 250
Ruscoe En-DUR-LON, 233
Stay-Tite Cement Patch, 35
Weldwood Concrete Patch, 254
CONCRETE SEALERS
Resin Systems Congard, 245
CONCRETE TOOLS
Dasco Concrete Point, 35; Target Head Brick Chisel, 253
Goldblatt Concrete Placer, 228
Union Atlas Mortar Mixer Hoe, 244
Weekender Products Cement Trowel, 229; Concrete Edger, 229
Congoleum Aztec Floor Tile, 42
Conoflex Decorative Laminate, 157
Con-Tact Tile Appliques, 52
Continental Bike Keeper, 196
CONTINUITY TESTERS
Lafayette Continuity Tester, 276
Conwed Gutter Guard, 241
Cook Varnish, 140
Cordomatic Reels Clothesline, 285; Dog Tenda Leash, 199
CORK
Decocraft Deco-Cork, 195
Corning Family Cooktop, 292
Coronado Petrified Forest Stepping Stones, 230
Cosco Solution 24, 273; Solution 26, 273
Coughlan Chimney Sweep Fireplace Powder, 274; De-Moist, 185; Permanent Concrete Patch, 250
CPM Solvent, 15
Craft Insulator Windows, 271
Craftman Wood Service Plastic Resin Glue, 128
Craftwood Moldings And Dowels, 158
Creative Tools Easydriver, 108
Crescent Tools, 209
Crown Chemicals Pest-Rid, 189
Cyclone Broadcast Spreader, 215
Dacor Miracle Bricks, 66; Stones, 67
Dalton Big John Tool Rack, 208; Hang-it-All Bracket, 221; Katy-Bar Sliding Door Lock, 145; Sawhorse Brackets, 205; Thrif-T Hanger Bracket, 221
DAP Derusto Little Job Spray Enamel, 122; Mitee Joint Compound, 11; '33' Glazing Compound, 87
Darworth Cuprinol Wood Preservative, 222; Fl:X Wood Patch, 176; Polyseamseal Adhesive Caulking, 100; Seamseal Acrylic Rubber Caulk, 100
Dasco Cold Chisel, 35; Concrete

Point, 35; Target Head Brick
Chisel, 253
Daubert Easy-Mask Tape, 118
Dayton Two-Tube Fluorescent Light
Fixture, 201
Dayton Walther Marvel All American
Refrigerator, 288
d-Con four/gone, 186
Deco-Cork, 195
Decro-Wall Paneling, 63; Wallpaper
In Squares, 69
Deflect-O Deflectors, 257; Vinyl
Weatherstripping, 96; 111
Deft Interior Clean Wood Finish,
141
DEGLOSSERS
Charles Paint Researchers Paint
Deglossers Paso, 116
Red Devil D.I.Y. Deglosser, 119
DEHUMIDIFIERS
Coughlan De-Moist Dehumidifier
And Air Freshener, 185
Malco Hum-i-dri, 273
Valley Dehumidifier, 185
Wizard Dehumidifier, 272
Del-Mar Woven Wood Shades, 97
Devoe Vinyl Acrylic Latex Paint, 114;
Mirrothane Polyurethane Var-
nish, 136
Dewey & Almy Colorundum
Dry-Shake Colors, 229
Dialoc Door Locks, 144
DIMMERS
GE Premier Dimmer, 25
Hemco Dimmer Switch, 24
Leviton Dimmer Socket, 26;
In-Line Dimmer, 25; Table Top
Dimmer, 25
DISHWASHERS
Frigidaire Electri-Saver Portable
Dishwasher, 287
Whirlpool SDU9000 Built-In Dish-
washer, 287
Disston Pruning Saws, 218; Retract-
able Steel Rule, 47; Teflon-
Coated Circular Saw Blades,
181
Dog Dor Magnetic Door, 199
Door Products Garage Door Rollers,
107
DOORBELLS
Nu-Tone Accent Chimes, 28;
Monticello Chimes, 28
DOOR HARDWARE
Hager Door Hinge, 102
Stanley Bi-fold Hardware, 104
Weiser Accent Ceramic Knobs,
171
DOORS
Allastics Cellwood Door Systems,
102
Como SF Bi-fold Door, 102
Dog Dor Magnetic Door, 199
Flex Port Two-Way Pet Door, 198
Reynolds Sunliners Glass Doors,
103
Urethane Arts Norwood Doors,
155
Double J. Systems Sparkledry Dish
Drainer, 164
Douglas Model A6690 Vacuum, 280
Dow Chemical Styrofoam TG, 266
Dow Corning Silicone Rubber Coat-
ing, 37
DOWELS
Arco Dowel Center, 127
Craftwood Moldings And Dowels,
158
Dowling Miner Magnetics Tool Stor-
age Bar, 206
Down Spout-O-Matic, 35
Drackett Drano Instant Plunger, 14;
Renuzit, 49
DRAINAGE SYSTEMS
Advanced Drainage System, 238
Nibcoware Drain System Kits, 8
DRAIN OPENERS
Clorox Liquid-Plumr, 15
CPM Solvent, 15
Drackett Drano Instant Plunger,
14
Spin-Thru Drain Cleaner, 14

DRAPERY HARDWARE
Marshall-McMurray Accent Fold
System, 98; Aluma Track, 98
DRAWERS
Freedman Artcraft Engineering
Drawermaster, 169
Rubbermaid Spacemaker Draw-
ers, 164
DRAWER SLIDES
Amerock Tri-Roller Drawer Slide,
195
Belwith Accuride Drawer Slides,
130
Knape & Vogt Drawer Slides, 131
Dremel Electric Engraver, 207;
Moto-Lathe, 127; Moto-Shop
Scroll Saw, 127; Variable
Speed Moto-Tool, 127
DRILL BITS AND BRACES
Century Drill & Tool Drill Stop, 161
Fuller Ratchet Bit Brace, 179
General Hardware Car-
bide-Tipped Masonry Bits, 51;
Drill Bit Case, 207; Set, 51
Irwin Auger Bits, 179
Plexiglas Drill Bits, 160
Trojan Wood Screw Countersink
Bit Set, 175
DRILL PRESSES
Shopmaster 24-inch Radial Arm
Drill Press, 203
Smithshop All-Purpose Power
Tool, 127
DRILLS
J. C. Penney Triple Action Drill, 168
Stanley Automatic Return Push
Drill, 155
Star Expansion Drill, 209
Vaco Ratchet Screwdriver, 105
Wen Variable-Speed Drill, 126
Dry-Mix Concrete Far-Go Cement
Colors, 229; Concrete
Krak-Kalk, 233
DRYWALL PARTITIONS
Standard Drywall Products
Thoro-System, 37
USG Drywall Partitions, 55
DUCTING
Leigh Ducting Kit, 284
Thermal Metalflex Ducting, 284
Duo-Fast Electric Staple Gun, 93
DuPont Corian Artificial Marble, 143;
Lucite Exterior Stain, 115; One
Step Polyurethane Stain And
Finish, 137
Dur-A-Flex Floor Covering, 42
Durham Rock Hard Water Putty, 108
Duro Art Stenciling Kit, 141
Eagle Cartridge Fuses, 22; Cord
Connector, 32; Grounded
Duplex Receptacle, 27; Elec-
trical Tape, 32; Handi-Mount
Transformer, 28; Jiffy
Push-Pull Plug, 29; Kwiklok
Plugs and Connectors, 29;
"O.K." Fuse, 22; Quiet Switch,
24; Solderless Connectors, 31;
Standard Socket Replace-
ments, 26
EAR PLUGS
Fibre-Metal Shoplyne Ear Plugs,
201
Easco Barracuda Bar, 90; Brick
Trowels, 253; Dyna-Mo, 90;
Hammers, 70; Screwdrivers,
110; Step-Edger Tools, 248
Easy Heat Heat Tape, 20
Eclipse Saw, 191
Elco Wood Screws, 160
ELECTRICAL OUTLETS AND
SWITCHES
Eagle Grounded Duplex Recep-
tacle, 27; Quiet Switch, 24
GE CO/ALR Fixtures, 24
Nelco Duplex Heating Recep-
tacle, 263
Switchpack Surface Switch, 25
Electricord Outdoor Extension
Cords, 242
Elephant Steel Wool, 44
Eller Spee-Dee Mitt, 122
Elmer's Acrylic Latex Blacktop Crack

Sealer, 251; Acrylic Latex
Caulk, 101; Carpenter's Wood
Glue, 125; Concrete Bonder,
250; Cove Base Adhesive, 62;
Heavy Grip Cement, 43; Latex
Base Contact Cement, 157;
Slide-All Spray Lubricant, 131;
Two-Part Waterproof Glue, 38;
Waterproof Glue, 38; Wood
Glue, 125
Emco Decorator Beams, 82; Modular
Furniture, 166
Emerson Portable Baseboard Heat-
er, 263
EMERY CLOTHS
Carborundum Emery Cloth, 6
Enderes Pry Bar, 85
End Stat, 48
ENGRAVERS
Dremel Electric Engraver, 207
ENM Tapeless Measure, 33
ESB Epoxybond Plumber Seal, 11
Esmay Spritzer, 186
Estwing Claw Hammer, 72;
Mini-Saw, 111; Shingling
Hatchet, 235; Trim Square, 152
Evans Aristocrat Chalk Line, 235;
Chalk-Mor Plumb Bob And
Chalk Line, 159; Thin Tapes,
153
Exact Aluminum Rule, 76; C-Clamp,
181; Level, 252
Excell Moth Protection Chemicals,
187
Exelon FillValve Unit, 17
EXHAUST FANS
Kool-O-Matic Attic Ventilator,
268; Cable Electric Ventilator,
268
Rittenhouse Exhaust Fan, 269
EXTENSION CORDS
Pacific-Electricord Outdoor Ex-
tension Cords, 242
E-Z Paintr Tray, 112; Paint Rollers,
124
EZ Plumb Flexible Copper Con-
nectors, 295; Ice Maker Or Hu-
midifier Installation Kit, 288;
Toilet Installation Kit, 16
Farberware Turbo-Oven, 292
FASTENERS
Power Products Remington
Fastening System, 208
FAUCET PARTS
Bowers Replacement Handles, 12
Bradley Faucet Valve, 13
Hancock-Gross Faucet Seats, 12;
Washers, 13
FAUCET TOOLS
Hancock-Gross Seat Wrench, 12;
Socket Wrench Set, 13
O'Malley Drip Stopper Kit, 13
Federal Housewares Mr. Twister
Wringer Bucket, 44
Ferum Plastic Pole Sockets, 162
Fibre-Metal Shoplyne Ear Plugs, 201;
Xtralite Softies Safety Goggles,
248
FILES
Nicholson Chainsaw File Guide,
224; File Pak, 210; Rasp, 178
Skokie Saw & Tools Mill File, 156
Filon Fiberglass Panels, 230
FINISHES, WOOD
American Art Clay Rub 'n Buff
Decorator Finish, 140
H. Behlen Shellac Sticks, 133
Behr Process Build 50 Finish, 141
Cook Varnish, 140
Deft Interior Clean Wood Finish,
141
DeVoe Mirrorthane Polyurethane
Varnish, 136
DuPont One Step Polyurethane
Stain And Finish, 137
Flecto Varathane Liquid Plastic,
139
GAF Brite-Bond, 42
General Finishes 1-2-3 Beautiful
Wood Kit, 139
Minwax Finishing Wax, 138
New York Bronze Powder Co.
Shellac, 130

Pierce & Stevens Fabulon
Finishes, 45
PPG Rez Water Based Varnish,
139
Sunnyside Linseed Oil, 138
United Gilsonite Wipe-On Zar, 139
Watco Danish Oil Finish, 138;
Teak Oil Finish, 138
William Zinsser Bulls Eye Shellac,
138
Zynolite Clear Spray Shellac, 142
Flashband Aluminum Tape, 237
Flecto Varathane Liquid Plastic, 139
Fletcher-Terry Gold Tip Glass Cut-
ters, 88
Flex Port Two-Way Pet Door, 198
Flintcoat Almeira Tiles, 43
Flood E-B Paint Conditioner, 115
FLOOD PREVENTION AND CON-
TROL DEVICES
General Wire Flood Guard, 9
Simer Pud-L-Scoop, 36
Fluidmaster Flusher Fixer Kit, 16;
400-A Ballcock Kit, 16; "Trou-
bleshooter's Guide To A Noisy
Toilet Tank," 17
FLUORESCENT LIGHTS
American Fluorescent Con-
vert-A-Lite, 30
Dayton Two-Tube Light Fixture,
201
L & L Fluorescent Fixture, 30
FLUORESCENT STARTERS
GE Watch Dog Fluorescent Start-
er, 30
Focal Point Moldings, 71
Formby's Refinisher, 135
Fort Steuben Shelving Units, 183
Franklin Concrete Adhesive, 246
Freedman Artcraft Drawermaster
Units, 169
Frigidaire Electri-Saver Portable
Dishwasher, 287
Fuel Sentry Automatic Thermostat
Control, 262
Fuller Ratchet Bit Brace, 179; Super
Quality Screwdrivers, 162
H. B. Fuller Silicone Sealer and Pol-
ish, 52
Fulton Pegboard Hooks, 65
FURNITURE LEGS
Gerber Wooden Replacement
Legs, 128
FURNITURE REPAIR COMPOUNDS
H. Behlen & Brother Shellac
Sticks, 133
Magic American Chemical
Scratch Magic, 132
Santash, 133
Vaseline Petroleum Jelly, 133
FUSE PULLERS
Bussman Fuse Pullers, 23
FUSES
Buss Fustat Type S Fuse, 23
Eagle Cartridge Fuse, 22; "O.K."
Fuse, 22
Montgomery Ward Mini Breaker
Fuse, 22
GAF Brite-Bond Floor Finish, 42;
GAFSTAR Flooring, 42
Galaxy Chemical Seep-Seal, 18
GALVANIZING
LPS Instant Cold Galvanize, 240
GARAGE DOOR PRODUCTS
Clopay Overhead Door Cables
And Pulleys, 106
Door Products Garage Door Roll-
ers, 107
Montgomery Ward Sliding Garage
Door Hardware, 106
Overhead Door Series 125 Garage
Door, 106
Sears Garage Door Digital Con-
trols, 105
Garco Stow Rack, 183
Garelick Roof Snow Rake, 242
Garrett Wade Danish Folding Bench,
204
GAS STOPS
Rockwell Gas Stop, 259
GATES
Johnson E-Z Tach Gate, 192

315

Gates Rubber V-Belt, 296
General Bathroom Crown Oval Medicine Chest, 172
GE Appliance Cords, 32; CO/ALR Fixtures, 24; Dishwasher Hook-Up Kit, 286; Electrical Tape, 32; Electrostatic Air Cleaner, 256; Executive Gas Furnace, 259; Heat Pump, 257; Home Sentry Timer, 144; Premier Dimmer, 25; Quick Clamp Plugs, 29; Sculpturesque Pushbutton Doorbell, 28; Silicone Bathtub Caulk and Seal, 53; Watch Dog Fluorescent Starter, 30
General Finishes 1-2-3 Beautiful Wood Kit, 139
General Hardware Carbide Tipped Masonry Bits, 51; Combination Square Drill Bit Case, 207; Scratch Awls, 94
General Products Recyclo-Heater, 256
General Wire Flood Guard, 9
Genova Rigid Vinyl Pipe, 7; Snap-Fit Roof Flashings, 237
Georgia-Pacific Denswall Wall Texture, 58; Vinyl Shield PVC Moldings, 71
Gerber Replacement Furniture Legs, 128
Gerson Child-Safe Razor Blade Scraper, 118; Paint Straining Kit, 117, Utility Knife, 80
GFA Nerak Coping Sections, 232
Gibson Gripper, 179
Gibson-Homans Black Jack Plastic Roofing Cement, 236; Handi-Gard Driveway Patching Compound, 251; Handi-Patch Tape, 241; Tile Grout With Silicone, 52
Gilbert & Bennett Hex Netting, 182
Giles & Kendall Flakeboard Cedar Panels, 177
Gill Tube Wringer, 101
Gilmour Air-O-Matic Sprayer, 187
GLASS CUTTING TOOLS
    T. A. Altender Straightedge, 88
    Fletcher-Terry Gold Tip Cutters, 88
    Red Devil Vacuum Cup, 88
GLAZING COMPOUNDS
    DAP '33' Glazing Compound, 87
Glidden Spred Gel-Flo Exterior Alkyd Paint, 114
Globe Venetian Blind Renew Kit, 99
GLOVES
    Boss Horsehide Work Gloves, 225
    Pioneer Bluettes Rubber Gloves, 201
    Wells Lamont White Mule Work Gloves, 255

GLUES, see ADHESIVES
Goddard Marble Stain Remover & Polish, 143
GOGGLES
    American Optical Safeline Safety Products, 201
    Fibre-Metal Shoplyne Xtralite Softies Safety Goggles, 248
    Vaughan & Bushnell Goggles, 209
Goldblatt Tool Concrete Placer, 228; Flex Metal Corner Tape, 57; Multi-Position Ladder, 89
Gold Bond Abstract Ceiling Tiles, 78; Ceiling Grid Kit 81; Clip-Strip Ceiling Tile Channels, 78
Golden Star Polish Mar-Glo Marble Polish, 143
Gold Seal Electrical Tape, 32
Goodyear Plio-Nail Panel Adhesive, 63
G.Q.F. Pet Watering Dish, 198
Granberry Rack-A-Tool, 221
Grayline Beverage Can Dispenser, 289; Freezer Storage Rack, 289; Vacuum Accessory Kaddy, 281
Great Neck Little Shaver Plane, 131;
316

Putty Knife, 72; Cold Chisel, 248; Hand-Drilling Hammer, 246; Stainless Steel Handsaw, 184; Swivel Snaps, 165
Greenford Happy II Radiant Heater, 260
GREENHOUSES
    Casa Mini Greenhouse, 227
    Redwood Domes Greenhouse Kit, 227
Greenview Arrow Combination Window Cleaner, 89
Greenview Crabicide Green, 214
GRILLS
    Hearth Craft Pow-Wow Portable Grill, 231
    Swaniebraai Newspaper Grill, 231
    Temco Regency Twin Gas Grill, 231
GROUT
    Bondex Tile Grout, 51
    Gibson-Homans Tile Grout With Silicone, 52
GROUT CLEANERS AND SEALERS
    H.B. Fuller Silicone Sealer And Polish, 52
    Magic American Tile, 'N Grout Spray, 52
Grrip Pipe Joint Compound, 11
Guardian Service Pre-Entry Door Alarm, 148
Gulfwax Paraffin, 130
GUTTERS AND DOWNSPOUTS
    AAA Up The Downspout, 239
    Down Spout-O-Matic, 35
    Reeves Style K Prepaint Gutters, 239
    Reynolds Colorweld Aluminum Gutters and Downspouts, 238
GUTTER GUARDS
    Conwed Gutter Guard, 241
GX International Space Age Caulk, 190
GYPSUM
    USG Sof 'n-Soil, 215
Hager Corner Braces, 41; Door Hinge, 102; Cabinet Hardware, 154
HAMMERS
    Easco Hammers, 70
    Estwing Claw Hammer, 72
    Great Neck Hand-Drilling Hammer, 246
    Plumb Hammers, 85
    Stanley Framing Hammer, 54
    True Temper Rocket Brick Hammer, 253
    Tru Test Supreme Hammer,175
    Utica Tool Bonney Rubber Tire mallet, 125
    Vaughan & Bushnell Ball Peen Hammer, 40; Hollow Core Handle Hammer, 108; Value Brand Drilling Hammer, 209
Hancock-Gross Boiler Repair Plugs, 9; Dishwasher Connector, 286; Disposer Clearing Wrench, 279; Faucet Seat Wrench, 12; Oil Burner Replacement Parts, 261; Replacement Disposer Splash Guard, 278; Socket Wrench Set, 13; Teflon Thread Dope, 10; Washers, 13
Handy Horses Sawhorses, 204
HAND SAWS, see SAWS, HAND
HANGERS
    Dalton Thrif-T Hanger And Hang-It-All Brackets, 221
    Gibson Gripper, 179
    Moore Hardwall Hangers, 74
    Platt Finger Grip Adjustable Clips, 179
    SMC Hang-It-Up Hanger, 221; No. 16 Utility Storage Hangers, 197
    Stik Tabs, 74
    USM Molly Bolts, 75
HARD HATS
    American Optical Safeline Safety Hat, 201
Harrington Tools Hawk, 254; Throw Away Spreader, 42
Hargrave Mitre Frame Clamp, 76

Hart Fireplace Furnishings, 274
Hartline Products Rockite, 249
HAWKS
    Harrington Tool Hawk, 254
    Red Devil Dry Wall Hawk, 56
HC Products Vent-A-Ridge System, 269
Hearth Craft Pow-Wow Portable Grill, 231
HEAT DEFLECTORS
    Aristo-Mat Deflex Deflectors, 257
    Deflect-O Deflectors, 257
HEATER FILTERS
    Amer-Glas Heater Filters, 259
    Phifer Air-Weave Filters, 258
Heath Heathkit V.O.M. Kit, 277
Heatilator Fireplace Ash Dump and Cleanout Door, 274
HEAT PUMPS
    Chrysler Air Temp Heat Pump, 257
    General Electric Heat Pump, 257
    Westinghouse Heat Pump, 257
HEAT REGISTERS AND DAMPERS
    Trol-A-Temp Registers And Dampers, 257
HEAT TAPES AND CABLES
    Easy Heat Tape, 20
    Thermwell Frost King Automatic Electric Heat Cable, 20
    Wrap-On Heat Tape, 20; Ice Guard Heat Cable, 242
Heirloom Crafts Decotiques, 141
Helistrand Mark II Bicycle Cable, 196
Hemco Dimmer Switch, 24; Model SAR-12 Appliance Roller Set, 241
Henkel Wallcovering Pastes And Adhesives, 84
Hercules SWIF Solder Paste, 287; U-can Make Roof Repairs, 241
Hide-A-Pipe Vanitique, 171
Hillwood Helyx Concrete Screws, 228
HINGES
    Acorn Butterfly Hinges, 168
    Chicago Specialty Toilet Seat Hinge, 19
    Hager Cabinet Hardware, 154; Door Hinge, 102
    Safe Cabinet Hinges And Catches, 171
    Soss Invisible Hinges, 194
HIP PADS
    McGuire-Nicholas Hip Pad, 243
HOBBY TOOLS
    Dremel Variable Speed Moto-Tool, 127
    X-PO Hobby Knife, 76
Homecraft Futura Hooks, 74; Locking Peg Panel Hooks, 65
Home Guide To Plumbing, Heating And Air Conditioning, 8
Honeywell Chronotherm Temperature Control, 262; Humidity Controller, 273
Hopkins Sevin Insect Control, 188
HOSE AND NOZZLES
    Armstrong LTG System Hose Nozzle
    Colorite Garden Hose, 250
HOT WATER DISPENSERS
    In-Sink-Erator Steaming H₂0 Tap, 295
Howard Hardware Sandpaper, 130; Wire Brushes, 86
Howmet Aluminum Valleys, 237
HUMIDIFIER CLEANER AND DEODORIZER
    Cosco Solution 24, 273; Solution 26, 273
HUMIDIFIERS
    Leigh Turbo-Flo Humidifier, 272
HUMIDISTATS
    Honeywell Humidity Controller, 273
Huron Products Doggie Dooley, 199
Hyde Century Trimmer, 68; Electric Paint Remover, 39; One Arm Paperhanger, 73; Putty Knife, 69; Side Arm Seam Roller, 73
Illinois Bronze Powder Chalk Board

Spray Paint, 200
Imperial Alarm Screens, 149
Independent Kolorpin Nails, 111; Screw-Tite Nails, 111; Stronghold Nails, 111
Indestro Classic Long-Nosed Pliers, 27; MPI Socket Wrench Set, 105; Stillson Wrench, 6
Indian Head Gold Metal Cotton Cord, 99
Industrial Petrolic Monkey Wrench Penetrating Oil, 212
Innovative Audio Tim-Can Kit, 195
INSULATION
    Certain-teed Duct Wrap Insulation, 258; Fiberglass Insulation, 267
    Dow Chemical Styrofoam TG Insulation, 266
    Johns-Manville Reinsul Fiberglass Insulation, 267; Water Insulation Kit, 294
    Masterworks Water Heater Overcoat, 294
    Owens-Corning Fiberglas Batts, 191; Fiberglass Blowing Wool, 266
    Teledyne Mono-Thane Pipe Cover, 191
Intertherm Baseboard Heater, 263
Ironworks Hill Hew-Do-It, 83
Irwin Auger Bit, 179; Strait-Line Chalk Line Reel, 59
Jack-Post Tiger Jack Posts, 34
JACK POSTS
    Adjusta-Post Telescoping Supports, 34
    Jack-Post Tiger Jack Posts, 34
    Montgomery Ward Heavy-Duty Jack Screw, 34
Jackson Ropes, 243
Jack The Stripper, 135
Jade Thermocouple, 275; Thermostats, 262
Jandy Leaf-Master, 233
JARS
    Wickliffe Handy Dandy Jars, 64
Jefco Wood Screws, 40
J-E Hearth-Flo Heater, 261
Jenn Air Grill Range, 292
Jer 'Lil' Red Barn Kit, 227
Jiffy Toilet Seat Bumpers, 19; Friction Catch, 175; Spring And Roller Catch, 174
Johns-Manville Reinsul Fiberglass Insulation, 267; Water Insulation Kit, 294; Whispertone Fiberglass Panels, 190
C. J. Johnson E-Z Tach Gate, 192
Johnson Shockproof Aluminum Level, 35
Johnson Waxes, 44
Jordan Handyman's Fastening Kit, 176; Jord-Eze Anchors, 74; Screw Hooks, 165; Shoulder Hooks, 65; Turnbuckle, 94
Jorgensen Band Clamp, 126; Handscrew Clamp, 126; Pony Clamp, 126
Judson Knee Pads, 213
Jupiter Pipe Joint Compound, 11
Kagil Spatter Shield, 113
E. A. Karay Quick-Link Chain Connector, 165
Kedman Quick-Wedge Screwdriver, 151
F. D. Kees Stur-D Bridging, 38; Timberlock Framing Anchors, 33
Kelley KC-5 Big Red Wheelbarrow, 246; Pail, 274
Kentile Delhi Tiles, 43
Kindergard Latches, 192
King Cotton Sash Cord, 90
Kirkhill Plumber's Pliers, 261; Replacement Disposer Stopper, 278
Kirsch Cranmere Shelving, 166
Klise Accent Picture Frame Moldings, 77
Knape & Vogt Drawer Slides, 131; Shelf Standards And Clips,

153; Shelf Units, 167; Tite-Joint Fastener, 128

KNEE PADS
Judson Knee Pads, 213

KNIVES
American Carpet Cutter Knife, 50
Arylan Industries Cutter, 157
BernzCutter Cutting Tool, 156
Buck Knives, 41
Gerson Utility Knife, 80
Marshalltown Iowa Broad Knife, 56
Schrade Cutlery Old Timer Pocket Knife, 95
X-PO Hobby Knife, 76

Kool-O-Matic Attic Ventilator, 268; Gable Electric Ventilator, 268
Koppers Fence Posts, 223
Korky Flapper, 17
Kwikset Exterior Alarm Bell, 149; Jig, 146
La-Co Pipe Joint Compound, 11

LADDER ANCHORS
Saf-T-Arm, 243

LADDERS
Bauer Aluminum Ladder, 33
Goldblatt Multi-Position Ladder, 89
Montgomery Ward Five-In-One Ladder, 182
Multi-Purpose Ladder, 62
R. D. Werner Saf-T-Master Ladder, 241

Lafayette Continuity Tester, 276
Lake Chemical Krak Stik, 10

LAMINATE CUTTERS
Arlyn Industries Ltd. Cutter, 157

LAMINATE ROLLERS
Minnesota Woodworkers Jay Roller, 156
Niemi Rollo Press, 156

L & L Fluorescent Fixture, 30

LATHES
Dremel Moto-Lathe, 127
Smithshop All-Purpose Power Tool, 127

Leigh Products Dryer Exhaust Kit, 284
Leigh Adjustable Steel Closet Shelves, 173; Klip-Lock Suspension System, 80; Brick Ventilator, 268; Light Diffusing Panels, 80; Mini Trio Medicine Chest, 172; Thermo-Base Duct Heating System, 263; Trio Medicine Chest, 172; Turbo-Flo Humidifier, 272

LEVELS
Exact Level & Tool Level, 252
Johnson Shockproof Aluminum Level, 35
Mayes Brothers Pocket Level, 239; Ultimate Level, 153
Pro Products Inclonometer and Level, 239; Ultimate Level, 153
Rathbone Chesterman Tuflite Level, 54
Ridgid Tool Line Level, 253
Skokie Saw & Tool Level, 34
Stanley 18-inch Lightweight Level, 155
Trophy Torpedo Level, 208

Leviton Decora Switches And Receptacles, 25; Dimmer Socket, 26; In-Line Dimmer, 25; Tabletop Dimmer, 25

LIGHT FIXTURES
American Fluorescent Convert-A-Lite, 30
Dayton Two-Tube Light Fixture, 201
L & L 18-Inch Fluorescent Fixture, 30

LIGHT SWITCHES
Eagle Quiet Switch, 24
Hemco Dimmer Switch, 24
Leviton Decora Designer, 25; Kwikwire Switch, 25
Switchpack Systems, 25

LINE BLOCKS
UB Tool Line Blocks, 252

Liquid Wrench, 212

Little Giant Workhorses, 93
Litton Model 630 Range, 293

LOCKS AND SECURITY DEVICES
Belwith Lock Plate, 144
Bowmar Digital Combination Entrance Control, 148; Trap Mat, 148
Dalton Katy-Bar Sliding Door Lock, 145
Dialoc Door Lock, 144
Heilistrand Mark II Bicycle Cable, 196
Imperial Screen Alarm Systems, 149
Lock Plate, 144
Loxem Door Chain, 148; Window Lock, 264
J. C. Penney Gard-Site Security System, 149
Schlage "G" Series Locks, 146
Sears Garage Door Digital Control, 105
Simplex Pushbutton Security System, 147
Sunbeam Stop Alarm, 145
Torch Side Lock, 107
Yale Bored Auxiliary Lock, 147; Disc Tumbler Window Lock, 264; Rim Lock, 147; 7200 Padlock, 145

Long-Bell Cabinet Components, 170
Loxem Door Chain, 148; Latch Window Lock, 264
LPS Instant Cold Galvanize, 240; Lubrication Sprays, 105

LUBRICANTS
American Grease Stick Sil-Glyde, 85
Arkansas Abrasives Indian Mountain Honing Oil, 210
Boyle-Midway 3-in-1 Lubricating Oil, 297
Cling-Surface TFE Dry Film Lubricant, 41
Elmer's Slide-All Spray Lubricant, 131
Gulfwax Paraffin, 130
Industrial Petrolic Monkey Wrench Penetrating Oil, 212
Liquid Wrench, 212
LPS Lubrication Sprays, 105
Panef Fan Belt V-Belt Dressing, 296; Lub-A-Lite, 38
Pennzoil Pennz-Guard Spray Lube, 277
Permatex Penetrating Oil, 212
Plasti-Kote Spray Belt Dressing, 296
*Radiator Specialty Liquid Wrench No.2, 212
Rockford Gas Stop Lubricants, 259
Seymour Lube Kit, 212
Seymour of Sycamore, 212
Superior Graphite Slip Plate No. 3, 217
WD-40 Spray Lube, 212
Woodhill Duro Belt Grip Belt Dressing, 296

Lufkin Mezurlock Power Tape, 54, 98; Folding Tape, 54; White Tape, 54
Macco Liquid Patch, 254; Liquid Seal Tub & Tile Caulk, 53; Spacko, 61; Super Caulk, 100
Magic American Appliance Magic Cleaner, 291; Magic Liquid Stitch, 99; Marble Magic Cleaner, 143; Rid 'O' Rust, 123; Scratch Magic, 132; Tile 'N Grout Spray, 52
Magic Chef Gas Ranges, 290
Magnolia Toilet Seat, 19
Malco Hum-I-Dri, 273

MALLETS
Utica Tool Bonney Rubber Tire Mallet, 125

Mantrose-Haeuser Room Groom, 84
Manhattan Brush Poxymix Concrete Repair Mix, 247
Marion Tool Tamper, 245
Marshall-McMurray Accent Fold System, 98; Aluma Track, 98

Marshalltown Iowa Broad Knife, 56; Taping Knife, 56; Bull Float, 244; Trowels, 244
Martin-Senour Antiquing Kit, 140
Masonite Marlite Paneling, 62, 63; Nails, 195; "Peg-Board," 65; "Peg-Board" Hooks, 64; Roofing Felt, 236; Roxite Brick Panels, 66
Mayes Brothers Pocket Level, 261; Squangle, 193
Mayhew Nailsets, 70; Steel Ambertuf Butt Chisels, 109
Maytag Model A608 Washing Machine, 283
McGill Mousetraps, 189
McGuire Bamboo Rake, 226
McGuire-Nicholas Hip Pad, 243
M-D Numetal Weatherstrip, 96; Thresholds, 110
Mechanical Plastics Perfect Patch Kit, 61
Mercer Plastics Universal Joiner, 47
Merix Anti-Static, 48
Metal Industries Screen Grills, 198
Michlin Caulking Gun, 100; Mr. Thinzit Concrete Crack Fix, 254; Mr. Thinzit Panel Adhesive MC-98, 82
Mico Caulking Tools, 53
Micro Lambda Electricity Miser, 294
Midget Louvers, 268
Millers Falls Hacksaw, 238; Mitre Box, 77
Miller Studio Magic Mount Hooks, 193
Milwaukee Contractors Saw, 161
Minnesota Woodworkers Jay Roller, 156; Paper-Cane, 142
Minwax Finishing Wax, 138

MITRE BOXES
Millers Falls Mitre Box, 77
Stanley Mitre Box, 72
Modern Methods Brickettes Mini-Panel, 67

Montgomery Ward Bike Rack, 196; Clothes Washer Screens, 282; Dryer Exhaust Kit, 285; Faucet Stem, 12; Five-In-One Ladder, 182; Heavy-Duty Jack Screw, 34; Mini-Breaker Fuse, 22; Powr Kraft Router, 194; Sliding Garage Door Hardware, 106
Moore Hardwall Hangers, 74
Mortell Automatic Door Bottom, 110; Garage Door Top & Sides Weatherstrip, 107; Garage Door Weatherstrip Cushion, 107; NoDrip Plastic Coating, 36; NoDrip Tape, 36; Transparent Weatherstrip Tape, 96; Windowseal, 265
M-P Safe-T-Disc, 226
M-R Products Mr. Chain, 165
MTI Rotarul, 191
Multi-Purpose Ladder, 62
Muralo Adhesium Wall Sizing, 69; Exterior Spackle, 113; Spackle, 113; Sta-Patch, 250
Murray-Black Electromatic Wallpaper Remover, 84; Paste-Bak, 73; Plaster-Stik, 61; Pointing Trowel, 255
My-Ro CarpeTape, 50; Tub 'N Wall Seal-A-Crack, 53

NAILSETS
Mayhew Nailsets, 70

NAIL STRIPPERS
Roofmaster Nail Strippers, 243
NanKee ST-100 Paint Thinner, 132
National Casein "DR" Powdered Resin Glue, 161
National Cup Pulls, 163
National Gypsum Clip Strip System, 79
National Recessed Cabinets Handy-Can Cupboard, 168
National Solvent Turpex, 136
National So-Soft Toilet Seat, 19
Nelco Baseboard Heating System, 263; Duplex Heating Receptacle, 263

New Delphos Gasoline Can, 226
Newell Caning Kit, 142
Newell Window Products Magic Fit Shades, 97
New England Masonry Cutting Blades, 247
New York Bronze Powder Clear Shellac, 130
Nibcoware Drain System Kits, 8
Nichols-Homestead Hy-Tensil Nails, 222
Nicholson Chain Saw File Guide, 224; Handyman's Home File Pak, 210; Nest of Saws, 169; Professional Cross Cut Saw, 55; Rasp, 178; Saws, 203
Niemi Rollo Press, 156
Northland Woods Ruff 'N Ready Shelving, 178
Normark Fiskars Scissors, 110
Norton Bear Sanders, 116
NuTone Accent Chimes, 28; Corner Vista Cabinets, 172; Monticello Chimes, 28

OILS, see LUBRICANTS
O'Malley Drip Stopper Kit, 13; Hair Snare, 14
Omega Utility Bar, 70
Onan Standby Power System, 23
C.S. Osborne Jointer, 254; Knee Kicker, 46
Overhead Door Series 125 Garage Doors, 106
Over-The-Rod Hanging Shoe Rack, 173
Owens-Corning Fiberglas Batts, 191; Fiberglas Blowing Wool, 266
Padco Corner Paint Pad, 113; Paint Box Bucket, 114; Paint Spreaders, 118; Wallpaper Smoother & Applicator, 68

PAILS AND BUCKETS
Federal Housewares Mr. Twister Wringer Bucket, 44
Kelley Pail, 274
Padco Paint Box Bucket, 114
Texamar Fortex Rubber Bucket, 255
Wooster MagiKoter Handy Bucket, 112

PAINTBRUSH CLEANERS
Red Devil D.I.Y. Sav-A-Brush Cleaner, 121
National Solvent Turpex, 136
Savogran Kwikeeze Brush Cleaner, 121; TSP Brush Cleaner, 121
Sunnyside Liquid Brush Cleaner, 120

PAINTBRUSHES AND ROLLERS
Adams Big Job Paint Kit, 114
E-Z Paintr Rollers, 124
H & G Ruff-Rider Masonry Brush, 124; Tynex Nylon Paint Brushes, 115
Wonder Color Brushes, 116
Wooster MagiKoter Brush, 112

PAINTER'S ACCESSORIES
Eller Spee-Dee Mitt, 122
E-Z Paintr Tray, 112
Gerson Child-Safe Razor Blade Scraper, 118; Paint Straining Kit, 117
Kagil Spatter Shield, 113
Padco Corner Paint Pad, 113; Paint Box Bucket, 114; Paint Spreaders, 118
Pour-Ezee Spout, 112
Preval Spraymaker Aerosol Power Unit, 122
Red Devil Brush Comb & Roller Cleaning Tool, 120; Dual Trim Guard, 119; Paint Scraper, 117; Plastic Drop Cloths, 119
Paint Master Poxymix Dry Paint, 124

PAINT REMOVERS
Formby's Refinishers, 135
Hyde Electric Paint Remover, 39
Jack The Stripper, 135
RAP Paint And Varnish Remover, 134
Savogran H$_2$0 Paint Remover,

134; Kutzit Paint Remover, 134; Stripeeze Paint Remover, 134
PAINTS
Armstrong Du-Kwik Acrylic Latex Enamel, 193
Benjamin Moore Regal Latex Enamel, 113
DAP Derusto Little Job Spray Enamel, 122
Devoe Vinyl Acrylic Latex Paint, 114
DuPont Lucite Exterior Stain, 115
Glidden Spred Gel-Flo Exterior Paint, 114
Illinois Bronze Powder Chalk Board Spray Paint, 200
Paint Master Poxymix Dry Paint, 124
Plasti-Kote Spray Paint, 182
Pliolite Waterproof Paint, 36
Pratt And Lambert Aqua-Satin Enamel, 118; Pool Shield Paint, 232; Vapex Flat Wall Paint, 118
Rust-Oleum Speedy Dry Aerosol Paint, 122
Sears Epoxy Concrete Enamel, 124
Seymour Epoxy Appliance Refinishing Kit, 282
Tru-Test Supreme Spray Paint, 180
Zynolyte 1000F Hi-Temp Spray Paint, 142, 231
PAINT THINNERS
NanKee ST-100 Paint Thinner, 132
National Solvents Turpex, 166
Sunnyside Specs Paint Thinner, 116
T & R Chemicals Nu-Turp, 121
Panef Fan Belt V-Belt Dressing, 296; Lub-A-Lite, 38
PANELING
Decro-Wall Tudor Panels, 63
Masonite Marlite Panels, 62; 63
Panel Magic, 62
Panelmatch Nails, 63
Park Carpenter's Tool Box, 207
PATCHING PRODUCTS
Durham Rock Hard Putty, 108
Hartline Rockite Patching Compound, 249
Hercules U-Can Make Roof Repairs, 241
Macco-Spacko, 61
Mechanical Plastics Perfect Patch Kit, 61
Murray-Black Plaster Stick, 61
Stay-Tite Roof Cement, 236
Tremco Instant Patch, 234
Tuff-Kote Krack-Kote, 60
PEGBOARD
Masonite "Peg-Board," 65
PEGBOARD HOOKS AND HANGERS
Fulton Perfix Pegboard Hooks, 65
Homecraft Locking Peg Panel Hooks, 65
Masonite Peg-Board Fixtures, 64
Wickliffe Handy Dandy Jars, 64
Pendleton Studios Stained Glass, 95
J.C. Penney Gard-Site Security System, 149; Textured Shade, 97; Triple Action Drill, 168
Pennzoil Pennz-Guard Spray Lube, 277
Pentapco Teflon-F Coated Sewing Machine Needles, 297
Permatex Penetrating Oil, 212
Pentapes Teflon-F Coated Sewing Machine Needles, 297
Peterson Vise-Grip Pliers, 129
Phifer Wire Air-Weave Filters, 258, Sun Screens, 93
Philstone Threaded Nails, 40
PICTURE FRAMES
Kise Accent Picture Frame Moldings, 77
Pierce & Stevens Fabulon Finishes, 45
Pioneer Bluettes Rubber Gloves, 201
Pipe Seal, 11
PIPE SEALERS
Chicago Specialty Shur-Seal

Pipe-Stik, 11
Dap Mitee Pipe Joint Compound, 11
ESB Epoxybond Plumber Seal, 11
Grrip Pipe Joint Compound, 11
Hancock-Gross Teflon Thread Dope, 10
Jupiter Pipe Joint Compound, 11
La-Co Pipe Joint Compound, 11
Lake Chemical Krak Stik, 10
Mortell NoDrip Plastic Coating, 36; NoDrip Tape, 36
Pipe Seal, 11
Pipette Pipe Joint Compound, 11
ProDope Pipe Joint Compound, 11
Schaul Clamp Leak Stopper Kit, 10
Sealmaster Pipe Joint Compound, 11
Slic-Tite Pipe Joint Compound, 11
PIPES
Cerro Copper Cinch Pipe, 7
Genova Rigid Vinyl Pipe, 7
Pipette Pipe Joint Compound, 11
PLANES
Arco 3-Way Plane, 109
Great Neck Little Shaver Plane, 131
Ironworks Hill Hew-Do-It, 83
Stanley Surform Plane, 157; Surform Shaver, 151
Trimmatool File & Plane, 109
Plaskolite In-Sider Storm Window System, 270
Plasplugs Mini Hacksaw, 60; Quiksand, 154; Plastic Shelf Supports, 166
PLASTIC PLUMBING COMPONENTS
Cerro Cinch-Pipe, 7
Genova Rigid Vinyl Pipe, 7; Novaweld Solvent, 7
Nibcoware Bath Kit, 8
Qest Magic Seal, 7
Plasti-Kote Spray Belt Dressing, 296; Spray Paint, 182
Platt Finger Grip Adjustable Clip, 179
Plexiglas Tools, 160
PLIERS
Channellock Model 415 Pliers, 12
Indestro Long-Nosed Pliers, 27
Kirkhill Plumbers Pliers, 261
Peterson Vise-Grip Pliers, 129
Stanley Electrician's Pliers, 26
Vise-Grip Locking Pliers, 209
Pliolite Waterproof Paints, 36
PLUGS
Eagle Jiffy Push Pull System, 29; Kwiklok Plugs & Connectors, 29
GE Quick Clamp Plug, 29
PLUMB BOBS
Evans Chalk-Mor Plumb Bob and Chalk Line, 14
Irwin Auger Bit Strait-Line Chalk Line Reel, 59
PLUMBING CONNECTORS
EZ Plumb Flexible Copper Connectors, 295
Plumb Craft Guide, 17
Plumb Hammer, 85
Plumbing Repairs Simplified, 8
PLUNGERS
U-Plumb-It Plunger, 15
Water Master Toilaflex, 18
POLISHES AND WAXES
Bon Ami POLISHING Cleanser, 288
Goddard Marble Stain Remover And Polish, 143
Golden Star Mar-Glo Marble Polish, 143
Johnson Waxes, 44
Magic American Appliance Magic Cleaner, 143, 219
Minwax Finishing Wax, 138
Panel Magic, 62
Rubin-Brite Metal Polish, 123
Scott's Liquid Gold, 62
Trewax Paste, 45
Woodhill Duro Aluminum Jelly, 123; Naval Jelly, 123

Pour-Ezee Spout, 112
Poolmaster Heet, 233
Power Products Remington Fastening System, 208
POWER SAWS, see SAWS, POWER
PPG Rez Water Based Varnish, 139
Practical Handbook of Plumbing and Heating, 8
Pratt and Lambert Aqua-Satin Enamel, 118; Pool Shield, 232; Vapex Flat Wall Paint, 118
Preval Spraymaker Aerosol Power Unit, 122
Prestolite Mower Tune-Up Kit, 216
Process Solvent Sure Klean Fireplace Cleaner, 274
Pro Dope Pipe Joint Compound, 11
Products Inclinometer and Level, 239; Ultimate Level, 153
PUTTY KNIVES
Great Neck Putty Knife, 72
Star Bronze Zip-Strip Putty Knife, 86
Warner Putty Knife, 39
Qest Magic Seal Plumbing Parts, 7
Quadmatic Safe-T-Guide Saw Guide, 208
Quaker CBW Window Channels, 91
Quaker Wall Storage Unit, 167
Quality Steel Fold-N-Store Legs, 174
Quickee Waterless Cream Hand Cleaner, 203
Quicker sticker, 119
Quikrete Concrete Mix, 247
Radiator Specialty Liquid Wrench, 212
Rain Bird Sprinkler Quick Connects, 213
Rain Jet Shower of Diamonds Fountain, 229
Rake-O-Matic, 216
RAP Paint and Varnish Remover, 134
Rathbone Chesterman Tuflite Level, 54
Raylor Brad Holder, 180
Ready Heat Roof Cable Kit, 242
Red Devil Brush Comb and Roller Cleaning Tool, 120; Corner Taping Tool, 56; D.I.Y. Deglosser, 119; D.I.Y. Sav-A-Brush Cleaner, 121; Dry Wall Hawk, 56; Dual Trim Guard, 119; Finishing Trowel, 56; Mud Pan, 56; Paint Scraper, 117; Plastic Drop Cloths, 119; "Roller Skate" Joint Raker, 255; Speed Demon Screen Painter, 94; Vacuum Cup, 88; Windo-Zipper, 85
Redwood Domes Greenhouse, 227
Reeves Style K Prepaint Gutters, 239
REFINISHERS
Formby's Refinisher, 135
Seymour Appliance Refinishing Kit, 282
Reflect-O-Lite Flex-Face Hand Sander, 151
REPAIR BOOKS
"How To Install Do-It-Yourself Carpet," 46
Home Guide to Plumbing, Heating & Air Conditioning, 8
Plumbing Repairs Simplified, 8
Practical Handbook Of Plumbing And Heating, 8
Super Handyman's Encyclopedia of Home Repair Hints, 120
Super Handyman's Fix and Finish Furniture Guide, 127
"Trouble Shooter's Guide to a Noisy Toilet," 17
Wiring Simplified, 31
Resin Systems Congard, 245
Reynolds Aluminum Storm Window Frames, 270; Colorweld Aluminum Gutters & Downspouts, 238; Sunliner Glass Doors, 103
Ridgid Aviation Snips, 237; Chain Wrench, 8; Fiberglass Folding Rules, 161; Line Level, 253; Metal Cutting Snips, 237; Strap Wrench, 8
Judd Ringer Compost Bin Kit,

220; Compost Maker Flakes And Tablets, 220; Killer Kane, 213
Rittenhouse Ceiling Light/Exhaust Fan, 269
Rockford Gas Stop Lubricants, 259
Rockford Products Wood Screws, 158
Rockwell Bandsaw, 202; Variable Speed Jig Saw, 173
Rockwell Gas Stop, 259
RODENT POISONS
Chempar Chemical RoZol, 189
Crown Chemicals Pest-Rid, 189
Roe Push-Pull Pocket Tape, 163
Ronson Varaflame Torch, 39
ROOF FLASHINGS
Genova Snap-Fit Roof Flashings, 237
ROOF HEAT CABLES
Ready Heat Roof Cable Kit, 242
ROOFING CEMENTS
Gibson-Homans Black Jack Plastic Roofing Cement, 236
Stay-Tite, 236
ROOFING FELT
Masonite Roofing Felt, 236
ROOFING PATCHES
Hercules U-Can Make Roof Repairs, 241
Tremco Instant Patch, 234
ROOFING VALLEYS
Howmet Aluminum Valleys, 237
Roofmaster Nail Stripper, 243
ROPES AND CORDS
Jackson Ropes, 243
King Cotton Nylon Center Sash Cord, 90
Rosco Screwdrivers, 181
Rotocrop Accelerator Compost Bin, 220
ROUTERS
Montgomery Ward Powr Kraft Router, 194
Skil Model 548 Router, 157
Rubbermaid Garden Carry Caddy, 221; Spacemaker Drawers, 164; Tool Organizer, 206
Rubin-Brite Metal Polish, 123
Rudolph Rudy-Door-Guide, 155
RUG, see CARPET
Ruscoe En-DUR-LON, 233; Permanent-Sealer, 233
Russell Harrington Dexter Mat Cutter, 76
Rust-Oleum 769 Damp-Proof Red Primer, 122; Speedy Dry Aerosol Paint, 122
RUST REMOVERS
Magic American Rid 'O' Rust, 123
Woodhill Duro Aluminum Jelly, 123; Duro Naval Jelly, 123
Rutt Design-A-Wall, 150
Sabre Saw Chain, 225
Safe Cabinet Hinges And Catches, 171
Saf-T-Arm, 243
Sakrete Black Top Patch, 251; Black Top Sealer, 251; Cement Mixes, 244
SANDERS
Black & Decker Finishing Sanders, 163
Norton Bear Sanders, 116
Reflect-O-Lite Flex-Face Hand Sander, 151
Skil Dustless Belt Sander, 45
Smithshop All-Purpose Power Tool, 127
SANDPAPER, see ABRASIVES
Sandvik Fish & Hook Chisel, 175
Santash, 133
Savogran H_2 Off Paint Remover, 134; Kutzit Paint Remover, 134; Kwikeeze Brush Cleaner, 121; Strypeeze Paint Remover, 134; TSP Brush Cleaner, 121
SAWHORSES
Bestop Super-Horse, 204
Dalton SawHorse Brackets, 205
Handy Horses, 204
Little Giant Work Horses, 93
SAW BLADES

Disston Teflon-Coated Circular Saw Blades, 181
New England Masonry Cutting Blades, 247
Simonds Si-Clone Saw Blades, 174
Skokie Chieftain Plywood Blades, 152
Trojan Coping and Jigsaw Blades, 162
SAWS, HAND
Allway Tools Master Saw, 170
Clay Tenon Saw, 180
Disston Pruning Saw, 218
Eclipse Saw, 191
Estwing Mini-Saw, 111
Great Neck Stainless Steel Handsaw, 184
Miller Falls Hacksaw, 238
Nicholson Nest of Saws, 169; Professional Cross-Cut Saw, 55; Saws, 203
Plasplugs Mini Hacksaw, 60
SBI Bushman Hand Saw, 219
Spear & Jackson Spearior Back Saw, 70
Stanley Panel Saws, 64
Trophy Keyhole Saw, 83; Rotater Keyhole Saw, 159
SAWS, POWER
Black & Decker Circular Saw, 55
DeWalt Deluxe Power Shop Saw, 202
Dremel Moto-Shop Scroll Saw, 127
Milwaukee Contractors Circular Saw, 161
Rockwell Bandsaw, 202; Variable Speed Jig Saw, 173
Sears Electric Chain Saw, 225; Craftsman Table Saw, 203
Shopsmith All-Purpose Power Tool, 127
Skil Circular Saw, 177
S-B Storm King Replacement Latch, 271
SBI Bushman Hand Saws, 219
Scandecor Photodoors, 103
Schaul Clamp Leak Stopper Kit, 10; Supreme Float Ball, 17
H.J. Scheirich Revolving Shelf Pantry-Pak, 164
Schlage "G" Series Locks, 146
Schrade Cutlery Old Timer Pocket Knife, 95
Schulte Dor-Wall Unit, 164; Stor-Wall Unit, 170
SCISSORS
Clauss Rug Shears, 47
Normark Fiskars, 110
Warner Paperhanging Shears, 73
Wiss Contura-Lite Shears, 59
Scotts Grass Seeds, 214
Scott's Liquid Gold, 62
SCRAPERS
Gerson Child-Safe Razor Blade Scraper, 118
Stanley Scraper, 89
S/V Tool Saf-T-Scrape, 87
SCREWDRIVERS
Creative Tools Easydriver, 108
Eastco Screwdrivers, 110
Fuller Super Quality Screwdrivers, 162
Kedman Quick-Wedge Screwdriver, 151
Roscoe Screwdrivers, 181
Stanley Strip-Driver, 27; Thrifty Screwdriver Set, 208
S-K Round Cabinet Blade Screwdriver, 38
S/V Tool Screw Ball, 150
Vaco Ratchet Screwdriver, 105; Reversible-Blade Screwdriver, 208; Screw Holding Driver, 194
SCREWS
Elco Wood Screws, 160
Hillwood Helyx Concrete Screws, 228
Jefco Wood Screws, 40
Rockford Products Wood Screws, 158

Sharon Bolt & Screw Wood Screws, 176; 182
U-Fasten-It Wood Screw Fix-It Kit, 153
VSI Wood Screws, 40
Sealmaster Pipe Joint Compound, 11
Sears Bike Storage Lift, 197; Craftsman Electric Chain Saw, 225; Craftsman Spading Fork, 220; Craftsman Table Saw, 203; Dishwasher Air Gap Kit, 286; Epoxy Concrete Enamel, 124; Garage Door Digital Controls, 105; Kenmore Dual-Agitator Clothes Washer, 283; Tack Strips, 46; Wall Framing Kit, 55
SECURITY DEVICES see LOCKS AND SECURITY DEVICES
SEEDS
Scott Seeds, 214
SEWING MACHINES
Singer Athena 2000 Sewing Machine, 297
Seymour Appliance Refinishing Kits, 282
Seymour Hercules Post Hole Digger, 223
Seymour Smith Snap-Cut Tree Pruner and Saw, 218
Seymour of Sycamore Lube Kit, 212
Sharon Bolt and Screw Wood Screws, 176, 182
SHEARS, see SCISSORS
SHEDS
Cluster Sheds, 227
Jer 'Lil' Red Barn Kit, 227
Shell Household Spray Insecticides, 188
SHELLAC, see FINISHES
Shepherd Saturn Casters, 129
Shopmaster 24-inch Radial Arm Drill Press, 203
Shopsmith All-Purpose Power Tool, 127
Shop-Vac Aqua-Vac Wet-Dry Vacuum Cleaner, 49
Simer Pud-L-Scoop, 36
Simonds Si-Clone Saw Blades, 174
Simplex Pushbutton Security System, 147
Singer Athena 2000 Sewing Machine, 297
Skil Circular Saw, 177; Dustless Belt Sander, 45; Model 548 Router, 157
Skokie Saw and Tool Chieftain Plywood Blades, 152; Level, 34; Mill File, 156
SKOTCH FASTENERS
Superior Skotch Fasteners, 200
S-K Round Cabinet Blade Screwdriver, 38
Slack Pole, 173
Slic-Tite Pipe Joint Compound, 11
SMC Hang-It-Up Hangers, 221; No. 16 Utility Storage Hangers, 197
Smooth-Aid Paint Conditioner, 117
Snapit Electrical Tape, 32
SNIPS
Channellock Aviation Snips, 80
Ridgid Metal Cutting Snips, 237
Wiss Metal Wizz, 236
SOCKETS, ELECTRICAL
Eagle Standard Socket Replacement, 26
Levitron Dimmer Socket, 26
SOCKET TOOLS
BernzOmatic Spark Plug Socket Set, 217
SOLDER
Canfield Quality Solder Roll, 6
Hercules SWIF Solder Paste, 287
SOLDERING IRONS
Weller Model W-60 Soldering Iron, 95
Spear and Jackson Spearior Black Saw, 70
Specialty Bag Butler, 219; Trash Kan Kart, 219; Yard n' Garden Cart, 219
Spin-Thru Drain Cleaners, 14

SPLINING TOOLS
Thermwell Frost King Splining Tool, 92
SPRAYERS
Esmay Spritzer, 186
Gilmour Air-O-Matic Sprayer, 187
SPRINKLERS
Burgess Fluidic Sprinkler, 215; Shower Stick Sprinkler, 215
SPRINKLER METERS AND TIMERS
Tru-Test Sprinkler Meter, 213
SQUARES
Estwing Trim Square, 152
Mayes Brothers Squangle, 193
STAINED GLASS
Pendleton Studios Stained Glass, 95
Worden Stained Glass Forms, 95
STAINS
Behr Spray Stain & Sealer, 137
Cabot Bleaching Oil, 223; Decking and Fence Stains, 223
DuPont Lucite Exterior Stain, 115; One Step Polyurethane Stain & Finish, 137
United Gilsonite Beverlee Satin Stain, 137
USG Durabond Latex Rustic Stains, 114
Standard Dry Wall Products Thoro System, 37
Stanley Automatic Return Push Drill, 155; Bi-fold Hardware, 104; Classic Brassware, 181; 18-inch Lightweight Level, 155; Electrichisel, 126; Electrician's Pliers, 26; Fastener Holder, 77; Framing Hammer, 54; Magnetic Stud Finder, 75; Mitre Box, 72; Panel Saws, 64; Scraper, 89; Strip-Driver, 27; Surform Plane, 109; Surform Shaver, 151; Thrifty Screwdriver Set, 208
STAPLE GUNS
Arrow T-50 Staple Gun, 78
Bostitch H2B Stapling Hammer, 267
Duo-Fast Electric Staple Gun, 93
Swingline Decorator 101 Staple Gun, 59
Star Blind Rivet Tool, 239; Drive Wallgrip Hollow Wall Fasteners, 81; Snapin Toggle Bolt, 75; Star Drill, 209
Star Bronze Zip-Strip Putty Knives, 86
Stat-O-Cide, 48
Stauffer Tontine Window Shade Cloth, 97
Stay-Tite Roof Cement, 236; Cement Patch, 35; Gutter Seal, 240
Steel City Work Bench Legs, 204; Tool Rack, 204
STEEL WOOL
American Steel Wool, 135
Elephant Steel Wool, 44
SunRay Steel Wool, 132
Stik Tabs, 74
STORM WINDOWS AND FRAMES
Plaskolite In-Sider Storm Window System, 270
Reynolds Aluminum Storm Window Frames, 270
S-B King Storm King Replacement Latch, 271
Stove Hospital, 293
STRIPPING COMPOUNDS
Jack The Stripper, 135
Savogran H₂ Off Paint Remover, 134; Kutzit, 134; Strypeeze, 134
Stroll-A-Mix Concrete Mixer, 244
Stove Hospital Range Parts, 293
Styrofoam TG Insulation, 266
Sunbeam Model 42-61 Vaccuum, 280; Stop Alarm, 145
Sunnyside Boiled Linseed Oil, 138; Liquid Brush Cleaner, 120; Specs Paint Thinner, 116
SunRay Steel Wool, 132
Supergraphic Wall Decoration, 69
Super Handyman's Encyclopedia of Home Repair Hints, 120

Super Handyman's Fix and Finish Furniture Guide, 127
Super Fastener Skotch Fasteners, 200
Superior Graphite Slip Plate No. 3, 217
Superior Insulating Super-Stik Tape, 200
SUSPENDED CEILING SUPPORTS
National Gypsum Gold Bond Ceiling Grid Kit, 79
S/V Tool Saf-T-Scrape, 87; Screw Ball, 150
Swaniebraai Newspaper Grill, 231
Swedlow Swedglaze Acrylic Sheeting, 86
SWIMMING POOL COPING
GFA Nerak Coping Sections, 232
Swingline Decorator 101 Staple Gun, 59
Switchpack Surface Switch, 25
Synkoloid Rottenstone, 137
TACK CLOTHS
Bond Chemical Crystal Tack-Cloth, 136
T & R Chemicals Nu-Turp, 121
TAPE DISPENSERS
Quicker Sticker, 119
TAPE MEASURES
ENM Tapeless Measure, 33
Evans Thin Tapes, 153
Lufkin Mezurlock Power Tape, 54, 98; Folding Tapes, 54; White Tape, 54
MTI Rotarul, 191
Ridgid Fiberglass Folding Rules, 161
Roe Push-Pull Pocket Tape, 163
Tappan Convectionaire Gas Range, 291; Over/Under Range, 290
TARPAULINS
Warps Carry-Home Coverall, 266
Teco Carpentry Connectors, 55
Teledyne Mono-Thane Pipe Cover, 191
TELEPHONES
Tel Products Extension Telephone, 202
Tel Products Extension Telephone 202
Temco Regency Twin Gas Grill, 231
Texamar Fortex Rubber Buckets, 255
Textron Homelite Safe-T-Tip, 224
Thermal Metal Products Metalflex Ducting Vent Systems, 284
THERMOCOUPLE
Jade Controls Thermocouple Unit, 275
THERMOSTATS
Chromalox Adapt-O-Matic Thermostat, 293
Fuel Sentry Automatic Thermostat Control, 262
Honeywell Chronotherm Temperature Control, 262
Jade Thermostat, 262
Thermotrol Thermotimer, 262
Thermotrol Thermotimer, 262
Thermwell Frost King Automatic Electric Heat Cable, 20; Pipe Wrap Insulation Kit, 21; Serrated Metal and Felt Weather Stripping Kit, 111; Splining Tools, 92
3M Press'N Sand Sanding Discs, 160; Resinite Sanding Discs, 45; Scotch Electrical Tape, 32; Scotchgard Fabric Protector, 192
TILLERS
Toro Tiller, 214
TIMERS
GE Home Sentry Timer, 144
TOGGLE BOLTS
Jordan Handyman's Fastening Kit, 176
Star Snapin Toggle Bolt, 75
TOILET PARTS
Exelon FillValve Unit, 17
EZ Plumb Toilet Installation Kit, 16
Fluidmaster Flusher Fixer Kit, 16; 400-A Ballcock Kit, 16

Galaxy Seep-Seal, 18
Korky Flapper, 17
Plumb Craft Guide, 17
Schaul Supreme Float Ball, 17
U-Plumb-It Toilet Tank Kit, 17
TOOL BOXES
Park Carpenter's Tool Box, 207
TOOL ORGANIZERS
Rubbermaid Tool Organizer, 206
TOOL RACKS
Dalton Big John Tool Rack, 208
Dowling Miner Magnetic Tool
Storage Bar, 206
Granberry Rack-a-Tool, 221
Steel City Tool Rack, 204
TOOL SETS
BernzOmatic 70-Piece Tool Set,
202
TOOL STORAGE
Akro-Mils Bench Mate, 205;
Drill-Mate, 206; Quik-Pik, 205;
Saw-Mate/Sander-Mate, 206
TORCHES
BernzOmatic Super Torch, 260
Ronson Varaflame Torch, 39
Turner Tornado Torch, 21
Wingaersheek Spitfire Tur-
botorch, 6
Torch Side Lock, 107
Toro Tiller, 214
Tower Wire Brads, 152
TRASH CAN CARTS
Specialty Trash Kan Kart, 219
Tremco Instant Patch, 234
Trewax Paste, 45
Trimmatool File and Plane, 109
Triplett Model 310 V.O.M., 277
Trojan Coping and Jig Saw Blades,
162; Wood Screw Countersink
Bit Set, 175
Trol-A-Temp Registers & Dampers,
257
Trophy Keyhole Saw, 83; Plastic Peg-
board Trays, 65; Rotater Key-
hole Saw, 159; Torpedo Level,
208
"Troubleshooter's Guide To Noisy
Toilet Tank," 17
TROWELS
Easco Brick Trowel, 253
Marshalltown Trowels, 244
Murray-Black Pointing Trowel,
255
Red Devil Finishing Trowel, 56
Weekender Cement Trowel, 229
True Temper Rake, 214; Rocket
Brick Hammer, 253; Rocket
Pruner, 218
Tru-Test Sprinkler Meter, 213; Su-
preme Hammer, 175; Supreme
Spray Paint, 180
TUBE CUTTERS
Utica Tool Bonney Tube Cutter, 6
Tuff-Kote Krack-Kote, 60
Tuffy Drain Cleanout Auger, 15
Turner Tornado Torch, 21
20-Mule Team Borax, 279
UB Tool Line Blocks, 252
U-Fasten-It Wood Screw Assortment
Fix-It Kit, 153
Union Fork and Hoe Atlas Hoe, 244
United Gilsonite Beverlee Stain
Stain, 137; Wipe-On Zar, 139
U-Plumb-It Flat Sewer Auger, 14;
Plunger, 15; Toilet Tank Kit, 17
Urethane Arts Norwood Doors, 155
U. S. Ceramic Quick Set Ceramic Tile
Adhesive, 51
U. S. Expansion Bolt Yellow Jacket
Drapery Hardware Anchor, 98
U.S. Floor Systems Steamex, 49
USG Acoustical Sealant, 190; Adjust-
able Shelving, 193; All-Purpose
Joint Compound, 58; Drywall
Partitions, 55; Durabond Acr-
ylic Caulk, 101; Durabond Butyl
Caulk, 101; Durabond Exterior
Carpet Adhesive, 228; Dura-
bond Latex Rustic Stains, 114;
Durabond Tub Caulk, 101;
Durabond Utility Caulk, 101;

Durabond Wallboard Kit, 58;
Durabond Waterproofing Coating, 36; Foil-Back Sheetrock,
57; Sof'n-Soil, 215; Thermafiber Sound Attenuation Blan-
kets, 190; Wal-lite Ceiling Pan-
els, 80; Wal-lite Ceiling Tile, 79;
Wal-lite Ceiling Tile Adhesive,
78
USM Ammo DrivePins and DriveTool,
75; Bostik Spray Glue, 200;
Molly Bolts, 75; Thermogrip
Electric Glue Gun, 180
Utica Tool Bonney Rubber Tire Mal-
let, 125; Bonney Tube Cutter, 6
Vaco Ratchet Screwdriver, 105; Re-
versible-Blade Screwdriver,
208; Screw Holding Driver, 194
Vacu-Static, 281
VACUUM CLEANER ACCESSORIES
Grayline Vacuum Accessory Kad-
dy, 281
Vacu-Static, 281
VACUUM CLEANERS
Douglas Model A6690 Upright
Vacuum Cleaner, 280
Shop-Vac Aqua-Vac Wet-Dry Vac-
uum Cleaner, 49
Sunbeam Model 42-61 Vacuum
Cleaner, 280
Val-A Tehr-Greeze Fabric Cement,
59
Valley Dehumidifier, 185
VANITIES
Commodore Vanity, 171
Hide-A-Pipe Vanitique, 171
VARNISH, see FINISHES
Vaseline Petroleum Jelly, 133
Vaughan & Bushnell Ball Peen Ham-
mer, 40; Goggles, 209; Hol-
low-Core Handle Hammers,
108; Value Brand Drilling Ham-
mer, 209; 249
V-BELTS
Gates V-Belts, 296
VENETIAN BLIND REPAIR KITS
Globe Venetian Blind Renew Kit,
99
VENTS
HC Products Vent-A-Ridge Sys-
tem, 269
Kool-O-Matic Attic Ventilator,
268; Gable Electric Ventilator,
268
Leigh Brick Ventilator, 268
Midget Louvers, 268
Rittenhouse Ceiling
Light/Exhaust Fan, 269
Wisper Cool Turbine Vent, 269
Ventwood Shelving System, 184
Vigilant Products D'Stat, 48
Viking Sauna Wine Vault, 178
Vise-Grip C-Clamp, 180; Locking
Pliers, 209
VISES
Columbian Long Jaw Hinged Vise,
7; Woodworker's Vise, 126
V.O.M.
Heathkit V.O.M. Unit Kit, 277
Triplett Model 310, 277
VSI Wood Screws, 40
WALL ANCHORS
Jordan Jord-Eze Anchors, 74
Star Drive Wallgrips, 81
WALLBOARD
Georgia-Pacific Denswall Wall
Texture, 58
USG Durabond Wallboard Kit, 58;
Foil-Back Sheetrock, 57
WALLBOARD COMPOUND
USG All-Purpose Joint Com-
pound, 58
WALLBOARD MUD PANS
Red Devil Mud Pan, 56
WALLBOARD TAPING TOOLS
Marshalltown Iowa Taping Tool,
56
Red Devil Corner Taping Tool, 56
WALL FRAMING
Sears Wall Framing Kit, 55
WALLPAPER
Decro - Wall Wallpaper In

Squares, 69
Supergraphic Wall Decoration, 69
WALLPAPER HANGING TOOLS
Hyde Century Trimmer, 68; One
Arm Paperhanger, 73; Side
Arm Seam Roller, 73
Padco Wallpaper Smoother and
Applicator, 68
Warner Paperhanging Shears, 73;
Tool Sets, 84
WALLPAPER REMOVERS
Mantrose-Haeuser Room Groom,
84
Murray-Black's Electromatic
Wallpaper Remover, 84
William Zinsser DIF Wallpaper
Stripper, 68
WALL STORAGE UNITS
Rutt Design-A-Wall, 150
Jim Walter Window Components
Screen Kit, 93; Xplora Sliding
Screen Door, 92
Warner Paperhanging Shears, 73;
Paperhanging Tool Sets, 84;
Push Points, 87; Putty Knife, 39
Warp's Carry-Home Coverall, 230,
266
WASHING MACHINES
Maytag Model A608 Washing Ma-
chine, 283
Sears Kenmore Dual-Agitator
Clothes Washers, 283
WASHING MACHINE VALVES
Chatham Brass Dual-Protector
Valve, 283
Watco Danish Oil Finish, 138; Teak
Oil Finish, 138
Water Master Toilaflex Plunger, 18
WATERPROOFING COMPOUNDS
AND KITS
Dow Corning Silicone Rubber
Coating, 37
Standard Dry Wall Products Thoro
System, 37
USG Durabond Waterproofing
Coating, 36
Woodhill Chemical Duro E-Pox-E
Waterproofing Kit, 37
WAXES, see POLISHES AND WAXES
WD-40 Spray Lube, 212
WEATHERSTRIPPING
Anchor Continental Weath-
erstripping Tapes, 111
Arvey Easy-Does-It Kit, 271
Deflect-O Energy Seal Rigid Vinyl
Weatherstripping, 96, 111
M-D Numetal Weatherstrip, 96;
Thresholds, 110
Mortell Automatic Door Bottom,
110; Garage Door Top &
Sides Weatherstrip, 107; Ga-
rage Door Weatherstrip Cush-
ion, 107; NoDrip Plastic Coat-
ing, 36; NoDrip Tape, 36;
Transparent Weatherstrip
Tape, 96; Windowseal, 265
Thermwell Frost King Weather
Stripping Kit, 111
WEED KILLERS
Greenview Crabicide Green, 213
Judd Ringer Killer Kane, 213
Weekender Products Bricklaying Kit,
252; Cement Trowel, 229; Con-
crete Edger, 229
Weil Adjustamatic Ratchet Wrench,
259
Weiser Accent Ceramic Knobs, 171
Wej-Its Expansion Bolts, 228
Weldwood Concrete Patch, 254;
Flexible Wood-Trim, 178
Weller Model W-60 Soldering Iron,
95
Wellington Puritan Gold Braid Nylon
Cord, 99
Wells Lamont White Mule Work
Gloves, 255
Wen Bench Grinder, 211; Vari-
able-Speed Drill, 126
R. D. Werner Saf-T-Master Ladder,
241
Wester Wire Pipe Hooks, 7
Westinghouse Heat Pump, 257

Westvaco Edgemate Strips, 150
WHEELBARROWS
Kelly KC-5 Big Red Wheelbarrow,
246
Whirlpool SDU9000 Dishwasher, 287
Wickliffe Handy Dandy Jars, 64
Williams Archcraft Ceiling Beams, 83
William Shine Couple-It, 183
Williamson Five-In-One System, 260
Willson Agri-Tox Mask, 201
Wilmod Nails Unlimited, 58
WINDOW SHADES
Del Mar Woven Wood Shades, 97
Newell Window Products Magic
Fit Shades, 97
J. C. Penney Textured Shade, 97
Stauffer Tontine Window Shade
Cloth, 97
WINE RACKS
Northlake Woods Ruff 'N Ready
Shelving, 178
Viking Sauna Wine Vault, 178
Wingaersheek Spitfire Turbotorch, 6
WIRE BRUSHES
Arco End Brush, 116
Howard Hardware Wire Brushes,
86
Wright Bernet Wire Brush, 116
WIRENUTS
Eagle Solderless Connectors, 31
Wire Products Grip-Tite Nails, 184
Wiring Simplified, 31
Wisper Cool Turbine Vent, 269
Wiss Contura-Lite Shears, 59; Metal
Wizz, 236
Wizard Dehumidifier, 272
Wonder Color Wonder Brushes, 116
Woodhill Chemical Duro Aluminum
Jelly, 123; Duro Belt Grip, 296;
Duro E-Pox-E Waterproofing
Kit, 37; Duro Naval Jelly, 123
WOOD PRESERVATIVES
Darworth Cuprinol Wood Pre-
servative, 222
Woodstream Victor Easy-Set Metal
Mouse Trap, 189
WOOD TRIM
Weldwood Flexible Wood Trim,
178
Westvaco Edgemate Strips, 150
Wooster MagiKoter Brushes, 112;
MagiKoter Handy Bucket, 112
Worden Stained Glass Forms, 95
WORKBENCHES
Black & Decker WorkMate, 205
Garrett Wade Danish Folding
Bench, 204
WORKBENCH LEGS
Steel City Work Bench Legs, 204
Wrap-On Heat Tape, 20; Ice Guard
Heat Cable, 242
WRENCHES
Hancock-Gross Disposer Clearing
Wrench, 279; Faucet Seat
Wrench, 12; Socket Wrench
Set, 13
Indestro Classic MPI Socket
Wrench Set, 105; Classic Still-
son Wrench, 6; Rigid Chain
Wrench, 8; Strap Wrench, 8
Weil Adjustamatic Ratchet
Wrench, 259
Wright Bernet Wire Brush, 116
Wrightway Toilet Tube Attachment,
18; Tuffy Closet Auger, 18; Tuf-
fy Drain Cleanout Auger, 15
X-PO Hobby Knife, 76
Yale Bored Auxiliary Lock, 147; Disc
Tumbler Window Lock, 264;
Rim Lock, 147; 7200 Padlock,
145
Yorktowne Athena Cutting Board,
159
Z-Brick 67
Zenith Model 96 Medicine Cab-
inet, 169
William Zinsser Bulls Eye Shellac,
138; DIF Wallpaper Stripper, 68
Zynolite Clear Spray Shellac, 142;
1000F Hi-Temp Spray Paint,
231; Rug-Mate, 49; Wallpaper
Protector, 68